AF608037

PARTITION'S LEGACIES

JOYA CHATTERJI

Partition's Legacies

with an Introduction by

DAVID WASHBROOK

Partition's Legacies by Joya Chatterji was first published by Permanent Black D-28 Oxford Apts, 11 IP Extension, Delhi 110092 INDIA, for the territory of SOUTH ASIA. First SUNY Press edition 2021.

Not for sale in South Asia

Cover design by Anuradha Roy.

Cover image: F. P. Mainprice and his wife at a Pakistan border post, 1950s. Reproduced courtesy of the Cambridge South Asia Archive, Mainprice Collection.

Published by State University of New York Press, Albany

Printed in the United States of America

For information, contact State University of New York Press, Albany, NY
www.sunypress.edu

Library of Congress Cataloging-in-Publication Data

Names: Chatterji, Joya, author
Title: Partition's legacies / Joya Chatterji, author.
Description: Albany : State University of New York Press, [2019] |
Includes bibliographical references and index.
Identifiers: ISBN 9781438483337 (hardcover : alk. paper) | ISBN
9781438483351 (e-book)
Further information is available at the Library of Congress.

10 9 8 7 6 5 4 3 2 1

Contents

Preface

Writing a preface for a collection of essays written over almost thirty years presents a challenge of a different order to cobbling together a preface for a book. It requires one to think back over one's entire scholarly life and the directions in which it has evolved. A daunting task. I feel a bit like Winnie the Pooh: let's begin by taking a smallish nap.

Or maybe I'll begin at the beginning, with Mrs Khanna at Welham Girls School. I must have been about eleven when Mrs Khanna read us a primary source, the first I had ever encountered: Ziauddin Barani's *Fatāwā-i Jahāndārī* (Mirrors for Princes), written in the mid-fourteenth century. It took my breath away. She was a small and serious woman who read quietly, but the words struck me so powerfully that they have stayed with me ever since. It was perhaps from this moment that I was starting to try to become a historian – by reading every historical work or novel I could lay my hands on.

But there was a problem. My father, who came from a respectable *bhadralok* family, thought that his academically minded daughter should become a doctor. In his own way he was a feminist and wanted me to become financially independent; he saw medicine as the route. I loved the sciences, but not as much as History. My first rebellion came when I was eighteen and joined Delhi's Lady Sri Ram College to read History. Next I went to Trinity College, Cambridge, where I read more History and took a PhD in History on Hindu communalism in Bengal. A book followed shortly after, *Bengal Divided* (in the old century we were encouraged to publish our PhD theses quickly. I try to persuade my doctoral students to do the same now, to no avail.) My son Kartik was a somewhat manageable three-year-old by then, leaving the question of what to do next.

My essay writing began as a young mother whose periods of work were constrained. Three or four hours in the archives were all that I could find. Visits to Calcutta were a great to-do. I would set off with Kartik on my hip from my home in Delhi to my research locations in West Bengal, for a month or six weeks at a stretch. By this time I was a Junior Research Fellow at Trinity College, so funding was not an issue. Logistics were. I stayed for long periods with friends and family who looked after Kartik while I worked in archives or wandered through graveyards (no necrophilia, only fieldwork) during the day. In the evenings there would be the pleasure of a shower that washed the dust and cobwebs of the archives out of my hair, and a quiet hour with the children while anticipating a dinner of fish curry and rice. Heaven in a nutshell. Not everyone's idea of heaven, to be sure: the *Statesman* archives at the time were at the top of the stately building in a lean-to with an asbestos roof. No fans allowed – the papers were crumbling. The Special Branch Archives had no ladies' loo. In the monsoon, Lord Sinha Road flooded and one waded through filthy water in Bata rubber chappals to get to the police archives. This was my perverse idea of bliss.

To begin with, I was feeling my way towards a new subject and found much in the archives that excited me. There was copious material on boundary-making, on refugees, on the surveillance of Muslims. I began to see fascinating patterns emerge. After a chat with Anil Seal, my former supervisor, I decided to follow his advice and write this material up as articles.

An article on the frontier emerged in this way. In 2000 or so, when Suvir Kaul asked me to contribute to a volume on the afterlife of Partition, I had enough notebooks on refugees to produce "Rights or Charity". (This was in the analogue age.) When Mushirul Hasan and Asim Roy asked me to think about a volume they were putting together on the theme of "Living together Separately", I had trudged through many of Calcutta's Muslim graveyards and read enough about Muslim flight and internal migration to write "On Graveyards and Ghettos". These articles went down well, and, judging by feedback and footnote citations, seemed quite influential, being seen as asking new questions and providing at least half-decent answers.

A few years down the line I began to see the connections between these essays and they formed the backbone to my next book, *The Spoils of Partition* (2007). In my head the relationship between articles and books has been quite intimate. After an article is done and dusted I feel a pressure to take the story forward, to find out more, to provide a larger context and an overarching argument within which its ideas eventually come to nestle. In this sense I am not an essayist like, for instance, David Washbrook or Sumit Sarkar, both historians who frequently deploy the genre to "solve" and "resolve" questions in long autonomous essays of great depth and importance, and then move on.

Given that the essay is a form which, in retrospect, I seem to have treated as a starting point for longer explorations, I think I have, in order to provide each of my essays with a semblance of wholeness, played about a bit with structure, particularly when starting out. In "The Fashioning of a Frontier" I imagined the shape of an onion, peeling off layer by layer until I got to the core. (That was fun.) In "Dispersal and the Failure of Rehabilitation" I sometimes thought of my structure as an hourglass or sand timer, wide at the top with a narrowly focussed centre, widening out again into a broad base. The image sedimented the notion in my head that my academic essays might begin with a range of ideas which should concentrate on a case study and then flow out into a broad set of expandable conclusions – both in my own books and in those by other scholars. With "Migration Myths and the Mechanics of Assimilation" I saw symmetry between apparently dissimilar texts, mirror images with their paradox of sameness and unfamiliarity. I think quite visually, I suppose, now that I come to reflect upon it, and my hope is that these formative images helped make my essays more elegant.

If I have improved as an essayist it is also because my years as editor of *Modern Asian Studies* were invaluable. Between 2009 and 2018 I read over 1800 readers' reports on essays submitted to the journal. Anonymous readers advised their authors on how to perfect their articles, and in the process taught me. If "On Being Stuck in the Bengal Delta" (my personal favourite) is technically better than the others, it is probably because I worked on it precisely in the way I did with authors who needed to improve their own submissions. Tough questions from my friend Prasannan Parthasarathi, who was then on the board of *American Historical Review*, were invaluable in the long process of refining and adding nuance. Prasannan's gaze, like that of the fabled basilisk, is pitiless and falls unfailingly on pretty writing, which he often manages to show up as a fig leaf covering substantive flaws. "South Asian Histories of Citizenship" also benefited from the careful reading of it by Peter Mandler, who was then editor of the *Historical Journal*. This is not a statistically significant sample, of course, but I have a strong hunch that editing journals makes one write better articles. Likewise, reading excellent articles has helped me write better in general.

If I have had favourite essays, I also have had favourite referees for my peer-reviewed articles. One, P.K. Datta, waived his anonymity for "Migration Myths", and my response to his terrific and challenging comments emerged in *The Bengal Diaspora* (2016). Another, who remains anonymous, pushed me very hard on "Dispositions and Destinations". Had I had more time then to reflect, read more widely, and take up the advice to be more overtly comparative, I think it would have been a stronger essay. But by then I was ill and preoccupied, so the essay lacks some facets it could have had.

Re-reading these essays – all written as solidly researched pieces, except one which is a literature-synthesising introductory essay –

I have been made more aware of the broad trajectory of my thinking. I started out, I think, as a political historian, though I take heart from the late Tapan Raychaudhuri's kindness in remarking that *Bengal Divided* (1994) represented a kind of "total history". But I have without question moved more and more into the terrain of the social. If I write about politics, it tends to be the politics of the street, or of the household, or of the network. I am constantly aware of the state, and I hope my understanding of Leviathan has grown more sophisticated, but by 2000 I was desperately bored by high politics, and that shows in *The Spoils of Partition* (2007). I have become more willing to borrow methods from other disciplines when my questions seem to demand it.

My concerns, though, have moved forward along a clear path. Partition, nation-making, frontiers, refugees, minority formation, and categories of citizenship have been my preoccupations. They remain so to this day. I am not really sure why. Perhaps the answer also goes back to my childhood. My ancestral home in North Bengal was a large household set within a great walled compound and dominated by my eldest *jethu* (paternal uncle). "Kalu *Daktaar*", as he was known in the area, helped fund the Naxalites, and both my aunt and father sheltered Naxals on the run. Yet for all their progressive zeal, I never once saw a Muslim enter our enclosed homestead. I never saw a Muslim at all, anywhere in the vicinity. I only realised that Bengal had been a Muslim-majority province when I went to Cambridge. The opacity at the heart of my childhood prompted questions I have spent my life trying to answer.

Will there be more essays? I am not sure. I am not exactly in the pink of health at the moment and have two books going. When they are done, if I still have petrol in my tank perhaps I will go back to writing articles and nurse them on into becoming books.

Cambridge, July 2018

Acknowledgements

Acknowledging debts is the best part of writing any book. Not only does it signal the end of a period of intense work, it allows one publicly to thank friends who would have been embarrassed to be recognised in person.

My first and largest debt is to Rukun Advani. I am amazed that anyone, let alone he, a particularly discerning editor, thought my essays worth reproducing in a collection. It seems an honour more significant than all other prizes and fellowships combined. It means that many of my essays will continue to be dipped into and read by students of history in South Asia. They are the future of our subject, and hence these articles will live on in a new form in a new century.

Rukun and I argued over which of my essays to include. Though I sent him my most substantive pieces, as asked to, I was not sure we should keep more than eleven. But in the end he won, as editors of stature often do, and there are now a baker's dozen.

I have accrued other debts. David Washbrook, who wrote the Introduction, has been the staunchest of friends and most percipient of critics since I first submitted my fellowship dissertation to Trinity College in 1989. Poor David has had much of my work inflicted on him since then. He has done much else to support me. Indeed, without his help at the Centre of South Asian Studies over the last five years, I would not have had the time to write the more recent articles in this volume.

Some of these essays were solicited by other scholars. I thank Martin Thomas, Andrew Thompson, Mushirul Hasan, Asim

Roy, Humeira Iqtidar, and Tanika Sarkar, Suvir Kaul, Al McCoy, Stephen Jacobson, and Naren Nanda for pushing me to set my ideas down on paper and think harder about them. Some of them pulled me well outside my comfort zone, and I am grateful to them for that.

Others I wrote off my own bat. Usually they were sparked off by a source, or by a life history which so upset or inspired me that I felt I had to write about it. A reviewer once remarked about one of these essays that it was written with "angry clarity". As I re-read them again for the first time, I recognise just how much anger about injustice has fuelled my writing, for all its calm and reasoned tone. I also seem to have done my best work at moments of deep personal suffering: I suppose I learned to sublimate emotion into productive channels. (The article on secularisation was written, for instance, while my mother was dying.) The friends who supported me through the dark times have my enduring love and gratitude: in no particular order, Shohini Ghosh, Sabeena Gadihoke, Sara Hossain, Shalini Sharma, Samita Sen, Sarah Pearsall (and Teddy for his hugs), Kamal Munir, Humeira Iqtidar, Tanika Sarkar, Sumit Sarkar, Tim Hochstrasser, Ornit Shani, Claire Alexander, Jennifer Davis, Gordon and Faith Johnson, Simon Longstaff, Chandra Mallampalli, Bob Frykenberg, Nikki and Dorothy Wagle, Ben Hopkins, Polly O'Hanlon, Partha Shil, and Prasannan Parthasarathi. Anjali Datta and Humaira Chowdhury helped in innumerable practical ways: I owe them much. And then there is Raj Chandavarkar, who cannot be thanked in person, but whose conversation and work has inspired me since I was a PhD student, and whose friendship made Cambridge feel more like home.

There is my family: my siblings, sisters-in-law, nieces and nephews, who don't know quite what I do all the time, and think I do "it" too much, but are proud of me nonetheless. There's also my growing family of doctoral students, present and past. They have given me a rich intellectual life, and have returned my strict supervision with affection. Thank you, wonderful people.

This book of essays was put together at a time when I was too ill to travel, and when even visits to a library were a challenge. A few people made it possible for me to work effectively from home. Above all I thank Rachel Rowe, Librarian of the Centre of South Asian Studies, Cambridge, for letting me borrow books on liberal terms. Ed Anderson, Anjali Datta, Humaira Chowdhury, and Patrick Clibbens ferried them across to me. Tina Bone's maps and Kevin Greenbank's work on the old photographs used here represented hours of work, well beyond the call of duty; they add much, I think, to the volume. I thank them both. Kevin's friendship has been a fabulous thing: not only has he pulled me out of endless computing disasters and magically transformed old printed articles into Word documents (how??), he has calmed me through countless computing meltdowns, saying "there there dear" in his inimitable soothing tone.

My consultants – Mel Lobo, Guy Leschziner, Nick Gall, and Serge Nikolic – literally pulled me through periods of agonising illness while I pulled these essays together. Paul Flynn, John Brown, and Shane Delamont have been wise friends whose medical knowledge we have often called upon in extremis, and Maria Flynn has tolerated all-too-many late-night calls. But for their counsel, and their careful watch and ward, there would have been no book. Tim Harper: friend, colleague and Chair of the History Faculty, and my colleagues at Trinity College could not have been kinder or more supportive. I have been extraordinarily fortunate.

And then there are the many people who have given me unstinting practical support and affection, which has made living and writing easier: Ingrid Freese, Mirka Cis, Dave ("Pinky") Roberts, Jimmy Jolland, Lucas Realli, Richard Chalklin, Saroj Tigga, Emmanuel Tigga, and Caitan Fernandez. Thank you for everything.

Above all, for the everyday, I thank Kartik, Ciara, and Anil. Anil and Kartik have accompanied me to hospital and consultations over five hundred times. I don't have the words to thank my little family for all the chats over cups of tea and coffee, for the rainy afternoons watching rubbish on TV, for talk and laughter over glasses of wine, for taking me to places on my bucket list, and for putting up with my moments of irritability and despair. They have been so generous in their love despite my relentless, unreasonable, focus on history, recognising that is my survival strategy.

Anil Seal read most of these essays at the time they were written. He has, with pride, watched me grow from a self-doubting doctoral student into a self-sustaining scholar. I could not have done any of this without his personal support and intellectual example. This book is dedicated to him.

I am grateful for permission from various journals and publishers to reproduce the articles in this book. Sources of first publication are given below.

"Decolonisation in South Asia: The Long View", in Martin Thomas and Andrew Thompson, eds, *Oxford Handbook of the Ends of Empire*, Oxford: Oxford University Press, forthcoming, December 2018.

"The Fashioning of a Frontier: The Radcliffe Line and Bengal's Border Landscape 1947–1952, *Modern Asian Studies*, vol. 33, issue I, 1999.

"The Bengali Muslim: A Contradiction in Terms?", first published in *Comparative Studies of South Asia, Africa and the Middle East*, vol. XVI, 2, 1996, reprinted in Mushirul Hasan, ed., *Islams, Communities and the Nation, Muslim Identities in South Asia and Beyond*, Delhi: Manohar, 1998.

"Secularisation and 'Constitutive Moments': Insights from Partition Diplomacy in South Asia", in Humeira Iqtidar and Tanika Sarkar, eds, *Secularisation and Tolerance in South Asia*, Cambridge: Cambridge University Press, 2018.

"Rights or Charity? The Debate over Relief and Rehabilitation in West Bengal 1947-1950", in Suvir Kaul, ed., *The Partition of Memory*, Delhi: Permanent Black, 2001.

"Migration Myths and the Mechanics of Assimilation: Two Community Histories from Bengal", *Studies in the Humanities and the Social Sciences,* vol. XVII, nos 1 and 2, 2010.

"Dispositions and Destinations: 'Mobility Capital' and Migration in the Bengal Delta", *Comparative Studies in Society and History,* vol. 55, issue 2, 2013.

"Dispersal and the Failure of Rehabilitation: Refugee Camp-dwellers and Squatters in West Bengal", *Modern Asian Studies,* vol. 41, issue 5, 2007.

"Of Graveyards and Ghettos: Muslims in West Bengal 1947–67", in Mushirul Hasan and Asim Roy, eds, *Living together Separately: Cultural India in History and Politics,* Delhi: Oxford University Press, 2005.

"On Being Stuck in the Bengal Delta: Immobility on the 'Age of Migration'", *Modern Asian Studies* (Special Issue: *New Directions in Social and Economic History*), vol. 51, issue 2, 2017.

"From Subjecthood to Citizenship: Migration, Nationality and the Post-imperial Global Order", in Alfred McCoy and Stephen Jacobson, eds, *Endless Empires,* Madison: Wisconsin University Press, 2012.

"Princes, Subjects, and Gandhi: Alternatives to Citizenship at the End of Empire", in Naren Nanda, ed., *Gandhi's Moral Politics,* Routledge: London and New York, 2018.

"South Asian Histories of Citizenship", *Historical Journal,* vol. 55, December 2012.

Introduction

DAVID WASHBROOK

It gives me great pleasure to introduce this collection of essays by Joya Chatterji. I first met Joya thirty years ago, not long after she arrived at Trinity College, Cambridge, to begin undergraduate studies for her second BA. She came from India with a stellar reputation which it did not take her very long to justify – walking off with Trinity's top prizes as undergraduate and post-graduate. From the beginning, she showed a passion for historical research which, I am delighted to say, has never diminished and has led her to many subsequent achievements: not least, election as a Fellow of the British Academy where she stands in rare company both as a woman and as an historian of something other than Britain. The "promise" that she offered all those years ago, when she passed under Trinity's Great Gate suitcase in hand, has been more than fulfilled.

In particular, that promise has realised itself in a series of projects that have changed the way that we think about Indian (and, more broadly, South Asian) history over the last century. Her first book, *Bengal Divided* (1994), shifted focus away from Islam and Muslim "fanaticism" in providing the driving force behind the Partition of India and on to supposedly "secular" Indian nationalism, middle-class aspiration, and the shadow of Hindu nationalism. Her second book, *The Spoils of Partition* (2007), rejected the idea of Partition as a breaking apart and took it more as a process of re-making – of both the social structure of eastern India and the nature of the post-colonial state. Her third (jointly written) *The Bengal Diaspora* (2016) challenged the idea of migration and (re-)settlement as exceptional conditions and viewed them in multiple dimensions as responding to precise and complex motivations. Her latest project on "citizenship", whose beginnings are reflected in essays included below, contrasts the rigidities of formal and legal "national" citizenship with the serendipitous and opportunistic political circumstances often lying behind its definition.

What is striking about this oeuvre, first and foremost, is its courage and originality. In all cases, it confronts received wisdoms which are often deeply held and capable of mobilising soldieries in their defence. Joya has never backed away from controversy and has proved herself capable of standing her ground even when coming under ferocious fire – be it from Kolkata's *bhadralok* intellectuals, whose historic culture she tarred with the charge of Hindu chauvinism, or the likes of David Starkey seeking to defend the narrowest idea of "Britishness". Moreover, the positions that she takes up tend to be justified by history itself since, over time, her heterodoxies usually become orthodoxies.

Also, she is usually among the very first to take them up. The lead-up time to publishing a "serious" history book is considerable and, if it is taken into account, Joya has a remarkable record of anticipating imminent shifts in both public sensibility and historiography. The work for her *Bengal Divided*, which reframed Hindu nationalism as a central feature of the Indian national experience, began in the mid 1980s – long before the destruction of the Babri Masjid and the rise of the BJP. The work for *Spoils* began in the late 1990s, long before the issue of eastern India's "soft" borders and ongoing Bangladeshi "infiltration" hit the headlines. Needless to say, the issues raised by international migration and citizenship, on which she began working in the 2000s, are now central to the politics (and identity) not only of diaspora, but of the USA and Europe themselves. As with all ground-breaking historians, Joya's sense of the links between past, present, and future is especially acute: if she backed racehorses, she would probably be a millionaire by now.

But also, and as with all visionary historians too, her work is deeply rooted in concern for a place and a people. While Joya's eye may roam across international movements, world wars, and global dispersions, it keeps coming back to Bengal whence both she and her adventures in history started out. Whether Divided, Spoiled, or Migrated, Bengal is the constant reference point for her judgements, comparisons, and perspectives. It is, however, a very idiosyncratic Bengal – especially in relation to that to which we are used. That Bengal is of the Kolkata *bhadralok*, the respectable, educated, Hindu middle classes who have provided many of India's leading intellectuals and written much of the nation's history. Indeed, it has sometimes seemed as if the history of modern India is their own history.

Yet, although with one foot in north Bengal, Joya has always stood somewhat apart. Born of an English mother, with family in Kolkata but raised in Delhi and colleged in Cambridge, she has a classic insider-outsider profile. While sensitive to the nuances of *bhadralok* culture, she is capable of sharp (self-)criticism and aware of the limitations of provincialism. Her Bengal is religiously plural and peopled as much by peasants, migrants, and paupers as an urban proto-bourgeoisie. Her Bengal is no less fractured and brutalised by colonialism, Partition, and the post-colonial state. However, it does not only stand as a field of negation and lament. In *Spoils*, and in several of the essays included here, she shows how even little people mattered, re-built their lives, challenged and re-made policies of the state, and acculturated themselves to new environments. Her subalterns are not divorced from elites but active with them in the world; and their violence, while recognised, is always seen as purposive. Her Bengal may have its tragedies, too, but it is also positively engaged in the epic struggles making this world. It does not just serve nostalgically as a surrogate for a world that has passed, if it ever was.

The essays gathered here represent but part of much wider work exemplified in Joya's other monographs and jointly written collections. In her preface, she disclaims her facility with the essay form. Yet, characteristically, she is over-modest. When commissioned to write on specified topics for themed collections, she shows great mastery – if it is still permissible to use such a gendered term. The essay on decolonisation provides a succinct account of its subject, explores nuances of concept, and draws together different strands of exegesis. However, in one regard, it may also illustrate her point. The essay uncovers increasing layers of complexity – decolonisation proceeds in different time dimensions – until the questions asked become questionable themselves and the conclusions reached necessarily provisional. QED are not three letters that can ever be put under a Chatterji essay.

Rather, as she herself notes, most of her essays represent either the beginnings of projects which she would later take on to study in greater depth; or else distinctive corners within them attracting separate exploration. Both types reflect her historian's craft, her passionate love of the archive, and her respect for detail and context. Many of the essays begin by rehearsing received understandings – of Partition demarcation or refugee settlement or "national" citizenship – but show that close readings of the archive reveal hiatuses and pose unanswered questions. She then begins to reconstruct events on the basis of better information, drawing out paradoxes, suggesting alternative conclusions, and pointing to the need for further research – in many cases, which she herself later supplies.

What emerges from the essays is often quite startling. The demarcation of Partition followed no master plan or even coherent strategy but was made up of myriad *ad hoc* decisions taken on the ground, often by obscure actors. Refugee policy, immigrant rights, and even definitions of national citizenship, again, were produced by no *deus ex machina* but out of day-to-day struggles on the streets and in the courts where the supposed omnicompetent power of the "modern state" was forced into compromise by the irrationality of its own bureaucracy and the recalcitrance of "the people". Joya's history has little time for Big Ideas or Great Men. It revels in the minutiae of events, which she sees unravelling Programmes and undermining Projects. Not only in war but also in politics, all battle plans would seem to dissolve on first contact with the enemy or, in this case, that between state authority and popular aspiration.

Similarly, events could undermine the most fixed of appearances and reverse the most obvious of truths. Pakistan and India may have been born in bitter hostility and proclaimed different goals of faith and secularism. However, she demonstrates that, in their dealings with each other, their governments became ever more convergent and even acquired each other's imagined vices and virtues. Over the refugee crisis, Pakistan found itself adopting increasingly secular policies, while over refugee property India found itself introducing religious criteria into its definition of citizenship. Indeed, the rarely remarked similarities between Pakistan and India represent an important general insight offered in these essays.

So, too, is the revelation that modern ideas of citizenship and nationality were not invented in "the West" and diffused to the Rest, but that they were in important ways re-fashioned out of the experience of decolonisation in the colonies themselves. Joya's essay "Citizenship in South Asia" stands at the start of what will be her latest major research project. But already some of the outlines of its trajectory are becoming clear: how Partition and post-imperial diaspora posed new problems to the concept of citizenship; how the ex-colonies came to strike back, forcing new ideas about identity and nationality onto the metropolis itself.

Other essays included here are more in the nature of explorations of nooks and crannies easily overlooked from the main vantage points of history, but containing valuable treasures. Two of the most thought-provoking concern "immobility" and those left behind by migration. We tend to think of processes of migration in terms of those who moved. But many who desperately wished to leave were prevented from doing so, trapped in situations becoming increasingly intolerable; and others who "stayed" behind continued to be part of networks connected to the mobile, still shaping the latter's social identities. Joya's work here immeasurably broadens the meaning(s) of migration, piecing together perceived fragments into whole processes again.

Elsewhere, she also considers the alternatives and the failures of history as the record actually turned out – and as historians have all too easily forgotten. The successful construction of Indian national identity and citizenship since 1947 has tended to blot out the contingency of the process and the many other possibilities existing at the time. It makes a modern and democratic India seem inevitable. Yet she shows strong leanings at the time towards a Balkanised subcontinent; towards the preservation of monarchical systems of order; even towards mystical and spiritual "Gandhian" polities. Understanding what did not eventuate is an important part of understanding what did, and why. Joya constantly reminds us of the many possibilities contained in the past, only some of which ever came to be realised.

Many historians are driven by the quest for self-understanding, for appreciation of the contexts that have given rise to themselves. In Joya's case, these are located in Bengal and most of the essays return to this focus again and again. Yet they reveal her to be anything but local in her breadth of vision and grasp of historical movement. They traverse countries and continents, deal with ranges of problems from state-building, to survival, to national, religious, and gender identity, and touch on several of the most critical international issues of our times. We see both Bengal in the world and the world in Bengal. They represent a marvellous introduction to her wider works and will more than serve their purpose if they take readers towards those studies and to her persistent questioning of why our world should have turned out as it has, and what possibilities there may be of making it again – and better.

Cambridge, August 2018

1

Decolonisation in South Asia

The Long View

DECOLONISATION WAS A global process whose scale, pace, and implications are not best captured by a regional study. So what, one might ask, is gained by approaching the process from the perspective of South Asia?

There are, I believe, compelling reasons for giving decolonisation in the region special attention. India was the first colony to achieve independence, albeit as two separate nation-states, India and Pakistan. Britain's abrupt withdrawal from India after the Second World War – so swift that many have denounced it as a scuttle – raised questions that have helped frame the debate about decolonisation, not just in India but elsewhere. Did Britain jump or was it pushed? If it jumped, was the prime agency of decolonisation situated in the metropolis, as some historians argue? In their view, Attlee's Labour government chose to "transfer power" to independent nations from a Britain battered by war and mired in debt, thereby engineering a convenient "escape" from their Indian empire, while retaining, so it was hoped, informal influence over the region.[1] Others who insist that Britain was pushed, by contrast, are more attentive to local or "peripheral" forces and pressures:

[1] Moore, *Escape from Empire.* Also see the eponymous *Transfer of Power* volumes I–XII, edited by N. Mansergh, E.W.R. Lumby, and Penderel Moon, and published by HMSO between 1970 and 1982.

widespread disorder during the Quit India Movement, communal riots and famine, demoralisation in the lower ranks of government, disorder in the ranks and on the streets, wave upon wave of strike action, and above all to nationalism on the road *Towards Freedom*.[2] For decades this debate, launched by political historians in the 1980s, seemed to be getting nowhere, stuck in a groove much like a needle in a vinyl record of that era, scratching away at the same refrains. That fundamental disagreement reverberated, as Shipway notes, through the study of decolonisation in other parts of the world.[3]

The independence of India and Pakistan has powerfully influenced this wider debate, if not always in a helpful way. In recent decades, however, a new generation of scholars has moved the subject forward. Taken together, their work shows – and this is an argument I will pursue here – that decolonisation cannot be reduced to one or other of these single drivers. It was a process simultaneously local and global. For one thing, in geo-strategic terms, India was never merely local or peripheral: the subcontinent always played a pivotal part in wider British imperial strategy. Even after India and Pakistan became independent, for the rest of the world they represented "exogenous factors" in their own right – for the colonised a beacon of hope of what they could achieve, and for colonisers a template of how they could manage retreat in parts of the world that were becoming too difficult, dangerous, or expensive to govern.[4] Posing the question in either/or terms does not advance our understanding. By eschewing these polarities,

[2] For these various themes, see Bhattacharya, *Propaganda and Information*; Kamtekar, "A Different War Dance"; Deshpande, "Sailors and the Crowd"; idem, "Hopes and Disillusionment"; Sarkar, "Popular Movements and National Leadership"; Ahuja, "Produce or Perish"; Mansergh, ed., *Towards Freedom*; Pandey, ed., *The Indian Nation in 1942*; Singh, *The Origins of the Partition of India*.

[3] Shipway, *Decolonization and its Impact*.

[4] Mazower, *No Enchanted Palace*.

I suggest that it was at conjunctures when local and global crises violently collided that decolonisation – never a smooth process – jolted forward.

The particularities of the process in this region are another compelling reason to focus on South Asia: above all the fact that decolonisation was achieved by a radical partition. In turn, the vivisection of British India would become a template for partitions elsewhere, notably Palestine in 1948.

But the Partition of India is also important because it has a profound bearing upon the second great issue of the subject – namely, what did decolonisation actually achieve? Did it merely involve the capture of the imperial state by local elites who perpetuated imperial "customs of governance" to secure their own dominance?[5] What, if anything, changed on the ground for the ordinary citizen (herself a product of the decolonising imaginary) after the transfer of power? Is there merit in "the continuity thesis" which holds that freedom in South Asia did not meaningfully transform colonial structures of power?[6]

I build upon recent scholarship to interrogate this powerful and durable thesis and challenge some of its conclusions, arguing that the imperial state was not some singular object, easily handed over, like a baton in a relay race, to local elites. Rather, it was an assemblage of power, "fluid, frequently irrational and often self-limiting", spread patchily over the various regions, articulated differently across different social spaces.[7] Decolonisation was therefore, and could only ever have been, an irregular process by which the imperial order was disaggregated – unevenly, haphazardly, and incompletely – and replaced, also incompletely, by two fragile and nascent national orders.

[5] Sarkar, "Popular Movements and National Leadership"; Chandavarkar, "Customs of Governance?"

[6] The boldest and most brilliant statement of this remains Chandavarkar, "Customs of Governance". Also see Brass, *The Politics of India after Independence*; Jalal, *Democracy and Authoritarianism in South Asia.*

[7] Sherman, *State Violence and Punishment in India*, p. 178.

Such a process was not, and could never have been, seamless. Acknowledging the incompleteness has led historians to revaluate the significance of 1947 and question the timing (and periodisation) of decolonisation. Did it occur, in some definitive way, in 1947? Or if it was indeed a more long-drawn-out process spread over about forty years or more, as Dipesh Chakrabarty has suggested, where does 1947 stand in that longer course of events?[8] I shall offer here some new ways of thinking about 1947, which suggest that while many (but not all) imperial structures of *governance* stayed in place after Independence, Partition saw off many of the old *social* structures. Another major change was that the independent states in South Asia had goals and purposes that their imperial counterparts had never envisaged. They derived their legitimacy from different sources and had to be seen to deliver different goods. They were subject, therefore, to far greater and very different pressures from the imperial regimes they replaced.[9] The way the nation-states evolved as they faced these new challenges is, I argue, a crucial part of decolonisation.[10] And by focussing on some of the questions raised by the recent historiography on South Asian decolonisation which have lent the subject fresh levels of empirical granularity and theoretical sophistication, I hope to pose new issues for the field as a whole.

1914–1922: From Flanders to Chauri-Chaura

Colonial rule in India was a bricolage. A congeries of complex and fluid relationships, it was never spread evenly across the subcontinent; it penetrated some regions more deeply than others, catching particular social groups more intensely in ever-shifting webs of collaboration and extraction.

[8] Chakrabarty, "Introduction", in Chakrabarty, Majumdar, and Sartori, *From the Colonial to the Post-Colonial*, p. 3.

[9] Gould, Sherman, and Ansari, "The Flux of the Matter".

[10] Shani, "Making India's Democracy".

For purposes of analysis, three types of relationship might be identified. First, there were the unequal and often uneasy alliances between the British imperial establishment and their so-called collaborators, drawn from the Indian elites: princes, landlords, so-called community leaders, mercantile elites, and high-caste or *ashraf* educated Indians who helped govern the empire. Second, there were relationships based upon the extraction of labour: peasants growing cash crops for export, workers in the public and industrial sectors, bonded and indentured labourers on the plantations, lascars who travelled the high seas in the service of the imperial economy, sepoys who manned the Indian army, as well as huge cohorts of lowly constables, village *chaukidars* and *patwaris* who represented "the realities of rule . . . closer to the ground."[11] Third, and at the broadest level, there were the connections that existed between the Raj and its ordinary subjects who, more or less, obeyed the law and paid taxes. These were fragile linkages and bonds. Some were built on face-to-face interactions between rulers and the ruled; but most were rather more intangible relationships, deriving from notions of subjecthood, or *namak*, fealty to the *hukum* or will of the British *sarkar*.[12] Given how thinly the British presence was spread on the ground, Indian intermediaries mediated between the Raj and its numerous subjects in almost every sphere of governance.

Decolonisation in South Asia is best understood as the intricate process by which these relationships unravelled, at different levels of imperial engagement and varying speeds, and across an array of locations. It was not, and could never have been, a smooth unilinear movement along the high road to freedom. Along the way there were starts and stops, spurts and lulls, with more crises and

[11] Shipway, *Decolonization and Its Impact,* p. 19. *Chaukidar*: village watchman, menial servant, or guard. See Giuliani, "Strangers in the Village?", pp. 1378–1404. Also see Shil, "Police Labour and State-formation", for a brilliant account of the labour that constituted the colonial state.

[12] *Namak*: literally, "salt"; idiomatically, denoting ties of loyalty between subject and ruler.

corners to be negotiated than open roads and clear destinations. It is only by recognising the intricacies and complex interplays, both temporal and spatial, that we can begin to grasp what decolonisation was, and still is today.

But when, and where, did that process begin? With no singular origin for a process of this complexity, I will focus instead on critical junctures, moments of acceleration and of crisis. The First World War and its aftermath – sadly still an understudied subject from Indian perspectives – was the first such major occasion when the concerns of Indians were propelled into an unprecedented confrontation with worldwide crises.[13] For one, the war drew Britain into a head-on collision with the Ottoman sultan and caliph of Islam in ways that deeply tested the loyalty to the Raj of India's Muslims. Not unlike the revolutionary Ghadar revolt, with which it was loosely connected, the Khilafat Movement was simultaneously local, national, and "global": its most expansive goals, as Maia Ramnath has noted, "could only really be imagined and enacted . . . outside the country."[14] But it was also substantially located within India, in local communities, rallied by ulema, students, and journalists writing for a buoyant Urdu press, in a formidable agitation against the government.

The war also sucked labour out of India and flung it abroad into strange lands. "Never before," says Ravi Ahuja, "had rural people from the Indo-Afghan frontier region and Nepal, from the Punjab and other military recruitment grounds of 'British India' engaged with European societies as intensively."[15] Many were non-combatants, but most were soldiers, and almost half of them were from the Punjab.[16] Ever since the Mutiny, the Punjab was the province on whose loyalty the Raj had relied most

[13] Although see Roy, *War and Society in Colonial India*; and Singh, *The Testimonies of Indian Soldiers*.

[14] Ramnath, *Haj to Utopia*, p. 169.

[15] Ahuja, "Lost Engagements?", p. 19.

[16] Singha, "The Short Career of the Indian Labour Corps"; and idem, "Finding Labour from India".

heavily, and from where hundreds of thousands of sepoys were now recruited for wartime duty outside India. In peacetime, annual recruitment into the Indian army was about 15,000 men; during the war it rocketed upwards to almost 1.3 million men over four years, about a million of whom were pressed into service overseas. "At no previous moment in history had South Asians entered Europe in comparable numbers," Ahuja reminds us, many of these sepoys being villagers from the Punjab, who by 1919 totalled a staggering 44.5 per cent of the entire Indian army, and who found themselves fighting at Flanders, the Somme, Ypres, Neuve Chapelle, and Gallipoli, in conditions for which they were hopelessly ill-prepared.[17] For the first time in the history of the sepoy armies of the Raj – other than the very different context of the Mutiny – they engaged white troops in battle.[18] Tens of thousands died. One Sikh sepoy from the Punjab, Santa Singh, wrote to his mother from the hospital in Britain where he lay wounded:

> Many sons of mothers, brothers of sisters, and brothers of mothers have been lying dead for a whole year on the field of battle. A year has passed and there they lie. He who sees them for the first time says there is no place empty. So many corpses are there, and all have perished in forty seconds . . . They too are the children of mothers.[19]

Like Santa Singh, many more were injured. While some were treated in Britain at the fanciful faux Indo-Islamic pavilion at Brighton, large numbers ended up in German prisoner-of-war camps where the potential for subversion was enormous. At these camps, the POWs learned, in the aphoristic words of Sib Singh, a Sikh peasant from Amritsar, about the frailties of empire: "The Angrez [Englishman] is *badshah* [Emperor] in India and we did

[17] Ahuja, "Lost Engagements?", p. 19; Mazumder, *The Indian Army*, p. 18, Table 1.5.

[18] Ahuja, "Lost Engagements?", p. 19.

[19] Santa Singh to his mother (translated from the Gurmukhi), 20 July 1915, in Omissi, *Indian Voices of the Great War*, p. 80.

not know there were other *badshahs* [elsewhere]. When the War began we heard of several badshahs. One flaw in India is that people are without *ilm* [knowledge] . . ."[20]

Returning from the front, they brought back from Europe this knowledge to the villages and towns of upper India, as well as other "seditious" ideas. For half a century, the Raj had done its utmost to insulate the Punjab – and above all, its soldiery – from the contagion of politics. But now, paradoxically, it was the Punjab which became a critical site from which the politics of decolonisation were set into motion, an epicentre from which protest radiated outwards.

In the Punjab and beyond, the burden of taxation upon Indians, already heavy before hostilities, grew ever more onerous during the war. In 1917, India had to contribute "an outright gift" to its imperial overlord of £100,000,000, which was nearly twice India's net annual revenue before the war.[21] Indian mercantile groups resented the heavy taxes on sales and "super profits" now slapped upon them. Even the Government of India, previously Westminster's compliant agency in Delhi, began to sense that this unremitting pressure on Indian taxpayers was simply too heavy to be borne and had begun to endanger its political purposes. In 1918, the army department in Delhi told the India Office in no uncertain terms that "the drain . . . in money and material on the resources of India cannot any longer be met without the gravest embarrassment."[22] In December 1919, the viceroy, Chelmsford, was even more blunt: "I must . . . point out to you that India [is] in this way being exploited by the War Office because they find that they can maintain Indian troops abroad without those extremely objectionable questions in Parliament which would be

[20] Cited in Ahuja, "Lost Engagements?", p. 44.

[21] General Sir H.V. Cox Montagu Papers, Trinity College, Cambridge, "Note on Finance", AS/I/56, cited in Jeffery, "India after the First World War", p. 374.

[22] Ibid., p. 376.

asked if they were British and not Indian forces."[23] This growing discord between the perspectives of HMG in London and the Government of India in Delhi, which came to a head after the war, is a striking and often overlooked dimension of decolonisation. In this period, a parting of the ways was reflected above all in India's increasing autonomy on tariffs, particularly on cotton. "Seemingly so omnipotent in the nineteenth century," Dewey notes, "Lancashire's ability to dictate Indian tariffs ended with the First World War."[24] In 1917, the Government of India more than doubled the duty on cotton imports, in the main from the United Kingdom, from 3.5 to 7.5 per cent; in the 1920s it rose further to 11 per cent, and in the 1930s it stood at approximately 25 per cent on all British piece goods (and 50 per cent on any goods from elsewhere).[25] Already by the end of the war, India was beginning to emerge as a distinct "national" market.[26] The army, Britain's imperial garrison in eastern seas, also faced serious questions about its future use, above all over who would pay – London or Delhi – when it was deployed outside India for imperial purposes.

Even before the war had ended, then, much had changed in the structure of colonial relationships, providing the context for the historic announcement by Montagu, secretary of state, in August 1917, promising "an increasing association of Indians in every branch of government." The significance of the government's failure to keep its word promptly must be set against this backdrop. Promises are dangerous things, particularly when they are as large and imprecise as the government's hint that (an undefined) "responsible" government was on its way. They unleashed hopes that the cautious reforms of the post-war Raj could never satisfy.

In March 1919 Gandhi launched a nationwide campaign – a hartal (strike). Against his intentions, it turned violent in some

[23] Chelmsford to Montagu, 17 October 1919, cited in ibid.

[24] Dewey, "The End of the Imperialism of Free Trade", p. 36.

[25] Ibid.

[26] Goswami, *Producing India*.

places, notably in the Punjab. The Raj was nervous, particularly about the loyalty of a province which had been the bulwark of its rule. The public mood turned ugly after the government reacted by "externing" popular political leaders from the province. The "Black" Rowlatt Bill, which extended the draconian powers of wartime government into an era of peace, was another flashpoint. On 13 April 1919 – Baisakhi day, the start of the Punjabi New Year and the anniversary of the birth of Sikhism – General Dyer ordered troops to fire on a peaceful crowd gathered at Jallianwalla Bagh, an enclosed walled park in Amritsar in the heart of the Punjab, just a stone's throw from the Golden Temple. Casualty figures remain in dispute, but in the carnage over five hundred people lost their lives.[27]

The event marked a profound and irreversible blow to the Raj's claims to legitimacy in their Indian empire, well beyond the Punjab where these atrocities took place. For a great many Indians outside that province – particularly the educated middle classes, who had valued the liberal possibilities of imperial subjecthood – that dream ended abruptly with Jallianwalla Bagh.[28]

Among those for whom this was a Damascene moment was Mohandas Karamchand Gandhi. Gandhi, it is well known, had served as a loyal subject of the king-emperor in the Imperial Ambulance Corps in South Africa during the Boer War, and as a staunch supporter, sometimes even a recruiting sergeant, of the Allied cause during the Great War. But after the war, a concatenation of global and local concerns – the Khilafat and Punjab "wrongs" as Gandhi described them – convinced him that Albion was perfidious and the Raj morally bankrupt. Gandhi's political message represented a frontal assault on the relationships of imperial collaboration and a clarion call to cut the ties of sentiment that underpinned British rule, and, as Gandhi well understood,

[27] Sherman, *State Violence and Punishment in India*, p. 16.

[28] Banerjee, *Becoming Imperial Citizens*.

this meant going for the jugular of the imperial project. In his seminal treatise *Hind Swaraj*, written in 1908 on board a ship to India from South Africa, he had insisted that British rule in India rested not on conquest but on the collaboration and collusion of Indians seduced by western materialism and the siren calls of modernity. If Indians withdrew their co-operation from the Raj, so Gandhi's thesis implied, it could not survive. Now, he signalled, the time had come for them to take that step.

At the 1920 Nagpur session of the Indian National Congress, Gandhi urged Indians not to co-operate with British rule, and to refuse non-violently to obey its "unjust" laws: "If . . . the acts of . . . the Government be wrong . . . it is clear that we must refuse to submit to this official violence. Appeal to parliament by all means if necessary, but if the parliament fails us and we are worthy to call ourselves a nation, we must refuse to uphold the Government by withdrawing co-operation from it."[29]

At Nagpur, Gandhi got his "non-cooperation" resolution through at a session packed with angry Muslim Khilafatists, backed also by all manner of politicians who calculated that, under a franchise carefully calibrated by the British to tilt the balance against them, they would not do well in the coming elections to the reformed councils. By skilful tactics and opportunism combined with a brilliant grand strategy, Gandhi captured Congress, outflanking many Congress leaders puzzled by his idiosyncrasies, alarmed by his alliance with Muslim Khilafat leaders, and unconvinced by the merits of his policy of standing back from elected councils in the provinces.

A year later, when he launched the Non-cooperation Movement, Gandhi promised to achieve swaraj (self-rule) within twelve months. He could not, of course, deliver. But the movement gained a far larger, more broad-based, and disparate following than anything the Congress had achieved before. In

[29] Brown, *Gandhi's Rise to Power*, p. 245.

part, this was because Gandhi had already enlisted powerful friends and constituents in regions outside the usual bases of the Congress – rich peasants, mill owners and mill-workers in Gujarat, prohibitionists in Karnataka, and Khilafatists in North India in Bengal – who were able to mobilise, albeit temporarily, their own networks behind local campaigns of unprecedented strength. In these campaigns they included social groups the Raj had previously relied upon to be neutral if not actively loyal to the imperial order. But the "winds of change" were blowing. Gandhi couched his political message in a language – both symbolic and semantic – which unlettered Indians understood and with which they could identify. When Gandhi discarded suits made from British cloth and instead wore a tiny strip of fabric he had woven on a simple spinning wheel, he advertised the predicament of India's weavers and artisans. For centuries in subcontinental statecraft, just rule had required the government to tax fairly and lightly, patronise handicrafts, and husband the resources of the land.[30] By adopting the spinning wheel and khadi (handloom cloth), Gandhi signalled to every Indian that British rule was failing in these duties and was hence illegitimate. By urging Indians to break the government's monopoly over the production of salt, Gandhi drew attention, again symbolically (since the cess on salt was minuscule) to the unjust burdens of taxation that British rule had placed on India. Since salt was a local metaphor for the symbiotic relations of obligation and loyalty between rulers and ruled, by urging the people to make their own salt Gandhi sent out a highly charged signal that the people of India should withdraw their fealty to the British. As Rajnarayan Chandavarkar suggested, India's working classes were often inspired by Gandhi's rhetoric because of his canny ability to develop "the blandest

[30] Modern nationalism took root so swiftly in an illiterate society, Bayly argues, because its proponents were able to appeal to widely held traditional ideas of ethics and political legitimacy. See Bayly, *The Origins of Nationality*.

metaphor and the most platitudinous axiom in a distinctly subversive direction."[31]

Ironically, however, Gandhi's success in becoming the Mahatma of the masses compromised his control over the direction of the movement he had started. The denouement came at Chauri-Chaura, a village in the North Indian district of Gorakhpur. Inhabitants of this hamlet, convinced that the new utopia was just over the horizon, burnt hapless Indian policemen alive for standing in their way, putting their little station to the torch.[32] This dramatic instance of violence prompted Gandhi abruptly to call off Non-cooperation. The movement of 1921–2 thus ended in confusion and disarray.

Of course, the politics of Non-cooperation floundered after this. And of course, as scholars have noted, the end of non-cooperation was followed by a decade of apparent calm. But the events between 1917 and 1922 represented a decisive shift in the relationship between rulers and ruled. Much had been damaged in the fragile web of imperial relationships. It was the first major crisis in the bumpy road to decolonisation.

The Interwar years – Deceleration?

The Raj responded by devising novel strategies to reassert its authority. It strove to hold on to power by building new alliances and afforcing old ones. The plan was to devolve, in two stages, a measure of power to some Indians in the provinces. The goal of both the Government of India Acts of 1920 and 1935 was to recruit new collaborators in the provinces and strengthen the hand of old friends. The British hoped to achieve this by giving certain provincial groups (men with wealth, land, and education) a share in provincial government, and the right to raise and spend

[31] Chandavarkar, *Imperial Power and Popular Politics.*

[32] Amin, *Event, Metaphor, Memory.*

local taxes, thereby fortifying their local power and patronage (and, it was hoped, their loyalty). Historians have observed that this "retreat to the centre" worked for a while, at least in terms of quelling major disturbances. Provincial parties and provincial questions dominated India's politics in the 1920s, much as the British had intended them to do. Until 1929, when Lord Simon's visit to India heralded a new round of reforms, politics at the all-India level appeared to have lost all momentum.

Yet the interwar interlude watered down British sovereignty over India in subtle but significant ways. To make its strategies work, the Raj had to concede to the provinces the right to certain heads of revenue, degrading substantially its powers of extraction. Under the 1920 constitution, the centre in New Delhi had to transfer about £6 million to the provinces.[33] It also began the "Indianisation" of government. In 1920, dyarchy, as this exercise in power-sharing was called, gave Indian politicians in the provinces some say over certain areas of governance that today would be described as "development" (whether schools, sanitation, or roads), which were of vital importance to Indian lives in the localities, but which the Raj regarded as secondary to its core purposes. After the Government of India Act of 1935, the vote was increased sevenfold, to about thirty-five million voters, who now could elect their own provincial governments presided over by Indian premiers. But the terms of the 1935 Act ensured that these governments would be dominated by "communal majorities". This raised fears of permanent minority status among increasingly bitter and vocal political minorities, Hindu and Muslim alike, in different provincial settings: notably in the Punjab, Bengal, and the United Provinces.[34]

In the elections of 1937 the Congress, revived by another round of civil disobedience led by Gandhi in the 1930s, won

[33] Gallagher and Seal, "Britain and India between the Wars", p. 400.

[34] See, for Bengal, Chatterji, *Bengal Divided*; for Pubjab, Nair, *Changing Homelands*; and for the United Provinces, Jalal, *The Sole Spokesman*.

the support of most Hindu voters and came into office in every Hindu-majority province in British India. In some Muslim-majority provinces, "loyalists" did rather better, particularly in the Punjab where the cross-communal Unionist Party came to power; but in Bengal, the largest province in India, the "Krishak Praja" party, backed by rural Muslims with anti-establishment views, seized control. This polarisation of provincial legislatures along communal lines would have far-reaching implications in the 1940s. The Indianisation of government in the provinces whittled away, meanwhile, at the morale of British civil servants, who, as Bhattacharya has shown, found it hard to take orders from Indian ministers.[35] The "iron frame" of the Indian Civil Service, on the face of it still intact, was becoming less secure under the surface. Among civil servants, the introduction of popular government challenged their singular focus of loyalty. Competing commitments to different political masters, the Raj on the one hand and provincial ministers on the other, forced government servants to make their allegiances "both more explicit and more flexible".[36] This did not bode well for the empire.

In the interwar years the Raj might have persuaded itself that it still controlled the "vital attributes of sovereignty" by beating a strategic retreat to the centre.[37] The viceroy continued to sit in splendour in his grand new viceregal lodge on Raisina Hill, apparently the commander of all he surveyed. But that was increasingly a chimera. The old balances had changed. By wresting fiscal autonomy from the treasury in London, Delhi had tipped the scales in India's favour. Meanwhile in the provinces British rule was starting to look rather less secure. In 1935 the British had given the vote to hundreds of thousands of richer peasants, confident that these rustic men would remain loyal to their "salt". But they

[35] Bhattacharya, *Propaganda and Information.*

[36] Gould, Sherman, and Ansari, "The Flux of the Matter", p. 219.

[37] Gallagher and Seal, "Britain and India between the Wars", p. 406.

got it badly wrong, as the votes for Congress and for the Krishak Praja Party suggest. This blunder revealed how patchy was the British understanding of the India they ruled – all their censuses and surveys notwithstanding – and how little they had grasped the impact of the Great Crash of 1929 and the global Depression which followed on the Indian countryside.

Already by 1939, J.S. Furnivall – colonial civil servant and historian of South East Asia – had concluded that the Depression

> marks the close of a period. For the crisis of 1929 brought to a head the changes due to the War in the economic relations between Europe and Asia, with their necessary reactions on social and political relations; it marks the close of a period of sixty years, beginning with the opening of the Suez Canal, and, although less definitely, the close of the period of four hundred years from the first landing of Vasco da Gama in Calicut.[38]

In his rare and valuable essays on the Depression, Christopher Baker showed how the finely balanced interdependence of the South and South East Asian region fell apart after 1928, with the most immediate and profound shock waves being experienced in those areas which grew produce for the global market.[39] In many localities of the Tamil countryside, landed magnates lost their former overweening dominance with their loss of control over the liquidity of the agrarian economy. Grain riots, protests against the government's revenue demands, and kisan and communist agitations suggested that the old structures of dominance, subordination, and deference were breaking down.[40] In Bengal, the world's largest producer of raw jute, high prices in the global marketplace had created a rich peasantry in the first decades

[38] Furnivall, *Netherlands India*, p. 428.

[39] Baker, "Economic Reorganisation and the Slump in South and Southeast Asia".

[40] Baker, "Debt and the Depression in Madras", p. 238.

of the century. Now, as prices tumbled, these men, known as *jotedars*, grew politically restive.[41] As for poorer peasants – whom the British had assumed to be simple law-abiding folk, loyal to *maa-baap* traditions of subservience – suddenly stopped paying interest, rents, and taxes.[42] Localised but shocking violence against moneylenders and landlords grew commonplace. Stepping back, we can see, in those parts of the country where the Depression hit hard, the assumptions of social control on which the British systems of collaboration rested coming unstuck. The "big men" on whom the British relied to impose order upon the countryside no longer seemed comfortably in charge.

There were warning signs also about the Raj's capacity to rely on other social groups whose loyalty it had once taken for granted. Indian businessmen began to join Congress in droves, if only to better influence it towards the path of moderation.[43] In 1930, in Peshawar, two platoons of the Royal Garhwal Rifles – which had won plaudits for their courage and loyalty during the war – refused to board buses into the city to contain rioting and disorder. At Jallianwalla Bagh, men from the Garhwal Rifles had obeyed Dyer's orders to shoot low, into the crowd, to kill. Now, the "warrior gentlemen" of British martial race theory were sending out a disturbingly different message to their paymasters.[44]

Even the princes, with their nominal sovereignty over a third of India, showed signs of restiveness. Despite British attempts to bend the principalities to their purposes, and to rule them firmly (if indirectly), rajas and nawabs found ways of resisting British intrusion into many areas of courtly life, religious affairs, and secular patronage by adapting or "inventing" new institutions, traditions, and "duties of kingship" – *rajadharma* – by which they

[41] Baker, "Economic Reorganisation and the Slump"; Bose, *Agrarian Bengal.*

[42] Chatterji, *Bengal Divided.*

[43] Markovits, *Indian Business and National Politics 1931–39.*

[44] Caplan, *Warrior Gentlemen.*

entrenched a sort of "monarchical modernity",[45] or established "minor sovereignty" over their subjects,[46] sometimes projecting their influence well beyond the boundaries of their states.[47] Frustrated in 1928 by the Indian States Committee's refusal to define paramountcy and to place limits on British interference in their durbars,[48] many princes began to see merit in parleying with nationalists in the run-up to the first Round Table Conference in London in 1930.[49] Significantly, they refused to join the federation the British offered them in 1935. Barbara Ramusack, the leading historian of the princely states, characterises the interwar era as a period of the dissolution of this "patron-client system" which had served the British so well for almost a century.

The social history of the interwar years, in particular the global Depression and its chequered impact across India, requires much more research. When that history is written, it may well show the era – often characterised as the calm before the storm – to be a time of gathering clouds. Much was changing, albeit at micro levels, where the impact of a global economic crisis hit hardest. Understanding these changes in all their vernacular intricacy will be crucial to achieving a more sure-footed grasp of the long history of decolonisation.

The Second War, Independence, and Partition

The Second World War brought with it another dramatic collision of Indian localities with global events. The Great War undoubtedly had had far-reaching repercussions on India, notably, but not only,

[45] Nair, *Mysore Modern.*

[46] Beverley, *Hyderabad, British India and the World.*

[47] Ramusack, *The Princes of India.*

[48] *Indian States Committee 1928. Replies Received to the Questionnaire issued by the Committee.*

[49] Ramusack, *The Indian Princes and their States*, pp. 245–57.

in the Punjab. The Second World War was a much more proximate crisis and its direct impact was felt across larger swathes of India. It was in large measure, as Bayly and Harper have reminded us, an Asian war.[50]

This time round, however, the government – which had taken India into the war without so much as a by-your-leave from its national leaders – encountered anti-recruitment propaganda even in regions that had traditionally produced fighting men. A political agent seeking to recruit Rajputs was told politely by one magnate, "Now there is not a single Rajput available for recruitment in the Indian Army."[51] In the Punjab "a small Muslim boy" was arrested in Lahore for singing an anti-recruitment song.[52] Popular support for the war effort beyond these parts was at best tepid, with large numbers preferring to tune into German radio broadcasts in Hindustani than to the All India Radio broadcasts in the Allied cause.[53]

The role of the eastern theatre was crucial to its outcome. Japan's occupation of Manchuria in 1937, and its bold advance between 1939 and 1942 through China, South East Asia, and the Pacific, followed by the fall of Singapore, sent shock waves around the world, provoking a "public outcry and bitter introspection by politicians in London."[54] As Harold Nicolson wrote in his diary, "The Singapore surrender has been a terrific blow to all of us. It is not merely the immediate dangers which threaten the Indian Ocean and the menace to our communications in the Middle East. It is said that we are only half-hearted in fighting the whole-hearted."[55]

When Japan then attacked Burma and took Rangoon in

[50] Bayly and Harper, *Forgotten Armies.*

[51] Khan, *The Raj at War*, p. 23.

[52] Ibid., p. 16.

[53] Ibid., p. 40.

[54] Bayly and Harper, *Forgotten Armies*, p. 154.

[55] Nicolson, *Diaries and Letters*, entry for 17 February 1942, cited in Bayly and Harper, *Forgotten Armies*, p. 154.

1942, this propelled India directly into the front line. Between January 1941 and October 1944, 1.3 million Indian recruits were persuaded or press-ganged into the army, and most were stationed on the eastern front. They were brought in from far and wide – the Punjab once again provided almost half the fighting forces – but were billeted mainly in Bengal, and to a lesser degree in Ceylon.[56]

To get troops to the front, the eastern region's infrastructure urgently needed to be improved. Japanese air strikes in the Bay of Bengal forced the closure of all ports on the eastern seaboard, and acute shortages of rolling stock crippled the railways. Road building, long neglected, finally came of age. Assam was connected to Bengal and Burma by a great new arc of metalled road thousands of miles long.[57] Government had to mobilise huge resources to pay for these public works: the budget of the engineering department increased 25-fold, from Rs 40 million in 1939–40 to Rs 1000 million in 1944.[58]

But roads, though necessary, were not sufficient: air power was essential to push back Japan. Before the war, Calcutta alone had an adequate airstrip. By the end of the war, the region was equipped with 145 aerodromes and runways.[59] In the same period, labourers had built "a fine network of . . . feeder roads" to the aerodromes. Protecting the health of American airmen, and British and Indian troops, required massive scrub clearance and anti-malarial programmes, all of which required labour.[60] To meet the demands of war work, specialised labour battalions were established, composed largely of "aboriginal tribes" recruited from Bengal, Bihar, and Orissa.[61] Bayly and Harper discovered that

[56] Jackson, "The Evolution and Use of British Imperial Military Formations", p. 28.

[57] Bhattacharya, *Propaganda*, p. 19.

[58] Ibid., p. 20, Table 1.1.

[59] Ibid., p. 19.

[60] *Census of India, 1951, Vol. VI, Part I-A,* pp. 75–8.

[61] Bhattacharya, *Propaganda*, p. 20.

the Indian Tea Association supplied 100,000 porters to work on roadworks between 1942 and 1945.[62] War work and its spectacular demands on labour were spread unevenly across the subcontinent, with the Punjab, North, and East India bearing the brunt.

But this was not all: the fall of Burma also pushed the government to intervene in the economy in other unprecedented ways. The "Limited Denial" policy, intended to starve the advancing Japanese army of essential resources, led the government to remove or destroy boats and vehicles which might fall into enemy hands, and to move foodgrains en masse from the coast to the interior. The Foodgrains Control Order of 1942 and the Bengal Rationing Order of 1943 are now widely deemed to have had disastrous effects: they are part of a chain of events that led to the catastrophic Bengal famine of 1942–3 in which between three and six million people died. These interventions, as the census commissioner, looking back, remarked in 1951, ended "free trade for the rest of the decade".[63]

These wartime measures on the eastern Indian front were the backcloth to a snowballing political crisis. Upon the outbreak of hostilities between England and Germany the viceroy, Lord Linlithgow, had declared war on behalf of India. Described by Nehru as a "slow" man, "as solid as a rock and with almost a rock's lack of awareness",[64] Linlithgow engaged India as a combatant without even the pretence of consultation with Indian politicians. Outraged, and ready to exploit Britain's wartime troubles, the Congress high command forced its ministries in the provinces to resign and demanded an immediate share of power at the centre, as well as a say in the defence of India. Churchill and Linlithgow had no intention of budging an inch, and so the British and the Congress were once more set on a collision course.

Conveniently for the British, however, Congress was also by

[62] Bayly and Harper, *Forgotten Armies*, p. 185.

[63] *Census of India, 1951, Vol. VI, Part I-A,* p. 84.

[64] Nehru, *The Discovery of India*, p. 446, cited in Khan, *The Raj at War*, p. 5.

this time caught up in a stand-off with the Muslim League, a party that had re-emerged on the national stage in 1937 under the leadership of the enigmatic Muhammad Ali Jinnah. Jinnah's ambiguous Lahore Resolution of 1940, calling for an ill-defined Pakistan, was his response to the 1935 Act and the permanent communal minorities it had created in provincial assemblies. It was also a reaction to the Congress' reneging on pledges to the Muslim League made before the 1937 elections.[65] The new demands of the League are properly understood as a consequence of earlier phases of decolonisation, as well as a significant force shaping its next stage.

None of this was appreciated at the time, of course. Churchill and his viceroy seized upon the excuse the Lahore Resolution presented them to put the question of India's constitutional future into cold storage during the war. For its part, the Congress leadership made the fatal mistake of underestimating Jinnah and his demands as an unwelcome and insignificant distraction. Those on the left of the Congress, Jawaharlal Nehru among them, tended to brush the League aside as unrepresentative, denouncing the Resolution as the self-serving, anti-democratic posturing of "backward-looking" Muslim elites. They ignored the growing – albeit dispersed and fractured – movements for Pakistan which, while imagined in a variety of ways, were attracting support in different regions from a wide range of constituents.[66] (Those on the right of the Congress, in a party increasingly polarised along a left–right axis, denounced Jinnah's demands as illegitimate – even treasonable – attacks on *Akhand Bharat*, the "integrity of the nation".) The British, meanwhile, gave tacit and opportunistic encouragement to Jinnah's claims to speak for a united "Muslim nation".[67]

[65] Jalal, *The Sole Spokesman*.

[66] For recent work that argues, contra Jalal, for the range and depth of the influence of the Pakistan idea, see Dhulipala, *Creating a New Medina*; Bose, "Purba Pakistan Zindabad"; Uddin, "In the Land of Eternal Eid". Also see Devji, *Muslim Zion. Pakistan as a Political Idea*.

[67] Jalal, *The Sole Spokesman*.

This stalemate ended with the Japanese attack on Pearl Harbor. It brought America into the war, and both Roosevelt and Chiang Kai-shek now began to put intense pressure upon Britain to mend fences with the Congress so as to bring India and its people more wholeheartedly behind the war effort. In 1942 Stafford Cripps flew out on a mission to make a deal with the Congress that would bring it on board. On behalf of Britain's National Government of the day he offered India dominion status after the end of the war and the right to draft its own constitution (also post-war). He promised the princes that Britain would protect their treaty rights when the British withdrew from India; and he also promised individual provinces the right to opt out of a federal union, in an apparent concession to the apprehensions of Jinnah and the Muslim League.

There was much in this "offer" to infuriate the Congress and it is the reason why historians have concluded that Churchill intended the Cripps Mission to fail.[68] If that was indeed Churchill's plan, it succeeded. Gandhi denounced the offer as "a post-dated cheque on a crashing bank". In his famous "Quit India" speech on 8 August 1942 he asked Indians to "do or die". But before they could do either, and before the August *kranti* (revolution) could begin, the police were ordered to swoop down and arrest the entire leadership of the Congress party and keep them in jail for the rest of the war.

This too was a dangerous mistake. Leaderless, the Quit India Movement (or, more properly, movements) proved far more violent and far less disciplined than anything Gandhi would have countenanced. Public meetings, strikes, and demonstrations were held in all the major cities of North India.[69] In Tamluk and Contai subdivisions of Midnapore in Bengal, local leaders sprang up who drove the British administration out altogether, establishing parallel governments of their own.[70] In Ballia,

[68] Ibid.

[69] Sherman, *State Violence and Punishment in India*, p. 121.

[70] Chakrabarty, "Political Mobilization in the Localities".

North India, people broke open a jail, released arrested Congress leaders, and established "independent rule". Several leaders who escaped arrest went underground and continued their struggle by broadcasting messages over clandestine radio stations. By the end of 1942, Taylor Sherman estimates, 250 railway stations had been destroyed and 550 post offices attacked, of which 50 were burnt to the ground; 3500 instances of wire cutting had shattered communications, and demonstrators had set upon 80 government buildings and 70 police stations and their outposts; 31 policemen and 11 military personnel had been killed, several by being burnt to death.[71] Linlithgow conceded that these protests, dispersed though they were, represented "by far the most serious rebellion since that of 1857."[72] It was only with a combination of aerial bombardment, shooting to kill protesters, public flogging, and collective fines on whole villages (in other words, applying the full arsenal of what Sherman describes as the Raj's "coercive network") that the British were able to re-establish control.[73]

Sadly, no major work has as yet been done on Quit India,[74] so it is hard to say with any degree of certainty who the "August revolutionaries" were. But these events, in conjunction with the deeply embarrassing – from the British point of view – uprising of the "Indian National Army" in Burma among soldiers captured by the Japanese, represented a point of no return for the Raj.[75] Wavell

[71] Sherman, *State Violence*, p. 121.

[72] Linlithgow to Churchill, 31 August 1942, in Mansergh, ed., *Transfer of Power, Vol. II*, Document 662.

[73] Sherman, *State Violence*.

[74] Although see Pandey, ed., *The Indian Nation in 1942*; Damodaran, *Broken Promises*; and Kamtekar, "The Shiver of 1942".

[75] With Japanese support, Subhas Chandra Bose, who escaped from India in 1941, revamped the Indian National Army (INA), then composed of Indian soldiers of the British Indian army who had been captured in the Battle of Singapore. To these, after Bose's arrival, were added enlisting Indian civilians in Malaya and Singapore. Despite Bose's drive and charisma, his military effort was short-lived. For fascinating depositions and accounts of some of the "INA" accused, see Singh, *The Testimonies of Indian Soldiers*.

replaced Linlithgow as viceroy. A thoughtful man, a soldier with a deep love of literature and poetry,[76] he had little stomach for a reconquest of India, which he believed would be unavoidable if the British were to stay on and rule after the war. He began to give thought to a planned exit.

Independence with Partition: Assessing "1947"

The Second World War shattered Britain's metropolitan economy and fundamentally altered the equations of profit and power that had for so long sustained the Raj in India. It destroyed both its capacity and its will to hold on to an empire in turmoil, ravaged by famine and by the swelling tides of communal violence and labour unrest.[77] Another casualty of the war was the Conservative faction in Britain that wanted to hold India at any price. After Labour won the elections in 1945, Attlee's government declared its intention to transfer power to Indians as soon as possible. The end game, as it has been characterised, had begun.

In that game, the power, priorities, and timetables of the key players underwent a volte-face. During the war, London had wanted to hang on to power in India and found the Muslim League's demands a convenient bulwark against Congress. So it had made promises to Muslims (and to the Indian princes) that their concerns would be addressed in the final constitutional settlement of India's future. After the war, however, when London wanted to get out of India as quickly as possible, these pledges were deeply inconvenient; and while it hoped to be able to brush assurances to the princes under the carpet, it could not ignore the "Muslim question".

For its part, the Congress leadership grew increasingly inflexible about making any concessions to the Muslim League which might

[76] Wavell, *Other Men's Flowers*.

[77] Ahuja, "'Produce or Perish'".

weaken the centre and encourage particularist demands by others. The Congress had always insisted that India was indivisible, but now, with the capture of the centralised apparatus of the British Raj almost within its grasp, it changed tack. In the swift but intricate tripartite negotiations for the transfer of power in 1946 and early 1947, the Congress high command settled for a limited partition that would cut out the troublesome Muslim-majority districts in the north-west and east, and allow them to inherit the rest of British India, with a union centre uncompromised by having to share power with the Muslim League.

In arriving at this historic decision, there was a rare unanimity between Congress leaders: liberals, socialists, and the hard men of the Hindu right all backed the high command's line. It also had the support of Hindu nationalists in Bengal – the largest Muslim-majority province – who refused to be subjected to "Muslim tyranny" and demanded a partition (ironically not dissimilar to Curzon's partition of 1905) that would give them a homeland of their own inside a divided India.[78] The departing viceroy, Mountbatten, lacked the vision or the will to resist a solution that offered Britain a quick exit from a desperate and dangerous situation. With his particular mix of opportunism and vainglory, he persuaded London to accept the Congress demand for a limited partition, pushed it through, and presented it to India and the world as his own idea.

In one of the great ironies of modern times, Pakistan was as much the product of Muslim aspirations for freedom (for "the Land of Eternal Eid",[79] in the words of the charismatic *alim*, Maulana Bhashani) as of Congress imperatives and the dramatic collapse of British power, and its will to rule India. The Congress party's single-minded unitarism forced a de-territorialised, variously imagined, "Muslim nation" into a "moth-eaten and

[78] Chatterji, *Bengal Divided.*

[79] Uddin, "In the Land of Eternal Eid".

truncated" state. Cyril Radcliffe may have tried to cleave to his remit,[80] but since this was influenced by Congress, in the end he carved Pakistan out like an inexpert butcher from those parts of the empire that the Congress leaders no longer wanted.[81]

Astonishing as it may seem in retrospect, no one expected the carnage that followed. No one anticipated the refugees, the looting, the mayhem, and the massacres. A state and army in the simultaneous process of a transfer of power, and dividing itself into two parts, was ill-prepared to cope with the riots that spread across the Punjab, killing three-quarters of a million people. Contrary to Devji's assertion that Pakistan was intended to be a "Muslim Zion",[82] there is little evidence to suggest that Jinnah expected all of India's Muslims to migrate there, or that he welcomed them, and mounting evidence to suggest that the governments of both Pakistan and India were desperate to stop the tides of refugees spilling over the new borders and engulfing their nascent states.[83]

These upheavals have been the subject of much scholarly attention. Some historians, notably Sekhar Bandyopadhyay, challenge what they see as an overdrawn emphasis on the impact of Partition, overshadowing the moment of freedom.[84] But the evidence for Partition's consequences continues to grow and cannot be ignored. By 1951, fifteen million people had crossed the western border between India and Pakistan.[85] By 1964, another ten million people had migrated between East and West Bengal.[86] Delhi, Mewat, Rajputana, Sindh, Assam, Kashmir, Tripura, Hyderabad (both in the Indian Deccan and in Pakistani Gujarat), Uttar Pradesh, and

[80] Chester, *Borders and Conflict in South Asia.*

[81] Chatterji, "The Fashioning of a Frontier"; and idem, *The Spoils of Partition.*

[82] Devji, *Muslim Zion.*

[83] Zamindar, *The Long Partition*; and Chatterji "South Asian Histories of Citizenship".

[84] Bandyopadhyay, *Meanings of Freedom in Post-Independence West Bengal.*

[85] Khan, *The Great Partition. The Making of India and Pakistan.*

[86] Chatterji, *The Spoils of Partition.*

Kutch were sites of mass migration. Literally hundreds of princely states, from the huge desert state of Bahawalpur to the tiny principality of Dholpur, were magnets which attracted refugees,[87] whose huge numbers are only just beginning to be measured.[88] Stayers-on in their millions, marginalised by political change but unable to move, and impoverished by this concatenation of circumstances, have only just begun to attract scholarly attention.[89]

Research has shown that in a myriad ways refugees drove change. In the Punjab (whose borders were redrawn), government redistributed agrarian land among the millions of peasant refugees, achieving land reforms in this deeply conservative province.[90] In West Bengal, where landed elites resisted reforms for all they were worth, refugees threw themselves behind communist agitations, propelling the communists to power in 1969. They seized and then squatted on vacant land, demanded full rehabilitation as a matter of right, pushing and stretching the vocabulary of "rights" in India's emergent democracy.[91] In Karachi, refugee *muhajirs* were no less militant, organising themselves into a formidable political force that still controls the city's streets and its politics.[92] In Delhi, refugee working women have feminised and commercialised the domestic and residential spaces of the city, subtly but irreversibly changing the structures and rhythms of family life and sociability.[93] In Calcutta they have gone to school and then to college, and joined the ranks of the clerical classes in their thousands.[94] Numerous studies have shown that family size and structure have changed, and changed fundamentally, as

[87] Moon, *Divide and Quit.*

[88] Chatterji, "Alternatives to Citizenship".

[89] Jaffrelot and Gayer, *Muslims in Indian Cities*; Chatterji, "On Being Stuck in the Bengal Delta".

[90] Tan and Kudaisya, *The Aftermath of Partition in South Asia.*

[91] Chatterji, "Right or Charity?"

[92] Ansari, *Life After Partition*; Gayer, *Karachi.*

[93] Datta, "Rebuilding Lives".

[94] Ray, "Growing Up Refugee".

a result. Even caste boundaries have been breached, at least to an extent, in some refugee areas, relaxing to the point where "love marriage" and exogamy have become everyday realities of life.[95]

Unquestionably, the states of South Asia bear the imprimatur of their colonial past – above all in their policies of "salutary neglect" towards public order.[96] But it would be a mistake to overstate these continuities. For good and ill, 1947 ushered in large changes to "the everyday states" of the subcontinent. Partition profoundly shaped and marked citizenship in India and Pakistan, and later in Bangladesh.[97] It framed notions of belonging, and coloured attitudes towards government servants and the state itself. As Gould, Sherman, and Ansari have pointed out, assumptions about the loyalty of officers and men were fundamentally altered by Partition everywhere in the subcontinent, even in its most remote district. Government workers who did not belong to the majority community were particularly vulnerable to charges of disloyalty and corruption, even as popular perceptions of corruption and partiality among bureaucrats grew more commonplace.[98] The discourses of "corruption" and "anti-corruption", Gould notes, were "often used as a means of creating or consolidating social advantage";[99] and in a context where flux and change intensified these struggles for advantage, the discourse of corruption undermined public faith in government itself. It quickly led to a mood of disillusionment and put a dampener on the euphoria of freedom, a mood brilliantly captured in R.K. Narayan's Malgudi novels. This is not to say that the colonial state was not political; of course it was. But the post-colonial state was political in a different

[95] E.g. De and Bhattacharjee, 'Social Consciousness and Fertility Patterns".

[96] Chandavarkar, "Customs of Governance".

[97] Zamindar, *The Long Partition*; Chatterji, "South Asian Histories"; Sherman, *Muslim Belonging in Secular India;* Redclift, *Statelessness and Citizenship*; Pandit, "From United Provinces to Uttar Pradesh".

[98] Gould, Sherman, and Ansari, "The Flux of the Matter".

[99] Gould, *Bureaucracy, Community and Influence in India*, p. 2.

way – the battles to capture its resources were more vocal, often more violent, and were couched in different terms, in which the discourse of loyalty, corruption (and anti-corruption), and group rights played an ever larger part.

The adoption in 1950 of universal adult suffrage was another remarkable and dramatic change in India. (Whether this would have been achievable so quickly without the changes Partition wrought is moot.) As Shani notes, this involved deliberate "ruptures from colonial practice" which had deemed full democracy "impracticable" in Indian circumstances.[100] Bold in imagining "all eligible adults as procedurally equal individuals",[101] with an equal right to vote, India's constitution-makers also made provisions for affirmative action to "uplift" the "downtrodden" scheduled castes and tribes. While scholars identified certain continuities in this approach with colonial constitutionalism and its communal safeguards,[102] many agree that the 1950 constitution, and the rights and redresses it gives citizens, have collectively assumed a status almost larger than life in India's public culture. Rohit De vividly describes how "a document with alien antecedents that was the product of an elite consensus" became "part of the lived experience of ordinary Indians", becoming "the dominant field for Indian politics".[103] The constitution's procedural provisions, which "empower citizens to challenge laws and administrative actions before the courts, and greatly enhance the powers of judicial review", have allowed the citizen to have her say in "an elite conversation". Writ petitions have forced state authorities to defend their policies before courts, and the government has suffered huge reverses in these bruising encounters. The courtroom, far from being a dreary and corrupt site which entrenched the social order

[100] Shani, "Making India's Democracy", p. 85.

[101] Ibid., p. 87.

[102] Bajpai, *Debating Difference.*

[103] De, "Litigious Citizens", p. 4.

and perpetuated "customs of governance" became, De concludes, "the space of the unexpected".[104]

Decolonisation "Beyond the Flags"?

How, in the light of this approach to decolonisation, might one rethink the significance of 1947 as being "beyond the flags"? Perhaps it is best understood as a year of crisis, not as the end of an era, nor a definitive moment in a revolution. Independence and Partition brought in yet another series of complex rearrangements of power – they did not mark a new beginning.

On 15 August 1947, in unseemly haste, the British quit India a year sooner than planned. Their physical surrender of formal rule had enormous significance, not least for "abandoned collaborators" who had to find their way and forge new alliances within new and often hostile dispensations, whether in India or in Pakistan.[105] Princes were the most visible losers. Bullied into signing instruments of accession with the successor states, they gave up most of their remaining powers and were forced into accommodation within the new order.[106] Other losers were Sikhs who were dispossessed of much of their land and many of their holy places by Pakistan: upon their migration to India they had no special status but had to make their way among the millions of other refugees who crossed the Radcliffe Line into India in search of shelter. Other erstwhile allies of the British found themselves wrong-footed by the abrupt departure of the Raj, at least temporarily, until they made adjustments with the new order: old Unionists, for instance, had to come to terms with the Muslim League's power in Pakistan.[107] By and large, the

[104] Ibid., p. 32.

[105] Talbot, "Deserted Collaborators".

[106] E.g. Sherman, *Muslim Belonging in Secular India*.

[107] Osman, "The Politics of the Landed Elite in West Punjab, 1937–58".

collaborating aristocracies of empire found their local standing compromised when the Union Jack came down. Yet lower down the scale, former allies of the British now simply switched allegiance. Landlords, magnates, and mercantile elites, having increasingly hedged their bets, now plumped for the new rulers of India and Pakistan as pragmatically as they had served the Raj in the past. Servants of the state in lesser and subordinate capacities – some of whom had been given the option to serve either India or Pakistan – rushed to serve the "right" new nations. Their support was gratefully received by the Congress and the League, both desperate to restore stability and secure law and order, which depended on having allies and functionaries in place. These new alliances with old allies of the Raj, and the admitted persistence of many imperial "customs of governance", explain the persistence of the "continuity thesis" – the view that nothing much really changed after Independence. This misses a great deal, however, at many levels.

On the wider global stage, the British hoped when they left India to retain informal influence over the subcontinent, and to cement this through the Commonwealth. But in this goal they were largely frustrated. Jinnah was so furious with Mountbatten for his bias towards Congress during the transfer of power negotiations that he rejected the latter's offer to be Pakistan's governor general, taking on that role himself. After the Qaid-i-Azam's death in 1948, Pakistan's governments were "rather grudging and unenthusiastic participants in Commonwealth proceedings", staying in mainly "to keep an eye on India".[108] India was more amenable, but not much. The role of British officers in the first Kashmir war had so infuriated Patel that he asked them all to resign.[109] The sterling balances question was another matter of considerable friction – not only between India and Pakistan, but

[108] Editorial, *Roundtable.*

[109] Dasgupta, *War and Diplomacy in Kashmir.*

between both countries and Britain.[110] Nehru's government, moreover, had a strong anti-imperialist and anti-racist agenda at the United Nations. As Mazower notes, this period saw the emergence in the General Assembly of "an entirely new conception of world order – one premised on the break-up of empire, rather than its continuation." The Assembly proved more unmanageable than the drafters of the UN charters had anticipated. And given the fact that the Security Council, which was designed to keep the Assembly in order, was hamstrung by Cold War rivalries, "for a time, it was more powerful too."[111] India used the Assembly to build the influence of the Afro-Asian bloc against the colonial powers, and also to build up its standing as a leader of the "non-aligned" nations. But British influence did persist in "soft ways", in the Anglophilia of Indian elites, the persistence of liberalism and the endurance of structures of thought embedded in the "colonial knowledge" in which these elites had been schooled. It was only in the 1990s that these really began to crumble against the countervailing intellectual influences of post-colonialism on the one hand, and religious fundamentalism on the other.

While giving "the meanings of freedom" their due, I have argued that Partition and Independence were twinned processes. In Pakistan, freedom and nationhood could not have been realised without a partition; in India, a strong centralised state and a largely unitary constitution could not have been achieved if Pakistan had not been cut out of it. The euphoria and agony of 1947 were two sides of the same coin.

Partition's upheavals, the death of three-quarters of a million people, and the massive migration of over twenty million people across (and millions more within) the new borders simply cannot be discounted in any survey of decolonisation in South Asia. The spatial impact of the migrations had its main focus on the northern

[110] Abreu, "Britain as a Debtor".

[111] Mazower, *No Enchanted Palace*, p. 185.

part of the subcontinent – but this was a vast swathe of territory. Sindh in the west, the Rajputana states, Bahawalpur, West and East Punjab, both parts of Kashmir, Uttar Pradesh, Delhi, Bihar, West and East Bengal, Assam, and Tripura were all in the front line, and were in many ways transformed by the mass migrations of Partition. Peninsular India too witnessed huge migrations when the premier princely state of Hyderabad was annexed and lesser (Muslim) principalities taken over.[112] The research on refugees confirms that there were monied elites and educated middle classes, and most government servants (up and down the social scale) who were given the option of serving either country. Poorer people, with few transferable assets, and tied into networks of dependence at home, tended to stay behind and were pushed into ever deeper poverty.[113] Mass migration created new forms of stratification, and new forms of poverty and powerlessness.

These movements (and countervailing immobilities) are proof that much changed, sometimes under the surface, and sometimes very visibly. The landed *ashraf* elites of North India left their estates and fled as refugees to Pakistan, mainly to Karachi, smaller numbers to Dhaka. In the main, they became service groups in their new country, but their efforts to dominate it did not succeed (or at least not for very long). That was also true of Hindu zamindars and rentiers fleeing East Bengal. Their estates were often grabbed by lesser folk – across eastern Bengal, *bhatia* peasants, who traditionally migrated each year in search of new land, grabbed much of the best land vacated by departing Hindus. In cities across the subcontinent, refugees swarmed into the vacant properties of emigrants, squatting illegally and refusing to move. Their militancy fuelled anti-establishment politics, whether of communism in Bengal, Hindu nationalism in Delhi, or the *mujahir qaum* in Karachi, their voices joining those of other groups

[112] Sherman, *Muslim Belonging in Secular India.*
[113] Chatterji, "On Being Stuck".

who expected much from freedom but who had been swiftly disenchanted by its *jhoothi azadi* (false freedom). Neither India nor Pakistan – simultaneously trying to deliver "development" to their people on a scale never dreamt of by the Raj – were able easily to counter the depth of disillusionment and frustration, which frequently turned into the open resistance of people against their governments. The state structures they had inherited or captured from the Raj were not suited to these new challenges. Small wonder, then, that both India and Pakistan have sought ever greater powers of repression and have developed, despite their differences, ever greater tendencies towards authoritarianism. These developments, too, must be understood to be part and parcel of the "long history" of decolonisation.

References

Abreu, M. Pavia, "Britain as a Debtor: Indian Sterling Balances, 1940–1953". *Economic History Review*, 2016.

Ahuja, Ravi, "'Produce or Perish'. The Crisis of the Late 1940s and the Place of Labour in Postcolonial India", *Modern Asian Studies*, forthcoming.

———, "Lost Engagements? Traces of South Asian Soldiers in German Captivity, 1915–1918", in Franziska Roy, Heike Liebau, and Ravi Ahuja, ed., *"When the War began We Heard of Several Kings". South Asian Prisoners in World War I Germany*, New Delhi: Social Science Press, 2011.

Alexander, Claire, Joya Chatterji, and Annu Jalais, *The Bengal Diaspora. Rethinking Muslim Migration,* Routledge: Abingdon, 2016.

Amin, Shahid, *Event, Metaphor, Memory: Chauri Chaura, 1922–1992,* Berkeley and Los Angeles: University of California Press, 1995.

Ansari, Sarah, *Life After Partition: Migration, Community and Strife in Sindh 1947–1962,* Karachi: Oxford University Press, 2005.

Bajpai, Rochana, *Debating Difference: Group Rights and Liberal Democracy in India*, New Delhi: Oxford University Press, 2011.

Baker, Christopher, "Debt and the Depression in Madras, 1929–1936", in Clive Dewey and A.G. Hopkins, ed., *The Imperial Impact: Studies in the Economic History of Africa and India,* London, 1978.

———, "Economic Reorganisation and the Slump in South and Southeast Asia", *Comparative Studies in Society and History*, 23, 03, 1981.

Bandyopadhyay, Sekhar, *Meanings of Freedom in Post-Independence West Bengal, 1947–52,* London: Routledge, 2009.

Banerjee, Sukanya, *Becoming Imperial Citizens. Indians in the Late-Victorian Empire,* Durham and London: Duke University Press, 2000.

Bayly, C.A., *The Origins of Nationality: Patriotism and Ethical Government in the Making of Modern India*, Delhi: Oxford University Press, 1998.

———, and Tim Harper, *Forgotten Armies. Britain's Asian Empire and the War with Japan*, London: Penguin, 2005.

Beverley, Eric Lewis, *Hyderabad, British India and the World. Muslim Networks and Minor Sovereignty, c.1850–1950,* Cambridge: Cambridge University Press, 2015.

Bhatia, Mohita, "Dominant Discourse and Marginal Realities: Hindus in Jammu", PhD dissertation, University of Cambridge, 2009.

Bhattacharya, Sanjoy, *Propaganda and Information in Eastern India. A Necessary Weapon of War*, Richmond: Curzon Routledge, 2001.

Bose, Neilesh, "Purba Pakistan Zindabad: Bengali Visions of Pakistan, 1940–1947", *Modern Asian Studies*, 48, 1, 2014.

Bose, Sugata, *Agrarian Bengal. Economy, Social Structure and Politics, 1919–1947,* New Delhi, 1987.

Brass, Paul R., *The Politics of India after Independence*, Cambridge: Cambridge University Press,1990.

Brown, Judith M., *Gandhi's Rise to Power: Indian Politics 1915–1922*, Cambridge: Cambridge University Press, 1974.

Caplan, Lionel, *Warrior Gentlemen. "Gurkhas" in the Western Imagination*, Oxford: Berghahn Books, 1995.

Census of India, 1951, Vol. VI, Part I-A, Simla: Government of India Press, 1952.

Chakrabarty, Bidyut, "Political Mobilization in the Localities: The 1942 Quit India Movement in Midnapur", *Modern Asian Studies*, 26, 4, 1992.

Chakrabarty, Dipesh, "Introduction", in Dipesh Chakrabarty, Rochona Majumdar, and Andrew Sartori, *From the Colonial to the Post-Colonial. India and Pakistan in Transition*, New Delhi: Oxford University Press, 2007.

Chandavarkar, Rajnarayan, "Customs of Governance? Colonialism and Democracy in Twentieth Century India", *Modern Asian Studies*, 41, 3, 2007.

———, *Imperial Power and Popular Politics*, Cambridge: Cambridge University Press, 1998.

Chatterji, Joya, "Alternatives to Citizenship at the End of Empire", B.R. Nanda Memorial Lecture, New Delhi, December 2015.

———, *Bengal Divided. Hindu Communalism and Partition, 1932–1947*, Cambridge: Cambridge University Press, 1985.

———, "On Being Stuck in the Bengal Delta: Immobility in the 'Age of Migration'", *Modern Asian Studies* (Special Issue: *New Directions in Social and Economic History*), March 2017.

———, "Right or Charity? The Debate over Relief and Rehabilitation in West Bengal, 1947–1950", in S. Kaul, ed., *The Partitions of Memory. The Afterlife of the Division of India*, Delhi: Permanent Black, 2001.

———, "South Asian Histories of Citizenship, 1946–1970", *The Historical Journal*, 55, 4, December 2012.

———, "The Fashioning of a Frontier: The Radcliffe Line and Bengal's Border Landscape", *Modern Asian Studies*, 33, 1, 1999.

———, *The Spoils of Partition, Bengal and India, 1947–1967*, Cambridge: Cambridge University Press, 1995.

Chattha, Ilyas, *Partition and Locality: Violence, Migration, and Development in Gujranwala and Sialkot 1947–1961*, Karachi: Oxford University Press, 2011.

Chester, Lucy, *Borders and Conflict in South Asia. The Radcliffe Boundary Commission and the Partition of Punjab*, Manchester: Manchester University Press, 2009.

Copland, Ian, "The Further Shores of Partition: Ethnic Cleansing in Rajasthan, 1947", *Past and Present*, August 1998.

Damodaran, Vinita, *Broken Promises: Popular Protest, Indian Nationalism and the Congress Party in Bihar, 1935–1946*, New York: Oxford University Press, 1992.

Dasgupta, C., *War and Diplomacy in Kashmir, 1947–48*, Delhi: Sage, 2002.

Datta, Anjali Bhardwaj, "Rebuilding Lives, Redefining Spaces: Women in Post-Colonial Delhi", PhD Dissertation, University of Cambridge, 2014.

De, Rohit, "Litigious Citizens: Constitutional Law, Everyday Life and the Making of the Indian Republic", PhD thesis, University of Princeton, 2013.

De, S.L., and A.K. Bhattacharjee, "Social Consciousness and Fertility Patterns of the Refugee Settlers in the Sundarbans", National Library, Calcutta, *c.* 1974.

Deshpande, Anirudh, "Hopes and Disillusionment: Recruitment, Demobilization and the Emergence of Discontent in the Indian Armed Forces after the Second World War", *Indian Economic and Social History Review*, 32, 2, 1996.

———, "Sailors and the Crowd: Popular Protest in Karachi, 1946", *Indian Economic and Social History Review*, 26, 1, 1989.

Devji, Faisal, *Muslim Zion. Pakistan as a Political Idea*, London: Hurst, 2013.

Dewey, Clive, "The End of the Imperialism of Free Trade: The Eclipse of the Lancashire Lobby and the Concession of Fiscal Autonomy to India", in Clive Dewey and A.G. Hopkins, ed., *The Imperial Impact: Studies in the Economic History of Africa and India*, London, 1978.

Dhulipala, Venkat, *Creating a New Medina. State Power, Islam and the Quest for Pakistan in Late-Colonial North India*, Delhi: Cambridge University Press, 2015.

Editorial, *Roundtable. The Commonwealth Journal of International Affairs*, 89, 354, 2000.

Furnivall, J.S., *Netherlands India. A Study of a Plural Economy*, Cambridge: Cambridge University Press 1939.

Gallagher, John, and Anil Seal, "Britain and India between the Wars", *Modern Asian Studies*, 15, 3, 1981.

Gayer, Laurent, *Karachi: Ordered Disorder and the Struggle for the City*, Oxford: Oxford University Press, 2014.

Giuliani, Erin M., "Strangers in the Village? Colonial Policing in Rural Bengal, 1861 to 1892", *Modern Asian Studies*, vol. 49, no. 5, September 2015.

Goswami, Manu, *Producing India. From Colonial Economy to National Space*, Chicago: University of Chicago Press, 2004.

Gould, William, *Bureaucracy, Community and Influence in India. Society and the State, 1930s–1960s*, Abingdon: Routledge, 2011.

———, Taylor C. Sherman, and Sarah Ansari, "The Flux of the Matter: Loyalty, Corruption and the 'Everyday State' in the Post-Partition Government Services of India and Pakistan", *Past and Present*, 219, May 2013.

Ibrahim, Farhana, *Settlers, Saints and Sovereigns: An Ethnography of State Formation in Western India*, Abingdon: Routledge, 2008.

Jackson, Ashley, "The Evolution and Use of British Imperial Military Formations", in Alan Jeffreys and Patrick Rose, ed., *The Indian Army, 1939–47, Experience and Development*, Farnham: Ashgate, 1988.

Jaffrelot, Christophe, and Laurent Gayer, *Muslims in Indian Cities: Trajectories of Marginalisation*, New York: Columbia University Press, 2011.

Jalal, Ayesha, *Democracy and Authoritarianism in South Asia: A Comparative and Historical Perspective*, Cambridge: Cambridge University Press, 1995.

———, *The Sole Spokesman. Jinnah, the Muslim League and the Demand for Pakistan*, Cambridge: Cambridge University Press, 1984.

Jeffery, Keith, "India After the First World War", *Modern Asian Studies*, 15, 3, 1981.

Kamtekar, Indivar, "A Different War Dance: State and Class in India, 1939–1945", *Past and Present*, 2002.

———, "The Shiver of 1942", *Studies in History*, 18, 1, n.s., (2002).

Khan, Yasmin, *The Great Partition. The Making of India and Pakistan*, London: Yale University Press, 2007.

———, *The Raj at War. A People's History of India's Second World War*, London: Penguin Random House, 2015.

Kothari, Rita, *Memories and Movements: Borders and Communities in Banni, Kutch, Gujarat*, Hyderabad: Orient Blackswan, 2013.

Mansergh, Nicholas, E. W. R. Lumby and Penderel Moon, *The Transfer of Power*, 12 vols, London: *HMSO*, 1970–1982.

Markovits, Claude, *Indian Business and National Politics 1931–39. The Indigenous Capitalist Party and the Rise of the Congress Party*, Cambridge: Cambridge University Press, 1985.

Mayaram, Shail, *Resisting Regimes: Myth, Memory and the Shaping of a Muslim Identity*, New Delhi: Oxford University Press, 2000.

Mazower, Mark, *No Enchanted Palace. The End of Empire and the Ideological Origins of the United Nations*, Princeton: Princeton University Press, 2009.

Mazumder, Rajit K., *The Indian Army and the Making of Punjab*, New Delhi: Permanent Black, 2003.

Moon, Penderel, *Divide and Quit. An Eyewitness Account of the Partition of India*, 1962; rpntd New Delhi: Oxford India Paperbacks, 1998.

Moore, R.J., *Escape from Empire. The Attlee Government and the Indian Problem*, Oxford: Clarendon Press, 1983.

Nair, Janaki, *Mysore Modern. Rethinking the Region Under Princely Rule*, Minneapolis: University of Minnesota, 2011.

Nair, Neeti, *Changing Homelands. Hindu Politics and the Partition of India*, Cambridge Mass: Harvard University Press, 2011.

Nehru, Jawaharlal, *The Discovery of India*, New Delhi: Penguin, 1960.

Nicolson, Nigel, ed., *Harold Nicolson, Diaries and Letters, 1930–1967*, London: Collins, 1967, rpntd New York: Atheneum, 1980.

Omissi, David, *Indian Voices of the Great War, Soldiers' Letters, 1914–18*, New York and Hampshire: Palgrave MacMillan, 1999.

Osman, Newal, "The Politics of the Landed Elite in West Punjab, 1937–58", Cambridge University doctoral dissertation, 2011.

Pandit, Aishwarya, "From United Provinces to Uttar Pradesh", Cambridge University doctoral dissertation, 2014.

Pandey, Gyanendra, ed., *The Indian Nation in 1942*, Calcutta: K.P. Bagchi and Sons, 1988.

Ramnath, Maia, *Haj to Utopia. How the Ghadar Movement Charted Global Radicalism and Attempted to Overthrow the British Empire*, Berkeley: University of California Press, 2011.

Ramusack, Barbara N., *The Indian Princes and Their States. The New Cambridge History of India*, III.6, Cambridge: Cambridge University Press, 2004.

———, *The Princes of India in the Twilight of Empire. Dissolution of a Patron–Client System, 1914–1939*, Columbus: Ohio State University Press, 1978.

Ray, Manas, "Growing Up Refugee: On Memory and Locality", *History Workshop Journal*, vol. 53, 1, 1 January 2002.

Redclift, Victoria, *Statelessness and Citizenship: Camps and the Creation of Political Space*, Abingdon: Routledge, 2013.

Roy, Kaushik, *War and Society in Colonial India, 1807–1945*, New Delhi: Oxford University Press, 2010.

Sarkar, Sumit, "Popular Movements and National Leadership, 1945–1947", *Economic and Political Weekly*, 17, 14/16, 1982.

Shani, Ornit, "Making India's Democracy. Rewriting the Bureaucratic Imagination in the Preparation of the First Elections", *Comparative Studies of South Asia, Africa and the Middle East*, 36, 1, 2016.

Sherman, Taylor C., "Migration, Citizenship and Belonging in Hyderabad (Deccan), 1946–1956", *Modern Asian Studies*, 45, 2011.

———, *Muslim Belonging in Secular India: Negotiating Citizenship in Postcolonial Hyderabad*, Cambridge: Cambridge University Press, 2015.

———, *State Violence and Punishment in India*, Abingdon: Routledge, 2010.

Shil, Partha Pratim, "Police Labour and State-formation in Bengal *c.*1860 – *c.*1950", PhD dissertation, University of Cambridge, 2016.

Shipway, Martin, *Decolonization and its Impact. A Comparative Approach to the End of Colonial Empires*, Oxford: Blackwell, 2008.

Singh, Anita Inder, *The Origins of the Partition of India, 1936–1947,* Delhi: Oxford University Press, 1987.

Singh, Gajendra, *The Testimonies of Indian Soldiers and the Two World Wars: Between Self and Sepoy*, London and New York: Bloomsbury, 2014.

Singha, Radhika, "Finding Labour from India for the War in Iraq: The Jail Porter", *Comparative Studies in Society and History*, 49, 2, 2007.

———, "The Short Career of the Indian Labour Corps in France, 1917–1919", *International Journal of Labor and Working Class History*, 87, Spring 2015.

Tan, Tai Yong, and Gyanesh Kudaisya, *The Aftermath of Partition in South Asia*, Abingdon: Routledge, 2000.

Uddin, Layli, "In the Land of Eternal Eid: Maulana Bhashani and the Political Mobilisation of Peasants and Lower-Class Urban Workers in East Pakistan, *c.* 1930s–1971", PhD dissertation, Royal Holloway, University of London, 2015.

Verkaaik, Oskar, *Migrants and Militants: Fun and Urban Violence in Pakistan*, Princeton: Princeton University Press, 2004.

Wavell, Lord Archibald, *Other Men's Flowers: An Anthology of Poetry*, 1944; rpntd London: J. Cape, 1977.

Zamindar, Vazira Fazila-Yacoobali, *The Long Partition and the Making of Modern South Asia: Refugees, Boundaries, Histories*, New York: Columbia University Press, 2007.

2

The Fashioning of a Frontier

The Radcliffe Line and Bengal's Border Landscape 1947–1952

THE PARTITION OF INDIA is customarily described in surgical metaphors as an operation, an amputation, a vivisection, or a dismemberment.[1] By extension, the new borders created in 1947 are often thought of as incision scars.[2]

At first sight, it seems unremarkable that this surgical imagery has been so central to the way in which the process of Partition has been represented. It is consistent with the British portrayal of their position in these events as one of clinical detachment. It also complements the anthropomorphic conception of the nation

[1] An early version of the first part of this article was presented (in absentia) at the South Asian Studies Conference in Copenhagen in August 1996. I am grateful for comments on that paper, as also for the critical suggestions on this version by Tanika Sarkar, Anil Seal, and Samita Sen.

[2] Medical and surgical analogies have been used to describe Partition ever since 1947. In fact, Jinnah first spoke of it thus in a meeting with Mountbatten in April 1947: "It would have to be a surgical operation." (Mountbatten replied, "An anaesthetic is required before the operation.") Campbell-Johnson, *Mission with Mountbatten*, p. 57. In 1969, Hodson described Partition as "a period of dissection", another variation on the surgical theme. See Hodson, *The Great Divide*, pp. 322–55. It was also very common to talk of communal violence as blood-letting, another expression that harks back to an earlier era of medicine.

(as mother) that was evoked so often in Indian nationalist discourse. From the standpoint of the independent Indian state, moreover, it is easy to see why it has been convenient to depict Pakistan as a diseased limb that had to be sacrificed for the health of the national body-politic.

The surgical analogy is, however, as misleading as it is vivid. For one, the deployment of medical phraseology has lent weight to the impression that Partition was a necessary part of a process of healing: that it was a surgical solution to the communal disease. Fifty years on, it is clear that Partition has not cured the subcontinent of communalism and the idea that Partition was a remedy has been widely challenged. The surgical metaphor suggests, furthermore, that Partition was something done to India: that she was the passive object of the surgeon's knife and therefore not responsible for the act or its consequences. This has accorded well with the nationalist version of Partition, which has been content to hold the British policy of divide and rule (and Jinnah's collusion with it) responsible for the events of 1947. Recent research has shown, however, that India's nationalist leaders were actively involved in the Partition and their agency and culpability in the tragic events of 1947 are increasingly coming to be recognised.

But there are other implications of thinking of Partition in this way, some of which have not seriously been questioned. One outcome has been the tendency to view Partition as a single definitive act, a clean-cut vivisection that was executed – with clinical precision – at a single stroke. By 17 August 1947, when Radcliffe announced his award, the operation is thought to have been concluded, all loose ends tied up. But in fact, as we shall see, Partition was a messy and long-drawn-out process. It was in no sense finally or tidily concluded in August 1947; indeed, one could argue that the process had just begun, and that it is still unfinished today.

The surgical metaphor has also supported the idea that the actual business of drawing the borderline was a technical affair informed by detailed specialist knowledge, just as the work of a surgeon is based upon specialist scientific knowledge. This could hardly contrast more sharply with the facts. Sir Cyril Radcliffe, author of the Boundary Awards, was a rank outsider to India. He had no background in Indian administration, nor any prior experience of adjudicating disputes of this sort.[3] If his appointment to the position of Chairman of the Boundary Commissions did not generate controversy it was because it was a tradition in British Indian civil administration to confer the most responsible and prestigious jobs upon the "confident amateur" rather than the "narrow technician".[4]

It does not follow from this, however, that the actual business of Partition was merely a matter of sorting out the administrative details once the politicians had made all the important decisions. Those who "implemented" Partition may have been, in their own eyes, disinterested professionals who simply carried out their orders to the best of their ability, who did their job in the best traditions of administrative professionalism – rationally, carefully,

[3] Sir (later Viscount) Cyril John Radcliffe (1899–1977) was, by 1938, "the outstanding figure at the Chancery bar". His "meteorical [*sic*] legal career" was interrupted only by the Second World War, when he joined the Ministry of Information, becoming its director general in 1941. This had been his only experience of administration when, in 1947, he was called upon to chair the boundary commissions in India. Subsequently, however, he chaired so many public enquiries in Britain that one critic was led to denounce "Government by Radcliffery"! Blake and Nicholls, *The Dictionary of National Biography 1971–1980*, pp. 696–7.

[4] In his discussion of the Indian Civil Service tradition, Potter observes that "the whole structure of the Raj celebrated generalist control and continuity, not specialist expertise and innovation." He argues that "the amateur ideal was linked to the older idea of a man of leisure, with the time and ability to engage in a wide variety of pursuits that were unremunerative. The professional, by contrast, was a narrow specialist paid for his technical skills . . ." See Potter, *India's Political Administrators*, pp. 34, 74–5.

and deliberately, without fear or favour.[5] Because they regarded themselves as non-partisan, it has been assumed that the process by which they partitioned India was apolitical. This assumption has bolstered the prevailing impression that while politics informed the decision to divide India, politics and politicians had little bearing on the execution of Partition. Chronologically speaking, 3 June 1947, the date of Mountbatten's Partition Plan, is assumed to be a dividing line. Before 3 June, politicians are known to have jockeyed to influence the terms of Partition and the transfer of power. After 3 June, the bureaucrats are believed to have taken over. As a result of this, historians of Partition, all of whom have been interested in the political rather than the administrative issues involved, have tended to end their stories with the 3 June Plan. Few have ventured beyond this date.

Yet the moment one crosses this Rubicon, the picture that emerges could hardly be more complicated. The politics and administration of Partition prove to have been too intricately intermeshed to be neatly separated into mutually exclusive domains. Political concerns were in play at every stage and at all levels of a very protracted process.

The object here is to unravel some of these complexities by looking at the making of the borderline between West Bengal and East Pakistan. The essay is divided into two parts. The first looks at the Bengal border from the top down, at the actual mapping out of the Radcliffe Line through Bengal. By investigating the Boundary Commission and its procedures, it asks how and why this line came to take the precise shape that it did. The second part looks closely at the Bengal border itself, as viewed from the ground. How did a line drawn on a map become a tangible geopolitical reality? How was it institutionalised and administered? How was

[5] The administrators of British India were accustomed to regarding themselves as "agents of justice and effective action, having the fairness and thoroughness to examine facts and the integrity to act upon [their] findings." Raven, *The English Gentleman*, pp. 58–9.

it given legitimacy? How did it affect the people who lived in its vicinity? How, in other words, did it work? The particular emphasis, dictated chiefly by the availability of source materials, is on West Bengal's experience.

I: The 3 June Statement

Before we begin to look at this process, it is worth recalling that certain significant political choices on the form that Partition would take had been written into the 3 June Plan itself. Though apparently leaving the entire question of Partition open, the Plan delimited the parameters within which a division could take place. According to the Plan, the Bengal legislative assembly was to divide itself into two parts, one consisting of the representatives of Muslim-majority districts and the other of the Hindu-majority districts. Each assembly was to meet separately to ascertain whether the majority of its members wished to partition their province. In the event that they did, they were to indicate whether they wished to attach their half of the province to India or to Pakistan.[6] Accordingly, on 20 June, these two provisionally partitioned units met to vote on the question of Partition. The majority of representatives of the Hindu-majority districts voted in favour of the partition of Bengal, while those of the Muslim-majority districts voted against it.[7] On the basis of this vote, it was taken that the will to Partition had been sufficiently established. It was only after

[6] "Statement by His Majesty's Government, dated the 3rd June 1947", *Partition Proceedings* (hereafter *PP*), vol. I, p. 2.

[7] The political background against which these votes were cast is discussed very briefly below. For further details on the political developments that led to the partition of Bengal, see Chatterji, *Bengal Divided.* The provisional West Bengal legislative assembly voted by 58 votes to 21 that the province should be partitioned and that West Bengal should join the existing constituent assembly. At a separate meeting later on the same day, members of the East Bengal Assembly voted against partition by 106 votes to 35. Burrows to Mountbatten, telegram of 2 June 1947, Document No. 278, in Mansergh

this vote that the Boundary Commission was set up to determine the real or final border between the two Bengals.

This procedure had some remarkable features, which become apparent if we consider the process by which the people's will to Partition was assumed to have been established. The vote that was taken to establish their will to Partition had been cast in an assembly temporarily or notionally divided into two parts. Before the Boundary Commission had given its award, there was no knowing to what extent these notional units would match the final shape of the two partitioned states. The Partition vote was therefore necessarily an imperfect one because members of the notional West Bengal Assembly voted for Partition without knowing for certain whether their constituencies would continue to be in West Bengal when the award was finally made. Whether or not such foreknowledge would have made a difference to the final outcome – the majority in the West Bengal assembly deciding in favour of Partition – must remain a matter of conjecture. But it is significant that the procedure for establishing the will on a question of such momentous import was dealt with so summarily.

It is also significant that the two voting blocs were divided, in the first instance, on territorial lines. This is noteworthy because everyone agrees that the basis for Partition was to satisfy a communal demand for autonomy; that its purpose was to ensure, for those who demanded it, a communal right to self-determination. But from the very start of the process of implementing Partition, this principle had to be tempered by a host of other considerations, amongst which territorial questions were paramount. The two voting groups into which the Bengal assembly was divided were composed of the representatives of territorial rather than communal units: Hindu-majority and Muslim-majority districts, respectively. Hindu and Muslim members were not

---

and Moon, *Constitutional Relations between Britain and India: The Transfer of Power 1942–1947* (hereafter *TP*), vol. XI.

invited to meet separately to determine their collective communal will on what was, in its primary form, a communal question. There is little doubt that the result of the voting (Hindus voting aye and Muslims nay) would have been the same. But it is interesting that the option of a communal vote was not raised by any of the parties concerned.

By this stage, therefore, the parties appear to have accepted that communal autonomy was to be realised by the creation of separate territorial sovereignties. There are subtle but significant differences between the notions of communal autonomy and territorial sovereignty. The first emphasises the rights of the people of a community to self-determination, rights which could in theory be achieved within a single state. The second stresses the bounded space within which a community is sovereign, and could be realised only by a territorial separation.[8] The tension between the two concepts is not always apparent but nevertheless it emerged quite sharply when the actual process of division began, as the focus of attention rapidly shifted from the question of how communal autonomy could be realised to the issue of how much territory was to be made available to each state.

The Constitution of the Bengal Boundary Commission

Once the will to Partition had been established in this singular fashion, the next step was to set up a Boundary Commission that would draw up the final or "real" border, on the basis of which power would be transferred to the two dominions.

The establishment of the commission, though on the face of it uncontroversial, reveals some of the priorities of the key players at this stage of the negotiations for the transfer of power. Jinnah had

[8] Indeed, it has been argued that it was precisely this ambiguity that Jinnah exploited when he refused to define Pakistan in precise terms. Jalal, *The Sole Spokesman.*

been in favour of a commission composed of three "impartial" non-Indians, appointed on the recommendation of the United Nations.[9] But his proposal had not found favour with the Earl of Listowel, then Secretary of State for India. Listowel was not only worried that "the Russian and other Slav states [might] create . . . difficulties"; he was also concerned that an appeal to the UN might "suggest that we ourselves had proved incapable of transferring power without recourse to that body . . ."[10] The Congress also opposed Jinnah's proposal, though for different reasons: Nehru feared that going to the UN would cause an unacceptable delay. He suggested instead that "each Commission should consist of an independent Chairman and four other persons of whom two would be nominated by the Muslim League and two by the Congress"; that they should all be "of high judicial standing" and should elect their own chairman.[11] Eventually, Mountbatten accepted this proposal word for word.[12]

The significance of all this lies not only in its demonstration of the extent to which, by this stage, Mountbatten was happy to take his cue from Nehru and the Congress.[13] The fact that the members of the Boundary Commissions were to be nominated by political parties indicates the degree to which party-political considerations were expected to play a part in the commission's

[9] Mountbatten to Listowel, telegram of 9 June 1947, *TP*, XI, no. 120.

[10] Listowel to Mountbatten, telegram of 13 June 1947, ibid., no. 195.

[11] Nehru to Mountbatten, 10 June 1947, ibid., no. 128.

[12] "Minutes of the Viceroy's Eighteenth Miscellaneous Meeting", ibid., no. 175.

[13] Mountbatten had initially agreed with Jinnah, telling Listowel that personally he "could think of no better proposal". Mountbatten to Listowel, telegram of 9 June 1947, ibid., no. 120. But he did a volte-face as soon as Nehru made his objections known. No doubt the arrangement recommended by Nehru suited his strategy better: it would give an Indian gloss to the commission while ensuring that the effective deciding voice would be that of an "independent" (non-Indian) chairman in whose appointment the viceroy should confidently expect to have a say.

findings. No one at the time appeared to have any doubt that the work of the commissions was *not* going to be simply technical. In the circumstances, the fact that the commissioners were to be judges of the highest standing was neither here nor there.

If the impartiality and professionalism of the commissioners had already been vitiated by the manner of their appointment, every effort was made to protect the credibility of Sir Cyril Radcliffe, whose name Mountbatten proposed as Chairman jointly of the Bengal and Punjab Boundary Commissions.[14] Perhaps one reason for this was that the Congress Party had initially objected to Radcliffe, apparently under the impression that he was a conservative and therefore likely to favour the Muslim League.[15] (Here was another example of the part that party-political bias was expected to play in these events.) Mountbatten took pains to ensure that Radcliffe as chairman "should not only be, but appear to be, free from official influence." He insisted, for instance, that Radcliffe should be housed neither in the governor's residence while at Calcutta nor in the viceroy's house in Delhi and refused to entertain any petitions on the boundary question before the award was made.[16]

None of this, however, appears to have had any effect on what one observer described as "the obstinate popular belief that Radcliffe [would] Award as HE [Mountbatten] dictates . . ."[17] And there are reasons to believe, despite all protestations to the contrary,[18] that this belief was not entirely unfounded. Mountbatten

[14] Radcliffe had been recommended to Mountbatten for the job by the secretary of state as a man of high integrity, legal reputation, and wide experience. Listowel to Mountbatten, 13 June 1947, ibid., no. 182.

[15] Viceroy's Personal Report No. 10, 27 June 1947, ibid., no. 369.

[16] Abbott to I.D. Scott, telegram of 5 July 1947, ibid., no. 529.

[17] Major Short to Stafford Cripps, 3 August 1947, ibid., no. 326.

[18] See, for instance, Alan Campbell-Johnson's defence of Mountbatten's "honour" in his *Mission with Mountbatten*, p. 308; also Hodson, *The Great Divide*, pp. 352–5.

did not influence the fine print of the award but he undoubtedly inspired some of its broader features. For one thing, it was Mountbatten's idea that Radcliffe should chair both commissions with the idea that a single chairman would keep the larger picture in mind.[19] No doubt with an eye to enhancing the palatability of the awards, he went so far as to advise Radcliffe to compensate each party's gains on one border with losses on the other.[20] So, although the two commissions were intended to be entirely independent, in fact they were not. This brought into play the prospect of a quid pro quo between Bengal and Punjab.

Radcliffe subsequently insisted that he paid no heed to Mountbatten's advice and treated each commission strictly independently.[21] Nevertheless, the parties framed their respective cases before the commissions under the impression that the two awards would be linked, and that some loose principle of balance between them would be followed. This certainly influenced the final contours of both borders.

It is also true that Mountbatten, by and large, left Radcliffe to interpret his own terms of reference.[22] But the terms themselves

[19] The suggestion that Radcliffe should chair both commissions first came from Jinnah. Record of meeting between Jinnah and Mountbatten, 23 June 1947, *TP*, XI, no. 311. Mountbatten was quick to take it up, explaining that one chairman could usefully make adjustments of losses and gains between the two borders. Meeting of the Special Committee of the Indian Cabinet, 26 June 1947, ibid., no. 354.

[20] Hodson, *The Great Divide*, p. 355.

[21] Ibid., pp. 354–5.

[22] With some notable exceptions: on the question of whether only those districts of Assam contiguous to Sylhet were to be considered for transfer to East Bengal, or whether all Muslim-majority areas in Assam be considered for transfer, Mountbatten informally advised Radcliffe in favour of the former interpretation, though he refused to give a ruling on the matter. Abell to Radcliffe, 2 August 1947, *TP*, XII, no. 318 (enclosure); no. 326. This drastically limited the scope for the transfer of territories from Assam to East Bengal. It has also been revealed by Christopher Beaumont, who acted

were set out by the viceroy, who once again saw fit to accept Nehru's advice on the subject. Nehru was clear that the work of the Boundary Commission was to be done as quickly as possible, believing (with characteristic naiveté) that "when the two States have been formed, those States will mutually consider modifications and variations of their frontiers so that a satisfactory arrangement is reached" and that "this was likely to be a fairly lengthy process involving the ascertainment of the wishes of the people concerned in those areas."[23] If, he argued, this was left to the Boundary Commission, its work would be "heavy and prolonged",[24] making it unlikely that the borders would be defined by 15 August. In these circumstances, the transfer of power would either have to be delayed or be carried out on the basis of the existing notional boundaries. Nehru was convinced that both these options were unacceptable and that, for the purpose of transferring power, a makeshift border would do. Mountbatten (at least on the face of it) agreed with him. So, when Nehru suggested that the Boundary Commission be instructed only "to demarcate the boundaries of the two parts of Bengal on the basis of ascertaining contiguous majority areas of Muslims and non-Muslims", taking "into account other factors",[25] Mountbatten accepted Nehru's

---

as private secretary to Radcliffe, that Mountbatten (allegedly under pressure from Nehru) persuaded Radcliffe to change the Punjab borderline in India's favour, so that Ferozepur tehsil was awarded to India instead of Pakistan. Statement by Christopher Beaumont (1989), Appendix VI, in Khan, *The Rediscovery of India*.

[23] Nehru to Mountbatten, 12 June 1947, *TP*, XI, no. 158. This was, incidentally, as close as he or anyone else came to recognising that the way in which the people's wishes had been ascertained under the terms of the Plan had been far from satisfactory. Nehru himself did not refer again to the need for any further investigations into the people's wishes once the award had been made.

[24] Nehru to Mountbatten, 12 June 1947, ibid., no. 158.

[25] Enclosure to ibid.

proposal to the letter.[26] The fact that the border was never intended to be anything other than a rough-and-ready improvisation was impressed upon Radcliffe,[27] and the result of his labours bore all the marks of the rush job that it was.

This insistence on speed flew in the face of the administrators' advice. The clearest warning came from Evan Jenkins, governor of Punjab, a man who was often described as being the best administrator in India. His assessment was that "in the time available it [would] be quite impossible to make a clean job of Partition, and even if . . . disorder [were checked] up to 15 August . . . there [would] be appalling confusion [afterwards] . . ." Making a pointed reference to Mountbatten's ignorance of civilian (as opposed to military) affairs, he stressed that "in civil administration, certain things cannot be done in a matter of days or weeks, and 'standstill' orders (most of which will be accepted very grudgingly by the Parties) do not really solve the administrative problem . . ."[28] But his counsel was not heeded by the viceroy, whose entire strategy for Partition appears to have been to rush it through without giving anyone a moment to pause for thought.[29] And the Indian leaders, perhaps tempted by the short-term gains that a speedy settlement seemed to offer, went along with him.[30]

[26] See the "Announcement by His Excellency the Governor General", 30 June 1947, *PP*, VI, pp. 8–9.

[27] Hodson, *The Great Divide*, pp. 347–8; Minutes of the Vicetoy's 54th Staff Meeting, 8 July 1947, *TP*, XI, no. 12.

[28] "Meetings of the Partition Committee," he said, "resemble a Peace Conference with a new war in sight . . . The Chairman of the Boundary Commission does not arrive until 14 July. His colleagues have given the Punjab Government an enormous questionnaire, the replies to which cannot be ready before about 20 July. Thereafter, if all the information is to be studied and transferred to special maps and if the parties are to be heard at any length it is difficult to see how the Commission can report by 15 August . . ." [Punjab] Governor's Appreciation, *TP*, XII, enclosure to no. 81.

[29] For a more sympathetic assessment of Mountbatten's game plan, see Brasted and Bridge, "The Transfer of Power in South Asia", pp. 93–114.

[30] Fifty years on, it is still impossible for the historian (at least for me)

Radcliffe's award was ready on 12 August, well in time for the transfer of power in Pakistan on the fourteenth. But in a remarkable last-minute about-turn, Mountbatten suddenly developed cold feet about publishing it. He brought his influence to bear upon Radcliffe, who agreed reluctantly to post-date the award for the thirteenth, by which time Mountbatten had already left for Karachi, and ultimately the award was only published on 17 August.

We cannot be certain whether Mountbatten genuinely changed his mind upon realising late in the day just how unpopular the award would be, or whether to delay the announcement had been his intention all along. Once again, he ignored administrative advice, this time from the supreme commander of the armed forces. Auchinleck warned that because it was already widely known that the award was ready, the delay in announcing it, by allowing "the wildest rumours" to gain currency, was "having the most disturbing and harmful effect".[31] But Mountbatten's concern to protect his government's image overrode all other factors. As he explained to the British government, although "from the purely

---

to comprehend the mad haste with which these decisions were taken. One might conjecture (uncharitably) that perhaps both the League and Congress leaders were in an inordinate hurry to assume office, or that the Congressmen in particular were anxious to wrap things up while a friendly viceroy, Mountbatten, was in command. A kinder view might be that they were all eager to avert a communal holocaust. Yet with hindsight one can see that in their very haste they hurtled blindly towards the scenario they wished to avoid: for there is little doubt that the Punjab violence was in no small measure a response to perceived injustices and irregularities in the Punjab Boundary Award. One can only share the bafflement of Maulana Azad when he writes: "Why was there such a hurry in taking a decision which almost everybody regarded as wrong? If the right solution to the Indian problem could not be found by 15 August, why take a wrong decision and then sorrow over it? Perhaps also the fixation of a date – 15 August – acted like a charm and hypnotised them into accepting whatever Mountbatten said . . ." Azad, *India Wins Freedom*, p. 226.

[31] Note by Auchinleck, 15 August 1947, *TP*, XII, no. 486.

administrative point of view there were considerable advantages in immediate publication so that the new boundaries could take effect on 15 August . . . it had been obvious all along that, the later we postponed publication, the less would the inevitable odium react upon the British . . ."[32] More personal considerations also appear to have been involved in this decision. By all accounts, Lord Mountbatten was a man who enjoyed pomp and circumstance more than most. So he was particularly anxious that no unpleasantness should mar the transfer of power celebrations in which he would play viceroy for the last time.

For reasons of this sort, power was transferred on the basis of the notional boundaries after all, and the hurry with which the Radcliffe Line was drafted turned out to have been completely – and as we shall see, tragically – unnecessary.

Claims and Counter-claims: The Bengal Boundary Commission

Political imperatives of the statesmen in Delhi and London thus profoundly shaped not only the character of the Boundary Commissions but also the nature of the awards and the timing of their announcement. In Calcutta too, the sittings of the Bengal Commission attracted the keenest political interest. The commission was supposed to arrive at its decision by studying closely the claims and representations put to it by members of the public. But, in fact, constraints of time meant that only the petitions presented by the key political parties could be examined with any degree of thoroughness. Also, as we have seen, the four presiding judges were party-political appointees, so it was only to be expected that their recommendations to the chairman would be deeply partisan.[33] And because Radcliffe arrived at his award

[32] Viceroy's Seventeenth Personal Report, 16 August 1947, ibid., no. 489.

[33] See the "Report of Non-Muslim Members" and the "Report of Muslim Members", *PP*, VI, pp. 29–70, 71–115.

essentially through evaluating their respective arguments, the claims and counter-claims of the political parties had a direct bearing on the final outcome.

The Bengal Boundary Commission's brief was to "demarcate the boundaries of the two parts of [the province] on the basis of ascertaining contiguous majority areas of Muslims and non-Muslims" while also taking into account "other factors".[34] The cases put before the Boundary Commission by the Muslim League and the Hindu "Co-ordination Committee" both used this last ambiguously worded clause to press for the inclusion of territory that could not conceivably have been claimed on the grounds of contiguous majority areas. But there were significant differences of emphasis between the two representations made before the commission. Within the Hindu Co-ordination Committee, inter-party disagreements broke out on the question of what constituted a reasonable claim. There are also tantalising hints of schisms within the Congress Party's ranks on the question of the shape and size of the new West Bengal. These dissensions throw light on the kind of concerns that were uppermost in the minds of the politicians when they lobbied before the commission.

One striking feature of both cases was the language in which they were couched. Both cases were written in a highly legalistic, technical style that could not have been more different from the hyperbole of the communal propaganda generated for popular consumption. Both were persuasive and insisted on the reasonableness of their respective demands. Both were backed with reams of "evidence" and called on "experts" to validate their arguments. The style in which the arguments were presented (and also much of their substance) calls to mind a property dispute being fought in a court of law. In addition, the fact that all the commissioners were judges and the chairman was a lawyer has

[34] "Statement by His Majesty's Government, dated the 3rd June 1947", *PP*, I, p. 2.

bolstered the widespread impression that the award and the cases on which it was based were the product of legal expertise, resting on judicial (rather than political) rationality; and by extension that the commission's rulings met the technical requirements of legal justice. But the picture that emerges from a closer reading of the commission's deliberations is not so clear-cut.

The "Muslim" case was the simpler of the two. For one thing, there was just one party involved; only the Muslim League came forward to represent the Muslims before the commission. The Bengal Provincial Muslim League was deeply divided by this time and the two main factions, led by Huseyn Shaheed Suhrawardy and Khwaja Nazimuddin respectively, were on the bitterest of terms. But these differences did not affect the Muslim League case before the commission, because only Nazimuddin's party took any interest in it. Suhrawardy and Abul Hashim had co-authored a proposal for a united and sovereign Bengal, independent of both India and Pakistan. Having made public their opposition to the partition of Bengal, the two men were not disposed to sit down to work out the details of a division they had already rejected.[35] And for obvious reasons, Congress-minded Muslims (such as Ashrafuddin Ahmed Chowdhury) who were staunchly opposed to Partition in any form took no part in the Boundary Commission's proceedings. Nazimuddin's group, on the other hand, supported the creation of a single Pakistan: they had opposed the partition of Bengal only because they wanted the whole of the province for Pakistan. Moreover, as the faction with the closest ties with Jinnah

[35] Hamidul Huq Chowdhury, who framed the Muslim League's case, thus recalls: "I did not receive any assistance from . . . Suhrawardy . . . [T]he group represented by . . . Suhrawardy was not on talking terms with me or my group . . . As a result, during . . . the Boundary Commission I was left entirely to my own resource[s] without any assistance or help from the [Suhrawardy] party. Not for one single day did any member of the party of the Ministry take any interest in the Boundary [Commission] proceedings in Sylhet or Bengal . . ." Chowdhury, *Memoirs*, pp. 118–19.

and the All-India Muslim League, Nazimuddin's group could confidently expect to take charge of East Pakistan after Partition and they therefore had the greatest stake in the commission's proceedings.[36] So, at the end of the day, Nazimuddin's party took charge of the "Muslim" case on its own.

But the Muslim case was also simpler in another sense: it had the single objective of extracting for East Bengal as much territory as possible, and to achieve this it insisted on particular principles. The first was that the scope of the term "contiguity" was to be limited to areas *within* Bengal, i.e. that if a Hindu-majority area was not contiguous to any other Hindu-majority area in Bengal it should go to East Bengal, even if it were contiguous to any other Hindu-majority outside Bengal in the Indian union. On this basis, the League claimed for East Bengal three districts where Muslims were a small minority of the population, namely the Chittagong Hill Tracts, Darjeeling, and Jalpaiguri.[37]

The next point that the League insisted upon was that the unit of Partition should be either the union or the subdivision. As the smallest units of administration, it was argued, they were cohesive and integrated in terms of politics and governance and could most easily be divided. Of the two, it favoured the subdivision, which would, it claimed, yield a straighter borderline. The League's spokesmen urged that the communal majority of each subdivision be worked out and that contiguous Muslim-majority subdivisions be allotted to East Bengal. Of course, there was merit in the argument that administrative and political units (such as unions) might have real advantages as units of Partition over *thanas*

[36] For more details on the differences within the Bengal Muslim League on the Partition issue, see Sen, *Muslim Politics in Bengal*, pp. 203–45.

[37] This description of the Muslim League representation before the Bengal Boundary Commission is based on the "Report of the Muslim Members" before the Bengal Boundary Commission, reproduced in *PP*, VI, *Reports of the Members and Awards of the Chairman of the Boundary Commission*, West Bengal Government Press, Alipore, 1950, pp. 71–82.

(police stations), which were merely criminal jurisdictions. But the point was more that a division based on contiguous majority subdivisions or even unions would give East Bengal more territory.

In addition, the Muslim League claimed huge territories for East Bengal on the basis of a variety of "other factors". The scope of the "other factors" clause was interpreted most liberally to make a bid for Calcutta. The League insisted that East Bengal must be given a share of the provincial revenue proportionate to its share of Bengal's population, and this could only be achieved if Calcutta went to the east.[38] On these grounds, not only did the League demand for East Bengal the whole of the Calcutta urban agglomeration, it also staked its claim to areas west of Calcutta where jute mills, military installations, ordnance factories, railway workshops, and lines were located on the ground that these facilities were essential for East Bengal's economy, internal communications, and defence.[39]

In effect, the Muslim League was asking for all the territory east of the Hooghly and Bhagirathi rivers.[40] Its representatives knew that this scheme would place roughly two-thirds of the Hindu population of Bengal in East Pakistan.[41] But they insisted that "the Partition [was] not to be effected on the basis of putting the maximum percentage of any class of population on one side or the other or balancing the populations in the two provinces.

[38] It asserted that "The total revenue of Bengal is about forty crores [rupees] of which thirteen crores are . . . contributed by Calcutta alone. If Calcutta goes to West Bengal, the result will be that West Bengal with about one-third of the total population of the Province will appropriate 66.9% of the revenue, while East Bengal with two-thirds of the population will have at its disposal only 33% of the revenue . . ." Ibid., p. 81.

[39] This very loose reading of the "other factors" clause contrasted sharply with the case presented by the judges nominated by the Muslim League for the Punjab Boundary Commission, who insisted on the narrowest possible interpretation of the same clause. See, for instance, the report of Mr Justice Muhammad Munir, 6 August 1947, in Singh, *Select Documents*, pp. 419–20.

[40] See Fig. 2.1.

[41] The exact figure was 66.89%. *PP*, VI, p. 78.

The basis is the determination of contiguous majority areas . . ."[42]

Hence, in order to claim for East Bengal the greatest possible amount of territory, the Muslim members of the commission were driven to insist that the aim of Partition was *not* to ensure self-determination for the largest possible numbers of each community, apparently reversing the Muslim League's proclaimed objectives. Their reasons for taking this position become clearer if it is borne in mind that the party had opposed the partition of Bengal. It had good reasons for this. Muslims constituted a majority of roughly 55 per cent in Bengal as a whole. If Bengal were not divided, a government elected by the Muslim majority would exercise sovereignty over the entire territory of Bengal. The 1946 elections had proved beyond doubt that this would be a Muslim League government.[43] A partition could only serve to reduce the extent of territory over which the League's sovereignty could extend. Once the partition of Bengal had been accepted in principle, the logical aim for Muslim spokesmen was to limit, as far as possible, the loss of territory and assets to West Bengal. By claiming almost four-fifths of the province, they had nothing to lose and everything to gain.

For the Hindu members of the commission, however, the position was not so straightforward. The Hindu members of the provisional West Bengal assembly had voted for a partition so as to secure a "homeland" for the Hindus of Bengal. They had wanted, in other words, to create a separate space within which Hindus, by virtue of their larger numbers, would determine their own future.[44] So it was crucially important to have a homeland with an outright and sizeable Hindu majority. Like their Muslim

[42] Ibid.

[43] The League had won a spectacular victory in the Bengal assembly elections, polling over two million Muslim votes and capturing 114 out of 121 Muslim seats. "Franchise, Elections in Bengal, 1946", File No. L/P&J/8/475, India Office Library and Records.

[44] For more details on the Hindu communal campaign for the Partition of Bengal in 1947, see Chatterji, *Bengal Divided.*

Fig. 2.1: The boundary line proposed by the Muslim League. (The shaded area shows the proposed limits of West Bengal.)

counterparts, on the other hand, they also wanted enough territory to accommodate the population and sustain a viable economy. The imperative for a communal majority had to be balanced against the requirements of space and economic rationality. How much territory was enough? How far could the communal majority safely be watered down? These were questions with no obvious or determinate answers. Inevitably, there were differences amongst the spokesmen for Hindu interests on what constituted the best possible solution.

These disagreements were accentuated by the fact that four parties jointly presented the Hindu case before the Boundary Commission. In addition to the Congress, the Hindu Mahasabha, the Indian Association, and the New Bengal Association were represented on the Central Co-ordination Committee.[45] The barrister Atul Chandra Gupta was appointed by the Congress president, J.B. Kripalani, as its chairman. He also led the Congress camp on the committee.

Differences emerged when the spokesmen of the four parties put their heads together to formulate the case to be argued before the commission. The representatives of the three smaller parties constituted a majority of ten in the twelve-member Co-ordination Committee. They insisted that the maximum possible extent of territory must be claimed. In addition to the ten Hindu-majority districts (Burdwan, Midnapore, Birbhum, Bankura, Howrah, Hooghly, 24 Parganas, Khulna, Darjeeling, and Jalpaiguri), they demanded that two entire Muslim-majority districts (Malda and Murshidabad), large parts of Nadia, Faridpur and Dinajpur, and selected *thanas* in Rangpur and Rajshahi, be given to West Bengal.[46] This would have given West Bengal roughly 57 per cent of the total area of Bengal (minus the Chittagong Hill Tracts, which were claimed for the Indian union but not for West Bengal).[47]

[45] The New Bengal Association was formed towards the end of 1946 to agitate for the Partition of Bengal. Government of [West] Bengal Intelligence Branch (hereafter GB IB), file no. 1009/47.

[46] See Fig. 2.2.

[47] *Memorandum for the Bengal Boundary Commission. Submitted by the Bengal Provincial Hindu Mahasabha and the New Bengal Association*, Dr S.P. Mookerjee Papers, Ist Instalment, Printed Material, file no. 17, serial no. 8, Nehru Memorial Museum and Library (hereafter NMML).

It made sense for the smaller parties, such as the Mahasabha and the New Bengal Association, susceptible as they were to pressure from Hindu extremist fringe groups, to put forward this maximum demand. Indeed, even this maximal claim fell far short of what was being demanded by some of their wilder supporters. The Arya Rashtra Sangha, for instance, insisted that as much as four-fifths of the territory of Bengal be made over to West Bengal, on the grounds that four-fifths of all lands were owned by Hindus; that every single town in Bengal should go to the West because over 75 per cent of their population was Hindu.[48] The New Bengal Association itself was a right-wing pressure group which had come into existence in 1946 as a forum to lobby for the partition of Bengal. Run by a self-styled major general, it was a front-runner in all subsequent campaigns to demand more Bihari areas for West Bengal.[49] Not much is known about the association or its leaders. But its pamphlets suggest that for "Major General" Chatterjee and his friends, Hindu Bengalis were a distinct race of people, and that they were of the view that for this people to fulfil its destiny it was crucial to have enough space.[50] Territory was clearly central to the association's vision of "New Bengal".

The Bengal Provincial Hindu Mahasabha, as a branch of a larger all-India organisation, could not advocate patently aggressive Bengali chauvinism of this sort, however much some of its members may have shared the New Bengal Association's worldview.

[48] Krishna Kumar Chatterjee, Arya Rashtra Sangha: Warning, undated, in AICC Papers, first instalment, file no. CL-14(D)/1948, NMML (hereafter AICC-I/CL-14(D)/1948, and so on).

[49] From September 1947, the New Bengal Association began a vocal campaign for the amalgamation of Bengali-speaking tracts of Bihar with West Bengal. It circulated several pamphlets which alleged that the Bihar government was systematically ill-treating Bengalis, in which it threatened to undertake "direct action" if its demands were not fulfilled. "A Brief Note on the New Bengal Association", 16 December 1948, GB IB file no. 1009/47.

[50] There was a distinctly fascist tenor to some of the New Bengal Association's fulminations. See "A Brief Note on the New Bengal Association", ibid.

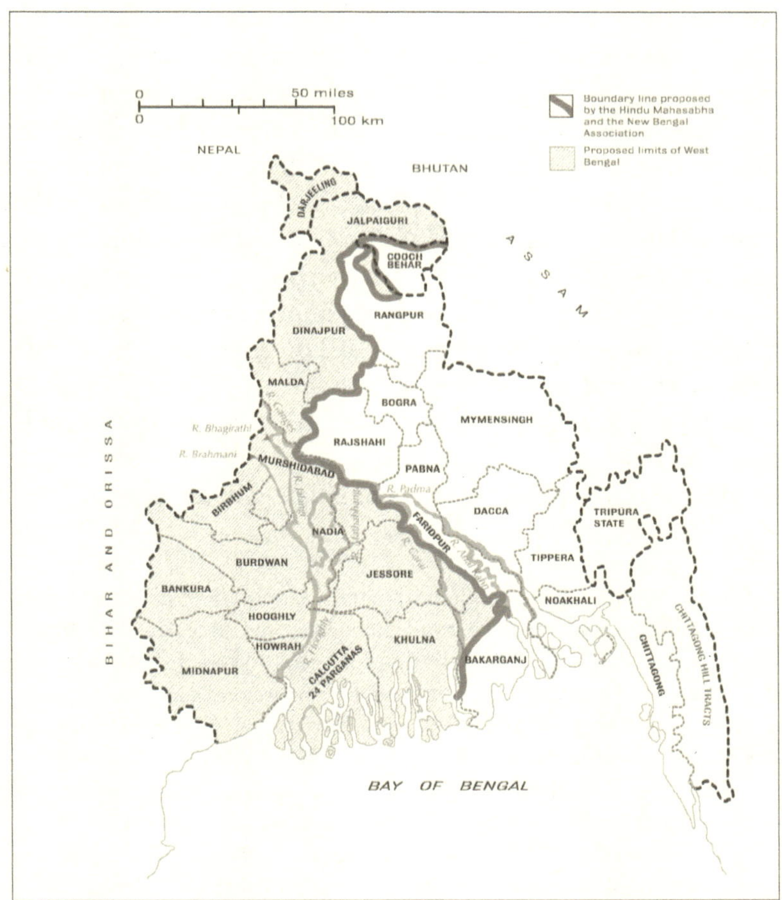

Fig. 2.2: The boundary line proposed by the Hindu Mahasabha and the New Bengal Association. (The shaded area shows the proposed limits of West Bengal.)

But there were other important party-political considerations that pushed the Bengal Mahasabha to make implausible demands for territory. Such inroads as the Bengal branch of the Mahasabha had been able to make in building an organisation were chiefly limited to the eastern districts, to Barisal and Dacca in particular.[51] The

[51] Writing in August 1945 Ashutosh Lahiry, the secretary of the Bengal

party had also worked hard to woo the Scheduled Castes into the Mahasabha fold through *shuddhi* and *sangathan* campaigns in the early 1940s.[52] The largest and most influential of these castes, the Namasudras, were clustered in the districts of Jessore and Faridpur: this was one persuasive reason for the Mahasabha to demand that these areas be included in West Bengal.[53] In the aftermath of the 1946 elections, in which the Mahasabha had been humbled by the Congress, it was understandably anxious to salvage as much of this base as possible. It also clearly hoped to recover some lost ground by winning the allegiance of Hindu refugees from East Bengal, who had begun to arrive in thousands after the Noakhali riots. So it justified its excessive territorial claims on the grounds that "the new State of West Bengal should be in a position to provide for the inclusion and accommodation of immigrants from

---

Provincial Hindu Mahasabha, claimed that there were 1400 branches all over Bengal. Ashutosh Lahiry to Rai Bahadur Surendra Nath Gupta Bhaya, 14 August 1945, Dr S.P. Mookerjee Papers, II–IV Instalment, file no. 90/1944–45. His claim cannot be substantiated, but the party's papers indicate that the most dynamic branch was in Barisal, while those in Narayanganj, Dacca, Sirajganj, Noakhali, Brahmanbaria, Pabna, and Chandpur were active.

[52] For further details on the Mahasabha's campaign for the allegiance of the Scheduled Castes, see Chatterji, *Bengal Divided*, pp. 195–203.

[53] The Mahasabha Memorandum insisted that "all the Scheduled Caste members from West Bengal had voted for the Partition of Bengal and had joined the Hindu campaign for a separate homeland. It is the universal desire of all sections of Scheduled Castes to remain as citizens of the Indian Union. The recognised leaders of the Scheduled Castes have in unequivocal terms demanded their inclusion in the West Bengal Province and declared their unwillingness to join the Pakistan State. For this reason we demand the inclusion of the Sub-Division of Gopalganj which is predominantly a Scheduled Caste area as well as the adjoining territory in the districts of Faridpur and Bakarganj . . ." Memorandum for the Boundary Commission submitted by the Bengal Provincial Hindu Mahasabha and the New Bengal Association, p. 4, Dr S.P. Mookerjee Papers (NMML), first instalment, printed matter, serial no. 8, file no. 17/1947.

Pakistan."[54] Though undoubtedly aware that it was very unlikely to succeed in persuading the Boundary Commission that its demands were fair or reasonable, its leaders probably calculated that it could do the party no harm to try. If they failed, as they almost certainly would, they could still claim to have fought for the Hindu cause until the bitter end. If, on the other hand, they succeeded in winning for West Bengal even the smallest piece of extra area (in excess of the Congress demand), they would come out as heroes who had stood up for Hindu rights, in contrast to the weak-kneed moderation of the Congress.

Atul Chandra Gupta, the lawyer who represented the Congress Party, took a very different view of the Hindu cases. He was convinced that to put forward this maximum demand, which claimed over 57 per cent of the land for 46 per cent of the population, would be suicidal because "no one seriously thinks that it will be accepted by the Commission."[55] It was, he argued, bad legal strategy to argue a case that could so easily be shot down. He held that it was more crucial for the Hindu side to present a patently reasonable case, because it was the Hindu side that had called for Partition in the first place. When the other Hindu parties refused to accept this argument, he offered to put two plans forward. The first, called the "Congress Scheme", outlined the Congress Party's maximum demand. Although it called upon "other factors" to demand a good number of Muslim-majority *thanas*, it still fell considerably short of the Mahasabha's more fantastic claims.[56] The second plan (known as the "Congress Plan") was a

[54] Ibid., p. 2. Indeed, even after the Radcliffe Award was announced, Dr Shyama Prasad Mookerjee continued to insist in parliament that more East Pakistani areas be seized so as to accommodate the refugees in West Bengal, and the issue remained one of the focal points of Mahasabha campaigns at least until the first general elections in 1952.

[55] Atul Chandra Gupta to J.B. Kripalani, 12 July 1947, AICC-I/G-33/1947–8.

[56] So, for instance, while the Mahasabha demanded the whole of Malda

lesser, more plausible claim drawn up strictly on the basis of contiguous majorities. As Gupta explained, the point of having two plans was tactical: he wanted to demonstrate the shortcomings of the Plan to strengthen the larger claims put forward in the Congress Scheme.[57] But the other parties felt this procedure was so complicated and devious that it was likely to fail, and they voted (by ten votes to two) to include only the maximum demand in the final memorandum. Gupta then threatened to resign from the committee.[58] At this point, the Congress leadership intervened: Dr Prafulla Ghosh wrote to Kripalani in support of the chairman's view,[59] Gupta retracted his resignation, and the two cases were presented side by side.

Why did the Bengal Congress dig in its heels, even to the extent of overruling the majority in the Hindu Co-ordination Committee? At one level, the party was merely following its lawyer's advice on the best strategy (and that it was sound advice was proved subsequently when the award was made). But would Atul Chandra Gupta's purely technical view of the case have prevailed had there not been good political reasons to support it? Dr Prafulla

(a Muslim-majority district), the Congress scheme did not claim its five eastern *thanas*. Similarly, while the Mahasabha wanted all of Jessore, the Congress asked only for those parts of that district that lay to the west of the River Gorai. In Rajshahi, the Mahasabha asked for three *thanas*, the Congress scheme asked for only one: namely Boalia. See the Memorandum on the Partition of Bengal presented on Behalf of the Indian National Congress before the Bengal Boundary Commission (filed on 17 July 1947), AICC-I/CL-14(D)/1947–8.

[57] As he explained to Kripalani, his purpose was "to show the defects of the plan to strengthen our argument for adopting the Scheme of Partition . . . this cannot be done by keeping Plan I up the sleeve and bringing it out only after the attack on the Scheme of Partition by the Muslim League and Muslim commissioners . . ." Atul Chandra Gupta to J.B. Kripalani, 12 July 1947, AICC-I/G-33/1947–8.

[58] Ibid.

[59] Prafulla Ghosh to J.B. Kripalani, 12 July 1947, AICC-I/G-33/1947–8.

Ghosh, as chief-minister-in-waiting and as leader of the shadow cabinet, was obliged to take a more responsible position than the Hindu opposition.[60] He was also alive to the security implications of the border and concerned that no demands be made that might jeopardise the safety of Calcutta.[61] But perhaps more importantly, the Congress leadership in Bengal was enjoying its first-ever taste of power. Like the all-India Congress leadership, it could see the logic of cutting out potential trouble spots where its writ might be challenged.[62] It could also see clearly that it was inadvisable to water down too much the Hindu majority of West Bengal, by including large Muslim-majority areas. From the point of view of those who would take over the reins of the West Bengal government, a compact state with a clear-cut Hindu majority would be the best guarantee for the future.[63] In other words, for Prafulla Ghosh and the Congress establishment, a bird in hand was worth two in the bush.

But there were also different sorts of rumblings within the Congress Party. Now that power was at last within reach, it was hard indeed to accept a smaller share in it. Once the decision to partition Bengal had been made, cracks began to surface in the

[60] He explained to Kripalani, "I do feel that it would be wrong not to put [the Plan] [forward]. In my humble opinion the Scheme of Partition can never be accepted. So Plan No 1 should be submitted as a proposal. Unreasonableness of the Scheme of Partition will be apparent and if we do not put this plan before the judges we shall lose our case . . ." Prafulla Ghosh to Acharya Kripalani, 12 July 1947, AICC-I/G-33/1947–8.

[61] As he pointed out, "According to Plan No. 1, the boundary of Pakistan will be 40 miles off from Calcutta. If we demand more than that, we shall have to concede that as far as the Pakistan capital is concerned . . ." Ibid.

[62] For similar sorts of reasons, for instance, there were those in the Congress who were not averse to surrendering Kashmir to Pakistan. Sheikh Abdullah clearly believed that Sardar Patel was amongst them. See the Patel–Abdullah correspondence in Das, *Sardar Patel's Correspondence*, vol. I, pp. 228–45. Also see Chandra, "The National Question in Kashmir", p. 50.

[63] See Fig. 2.3.

alliance that had led the Jatiya Banga Andolan (or the "Bengal National Movement" as the Congress described the movement for Partition it had led). In May 1947, the West Bengal Provincial Committee published a pamphlet entitled *The Origin and Progress of the Partition Movement in Bengal.* The Provincial Committee was a Congress-sponsored body which had been set up in December 1946 at Calcutta with the object of mobilising support for Partition.[64] The pamphlet alleged that in January 1947, dissension had emerged within the committee on the question of the boundaries of the proposed new West Bengal state. The dissidents within the committee had formed the Jatiya Banga Sangathan Samiti, with Jadabendranath Panja of the Burdwan District Congress Committee as president and Atulya Ghosh, secretary of the Hooghly Congress, as secretary. This Samiti lobbied for the *exclusion* of the entire Muslim-majority districts of Nadia, Jessore, and Murshidabad, and also of the Hindu-majority districts of Jalpaiguri and Darjeeling in North Bengal.[65] It also opposed plans to demand the inclusion of Bengali-speaking areas of Bihar in the new West Bengal state.

This fascinating proposal points to the existence, within the Congress party, of minimalist pressures for the creation of a small and territorially compact state that would include *only* the districts of south-west and central Bengal. This is significant in itself, particularly as a counterpoint to the wild claims of the Mahasabha and other parties, and also to the expansionism of the West Bengal Congress in later years.[66] But it is also revealing to look at the particularities of the plan: at what areas it proposed to include and what it wanted to jettison.

[64] Hemanta Kumar Sarkar was its general secretary and Upendranath Banerjee its president. The Origin and Progress of the Partition Movement in Bengal, West Bengal Provisional Committee, Calcutta, 1 May 1947, AICC-I/CL-14(D)/1946.

[65] See Fig. 2.4.

[66] For details on the West Bengal Congress Party's role in the movement for a greater Bengal, see Franda, *West Bengal and the Federalizing Process.*

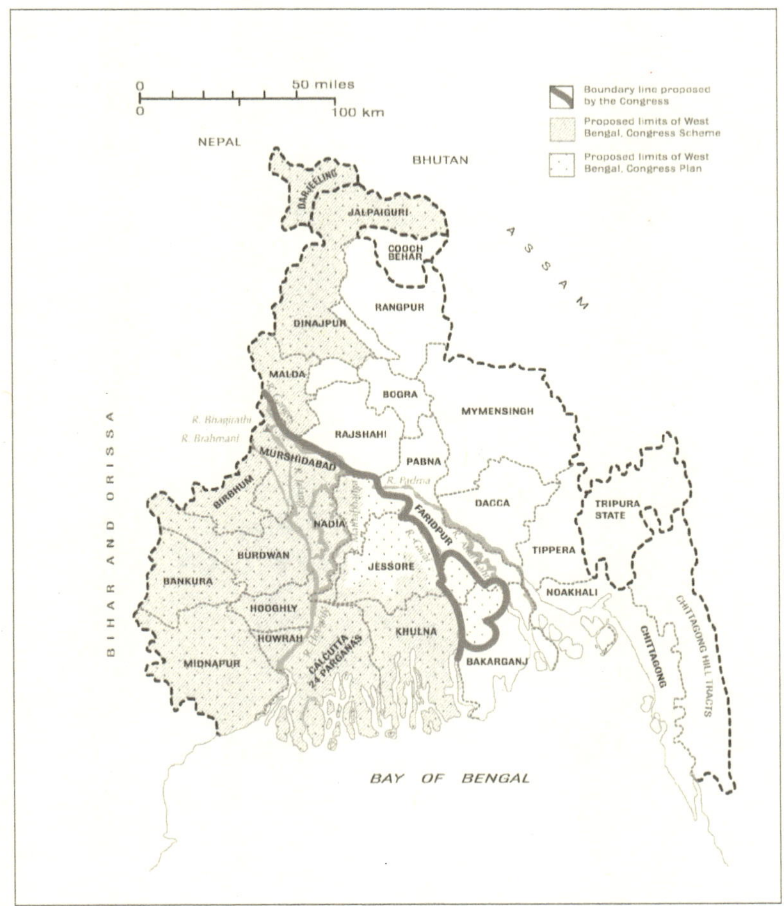

Fig. 2.3: The boundary line proposed by the Congress. (The shaded area shows the limits of West Bengal proposed in the Congress Scheme. The dotted area shows the limits of West Bengal proposed in the Congress Plan.)

The demand to exclude North Bengal was particularly significant. North Bengal was something of a frontier region, ethnically and culturally distinct from the Bengal heartland.[67] It had long

[67] For an excellent ethnography of the area, see Das Gupta, *Economy, Society and Politics in Bengal*, pp. 5–26.

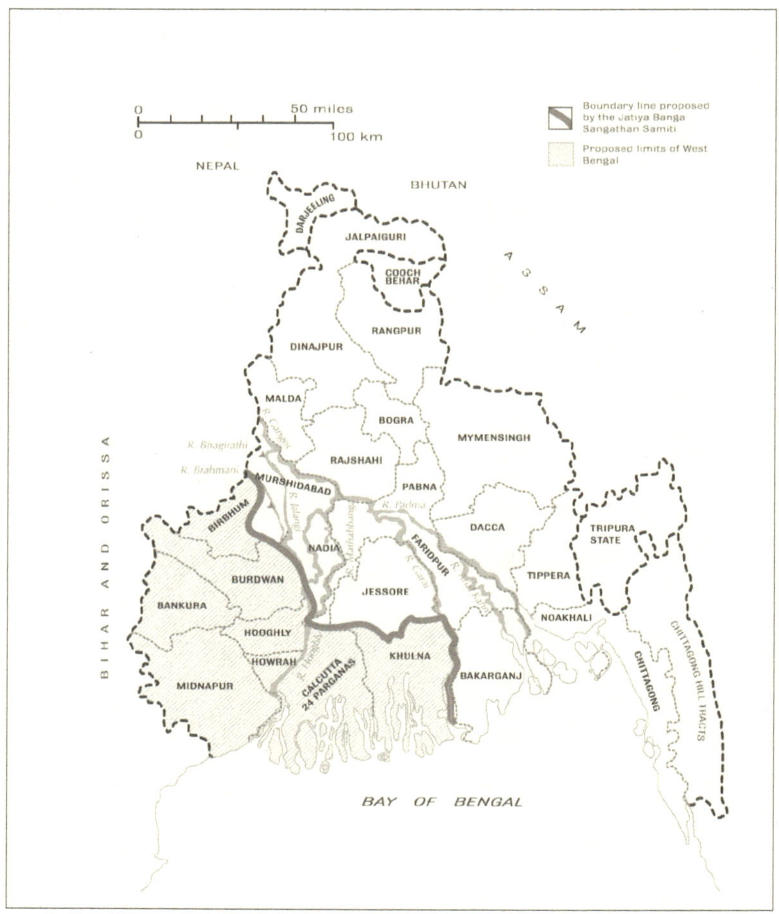

Fig. 2.4: The boundary line proposed by the Jatiya Banga Sangathan Samiti. (The shaded area shows the proposed limits.)

been a political backwater, although in recent years it had been the locus of communist campaigns among sharecroppers and plantation labour. But from the economic point of view, North Bengal was enormously important. Darjeeling and Jalpaiguri produced practically all of Bengal's fine teas and were destined to be key revenue earners for the new state. Indeed, so great was the economic potential of these two districts that neighbouring states coveted them for themselves. In September 1947, there were reports that Assamese politicians were encouraging anti-Bengali movements in North Bengal. In Darjeeling, the Gurkha League demanded independence from West Bengal, allegedly with the backing of Assamese politicians and British tea planters (the latter no doubt could see the advantages of having their estates in the less volatile state of Assam, safe from the communist menace). At the same time the raja of Cooch-Behar began a campaign against Bengali *bhatias* (outsiders), insisting that the autochthonous Rajbangshi tribals of Jalpaiguri and Cooch-Behar had more in common with their neighbours in Assam than with the Bengali babus.[68] If Cooch-Behar could not be allowed to exist as a separate state, he insisted that it must go to Assam rather than to Bengal. Not long afterwards, when the boundary disputes between West Bengal and Bihar began to gain ground, the police reported secret meetings between Bihari and Gurkha leaders, at which they discussed the possibility of Darjeeling's transfer to Bihar.[69] It was plain to all, therefore, that North Bengal was a glittering prize. Yet there were Congressmen in West Bengal who would gladly have thrown it away.

Murshidabad also had a special significance as the site of the headwaters of the Hooghly. It was widely accepted that the survival of Hooghly as a port (and of Calcutta as an entrepôt of trade) depended on its link with the River Ganges, which flowed through the northern edge of Murshidabad. The representatives of all four Hindu parties had therefore insisted that Murshidabad be included in West Bengal, even though it was a Muslim-majority district. There appears to have been an unspoken understanding that if it came to a trade-off, they were prepared to exchange Khulna, a large Hindu-majority district to the east of the 24 Parganas, for

[68] Secretary, Dacca District National Chamber of Commerce to Prafulla Chandra Ghosh, 5 September 1947, AICC-I/G-30/1947–8.

[69] Superintendent of Police (Intelligence Branch), Darjeeling, to Special Superintendent of Police (Intelligence Branch), West Bengal, 15 July 1953, GB IB file no. 1034/48.

Murshidabad.[70] So the Jatiya Banga Sangathan Samiti's case went against the tide of opinion on the Hindu side. If, moreover, these three districts were sacrificed, it would mean that the claim to parts of Dinajpur and Malda (and eventually Cooch-Behar) on the grounds of contiguity would also have to be given up. All in all, six districts (Darjeeling, Jalpaiguri, Cooch-Behar, Dinajpur, Malda, and Murshidabad) were being written off in exchange for one: Khulna. Three of the six (Darjeeling, Jalpaiguri, and Cooch-Behar) had outright, unequivocal, Hindu majorities. What imperatives could have prompted this remarkable demand?

One obvious answer is that Khulna Congressmen were involved in this move. From their point of view, any territorial or economic losses that the state might have to suffer in the future would be preferable to the immediate loss of Khulna to Pakistan. But neither of the office holders of the Samiti was from Khulna, nor is there any evidence that Khulna men were particularly strongly represented on the Samiti. So clearly this was not the only consideration.

It seems very likely that the formation of the Samiti was the first phase in the process by which territorial factionalism emerged as a powerful force within the West Bengal Congress. The notorious fractiousness of the Bengal Congress had not been much in evidence during the 1940s. Once Subhas Bose and his supporters had been expelled from the party, the Congress leadership that had taken over the party had displayed a rare cohesiveness and unity of purpose, particularly during the campaign for the partition of Bengal. But immediately after Independence, groupism re-emerged with a vengeance. For three or four years afterwards, Congressmen in West Bengal would engage in a rancorous contest for control of the party organisation, in which the battle lines were

[70] Murshidabad had a Muslim majority of 56.55 per cent. Atul Gupta, in his letter to Kripalani, insisted that this district had to be claimed for West Bengal "in any event". Atul Chandra Gupta to J.B. Kripalani, 12 July 1947, AICC-I/G-33/1947–8.

drawn on territorial lines. Partymen from the West Bengal heartland (chiefly Hooghly, Burdwan, and Midnapore) would form themselves into an alliance in order to wrest control of the party from the refugee Congressmen from East Bengal who, by virtue of their larger numbers, continued to dominate the organisation after Partition, despite the fact that they had left their constituencies behind in Pakistan. Atulya Ghosh of Hooghly and Jadabedranath Panja of Burdwan were key players in this battle in which the stake was nothing less than the capture of political power.[71] The involvement of these two men in the Jatiya Banga Sangathan Samiti suggests that the nucleus of the new alliance had begun to crystallise well before 15 August 1947. The move to limit the boundaries of the new state to the West Bengal heartland may well have been a pre-emptive strike by Atulya Ghosh, a man whose foresight and ruthlessness would win him the secretaryship of the West Bengal Congress in 1950. By January 1947, when the Jatiya Banga Sangathan Samiti was formed, it must have been clear to him that while nothing could stop the Congress Party from taking office in West Bengal after Partition, it was not clear which Congressmen would seize power in the divided party. If the state boundaries were drawn so as to include only the districts of the Burdwan and presidency divisions in the new West Bengal, Congressmen from these districts would have the best chance of controlling the party and government after Partition and Independence. Atulya Ghosh and the members of the Sangathan Samiti seem not to have been unduly concerned about the fact that such a Partition would involve sacrificing to Pakistan the sizeable Hindu population of six northern districts.

If this is correct, it would seem that canny politicians had realised very early on that the Radcliffe Line would do much more than demarcate the boundaries between two nations. It would

[71] Some details on this struggle within the West Bengal Congress are available in Sengupta, *The Congress Party in West Bengal.*

shape the very contours of control and influence in the divided successor states. It would help to define not only the political futures of political parties in the two successor states, but also of the individuals and factions within the parties that would rule them. The disputes between the Congress and the Mahasabha on the boundary question indicate that their leaders could see that the shape of the border would have implications for the future of their respective parties. Within the Congress, equally, at least some partymen seem to have been keenly conscious of the part which the borderline would play in determining who would capture the organisation.

The Hindu and Muslim cases presented before the Boundary Commission thus reflected concerns and aspirations that had little to do with a communal vision of the welfare of the "communities". In the making of the Radcliffe Award, questions of economic rationality, geographical coherence, and strategic necessity were not the only "other factors" that tempered the fundamental principles of contiguity and communal majority on which Partition was supposed to be based. Party-political, factional, and personal ambitions were also very much in evidence in the list of issues that influenced the final shape the border would take.

To return to the metaphor of the surgical operation, this would suggest that by the time the surgeon had begun his task, the original problem he had been called in to solve had been so overlaid with secondary factors that it had been all but forgotten; or if not forgotten then certainly pushed far into the background.

Radcliffe's Award

These were some of the pressures and counter-pressures that Radcliffe had to weigh while making his award. He had to appear to be even-handed while keeping in mind the imperatives of British policy for the future of the subcontinent. Inevitably, his award pleased no one entirely, but there is little doubt that it displeased some less than others.

The award gave West Bengal an area of 28,000 square miles, containing a population of 21.19 million people of which nearly 5.3 million (or 29 per cent) were Muslims. East Bengal got 49,000 square miles for a population of 39.11 million, of which 29.1 per cent (11.4 million) were Hindus.[72] West Bengal got 36.36 per cent of the land to accommodate some 35.14 per cent of the people, while East Bengal got 63.6 per cent of the land to accommodate 64.85 per cent of the population.[73] These figures make it immediately obvious that Radcliffe accepted the two "cardinal principles" of the Congress case: firstly that the two parts respectively were to contain as large a proportion as possible of the total Muslim and non-Muslim population of Bengal, and secondly that "the ratio of Muslims to non-Muslims in one zone must be as nearly equal as possible to the ratio of non-Muslims to Muslims in the other."[74] Radcliffe's award created two states in which the ratio of the majority to the minority population was almost exactly the same.

Radcliffe also conceded the Congress argument that *thanas* (police stations), as the smallest units for which census figures had been published, were the most acceptable units of Partition.[75] He accepted the Congress argument about the importance of the Murshidabad and Nadia river system for the survival of the Hooghly and gave the whole of Murshidabad to West Bengal. Khulna went to Pakistan except for those parts of it that fell to the east of the River Mathabhanga. It goes without saying that Calcutta went to West Bengal. The tea-producing districts

[72] Chakrabarty, *With Dr. B.C. Roy*, pp. 59–60.

[73] See Fig. 2.5.

[74] See The Memorandum on the Partition of Bengal presented on Behalf of the Indian National Congress Case before the Bengal Boundary Commission (Calcutta, 1947), AICC-I/CL-14(D)/1946; and "Report of the Non-Muslim Members", *PP*, VI, p. 30.

[75] The Memorandum on the Partition of Bengal presented on Behalf of the Indian National Congress Case before the Bengal Boundary Commission, p. 27.

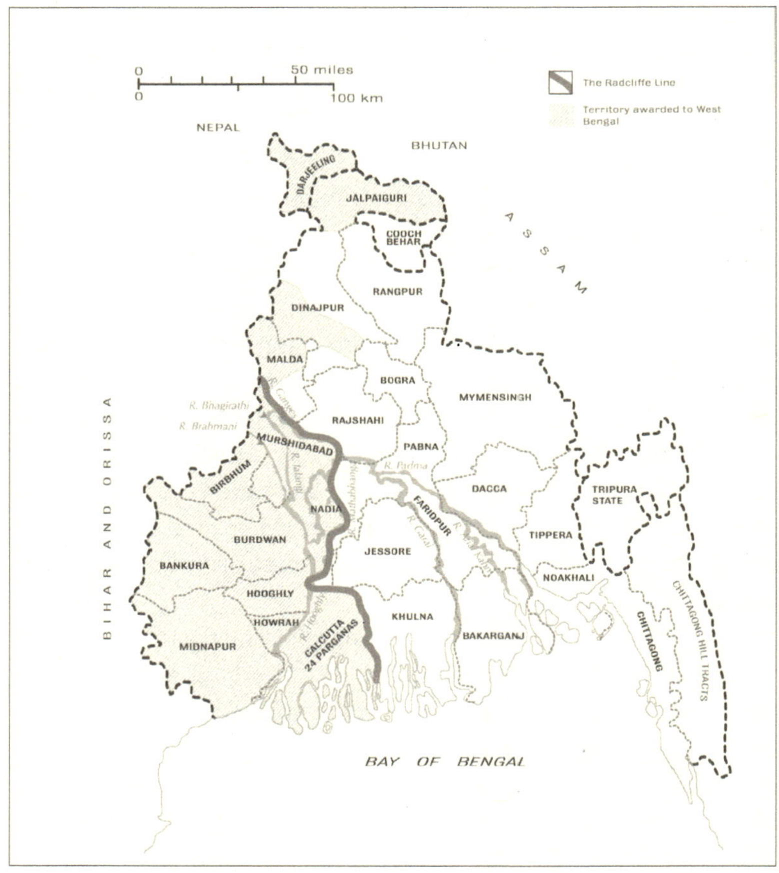

Fig. 2.5: The Radcliffe Line. (The shaded area shows the territory awarded to West Bengal.)

of Darjeeling and Jalpaiguri also went to West Bengal,[76] with the exception of the five Muslim-majority *thanas* of the Boda–Debiganj–Pachagarh area.[77] In awarding these areas to West

[76] "The Schedule", Sir Cyril Radcliffe's Award, 12 August 1947, *PP*, VI, p. 119.

[77] See the telegram from Kaviraj Satish Chandra Lahiry to J. B. Kripalani, 4 September 1947, AICC-I/G-33/1947–8; and Das Gupta, *Economy, Society and Politics in Bengal*, pp. 237–9.

Bengal, Radcliffe rejected the first principle of the Muslim League's case: namely that the scope of the term "contiguity" was to be limited to areas *within* Bengal.

In its broad principles, therefore, the Radcliffe Plan looked remarkably like the Congress scheme. The only major point that the Congress did not win was its insistence that the boundary must be continuous.[78] Radcliffe would not allow this, so there were in effect *two* Radcliffe lines. A continuous boundary would have given West Bengal a corridor connecting the two North Bengal districts with the rest of the province: as it was, the two halves were separated from each other by a substantial stretch of foreign (and for the most part), hostile, territory.[79] This awkward arrangement was not put right until 1956, when the States Reorganisation Committee awarded a narrow piece of Bihar to West Bengal.[80]

Nor would Radcliffe allow the principle of contiguity to be compromised too much: so the *thana* of Boalia in Rajshahi, the four *thanas* in Bakarganj, and the areas of Faridpur claimed for West Bengal by the Congress all went to East Bengal. Despite this, Radcliffe's package was very similar, on the whole, to the Congress proposal. The award placed 71 per cent of the Muslim population in East Bengal and 70.8 per cent of the Hindu population in West Bengal. Had the Congress Scheme been followed in its entirety, the figures would have been 73 per cent and 70.67 per cent, respectively.[81]

[78] See point number two of the "Guiding Rules" set out in The Memorandum on the Partition of Bengal presented on Behalf of the Indian National Congress Case before the Bengal Boundary Commission.

[79] It would have been difficult to justify giving West Bengal a corridor after Nehru himself had denounced Jinnah's demand for a corridor to link West and East Pakistan as "fantastic and absurd". Campbell-Johnson, *Mission with Mountbatten*, pp. 94–6.

[80] *Report of the States Reorganisation Committee*, pp. 174–80.

[81] See The Memorandum on the Partition of Bengal presented on Behalf of the Indian National Congress before the Bengal Boundary Commission, p. 4.

Why did Radcliffe accept so much of the letter and spirit of the Congress Scheme? Was he simply guided by his legal training to accept what was undoubtedly the soundest and best-reasoned case? The award itself, brief and baldly stated as it is, gives no indication of Radcliffe's mind. Moreover, since Radcliffe refused steadfastly to elaborate further upon, supplement, or discuss his awards once they had been made, perhaps we shall never know the reasons for certain.[82] But if it is recalled that Mountbatten had allowed the Congress leadership not only to determine the structure and composition of the Boundary Commissions but also to draft their terms of reference, it is not entirely surprising to find that the commission awarded, to such extent as it did, in the Congress Party's favour.

II: Ambiguities and Errors in the Award

Saroj Chakrabarty, whose memoirs are a key resource for the study of West Bengal in this period, writes that "there was considerable resentment particularly among Hindus, over certain features of the Award."[83] If the Congress had got more or less what it wanted from Radcliffe, how do we explain the extent of discontent with the award in West Bengal? Why is the award remembered as a monument of folly?

Much of the most vocal discontent with the award was specific rather than general: while particular aspects of it were criticised in the strongest terms, the award as a whole was not challenged. This sort of discontent was voiced chiefly by Hindus and Muslims who believed that their particular *thanas*, subdivisions, and districts had reasonable grounds to demand inclusion in West and East Bengal respectively, but who found themselves in the wrong country

[82] Hodson, *The Great Divide*, p. 353.

[83] Chakrabarty acted as personal secretary to three successive chief ministers of West Bengal: Dr Prafulla Ghosh, Dr B.C. Roy and P.C. Sen. See Chakrabarty, *With Dr. B.C. Roy*, p. 60.

after Independence. They belonged mostly to areas immediately to the east or south-east of the Radcliffe Line. So while Muslims in Murshidabad and Nabadwip were furious to find that their districts had gone to West Bengal, the Hindus of the five southern *thanas* of Jalpaiguri protested bitterly against their inclusion in East Pakistan.[84] So did the Hindus who found themselves in the wrong part of Dinajpur.[85] In Nadia, particularly in Meherpur,

[84] A police officer reported that because under the notional division Murshidabad had been included in East Bengal, when Radcliffe awarded the district to West Bengal "underground and open activities started for the inclusion of Murshidabad in East Pakistan . . . [and] communal tension ran high . . ." "Note showing the developments in Murshidabad district since the Partition of Bengal", 1 December 1948, GB IB file no. 1238/47 (Murshidabad). Particularly in Karimpur *thana*, where the Muslims constituted over 80 per cent of the population, "the Muslims . . . had high hopes that their area would be included in Pakistan and as such they had hoisted the Pakistan Dominion flag . . ." Special Superintendent's report, 23 September 1947, GB IB file no. 167/47 (Nabadwip). At a public meeting in Jalpaiguri, the people of Patgram, Boda, Pachagarh, and Debiganj *thanas* demanded the return of their respective *thanas* to West Bengal, if not with Pakistan's consent, then through a UN-sponsored plebiscite or referendum. Telegram from Satish Chandra Lahiry to J.B. Kripalani, 4 September 1947, AICC-I/G-33/1947–8. Also see the memorial by the people of Jalpaiguri and Thakurgaon subdivisions, 27 August 1947, AICC-I/CL-14/1946, and the telegram from Nagendra Sarkar of Pachagram to Kripalani, 30 August 1947, AICC-I/G-33/1947–8.

[85] The president of the Patnitola Congress Committee in Balurghat wrote objecting to the exclusion of the *thanas* of Porsa, Patnitola, and Damurhat from West Bengal so as to tag them on to Bogra in East Pakistan. President, Patnitola Congress Committee to the members of the Boundary Commission, 12 September 1947, ibid. A public meeting in Thakurgaon denounced the award as "highly unjust, unfair and inequitable". "Resolution of the Public Meeting held by Thakurgaon subdivisional Public", 22 August 1947, AICC-I/CL-14/1946. Nishithanath Kundu, MLA from Dinajpur, petitioned the Boundary Commission against the exclusion of five non-Muslim-majority *thanas* from West Bengal, pointing out that valuable sugar and rice mills owned by Hindus had in the process been lost to Pakistan. Memorial by

Gangni, and parts of Chuadanga west of the River Mathabhanga, Hindus took the view that their inclusion in East Bengal violated the spirit of the award itself.[86] But the most trenchant and bitter (albeit partial) attack on the award came from Khulna. Khulna was a Hindu-majority district, covering an area of roughly 4800 square miles to the east of the 24 Parganas. Under the provisional cabinet arrangements it had been included, in its entirety, in West Bengal. Now, after the award, the whole district went to Pakistan in what was widely believed to be an exchange for Murshidabad. This did not, as we have seen, come as a complete surprise: nevertheless, feelings in the district ran so high that even the Khulna District Congress Committee petitioned that Khulna be exchanged back for Murshidabad.[87] Justices Mukherjee and Biswas, the two Hindu members of the Bengal Boundary Commission, were forced to make a public declaration to the effect that no territory had been "exchanged" in the first place,[88] but Khulna's Hindu spokesmen found this denial hard to believe.[89] Murshidabad's Hindu leaders, for their part, reacted fiercely against what they described as the "utter selfishness and lack of perspective" of the Khulna Congress and urged the party leadership to "cry halt to this sinister move".[90]

Nishithanath Kundu and others to the Boundary Commission, 27 August 1946, ibid. The Merchants Association of Thakurgaon also protested at the inclusion of Thakurgaon in East Pakistan. Secretary, Thakurgaon Merchants Association to Acharya Kripalani, 28 August 1947, ibid.

[86] Secretary, New Bengal Association, Meherpur, Nadia, to Acharya Kripalani, 11 September 1947, AICC-I/G-33/1947–8.

[87] Associated Press of India report, cited in Ramagopal Banerjee to Acharya Kripalani, 10 September 1947, ibid.

[88] Ramagopal Banerjee to Acharya Kripalani, 10 September 1947, ibid.

[89] Memorials, resolutions, and all manner of petitions poured in from Nangla, Sujanshahi, Nagarghat, Tala, Mashaldanga, and Sakdali (see AICC-I/G-33/1947–8); from Bagerhat, Kamira, Katipara, and Gangarampur (see AICC-I/CL-14(D)/1946).

[90] Ramagopal Banerjee to Acharya Kripalani, 10 September 1947, AICC-I/G-33/1947–8.

They insisted that any agitation for the modification of the Radcliffe Award must demand territory *in addition to* that which had already been placed in West Bengal.[91] Each aggrieved district and *thana*, in other words, was looking out strictly for itself.

It would seem, therefore, that as the reality of Partition hit them, Hindu politicians east and west very quickly forgot about the putative brotherhood that had inspired their demand for a homeland. But new, equally unattractive particularisms now rose in its stead – suddenly, the district emerged as a new locus of political solidarity. So while Hindus in Khulna resented being "sacrificed" for the Hindu homeland, they were quite happy to demand that someone else (Murshidabad Hindus) be offered up at the altar instead. (The same spirit characterised the Murshidabad Hindu leadership's defence of the new status quo.) It is fair to say that this sort of criticism of the Radcliffe Line was far from being a critique of Partition, or even of the award as a whole. It was the panic-stricken response of people who realised, too late, that they had been shut out of their promised land.

But there were also a number of more general and fundamental problems with the award, which emerged only gradually with the first efforts to implement and administer it. Despite its appearance of thoroughness and finality, the award was surrounded by uncertainty. A good part of this was the result of misinformation.

[91] Powerful Hindus of Murshidabad issued a statement in which they agreed that the award was "unfair, illogical and full of inconsistencies". But they insisted that "any attempt to have an area now placed in the Indian Union exchanged for a non-Muslim majority area placed in Pakistan . . . is bound to encourage rebellious conditions in a number of border districts" and advised the public of East and West Bengal "to peacefully permit the operation of the Boundary Commission's award . . ." Statement issued by Maharaja Sris Chandra Nandy, MLA of Cossimbazar, Dr S.K. Ganguly (president of the New Bengal Association), Dr Radhakumud Mukherjee, Syamapada Banerjee (MLA and Secretary of the Murshidabad District Congress Committee), Bejoy Singh Nahar (zamindar), Nalinakshya Sanyal and others, enclosed in a letter from S.K. Ganguly to J.B. Kripalani, 2 September 1947, in AICC-I/G-33/1947–8.

Most people simply did not have access to the printed document and did not know what it contained.[92] The controversy that surrounded the award, the strong (if localised) campaigns against it, and the confusion about the scope of the Arbitral Tribunal that had been appointed to referee disputes about the division of assets,[93] all created the impression that the award might substantially be amended. For more than a year after the award was made, rumours that this or that district was going to be exchanged for the other fuelled hopes and fears among many people on both sides of the border. A "strong rumour throughout Nadia district to the effect that Nadia and Murshidabad would be included in Pakistan in exchange with Khulna", for instance, was reported to have sparked off panic amongst Nadia Hindus; no doubt it also was the cause of vain hope for Hindus in Khulna.[94] People of bordering areas lived in a state of anxiety, believing that any day they could wake up to find themselves in India where they had been in Pakistan, as part of a majority where they had once been minorities, and vice versa. This wildly unstable equilibrium between the communities strained communal relations to breaking point. The pettiest incidents sparked off brutal killings and the

[92] In his short story "The Champion of the People", the Bengali writer Satinath Bhaduri has portrayed vividly the confusion and uncertainty surrounding the precise terms of the Boundary Commission's Award. An English translation of the story is included in Bhalla, *Stories about the Partition of India*, vol. I.

[93] The Arbitral Tribunal, chaired by Sir Patrick Spens (Chief Justice of the Federal Court), was to make awards on the division of assets and liabilities between India and Pakistan, and on the apportionment between the two dominions of expenses incurred by the Joint Defence Council. It was also to decide "other matters arising out of Partition". It was perhaps this last clause that encouraged hopes that the tribunal would consider border disputes. See "The Arbitral Tribunal Order, 1947", 12 August 1947, *PP*, I, pp. 58–9.

[94] Memo from the Superintendent of Police, Nadia, to the Inspector General of Police, West Bengal, 31 March 1948, in GB IB file no. 1238/47 (Nabadwip).

most unsubstantial rumours caused people to flee their homes in their thousands. For both governments, this became a problem of unmanageable proportions. On 14 December 1948, Nehru and Liaquat Ali Khan signed the Inter-Dominion Agreement in a desperate bid to bring calm to the troubled borders.[95] Both sides agreed to set up a tribunal that would resolve, once and for all, boundary disputes "arising out of the interpretation of the Radcliffe Award". This tribunal, chaired by the Swedish judge Algot Bagge, announced its decisions in February 1950.[96] In it, Justice Bagge interpreted and clarified those parts of Radcliffe's notification which had been ambiguously worded.

The Boundary Disputes Tribunal's decision cleared up some of the doubts and misinformation about the correct interpretation of the award. But there was another whole order of problems that it did not begin to address. Even where there was no room for doubt about what Radcliffe meant, there were still enormous difficulties in first defining and then administering the border.

When he drafted the border line, Radcliffe based it upon physical or natural markers and pre-existing administrative borders. Parts of it were traced over the boundaries between *thanas* and districts, other parts followed the course of large rivers and their tributaries. On paper the result was a clear and tidy line.

[95] Proceedings of the Inter-Dominion Conference held at Calcutta, 15–18 April 1948, Government of West Bengal Home (Political) Department Confidential Files (hereafter GWB HPC) for the year 1948 (no file number), West Bengal State Archives.

[96] The tribunal's brief was limited: it was only to demarcate the boundary between Murshidabad and Rajshahi districts, and to settle disputes about the course of the Mathabhanga river. Justices Chandrashekhar Aiyer and Shahabuddin represented India and Pakistan respectively. See the "Decisions given by the Indo-Pakistan Boundary Disputes Tribunal in conformity with the agreement concluded at the Inter-Dominion Conference at Delhi on December 14, 1948 between the Dominion of India and the Dominion of Pakistan relating to the interpretation of the report of the Bengal Boundary Commission, August 12 and 13, 1947", *PP*, VI, pp. 315–21.

But as Radcliffe would have realised had he visited the border areas himself, the picture on the ground was very different. The frontiers between *thanas*, and even between districts, were not physically marked out. Actual administrative boundaries could only be established with reference to survey and settlement maps, which were often inaccurate and almost always outdated. "There is nothing to demarcate the boundary line except an imaginary one supported by settlement maps showing the border of villages," complained one intelligence branch officer of the Nadia border. "In the event of encroachment . . . the matter will remain disputed until it is . . . amicably settled by both Dominions or decided by a court of law by reference to the Settlement documents, which may or may not be accepted by both Dominions . . ."[97] Such disputes could only be resolved by goodwill on both sides, which, in the strained aftermath of Partition, was not often to be had.

The problem became even more complicated in cases where settlement maps differed from the crime maps used by the local police stations to establish their jurisdiction. Radcliffe had settled on the *thana* as the smallest unit of Partition, but he used settlement maps (rather than police maps) to mark out the border. Contradictions between the two maps were sought to be exploited by both sides, each insisting on whichever interpretation would give it more territory.[98] On the border between Khulna and the 24 Parganas, for instance, just to the east of Hasnabad, lay a village called Rajnagar. Until October 1945, this village had been

[97] Inspector's "Report on Border Intelligence of Nadia district", 23 April 1948, in GB IB file no. 1238–47 (Nabadwip).

[98] Settlement maps were the basis on which revenue was extracted, and a settlement "zone" could be, and in fact often was, much larger than a "police" or "criminal" zone, which covered the area physically controlled by a single police station. Trying to reconcile the two maps would have been a nightmare even if Radcliffe understood these differences and had had the time; not surprisingly, he was bewildered, and never quite got his head round the problem.

included within the jurisdiction of the Debhatta *thana* police in Khulna district. But in 1945 the Land Record and Surveys Department had decided to add the village on to Hasnabad *thana* in the 24 Parganas. This change had not, however, been marked on to the relevant crime maps. In August 1947, it had been included, *de facto*, in West Bengal. Muslims in Khulna challenged this,[99] and the village became the scene of a protracted and bitter stand-off between the two states.

Nor did geographical or "natural" boundaries work any better as border posts. If anything, they were even more ambiguous. Some of the rivers which were a part of Radcliffe's line were fed by the melting Himalayan ice-caps and flowed all year round. Others were rainfed, and, except for the monsoon months, dried up to a trickle. The Mathabhanga River, for instance, which was the dividing line between the two halves of Nadia, "lies totally dry throughout the year except during the rainy season . . ." But once the rains began, it would burst its banks and flood large tracts, obscuring the border completely. "During the heavy and constant downpour, the western portion of the district [would] be practically cut off from the district headquarters," noted one observer, and "the only way of transport and communication [would become] impassable."[100] So not only was this section of the border invisible for several months of the year, it was also unapproachable; with disastrous effects on border security and administration.

Even the more perennial rivers created difficulties when they stood in as the border. For one thing, they were apt suddenly to change their course. Radcliffe had designated the River Mathabhanga as the border for the north-western part of Nadia, starting from the point at which "the channel of the river Mathabhanga

[99] Extract from the report of the Chief Inspector of Police, Basirhat, 31 December 1947, in GB IB file no. 1238–47 (24 Parganas).

[100] Inspector's "Report on Border Intelligence of Nadia district", 23 April 1948, in GB IB file no. 1238–47 (Nabadwip).

takes off from the river Ganges . . ."[101] The problem was that the erratic Mathabhanga had already changed its path, starting off at a new point some distance to the west of the old source. The new course had not been depicted on the Bengal Government Press map which Radcliffe had used (although it had been shown correctly on the updated Revenue and Survey Department map). The result of this error was that almost 500 square miles of territory went to Pakistan when it should have gone to India.[102]

Nor was there any guarantee that Bengal's volatile rivers would stick to the course they were following at the time of Partition. In January 1948, a police officer reported that the River Ichhamati,

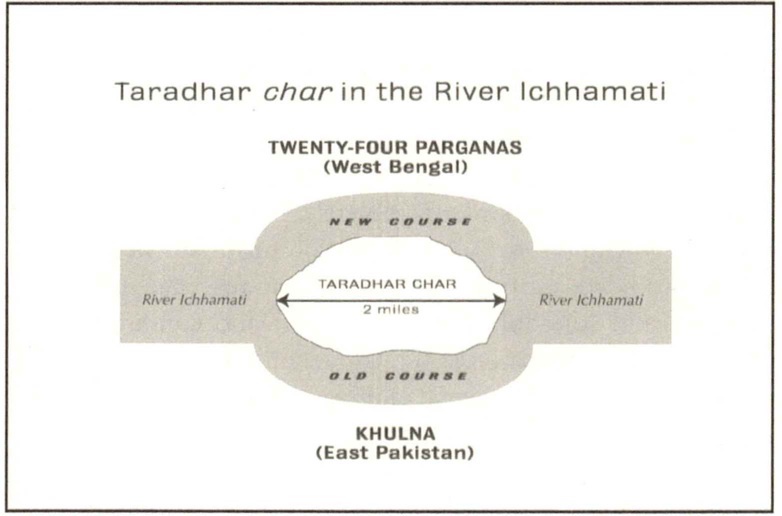

Fig. 2.6: Taradhar *char* in the River Ichhamati.

[101] Sir Cyril Radcliffe's award, *PP*, VI, pp. 119–20.

[102] Secretary, New Bengal Association, Meherpur, Nadia, to Acharya Kripalani, 11 September 1947, AICC-I/G-33/1947–8. The Mathabhanga issue was one of those clarified by Justice Bagge in 1950: the starting point of the river was fixed at a point in the Ganges south-west of Jalangi village. "Decisions given by the Indo-Pakistan Boundary Disputes Tribunal", *PP*, VI, p. 321.

which defined the boundary between Khulna and the 24 Parganas, had taken a new course sixteen miles south of Hasnabad. "The new stream, after taking a crescent course, now joins the original river at Ghumti . . . about twenty miles south of Hasnabad." The old course was no longer navigable except during the flow tide: during the ebb tide all boats would have to use the new stream. In between the old course and the new stream was a piece of uninhabited land which had become a *char* (the Bengali word for a strip of sandy land rising out of the river bed above water level). The new *char* in the Ichhamati, called Taradhar *char*, was about two miles long and almost a mile wide.[103] This tiny tract was submerged during flow tide, but during ebb tide was of enormous strategic significance. By virtue of its position, it was the key to the control of the entire river.[104] Both sides were quick to realise this, and Taradhar *char* became a flashpoint as each tried forcibly to claim it.

Radcliffe had not given any thought to the possibility of rivers changing course; a serious lapse in a province whose rivers were notoriously wayward. Nor had he paid attention to the question of the *chars* which were a common feature in all the large rivers of Bengal. In all likelihood he did not know that they existed, else he would surely have foreseen the difficulties they would create. The River Padma, which divided Murshidabad and Rajshahi, was dotted with *chars*. These "became a bone of contention and a source of constant trouble from the latter half of 1947", which continued until the first war between India and Pakistan.[105] Both sides had agreed, after the Inter-Dominion Conference, to leave

[103] See Fig. 2.6.

[104] Superintendent of Police (DIB), 24 Parganas, to the Assistant Inspector General of Police, West Bengal, 14 January 1948, GB IB file no. 1238–47 (24 Parganas).

[105] "Note showing the developments in Murshidabad district since the Partition of Bengal", 1 December 1948, GB IB file no. 1238–47 (Murshidabad).

existing *chars* unoccupied and to treat them as no-man's land.[106] But this agreement was often violated, particularly as it did not cover the new *chars* that came up every year as water levels fell off. Both countries scrambled to occupy them, adding to the ill will between India and Pakistan.

Some of the *chars* in the River Padma were so large that they had whole villages built upon them, and the people who inhabited these little islands became victims of a protracted tug-of-war. Biren Mandal lived on Rajnagore *char* in the Padma river.[107] As was typical of Bengali villages, his homestead was made up of several thatched huts, two of which fell in Rajshahi in Pakistan, while the other huts were in Murshidabad in India. According to a police report, both Indian and Pakistani troops periodically "claimed his allegiance". What this meant in real terms can only be guessed at. We do know that one of his neighbours, Bishnu Pramanik, died in the crossfire.[108] Like Toba Tek Singh in Sadat Hasan Manto's celebrated story, Rajnagore *char* belonged neither here nor there and its inhabitants paid a heavy price for the Boundary Commission's oversight.

Tragedies of this sort could have been avoided, or at least minimised, had Radcliffe and the boundary commissioners done their job with greater care and sensitivity. Indeed, one is struck by the audacious haste with which they executed their task. Radcliffe did not come out to India until 8 July; the sittings of the Bengal Boundary Commission were held between 16 and 24 July, and Radcliffe gave his decision on 12 August. Radcliffe did not attend

[106] Memo no. S. 50–51, 17 February 1951. Ibid.

[107] The names of all individuals involved in border incidents referred to here have been changed, in compliance with the wishes of the Deputy Inspector General of Police, Intelligence Branch, West Bengal. The aliases used here have been chosen carefully to reflect the caste, community, and class locations of the individuals they refer to.

[108] "A report on the incident in *char* Munshipara", GB IB file no. 1238–47 (Murshidabad).

any of its public sittings in person, he merely examined the papers presented to the commission by all parties.[109] He made no effort to survey the areas he had been asked to carve up. An aerial view of the Murshidabad and Nadia rivers could have revealed some of the more obvious problems, such as the new course of the Mathabhanga and the existence of *chars*. But it seems that no one, not even the Congress and Muslim League leaders, thought such a survey necessary. Policemen, revenue officers, and bureaucrats in the border districts were not consulted: they undoubtedly would have given the commission valuable advice on the conditions on the ground. It is no surprise that an award drafted with so little attention to detail was so slipshod, so full of gross inaccuracies. All those involved in its making must bear culpability for the sheer human cost of their astounding negligence.

The Border and Everyday Life

But if we look to yet another level – to the everyday operation of the Radcliffe Line – it becomes clear that no such award, however carefully and sensitively worked out, could ever have been just or rational in the way that it impinged upon the lives of people.

The border cut a channel several hundred miles long, mostly through settled agricultural land. The Bengal countryside was a dense patchwork of small and large holdings, rights over which were shared in a variety of ways. Landlords, *jotedars*, tenant proprietors, sharecroppers, and a host of other intermediaries all claimed a part of the produce of each plot of land. The same person often sharecropped one plot, held tenurial rights over another, cultivated part of this with the help of his family, and let the other part out to be sharecropped by someone else.

[109] Because the sittings of the Punjab Boundary Commission, which Radcliffe also chaired, were held at the same time as those of the Bengal Boundary Commission, he attended neither. Sir Cyril Radcliffe's Award, *PP*, VI, p. 116.

A zamindar, in the same way, might have owned one or two estates outright, but held *taluqdari* and *jotedari* rights over several other plots scattered over large areas.

The line which severed this landscape was bound to disrupt every aspect of existence for the rural community, criminalising the routine and customary transactions by which it survived. It separated the peasant's homestead from the plot he had share-cropped in the last season and the peasant-proprietor from his holding. It cut creditors off from debtors; landlords from tenants. When a *bhag-chashi* (sharecropper) crossed the line to bring home his share of the standing crop, he risked arrest and beatings. So, for instance, when a peasant of Kumarganj in West Dinajpur was returning from Phulbari across the border with a maund of paddy that he had earned, he was arrested by the East Pakistani border militia.[110] A Hindu zamindar of Kazipur in Nadia, who in January 1950 crossed over to Damurhuda "to realise rents from his tenants . . . was arrested by the Pakistani border patrol and released with a warning never to return."[111] That October, a resident of Dinhata in Cooch-Behar, while returning from Rangpur with money he had reclaimed from a creditor, was robbed at the border of forty-five rupees.[112] In another similar incident, Subroto Dutta and his servant Narendra Ghosh of Puthikhali in Nabadwip, went to Medinipur across the border to reclaim a grain loan. Narendra was carrying thirty-five seers of paddy back to Puthikhali for his master when he was caught and severely beaten by a Pakistani constable.[113] The same thing happened on the western side of the border. In March 1951 some Muslims of Balabari in Cooch-Behar,

[110] Report for the second half of August 1950, Fortnightly Reports on Border Incidents in West Bengal (hereafter FRBI), GB IB file no. 1238-A/47.

[111] FRBI for the second half of January 1950, ibid.

[112] FRBI, October 1950, ibid.

[113] This incident created so much ill will that it prompted a mass exodus of Medinipur Hindus to Malda. Report of the Assistant Sub-Inspector of Tungi camp, P.S. Krishnaganj, 7 February 1948, GB IB file no. 1238–47 (Nabadwip).

who had sought shelter across the border during a communal flare-up, returned to reap the paddy they had sown on their own plots. As one of them told the police: "Sometime after we proceeded with harvesting, I noticed four soldiers along with [a member of the] Panchayat coming towards us. I informed my companions and asked them to run away . . ." But the Indian police shot one of them dead as he tried to cross back to safety.[114]

The border thus ruptured agrarian communities all along its lengths. Now it is important to recall that these communities were by no means always harmonious ones, and the relations between their members were often bitterly antagonistic. During the 1940s, particularly in parts of north and deltaic Bengal, sharecroppers were engaged in a protracted and often violent struggle to retain a two-thirds share of the produce (*tebhaga*). Where the border cut through *tebhaga* areas, its impact on such local battles could be momentous. If it cut a *jotedar* off from the land he had given out to sharecroppers, it became almost impossible for him to insist on his share. Conversely, it was greatly to the disadvantage of sharecroppers if the lands they held in *barga* fell on the wrong side of the border. If they insisted on crossing over to reap their "rightful" share, the concerned *jotedar* could appeal to the border security patrols for protection. For their part, the sharecroppers could and did ask for the support of border patrols from their side to assist them in harvesting their crop and the policemen often obliged. Every harvesting season (at least until 1952), cases of "forcible harvesting of paddy by Pakistani Muslims" were reported in large numbers; so much so that in December 1950 the West Bengal inspector general of police issued a special notice to all border superintendents to be vigilant in preventing such incidents.[115] In this way, border policemen and militias were

[114] Statement of Emam Ali Khondokar, 28 March 1951, GB IB file no. 1238–47 (Cooch-Behar).

[115] FBRI for the first fortnight of November 1950, GB IB file no. 1237(A)–1947.

drawn into agrarian conflict along the length of the border, and local struggles assumed international dimensions.

In the same way, livestock could become the cause of international incidents. Cattle were not allowed freely to cross the border. It had been a common practice for poorer sharecroppers (*adhiars*) to enter into agreements with *jotedars* in which the latter would lend them the seed-grain, ploughs, and bullocks with which they would sow and till the land. But now, if the *adhiar* was on the wrong side of the boundary, it could be difficult to get the cattle and implements across to him. So, when a Hindu resident of Mathabhanga in Cooch-Behar tried to send a pair of bullocks across the border to his *adhiars* at Balarhat, they were snatched away by militiamen and he never saw them again.[116]

Grazing one's herds along the border also became a risky business. If they strayed across the line, they could be seized by the police or stolen by villagers on the other side. Cattle theft was particularly common on the stretches of dry border between Cooch-Behar and Rangpur, between Malda and Rajshahi, and between Nadia and Kushtia. In one week in May 1950, as many as 250 head of cattle were stolen from English Bazar.[117] It was difficult and dangerous to try and recover lost livestock. In one incident, an Indian Muslim of Sitalkuchi crossed over to Hatibandha to retrieve a cow that had strayed across to Pakistani territory. He was caught by a Pakistani patrol party. They beat him to death.[118]

Where rivers formed the borderline, fishermen who customarily fished in their waters found that their traditional occupation was now regarded as an offence. Those who fell into the hands of the river patrols were not only threatened and abused, their nets, boats, and even their catch were confiscated. A fisherman of Karimpur was fishing in his boat on the Mathabhanga when he was captured by the Pakistani police. They harassed him and

[116] FRBI for the second fortnight of July 1950, GB IB file no. 1238-A/47.
[117] FRBI for the first fortnight of May 1950, ibid.
[118] FRBI for the second fortnight of April 1951, ibid.

relieved him of his catch.[119] Some fishermen of Gaighata in the 24 Parganas were fired at while they fished in the Ichhamati. They jumped into the river and swam to safety, but their boats were seized by the police patrol.[120] The communities that fished in the many *bils* (shallow ponds or lakes) that spanned the border faced similar difficulties. In Dinajpur, the boundary line between Porsa and Tapan *thanas* passed through a large *bil* that was almost three miles wide. Fishermen from both *thanas* who depended on this *bil* for their survival now risked their lives every time they went out to fish.[121] Border patrols and vigilantes were not the only source of danger. Sometimes fisherfolk of one side attacked fishermen from across the border. In April 1950, two hundred Pakistani fishermen attacked Indian fishermen who were casting their nets on the Indian side of Panchbar *bil* and drove them out by force.[122] Here was another case of the border being exploited to settle older political scores: one section of this fishing community made the most of the opportunity to claim the sole right to fish in a *bil* that they had shared with other fisherfolk before Partition.

Even people who lived at some distance from the border found that it disrupted their lives in all sorts of ways. Few villages had their own shops. Most depended on weekly *haats* and bigger markets several miles away. The border cut many villages off from the markets that served them. This meant that villagers now had to brave crossing the border to purchase salt, cloth, oil, and other daily essentials. It also meant that the local trade on which whole regions depended was seriously hampered. The border divided towns from the hinterland that habitually supplied their needs.

[119] FRBI for the second fortnight of August 1950, ibid.

[120] FRBI for the first fortnight of August 1951, ibid. In another such incident, five Indian fishermen were arrested and their boats were seized when they were found fishing midstream in the Ichhamati near Sodepur. FRBI for the second fortnight of May 1950, ibid.

[121] President of the Patnitola Congress Committee, Balurghat, to members of the Boundary Commission, 12 September 1947, AICC-I/G-33/1947–8.

[122] FRBI for the first fortnight of May 1950, ibid.

For instance, oilcakes, green vegetables, potatoes, brinjals, and pulses were not grown or produced in the villages surrounding Rajshahi town. "Since time immemorial" these had been supplied by villagers living on the southern bank of the Padma in Murshidabad. Prices were substantially lower in Murshidabad than in Rajshahi, so it had been worth their while to cross the river and carry their produce all the way to Rajshahi to sell in the markets there. After Partition, the Padma became the border and people were not allowed to cross it with commodities. As a result, a whole sub-economy was destroyed.[123]

The suffering that resulted from the loss of markets must have been widespread. By this time, Bengali villagers had become fully integrated into the market economy. Because they all had to pay their rents and other dues and service their debts in cash, they had to sell at least part of their produce in the market.[124] After Partition, they naturally continued to try to get to their regular markets, often with grave consequences. A *goala* (milkman) of Kushtia, now in East Pakistan, was shot dead as he crossed the border to Nadia with milk for his customers.[125] Border policemen drove a potter of Chapra (Nadia) away as he crossed the border to sell earthenware goods at Thakurpur, but only after they had robbed him of all his pots.[126] Two Indians were arrested while they were returning home to Karimpur in Nadia after buying a maund of paddy at Brajanathpur *haat* in Kushtia.[127] A vegetable vendor was beaten up and robbed as he returned from Daulatpur to Jalangi in Murshidabad.[128]

[123] President, Rajshahi District Congress Committee to Dr P.C. Ghosh, 18 October 1947, AICC-I/G-5/1947–8.

[124] Sugata Bose has argued the case for a highly monetised agrarian economy in twentieth-century Bengal. See his *Agrarian Bengal*, pp. 34–97.

[125] FRBI for the first fortnight of May 1950, GB IB 1238-A/47.

[126] FRBI for the second fortnight of August 1950, ibid.

[127] FRBI for October 1950, ibid.

[128] FRBI for the second fortnight of May 1950, ibid.

Even when villages and their respective markets were fortuitously on the same side of the boundary, there were problems when the roads or railheads that served them were on the wrong side. The *thanas* of Porsa and Patnitala, which went to Bogra in East Pakistan after Partition, produced two million maunds of surplus paddy every year. This paddy was sold at Nithpur *haat*, also in Pakistan. But the railhead connecting Nithpur went to West Bengal. The nearest line in East Pakistan was over forty miles away. The paddy now had to be transported this distance by bullock-cart or lorry, raising its price substantially.[129] While Radcliffe made an effort to preserve, as far as possible, the integrity of major highways and railway lines, smaller roads and lines were fragmented and many markets suffered the same fate as Nithpur.

Of course, the most serious disruption to transport, communications, and trade was caused by the separation of North Bengal from the rest of West Bengal. Between Rohanpur railway station and Godagharighat, people had to suffer "the hardship and humiliation of passing through Pakistani territory, where they were subjected to searches." To get to Calcutta from Malda, they had to take a circuitous route via Rajmahal in Bihar, with numerous changes and long waits.[130] All this caused a major setback to the multi-million-rupee tea trade.[131] Not surprisingly, months after Partition the Indian Tea Planters' Association submitted a detailed road-cum-rail plan that would connect Jalpaiguri, Darjeeling, Malda, and West Dinajpur with Assam and the rest of West

[129] President, Patnitola Congress Committee, Balurghat, to the members of the Boundary Commission, 12 September 1947, AICC-I/G-33/1947–8.

[130] Resolution passed at a public meeting at Malda on 18 February 1948, AICC-I/G-5/1947–8. Also see the letter from Surendra Mohan Ghosh to Balvantrai Mehta (AICC General Secretary), 18 November 1953, AICC Papers Second Instalment, Parliamentary Board file no. 21 of 1953 (hereafter AICC-II/PB – followed by the relevant file no. and year).

[131] Tea was grown only in Darjeeling and the Jalpaiguri Dooars. It was packed mostly in Calcutta, whence much of it left by ship to markets all over the world.

Bengal. The West Bengal government naturally took this plan very seriously and regarded the task of re-establishing the link as an urgent priority. But the problems of smaller roads and markets were never addressed, with long-term effects on the economy of the border zones.

Towns were not only major markets of rural produce, they were also administrative headquarters and housed public institutions. Their hospitals, dispensaries, and law courts drew people from miles around. The Radcliffe Line cut many of them off from the people they were designed to serve. A constable of Malda who took ten days' casual leave to go home to Faridpur to attend the hearing of a civil suit was arrested, locked up for several hours, and prevented from attending the hearing.[132] In cases such as this, litigation already under way had to be abandoned by appellants from the wrong side of the border. In many more, legal cases could not be instituted at all because the border had made the old district headquarters inaccessible, and the nearest court on this side of the line was too far away. The border also sometimes set these institutions apart from the staff that manned them, as in the case of the doctor who lived in Karimpur but worked at the dispensary in Kazipur Bazar across the Nadia border. Every day he walked half a mile from his home to the dispensary and returned in the evening. One evening he was arrested as he was walking home. He was searched and detained for two days, all the medicines and instruments he had kept in his bag were confiscated, and he was forced to pay a fine of Rs 2000.[133] He lost his job and much of his practice; the dispensary lost a skilled and qualified employee and the people of Kazipur Bazar lost access to their doctor. It would take years, even decades, before problems of this sort were even addressed.[134]

[132] Fortnightly appreciation of the border situation in West Bengal for the second fortnight of March, 1948, GB IB file no. 1238-A/47 (KW).

[133] English translation of the petition of Dr Gaur Chandra Ray of Fulbari, P.S. Karimpur, Nadia, 16 March 1948, GB IB file no. 1238–47 (Nabadwip).

[134] The effect of Partition on institutions, particularly in the east, was com-

And finally, the border separated people from their families. Particularly for those unfortunate women whose natal and affinal homes were on opposite sides of the boundary, the rare visits home to their parents became a difficult and dangerous proposition. One woman was robbed at Jadabpur on the border as she tried to go home to her family in Meherpur. In all likelihood, few others dared (or were allowed) even to try.[135] Their stories are not recorded in the police archive but their experiences are a part of lived memory and Partition folklore.

The Evolution of New Ways of Life

One reason why the Bengal border continued to be troubled by incidents of this sort years after Partition was a confused and

---

pounded many times over by the massive exodus of refugees from both sides of the border. The first wave of refugees from east to west was predominantly composed of middle-class Hindus: and amongst them were many of the doctors, lawyers, teachers, clerks, and white-collar employees who had manned public institutions in East Bengal. Of the 1.1 million refugees who migrated to West Bengal by June 1948, 350,000 belonged to the urban *bhadralok* and 550,000 to the rural *bhadralok*. Chakrabarti, *The Marginal Men*, p. 1. East Pakistan lacked people qualified to take over from them, it lacked the universities and technical institutes that could train another generation to take their place and so its hospitals, courts, schools, and offices would run below par for decades. West Bengal, on the other hand, was inundated with skilled, qualified, and educated people for whom no jobs were available. They would join the ranks of the unemployed and disaffected, creating enormous problems for future governments. The refugee issue is a rich and complex subject in itself, and I will not attempt to discuss it here. For details, see Chakrabarti, *The Marginal Men*.

[135] FRBI for the second fortnight of June 1950, GB IB file no. 1238-A/47. The border also interfered with the customary visits of the son-in law (*jamaibabu*) to his in-laws on the occasion of Jamai-shoshti. Kishori Mohan Sarkar of Jalangi in Murshidabad was arrested while trying to visit his father-in-law at Bagwan. The same fate befell Jadunath Mistri of Lalgola. Extract from the Murshidabad district Weekly Confidential Report for the week ending 27 November 1948, GB IB 1238-A/1947.

contradictory government policy. In Punjab, both governments had agreed in principle to compensate all migrants for property that they had left behind, thereby ensuring that they would not return to reclaim it. Nehru's government also undertook a fairly vigorous scheme to resettle and rehabilitate Punjabi refugees.[136] These policies were a clear indication that both India and Pakistan intended to treat the partition of Punjab as final and irrevocable.

But because conditions in Bengal were not as volatile at the time, and because the flow of refugees across the eastern border was not as sudden and torrential, the two countries took the view that normalcy in Bengal could be restored more easily. To this end they agreed that Bengalis could retain their title to land on both sides of the border and undertook to safeguard evacuee property for its owners until such time when they could safely come back to claim it.[137] This meant that, in theory, many West Bengalis continued after Partition to own land in East Pakistan and vice versa. It also meant that, officially, the Bengal border was to be porous. Government policy decreed that people were to be allowed freely to cross the Radcliffe Line to attend to their legitimate business on the other side.[138] At a meeting in Dacca in February 1948, government representatives of East and West Bengal "agreed to ensure the implementation of the two Premiers' agreement allowing nationals of one state to move the produce of his land lying in another State in the border areas . . ."[139] For

[136] See Kudaisya, "The Demographic Upheaval of Partition", pp. 73–94.

[137] At the Inter-Dominion Conference, Nehru and Liaquat Ali Khan agreed to set up evacuee property management boards on both sides of the Bengal border. Proceedings of the Inter-Dominion Conference held at Calcutta, 15–18 April 1948, GWB HPC for the year 1948 (no file number), West Bengal State Archives.

[138] Until March 1948, this right was guaranteed by the Standstill Agreement between India and Pakistan.

[139] Proceedings of the Conference of Representatives of the Governments of East Bengal and West Bengal, held at Dacca on 14 February, 1948, GWB HPC file no. 62 (1–20)/48. The Inter-Dominion agreement reaffirmed this right for the citizens of the two Bengals.

those who migrated to the other side from places that were far from the border, these rights remained on paper. But people who lived beside the border could and did try physically to exercise the right to their property and its produce that had been guaranteed to them.[140]

These arrangements were inspired by a genuine belief that peace would return to Bengal if Hindu and Muslim refugees were encouraged to return to their homes.[141] But in the border areas, things turned out very differently. Two factors prevented the government's design to achieve a porous but peaceful border from having the desired effect. The first was the drive to stop smuggling. The second factor was the difficulty of impressing the official policy of openness upon border police and militias. In the turbulent aftermath of Partition, local policemen and vigilantes on both sides of the border were inclined to be vicious and vindictive towards minorities and overzealous in guarding the frontier. People who were brave or foolhardy enough to cross over regardless ran the risk of being robbed, of being arrested on trumped-up charges, being beaten or even, as we have seen, being killed.[142]

Immediately after Partition, the Standstill Agreement between the two dominions had provided for the joint administration of currency, trade, imports and exports.[143] But after it lapsed in

[140] So, for instance, every year Pakistani Muslims would cross the Bongaon border to farm the 200 *bighas* of land they owned at different points along the border. District Inspection Officer's Report, 14 December 1948, GB IB file no. 1238–47 (24 Parganas).

[141] Nehru was convinced that all that was needed in Bengal was a "psychological" approach – if the right psychological conditions were created, people would return to their homes. Jawaharlal Nehru to Bidhan Chandra Roy, 2 December 1949, cited in Chakrabarty, *With Dr. B.C. Roy*, p. 143.

[142] Government representatives recognised that most incidents of this sort arose out of the "misrepresentation of Government policy by overzealous, misinformed or tactless petty officials on either side . . ." Proceedings of the Conference of Representatives of the Governments of East Bengal and West Bengal, GWB HPC file no. 62 (1–20)/48.

[143] The agreement retained controls over essential commodities such as

March 1948, the Radcliffe Line became an economic frontier across which trade, particularly in certain key commodities, was strictly controlled. This had the effect of notifying as criminal a whole range of customary economic activities along the border. Even though the two governments agreed at the Dacca Conference to make an exception for the inhabitants of the border areas, we have seen above that this provision was largely disregarded by officials on the spot. So, in fact, by the middle of 1948 there were three different and conflicting directives regarding economic activity on the border. First, citizens of one dominion could legally own property in the other; second, the government would control all trade in commodities between the two countries; and third, inhabitants of the border area would be allowed to continue to buy their personal requirements and sell their individual produce across the border.

The result, as we have seen, was messy. Officials on the spot were left with the discretion to decide which particular policy prevailed in each individual case and were usually harsh in dealing with border crossing by border-dwellers on genuine and legitimate business. On the other hand, this somewhat confused policy created space for the emergence of smuggling as a thriving enterprise in the border areas, usually with the connivance of the border police.

Smuggling across the Bengal border was an attractive proposition. The price of food was higher in East Bengal than anywhere else in India,[144] and there was a huge demand in West Bengal for East Bengali raw jute. Anyone could see that there was a fortune to be made in smuggling rice across the border for sale in the markets

---

steel, coal, and textiles, provided for the free movement of goods and persons between the two dominions and for the retention of existing customs, tariffs, currency, and coinage until 31 March 1948. *The Statesman*, 8 July 1947.

144 "The Viceroy's Visit to Bengal: Note by the Viceroy", *PP*, I, p. 188(C).

of East Bengal,[145] and in bringing jute into West Bengal. The Indian government, struggling as it was against severe and chronic food shortages, was anxious to prevent foodgrains from being lost to government procurement schemes. The government of East Pakistan was equally concerned to prevent raw jute from being spirited across the border. Jute was one of its key trading advantages over India, and East Pakistan could not allow it to be squandered.[146] So both governments made arrangements to secure the border against smugglers.[147]

Despite this, smuggling was widespread. In April 1948, border secret police reported that the "smuggling of foodgrains, textile goods and all kinds of commodities from West Bengal to East Bengal territory by all conceivable and ingenious means continues unabated . . ."[148] Rice, cloth, kerosene oil, and salt figured at the top of the list of goods smuggled eastwards. Consumer goods such as soap, matches, tobacco, cigarettes, soda, and torch cells also regularly made their way across the border to East Bengal.[149]

[145] On the Nadia–Kushtia border, the difference in the price of a maund of paddy could be as high as Rs 6. In Shikarpore, for instance, in Nabadwip, paddy sold at Rs 8 per maund, whereas at *Char* Pragpur across the border it could command as much as Rs 14. District Sub-Inspector's Report, 20 December 1947, GB IB file no. 167/47 (Nabadwip).

[146] Jalal, *Democracy and Authoritarianism*, p. 24.

[147] For instance, at the end of September 1950, the border patrol at Ramkrishnapur was reportedly strengthened to prevent the smuggling of jute. Extract from the Weekly Confidential Report for Murshidabad district for the week ending 30 September 1950, GB IB 1238–47 (Murshidabad). On the Indian side, efforts were made to strengthen police presence at points such as Augalbari in Karimpur which was an entrepôt for the illegal export of foodgrains and cotton to East Bengal.

[148] Fortnightly Appreciation of the Border Situation in West Bengal (hereafter FABS) for the first fortnight in April 1948, GB IB file no. 1238-A/47 (KW).

[149] See the FRBIs for the first fortnight in April 1950, the first fortnight in May 1950, the first fortnight in August 1950 and the first fortnight in February 1951, all in GB IB 1238-A/47.

Jute dominated the list of clandestine exports from east to west.[150] Betel nuts and chillies, which were substantially cheaper in East Bengal, were also routinely smuggled westwards.[151]

How did all of this affect everyday life on the border? It would appear that a good many border-dwellers became involved in this clandestine trade. Of course, many of them were treated as smugglers even when they were merely conducting their habitual business across the border, selling their wares and buying a few goods to meet their personal needs. But there seems little doubt that many individuals and even entire village communities took deliberately to smuggling on a regular basis. This was, in a sense, the one door of opportunity that had been opened to them when Partition shut all others. As border-dwellers they were formally entitled to cross over with their individual produce: this made them the only nationals of one state who had the right to enter the other with goods of any description. They could exploit this position to conduct their own petty illegal trade in locally produced commodities, or act as covers or delivery-men for wider smuggling networks. One intelligence officer was surprised to find "no disorder and very little bad feeling among the people of the two dominions" when he surveyed conditions in border villages in the 24 Parganas. His assessment was that "the expected bad feeling is probably nipped [in the bud] by the self-interest of both the people of India and Pakistan. They are too busy with their own smuggling of chillies, mustard oil, cloth, black pepper etc. . . ."[152]

For these villagers the exigencies of survival outweighed the

[150] So, for instance, the Pakistani police stopped two boats carrying over 200 maunds of jute across the Padma from Shibgunje in Rajshahi to Suti in Murshidabad. Telegraphic message from the Superintendent of Police, Murshidabad, to the Deputy Inspector General of the Intelligence Branch, 3 October 1950, GB IB file no. 1238/47 (Murshidabad).

[151] FRBI for the first fortnight in August 1950, GB IB file no. 1238-A/47.

[152] Report on border affairs, 20 March 1950, GB IB file no. 1238–47 (24 Parganas).

exhortations of the ideologues against dealing with the enemy. Patriotism and communalism were luxuries that they could ill afford now that Partition had ruptured so many of their traditional subsistence networks. The district magistrate of Khulna in Pakistan recognised this when he held a meeting at Kaliganj to warn its inhabitants against smuggling. He reportedly said that "all sorts of exports to India were stopped now, especially the export of jute." He warned them that the Pakistan government would not hesitate to shoot smugglers. He added that "*Muslims should realise that Pakistan is their own dominion* and requested them to check all sorts of corruption and smuggling . . ."[153] His appeal to Pakistani nationalism was realistically backed up with the threat of force, a sign that the communal and nationalist argument alone was not enough to persuade his audience. In other words, border villagers appeared to be developing an attitude of rough-and-ready cynicism towards the official ideologies of their respective states: an attitude which the authorities were inclined to regard as subversive.

To cope with this kind of mass subversion, it was not enough simply to beef up border patrols, although both governments did their best to strengthen and invigorate border security.[154] In all likelihood, the idea of setting up border militias was first proposed to deal with the enemy within. In February 1948

[153] Report of the Assistant Sub-Inspector of Himulganj of a meeting held on 28 November 1949; report on border incidents for the week ending 17 December 1949, GB IB file no. 1238/47 (24 Parganas), emphasis added. Similarly in October 1947 the East Bengal minister for public health and local self-government announced that only "loyal citizens" were wanted in Pakistan, and that "the unscrupulous men who are gambling with the food of the nation for their individual gains" would be severely punished. *The Statesman*, 8 October 1947.

[154] By the end of 1949, Indian border police had begun regularly to complain that Pakistani officials were being "over-zealous" in their drive to check smuggling. See the weekly reports of border incidents in the 24 Parganas for the latter part of 1949, GB IB file no. 1238/47 (24 Parganas).

"the Pakistan government was reported to have given a call to Muslim youths to build up a 150,000 strong non-official Muslim military organisation" to be called the Ansar Bahini. An expensive recruitment campaign using cinema slides and magic lantern shows was taken up in earnest.[155] The idea clearly was to draw motivated youths into the campaign against smuggling. They would act as a vigilante force, rooting out the bad eggs in the home camp and injecting a healthy dose of the state's political ideology into the border-dwelling communities. There were plenty of suitably indoctrinated young men out on a limb now that organisations such as the Muslim National Guard had become defunct. They flocked to the new Muslim militia and within months, lathi-wielding Ansars had become a familiar and dreaded sight all along the border. Not only were they involved in many of the crimes committed against border crossers, they were also responsible for raising the communal temperature along the border. Ansars seem to have been behind a new trend which emerged after 1950, in which Muslims from border-lying villages in West Bengal would cross over to Pakistan after burning down their homesteads. Presumably this was to prevent Hindu refugees from occupying evacuee Muslim property. If they were not able to set fire to their homes before crossing, Ansars would do the job for them.[156] Before this, it had not been uncommon for Muslims intending to migrate to Pakistan to enter into informal agreements to exchange some property with Hindus crossing the other way. It was also quite common for Muslims who left for Pakistan when the communal situation was fraught, to return to their homes in India later when the air had cleared a little.[157] But once the Ansars began to display a dog-in-the-manger attitude towards Muslim evacuee property in India, communal attitudes hardened

[155] FRBI for the second fortnight of February 1948, GB IB file no. 1238A/47 (KW).

[156] See, for instance, the FRBIs for April 1950, GB IB file no. 1238-A/47.

[157] Several examples of this are cited in the FRBI for the second fortnight in September 1950, ibid.

and informal and temporary arrangements such as these became much harder to achieve. In one typical incident, Ansars arrested a Hindu of Gadra in Jalpaiguri on a border road for plucking mangoes from a tree (on the Indian side of the road) that had belonged to a Muslim who had left for Pakistan. In retaliation, the man's brother attacked a Pakistani Muslim when he crossed over to graze his cattle. Communal tempers were frayed for a good while afterwards as a result.[158]

The West Bengal government did not lag behind in setting up a militia of its own. In February 1948 Dr B.C. Roy announced his government's plans for the prevention of smuggling along the frontier. These included arrangements not only for the establishment of a volunteer corps but also for "training villagers in border areas to defend themselves [and] to act in collaboration with the police in the neightbourhood [to] assist them in stopping smuggling."[159] On 16 March 1948 the Bangiya Jatiya Rakshi Dal (the Bengal National Protection Brigade) was formed. It was a provincial volunteer force of a "semi-military nature", made up of trained youths from the six border districts: Jalpaiguri, West Dinajpur, Malda, Murshidabad, Nadia, and the 24 Parganas.[160] The Rakshi Dal was exempted from the ban against holding parades and wearing uniforms that had been imposed upon private organisations in the wake of Gandhi's killing. It was administered in each district by a high-powered committee consisting of the magistrate, the superintendent of police, the president of the District Congress Committee and the local assembly member. The government's instruction was that "the administration of the Bangiya Jatiya Rakshi Dal should take the highest priority over routine administration."[161]

[158] FRBI for the first fortnight of June 1950, ibid.

[159] *The Statesman*, 4 February 1948.

[160] Chief Secretary to the Government of West Bengal (Home Political) to District Officers, 16 March 1948, GB IB file no. 769/48.

[161] Ibid.

Not much information is available about the Rakshi Dal's activities. But one horrific incident is perhaps indicative of the general pattern. In March 1950, Muslims from various parts of Dinhata *thana* in Cooch-Behar began to leave their homes and take shelter in Pakistani enclaves along the border. Masaldanga was one of these enclaves, into which about 1500 Muslims crowded together seeking security in numbers. Sometime at the end of March, the local Rakshi Dal led by the secretary of the Nazirhat Congress Committee began to drive them out. In a campaign that resembles ethnic cleansing, they besieged the little enclave, cutting its inhabitants off from access to food and other essential supplies. The people of Masaldanga decided to shift wholesale across the border to safety. On 28 March they made their way to the checkpost under the protection of a Hindu mercenary who had collected a ransom from them as the price for his services. When they reached the border, they found the local Congress secretary waiting for them in the company of excise inspectors who insisted on searching them and their belongings. This added insult infuriated the Pakistani Muslims who had collected on the other side of the border to watch. They forced their way through and a riot broke out. The Congressman, who was armed with a dagger, stabbed one of them to death, whereupon the mob turned on him and killed him with his own weapon. His body was dragged across the border so as to deny the dead man the dignity of a suitable cremation.[162]

Incidents such as these suggest that the presence of armed border militias did much to rekindle communal hostilities along the border. If this is correct, it would seem that they played an important part in strengthening the border and making it more impregnable. This was not just because they carried lathis (and even guns) and tended to use them indiscriminately. In this they merely supplemented the already considerable physical force wielded

[162] Note of 19 April 1950, GB IB file no. 1238/47 (Cooch-Behar).

by the official border security force. Their special contribution was to act as an ideological bulwark, not only against outsiders but against the fifth columnists within. Their presence in the community served as a warning to the so-called anti-nationals who would trade with the enemy. And for ordinary law-abiding villagers they acted as teachers in citizenship, preaching patriotism and loyalty to the new nation-state, and defining the neighbour across the border as the enemy.[163] Villagers were encouraged to keep their eyes open and report suspicious activities to them: in other words, to carry tales against fellow villagers and neighbours to the authorities. So it is significant that it was Banaphool Panchayat, head of the village council of Jaigir Balabari, who betrayed his neighbour Ershad Ali Khondokar and his companions when they crossed the border to reap the crop on their own plots in March 1951: Banaphool actually led the soldiers to the spot and pointed the culprits out to them.[164] There was also an important symbolism in the Ansars' act of burning down houses evacuated by Indian Muslims who crossed the border to Pakistan. It was not just that the Muslim refugee now no longer had anything to which to return, although this was undeniably important. By encouraging him to set fire to his home, the Ansar was asking the Muslim refugee to repudiate his entire Indian past, to be "born again" as a Pakistani. It was almost a rite of passage which made migration to the new state a final and irrevocable act.

This flew in the face of the official policy of openness, just as the Rakshi Dal's effort at ethnic cleansing in Cooch-Behar defied Nehru's "psychological" approach of guaranteeing security to minorities. The militias ensured that life could not go on as usual

[163] The Commandant of the Pakistan National Guard thus announced that one of its main objects "was to enable the people to serve their country better by training them in citizenship and discipline . . ." *The Statesman*, 23 December 1947.

[164] One man was shot dead in this incident. GB IB File No. 1238–27 (Cooch-Behar).

on the border. We cannot be certain how far this was the result that the two governments intended to achieve. On the Indian side, we know that there were differences of opinion between Nehru and Dr B.C. Roy, the premier of West Bengal. The latter favoured a hard-line approach towards Pakistan and would have preferred to seal the border completely, even to Hindu refugees from the east. He also recommended that the border zones be cleared of Muslims and resettled with "loyal" Hindus, but Nehru would have none of it.[165] It is perhaps significant that the decision to set up the Rakshi Dal was taken by the West Bengal (rather than the Indian) government. On the Pakistani side, we know only that from the middle of 1951 the border was further fortified in preparation for the threat of war between India and Pakistan. In August 1951 Khulna Hindus were reportedly shifted out from areas within a radius of three miles from the border, and the entire population, Hindu and Muslim, was evacuated from the Jalpaiguri border. Jungles in the border zone began to be cleared and the booking of goods between Rajshahi and Godagari was stopped. In September, Section 144 of the Criminal Procedure Code was declared along the entire Nadia border, and in October *haats* along the entire length of the border were closed down.[166]

All of this changed life on the border beyond recognition. Long

[165] Nehru wrote: "I have had some reports about the border areas of Nadia district. It is stated that large number[s] of Muslims living on our side of the border are being uprooted and taken elsewhere. Presumably, the policy is to clear those areas, up to a certain depth, of Muslims because it is thought that they might be unreliable elements in case of trouble. I feel that such a policy would be definitely wrong and harmful even from the narrowest view of expediency. It would, of course, be against any general principle that we follow . . . Any such attempt would do us injury in many ways . . . I should like you to look into this matter and take steps to rectify any such action which might have been taken . . ." Jawaharlal Nehru to Dr Bidhan Chandra Roy, 15 September 1951, cited in Chakrabarty, *With Dr. B.C. Roy*, pp. 192–3.

[166] Report of the Superintendent of Police (Intelligence Branch), Nadia, 26 September 1951, GB IB file no. 1238-A/47.

before war actually broke out, the little villages and once-sleepy hamlets had become busy centres of militia activities. People whose closest contact with the state had once been the local chowkidar now became accustomed to seeing armed men in uniform. Where they had once lived off the land as best as they could, earning a little cash by selling their wares at the weekly market, now they could, if they dared, turn to smuggling instead, or else offer to supply the needs of the nearest police picket or army barracks. Village politics that had, so far as we know, revolved around caste councils, union boards, and tenancy disputes, now began to be the site where citizenship and patriotic duty were propagated, where ideological battles between nations were fought.

This suggests that even if the border zones were geographically on the periphery of the new state, politically they were not. Once these regions had been quiet backwaters where the state was a distant presence. But now, paradoxically, the border catapulted them into the closest proximity with the state. It has been customary to think of borders as being peripheral to the state. If the centre is the core of the state, where its political, economic, and cultural hegemony is strongest, the border has been generally thought of as its opposite, as a terrain where the political power of the state is most compromised.[167] But as we have seen, on the Bengal frontier the relationship between the nation-state and its borders was far more complex, intense, and direct than the centre–periphery model would have us expect.

Conclusion

In the first part of this essay we saw how the Radcliffe Line came to take its final shape, how the making of the border was influenced by calculations that often had little to do with communal or even national interest. The arguments and appeals presented before the

[167] See the introduction by Julian Minghi in Rumley and Minghi, *The Geography of Border Landscapes*.

Boundary Commission demonstrated, if anything, how quickly communal solidarity could fall apart along lines of territory, party, faction, and personal ambition when it ran into the reality of Partition. If the original purpose of the Bengal Partition was indeed to wrest a separate homeland for the Hindu community, it is striking how many Hindus were sacrificed in order to achieve it, and how readily these sacrifices were made.

Yet the myth of the homeland had to be kept alive, especially at the border. We saw in the second part how the border, once defined, quickly became sacrosanct. And it had to be honoured as such by the ordinary village people who happened to live along its path, even at the expense of their homes, their lands, their livelihood, and their very lives. If heavy-handed persuasion and even force were necessary to extract their compliance, it was justified "in the national interest".

To return to the discussion of the surgical metaphor with which I began: the first half of the essay shows how inappropriate it is to consider the drawing of the border as a purely technical affair. The border was not drawn dispassionately, with clinical precision and attention to detail. It was a hastily and ignorantly drawn line in whose drafting political pressures played no small part. Moreover, the political considerations that shaped the drawing up of the border were substantially different from the concerns which had influenced the 3 June Plan. In this sense, the politics of Partition was far from being over and done with on 3 June or even on 17 August 1947. Partition was a political process which continued to unfold long afterwards, and indeed continues to unfold even today.

So Partition was in no sense like an operation that was concluded in August 1947. The border is far from being the trace of an event long over, like a healed and fading incision scar. It is still in the process of being formed. Its creation was not merely a matter of drawing a line through a map by a qualified technocrat: it was created again and again by a number of different agencies on the ground through which it ran. Its shape, both literally and metaphorically, has varied, and continues to vary, through time.

In the second part I have tried to suggest what is really wrong with the surgical metaphor by showing how extraordinarily violent and crude an instrument the border was. Looked at from the ground, from the eyes of those whose lives it shattered, this violence was the more terrifying because it was irrational, because there was no sense in which it could ever have been rational. Even if in one place the Radcliffe Line had not cut this sharecropper off from his field, or separated that woman from her parental home, they would have been the lucky exceptions and their lives undoubtedly would have been damaged in a thousand other ways. The idiom of surgery puts a gloss on this experience. Surgery is painful and bloody, but it serves a purpose – it makes things all right in the end – and the pain of surgery is comprehensible and endurable because of this. By describing the creation of the border in these terms, the violence that was involved in this process (and the destruction that could never be put right) has been contained within an acceptable, comprehensible, and even meaningful idiom. The surgical metaphor has thus worked to lend legitimacy and credibility not only to the Radcliffe Line but to the very idea of Partition itself.

References

Azad, Maulana Abul Kalam, *India Wins Freedom*, New Delhi, 1959, rpnt 1988.

Bhaduri, Satinath, "The Champion of the People", in Alok Bhalla, ed., *Stories about the Partition of India*, vol. I, New Delhi, 1994.

Blake, Lord, and C.S. Nicholls, eds, *The Dictionary of National Biography 1971–1980*, Oxford and New York, 1986.

Bose, Sugata *Agrarian Bengal. Economy, Social Structure and Politics, 1919–1947*, Cambridge, 1986.

Brasted, H.V., and Carl Bridge, "The Transfer of Power in South Asia: An Historiographical Review", *South Asia*, vol. XVII, no. 1 (1994).

Campbell-Johnson, Alan, *Mission with Mountbatten*, London 1951, rpnt 1985.

———, *Mission with Mountbatten*, London, 1951; rpnt 1985.

Chakrabarti, Prafulla, *The Marginal Men. The Refugees and the Left—Political Experiment in West Bengal*, Calcutta, 1990.

Chakrabarty, Saroj, *With Dr. B.C. Roy and Other Chief Ministers (A Record up to 1962)*, Calcutta, 1974.

Chandra, Prakash, "The National Question in Kashmir", *Social Scientist*, 13, 6 (June 1985).

Chatterji, Joya, *Bengal Divided. Hindu Communalism and Partition, 1932–1947*, Cambridge, 1994.

Chowdhury, Hamidul Huq, *Memoirs*, Dhaka, 1989.

Das Gupta, Ranajit, *Economy, Society and Politics in Bengal: Jalpaiguri 1869–1947*, Delhi, 1992.

Das, Durga, ed., *Sardar Patel's Correspondence 1945–1950*, vol. I, Ahmedabad, 1971.

Franda, Marcus, *West Bengal and the Federalizing Process in India*, Princeton, 1968.

Hodson, H.V., *The Great Divide: Britain–India*–Pakistan, Karachi, 1969, rpnt 1993.

Jalal, Ayesha, *Democracy and Authoritarianism in South Asia. A Comparative and Historical* Perspective, Cambridge, 1995.

———, *The Sole Spokesman. Jinnah, the Muslim League and the Demand for Pakistan*, Cambridge, 1985.

Khan, Ansar Hussain, *The Rediscovery of India. A New Subcontinent*, Hyderabad, 1995.

Kudaisya, Gyanesh, "The Demographic Upheaval of Partition: Refugees and Agricultural Resettlement in India, 1947–67", *South Asia*, vol. XVIII, Special issue (1995).

Mansergh, N., and P. Moon, eds, *Constitutional Relations between Britain and India: The Transfer of Power 1942–1947*, London, 1970–82.

Partition Proceedings, vol. I, New Delhi, Government of India Press, 1949.

Potter, David C., *India's Political Administrators. From ICS to IAS*, Delhi, 1966.

Report of the States Reorganisation Committee, New Delhi, Manager of Publications, 1955.

Raven, Simon, *The English Gentleman*, London, 1961.

Rumley, Dennis, and Julian Minghi, eds, *The Geography of Border Landscapes*, London and New York, 1991.

Sen, Shila, *Muslim Politics in Bengal, 1937–1947*, New Delhi, 1976.

Sengupta, Prasanta, *The Congress Party in West Bengal. A Study of Factionalism 1947–86*, Calcutta, 1986.

Singh, Kirpal, ed., *Select Documents on Partition of Punjab – 1947, India and Pakistan*, Delhi, 1991.

3

The Bengali Muslim

A Contradiction in Terms? An Overview of the Debate on Bengali Muslim Identity

THE BENGALI MUSLIM has long been regarded as a living oxymoron, his Muslimness vitiated to the extent that he is a Bengali. The idea that, outside the Middle East, Islam exists in contradistinction with a "host" culture is widely accepted and pervades much of the literature on Islam in South and South East Asia. It is certainly not unique to the discussion of Islam in Bengal. But in the case of Bengal it is particularly powerful because it appears to have been vindicated by history. The formation of Bangladesh is widely interpreted as the reassertion of a latent Bengali identity, hitherto suppressed by the triumphant pan-Islamism of the Muslim League political alliance.[1]

Bengali Muslim identity is thus commonly perceived as being riven by a faultline, with Bengaliness and Muslimness coexisting uneasily on the opposite sides of a deep and fundamental divide. Bengali Muslim culture is almost invariably written about in terms of a series of binary opposites which loosely correspond to the primary Muslim *versus* Bengali opposition: *ashraf* (Muslims of

[1] See, for instance, Ahmed, "Conflicts and Contradictions in Bengali Islam: Problem of Change and Adjustment", pp. 138–9,

foreign ancestry) *versus atrap* (Muslims of regional origins); orthodox *versus* heterodox; *sharia* (Muslims who adhere to the *shariat*) *versus basharia* (those who follow practices such as *pir* worship,[2] not sanctioned by the shariat), Urdu-speaking *versus* Bengali-speaking, elite *versus* popular, pan-Islamic *versus* regionalist, and so on. Moreover, it is readily assumed that each corresponding series of attributes – Muslimness, foreign antecedents, orthodoxy, shariat-following, Urdu-speaking – are clustered together, so much so that their relationship with each other is deemed to be one of continuity, even interchangeability. In other words, if one were told that a certain group of people were of *atrap* (or local) origin, it would be considered safe to assume that they were also Bengali-speaking, *pir*-worshipping, heterodox in religious practice, and all in all more "Bengali" than "Muslim".

Corresponding to this paradigm, the history of Bengali Muslims until 1947 has been understood as a history of Islamisation: as the history of a process by which the first series of attributes (Muslimness, *ashrafism*, orthodoxy, shariat-following, Urdu-speaking) gradually replaces the second (Bengaliness, *pir* worship, heterodoxy, idolatry, Bengali-speaking). In other words, it is perceived as linear progress, albeit partial and halting, towards the Islamic ideal. Conversely, the history of East Pakistan between 1947 and 1970 is written as a history of a triumphant "Bengaliness".[3]

This sort of narrative rests, in turn, on a particular understanding of "Islam" as a pure, transcendent idea, the "essentials" of which

[2] A *pir* is (literally) a mystic saint of a Sufi brotherhood. As we shall see later, this was not the only meaning of the word in Bengal.

[3] So, for instance, one scholar argues that immediately after Partition, *Bengali distinctiveness* was asserted within the Pakistani structure, that the struggle for language drew fresh attention to the *other* tradition (the first being Islam) both liberal and secular, the tradition of Bengali culture nurtured in the course of 2500 years. Anwar, "Muslim Mind and Society in Bangladesh". Also see Ahmed, "Contradictions in Bengali Islam", pp. 138–9; Murshid, *The Sacred and the Secular*, p. 443; Harun-ur-Rashid, *The Foreshadowing of Bangladesh*, p. 346.

are indisputable. Traditionally, these "essentials" are understood as being inscribed in certain core texts of Islam: whether the Koran, *sharia, sunnat,* or *hadith*. Not only are they obvious and indisputable, their true meaning, for many scholars, is unproblematic. For one historian, "the moral ideal established by the Koran is at once objectively knowable [and] universally applicable to all people and all times . . ."[4] Even Clifford Geertz, more sceptical than most scholars of the value of treating Islam as a single unified religion, tends to slip back into describing Islam as "a universal, in theory standardised and essentially unchangeable system of ritual and belief."[5] More recently, scholars have attempted to uncover in the diversity of Islamic practice certain "core values" which reflect a universal Islamic code of conduct or *adab*.[6] In her introduction to a collection of essays devoted to defining and describing *adab*, Barbara Metcalf speaks of her "wonder at having approached . . . the core of what has given the Islamic tradition its resilience throughout times and places of such increasing diversity . . ."[7] She insists not only that there is one Islam ("the teachings of Islam are one"),[8] but that "there is a general *adab* shared widely in Muslim society."[9] This general moral essence can be distilled, by careful scholarship, out of the medley of Islamic practice.

Following from this definition of Islam as having a pure, irreducible kernel, the process of conversion to Islam has often been explained with the analogy of implantation. It is frequently described as the process by which the pure seed of Islam was implanted in the "soil" of the host society. Biological metaphors of

[4] Eaton, "The Political and Religious Authority of the Shrine of Baba Farid", p. 333. As we shall see later, Eaton has moved away from this position in his recent work.

[5] Geertz, *Islam Observed*, p. 14.

[6] Metcalf, *Moral Conduct and Authority*.

[7] Metcalf's "Preface", ibid., p. viii.

[8] Ibid., "Introduction", p. 9.

[9] Ibid., p. 4.

insemination, implantation, and germination abound in scholarly writing on conversion to Islam.[10] Inevitably, the role of the host society is seen as passive,[11] merely receiving the living seed which takes root, grows, and struggles to survive. And where the cultural distance between the host society and western Asiatic cultures is great, the "soil" is deemed to be too poor to sustain a healthy tree: the Islam that grows in such soil will inevitably be a poor, debased sort of faith. In medieval Bengal, a humid, tropical, riverine, frontier society on the farthest eastern reaches of Gangetic civilisation, the product was "inevitably" a grossly distorted, almost unrecognisable version of Islam.

Another popular variation on this theme is the idea of "local accretions" which are believed to have obscured the pure Islamic core beneath. The metaphor of accretion or sedimentation of layers of local (cultural) matter is used to explain, for instance, the "invisibility" of Islam in Bengal.[12] So, for instance, the story of the first British census officers who were surprised to find so many Muslims in Bengal is told and retold to demonstrate the density of the local accretions that hid Bengali Islam from British view.

Yet for all this the fact remains that it is this very "stunted", "unrecognisable" version of Islam which prevails amongst the second-largest Muslim society in the world. Bengali-speaking Muslims are second only to Arab Muslims in number.[13] If their version of Islam is an exception to the rule, it is indeed a massive exception. As one scholar has remarked in a different context, rules which require such gigantic exceptions to sustain themselves can only have the most limited power to explain.[14]

This paradigm has limited the discussion of the history of Bengali Muslim society to a static and increasingly sterile reaffirmation

[10] See, for instance, Geertz, *Islam Observed*, p. 14.

[11] Ahmed, *The Bengal Muslims*, p. 8.

[12] Ahmed, "Conflicts and Contradictions in Bengali Islam", p. 127.

[13] Weekes, *Muslim Peoples*, p. 137.

[14] Chandavarkar, *The Origins of Industrial Capitalism in India*, p. 1.

of the "basic contradictions" and "inherent ambiguities" between true Islam and the Bengali reality. Moreover it has forced us for too long into the untenable position of regarding the Bengali Muslims as victims perpetually trapped in a dilemma of identity, forever torn between their (irreconcilable) Bengaliness and Muslimness. We cannot but help see this dilemma as being engendered by their own failure to grasp what we scholars comprehend so easily, i.e. the true meaning of Islam. From the traditional standpoint, the very density of "local" Bengali culture makes it opaque: Bengalis cannot see through it into the heart of Islam. So it is their lot to be Muslims only in name, or else Bengalis only in name.

This is, of course, a position that none of the scholars involved in the discussion would explicitly take. There is an element of parody in my description of what is undoubtedly a very rich and informed body of scholarship. But the parody is deliberately intended to bring out what I would argue is the underlying rationale within which the subject has been defined. Rafiuddin Ahmed, in his enormously influential and learned study of the Bengali Muslims, actually insists that "a Bengali identity was in no way inconsistent with their faith in Islam."[15] Yet his avowal is unconvincing because Ahmed accepts the main features of the model I have set out above: that there are certain "basic tenets of faith" that characterise Islam,[16] that Bengali Muslims, for the most part, "were semiliterate with a bare knowledge of the rudiments of Islam",[17] their faith was dominated by "un-Islamic" practices – such as *pir* worship,[18] and idolatry[19] – and that, despite a century of reformist efforts, they are very little closer to seeing the light today.[20] Inevitably, for Ahmed, "there was something

[15] Ahmed, *The Bengal Muslims*, p. 113.

[16] Ibid., p. 57.

[17] Ibid., p. 29.

[18] Ibid., p. 60.

[19] Ibid., p. 186.

[20] Ibid., pp. 186–90.

curiously self-contradictory in the Muslim masses' quest for an Islamic identity.[21] And Geertz, whose writings on Indonesia and Morocco have deeply influenced scholarship on Islam outside western Asia, goes even further to conclude that Muslims in these cultures are "rather thoroughly mixed up".[22]

Is this a tenable point of view? Can one be comfortable with a paradigm which regards the people who are its subjects as somehow unable to see the main point? If Geertz, Ahmed, Metcalf, and a host of other scholars, writing from cultural positions no closer to the Arabia of the Prophet, can easily and unproblematically grasp the "core" values and "basic tenets" of Islam, why have Bengali Muslims failed to do likewise? Surely no one would argue that as a "race" they lack the mental equipment. Nor would I suggest for a moment that any of the scholars cited here would take such a stance. Yet the way in which they have argued the issue leads us, albeit unwillingly, into this position. How are we to extricate ourselves from it?

This essay aims critically to examine the paradigm within which the discussion of Bengali Muslim identity has been circumscribed. It will suggest more fruitful ways of looking at the subject and point to recent research which is beginning to engage with these questions in a new and dynamic way. I should stress at the outset that this essay is not based on original historical research and makes no claims to specialist competence in this area. It is no more than an idiosyncratic overview of the literature by a reviewer whose entry into the subject has been by a circuitous route.

I

The first and most obvious problem with the traditional paradigm is its deployment of a profoundly idealistic notion of "Islam". In the framework outlined above, Islam appears an autonomous subject which acts on society. This is clearest in the discussion

[21] Ibid., p. 184.

[22] Geertz, *Islam Observed*, p. 18.

of conversion, where Islam appears as the living seed and society as the inert soil in which it grows. In other words, Islam is treated as a subject or agent and Bengali society as merely a passive predicate.[23]

This gives rise to a particular problem. If we think of Bengali society as a "thing" that was acted upon by Islam, it encourages us to regard that society as a fixed entity with a given structure. This is to think in a way that deprives the Bengalis of agency and also to dehistoricise Bengal, to reduce it to a context whose basic elements are unchanging. This has led to some extraordinarily careless history-writing by otherwise painstaking scholars. For instance, Rafiuddin Ahmed writes that "Bengal, particularly the low-lying districts of eastern and southern Bengal where Islam found most of its adherents, *has been a peasant society for the whole of her recorded history*, agriculture . . . has [always) provided the foundations of the region's distinctive culture."[24] The point about this is not so much that it is incorrect (as we shall see later, the areas where Islam has flourished in Bengal were brought under the plough much more recently), but that the author is so comfortable with this picture of an unchanging peasant society because the uncritical idealism of his paradigm predisposes him to think of society as an inert object.[25] If Bengal appears to have had no history, it is because history itself – in the sense of diachronicity and change – is not a dynamic variable in this model.

[23] The theoretical difficulties of this approach were pointed out a long time ago, though in a different context. See Marx's polemic against Hegel in his "Critique of Hegel's Doctrine of the State" (1843), in Marx, *Early Writings*.

[24] Ahmed, "Conflicts and Contractions in Bengali Islam", p. 115. Emphasis added.

[25] Similarly, he speculates that "a plausible explanation for such a massive Muslim population . . . is the *possibility* of large-scale conversions of indigenous tribes who *probably* have never been fully Hinduized, either professing a localized form of Buddhism or adhering to the animistic rituals and beliefs of their ancestors", ibid., p. 119. Here again, we sense that it would make little difference to the author's argument if these assumptions actually turned out to be wrong.

If we turn to the second part of this binary, i.e. Islam, the problem is slightly different. Problems arise from the tendency to think of Islam as a set of "core values" with an unambiguous meaning.

There are two ways in which this notion is problematic. It does not allow for the possibility that Islam's "core values" might be historically constituted: in other words, that at different places and times in history, and in response to different sorts of challenges, different constellations of ideas might have been represented as being the "core values" of Islam. It does not grant that this terrain might in fact be a contested one, in which different and even contradictory readings of Islam compete for hegemony. And yet even a cursory reading (against the grain) of the history of Muslims in Bengal suggests that it is possible to argue this case. So, for instance, one might argue that the early battles between the ulama and the Sufis were actually a debate about the "true meaning" of Islam; with the ulama insisting that dualism, the transcendence of God and the shariat laws were the non-negotiable truth of Islam, while the Sufis who argued for God's immanence and monism, asserted that the shariat was only a primer for the uninitiated and that there was a higher truth revealed only to those who pursued the mystic path. Similarly one could argue that the subsequent Tariqah and Fairazi campaigns against the "corrupted" practices of both the ulama and the *pirs* were actually reinventing the "fundamental tenets" of Islam in ways that allowed for no intermediaries between man and God. Yet even the reformers themselves did not agree about the key texts (some argued that "only" the Koran and *sunnat* were the core texts of Islam, others insisted that the hadith be included). The Wahabis did not accept any of the four established schools of Islamic jurisprudence, the Fairazis accepted the Hanafite school,[26] and so on. One might extend this further to argue that in the modern period, when communal friction with "Hindus"

[26] Ahmed, *The Bengal Muslims*, pp. 58–60.

increasingly dominated religious discussion, non-Hindu practices (such as cow slaughter, silence before mosques, iconoclasm) were elevated by some Muslims (such as Pir Abu Bakr) to the status of core values, while others argued that universal brotherhood, equality, and tolerance were the "true" meaning of Islam.[27]

This is not to suggest that this scheme or history is the correct one. It is merely to argue that it is one among many readings opened up once we give up our habit of regarding Islam's core values as an unchanging, universal, and standardised essence about which there can be (and has been) no dispute.

The second order of problems arises from thinking of Islam (and Islamic texts) as having an unambiguous, fixed meaning. It is a little surprising to have to raise this point *vis-à-vis* a body of scholarship so deeply influenced by Geertz. After all it was Geertz who so eloquently argued for the impossibility of a correct or final interpretation of culture.[28] And yet Geertz himself lapses from his own position when it comes to discussing what Islam *is*.[29]

The arguments against the possibility of establishing the "true meaning" of any text are well known in the social sciences and I will not go over this ground here. But it has important implications for any discussion about Bengali Muslim identity. If (as has generally been the case) the core texts of Islam are credited with a

[27] Datta, "Hindu–Muslim Relations in Bengal in the 1920s", pp. 132, 134.

[28] See, for instance, "Thick Description: Towards an Interpretive Theory of Culture", in Geertz, *The Interpretation of Cultures*.

[29] The isolation of the study of Islam from the main currents of the social sciences is remarkable. But as Edward Said has pointed out, this isolation has a long history. He argues that "the history of Islamic Orientalism is relatively free of sceptical currents and almost entirely free from methodological self-questioning. Most students of Islam in the West have not doubted that despite the limitations of time and place, a genuinely objective knowledge of Islam . . . is achievable . . . I have been unable to find any contemporary example of the Islamic scholar for whom the enterprise of 'knowing' Islam was itself a source of doubt . . ." Said, *Covering Islam*, pp.128–9. Perhaps Geertz's lapse from his hermeneutic position can be understood in the context of this tradition of scholarship.

fixed and unambiguous meaning, then "true" conversion must be regarded as the process of correctly apprehending their message. Conversely, "false" conversion is failing to comprehend the true meaning. When there is only one possible meaning, you either get it or you don't. In this sense, it has been argued the Bengali masses were not proper Muslims because they failed to understand the true meaning of Islam. This is explained partly as a failure of pedagogy (those who tried to teach them – the rural *ulema* – did not understand "it" themselves);[30] and partly as a failure of translation (Bengali culture was so different, in essence, from Islam that all attempts at translation failed). But for whatever reason, goes the argument, the Bengali Muslims did not (and still do not) get "it", while to us scholars "it" is as obvious as "it" is indisputable.

Now the problem with this is not only that this is an uncomfortable argument to justify. It also lends weight to fundamentalism. If there is only one true meaning of Islam, then the fundamentalist reformers must be understood on their own terms as pedagogues who were trying to teach people this true meaning. We cannot help inferring that they were right. So, for instance, Rafiuddin Ahmed cannot help but reach the conclusion that the fundamentalists launched the process of true "Islamisation" in Bengal,[31] however much he might deplore fundamentalist politics.

If, on the other hand, we accept as valid the idea that "meaning" is impossible to fix, the whole picture changes. Conversion then becomes an act whose agents are the converts themselves. They become, like Barthes' readers, creative agents who write the text anew with each reading.[32] From this standpoint, fundamentalism is not an effort to impart "true meaning" but an effort to foreclose

[30] Ahmed, *The Bengal Muslims*, p. 29.

[31] He thus argues that the process of Islamization in Bengal began only in the nineteenth century with the rise of fundamentalist movements. Ahmed, "Conflicts and Contradictions".

[32] Barthes, "The Death of the Author".

the possibility of reading itself by valorising one reading above all others. Islamisation can then be understood not as a process of gradual purification of belief, or as a movement in the direction of the truth that Islam actually is, but as a project of imposing on society one construct or reading of Islam as the correct one.

In other words, it opens up the whole field of discussion in a historical way. Or rather, it allows one to write history differently. When seen from the old standpoint of Islamisation, Islam itself – eternal, essential, and unique, standing outside time – was the subject of history, and history could be written in only one way, as "an alternate in a continuity of decadence and health".[33] In Bengal, this meant that history could only be a narrative of gradual (and still incomplete) recovery of an Islam rendered diseased by the hostile local culture of Bengal.

But if we can accept that what is put forward as true Islam is itself a social construct, we can then begin to think about when, how, and why that construct was fashioned. We can begin to consider the processes by which it came to exercise hegemony, shutting out alternative readings. We could see these alternative readings not as "accretions" or corruptions but as powerful and compelling creations with a rich history of their own. We can think about how particular readings of Islam came to be bound up, at different times, with power and privilege. We would have to seek the answers to these questions in Bengali society itself, in its history. We would have to think, in other words, about these issues in ways that break down the dichotomies between religion and society, "Islam" and "Bengal", "Muslimness" and "Bengaliness".

II

Two recent books have made a breakthrough in this direction: Asim Roy's history of Islamic syncretism in Bengal,[34] and Richard

[33] Al-Azmeh, *Islams and Modernities*, p. 42.

[34] Roy, *The Islamic Syncretistic Tradition in Bengal.*

Eaton's study of the rise of Islam in Bengal.[35] Both are histories of the origins and growth of Islamic society in Bengal. Essentially they cover the same period, the thirteenth to eighteenth centuries, and complement each other. Eaton's is the more ambitious, including in its ambit the consideration of socio-political, geographical, technological, as well as ideational changes which accompanied the rise of Islam in Bengal. Roy's focus is more specifically on culture, on the emergence of a syncretistic Islamic tradition in Bengal. Neither extends further in time than the eighteenth century. Neither deals, therefore, either with the rise of fundamentalist movements in the nineteenth century or with the emergence of modern (twentieth-century) Muslim identity politics in Bengal. Yet both books, read together, throw new and (in my view) significant light on the whole question of Bengali Muslim identity.

Eaton's is the first work to seriously engage with the question of the exceptional expansion of Islam in Bengal. How did it come to pass that the people of a far-flung delta, never thoroughly subjugated by Delhi, embraced Islam in such large numbers, while those of the north Indian heartland, more closely integrated into the political and cultural systems established by successive Muslim monarchs, did not? This is a paradox that has long baffled observers. Eaton provides, at long last, some persuasive answers.

The great strength of Eaton's work is that it deploys the terms "Islam" and "Bengal" in a remarkably open-ended and dynamic way. In his analysis, neither are closed or discrete cultural systems: they are constantly in flux. For Eaton, deltaic Bengal was far from being *a peasant society for the whole of her recorded history*, with an ancient (primordial) culture founded in agriculture.[36] Instead he describes the Bengal delta as frontier zone in which different frontiers – each moving by its own dynamic gradually from west to east – overlapped. The first and oldest frontier defined

[35] Eaton, *The Rise of Islam and the Bengal Frontier.*

[36] Ahmed, "Conflicts and Contradictions", p. 115. Emphasis added.

the long-term eastward movement of Sanskritic civilisation. The second, agrarian, frontier divided settled agricultural zones from the uncultivated marshes and forests. The third was the political frontier, which defined the territories within which the sultans and Mughal governors "minted coins, garrisoned troops and collected revenue". And the fourth was the porous Islamic frontier between Muslim and non-Muslim communities.[37] Eaton explains the growth of Islam in Bengal as the product of a complex interaction between each of these dynamic frontiers.

His argument is a complex and sophisticated one, and I will not attempt to summarise it here. Instead, I will draw upon it in parts to bring out themes which are significant to any discussion of modern Bengali identity.

Briefly put, Eaton argues for two stages in the advance of the Islamic frontier in Bengal. The first began when Mohammed Bakhtiyar led his Turkish cavalry into Bengal in the beginning of the thirteenth century, ending with the consolidation of Mughal power over Bengal at the end of the sixteenth century. In this period, the sultans of Delhi struggled to keep Bengal in their ken, but with very little success. In 1359, Firuz Shah Tughlaq's effort to establish his hold over Bengal failed, and after this Delhi left Bengal alone for two and a half centuries. Successive ruling dynasties established their capitals in the older, more settled areas of western Bengal and governed them, always with one eye on the threat from Delhi. It was a period characterised by conflict, whether intense or simmering, between the rulers of Bengal and the court at Delhi.

In this first phase, Islam came to Bengal as a religion of the court capital and garrison towns where Turks, Arabs, and Afghans settled. Most of the important Sufi brotherhoods grew in the capital cities and for the most part shared ties of mutual patronage and dependency with the courts. Islam did not become a mass religion in this period. Nevertheless, some crucial themes of

[37] Eaton, *The Rise of Islam*, p. xxv.

Bengali Islam were born in this period: the most significant being Ashrafism or the cult of "foreign origins" that is still so much in evidence in modern Bengal.

Eaton's work suggests that as the Bengal sultans struggled to break free of Delhi, they sought ways of articulating their political authority without reference to the sultanate. One strategy was to claim a direct relationship with the "centre" of Islam and with the caliphate. In the titles they adopted, the coins they minted, and the grand mosques they built, they used motifs that deliberately replicated Sassanian and Iranian traditions. This was a strategy that sought to bypass the authority of Delhi and to appeal over its head directly to the "highest" authorities of Islam in Persia. They cultivated a version of Persio-Sassanian culture so as to distance themselves from their would-be overlords at Delhi.[38] Gradually, as the threat from Delhi grew weaker and the need grew to co-opt local "Hindu" notables into their political system, local motifs were incorporated into the paraphernalia of power. It was this cultural complex that survived as Ashrafism: in the valorisation of Persian, the insistence on foreign origins, the habit of tracing lineages back to the Khalifat, in a version of pan-Islamism that ignored Delhi and looked only towards Mecca-sharif and the Khalifa.

Several points emerge from this that bear upon the question of modern Bengali Muslim identity. The first is that Ashrafism was a construct, born of the political history of medieval Bengal. Later attempts to impose *ashraf* culture as genuinely Islamic culture must be seen in this context. Ashrafism was in no sense congruent with what passes for "Islamic orthodoxy": indeed the earliest (and some of the most popular) Sufi orders were patronised by *ashraf* kings, courtiers, and soldiers. There is a real tendency in scholarly writing to mistake Ashrafisation for Islamisation.[39] Eaton's work cautions us against this error.

[38] Ibid., pp. 47–50.

[39] This perspective is particularly pervasive in all of Rafiuddin Ahmed's writings.

The second point is that Ashrafism is quite as much Bengali as the more popular sorts of Islam that emerged at a later date. It was born in Bengal, in response to very local and particular political contingencies. Despite its deployment of foreign pan-Islamic idioms, it was basically the ideology of a regional elite seeking to protect and legitimate its regional power against the centre. In its first incarnation, therefore, Ashrafism was not fashioned in opposition to popular *atrap* Islam. There were in fact no *atrap* Muslims to speak of at the time when Ashrafism was first elaborated. So the scholarly habit of posing *ashraf* and *atrap* as eternal opposites is ahistorical.

Atrap Islam, according to Eaton, is a recent development. He argues that mass conversion only began in the Mughal era, in the seventeenth and eighteenth centuries. Several things happened simultaneously, "by momentous coincidence", to create the conditions for the rise of Islam in the delta. The first was the change in the course of the Ganga, so that its main channel now met the Padma. Its main discharge, which had hitherto been into the Bhagirathi-Hooghly river system in the west, now surged through the eastern land mass into the sea. This meant that for the first time a channel of communication was opened up directly linking eastern Bengal with the Gangetic heartland. It also meant that as the active delta moved eastwards, it created new possibilities for intensive settled cultivation in the marshy and forested tracts of the east.

It so happened that these natural changes took place at about the same time that Akbar launched his campaign to integrate the entire delta into the Mughal revenue system. The spread of settled cultivation went hand in hand with the spread of Mughal authority, and according to Eaton the via-media for both were pioneer-saints. These men (some but by no means all of whom claimed divine inspiration) organised the clearing of the forests and the sowing of the first rice crop. They did so with the backing of the Mughal state, which gave them titles to the land they cleared in expectation of enhancing its agricultural output and revenue collections. These pioneers were the first *pirs* who brought Islam to this frontier zone together with the axe and the plough. They were remembered by later generations of east Bengali Muslims as much for their power over nature as for their Islamic teaching. The shrines that were built in their memory, together with the rough mosques that they erected, were the social and cultural nuclei of new communities that grew up around them.

So Islam did not descend upon a ready-made ancient agrarian civilisation (as Rafiuddin Ahmed contends). On the contrary, it advanced hand in hand with a new agricultural civilisation. It developed in eastern Bengal as a vector not only of religious change, but of social and technological revolution. It was "locally understood as a civilisation-building ideology", a religion of the axe and the plough and was analogous with economic development and agricultural prosperity.[40] It is in this context that one must interpret the extraordinary popularity of Islam in rural Bengal, as also its depth and tenacity.

Most of the first Muslim converts were tribal forest-dwellers only weakly influenced by Sanskritic civilisation. They did not convert from Hinduism to Islam: instead they incorporated Islamic superhuman agencies into dynamic local cosmologies. Eaton and Asim Roy both give us some fascinating insights into this process. Roy argues for an "orthogenetic" model of interaction between the two cultures, with each acting as a stimulus in the generation of growth and change in the other.[41] Islamic belief in Bengal was born of the interaction between two vigorous systems, so that by now it is impossible to extricate the foreign from the indigenous elements in popular rituals and beliefs.

Eaton and Roy both stress the crucial importance of the *pir* cults in the creation of popular Islam. Both argue, however, that it is

[40] Eaton, *The Rise of Islam*, p. 308.

[41] Roy, *The Islamic Syncretistic Tradition*, p. 250.

unhelpful to regard the *pir* tradition in the standard way as simply the veneration or worship of mystic guides and holy men, though some *pir* cults did begin in this way.[42] Many other founder-*pirs* were leaders of men canonised for the secular part they had played in the taming of the forest.[43] As Eaton argues, "in such cases, the vocabulary of popular Sufism stabilised in popular memory those persons who had been instrumental in building new (agricultural) communities", persons who often had little acquaintance with the intricacies of Islamic mysticism.[44] In other cases, *pir* cults grew up around older (pre-Muslim) mythical figures attributed with special superhuman powers. Even inanimate objects, venerated for their particular powers over nature, over the forest, snakes, crocodiles, tigers and diseases, were "pirified".[45] Eaton suggests that these forces were Islamised as Islam itself came to represent the force of civilisation (agrarianisation) against the vagaries of nature.

If Eaton and Roy are correct, their works have important implications for the discussion of modern Muslim Bengali identity. They demonstrate, for one, that the growth of folk or popular Islam went hand in hand with the extension of Mughal authority in the southern and eastern deltaic tracts of Bengal. The Mughal state was a key player in the process by which forests were cleared, lands brought under the plough, little mosques and shrines constructed, and peasant civilisation built up in these areas. The early pioneers in these frontier regions were patronised by the Mughal court, receiving from it land titles, grants-in-aid, and religious endowments. The revenue-paying Muslim peasant communities that emerged in these areas were thus integrated into the centralised state structure. In this sense, these Muslim communities were far less parochial than their predecessors in Bengal,

[42] Ibid., p. 208.

[43] Ibid.

[44] Eaton, *The Rise of Islam*, p. 257.

[45] Roy, *The Islamic Syncretistic Tradition*, p. 208.

the *ashraf* Muslims of the towns. The latter might have had foreign ancestors and might have looked to Iran and Mecca for the symbols of their authority, but their political allegiances were the more strongly regional.

This picture shakes some of our deepest assumptions about the sources of the regional identity of Bengali Muslims. For too long, a continuity has been readily assumed between the adherents of folk Islam or the *atrap* Mussalmans, and a sense of regional Bengali identity. The *atrap* Mussalmans had Bengali ethnic origins: they spoke Bengali dialects and followed a heterodox local version of Islam, hence the argument that they must have had a strong sense of regional Bengali identity (which was "ready-made" for mobilisation during the struggle for Bangladesh).[46] Conversely, it is assumed that because *ashraf* Muslims had non-Bengali ancestors, spoke non-Bengali languages, and followed (though this is debatable) a more orthodox sort of Islam, they must have had a more trans-regional, pan-Indian, and pan-Islamic worldview (which was "readymade" for mobilisation by the Muslim League). Yet the arguments outlined above turn these assumptions on their heads. If nothing else, they force us to question these assumptions and to think afresh about the processes (political as well as cultural) by which a regional Bengali identity was constructed.

This work also throws new light on another hoary shibboleth in the discussion of Bengali Muslim identity: the class–community paradox. Scholarly discussion of Muslim communalism in Bengal has almost invariably drawn attention to the ways in which agrarian (class) issues were "given a communal colouring" in twentieth-century Bengal. There has been a search for the culprits responsible for this unfortunate twist, and the so-called *kath mullah*, the itinerant Muslim preacher, has been a handy peg on which to hang the blame.[47] Increasingly, there has been dissatisfaction with this

[46] See, for instance, Murshid, *The Sacred and the Secular*, pp. 440–4.

[47] Taj ul-Islam Hashmi, for instance, writes that "as agents of orthodoxy and Islamic revivalism, the *pirs* and other categories of *ulama* aroused religious

paradigm, as more and more scholars ask why it is that class interests have lent themselves so easily to communalisation.[48] If Eaton is right, then we have the beginnings of an answer. If Islam was a part of the very process by which agrarian civilisation was born, if Islam was a vector of social and technological transformation, if it was indeed the "world-building ideology" of a nascent agrarian civilisation, we can see how the hard distinction between class and community ideologies might break down.

This is not to suggest that "Islam" was the same thing for the peasant-pioneers of the eighteenth century as it was for the *jotedars* and *adhiars* of twentieth-century Bengal. What Islam signified for Bengali peasants must undoubtedly have been transformed and reinvented countless times even as agrarian society grew more complex and stratified with the onset of colonial rule and the elaboration of intricate tenurial hierarchies under the Permanent Settlement. But there are suggestions, for instance in the work of Pradip Datta, that in the twentieth century being a Muslim was imagined in ways that sought to tie Islam to notions of a peasant ethic. Datta describes the emergence of a genre of writing by rural Muslims that preached peasant improvement in ways that combined practical advice on day-to-day agriculture with ethical (Islamic) exhortations. Their message was that the path to collective (Muslim) betterment lay in pursuing individual economic advancement and piety. In these texts, Muslim peasants were given practical advice, for instance on how to form co-operative banks and credit societies in order to pursue more capital-intensive improvements in their agricultural practice.[49] They were also warned – always with reference to appropriate parables from the life of the Prophet – against the dangers of

solidarity and fanaticism among a large section of the peasantry . . ." Hashmi, *Pakistan as a Peasant Utopia*, p. 127.

[48] Datta, "Hindu–Muslim Relations", p. 78.

[49] Ibid., p. 99.

extravagance and improvidence.[50] We can see how, in their emphasis on agricultural pedagogy, they might have resonated powerfully with older, perhaps still familiar, images and messages of Islam.

Datta points out that the discourse of improvement was not intentionally communal, although it did cast the Hindu moneylender in the role of enemy, setting him up as a corrupt figure of temptation who lured hard-working Muslim peasants into the trap of debt.[51] But in the hands of a powerful thinker and organiser such as Abu Bakr (who, interestingly enough, called himself a Sharia-*pir*) improvement could be reworked so as to make it, without too much difficulty, available for absorption into a more deliberately communal agenda.[52] Here then was yet another version of "true Islam", which raised cow slaughter, iconoclasm, and silence before mosques to the status of "core values" for an idealised Muslim peasant community.[53]

Where does all of this leave the question of Bengali Muslim identity? We can see that very little might remain of the familiar "crisis of identity" paradigm if scholars of Bengali Muslim history were to give up their idealist and essentialist assumptions, the most tenacious of which is the idea of a true and fundamentally knowable Islam. If this lynchpin is removed, the entire structure built around the idea of oppositional essences of Bengali Islam-Muslimness *versus* Bengaliness, *ashraf versus atrap*, elite *versus* popular, *sharia versus basharia*, collapses. All of these become porous concepts which have overlapped with each other at different times and in a variety of ways. So in the early twentieth century, Pir Abu Bakr could describe himself as a Sharia-*pir*, straddling orthodoxy and heterodoxy by means of a new rendition of Islam. Similarly, as we have seen, Ashrafism could and did overlap with Bengali regionalism and with *basharia* practices. It is clearly

[50] Ibid., pp. 87–70.

[51] Ibid., p. 95.

[52] Ibid., pp. 120ff.

[53] Ibid., pp. 132, 134.

time to dispense with a model that insists on presenting Bengali Islam itself as a paradox. In its stead, we need to fashion a new historiography which takes very little for granted and subjects even the most cherished notions to sceptical scrutiny and doubt.

The recent breakthrough that scholars have made in this direction may not be only of academic or historiographical interest. It might also have implications for our understanding of contemporary political questions. If, as I have tried to show, "true Islam" has always been a matter of dispute, whose outcome (always temporary) has been bound up with power, it follows that there is no authentic soul or spirit of Islam, or indeed of the Muslim community. From this standpoint, authenticity can only be a fundamentalist claim that seeks to standardise, essentialise, and sentimentalise a past which has been characterised by plurality, multivocality, and conflict.

References

Ahmed, Rafiuddin, "Contradictions in Bengali Islam: Problem of Change and Adjustment", in Katherine P. Ewing, ed., *Shariat and Ambiguity in South Asian Islam*, Delhi, 1988.

———, *The Bengal Muslims 1871–1906: A Quest for Identity*, Delhi, 1981.

al-Azmeh, Aziz, *Islams and Modernities*, London, 1993.

Anwar, Ali, "Muslim Mind and Society in Bangladesh: A Historical Retrospect", in Asghar Ali Engineer, ed., *Islam in South and South-East Asia*, Delhi, 1985.

Barthes, Roland, "The Death of the Author", in idem, *Image Music Text*, London, 1977; translated edn 1990.

Chandavarkar, Rajnarayan, *The Origins of Industrial Capitalism in India: Business Strategies and the Working Classes in Bombay, 1900–1940*, Cambridge, 1994.

Datta, Pradip Kumar, "Hindu–Muslim Relations in Bengal in the 1920s", Delhi University, Ph.D. thesis, 1995.

Eaton, Richard M., "The Political and Religious Authority of the Shrine of Baba Farid" in Barbara Daly Metcalf, ed., *Moral Conduct and Authority: The Place of Adab in South Asian Islam*, Berkeley, 1984.

———, *The Rise of Islam and the Bengal Frontier, 1204–1760*, Delhi, 1960.

Geertz, Clifford, "Thick Description: Towards an Interpretive Theory of Culture", in idem, *The Interpretation of Cultures*, New York, 1973.

———, *Islam Observed: Religious Development in Morocco and Indonesia*, New Haven and London, 1968.

Harun-ur-Rashid, *The Foreshadowing of Bangladesh: Bengal Muslim League and Muslim Politics, 1936–1947*, Dhaka, 1987.

Hashmi, Taj ul-Islam, *Pakistan as a Peasant Utopia. The Communalisation of Class Politics in Bengal, 1920–1947*, Boulder, San Fransisco and Oxford, 1992.

Marx, Karl, "Critique of Hegel's Doctrine of the State" (1843), in Karl Marx, *Early Writings*, London, 1975.

Murshid, Tazeen, *The Sacred and the Secular: Bengali Muslim Discourses 1871–1977*, Calcutta, 1995.

Roy, Asim, *The Islamic Syncretistic Tradition in Bengal*, New Delhi, 1983.

Said, Edward W., *Covering Islam: How the Media and the Experts determine how we see the Rest of the World*, New York, 1981.

Weekes, Richard V., ed., *Muslim Peoples: A World Ethnographic Survey*, Westport, 1984.

4

Secularisation and Constitutive Moments

Insights from Partition Diplomacy in South Asia

THIS ESSAY PROPOSES an argument – on the face of it, paradoxical – that the violent upheavals of Partition, which divided British India along religious lines, encouraged trends towards secularisation in India and Pakistan.[1] In the very months when the subcontinent was engulfed in religious conflict, both countries took significant steps to produce common institutions – indeed a common statecraft – to manage mass migration and lawlessness across the new borders that divided them. I suggest this process secularised both states simultaneously in specific, admittedly partial, but remarkably similar, ways.

This is not to claim, as others have done, that Partition "solved" the communal problem by creating conditions in which (at least in

[1] I am grateful to Humeira Iqtidar for persuading me to engage with the history of secularisation. Her candid feedback helped me tighten the argument. Tanika Sarkar, and the participants of the workshop on secularisation held at King's College London in 2014, as well as the anonymous referees, have my gratitude for their helpful comments on an early draft. Simon Longstaff deserves warm thanks for his encouragement of these ideas at an embryonic stage. Kartik Upadhyaya, and his thoughts on Rawls, were a powerful influence.

India) it was easier for secularism to flourish. I argue instead that the process of secularisation occurred while communal attitudes remained pervasive – sometimes despite and sometimes because – of extreme violence. I hope to show that in seeking to contain the threat that communal disorder posed to their ability to govern, elites at the helm in both countries took measures that "secularised" their approach to communalism, to religious communities, and to the "enemy" across the border.

To make this case, I deploy a conception of secularisation that is supple but not controversial. I use the term to mean a tendency towards differentiation not only between the secular spheres – the state and the market – and the religious sphere, but also between state and society, society and the individual, and state and religious communities. This notion of secularisation draws attention to the growing institutional autonomy of these spheres. In addition, it notes that internal differentiation and stratification within these separate spheres is a feature of secularisation. "Secularisation as differentiation" is a concept that many sociologists have used and continue to find helpful: indeed, as Jose Casanova has famously stated, this thesis remains "the valid core of the theory of secularisation".[2]

Periods of crisis and emergency, this essay proposes, can throw up conjunctures in which these separations are crystallised in one or more sphere, encouraging forms of secular practice to emerge.[3] It suggests that in both India and Pakistan, the post-Partition crisis was one such moment in the history of secularisation.

[2] Casanova, *Public Religions in the Modern World*, p. 212. Also see Martin, *On Secularization*.

[3] I am not suggesting that the state did in fact separate itself from society in any simple sense. It will become clear below that I see this distinction rather as Timothy Mitchell does, as an internal (and often notional) border within the wider network of institutional mechanisms through which a social and political order is maintained. Mitchell, "Society, Economy and the State Effect", p. 170.

That the relationship between India and Pakistan after 1947 became mired in intractable conflict – as India pursued a policy of secularism, while Pakistan sought to build a state whose laws conformed to Islamic principles – has long been a cornerstone in South Asian Studies.[4] Recently, however, this consensus, rock solid for decades, has begun to crumble. Scholars are coming to identify much "mutuality and co-operation" between the two states in the aftermath of Partition, whether in the areas of refugee relief and rehabilitation, citizenship regimes, or inter-dominion relations.[5] This essay builds upon such scholarship but takes its conclusions in rather different directions. In particular, it investigates the hesitant, but nonetheless significant, conformity of policy and practice in tackling borderlands and border crossings in the late 1940s and early 1950s. It regards these as processes by which, on both sides of the Radcliffe Line, the state withdrew from its commitment to safeguard the welfare of a particular religious community in favour of policies that promoted order and stability more broadly. In this process, it suggests, the authorities in both India and Pakistan began to regard (and perhaps construct) the interests of the post-colonial state itself, and also of property and the private citizen, as distinct from the interests of the religious communities with which one or other nation-state was (and to a great extent remained) strongly identified. They also began to conceive of society as being an arena separate from the state. At these historical junctures, key actors on both sides took the view that the separation of state from society was vital for the survival of both state *and* society.

In focussing tightly on specific historical *moments* of post-colonial state formation, this essay, I am aware, might be seen as

[4] E.g. Paul, *The India–Pakistan Conflict*; Blinkenberg, *India-Pakistan*, vol. 1; Lamb, *Incomplete Partition*; Ganguly, "Wars Without End".

[5] Chatterji, "Mutuality and Co-operation"; Zamindar, *The Long Partition*; Chatterji, "South Asian Histories of Citizenship", pp. 1049–71; Raghavan, "The Finality of Partition"; Bajpai, *et al.*, *Brasstacks and Beyond*.

going against the grain of scholarship on the subject. That rich and illuminating body of work suggests that secularisation (in the modern West) occurred slowly, over a period of centuries, as the result of complex social change.[6] My aim is not to challenge the gradualist account of secularisation. It is rather to investigate the relationship between critical events and more leisurely historical transformations. The question it addresses is: what insights into that longer process of secularisation can be gained from the perspective of "constitutive moments"?

In periods of crisis, this essay suggests, trends and tendencies with long histories can rapidly crystallise into new institutional practices with a wider secularising impulse. But it shows, too, that these new institutions did not always survive, and when they did their foundations often remained insecure. Reversals were as significant as gains, and incoherence was more common than ideological unity of purpose. In other words, while secularisation might appear (from the comfortable distance of hindsight) to have been a seamless, unilinear process with powerful philosophical underpinnings, looked at from up close it proves to have been formed by more fragile moments, with tenuous outcomes and uncertain directions. By looking closely at historical moments during which, metaphorically speaking, the hyphen between the (religious) "nation" and the "state" was partly erased, and the interests of the state took precedence over the nation (and the national "community"), this essay draws attention to trends towards secularisation that are hardly discernible, and have rarely been discussed, but which, I argue, call to be better understood.

The essay analyses two such junctures, both at the earliest stages of the development of third world diplomacy. Both case studies concern the management of the eastern and western frontiers, respectively, between India and Pakistan. One of my examples

[6] The classic statement of this position is set out in Taylor's magisterial *A Secular Age*.

is drawn from the highest levels of India–Pakistan diplomacy, at the moment of its very birth; the other is based on evidence garnered at local levels, to do with everyday policing of the new border that separated the two countries. These cases proved to have fascinating and surprising interconnections. Historians of India's Partition take the view that Partition in the east was fundamentally different from Partition in the west, a consensus to which my own work has contributed.[7] The two cases looked at below challenged my assumptions and throw a different light on Partition Studies as a whole. But there is also a remarkable subtext. Teasing that out, as I try to do in this essay, reveals much about the history of secularisation in South Asia.

I

In several important respects, Radcliffe's borders were governed differently in the east and the west. To summarise briefly a complex history: in August 1947, in the west, the two governments and their armies became involved in the rescue and transfer of minority populations and the recovery of abducted women.[8] India committed troops to arrange the evacuation of Hindu and Sikh minorities from Pakistan,[9] and created a special unit to track down and recover Hindu and Sikh women abducted by Muslim men.[10] Pakistan did the same for Muslim refugees and abductees. These arrangements were intended to apply to both parts of the divided Punjab. But after the September 1947 riots in Delhi, and mass

[7] E.g. Chatterji, "Rights or Charity?", and Chatterji, *The Spoils of Partition*. Also see Samaddar, *Reflections on Partition*.

[8] Jeffrey, "The Punjab Boundary Force"; Kamran, "The Unfolding Crisis in Punjab", pp. 187–210; Menon and Bhasin, *Borders and Boundaries*.

[9] Rajendra Prasad to Patel, 10 September 1947; and Patel's reply to Prasad, 12 September 1947, in Das, *SPC*, vol. IV, pp. 340–1.

[10] Government of India (GOI), Ministry of External Affairs (MEA), CAP Branch/F.8-CAP(AP)48.

exoduses across North India and Sind,[11] the Punjab agreements had to be extended first to Delhi; and, following the anti-Meo pogroms, to Bharatpur, Alwar, and Bikaner.[12] After troubles broke out in Sind and Bihar, these rules began to be applied there too,[13] and were extended to the princely state of Hyderabad after India's "police action" in 1948.[14]

At this point, India took measures to discourage the return home of evacuees of the "wrong" religious denomination: first, by introducing a permit system in June 1948,[15] and then, by draconian ordinances in 1949, taking over the property of all Muslim evacuees from "the affected areas" – now extended to include all of India, except West Bengal, Assam, and Tripura – who were deemed to have migrated to Pakistan.[16] The evacuee property of Muslims was then deployed by the Government of India as the cornerstone of its projects to house and rehabilitate Hindu and Sikh refugees.[17] Soon afterwards, Pakistan followed suit, taking over abandoned Hindu and Sikh property in western Pakistan for allocation to Muslim refugees.[18] By threatening would-be migrants with dispossession, these reciprocal measures stabilised

[11] I have used throughout the contemporary (1948–50) spellings of place names, which subsequently changed several times, to avoid confusion.

[12] Copland, "The Further Shores of Partition", pp. 203–39; Mayaram, "Speech, Silence and the Making of Partition Violence".

[13] Chatterji, "South Asian Histories of Citizenship". The regions where the rules applied were known as the "agreed areas". Chattha, *Partition and Locality*.

[14] Sherman, "Migration, Citizenship and Belonging", pp. 81–107; Sherman, *Muslim Belonging in Secular India*.

[15] GOI/ Ministry of Home Affairs (MHA)/F. 6/62/48-FI; GOI/MEA/ F.21/48-Pak I; GOI/MEA/F.2-1/48-Pak I; Zamindar, *The Long Partition*; Chatterji, "South Asian Histories of Citizenship".

[16] "An ordinance to provide for the administration of evacuee property and for certain matters connected therewith", Ordinance No. XXVII of 1949, *The Gazette of India*, 18 October 1949, GOI/MEA F. 17-39/49-AFRI.

[17] (India) Act XXXXIV of 1954, 9 October 1954.

[18] GOI/MEA/F.11-21/49-Pak III/ Secret.

populations and stemmed the massive flows of refugees that had challenged the capacity of the state to handle and absorb these people both in north, west, and south India, and in west Pakistan. They produced a relatively impervious border between the two countries in the west, across which flows came to be strictly regulated. Later, the diplomatic corps of both countries were charged with exercising oversight over the welfare of "their" minorities in the other country.[19]

So in western Pakistan, as well as in large parts of north, west, and south India, the two states evolved policies for the welfare of refugees, evacuees, and abductees which were reciprocal, but which nonetheless identified each of them strongly with the interests of the particular community (or communities) at the core of their conception of nationhood. In the immediate aftermath of Partition, it was Hindu women, Hindu property, Hindu refugees, and Hindu and Sikh minorities whom India sought to protect. Pakistan did the same for Muslims. Scholars have remarked, rightly, upon the implications of these policies for national identity, citizenship, and belonging on both sides of the Radcliffe Line.[20]

But there were large and significant exceptions to these rules. In Pakistan, the entire eastern wing (East Bengal, latterly East Pakistan), which made up the majority of Pakistan's entire population, was left out of these arrangements. In India, three entire provinces – West Bengal, Assam, and Tripura – were excluded. In concert, India and Pakistan agreed to adopt a very different policy towards cross-border migrants across the entire eastern region of the subcontinent than they had established in the west. The border here, they agreed, was to be left porous. There would be no state-

[19] GOI/MEA/F.12-16/49-Pak A; Chatterji, "South Asian Histories of Citizenship".

[20] Zamindar, *The Long Partition*; Chatterji, "South Asian Histories of Citizenship"; Menon and Bhasin, *Borders and Boundaries*; Raghavan, "The Finality of Partition"; Sherman, "Migration, Citizenship and Belonging"; Sherman, *Muslim Belonging in Secular India*.

assisted evacuation of refugees. The vacant property of emigrant minorities would not be deployed for the rehabilitation of incoming refugees. Instead, it would be held in trust for its original owners and managed by special Evacuee Property Management Boards, set up specifically for this purpose.[21] Incoming refugees would largely be left to fend for themselves.

These policies might be described in some senses as secular. In contrast to the west, in the east, the state in both India and Pakistan appeared to dissociate itself from their responsibilities towards "core" national (but religiously defined) communities which had fled – in both directions – across the eastern borders in search of shelter.

How do we make sense of these arrangements which, taken together, produced the specificities of "Partition in the east"?[22] Might they be understood as efforts by the state to step back from the arena of "community", and hence as a form of secularisation? And if this occurred, how and why did it come about? How did the participants in these processes understand or justify them?

Fortunately, a detailed record of the first Inter-Dominion Conference between India and Pakistan in Calcutta in April 1948, at which the representatives of India and Pakistan hammered out these arrangements, has survived. Rather like the scribes in a court of law, a small army of stenographers recorded every single word that was spoken at the conference, over the course of three days, in Calcutta's Writers' Building. This transcript, only recently released for scholarly scrutiny, yields a fly-on-the-wall view of Indo–Pakistan diplomacy at this embryonic stage of that relationship. But more importantly for our purposes here, it also gives a hint of why this new policy for the east, so different from that recently adopted in the north and west of the subcontinent, appealed to policy-makers on both sides.

[21] Chatterji, "Rights or Charity?"; Roy, *Partitioned Lives.*

[22] Samaddar, *Reflections on Partition in the East.*

Before addressing this source in detail, some background information is needed to grasp its full significance. By December 1947, the Military Evacuation Organisation, established in September, had rescued and evacuated most of the refugees stranded in the two Punjabs. A semblance of order was returning to the divided Punjab, to Delhi and to the towns and villages of the north and west of the subcontinent that had witnessed the worst violence. To the relief of government on both sides, the huge migrations in the west of the subcontinent appeared to have ceased. It seemed that the crisis was finally over.

But no sooner had things begun to settle down in the north-western tracts than trouble broke out in the east. In the summer of 1947, Calcutta and its surrounding townships had remained tense but largely peaceful.[23] Yet despite the uneasy calm, over a million Hindu refugees from eastern Bengal had made their way across the border to Calcutta between August and December 1947 and perhaps half as many Muslims had fled from West Bengal, Assam, and Bihar, crossing the border into East Bengal.[24] In February 1948, however, localised violence sparked off fresh exoduses across the eastern border between India and Pakistan. Soon after, the Standstill Agreement between India and Pakistan on trade broke down, after Pakistan decided to impose an export levy on jute.[25] On 1 March 1948 the two countries declared "each other [to be] foreign country as regards customs and excise duty."[26] Tensions escalated in the two Bengals and Assam, and frightened people of the minority communities once again began to flee their homes in search of security.

This was the context in which the first Inter-Dominion Conference

[23] Although see Mukherjee, "Agitations, Riots and the Transitional State", who makes a strong case for continued, if low-grade, violence, throughout the period in Calcutta.

[24] Chakravarty, *The Marginal Men*; Chatterji, *The Spoils of Partition. Bengal and India, 1947–67*; Kamaluddin, "Refugee Problems in Bangladesh".

[25] Tyagi, "The Economic Impact of Partition".

[26] Blinkenberg, *India–Pakistan*, p. 135.

was held in Calcutta in April 1948. The conference was quite different from the numerous previous meetings that had been held to discuss arrangements about refugees in Punjab. There, agreement between India and Pakistan had been achieved within the joint institutional structures established by the Partition Council, with the meetings chaired by Auchinleck or by Mountbatten. The Calcutta Inter-Dominion Conference was, in this sense, the first properly "international" encounter between the leaders of India and Pakistan, at which delegates from the two countries faced each other across the table without a British viceroy or his deputy in the chair; and this in the broader context where a new international order was just beginning to emerge,[27] and widespread scepticism about the prospects of Asia's two newest countries surviving as sovereign states.[28]

At Calcutta, K.C. Neogy and Ghulam Muhammad, Refugee Rehabilitation ministers of India and Pakistan respectively, led the two delegations. The Indian deputation also included Syama Prasad Mookerjee (then Cabinet Minister for Industry and Supply) and Sri Prakasa (the Indian High Commissioner in Pakistan) as well as the chief ministers of West Bengal (Dr B.C. Roy) and Assam (Gopinath Bardoloi). Pakistan's team included Khwaja Nazimuddin (Chief Minister, East Bengal), and Hamidul Huq Choudhury (East Bengal's Minister for Finance, Commerce, Labour & Industries, later the third Foreign Minister of Pakistan). Politicians of long standing for the most part, these men inevitably had elite backgrounds – B.C. Roy was a wealthy society doctor in Calcutta, Sir Ghulam Muhammad, an Aligarh alumnus, had been Accountant for the Ministry of Finance; Khwaja Nazimuddin, a prosperous landlord, was a scion of the Nawab of Dhaka's family; Syama Prasad Mookerjee, son of Sir Ashutosh Mukherjee, had been called to the bar at Lincoln's Inn, and went on to become the youngest vice chancellor of Calcutta University. But few of

[27] Mazower, *No Enchanted Palace*; Raghavan, "The Finality of Partition".
[28] Ali, *The Emergence of Pakistan*.

these men had worked for government (Ghulam Muhammad was an exception in this regard) and none of them had any experience of international negotiations.

The agenda before them was "to discuss the causes of the present exodus of non-Muslims from Eastern Pakistan and Muslims from West Bengal and action necessary to create conditions in Eastern Pakistan and West Bengal which will make it possible for non-Muslims and Muslims respectively to continue to live there"; and "to discuss steps necessary to induce evacuees from Eastern Pakistan and West Bengal to return home and other ancillary action."[29] The agenda makes it plain that neither government felt able to cope with another exchange of population on the scale of Punjab, and each wanted to head off the looming crisis before it was engulfed by another tide of refugees.

Thus, the common goal for the delegates from India and Pakistan was to agree on ways to restore order on both sides of the border, which in turn would persuade members of minority communities in East and West Bengal to stay on where they were, and encourage evacuees who had already fled to go back to their homes. The verbatim transcript gives us a candid camera of the conference, and see how both sides went about the business of producing peace.

Reading through the transcript, the reaction of the historian is just how remarkable it was that they succeeded. Minutes after the conference began, members of the two delegations reacted with rage when the subject of Muslim migrants forced to leave Assam was first mentioned.[30]

[29] "Proceedings of the Inter-Dominion Conference held at 2.15 p.m. on the 18th April, 1948, at the Writers' Buildings, Calcutta", GOI/MEA/ Pak-I Branch, file no. 8-15/48.

[30] Since the late-nineteenth century, Muslim peasants from Bengal, chiefly from Mymensingh district, had begun to migrate in increasing numbers up the Brahmaputra River into Assam, and colonise empty land in the Brahmaputra valley for agriculture. Chattopadhyay, *Internal Migration in India.* Tensions had begun to rise between local Assamese people and the Bengali

The Hon'ble H.H. Choudhury: Let the [Assam] Government not force [Muslims] out.

The Hon'ble Mr Bardoloi: I am not forcing anybody out. If you go on talking like this, I refuse to take part in this conference.

The Hon'ble Mr Ghulam Muhammad: Then let us agree that pending the discussion at the next Inter-Dominion Conference Assam government will not do anything to force the immigrants out . . .

The Hon'ble Mr Bardoloi: I do not agree to that . . .

The Hon'ble Mr Ghulam Muhammad: We are trying to give and take and not dictate.

The Hon'ble Mr Neogy: Then we better call a separate inter-dominion conference.

The Hon'ble Mr Ghulam Muhammad: Let the resolution be like this: It is recommended that a separate inter-Dominion conference should be called at an early date . . . to discuss the question of migration of Muslims from East Bengal to Assam . . . Pending this conference both sides agree not to take any action to force or precipitate exodus on a mass scale from one province to the other.

The Hon'ble Mr Neogy: Let us get on with the rest of the work.[31]

In effect, both sides decided to shelve for the time being talking about issues in Assam that so infuriated members, Indian and Pakistani alike, in order to get on with "the rest of the work". They achieved this by separating the Assam question from all the others that had to be addressed. What had previously been seen as a single "communal" question, conceived as being a conflict

---

migrants in the 1930s, escalating sharply in the 1940s when the Congress and the Muslim League became involved in the issue. Guha, *Planter-Raj to Swaraj*. The conflict had assumed ethnic and communal dimensions well before the partition of India, but these were exacerbated after 1947. GOI/MEA/ F.39-NEF/47/Secret. Also see Sharma, *Empire's Garden*.

[31] "Proceedings of the Inter-Dominion Conference, 16–18 April 1948, at the Writers" Buildings, Calcutta", GOI/MEA/ Pak-I Branch, file no. 8-15/48. Emphasis added.

between monolithic Hindu and Muslim communities, was thus broken down (or differentiated) into discrete, regionally defined, questions, each requiring a distinct approach.[32]

Indeed, deferral was a device that the delegates used more than once when the conference ran into troubled waters. When matters came up that prompted one or other incensed delegate to threaten to walk out, the other members quickly agreed to put the matter off, to be discussed at a future conference. This was an interesting tactic (it was frequently deployed at subsequent Indo-Pakistan negotiations) because it assumed – and thus laid the basis for – *continued* dialogue. It presumed that the two sides would continue to talk to each other and settle differences between themselves through discussion, albeit at some later date. It also ensured that in these ways the agenda for a future conference, and further dialogue, had been mutually established.

But at another level, the deployment of this tactic can be seen as a secularisation of the process. By disaggregating "communal" issues into separate parts, by postponing the discussion of matters about which delegates were "passionate" (as opposed to reasoned and rational), and by first settling matters over which the two sides had achieved (in a Rawlsian sense) a kind of "overlapping consensus", the two delegations were creating a secular practice of international diplomacy that would endure well beyond the crisis of 1948.[33]

Substantial agreement was even more swiftly achieved once delegates began to speak to each other quite openly as members of the same social class, with common material interests and a common stake in a mutually beneficial settlement. One such instance was settling the scope of the proposed Evacuee Property Management Boards.

[32] The fact that Ghulam Muhammad had experience as a public servant in the railways in British India may or may not be relevant to his readiness to agree a solution to the problem. Neogy had no such experience.

[33] Raghavan, "The Finality of Partition".

Again, a word of clarification will be useful here. The two sides had intended to set up these boards, as their name suggests, for the express purpose of protecting and managing the property of distressed evacuees who had abandoned their homes during the riots. Both governments were clear that it was imperative to restore the confidence of minorities if they were to prevent another mass exodus on the scale of Punjab, and to persuade those who had fled to return home. To ensure these twin purposes, H.M. Patel – a model career bureaucrat on the Indian side – proposed that the rather general term, "minority", in the proposed agreement be replaced with the word "evacuee", which, by this time, had acquired a very specific legal meaning.[34]

Patel had represented India on the steering committee that had dealt with these issues in the west, so he knew well that this was a critically important distinction. Precedents in the Punjab and the north-west had established that the word "evacuee" meant quite specifically those who had fled from one country to the other during the troubles and had abandoned property in the land of their birth and residence. But most delegates – who were surprisingly ill-informed about what had happened in Punjab – misunderstood Patel's intent. The exchange which followed is funny as well as telling:

> **The Hon'ble Mr Hamidul Huq Choudhury:** I have got some property in Kalimpong [in Indian West Bengal]. Will this Committee manage that property?

[34] H.M. Patel, graduate of St Catherine"s College, Oxford, and a distinguished member of the Indian Civil Service, served until 1950 as cabinet secretary to the Ministry for Home Affairs under Vallabhbhai Patel in 1946. He worked with Chaudhry Muhammad Ali, the future prime minister of Pakistan, on the implementation of Partition. He was the head of the Emergency Committee administering Delhi during the outbreak of violence in September 1947. He continued as one of India's highest ranking civil servants until 1959. *Times of India* (Ahmedabad), 26 August 2004.

The Hon'ble Mr Neogy: Yes, certainly . . . Do not discriminate between the different classes of people we have in view . . . I know of any numbers of landlords and businessmen who have never crossed the [River] Padma, although they own property in East Bengal.

The Hon'ble Mr Ghulam Muhammad: We are considering here [how] to safeguard the property of those people who have left against their wishes. You want to bring in all sorts of people . . .

The Hon'ble Mr Neogy: I have some personal property.

The Hon'ble Mr Ghulam Muhammad: Men like you would have served us in a higher position and we are being deprived of that benefit. So we think these cases should be punished! (Laughter).[35]

Not surprisingly, this was quickly agreed among fellow landlords, despite H.M. Patel's quiet protest. The Evacuee Property Management Boards, which had been established to protect the abandoned homes only of genuine evacuees, would now extend their jurisdiction to *all* property owners who belonged to the minority community, whether or not they had actually set foot in these estates, and regardless of whether they were actually evacuees or not. The boards would thus be empowered to act as state-backed estate managers for large private landowners who were in fact *not* evacuees, at a time when private property everywhere had been rendered insecure. Once again, we see the delegates retreat from a commitment to specifically communal welfare to a pursuit of beneficial arrangements for propertied groups on both sides. This is an interesting example of how private interests worked with and through the state to buttress both themselves and the state's secular authority, while appearing to create official institutions (the boards) sharply distinct from society.[36]

A similar drift is perceptible in the discussion of measures to

[35] "Proceedings of the Inter-Dominion Conference, 16–18 April, 1948, at the Writers' Buildings, Calcutta", GOI/MEA/ Pak-I Branch, file no. 8-15/48. Emphasis added.

[36] Also see Mitchell, "Society, Economy and State Effect", p. 175.

alleviate the "economic boycott and strangulation" of vulnerable minority groups. These measures were intended to alleviate the hardship faced by vulnerable persons who were left behind – such as, for example, Hindu *goalas* (milkmen) in East Bengal who had earned their livelihoods by selling milk locally, or Muslim artisans in West Bengal – who faced economic boycott by members of the majority community. Instead, the discussion quickly turned to cases, on both sides, of "unfair" and "excessive" income-tax demands levied upon individual (and famously wealthy) members of those minority communities. Some of them happened to be delegates at the conference.[37] Once again, there was much laughter and mutual leg-pulling, references to common acquaintances who had fallen foul of the taxman, and jokes about rapacious finance ministers. ("The Hon'ble Mr Nazimuddin: You don't know what the finance ministers have [up] their sleeves!") Not surprisingly, it did not take long for the two sides to achieve "absolute agreement in the matter".[38] By the end of the first day of the conference, the parties who had started out at each others' throats as angry spokesmen of violated and embattled rival communities were acting as "rational, sociable agents who meant to collaborate in peace to their mutual benefit."[39]

Significantly, both sides also helped defuse any remaining tensions by distancing themselves (and the wider social class to which they all belonged) from any responsibility for the communal violence and discrimination against the minorities in both countries. The delegates insisted that it was people lower down the social scale, Hindus and Muslims alike, who were to blame for the mess. As Hamidul Huq Choudhury put it, "nobody occupying

[37] Khwaja Nazimuddin had considerable landed property spread over many districts. Hamidul Huq Choudhury and K.C. Neogy also had substantial landed interests.

[38] "Proceedings of the Inter-Dominion Conference, 16–18 April, 1948, at the Writers' Buildings, Calcutta", GOI/MEA/ Pak-I Branch, file no. 8–15/48.

[39] Taylor, *The Secular Age*, p. 159.

high position can ever think of molesting or injuring the interests of the minorities . . . It is generally the petty officers who being misled by a false patriotic feeling [who] are responsible for all this mischief . . ." This theme crops up again and again, and at later conferences as well – the idea that it was lowly functionaries at the bottom of the food chain who spread the "contagion" of communalism, while their enlightened superiors looked on in horror. Also interesting here is the reference to "false patriotic feeling", presumably the passionate and irrational attachment towards the nation or community felt by the lower ranks, in contrast to the sensibly measured attitude of the elites to their respective communal affiliations. There was also a tendency on both sides of the table to blame *some* refugees for their own plight – those impoverished and in distress (as opposed, presumably, to the wealthiest, who had managed to transfer many of their assets in good time): "It is only some people who have gone from the Indian Union and *who are themselves in difficulty about their own prospects, who are irritated for the sufferings* they have undergone – it is they who are contributing . . . to the problem."[40]

By the evening of the second day of the conference, the delegates appeared to be relaxing into a mood of mutual trust and good-humoured ease. Indeed, at several points that afternoon, they appear to have forgotten that they were at a serious international meeting and not at a social occasion in the company of friends and social equals. That night, when the meeting broke off for dinner, the serious business was all done, bar the shouting – which was no longer the order of the day. The conference ended early the next day, several hours before the appointed time.

Yet all the laughter and bonhomie should not blind us to the very serious decisions that were made at this conference (see Appendix 4.I). Nor should we avoid recognising *how* – at a time

[40] "Proceedings of the Inter-Dominion Conference, 16–18 April, 1948, at the Writers' Buildings, Calcutta", GOI/MEA/ Pak-I Branch, file no. 8-15/48. Emphasis added.

of great tension and conflict – these decisions came to be agreed. First, both sides believed that it was imperative for their respective states' survival to do everything they could to stem cross-border flows. Second, individual members of both delegations believed that the restoration of order and the security of property was vital to their own interests, and that of their social class. If, in order to achieve this greater good, they had to retreat from commitments to the welfare of their more vulnerable co-religionists who had already fled their homes and were reluctant to return, so be it: that was the price they were prepared to pay.

Third, arriving at agreement had required the delegates to take a view about *who* was responsible for the violence against minorities on both sides of the border. They quickly agreed it was not themselves, or members of the wider social stratum to which they belonged. They distanced themselves from the "unfortunate" or "misguided" (or "irrational") actions of their inferiors, on whom they placed the blame. They simultaneously and rhetorically separated the "community" into two groups – the enlightened elite (to which they themselves belonged) and whose interests were closely aligned with the interests of both states in the restoration of order; and the unenlightened popular classes who had been swayed by the passions of misguided "patriotic" and communal fervour, and who were the cause of disorder. They also, as we have seen, disaggregated the "communal question" into discrete local and regional questions. These processes of simultaneous (though not necessarily intellectually coherent) differentiation helped to secularise a space and a moment, and that in turn allowed the Calcutta agreement – which would have profound and complex legacies – to be signed.

But it is also noteworthy that all of this happened without anyone professing any ideological commitment to "secularism". Indeed, we can presume that at least some of the delegates (such as the Hindu nationalist Syama Prasad Mookerjee and K.C. Neogy on the Indian side, and possibly Nazimuddin for

Pakistan), if tested, would have protested that far from being committed secularists, they were in favour of giving religious values a prominent role in shaping state institutions, and indeed, international relations.[41]

Yet so much was agreed, by so many, with so little needing to be said, through jokes and teasing asides that all the delegates immediately seemed to understand. Hence in order to understand how secularising institutions were created by religious men at the Calcutta conference, we have perhaps to fall back on Bourdieu's notion of habitus: the unexamined and shared predispositions, or common-sense assumptions about the "obvious" good, of members of a post-colonial elite who arrived at much the same conclusions from different starting points – and achieved an "overlapping consensus" – without necessarily knowing how or why. This also might throw some light on the tricky question of how long-term social change impacted upon a discrete governmental (and inter-governmental) process of decision-making. What we are observing, perhaps, were the outcome of long-term changes that had predisposed South Asian elites, whether Hindu or Muslim, Indian or Pakistani, to understand "the obvious good" in the same way.

II

Once this key idea is given its due, it should no longer come as a surprise that the apparently intractable disputes over jute which had threatened trade between India and Pakistan in March 1948 were settled at a new trade agreement in May 1948;[42] and that in

[41] Chowdhury had played a key role in presenting the Muslim case before Sir Cyril Radcliffe, and was not at this point in his life well known for a conciliatory approach towards India. Chowdhury, *Memoirs*. For his part, Mookerjee would soon resign from the cabinet and famously demand that India go to war with Pakistan.

[42] Blinkenberg, *India–Pakistan*, p. 135.

the matter of minority rights and refugee rehabilitation the two countries went on to produce a whole series of entirely identical laws and regulations, in tandem (see Appendix 4.II).

Nor should it surprise us to find that after Calcutta the same logic would be extended to other regions and other areas of governance. Soon afterwards, both sides would begin actively to co-operate with the other, first to realise, and then to bolster, the sovereignty of its counterpart in the *western* border zones.

After the exchange of populations had been "completed" across the western border, the border itself remained largely undefined, undemarcated, and unsettled. This came to be a worrying issue for both governments, particularly where the border cut through sparsely inhabited and poorly policed desert tracts. Before December 1948 India and Pakistan had authorised the inspectors general of police in East and West Punjab, the epicentre of the troubles, to devise common measures "to bring under control the border incidents between the two states."[43] But in 1949 a new series of arrangements were put into place for the police forces of the two countries to co-operate in managing "ordinary" crime in remote border areas, well beyond the killing fields of Punjab. A new problem had arisen, becoming marked by the winter of 1948: policemen on both sides began to report increasingly frequent cross-border raids, particularly along the border between Bikaner, Jodhpur, and Jaisalmer on the Indian side, and Bahawalpur, Khairpur, and Sind in Pakistan. Men on horseback (often dressed in police or army uniforms) would come sweeping across the border and loot isolated villages on the other side, retreating with their booty across the border. In one typical incident on 12 November 1948, the police reported that "at 5 p.m. about 150 armed Muslims consisting of pathans from Bahawalpur state raided village Khilliwala on the border of Bikaner state." The raiders, who were armed, broke up into three groups

[43] NAI/MEA/27-16/49 Pak III.

and encircled the village, attacking the villagers and "looting the whole village to their hearts' content." Eleven armed policemen of the princely state of Bikaner were stationed in the village, but most of them fled when the first shots were fired. Two people were killed. The residents of this village, and four neighbouring villages on the Indian side, abandoned their homes.[44] By 1950, the inspector general of the Sind police reported that 168 incidents of this sort had taken place, most of them concentrated in the sector between Khokropar and Gadro. "It was obvious that these raids have become common since partition," he reported, "and were a regular menace to both sides." His Indian counterpart, the inspector general of the Rajasthan police, agreed with him, reporting 193 similar incidents in Rajasthan alone. "He stressed the raiders in several instances came in uniform and equipped with modern weapons."[45]

Preserved in the archives is a fascinating set of reports of these meetings, at which measures to manage and contain these raids were agreed by local policemen from the affected zones of India and Pakistan. These reveal the depth and range of the "overlapping consensus" – often at humble and quotidian levels – between the two countries across a whole range of questions. But, for our purpose here, what is significant is the gradual shift in the police's perception of these raids.

To begin with, the local police viewed these raids in unequivocally communal terms. So, for instance, in their first report on the Khilliwala incident described above, the police insisted that the perpetrators were "150 *Muslims*", without any evidence to support that claim. Less than three months later, in respect of an almost identical incident on 5 February 1949, in which five people were murdered in the village of Ragri (also in Bikaner), the police

[44] Extract from Daily Situation Report, 20 November 1948, from the Central Intelligence Office, Ajmer, NAI/MEA/36-15/49 Pak III.

[45] "Minutes of the border conference held in the office of the S.P. Sind C.I.D. Karachi on 13 October 1950 at 15.30 hours", ibid.

were a little more agnostic about the religious affiliation of the perpetrators, describing them simply as "Pakistanis". By the time the chief secretary reported the event, he cautiously described the raiders as "*alleged* Pakistanis".[46]

Gradually, over the next twelve months or so, officials increasingly began to see these raids as secular crimes against persons and property. They made fewer and fewer assumptions about either the communal (or national) identity, or communal motives, of the raiders. Instead, they began to refer to the perpetrators in the more traditional language of colonial policing,[47] as "bad characters".[48] They spoke of the fact that "people residing within easy reach of the border in both India and Pakistan [were] very closely connected." Indian and Pakistani officers agreed that "there [were] certainly some undesirable characters on both sides who encourage[d] the commission of many forms of crime, including dacoity, robbery and cattle theft." They recognised that they had to work together to police these "*badmashes*".[49]

The police also increasingly distinguished between the majority of "law abiding citizens" who were "naturally disturbed" by these crimes, and the "bad characters" who committed them.[50] Both sides agreed on the importance "for the Police on both sides to exchange lists giving names and necessary particulars of such persons to ensure that all are suitably dealt with."[51] The criminals were thus understood as individuals, with names and personal particulars, rather than as innominate representatives of entire

[46] Telegram no. 940, 7 February 1949, from Chief Secretary, Bikaner State, to Prime Minister, Bikaner, NAI/MEA/36-15/49 Pak III. Emphasis added.

[47] Chandavarkar, "Customs of Governance", pp. 441–70. Also see Sherman, *State Violence and Punishment.*

[48] "Minutes of the border conference held in the office of the S.P. Sind C.I.D Karachi on 13 October 1950 at 15.30 hours", NAI/MEA/36-15/49 Pak III.

[49] Loosely, career criminals.

[50] Ibid.

[51] Ibid.

communities. Their crimes were viewed as secular crimes (robbery, dacoity, cattle-theft) against "law abiding citizens". The victims of crime, too, were simultaneously secularised: they were seen as upright, individual, property-owning members of "the public" or "society", rather than as a part of a homogeneous and united, but essentially faceless, community/nation.

This is not to suggest that the police or administration in the area abandoned a communal view of identity, or of national belonging. They did not. We see this plainly in the exchanges between the chief commissioner of Kutch and the Government of India at the centre on the wisdom of extending to Kutch the mutually agreed cross-border policing arrangements set out in Appendix 4.III. Kutch, a sparsely populated region situated on the Indian side of the western border between India and Pakistan,[52] had a large number of Muslims. The chief commissioner of Kutch reported that no similar incident had ever occurred in Kutch, so extending these arrangements to Kutch was unnecessary. Moreover, he argued, to do so represented a real threat to India's national security, as "the population on our side of the border [being] mostly Muslim . . . [it] cannot be relied upon in times of emergency." He concluded that "it would not be advisable to allow any Pakistani officer to visit Kutch and get an idea of the existing conditions in Kutch."[53] His implication was clear: Kutchi Muslims were not reliable and their loyalty to India was uncertain; and if a Pakistani officer got wind of this, he might encourage his government to stir up trouble in the region, already the site of a border dispute between the two countries.[54]

What is particularly revealing is the central Ministry of State's response to this missive. The deputy secretary in Delhi denied

[52] Ibrahim, *Settlers, Saints and Sovereigns.*

[53] "D.O.C. No. C-129/49, 9 May 1950, from the Chief Commissioner, Cutch, to the Deputy Secretary, Ministry of States, Government of India", NAI/MEA/36-15/49 Pak III.

[54] On the Sir Creek dispute, see Raghavan, *War and Peace in Modern India.*

Kutch permission to stand apart from its neighbouring border zones, insisting that "we do not need to wait for the actual occurrence of serious incidents to create such a machinery in Kutch." And "as for . . . the presence of an unreliable Muslim population, we feel that the visit of one or two officers for a meeting, which will be pre-arranged, will not in itself be a source of danger . . . Other security arrangements should be able to meet such dangers."[55] Note that the deputy secretary in Delhi did not challenge the Kutch commissioner's claim that "such dangers" indeed existed, or question the assumption that the Muslim population was "unreliable". He took for granted the "fact" that Muslim loyalty was shaky. But he was clear that this was not in itself a ground to depart from established procedure.

Here we catch another glimpse of the process of secularisation at work. Secularising institutional practice in one arena of government (inter-dominion relations and cross-border migration in the east) could and did influence the official approach to very different issues in a very different region and level of governance. So much so that the institutional practices set up by the Calcutta Agreement could reverse, at least in part, established aspects of border management in the west. Practices agreed at exceptional moments of crisis by elites could spread, and eventually came to affect more quotidian, but nonetheless significant, cultures of governance at more humdrum levels. This spread did not, however, represent an abandonment of communal stereotypes or ideologies on the part of the men who implemented them. The two sets of dynamics, contrary though they were, existed side by side.

Creating secularising practices that helped to promote peace and enable Indo-Pakistan co-operation was not, then, all about motherhood and apple pie. Nor was it incompatible with communal

[55] GOI/MEA/36-15/49 Pak III; GOI/MEA U/C No. D.4507-P/50, 16 May 1950.

perceptions and conflict. Co-operation between India and Pakistan drew heavily on their officials' fear of anarchy and disorder, and their elites' powerful and shared perception that the survival of both states, and the social order that sustained their own power, was threatened by uncontrolled flows of people across unmanageable borders. It thus drew eclectically upon a shared (but shifting) legacy of colonial bureaucratic mind-sets and a common elite "habitus".[56] As Gould, Sherman, and Ansari have noted, the transition to Independence and Partition created stresses that "altered conceptions of loyalty among government servants, particularly with respect to minorities and political opponents",[57] and these new perceptions cannot be ignored. Yet, remarkably, we find police in the borderlands slipping easily from seeing all crime as "communal", to a familiar preoccupation with "bad characters" (seen as habitually criminal individuals, distinct from "bad religious communities"), "conniving villagers", and "harbouring villages" (as opposed to homogeneous communal groups). From the fascinating vignettes that emerge from the archives, it seems that Indian and Pakistani elites high and low, who also had the role of agents of these states in their negotiations with each other, shared an unexamined commitment to preserving social hierarchy and state authority by coercion, if necessary, and took it for granted that this was the "obvious" thing to do.

My aim in this essay has been to investigate the relationship between "critical" or "constitutive" moments, and the long arc of history. If one can draw on these particular moments to make observations about longer processes of secularisation, the first thing to be said is that they were ideologically incoherent. Their "progress", if one can so describe it, was piecemeal and illogical. It had many rationales – whether to promote local order, bureaucratic efficiency, social hierarchy, or elite interests – and they sometimes

[56] Chandavarkar, "Customs of Governance"; Sherman, *State Violence.*

[57] Gould, Sherman, and Ansari, "The Flux of the Matter".

contradicted one another. In one case, the imperative of orderly bureaucracy might trump local exception; in another, where the exception was more expedient, it trumped the rule. We get no sense of a clear linear progression in a single direction towards a predetermined goal. Secularisation involved differentiating between the state and the community, the community and the individual, national and regional interests, the community and class. But in the subcontinent's post-Partition crises, these differentiations did not occur in the same time, in the same way, with the same intention – or indeed any coherent intent at all, other than the immediately and "obviously" expedient.

Reversals, too, were frequent. Large parts of the Calcutta Agreement 1948 did not endure for very long after the ink was dry. Safeguarding the life, property, and cultural rights of minorities was observed more in the breach than in the substance.[58] In 1950, terrible rioting required a whole new agreement (the Nehru–Liaquat Pact) to be drawn up in another attempt to restore peace and stem migration. Passports were introduced for cross-border travel in 1952, and in 1965 the application of the Enemy Property Act of that year made a nonsense of the substantive goals of the 1948 Agreement.[59]

Yet institutions, and bureaucratic practices, introduced in 1948, proved to be less ephemeral. The Evacuee Property Management Boards established in that year survived for decades, and cross-border consultative processes of this kind (such as Joint Riot Enquiry Commissions, Joint Border Working Groups, monthly inter-Dominion meetings, Provincial and District Minority Boards, and Inter-Dominion Consultative Committees) proliferated in the aftermath. Many of them have proved resilient. When Willem van Schendel conducted anthropological research in Bengal's borderlands in the 1990s and early 2000s, he found

[58] Chatterji, *The Spoils of Partition*; Roy, *Partitioned Lives*.

[59] E.g. Farooqui, *The Law of Abandoned Property*.

that "in their pursuit of border stability, officials in border districts often quietly employed practices of cross-border cooperation and conflict management that flew in the face of the confrontational policies of territoriality employed by their superiors in the capital."[60]

If secularising institutions were created with tenuous outcomes and contradictory purposes, peace between neighbouring states – and thus "the international order" – was sometimes the outcome of secularisation. However, peace was not necessarily the goal of any individual actor. The protagonists in our story were, in one way or other, all agents of the state, and secularisation occurred when they found it appropriate to place the interests of the state above the interests of their (religious) "community" or "nation". But often they were driven to do so more by threats to local order, or to their own social group, than by commitment to any abstract conception of the state, or the international order, or a peaceful South Asian neighbourhood.

None of this is intended to suggest that conflict was no part of the relationship between India and Pakistan. Of course it was. Kashmir was already a huge bone of contention in the early months of 1948. Junagarh, Hyderabad, and the Indus Waters dispute would soon deeply compromise the fragile trust between these two nations. But the point here is that both sides had developed a pragmatic understanding that each of these conflicts had to be resolved, or if that was not possible, at least contained. Moreover, these areas of conflict must be understood alongside the very significant areas of agreement between the two sides. The contrapuntal relationship between the notorious disagreements which have dominated the conventional narrative on Indo-Pakistan affairs and their less well known, but arguably more substantial agreements, calls, as this essay has suggested, to be explored more fully, and to be better understood.

[60] van Schendel, *The Bengal Borderland*, p. 394, n. 83.

Appendix 4.I

Calcutta Inter-Dominion Conference, April 1948: Agreements Reached

to protect life and property of minorities

to safeguard their civic and cultural rights

to discourage propaganda for the amalgamation of India and Pak

to warn Govt servants against dereliction of duty towards minorities, towards creation of fear and apprehension in their minds

to curb tendencies towards economic boycott and strangulation of their normal life

Setting up of Evacuee Property Management Boards in districts or areas from which a substantial exodus had taken place

to postpone discussion of the question of Muslim migration between Assam and East Bengal to a separate Inter-Dominion

Pending this, not to taken any action to force or precipitate migration to one province from the other on a mass scale

Appendix 4.II

Key Legislation and Agreements Regarding Refugees and Evacuees in India, Pakistan, and Bangladesh 1947–72

Declarations establishing custodians of evacuee property	India, September 1947	Pakistan, September 1947
Joint Defence Council decision to establish the MEO	India, September 1947	Pakistan, September 1947
Calcutta inter-dominion agreement	India, April 1948	Pakistan, April 1948
Permit ordinances	India, 14 July 1948	Pakistan, 15 October 1948
Evacuee Property Ordinance	India, June 1948	Pakistan, October 1949
Karachi Agreement	India, January 1949	Pakistan, January 1949
Evacuee Property Act	India, April 1950	Pakistan, April 1950
Liaquat-Nehru Pact	India, 1950	Pakistan, 1950
Passports	India, October 1952	Pakistan, October 1952
Displaced Persons (Compensation) Act	India, 1954	Pakistan (NADRA rules) 1949-55
Enemy Property Act	India, 1968	(Ordinance) Pakistan, 1969
Vested Property Ordinance		Bangladesh, 1972

Appendix 4.III

Protocol Agreed between Police Officers in the Event of Border Incidents

- Exchange of First Information Reports and Daily Reports of all incidents of raids.
- In the event of raids, police of both sides to exchange information, by wireless, where possible, or telegram.
- "Earnest efforts" to be made to recover stolen property. "This is imperative in the case of abducted persons particularly women."
- When a raider has been identified by name, "strong and effective action" to be taken "to run him to earth".
- Exchange of lists of "notorious persons" strong and effective action against "these individuals".
- Collective penal action "in the shape of collective fines or otherwise" against villages conniving with border raids.
- Superintendents of Police (SPs) and their gazette officers to "keep an eye" on "the harbourers of the raiders".
- Where possible, permanent permits to be issued to concerned SPs and gazetted officers to enable them to meet their opposite numbers without delay.
- Warnings to be issued to all border police, village defence societies, national guards and troops "to refrain from giving any direct or indirect assistance to the raiders".
- Steps to be taken to publicize these decisions so that miscreants and raiders on both sides are aware that "adequate steps" would be taken against them

Source: "Instructions relating to meetings between police officers of Rajasthan and Pakistan to prevent border incidents", NAI/MEA/36-15/49 Pak III.

References

Ali, Chaudhri Muhammad, *The Emergence of Pakistan*, New York and London: Columbia University Press, 1967.

Bajpai, Kanti, *et al.*, eds, *Brasstacks and Beyond: Perception and Management of Crisis in South Asia*, New Delhi: Barnes and Noble, 1995.

Blinkenberg, Lars, *India–Pakistan. The History of Unsolved Conflict. Volume I. The Historical Part*, Odense: Odense University Press, 1998.

Casanova, Jose, *Public Religions in the Modern World*, Chicago: University of Chicago Press, 1994.

Chandavarkar, Rajnarayan, "Customs of Governance: Colonialism and Democracy in Twentieth Century India", *Modern Asian Studies*, vol. 41, no. 3 May, 2007.

Chatterji, Joya, "Mutuality and Co-operation in South Asia: An Alternative History of India–Pakistan Relations", unpublished lecture, Royal Asiatic Society, March 2012, http://backdoorbroadcasting.net/2012/03/joya-chatterji-an-alternative-history-of-india-pakistan-relations.

———, "Rights or Charity? Government and Refugees: The Debate over Relief and Rehabilitation in West Bengal, 1947–1950", in Suvir Kaul, ed., *Partition of Memory*, Delhi: Permanent Black, 2001.

———, "South Asian Histories of Citizenship, 1946–1970", *The Historical Journal*, 55, 4, 2012.

———, *The Spoils of Partition. Bengal and India 1947–1967*, Cambridge: Cambridge University Press, 2007.

Chattha, Ilyas, *Partition and Locality: Violence, Migration, and Development in Gujranwala and Sialkot 1947–1961,* Karachi: Oxford University Press, 2011.

Chattopadhyaya, Haraprasad, *Internal Migration in India: A Case Study of Bengal*, Calcutta: K.P. Bagchi, 1987.

Chowdhury, Hamidul Huq, *Memoirs*, Dacca: Halima Hamid Trust, 1989.

Copland, Ian, "The Further Shores of Partition: Ethnic Cleansing in Rajasthan 1947", *Past and Present*, no. 160 August, 1998.

Das, Durga, ed., *Sardar Patel's Correspondence* [*SPC*], 10 vols, Ahmedabad, 1971.

Farooqui, M.I., *The Law of Abandoned Property*, Dhaka: Khaja Art, 2000.

Ganguly, Sumit, "Wars Without End: The Indo-Pakistani Conflict", *Annals of the American Academy of Political and Social Science*, 541, September 1995.

Gould, William, Taylor C. Sherman, and Sarah Ansari, "The Flux of the Matter: Loyalty, Corruption and the 'Everyday State' in the Post-Partition Government Services of India and Pakistan", *Past and Present*, 219, May 2013.

Guha, Amalendu, *Planter-Raj to Swaraj. Freedom Struggle and Electoral Politics in Assam, 1826–1946*, New Delhi: Indian Council of Historical Research, 1977.

Ibrahim, Farhana, *Settlers, Saints and Sovereigns. An Ethnography of State Formation in Western India*, London: Routledge, 2009.

Jeffrey, Robin, "The Punjab Boundary Force and the Problem of Order, 1947", *Modern Asian Studies*, 8,4 1974.

Kamaluddin, A.F.M., "Refugee Problems in Bangladesh", in L.A. Kosinski and K.M. Elahi, eds, *Population Redistribution and Development in South Asia*, Dordrecht: D. Reidel Publishing, 1985.

Kamran, Tahir, "The Unfolding Crisis in Punjab, March–August, 1947: Key Turning Points and British Responses", *Journal of Punjab Studies*, 14, 2007.

Lamb, Alistair, *Incomplete Partition. The Genesis of India's Kashmir Dispute*, Roxburg, 1997, and Karachi: Oxford University Press, 2002.

Martin, David, *On Secularization: Toward a Revised General Theory*, Aldershot: Ashgate Publishing Company, 2005.

Mayaram, Shail, "Speech, Silence and the Making of Partition Violence in Mewat", in Shahid Amin and Dipesh Chakrabarty, eds, *Subaltern Studies X*, New Delhi: Oxford University Press, 1996.

Mazower, Mark, *No Enchanted Palace: The End of Empire and the Ideological Origins of the United Nations*, Princeton: Princeton University Press, 2013.

Menon, Ritu, and Kamla Bhasin, *Borders and Boundaries: Women in India's Partition*, New Delhi, 1998.

Mitchell, Timothy, "Society, Economy and the State Effect", in Aradhana Sharma and Akhil Gupta, eds, *The Anthropology of the State: A Reader*, Oxford: Blackwell Publishing, 2006.

Mukherjee, Ishan, "Agitations, Riots and the Transitional State in Calcutta, 1945–50", Doctoral dissertation, University of Cambridge, 2017.

Paul, T.V., ed., *The India–Pakistan Conflict. An Enduring Rivalry*, Cambridge: Cambridge University Press, 2005.

Raghavan, Pallavi, "The Finality of Partition: Bilateral Relations between India and Pakistan, 1947–1957", Doctoral dissertation, University of Cambridge, 2012.

Raghavan, Srinath, *War and Peace in Modern India*, London: Palgrave Macmillan, 2010.

Roy, Haimanti, *Partitioned Lives. Migrants, Refugees, Citizens in India and Pakistan, 1947–65*, New Delhi: Oxford University Press, 2013.

Samaddar, Ranabir, ed., *Reflections on Partition in the East*, New Delhi and Calcutta: Vikas Publishing House and Calcutta Research Group, 1997.

Sharma, Jayeeta, *Empire's Garden. Assam and the Making of India*, Duke University Press: Durham and London, 2011.

Sherman, Taylor C., "Migration, Citizenship and Belonging in Hyderabad Deccan, 1946–1956", *Modern Asian Studies*, 45, 2011.

———, *Muslim Belonging in Secular India: Negotiating Citizenship in Postcolonial Hyderabad*, Cambridge: Cambridge University Press, 2015.

———, *State Violence and Punishment in India*, London and New York: Routledge, 2010.

Taylor, Charles, *A Secular Age*, Cambridge, Mass.: Harvard University Press, 2007.

Tyagi, V.V.S., "The Economic Impact of Partition on Indian Agriculture and Related Industries", Unpublished doctoral dissertation, American University, Washington DC, 1958.

van Schendel, Willem, *The Bengal Borderland. Beyond State and Nation in South Asia*, London: Anthem Press, 2005.

Zamindar, Vazira F., *The Long Partition and the Making of Modern South Asia: Refugees, Boundaries, Histories*, New York, 2007.

5

Rights or Charity? The Debate over Relief and Rehabilitation in West Bengal 1947–1950

In the half-century since India was partitioned, more than twenty-five million refugees have crossed the new frontier mapped out by Radcliffe between East Pakistan and the state of West Bengal in India. The migration out of East Bengal was very different from the rush of refugees into India from West Pakistan, which was immediate and immense, as was the way the dispossessed were received by the country to which they fled. Unlike those from the west, the refugees from the east did not flood into India in one huge wave; they came sometimes in surges but often in barely perceptible trickles over five decades of Independence.[1]

[1] The table below on refugees coming into West Bengal between 1946 and 1962, based on official sources which always underestimated the numbers of refugees entering, nevertheless gives an indication of the ebb and flow of the migration.

Migration of Refugees from East Pakistan to West Bengal, 1946–1962

1946	58,602
1947	4,63,474
1948	4,90,555
1949	3,26,211

The elemental violence of Partition in the Punjab explains why millions crossed its plains in 1947. By contrast, the causes of the much larger migration out of East Bengal over a much longer time span are more complex. That migration was caused by many different factors: minorities found their fortunes rapidly declining as avenues of advancement and livelihood were foreclosed; they also experienced social harassment, whether open and fierce or covert and subtle, usually set against a backcloth of communal hostility which, in Hindu perception at least, was sometimes banked but always burning. Another critical factor was the ups and downs in India's relationship with Pakistan which powerfully influenced why and when refugees fled to West Bengal.[2]

1950	11,72,978
1951	47,437
1952	5,31,440
1953	76,123
1954	1,21,364
1955	2,40,424
1956	5,81,000
1957	6,000
1958	4,898
1959	6,348
1960	9,712
1961	10,847
1962	13,894
Total	42,61,257 (4.26 million)

Source: Reports of the Committee of Review of Rehabilitation Work in West Bengal.

[2] The police action in Hyderabad in August 1948, the Bagerhat riots in East Bengal in 1950, the renewed agitation in Pakistan over the Kashmir issue in May 1951, and the introduction of a passport system between India and Pakistan in October 1952 each triggered off large-scale migration from East Pakistan into West Bengal. See *Report on How the Millions*, pp. 1–2. On the other hand, migration slowed down markedly after the signing in 1948 of the Inter-Dominion Agreement between Pakistan and India. It fell

Given this context, the strikingly different way in which the Government of India viewed the refugee problem in the east and in the west is not altogether surprising, although the refugees from the east paid dearly for it. The crisis in Punjab, Government decided, was a national emergency, to be tackled on a war footing. In September 1947, Government set up the Military Evacuation Organisation to get Hindus and Sikhs out of Pakistan in a swift and orderly fashion. By 15 November, within just two months, the Government of India had escorted 1.7 million Punjab evacuees into its refugee camps.[3] From the start, Government accepted that a transfer of population across the western border with Pakistan was a fact of Partition, inevitable and irreversible. So it readily committed itself to the view that refugees from the west would have to be fully and permanently rehabilitated. It also quickly decided that property abandoned by Muslims who had fled to Pakistan would be given to the refugees as the cornerstone of its programmes of relocating and rehabilitating them.[4]

The influx of refugees into Bengal, on the other hand, was seen in an altogether different light. In Nehru's view, and this was typical of the Congress High Command, conditions in East Bengal did not constitute a grave and permanent danger to its Hindu minorities. It was convenient for Delhi to regard their flight westwards as the product of fears, mainly imaginary, and of baseless rumours, rather than the consequence of palpable threats to life, limb, and property. Well after it had begun, Nehru continued to believe that the exodus could be halted, even reversed, provided

---

off again – after a sharp rise in February and March 1950 which coincided with the Bagerhat riots – once the Delhi Pact was signed in April of that year.

[3] See Rao, *The Story of Rehabilitation*, p. 15.

[4] The official history of the relief and rehabilitation measures undertaken *vis-à-vis* the refugees from West Pakistan is set out in *After Partition*; and Rao, *The Story of Rehabilitation*. A more scholarly assessment may be found in Kudaisya, "The Demographic Upheaval of Partition", pp. 73–94.

the Government in Dacca could be persuaded to deploy "psychological measures" to restore confidence among the Hindu minorities.[5] The Inter-Dominion Agreement of April 1948 was designed, Canute-like, to prevent the tide coming in.[6] In the meantime, Government saw the giving of relief to refugees from East Bengal as a stop-gap measure since permanent rehabilitation was judged to be unnecessary; indeed it was something to be positively discouraged. So it set itself against the redistribution of the property of Muslim evacuees from Bengal to incoming Hindu refugees; the policy was to hold it in trust for the Muslims until they too came back home, *pace* NATO's latter-day plans for Kosovo. The official line was grounded in the belief that Bengali refugees crossing the border in either direction could, and indeed should, be persuaded to return home. Government clung to this view, in which optimism triumphed over experience, long after it had become patently obvious that the refugees in Bengal had come to stay and that their numbers would only increase. It was several months before the Government of West Bengal accepted that it had to do something for the refugees. When it belatedly set up a rehabilitation board, it was never given adequate resources to do the job. Even after the number of refugees in Bengal had outstripped those from Punjab, such relief and rehabilitation measures as Government put into place still bore the mark of its stubborn unwillingness to accept that the problem would not simply go away on its own.[7]

[5] Jawaharlal Nehru to Dr B.C. Roy, 2 December 1949, cited in Chakrabarty, *With Dr B.C. Roy*, p. 144.

[6] The first Inter-Dominion Agreement was signed in April 1948 and provided for the setting up of minorities boards and evacuee property management boards comprising members of the minority communities in East and West Bengal. Proceedings of the Inter-Dominion Conference, Calcutta, 15–18 April 1948, Government of West Bengal, Home (Political) Department Confidential File for the year 1948 (no file number), West Bengal State Archives.

[7] By the end of 1951, the number of refugees in West Bengal was estimated

This was what led the refugees to organise and demand that Government give them what they regarded as their "right". Their movement of protest embroiled refugees and Government in a bitter and long-drawn-out battle over what legitimately could be expected from the state. These increasingly entrenched positions were set out in official policy decisions and the campaigns against their implementation launched by refugee organisations. The nub of the matter, however, was quite simple: did the refugees have rights to relief and permanent rehabilitation, and did Government have a responsibility to satisfy these rights? As both sides argued their corner, they were forced to spell out their own (often unexamined) assumptions on a range of critically important issues about the ethical prerogatives of citizenship and the imperatives of *realpolitik*.

This essay looks at the main arguments that emerged from the confrontation and tries to tease out their inwardness. In examining what divided Government and the refugees, it assesses how far apart their positions were and how different the premises on which they were based. It also locates the common ground, if any, that they shared. In so doing, this enquiry may contribute to a better understanding of the ideological underpinnings of Independent India and the role that marginal groups, notably refugees, have played in creating notions of legitimacy and citizenship which came to challenge India's new orthodoxies.

Government Directives: The Construction of Relief as "Charity"

Campaigns by refugees against Government *diktat* were a persistent and highly visible feature of political life in West Bengal well

---

to be 2.51 million, while those in Punjab only 2.4 million. By the beginning of 1956, the numbers in Bengal had grown to about 3.5 million. *Relief and Rehabilitation of Displaced Persons in West Bengal.*

into the 1960s.[8] But their formative period coincided with the initial wave of migration between 1947 and 1950, which is the focus here. The issues began to crystallise after the Government of West Bengal decided, quite early on, to deny relief to "able-bodied males" and to phase out relief camps. As soon as refugees demanded a say in their rehabilitation, the battle lines had been drawn.

Stopping free relief to able-bodied males was only the first of a series of measures to limit Government's liability towards the refugees. The essence of the policy was to whittle down, by one device or another, the numbers eligible for help from the state. By November 1948, the surge in migration caused in large part by events in distant Hyderabad began to tail off.[9] As soon as the number of refugees entering West Bengal had slowed, Government was quick to claim that the worst was over and some officials, adding their two-*anna* bit, even argued that the lure of handouts in the relief programmes was itself attracting migrants – a convenient justification when Government decided to stop providing the pitifully meagre relief it had reluctantly given.[10]

In late 1948, Government began to put a new and harsher policy into place. On 25 November 1948 Calcutta announced that only refugees, narrowly defined as persons ordinarily resident in East Bengal who had managed to get to West Bengal between

[8] The last of the major refugee campaigns against Government began in 1961, when the West Bengal Government ordered camp refugees to move to Dandakaranya in Madhya Pradesh. The order was vigorously resisted by 10,000 camp dwellers who simply refused to go.

[9] The threat of conflict between India and Pakistan over the accession of Hyderabad had reverberations in East Bengal, where Hindus feared that in the event of war they would face persecution. This fear prompted a sudden and sharp rise in the number of refugees fleeing East Bengal.

[10] In 1947 and 1948, acute foodgrain shortage and high prices were endemic in East Bengal and led to famine conditions in at least three districts: Barisal, Noakhali, and Chittagong. See, for example, the reports in *The Statesman*, Calcutta, on 14 and 16 July 1947, and 9 August 1947.

the precise dates of 1 June 1947 and 25 June 1948, "on account of civil disturbances or fear of such disturbances or the Partition of India", were entitled to relief and rehabilitation.[11] A second order published in December 1948 declared that refugees would not be registered after 15 January 1949, further cutting back the official definition of a "refugee".[12]

A month earlier, on 22 November 1948, the Government of West Bengal had decreed that "no able-bodied male immigrant . . . capable of earning his own living [would] be given gratuitous relief either in cash or in kind for himself as well as members of his family for more than a week from the date of their arrival at . . . camps."[13] Relief with no questions asked would be given for just one week. After that, relief would be conditional "only against works" – shades of the much criticised famine relief policy of the British Raj; indeed Samuel Smiles could hardly have done better.

It was all very well for Government to offer relief "against works". But there were no such "works" to employ the able-bodied in need of relief, and Government gave no assurance that it would create them. Instead, the official line was that the immigrant himself "through his own effort [must) find work suitable to

[11] An exception was made for refugees arriving from Noakhali and Tippera, for whom it was decreed that "the time of leaving such residence shall run from the lst day of December 1946" (i.e. when the communal rioting first began in these districts). Memo No. 5691 F.R./I0M-87/48, from the Assistant Secretary, Relief and Rehabilitation Department, Government of West Bengal, to the Relief Commissioner, West Bengal, 25 November 1948. This and other Government memoranda cited below have been culled from the voluminous *Weekly Reports on Relief and Rehabilitation of Displaced Persons from East Bengal*, contained in Government of Bengal, Intelligence Bureau (hereafter GB IB), File No. 1838/48.

[12] Relief and Rehabilitation Department, Government of West Bengal, Memo, 20 December 1948, in GB IB 1838/48.

[13] Memo No. 5610 (13) F.R., from the Secretary, Relief and Rehabilitation, Government of West Bengal to all District Officers, 12 November 1948, ibid.

himself."[14] Male refugees who were physically capable of working had, somehow or the other, instantly and miraculously to find themselves jobs sufficiently remunerative to feed, clothe, and house themselves and their dependent families, all within seven days of setting foot across the border. In this triumph of fantasy over fact, Government outdid itself by urging refugees go anywhere in Bengal except to Calcutta and its suburbs, where casual employment was most easily to be found.

To begin with, Government had allowed camp offices discretion to make an exception in those cases where they felt that free relief (or "doles", as they were called in terminology unattractively reminiscent of the Poor Law) was "essential for preservation of life". Put bluntly, Government realised that it would not look good if people starved to death in its camps. Two months later, however, in the wake of refugee hunger strikes against its Gradgrind directives, it hardened its heart. On 15 February 1949, a Government brought to office by the sacrifices of generations of freedom fighters, decreed that "Such able bodied immigrants as do not accept offers of employment or rehabilitation facilities without justification should be denied gratuitous relief *even if they may be found starving*."[15] This breathtaking decision was reiterated towards the end of March 1949. In a directive aimed at "soft" camp superintendents suspected of being susceptible to pressures from refugees (or indeed to the imperatives of humanity), it laid down that free relief must not be given to anyone "merely because he was found starving once, the underlying principle being that *an able-bodied male must earn his own living, and should not be made to feel, under any circumstances, that he can at any time be a charge on the state*."[16]

[14] Ibid.

[15] Memo No. 800 (14) R.R., from the Secretary, Relief and Rehabilitation Department, Government of West Bengal, to all District Officers, 15 February 1949. Emphasis added.

[16] Memo No. 1745 (10) R.R./18R-18/49, from the Secretary, Relief and

In July 1949 Calcutta announced that all relief camps in West Bengal must be closed down by 31 October 1949, just three months down.[17] A little later, the deadline was grudgingly extended by a further three months until 31 December 1949, "with a clear direction that rehabilitation of the inmates of the camps be completed by that date and the camps be closed with effect from that date." This time, the Government of West Bengal took pains to make it clear that while "there may be cases where refugees may show disinclination to move . . . [t]hat should not be any reason why the closing of camps . . . should be delayed. As soon as lands have been allotted and rents offered and railway warrants issued, refugees are expected to move to their new places of settlement. If they do not, they unnecessarily hold up rehabilitation. It should be made clear to them that by doing so they cannot continue the life of the camp which shall positively be closed."[18]

In this step, Bengal's first national Government spelled out its draconian solution. It asserted that it had fulfilled its responsibility to provide "relief" to the refugees. From now on it would only "rehabilitate" those few persons it chose to define as refugees. Refugees had to be made to understand that they should expect no further relief and that they would be entitled only to whatever crumbs by way of rehabilitation Government decided to offer them. This was the first in a series of official announcements by which it was made unequivocally clear that refugees had no choice in the matter. They had to take what was offered or get nothing at all.

Rehabilitation Department, Government of West Bengal, to all District Officers, 29 March 1949. Emphasis added.

[17] Memo No. 4482 (13)-Misc.l6B-3/49, from the Secretary, Relief and Rehabilitation Department, Government ofWest Bengal, to all District Officers, 11 July 1949.

[18] Memo No. 8637 (13) Rehab., from].K. Sanyal, Assistant Secretary to the Government of West Bengal to all District Officers, 9 December 1949.

The thrust of what Government set out to do, at least in the prospectus, was to encourage refugees to be self-employed. Categorised by their social background and training, they were to be offered soft loans of varying amounts to enable them to buy equipment, tools, or supplies in order to set themselves up as entrepreneurs.[19] Those who felt they had neither the training nor the talent for entrepreneurship but wanted "proper jobs" instead, those who preferred to stay on in camps and those who "deserted" from the concentration camp-like conditions of "rehabilitation colonies", were given no choice. They had to do as they were told or lose all claim to the meagre rehabilitation benefits on offer. Hardly surprisingly, this unattractive policy brought Government into repeated conflict with the refugees.

These directives give an insight into Government's view of its responsibilities towards its refugee citizenry. The policy of the centre and the state of West Bengal may have differed in emphasis, but more significant is the measure of consensus between them on this question. The core assumptions that underpinned their common position need to be examined as they have an importance that goes beyond the issue around which their thinking crystallised.[20]

By attempting repeatedly to restrict the definition of who could claim to be a "refugee", Government showed that it had

[19] "Professional loans" of Rs 2600 and Rs 2100 were offered to doctors and lawyers respectively to set up practice; "business loans" (of up to a maximum of Rs 100,000) to those who could persuade the authorities that they had the knowhow and contacts required to set up industries; "business or small-trades loans" and "loans for artisans" of up to Rs 500 were offered to aspiring petty entrepreneurs in the rural areas. In addition, loans were on offer to weavers (Rs 600); there were also "paddy-husking loans" of Rs 122 (intended especially for rural women) and "horticultural loans" of Rs 630 and a *bigha* (a fraction of an acre) of land, which were designed "especially for middle-class families" to live in reduced *bhadralok* circumstances, growing their own fruit and vegetables! *Report on How the Millions*, pp. 29–30.

[20] In the section that follows, unless otherwise specified, the term "Government" is used to denote this common official position.

to accept, however grudgingly, that it could not altogether avoid responsibility for those displaced by Partition and to acknowledge that it had some obligations towards the "victims" of India's vivisection. The fine sentiment, frequently and platitudinously voiced in the documents of the Rehabilitation Department, was that "to succour and rehabilitate the victims of communal passion is an obligation the country is solemnly pledged to honour."[21]

In practice, however, Government strove officiously to limit its liability and did so by cutting its definition of the term "refugee" to the bone. A refugee, Calcutta declared, was a person who had migrated before the end of June 1948; to be classified as a refugee, he was also required to have registered himself as such before January 1949, and the small print further narrowed this straitened path for those who sought the status of refugee. In this enterprise, many were called but few chosen. A key device by which Government was able to achieve its objective was by limiting its definition not only of refugees but also of "Partition" itself, the *fons et origo* for such responsibility for refugees it felt it had to accept. By its own narrow edict, Partition was defined by official decree to be occurrences which began in June 1947 (or six months earlier in December 1946 if the refugee had happened to live in Noakhali or Tippera) and abruptly came to an end one year later in June 1948. That Partition was a process which began in 1947 but whose impact continued to unfold long after June 1948 was obvious to everyone outside the Writers' Building. But blinded by their own self-serving definitions, Bengal's new rulers' myopia deprived them of the ability to anticipate and effectively to react to the ongoing problems caused by Partition and its aftermath. Not surprisingly, they were caught off guard by each new crisis.[22]

[21] This quotation (from Rao, *The Story of Rehabilitation*, p. 229) is so typical an example of the dominant sentiment in the official record that it would be otiose to give detailed citations of other examples of this genre.

[22] In practice, Government found it repeatedly had to extend the time limit as each new horde of refugees entered Bengal. Time and again, camps were

The stance taken by Government also prevented it from seeing that the refugee problem was affected in vitally important ways by developments outside the two Bengals. Its choice of dates, by which only those who crossed the border before the end of June 1948 were recognised as refugees, was a deliberate act of policy intended specifically to deny refugee status to the hundreds of thousands who had crossed over to India between July and October 1948 after the Hyderabad crisis. Government clearly planned to limit, in spatial terms, the scope of what it would accept as direct consequences of Partition. For officials in distant Delhi and those closer at hand in Calcutta, only events in East Bengal itself were to count as bona fide consequences of Partition for those who decided to flee that territory. But outside Lutyens' palaces and the rabbit warrens of the Writers' Building, refugees continued to be driven from their homes by happenings many hundreds of miles away, whether in India or in Pakistan, the consequences of faraway events which nonetheless had powerful reverberations upon communal relations in the towns and countryside of East Bengal.[23]

In a similar vein, the Government decided to define in the strictest possible way what could be deemed to be the *effects* of Partition. According to its taxonomy, "civil disturbances" alone – that is communal violence or blatant discrimination against minorities – were accepted as genuine "effects" of Partition. Only those who could prove that they had fled communal violence

---

closed down only to be reopened to take them in. But on each occasion the same charade was played out of announcing cut-off dates, declaring camps closed once and for all, categorising refugees according to those who arrived before (or after) certain dates, and all the other well-established devices. For details, see Chakrabarti, *The Marginal Men*; and Chatterjee, "The East Bengal Refugees".

[23] This is true even today: the demolition of the Babri mosque in Ayodhya prompted a wave of refugees into India from Bangladesh. This is, of course, one of the central themes of Amitav Ghosh's novel *The Shadow Lines*.

directed against themselves personally were regarded as genuine victims of Partition and therefore as proper refugees entitled to protection (in however small measure) from the Indian state. But economic hardship in East Bengal, where famine stalked the land and where food cost much more than anywhere else in India,[24] was not accepted as a consequence of Partition. It may have been obvious to others that Partition had directly and disastrously affected the livelihoods of millions of people, Hindus and Muslims, in both Bengals,[25] but migrants tossed across borders in search of work and food were not deemed by Government to be "genuine" victims of Partition or as "true" refugees. So it followed that they were not in any sense the responsibility of the Indian state. This helps to explain why the Government of India treated the refugees from Punjab, where communal violence came close to being genocide, so differently from the refugees from East Bengal, where the violence was never remotely on that scale.[26] Such devices enabled the state to accept minimal responsibility, whether moral or practical, for the "victim of Partition".

But the official definition of the refugee as *victim* also deserves closer scrutiny, since this provides another key to assess the tenuous morality behind Government's attitude towards the refugees. Only bona fide "victims" were entitled to relief and rehabilitation. To be eligible for relief, a refugee family had to register itself. This required giving "detailed information", much

[24] "The Viceroy's Visit to Bengal", vol. I, p. 188 (C).

[25] For a brief account of the havoc caused for the economic life of the border districts, see Chatterji, "The Fashioning of a Frontier", pp. 185–242.

[26] The prime minister justified to the chief minister of West Bengal the striking difference in expenditure per capita on refugees in the West and East by arguing that while "there was something elemental" about the situation in West Pakistan, "where practically all Hindus and Sikhs have been driven out", in the East it was more gradual, and many Hindus had been able to remain. Jawaharlal Nehru to Dr B.C. Roy, 2 December 1949, cited in Chakrabarty, *With Dr B.C. Roy*, p. 143.

of which was not readily at hand, to the registration officer. In December 1948, when Government made public its decision to shut down registration offices by 15 January 1949, it justified the edict by arguing that refugees who were "genuinely interested" had been given "ample time" to register.[27] This introduced a new refinement to the horrors of Partition – what might be described as a "desperation index" in the procedures by which a refugee was prevented from claiming the benefits of that status. If a refugee was truly desperate, so Government argued, he would have found his way to a registration office by mid January 1949. If he did not get to the office on time, that was proof positive that the person claiming refugee status could not have been sufficiently desperate (or destitute enough) to require relief. QED: such dilatory persons were not "victim" enough to be classed as refugees. By laying down as the precondition for receiving state help that a person had first to be registered as a legitimate victim, Government at a stroke cut down a huge problem to a size it felt it could handle. It mattered not a whit that in so doing it slammed the door in the face of so many refugees who had nowhere else to turn.

This had far-reaching implications for the way in which Government responded to refugee demands once they came to be voiced in an organised way. By definition, since they are not the commanders of their own fate, victims are not agents. Rather they are the innocent, the passive: objects of persecution, casualties of fate. Significantly, the state's favourite euphemism for refugees was "displaced persons", with connotations of innocent victims dislocated by events in whose shaping they had played no part. This helped Government to justify treating the refugees from West Pakistan and East Bengal with such an uneven hand. Nehru's point was that the Punjabis had been "driven out" from their homes. Bengalis, by contrast, by migrating in fits and starts, proved that

[27] Relief and Rehabilitation Department, Government of West Bengal, memo, 20 December 1948, in GB IB 1838/48.

they had the option of staying or leaving. According to the official line, a true refugee or "victim" had no choice and was not a free agent. He could therefore not be expected to exercise volition, or have any choice over where or how he was to live in the country in which he sought refuge. These were the only terms on which Government was prepared to offer the refugees its helping hand.

By defining refugees in this way, Government, without having to cross the road, could persuade itself that it had been a Good Samaritan. Furthermore, it could argue that it helped refugees not because of any binding obligation but voluntarily, out of the goodness of its heart. In this way it could claim the moral high ground while acting in ways that made a mockery of the ideals trumpeted in India's new charters and constitution. There is an unattractive undertone of self-congratulation in many of the official accounts of refugee rehabilitation programmes. Bhaskar Rao, himself a worker in this barren vineyard, thus describes the "saga" of rehabilitation in smug hyperbole:

> the indefatigable effort to bring healing to these bruised masses of humanity, to wipe their tears, apply balm to their wounds, assuage their hunger and thirst, clothe their nakedness. And more, to set them on their feet and restore to them the dignity of man . . . What one needed here were virtues alien to bureaucratic routine – sympathy, understanding, great compassion, the urge to succour and sustain, attributes almost of divinity . . . [28]

Others may not have made such extravagant claims to godliness. But terms such as "heroism" and "courage" were frequently used by apologists to describe the efforts of rehabilitation officials who spent sleepless days in this endeavour, "unflinching in the face of indomitable odds", and other sanctimonious variations on the same theme.[29]

[28] Rao, *The Story of Rehabilitation,* pp. 2–3.

[29] For instance, the (unnamed) author of *They Live Again* writes: "statistics cannot describe this story of misfortune, of mass human upheaval. It is too

Stripped of its trappings, the message from on high was that the state had no obligation to give relief, but gave graciously at its pleasure. The refugee had no right to receive. Rather he had a duty to accept with humble gratitude whatever crumbs he was given. In effect, what the refugee received was charity. Since the recipient of charity has no right over how much or what he is given, so too the refugee had no moral right to relief, nor any say over what was doled out to him.

This construction of relief and rehabilitation as charity is seen most explicitly when Government decided at a stroke to stop "doles" for able-bodied males and shut down its camps. In its defence, Government insisted that doles were simply a form of official charity. If able-bodied men accepted these handouts, this would erode their moral fibre and get them accustomed to a culture of dependency. "Living on the permanent charity of doles" would, it was argued, make them "sink into a state of hopeless demoralisation". Camps, likewise, were seen as "symbols of permanent dependence".[30] At least to begin with, the Government of West Bengal had the candour to admit that it had other reasons for its stance, particularly hard calculations to do with money. It admitted that its "financial resources would not permit a continued expenditure of Rs 24 lakhs a month on doles alone for an unlimited period." But from the outset, Government claimed that it was not shortage of cash that determined its policy but an overriding concern for the refugees' own good. In a press note worthy of an Orwellian state, Calcutta defended its order on the grounds that "the Government of West Bengal feels further that grant of gratuitous relief for any length of time would be demoralising to the individual and would affect his self-respect."[31]

tragic for words. Nor can mere facts and figures relate the *magnificent* task of their rehabilitation . . ." *Report on How the Millions*, p. 1.

[30] Rao, *The Story of Rehabilitation*, p. 160.

[31] Press Note, 26 November 1948, GB IB 1838/48.

In time, official reconstruction of the Government's rehabilitation efforts came to avoid any reference to the financial constraints which may have lain behind its decisions, and kept on the safe ground of high morality. So by 1956 it was commonplace for it confidently to be asserted in the publications of the Relief and Rehabilitation Department that it was "in order to counteract the demoralising effect of prolonged stay in camps [that] Government introduced the scheme of keeping able-bodied men engaged in useful work . . ."[32]

While the refugees starved, or at best survived on the barest rations, Government was thus able to have its cake and eat it. It had, after all, a double-edged sword in its armoury. The state was able to represent its relief to the refugees as "charity" (and to congratulate itself for being so charitable), and at the same time it was able to reprimand the refugees (or at least several large categories of them) for daring to *demand* "charity".

It might be tempting to see all of this as little more than a cynical tactic adopted by servants of the state to circumscribe, as far as possible, its responsibilities. But this would be to miss the point. The theme so dominates official thinking that it suggests it was the very touchstone of rehabilitation policy. In official pronouncements, the notion that charity breeds a demoralising "dependence" which is inconsistent with manly self-respect was seen as an obvious truth and elevated to the status of a self-evident, generally accepted, and quotidian value in Indian culture.

But was this view of charity in fact a truism in a social milieu where *dana, dakshina,* and *bhiksha* had long been carefully regulated and vital elements of religious and social life,[33] and where the

[32] *Relief and Rehabilitation.*

[33] See, for instance, Thapar, "*Dana* and *Daksinaas*", pp. 105–21. Even if one accepts Raheja's arguments that a "poison in the gift" tainted the (usually priestly) receiver in caste Hindu society, it does not follow that India had a tradition of contempt for those who received charity. See Raheja, *The Poison in the Gift.*

renouncer who lived on alms was customarily venerated at least as much as the householder?[34] It is by no means clear that it was.[35] By all accounts, these views were of recent origin, not hallowed by Indian tradition. Even in Europe, "in the old days, the beggar who knocked at the rich man's door was regarded as a messenger from God, and might even be Christ in disguise." According to Braudel, the origins of European attitudes which drove a distinction between the "worthy poor, looking for work . . . whom one should succour" and the "unworthy poor not seeking a living", the miscreants, vagrants and beggars who were "idle, good-for-nothing, dangerous", deserving slavery and exile, are as recent as the seventeenth century.[36] By the late-eighteenth century accepting

[34] On the distinctive role of the renouncer in Hindu society, see Dumont, "World Renunciation", Appendix B, in Dumont, *Homo Hierarchicus*, pp. 267–86. A critical reappraisal of Dumont's argument can be found in Madan, *Non-Renunciation*. C.A. Bayly suggests that as late as 1880 religious mendicants of all sorts accounted for five people out of every hundred in northern India; in Banaras alone, the 40,000 or so Brahmins living on charity in 1810 accounted for almost one person in five of the city's population. Bayly surmises that in the last decade of the eighteenth century there were as many as half a million Shaivite and Vaishnavite ascetics in North India, all living off alms. Nor were mendicant groups, such as the Gosains and Bairagis, in any sense marginal: indeed they played a critically important role in the economic life of the post-Mughal successor states and were respected as much for their ritual status as for their commercial success. See Bayly, *Rulers, Townsmen and Bazaars*, pp. 126, 183; Haynes, "From Tribute to Philanthropy"; and Kozlowski, *Muslim Endowments*, show that traditional forms of charity and philanthropy persisted in the late-colonial period.

[35] The description of *dana* and *dakshina* in middle-period Bengal suggests that these practices were very much a part of the religious life of Bengal. See Inden, *Marriage and Rank in Bengali Culture*, pp. 83–92. Tapan Raychaudhuri has shown that amongst Hindus of high status in early-modern Bengal the traditional norms of morality required them "never to run away a suitor for charity". Raychaudhuri, "Norms of Family Life", p. 21.

[36] Braudel, *Civilisation and Capitalism*, pp. 506–8. The literature on charity, philanthropy, and welfare in early-modern and modern Europe is rich

"charity" had already begun to attract social odium; a century later, the wheel had come full circle and charity was seen as "injuring" those it was intended to aid.[37]

Similarly, in industrial Europe "dependency" came to denote a stigmatised condition appropriate only for women, children, and the infirm. When England put its New Poor Law onto the statute book in 1834, this attitude informed the amendment which aimed "both to deter the poor from resorting to public assistance and to stigmatise those who did."[38] By the early twentieth century, dependency had come to be taken as a mark of debility of character rather than a function of poverty.[39] So an able-bodied male who came to be dependent was seen as the epitome of the "undeserving poor",[40] since it was not poverty but a man's lack of self-respect that caused his dependence. Dependence was thus a subjective condition. And because it was only acceptable for women and children to be dependent, an able-bodied dependent man was seen to have the perceived attributes of women and children: weakness, idleness, passivity, and irresponsibility.

If India's new policy-makers deployed these imported European attitudes towards charity and dependency with such great effect, it was because in their passage to Bengal they assumed highly charged local inflections and particular resonances of their

---

and voluminous; Cunningham and Innes, *Charity, Philanthropy and Reform*, provides a useful and comparative overview of the subject.

[37] Williams, *Keywords*, pp. 54–5.

[38] Hirschman, *The Rhetoric of Reaction*, p. 30, argues that the notion of well-intended welfare measures inevitably bringing about results quite the opposite of those intended has been a central pillar of reactionary thought since Burke's reflections on the French revolution. The idea that welfare assistance, which is intended to alleviate poverty, actually creates the conditions that entrench poverty more deeply, belongs to this tradition, described by Hirschman as the 'perversity thesis'. Ibid., pp. 11–42.

[39] See Fraser and Gordon, "A Genealogy of Dependency", pp. 309–36.

[40] Williams, *Keywords*, p. 55.

own. In one of the deeper ironies of Bengal's modern history, this way of thinking happened to fit neatly with a pre-existing tradition among its colonial masters about the flawed character of the Bengali Hindu male, a hurtful caricature which now came to gain a new lease of life as the accredited political wisdom of the very people whom it had so cruelly mocked. In the nineteenth century, British officials had conventionally regarded physical weakness and lack of vigour, lethargy, effeminacy, and (not to put too fine a point on it) an absence of moral backbone as the very essence of the Bengali babu's being.[41] By the mid-twentieth century even the babu's brave forays into terrorism, far from metamorphosing him into an intrepid fighter, only underlined the weakness of his character in British eyes: the attributes of volatility, irresponsibility, immaturity, and cowardice were simply added to the list of his irredeemable flaws. In gross stereotype, the Bengali Hindu male was thus seen by his imperial critic as a deplorable combination of the worst possible feminine and childish qualities.

Writing on rehabilitation by officers in Delhi and Calcutta unconsciously aped the prejudices of their erstwhile masters, thus bringing together two borrowed traditions – one from Europe and the other from colonial India's recent past – to produce a new and potent stereotype of the Bengali refugee. This characterisation was drawn in counterpoint to an equally hackneyed, but far more flattering, picture of the Punjabi refugee whose "toughness . . . sturdy sense of self-reliance . . . [and] pride" never let him "submit to the indignity of living on doles and charity". Even in their "hour of supreme trial", the doughty Punjabi refugees

> . . . would not stoop to accept charity, never would their proud hands be stretched out to receive alms. No work, however seemingly low, would they despise . . . They represented the fine core of the Punjabi peasantry, to whom honest labour is the flower of human dignity. Rehabilitation, in their case, was easy, for they met the Government's

[41] See Rosselli, "The Self-Image of Effeteness"; and Sinha, *Colonial Masculinity*.

> efforts half-way . . . They were of the breed of heroes, though their stories have not been told in epic and song . . .[42]

The Punjabi refugee, heir of the martial races who were the darlings of the post-Mutiny Raj, was thus held up by independent Indian officialdom as the model of the "deserving poor". The outrageousness of this statement – given that Government allocated many thousand acres of land to the Punjabis, disbursed Rs 11 million among them for the purchase of livestock, and gave them a further Rs 44 million in grants, loans, and advances – does not need to be underlined.[43]

The contrast drawn by officials between the Punjabi and the Bengali refugee could hardly have been sharper. Blaming the "character of the refugees themselves" for the failings of the rehabilitation effort in West Bengal, the same author who lavished praise on the Punjabis, admittedly no Bengali himself, condemned the Bengalis in prose reminiscent of the *Koi Hais* of Victorian India:

> In the Western region they were tougher, more resilient of spirit and much more adaptable . . . But the refugees in the East came from a different milieu; the influences that moulded their lives were different. East Bengal was a comparatively poor agricultural region, with an economy less diversified than West Punjab's. Also, what is more significant, the person displaced from East Pakistan had been exposed to devitalising, demoralising forces much longer than his western counterpart had been . . . he was completely shattered in body and spirit, all initiative, all capacity for self-adjustment drained out of him . . .[44]

Describing the West Bengal Government's repeated but unsuccessful attempts to shut down the camps, Bhaskar Rao almost outdid Macaulay in the fatuousness of his sentiments:

[42] Rao, *The Story of Rehabilitation*, p. 38.

[43] See Kudaisya, "The Demographic Upheaval of Partition".

[44] Rao, *The Story of Rehabilitation*, p. 147.

> The more serious difficulty arose out of a certain psychological weakness or deficiency among a fairly large section of the camp population. Many showed a reluctance to forgo the advantage of gratuitous relief, a disinclination to embrace the rigorous discipline of independent existence . . . Whether it was because the refugee sought sanctuary in India already broken in spirit as well as in body, or whether because long exposure to doles had demoralised him, here was a mood most frustrating to the rehabilitation effort . . .[45]

The official view was that his very disposition rendered the Bengali male refugee prone to fall into a state of dependency and therefore incapable of breaking out of it. This, it was argued, made the task of Government in West Bengal impossibly difficult and indeed justified policies that might, in other circumstances, be seen as ruthless or harsh. Whereas "in the West, the refugee matched Government efforts on his behalf with an overwhelming passion to be absorbed into the normal routine of living", in Bengal "the Government had to supply the initiative as well as the motive power. To overcome the apathy, even the sullenness, of the displaced person was itself no small task. It called for patience and tact, endless sympathy joined to occasional firmness . . ."[46] In other words, India's new breed of self-appointed guardians had no option but to be "firm" in the male refugees' own "best interests".

Here, the thesis – if it deserves to be elevated to that status – brought together two different lines of argument. The first was that their qualities of character inculcated a psychological dependency amongst Bengali males. In turn, this rendered them incapable of making rational decisions for themselves.[47] Because they were dependent, any judgement of their own about themselves and their

[45] Ibid., p. 155.

[46] Ibid., p. 157.

[47] This was reasoning similar to that which had informed the French Constitution of 1791, which excluded all categories of dependent individuals (including wage workers) from the suffrage "because poverty and dependency were thought to be obstacles to the possession of a reasonable will. See Offe and Preuss, "Democratic Institutions and Moral Resources", p. 161.

lives and times had no value: it was as feeble and untrustworthy as the judgement of women and children.

The second line of argument, again borrowed from the vocabulary of the Raj (albeit with unconscious plagiarism), was that the state's relation to this dross of humankind was that of surrogate *pater familias* or benevolent despot. Because the refugees had placed themselves in its care, Government could decide – indeed it had a duty to decide – what was best for them. In this role, Government assumed the moral authority to determine their fate; if need be by overruling the judgement of adult voting males about what they thought was best for themselves. In this same role, the state also accepted (albeit without much enthusiasm) responsibility for single "unattached" women, the elderly, the infirm, and their dependants. These categories of refugees were, it acknowledged, "more or less a permanent burden on the Government" because they had no able-bodied male relative to support them.[48] In the case of the infirm, women, and children, the state accepted "permanent liability". In other words, it saw itself as standing in for the male bread-winner in relation to these unfortunates and therefore entitled to assert all the moral authority over them that a male bread-winner enjoys over his dependants.

The offcial discourse moved easily between these two different positions. On the one hand it claimed that the state was the fountainhead of charity and on the other it played the part of family patriarch, hardly missing a step as it straddled the divide between these very disparate positions. Indeed, often in the same paragraph, certainly within the text of a single directive, both arguments and models were deployed side by side. But of course, there are glaring contradictions between these two positions. The role of *pater familias* entails a far greater acknowledgement of responsibility and obligation (albeit of a patriarchal variety)

[48] Memo No. 8637 (13) Rehab., from J.K. Sanyal, Assistant Secretary to the Government of West Bengal to all District Officers, 9 December 1949.

than does the role of dispenser of charity. The material support extended to a dependent family member can in no circumstances be constructed as "charity", which, by contrast, is purely voluntary. Unlike those at the receiving end of charity, dependent members of the family have socially sanctioned and legally enforceable rights to maintenance.

Yet the refugees never made an issue of these contradictions. One reason might be that from the point of view of a refugee the impact of both constructions on their rights tended to be much the same in practice. If refugees were to be seen as dependent members of the national family, they could claim rights to maintenance only by virtue of their dependent status, and as dependants they were denied any other rights. If they were represented as recipients of voluntary charity, they had no claims whatever over the source of the charity. Indeed the very fact that they took charity showed them, in the official view, to be so "psychologically dependent" that they were not fit to determine their own destinies. So the net effect of bath positions – however mutually inconsistent – on refugees' rights, could be seen as not being significantly different.

But it is also possible that the refugees chose not to make much of this inconsistency because they saw opportunities in exploiting the grey areas in the official position to their advantage. If they had forced Government to take a consistent line, that line – however Government chose to define it – might have been so tightly drawn that the state could have disclaimed responsibility for refugees altogether. By leaving the ambiguity unchallenged, the refugee movement, whether by accident or by design, kept some room for manouevre in constructing its own definition of refugee claims as "rights", and this eventually enabled it to wrest significant concessions from a reluctant Government.

Refugee Claims: The Notion of "Rights"

Perhaps because the first wave of East Bengal refugees were largely drawn from the *bhadralok*, with lively traditions of political activism, they were quick to organise themselves into pressure groups.[49] Middle-class refugees from the east who had neither homes nor jobs in Calcutta were particularly hard hit by Partition. In East Bengal they had been respectable people, with homes, lands, secure jobs, and a distinctive way of life – even if its advantages had been eroded in the decades before Partition. Now as refugees they often had no more than the clothes in which they stood. They were forced to jostle cheek by jowl with other destitutes of inferior status (as they saw it) on the filthy platforms of Sealdah station, where they waited to be transported to squalid, overcrowded camps. There, herded into barracks that robbed them of any semblance of privacy, they survived (for only as long as Government permitted) on dry rations of stinking, inedible rice, or were left to die without dignity.[50] It is small wonder that they began so swiftly to organise themselves in protest against these appalling conditions.

To begin with, these new groupings were a very mixed bag, heterogeneous in leadership and political affiliation. Each camp or colony tended to set up its own Bastuhara Samiti (Refugee Committee) or Parishad (Council). By the middle of 1949, these numerous camp committees had begun to make the significant transition of forming themselves into larger umbrella organisations. Two such organisations, rivals to each other, were formed in 1950, the United Central Refugee Council (UCRC) and the Refugee Central Rehabilitation Council (RCRC). Although the Communist Party of India (CPI) and the Revolutionary Socialist

[49] Of the 1.1 million refugees who arrived in West Bengal before June 1948, it has been estimated, deploying the broadest of brushes, that 350,000 were members of the "urban *bhadralok*", 550,000 of the "rural *bhadralok*", 100,000 were "peasants" and 100,000 were "artisans". Chakrabarti, *The Marginal Men*, p. 1.

[50] Descriptions of the unspeakably degrading conditions in camps and colonies are commonplace in the newspapers and literary writings of this period. A brief and shocking account can be found in Chakrabarti, *The Marginal Men*, pp. 156–61.

Party (RSP) quickly began to try to establish their respective influence over these organisations, in 1950 they were still far from being party fronts.[51] In the period between 1947 and 1950 refugee organisations, as far as their political affiliations went, remained free-floating and disparate. Many had no allegiance even to the two umbrella organisations. Amongst those committees that did, a good number possessed no party-political affiliation. Moreover, those parties which claimed support from the refugees were themselves ranged across the entire political and ideological spectrum, from the Hindu Mahasabha on the Right (which in these early days had a great deal of influence over several camp committees), to the Revolutionary Communist Party on the Left, which had yet to capture a mass following among the refugees.

It would therefore be wrong to suggest that the refugees had a united and homogeneous programme in ways analogous to the Government's policy and practice. Nevertheless, out of the somewhat amorphous refugee movement there came a distinguishable stance on the questions of relief and rehabilitation. This position, which evolved during the course of many campaigns and was spelled out in endless slogans, pamphlets, and demand charters, was quite simple – as refugees they claimed a right to relief and full rehabilitation, as well as the right to decide what form of rehabilitation they preferred.

In the early days of the refugee movement, its claim to rights was usually defined and defended in a limited and rather sectional way. These rights were seen as deriving from a specific if unwritten

[51] The UCRC Central Council, formed in August 1950, included representatives from the CPI, the Forward Bloc, the Marxist Forward Bloc, the Socialist Unity Centre of India, the Revolutionary Communist Party of India (RCPI: Pannalal Dasgupta's group), the Democratic Vanguard, the Bolshevik Party, the Socialist Republican party and the Hindu Mahasabha: ibid., p. 76. The RCPI was composed of representatives from the RSP, the RCPI (Saumyen Tagore's group), the Forward Bloc (Leela Roy's group), the Kisan Mazdoor Praja Party, and the Socialist Party: ibid., p. 88.

bargain made before Partition between the Hindu leaders of western Bengal and the Hindu minorities of eastern Bengal. The refugees argued that both the state Government and the centre owed them a special debt, because the Hindu minorities of eastern Bengal had deliberately and unselfishly sacrificed their own well-being to create a separate province of West Bengal from which their brethren in the Hindu-majority districts had mainly benefited.[52] As one pamphleteer put it:

> The East Bengal Hindus have endured untold hardships in the cause of India's independence. When the freedom struggle had at last brought freedom within our grasp, then the scheming British imperialists together with the Muslim League put forward the Pakistan demand as an obstacle in the path of India's independence and worked to divide India. To foil their design, and to bring about India's freedom, the Hindus of East Bengal and West Pakistan resolved to sacrifice everything – like Dadhichi, they worked against their own interests to enable India to become free. At that time the leaders of the Congres, the Hindu Mahasabha, the Ramakrishna Mission and the Bharat Sevashram Sangha and many other organisations repeatedly promised to protect the life, dignity and property of East Bengal Hindus, and guarantee them full citizenship rights [*nagrik adhikar*], birth rights [*janmagat adhikar*] and complete rehabilitation in India. Taking them at their word, we all threw out weight behind the campaign to divide Bengal, so as to prevent the whole of Bengal and the city of Calcutta . . . from falling into the hands of the Muslim League and Pakistan. After the Partition of Bengal, we arrived in West Bengal, the independent homeland for whose creation we had sacrificed everything. For fourteen long months, we have waited in vain for that symbol of our hopes and aspiration, "the Congress national Government" [to come to our aid] . . .[53]

[52] For an account of the Hindu campaign for the Partition of Bengal in 1947, see Chatterji, *Bengal Divided*.

[53] "*Amar Sankalp*" (My Resolve), Nabadwip, 6 Agrahayan, 1355 B.S. This pamphlet was issued by Nagendranath Das of the *Purbasthali Thana Punarbasto o Palli Unnayan Samiti* [The Purbasthali Thana Rehabilitation and

Here, the claim to rehabilitation as a right was grounded in the notion of a pre-existing covenant between the Hindus of East Bengal and the political leadership of undivided Bengal, and, by extension, underwritten by the Congress High Command. According to this "pact", the Hindus of East Bengal had agreed to support the cause of a separate West Bengal that was self-evidently antithetical to their own interests, and they had done so on the understanding that once Independence came, the state would compensate them for whatever losses they had suffered as a result of being dispossessed in the East. In this construction, the Government of West Bengal owed the refugees relief and full rehabilitation as compensation or damages. By failing to fulfil its promises, Government had reneged on its pledge. This was a breach of contract, no more and no less, even though the contract was unenforceable except in terms of a moral commitment.

This line, whatever its emotional appeal, was hardly a sufficient foundation on which to base a secure claim to "rights". The argument was, first, that the state owed refugees from East Bengal certain goods that it owed to no other class of its citizens. In other words, it could be seen as special pleading that gave the state scope to avoid accepting a *general* responsibility towards all refugees. In this sense, this was an even narrower definition of its liabilities than the Government itself, however notionally or grudgingly, accepted. This portrayal of refugee "rights" as a special or sectional claim was never entirely abandoned by its protagonists. But as the movement gained momentum, it gradually came to be overlaid with other, more open-ended, meanings. The battle against the cutback in the grants of doles to able-bodied male refugees provided a context in which refugee activists were forced to think afresh on the question of rights. In effect, the cutback created two classes of camp refugees, those who were entitled to some benefits and those who were not. Those who resisted the Government

---

Village Development Committee], to announce his decision to fast unto death if Government did not fulfil his demands.

order insisted that dividing refugees into "haves" and "have-nots" was wrong, and they challenged it with a wave of hunger strikes and hartals in camps all over West Bengal. But in the course of these struggles they learnt how difficult it was to carry the haves along with the have-nots in a unified campaign. For example, in the Chakdah camp of Nadia district, the 200 families headed by able-bodied males who were affected by the order launched a hartal. But, as the officer on the spot reported, "the attempts to dissuade persons from taking their legitimate doles by the refugees who are not eligible by the Government Order were made but without success."[54] In effect, the refugee leaders found themselves waging war on two fronts, one against Government for creating two classes of refugees – the dole receivers and the rest – and the other against those of their own dole-receiving brothers who took what they could and looked the other way.

The series of Government orders which followed presented similar problems for refugee activists trying to bring about a measure of unity in their response. The thrust of the Government's rehabilitation measures was to lump refugees into several different categories – able-bodied males, widows, the handicapped, Government servants, medical practitioners, lawyers, etc. – and to offer each category a different rehabilitation package by way of help. Inevitably some refugee families who were against the decision to shut down their camp had to contend with the difficulty that at least some refugee families in the camp were "willing to leave the camp and go to their places of rehabilitation and to be settled on their land . . ."[55] And again in Nadia, when "the majority" of refugees at the Goushala and Chandmari camps refused to leave their camps for a rehabilitation site at Gayeshpur, they found that there were some refugees "who [were] willing to accept the Government project . . ."[56]

[54] Copy of a report, 17 December 1948, by the Officer-in-charge, Chakdah Police Station, in GB IB File No. 1809–48 (Noida).

[55] Report by P.K. Bhattacharjee, 13 December 1949, GB IB 1809–48 M.F.

[56] Report on the political activities of refugees and corruption in refugee

These circumstances forced refugee activists to begin to recognise the strategic necessity of arguing that the rights they claimed were held *equally* by *all* refugees. In this period, refugee organisations increasingly came to put forward the stronger line that the "rights" of refugees were absolute and indivisible. The argument that these rights derived from a specific contract was gradually replaced by the claim that these were "fundamental rights". So, for example, at a meeting of 1500 refugees at Karbagan, organised under the aegis of the RCRC on 5 August 1950, "the speakers criticised the Congress Government for its utter failure to solve the *fundamental rights* of the refugees [*sic*]. . . ."[57] The following day, at a meeting organised at Hazra Park by the Dakshin Kalikata Bastuhara Sangha, resolutions were passed making the usual demands – for free rations, free schooling, medicines, and adequate sanitary arrangements in the colonies. Leaflets distributed at the meeting urged refugees "not to make any compromise with the Government but to fight unto death for the vindication of their *rights* . . ."[58] Inevitably, it became increasingly untenable for refugee organisations to insist that *only* refugees were entitled to these "fundamental rights", and not every citizen.

In turn this raises the question of what specifically these rights were. Just as rights were asserted increasingly on the basis of an absolute and indivisible entitlement by all, so also there was a trend for the rights themselves to be interpreted more and more broadly. A perceptible shift can be seen, as time passed, from the assertion of specific, exclusive and sectional entitlements to more general exclusive rights. The list of demands put forward at various meetings and during successive campaigns have a familiar ring to them. Invariably they included both political and economic rights. Amongst the political rights claimed,

---

camps for the week ending 4.12.1949 (hereafter RPAR W/E 4.12.1949, and so on), in GB IB 1809–48 (KW).

[57] RPAR W/E 13.8.1950, in GB IB 1809–48 (KW).

[58] Ibid.

two were common to every agitation by refugees. The first was their right to organise themselves politically. This was a response to the growing high-handedness of camp superintendents who picked on and punished those they saw as "ring-leaders" of the agitations.[59] As the refugee movement became more and more closely associated with the left-wing political opposition, this developed into a more general protest against the constraints on political freedom in independent West Bengal, particularly the Security Act and the Special Powers Act – which hurt all citizens, not refugees alone. So refugee pamphlets contributed to make specific demands for the removal of a particular camp superintendent or the release of a particular refugee leader who had been detained, but increasingly these demands were linked with the broader campaign for the repeal of the so-called "Black Acts". Particularly after they fought pitched street battles with the police during Nehru's visit to Calcutta in January 1949, refugees formed increasingly visible and vocal contingents at protest marches in the city which denounced police "*zulum*" and raised the slogan "*Yeh azadi jhootha hai*" (this Independence is a sham).[60]

[59] The most spectacular incident occurred at Dhubulia camp in Nadia. In September 1950, after some fifty refugees of the camp set up a central committee, the infuriated camp superintendent dragged four of its leaders away from a meeting and held them captive in his office. In the resulting melee, several refugees were badly beaten and one, a young boy named Anakul Brahma, was shot dead by the police. The case gained wide publicity and became the focus of several refugee campaigns. "Secret Report re: the incident at Dhubulia Camp on 19.9.1950", 25 September 1951, GB IB File No. 1809–48 (Nadia).

[60] So on 15 August 1950 "a procession of about 500 refugees from different refugee colonies such as Jadabpur, Tollygunj, Garia, etc., . . . converged at Deshapriya Park where two meetings were held in succession under the auspices of the two factions of the Forward Bloc-Marxist and non-Marxist – to decry the Congress Government for the allegedly fake Independence achieved. . . ." On the same day, another refugee procession ended up at Hazra Park to celebrate "Anti-Independence Day". RPAR W/E 20.8.1950, GB IB File No. 1838–48 (KW).

The second demand made by practically every refugee organisation was the right to determine how, when, and where they were to be rehabilitated. They demanded that families be given adequate notice before they were moved to rehabilitation colonies, and more importantly that refugees should not be sent to "rehabilitation sites" against their will. This eventually hardened into the demand that all refugees be rehabilitated within West Bengal. But here too a trend towards expansion and inclusion can be detected in the way that the right came to be asserted. The refugee campaigns linked their demand that refugees be rehabilitated in West Bengal with a call for a state-driven programme to achieve economic reform and greater equality in West Bengal society as a whole. The same trend towards greater inclusiveness can be seen in the demand for specifically *economic* rights. Every meeting reiterated the demand for certain basic economic rights: the provision of relief to all refugees, full rehabilitation, and entitlement to relief grants until rehabilitation had been achieved. In elaborating these demands, the refugees showed that they defined both "relief and "rehabilitation" in a broader way than Government did. In their view, relief not only meant doles for all, but also free education for refugee children, free medical care and clothing, as well as clean and sanitary camps. Rehabilitation meant a brick-built "pucca" house for each refugee household and regular, paid employment.[61] This particular demand went diametrically against the thrust of Government policy on rehabilitation, since its central purpose was to encourage refugees to find self-employment, and not look to the *sarkar* for jobs.

But here too, the trend in the refugee movement was to assert that these were not specifically refugee rights but the rights of *all* members of society. For instance, one pamphlet issued by the

[61] For example, a meeting of refugees in Srirampur at Purbasrhali demanded that the Government set up a mill at Nabadwip "to enable the refugees to find employment". RPAR W/E 10.9.1950, GB IB 1809–48 (KW). Similarly, at a meeting of refugees at Balurghat in August 1950, "demands were made for employment of refugee youths", ibid.

Nikhil Banga Bastuhara Karma Parishad appended the following "long-term demands" (*deerghameyadi dabi*) to a list of demands specifically to do with refugees:

1. The zamindari system must be abolished without compensation, and the land must be distributed to the poor peasants, the landless and the poor refugees according to their needs.
2. . . . [Illegible] arrangements must be made to ensure regular employment and livelihood for refugees and all other members of society [*ananya janata*] and to give their lives greater dignity [*jeebanmaan unneet korite hoibe*].
3. Free primary education must be provided and teachers must be paid a living wage . . .[62]

In the same way, the demand for free rations for refugees was increasingly linked to a more general critique of the Government's food policy and its failure to guarantee security of rations for the public at large.[63]

In these ways, the construction of rights which evolved out of the successive refugee campaigns came to be part of an increasingly broad-based and inclusive political programme in a welfarist and even socialist mode, breaking with liberal and bourgeois traditions. This was only partly due to a movement by the Left to attract refugees, which (as Prafulla Chakrabarti has shown) only began in earnest after 1951 and was not achieved in full measure until 1959.[64] So the explanation has to be sought

[62] *Desher janayana o bastuhara bhaiboner prati Nikhil Banga Bastuhara Karma Parishader dak* (The Call of the All Bengal Refugee Council of Action to the People of the Country and to Refugee Brothers and Sisters), no date but clearly published in or before July 1949, probably in Calcutta, GB IB File No. 1809–48 M.F.

[63] The UCRC Working Committee organised meetings all over West Bengal on 3 September 1950 to discuss the "food problem". Similarly, at a meeting of refugees at Shraddhananda Park on 27 August 1950, "speeches were delivered criticising the food and rehabilitation politics of the Government." RPAR W/F. 27.8.1950, GB IB File No. 1838–48 (KW).

[64] Chakrabarti, *The Marginal Men*, p. 407.

in the internal dynamics and logic of the refugee movement itself. To some extent, this logic was more semantic than substantial: in theory and in historical fact, the notion of "rights" is based on the premise that all men are equal. So the rhetoric of "rights" is a natural bedfellow of egalitarianism, since it is hard to sustain a claim to rights without claiming them *equally* for all.[65]

The refugee movement also soon realised that its own demands took it down the egalitarian path. Much of what the refugees claimed as of right was economic in nature: food, clothes, medicine, housing, education, and jobs. It would have been difficult, if not impossible, to justify the argument that refugees had an entitlement to these economic "rights" whereas other equally destitute Indians did not.

Practical considerations also encouraged the refugees to link their demands with a call for wider social change in an egalitarian direction. If they had insisted on fighting alone for their own particularist demands, they would have found themselves politically isolated and socially vulnerable. More to the point, social and political transformation in Bengal was the necessary precondition for the realisation of some of the refugees' most basic and unnegotiable demands. One example was their insistence that they be rehabilitated in West Bengal.[66] Government claimed that

[65] For a discussion of the history of the concept of rights and its historical and theoretical association with notions of equality, see Dagger, "Rights", pp. 299–300.

[66] This demand appears to have evolved spontaneously among the refugees, although it later came to win support from many political parties. For instance, a secret report on the objections of refugees in Nadia against leaving Bengal observed that "this is purely their voluntary and sentimental objection. They say that they have been born in Bengal and will die in Bengal. There is no provocation or incitement from outside. Some of the refugees have even fled from the camp for fear of being transferred outside Bengal . . ." Copy of a report of a District Investigating Officer of Nadia District, 23 April 1950, GB IE File No. 1808–48 (Nadia). After the summer of 1950, the refugees' worst fears were realised when those who had been sent to camps in Bihar and

West Bengal was already too overcrowded to accommodate millions of refugees and that the state simply did not have enough uninhabited land to go around. If there was to be more land available for redistribution to the dispossessed, it could only come as the result of quite fundamental land reforms. So it is not surprising that refugees called for radical land reform, for the abolition of the *zamindaris*, and for more equitable laws which imposed ceilings on the amount of urban land which the privileged could own.

In much the same way, in their campaign against the eviction, refugees challenged entrenched rights to private property. From late September 1949, when Government ordered camps to be shut down, groups of refugees began forcibly to occupy vacant plots and garden houses, chiefly in suburban Calcutta, in Dumdum, Naihati, and Baranagar. They would stealthily enter these plots at night and under cover of darkness rapidly put up makeshift shelters. They would then refuse to leave, while offering in many instances to pay a fair price for the land.[67] To evict them from these patently unused plots would have been particularly embarrassing for a Government which had loudly proclaimed that there was no land available for redistribution. When it tried to evict the refugees, this inevitably led to ugly incidents. One which attracted wide publicity took place at Mahesh in Hooghly, where police were summoned to help a landlord repossess his vacant land which had been occupied by refugees. Characteristically, the police were brutal in enforcing the landlords's right of access but turned a blind eye when the landlord used thugs to

---

Orissa began to "desert" in large numbers, bringing back horror stories of the conditions in the colonies from which they had fled. After this, the demand for "rehabilitation in Bengal" became one of the central planks of the refugee movement's platform.

[67] For example, the fifty refugees who occupied four *bighas* of private land at Jhil Road in Jadavpur "were agreeable to pay a fair price for the lands occupied by them . . ." RPAR W/E 8.1.1950, GB IE File No. 1838–48 (IV).

oust the squatters.[68] The refugees could see only too clearly the galling contrast between the alacrity with which the state and its law-enforcement machinery responded to defend the rights of property owners, and its vigorous denial that destitute refugees had any rights at all. Inevitably, refugees who had started out by acknowledging the right of the landlord to be paid for plots they had occupied ended up taking a more jaundiced view of the right to private property. Confrontations of this sort, which began with limited aims – often simply for a little space within the system in which individuals could survive – thus often rapidly developed into passionate indictments of the established order.[69]

The battle against eviction, which by implication was also a campaign against rights to private property, became fiercer after the public found out, through a leak in March 1951, about the secretly drafted clauses of the Eviction Bill. The bill, as the chief minister admitted at a press conference on 20 March, was essential if his Government was to have the power to deal with squatter colonies which violated the right to private property enshrined in the Indian Constitution. But faced with a sustained campaign against the Eviction Bill and its no-longer secret provisions, the Government of West Bengal was forced to retreat: the bill was redrafted to include two significant new provisions. The first, Section 4, was reworded to include a pledge that a "Displaced Person" in unauthorised occupation of land would not be disturbed "until the Government provides for him other land or house . . . in an area which . . . enables the person to carry on such occupation as he may be engaged in for earning his livelihood at the time of the order." The second was a new definition of the term "bona fide refugee", which was broadened to include families

[68] Chakrabarti, *The Marginal Men*, pp. 80–2.

[69] Sunil Gangopadhyay develops this theme in his novel *Arjun*, which traces the radicalisation and politicisation of one refugee youth in the course of a property dispute between neighbouring landlords and the refugee squatters' colony.

who arrived in West Bengal before 31 December 1950.[70] This represented a major victory for the refugee movement, because it acknowledged that refugees had an absolute, inalienable, right to shelter, and that Government had a duty to provide it. It was also an admission that there were circumstances in which the right to private property could not be enforced.

It was also a great victory for West Bengal's left-wing opposition. The communist parties (particularly the CPI) successfully refined the tactic of using refugee demands as the thin end of the wedge in their wider struggle. First they would press the case for the rights of refugees, whether to food, shelter, or employment. And once Government (which acknowledged, Government however half-heartedly, that it had some special obligations towards refugees) had been forced to accept that the refugees did indeed have these rights, the left-wing parties would demand the same rights for everybody. To change the metaphor, the left used the refugees and their rights as a toe in the door that Government was trying to keep firmly shut.

This also explains why the sectional basis for the claim to refugee rights was never wholly given up. The very same pamphlet which demanded the abolition of the zamindari system began by asserting that "before the Partition was brought about by the conspiracy of a pro-rich Congress, the leaders made pretty speeches promising that the refugees in West Bengal, in their capacity as free citizens would be able to live in comfort . . . it is clear that the Congress has completely betrayed this pledge."[71] In one and the same sentence, both the sectional and the general cliam to rights is asstert-ed. The Congress is alleged to have made a promise, and that was all and well, but it was "*in their capacity as free citizens* that the

[70] *West Bengal Act XVI of 1951. The Rehabilitation of Displaced Persons and Eviction of Persons in Unauthorised Occupation of Land Act 1951.*

[71] *Desher janagana o bastuhara bhaiboner prati Nikhil Banga Bastuhara Karma Parishader dak* (The Call of the All Bengal Refugee Council of Action to the People of the Country and to Refugee Brothers and Sisters).

refugees would live in comfort . . ." This could be interpreted either to mean that the refugees were rightfully demanding that the Congress fulfil its promises to them or to imply that all free citizens had the right to live in comfort. Here was the convenient ambiguity upon which the left-wing leadership could, and did, capitalise, first asking for the fulfilment of the special obligation, and then quickly changing tack to demand the same treatment for all citizens. The refugee movement was thus the Trojan horse in the siege laid by the left around the bastions of Government in its battle to achieve a broader, more egalitarian, definition of citizenship.

Conclusion

In the chronicles of political science it is a commonplace that the refugees from East Bengal played a key role in the development of left-wing politics in West Bengal. Yet the relationship between the refugees and the communist parties has usually been described in purely instrumentalist terms. The communists are accused of having used the refugees as cannon fodder in their campaigns. In his seminal study of the refugee movement in West Bengal, Prafulla Chakrabarti asserts that the communists used the refugees as "plastic material" in their struggle for power, or as a mere "footstool to mount the *gaddi*."[72] This essay has shown how misleading these analogies can be. In the volatile 1950s, the refugees undoubtedly helped to advance a great many left-wing campaigns in Bengal. Yet the crucial importance of their role was that they served as a test case for the whole question of rights. It was precisely because Government admitted, albeit in as narrow a way as possible, that it had some special obligations towards refugees, that the left-wing opposition was able to push forward so many of their general claims for the citizens of India as a whole.

[72] Chakrabarti, *The Marginal Men*, pp. 426, 433.

As this article has shown, there was *some* common ground between the Government and the refugees: even if its extent was very limited. But this was the very ground on which the refugees stood when they successfully campaigned for their "rights". Once Government had conceded the justice of some of their claims, the same claims were extended further and further by their left-wing allies. In the process, more and more concessions were wrested from a reluctant Government. And upon this ground, the communists and radicals would skilfully erect the claim that everybody had the same rights and entitlements.

It follows that the relationship between the refugee movements and the wider politics of the left in West Bengal was more complex and symbiotic than the metaphors of cannon fodder, plastic material, or footstools would suggest. It will certainly not do to argue that the refugee movement was simply subsumed and exploited by the left. The shift in their politics towards the left was, to a substantial degree, a considered response by refugees to their distinctive experience as they organised their fight for survival. It was this experience, and not some unthinking adherence to a borrowed communist ideology, which persuaded them to articulate their demands in the particular ways that they did. In the final analysis, it was this experience, moreover – the public spectacle of their wretchedness and their incessant campaigns for rehabilitation and for a measure of human dignity – that created the moral and political climate in which so many aspects of communist ideology found a more general acceptance in West Bengal in the formative decades after Independence.

References

After Partition, Delhi: Government of India, Publications Division, 1948.

Bayly, C.A., *Rulers, Townsmen and Bazaars: North Indian Society in the Age of British Expansion, 1770–1870*, Cambridge, 1983.

Braudel, Fernand, *Civilisation and Capitalism, 15th–18th century, Vol. II. The Wheels of Commerce*, London, 1985 edn.

Chakrabarti, Prafulla, *The Marginal Men: The Refugees and the Left Political Syndrome in West Bengal*, Calcutta, 1990.

Chakrabarty, Saroj, *With Dr B.C. Roy*, Calcutta, 1974.

Chatterjee, Nilanjana, "The East Bengal Refugees. A Lesson in Survival", in Sukanta Chaudhuri, ed., *Calcutta, The Living City*, vol. II, Calcutta, 1990.

Chatterji, Joya, "The Fashioning of a Frontier: The Radcliffe Line and Bengal's Border Landscape, 1947–52", *Modern Asian Studies*, vol. 33, I (1999).

———, *Bengal Divided. Hindu Communalism and Partition, 1932–1947*, Cambridge, 1994.

Cunningham, Hugh and Joanna Innes, ed., *Charity, Philanthropy and Reform from the 1690s to 1850*, London, 1998.

Dagger, Richard, "Rights", in Terence Ball, James Farr, and Russell Hanson, ed., *Political Innovation and Conceptual Change*, Cambridge, 1989.

Dumont, Louis, "World Renunciation in Indian Religions", Appendix B, in Louis Dumont, *Homo Hierarchicus. The Caste System and its Implications*, trans. Mark Sainsbury, Louis Dumont, and Basia Gulti, Chicago, 1980 edn.

Fraser, Nancy, and Linda Gordon, "A Genealogy of Dependency: Tracing a Keyword of the U.S. Welfare State", *Signs: Journal of Women in Culture and Society*, vol. 19, no. 2 (1994).

Haynes, Douglas, "From Tribute to Philanthropy: The Politics of Gift Giving in a Western Indian City', *Journal of Asian Studies*, vol. 46, 1987.

Hirschman, Albert O., *The Rhetoric of Reaction, Perversity, Futility, Jeopardy*, Cambridge, Massachusetts, 1991.

Inden, Ronald, *Marriage and Rank in Bengali Culture: A History of Caste in Middle-Period Bengal*, Delhi, 1976.

Kozlowski, Gregory C., *Muslim Endowments and Society in British India*, Cambridge, 1985.

Kudaisya, Gyanesh, "The Demographic Upheaval of Partition: Refugees and Agricultural Resettlement in India, 1947–67', *South Asia*, vol. XVIII, Special Issue, 1995.

Madan, T.N., *Non-Renunciation: Themes and Interpretations of Hindu Culture*, Delhi, 1987.

Offe, Clause, and Ulrich K. Preuss, "Democratic Institutions and Moral Resources", in David Held, ed., *Political Theory Today*, Cambridge, 1991.

Raheja, Gloria Goodwin, *The Poison in the Gift: Ritual, Prestation and the Dominant Caste in a North Indian Village*, Chicago, 1988.

Rao, U. Bhaskar, *The Story of Rehabilitation*, Faridabad: Government of India, Department of Rehabilitation, Ministry of Labour, Employment and Rehabilitation, 1967.

Raychaudhuri, Tapan, "Norms of Family Life and Personal Morality Among the Bengali Hindu Elite, 1600–1850', in Rachel Van M. Baumer, ed., *Aspects of Bengali History and Society*, Hawaii, 1975.

Relief and Rehabilitation of Displaced Persons in West Bengal, Government of West Bengal, Refugee Relief and Rehabilitation Department, 1956.

Report on How the Millions Who Came from Eastern Pakistan Live Here. They Live Again, Government of West Bengal, 1954.

Rosselli, John, "The Self-Image of Effeteness: Physical Education and Nationalism in Nineteenth-Century Bengal", *Past and Present*, vol. 86, February 1989.

Sinha, Mrinalini, *Colonial Masculinity: The 'Manly Englishman' and the 'Effeminate Bengali' in the Late Nineteenth Century*, Manchester, 1995.

Thapar, Romila, "*Dana* and *Daksina* as Forms of Exchange", in idem, *Ancient Indian Social History*, New Delhi, 1987 edn.

"Viceroy's Visit to Bengal: Note by the Viceroy", in *Partition Proceedings*, New Delhi: Government of India Press, 1949.

Williams, Raymond, *Keywords. A Vocabulary of Culture and Society*, London, 1983 edn.

6

Migration Myths and the Mechanics of Assimilation

Two Community Histories from Bengal

Assimilate; do not be assimilated.

– Leopold Senghor

IN 1993, THE Sylheti Social History Group in London published a little book entitled *The Roots and Tales of Bangladeshi Settlers*. Ten years later, in 2003, *Biharis. The Indian Emigres in Bangladesh: An Objective Analysis*, was brought out by the Shamsul Huq Foundation, a non-governmental organisation based in the old railway town of Syedpur in Bangladesh. The former, *Roots and Tales*, is an account of the Sylheti diaspora in the United Kingdom. Written in the first person by Yousuf Choudhury, who migrated to Britain in the 1950s as a bachelor in his twenties, it purports to be the view of the migrant-insider and its style is personal and confessional. The latter, *Biharis*, tells the history of a community twice displaced by violence, the so-called "Biharis" of Bangladesh. Although its author – the journalist, social worker, and poet Ahmed Ilias – is himself a "Bihari" who migrated from Calcutta in 1953 to what was then East Pakistan, he strives, as the subtitle of the book suggests, to write as "objectively" as a professional historian might, supporting his narrative with references to primary and secondary sources.

On the face of it, the two texts appear to have very little in common. One, *Roots and Tales*, is apparently a classic story of economic migration. It chronicles the temporary sojourn and eventual settlement in the United Kingdom of people largely drawn from a single region in the Bengal delta, the lowland districts of Sylhet, who now number about 300,000, living mainly in defined localities in the East End of London and Greater Manchester. Choudhury traces their history back to the heyday of the Raj, when young men from Sylhet worked as lascars in the British merchant marine, some jumping ship in London in search of better working conditions. Others followed their lead, and gradually through typical chain migration quite significant clusters of Sylheti migrants developed within working-class neighbourhoods of London's East End, Manchester, and also in Birmingham. In due course, these men were joined by elderly parents, by wives and children and other relatives, and became a typically self-sustaining diasporic community. Choudhury's is an optimistic story of (upward) mobility: of people who used their connections and wits to survive, and who, through hard work and sacrifice, prospered and built a better life for themselves and their children.

Ahmed Ilias' *Biharis*, in contrast, is a stark account of forced migration. It tells the grim tale of how in 1946, just before India was partitioned, Urdu-speaking Muslims fled from the deadly communal violence in Bihar. They sought and were given shelter first in Bengal (a province then run by a Muslim-dominated government). After Partition, they fled to Bengal's eastern wing, which now became East Pakistan, only to become, once again in 1971, the victims of genocidal violence. This was when Bangladesh gained independence from Pakistan in a civil war of unspeakable brutality. Today, perhaps 300,000 "Biharis" remain in Bangladesh, most of them still living in the squalid and desperately overcrowded camps where they took shelter during the war and in its aftermath. This is the story Ahmed Ilias attempts to tell in *Biharis*, "objectivity" being his declared aim. But inevitably it is a much darker work than *Roots and Tales*, reflecting as it does on the defeat of a once-proud community and the death of its culture.[1]

Yet a closer look at these two very different works reveals interesting parallels between them. Both are written in English, although for Choudhury and Ilias it is quite evidently their third language. Both authors are thinking men who might be described as "organic intellectuals", members of the group or community whose experience they sought to articulate, though Choudhury's comes from a working-class background while Ilias is a product of a North Indian Urdu-speaking service elite. Both began their research and writing at roughly the same time, Choudhury in 1981 and Ilias in 1978. Both works were published by community groups. On scrutiny, the two books prove to have similar themes, similar internal structures, and similar patterns of emphasis. I argue here that both texts produce "origin myths" as well as "migration myths" which have many tropes in common. By teasing out the features which the two books share, I will explore the inwardness of how, when, and why migrant groups come to write their own histories. I will suggest that both these histories were written with a view to enabling the "assimilation" of the community they claimed to speak for, and to seek rights and recognition for that "community" in its place of settlement. It suggests that reading these texts in a comparative and historical way throws light on the complex processes by which migrant communities try to "assimilate" into "host" cultures.

"Assimilation" itself is a controversial concept. Since the early 1970s, it has been subjected to a sustained critique. Scholars have

[1]The research on which this essay is based was funded by the UK Arts and Humanities Research Council under the auspices of the "Bengal Diaspora Project" and the "Diasporas, Identities and Migration" programme. I am grateful to my colleague Claire Alexander for her advice; and to Alan Strathern, Tim Hochstrasser, David Washbrook, Peter Mandler, and Rosamond McKitterick for pointing me to relevant historical literature.

In this context, it is an excellent example of the histories of the vanquished which Schivelbusch describes in *The Culture of Defeat*.

rejected the classical portrayal of assimilation as a one-sided process by which alien communities are incorporated into an apparently homogeneous host culture, gradually (and inevitably) shedding their foreign ways and increasingly adopting the cultural values and mores of their hosts. As Rogers Brubaker has argued, this perspective was "analytically and normatively Anglo-conformist. It posited, endorsed and expected assimilation towards an unproblematically conceived white Protestant 'core culture'."[2] In challenging this perspective, the "differentialist" critique has informed (and was in turn inspired by) the politics and practices of multiculturalism. It was supported by a growing body of evidence that ethnic diversity persists and survives among the "new migrants" in the West, so much so that the new orthodoxy is that the melting pot "never happened".[3]

In recent times, studies of migration have come to recognise the transnational networks of migrant communities[4]. It is increasingly well understood that migrants remain embedded simultaneously in a variety of locations and "networks".[5] They are seen to maintain and deploy these networks to "circulate" between locations, rather than permanently to settle in one.[6] Many scholars now see migrants as cosmopolitans who constantly and creatively renegotiate "hybridity", rather than as conformists who either maintain their "traditional" culture or aspire to or adapt to the lifestyles of the host countries in the West.[7] These studies regard the practice

[2] Brubaker, "The Return of Assimilation?", p. 540.

[3] Glazer and Moynihan, *Beyond the Melting Pot*, cited in Brubaker, "The Return of Assimilation", p. 532.

[4] Levitt, *The Transnational Villagers*; Tololyan, "Elites and Institutions in the Armenian Transnation"; (also see Alejandro Portes' concluding remarks in the same special issue of *IMR*); Ballantyne, *Between Colonialism and Diaspora*.

[5] *Migration: A Welcome Opportunity*.

[6] Markovits, *et al.*, eds, *Mobile People and Itinerant Cultures*.

[7] Bhabha, "The Third Space"; idem, *The Location of Culture*; Brah, *Cartographies of Diaspora*; Appadurai, *Modernity at Large*. For a critical discussion of the concept of "hybridity", see Alexander, "Diaspora and Hybridity".

of "hybridity" as challenging and unsettling the logic of modernity and its vehicle, the nation-state.[8]

These are valuable insights. Yet they gloss over the harsh realities of the contemporary world, where nation-states monopolise "the legitimate means of movement", control their borders ever more stringently, and erect ever higher barriers against entry and naturalisation, making it ever more difficult for migrants to "circulate", let alone enter and stay on with full rights of citizenship.[9] This is as true not only of the West (which implicitly or explicitly has been the focus of these new theories of diaspora), but also of states in the global South which, as Zolberg and Shmeidl have shown,[10] have since 1945 absorbed the vast majority of the world's migrants.[11] For many compelling reasons – which in turn have much to do with the constraints upon their options – many migrants today, whether in the West or elsewhere, seek permanently to settle in the locations where they presently dwell. Like Yousuf Choudhuri's "Bangladeshi settlers" and Ahmed Ilias' "Bihari emigres", they aspire to live with dignity and in security in their new homelands. By examining the circumstances in which two migrants seek to negotiate assimilation in two very different national contexts, in Britain and Bangladesh respectively, I throw light on concepts of assimilation which are still not well understood, and reveal the complex and textured quality of "hybrid" subjectivities.

But first an important caveat. One of the authors of the works discussed here is still alive and well, and both have living children and families. *Roots and Tales* and *Biharis* are important works, not only for the communities they describe, but also for scholars of

[8] Clifford, *Routes*.

[9] Torpey, *The Invention of the Passport*. Also see Salter, *Rights of Passage*; and Turack, *The Passport in International Law*.

[10] On the control of borders and membership in South Asia, see Zamindar, *The Long Partition*; and Chatterji, *The Disinherited*.

[11] Zolberg and Benda, eds, *Global Migrants, Global Refugees*.

migration. Both contain much vital information. By suggesting that these works construct myths which deserve close analysis, I am not impugning their value or their sincerity of purpose. Rather, I underline the fact that these books have a great deal to tell us, indeed much more than meets the eye.

Mythical Pasts and Sacred Origins

Both books begin, as well they might, with an account of the origins of "their community". But both represent these origins using tropes that betray their intent to invest them with a special moral quality and purpose. Choudhury's *Roots and Tales* is the more obviously fabulous: indeed in places it resorts to the style of magical realism. The author traces the origins of the "Bangladeshis" who are the subject of his book back to the central lowlands of Sylhet at the beginning of the thirteenth century. In ancient times, he tells us, this low-lying territory to the south of the kingdom of Kamrup in Assam lay partially submerged under the waters of the Bay of Bengal. But a swan-shaped gulf rose out of the sea and nestled among "low hills covered with lush monsoonal forest, in an area rich in natural beauty . . . full of exotic fruit trees, splendid flowering plants and birds such as parrots, mynahs and seagulls." This came to be the site of a market-town and port, known on account of its rare beauty as "Sri Khetro" or "Beautiful Field". It served as a commercial centre "for traders from many nations . . . Seafaring Arab merchants used to call at that port regularly for silk, spices and other oriental products."[12]

In a work written in a rather prosaic style – as the Foreword by the Oxford theologian Clinton Bennett puts it – Choudhury "makes no claim to literary finesse in his third language, although he is an accomplished writer in Bengali,"[13] this passage stands

[12] Choudhury, *Roots and Tales*, p. 10.

[13] Ibid., p. viii.

out for its almost lyrical quality.[14] Home is, first and foremost, a landscape of extraordinary loveliness, a veritable Garden of Eden. But it is significant that Choudhury chooses to stress Sylhet's ancient and original connection with the sea. Though present-day Sylhet is far from the Indian Ocean, the sea plays a crucial part in his story. The ancient Sylhet of *Roots and Tales* is a hub of trade and exchange; Choudhury's Sylheti ancestors in a long-distant past were already itinerant seafaring cosmopolitans.

In 1209 and 1300, according to Choudhury, two earthquakes changed the landscape around "Sri Khetro", lifting the gulf out of the deep and severing its connection with the sea.[15] At that time, the land around the town was still partly submerged and remained largely uninhabited. But in 1313 it was conquered by Gour Gobindo, "a cruel Hindu king who had no mercy for anyone."[16] At this juncture in its early history, so we are told, there were only thirteen Muslim families in the area, descendants of seafaring merchants and Islamic missionaries, and they lived together in a village by the River Surma, a waterway which connected the hills of Assam to the Bengal delta. In 1340, the wife of one of these Muslim pioneers, Borhanuddin, gave birth to a baby son, and to celebrate, the proud father slaughtered a cow. On hearing of this, Raja Gour Gobindo ordered that the baby be beheaded and the arms of the mother be cut off. After the death of mother and child, Borhanuddin sought the protection of neighbouring Muslim rulers in Bengal, and travelled to Delhi to raise an army to challenge and defeat the "cruel king".

It was in Delhi, Choudhury says, in the presence of the great Sufi mystic Nizamuddin Auliya, that a fateful meeting took place between brave Borhanuddin and the "leading Muslim saint" Shah

[14] Deliberately or otherwise, it evokes Bankim Chandra Chatterjee's famous verse *Bandemataram,* which describes the "motherland" as a place of sweet waters, ripe fruit and cool breezes (*sujalam, suphalam, malayaja sheetalam*).

[15] *Roots and Tales*, p. 11.

[16] Ibid., p. 12.

Jalal, who had travelled to Delhi from Yemen with 313 followers. On hearing Borhanuddin's story, Shah Jalal "decided to volunteer himself along with his followers" to fight Gour Gobindo.[17] Together with an army of 360 saints, Shah Jalal marched eastwards into Bengal and defeated Gour Gobindo in a battle replete with miracles in which the saints deployed supernatural powers and witchcraft to bewitch and destroy the enemy.

And then Sylhet revealed its sacred destiny. Before he set out on his mission in Al-Hind, Shah Jalal had been given a clod of Arabian earth by his spiritual mentors who instructed him to settle wherever he found similar soil. Miraculously, the marshy soil of Sri Khetro exactly matched this sacred lump of earth from dry and distant Arabia. So Shah Jalal settled permanently in "Shil-hotto", and the 360 saints "spread all over Sylhet" to propagate Islam. They also set to work reclaiming the land, building simple structures as their mosques, fishing in the waters and farming the land:

> Most of the saints got married, and many of them had a farm and a family. They worked all day long, growing crops or vegetables, looking after their cattle and catching fish. When the work was done they swam in the open clean water, then they sat and had some food. At the end of the day, they could go to their own straw built mosque and pray to their heart's content. Many of the saints were married to the new converts, had families, ran farms by themselves . . . but the saintliness of the working saints was never washed away or wasted. Their faith was always with them and passed on to their descendants.[18]

Here the story of conversion deploys sexual metaphors of fertility and insemination so prominent in descriptions of Islam's spread in Bengal.[19] But whereas in other parts of Bengal, the exotic "soil" (or host society) produced a version of Islam distorted by caste hierarchy and contaminated by other Hindu manners and

[17] Ibid., p. 14.
[18] Ibid., p. 17.
[19] Chatterji, "The Bengali Muslim".

customs, Sylhet's wondrous soil, in Choudhury's account, nourished the true faith. The homeland emerges from *Roots and Tales* as a beautiful green paradise adorned by the graves of saints. It is a land of plenty which sustains a casteless society of hard-working, peace-loving, and god-fearing peasants, a truly Islamic brotherhood governed by the simple but robust moral values of their forefathers.[20]

Some of these themes recall other better-known foundation myths,[21] and the story as a whole powerfully echoes Eaton's classic account of the role of *ghazi-pirs* (soldier-saints) in establishing Islam and settled agriculture on the Bengal frontier.[22] But the point here is a rather different one. Choudhury's story is not only a myth of origins, it is also a parable about settlement. In ascribing this cosmopolitan origin to the "Bangladeshi settlers" in Britain, Choudhury constructs them as living descendants of saints from all over the Muslim world who long ago settled in Sylhet, bringing their faith with them and establishing Islam in the delta. By tracing the community's roots back to these pioneers, it validates the struggles and journeys of present-day migrants and sets them up as vectors for the expansion of the Islamic frontier in the western world. Implicitly, it imbues their story of migration *and settlement* not only with legitimacy derived from this origin myth, but also with a deeper moral and religious purpose.[23]

But there is also another process at work in this account of origins: the construction of the notion of a single "Bangladeshi community". That process begins, of course, with Choudhury's choice of title, which alludes to "Bangladeshi settlers". In his preface or

[20] *Roots and Tales*, pp. 20, 26.

[21] Gour Gobindo's act of infanticide resembles, of course, the evil acts committed by King Herod and also the wicked King Kansa of Mathura in Hindu mythology. Kansa, the maternal uncle of Lord Krishna, imprisoned his sister and killed each one of Krishna's siblings at birth.

[22] Eaton, *The Rise of Islam.*

[23] Also see Ho, *The Graves of Tarim.*

introduction, the author admits that his story is "mostly about the settlers from Sylhet as . . . they are 95% of Bangladeshi settlers. The remaining 5% came from other places. I have tried my best to cover these people too."[24] Yet he makes hardly any reference to these "other people", and when he does, as we shall see, his remarks are disparaging and dismissive. But by describing his subjects as "Bangladeshis" rather than Sylhetis, and then by assigning a single foundation myth set in ancient Sylhet to all of them, the work launches the enterprise of incorporating (and indeed assimilating) different groups with disparate histories into a single national "community" with shared origins and with a destiny in common.

Ahmed Ilias' account of the origins of the "Biharis" is not as colourful as Choudhury's tales of Sylhet; nonetheless it shares with it some significant features. *Biharis* begins with a description of "The Home and Culture" which sets out, in ten pages, "the glorious history of Bihar". Even though, in the second paragraph of his preface, Ilias states (accurately) that "Biharis did not come from the Indian state of Bihar alone", a few pages later he contradicts himself and states that "the Biharis are proud of their ancient history" which he locates in the state of Bihar.[25] This is reminiscent of Choudhury's strategy where he first admits that all Bangladeshi settlers in Britain are not in fact from Sylhet, but then proceeds to give the whole community a single foundation myth located in ancient Sylhet.

Ilias constructs "the home" of the Biharis not only as a place lost forever, but as a vanished golden age of Indian achievement. The thrust and tone of his argument appear thus: "Historically, Bihar is a land of faiths and religions, myths and mysticism, parables and legends. Islam began to spread in this part of India from around the twelfth century. Both its Hindus and Muslims were always seen at the forefront of every movement launched for the glory

[24] *Roots and Tales*, p. xii.

[25] *Biharis*, p. ix.

and greatness, liberty and independence of India."[26] At "home", the "Muslim minority lived scattered in villages and towns with all their [pride] and [prejudice], with the low standards of skills and education and the high esteem of old orthodox society. They were happy with their own way of life, culture, customs and traditions."[27]

In the same way that Choudhury's Sylhet is idealised, Ilias' "Bihar" is also a rich and bountiful land. Indeed, readers might be surprised by Ilias' confident assertion that "as a geographical unit, Bihar is the richest State in India"[28] (in fact it is one of the poorest). It is also, like Choudhury's Sylhet, a land sanctified by faith. Ilias describes Bihar as a sacred site where Islam first took root in the subcontinent:

> Long before the arrival of Muslim rulers, many Sufis and saints came to Bihar to preach Islam among the cast-ridden [*sic*] Hindu community . . . Hazrat Shahbuddin reached Bihar before the attacks on Punjab by . . . Mahmud Ghaznavi (999–1027). Imam Mohammed Taj Fakir, another Muslim saint[,] came from the Middle East in 1104. His grandson Makhdum Sharfuddin Yahia Muniri belonged to the oldest and most widely dispersed Sufi orders in Bihar, the Suhrawardy and Chisti. A branch of the Suhrawardy order later emerged [and] was known as Firdausia under Yahia Muniri . . .[29]

So far, so similar. Both accounts trace the origins of the migrant community back to a single place; both describe that place as a land of peace and plenty; both locate the ancient "homeland" as a sacred site which witnessed the birth of Islam in the Indian subcontinent; both claim cosmopolitan and saintly ancestors who played a key role in expanding the frontiers of the Islamic world.

[26] Ibid., p. 17.
[27] Ibid., p. 25.
[28] Ibid., p. 16.
[29] Ibid., p. 18.

But there are also differences between Ilias' account and Choudhury's, and their signficance will become apparent when the authors' political intentions are considered. Ilias situates his "Bihar" within a robust tradition of syncretism and constructs it as a place where, as well as Islam, Hindu, Muslim, Buddhist, and Jain cultures and polities thrived. *Biharis'* understanding of culture is more ecumenical than that of *Roots and Tales*, claiming as part of the community's "glorious history" the achievements of other religions besides Islam. Ilias takes pains, for example, to inform his readers that "the two founders of Buddhism and Jainism inspired the world from this land. Ram's wife Sita, the most significant character in Hindu mythology [,] was born in this land of faiths and religions."[30] He also repeatedly insists on a powerful Bihari tradition of "anti-imperialism", claiming that "Bihar gave birth to many valiant sons, who fought for the liberation of India from the yoke of British Empire." From the earliest times, he tells us, Bihar's rulers have repelled invaders. Chandragupta Maurya "put an end to Greek rule in India."[31] Mir Quasem "shifted his capital from Murshedabad [*sic*] to Munghyr to defend his rule against the forces of the East India Company."[32] To a far greater extent than Choudhury, Ilias claims for his community a history of political sacrifice and leadership in the national struggle against British rule. By contrast, Choudhury's text is far more muted in its criticisms of British rule, for example, glossing over an uprising in Sylhet against the Raj in 1782.[33] Its heroes are not rebels who fought the British, but trade unionists like Aftab Ali who organised and defended Sylheti seamen, and community leaders like Ayub Ali "Master", who helped illiterate lascar migrants to cut through the red tape in Britain. Ilias' emphasis on Bihar's traditions of high culture has no counterpart in Choudhury. Unlike Choudhury's idealised

[30] Ibid., p. 17.
[31] Ibid., pp. 17–19.
[32] Ibid., p. 18.
[33] *Roots and Tales*, p. 21.

but rustic Sylhet, Ilias' Bihar was "an ancient seat of learning which attracted people from far and wide, ever since Kumaragupta founded the Nalinda [*sic*] university near the capital Patna. This was a great seat of learning where more than a thousand teachers and scholars used to teach about ten thousand students drawn from middle and Far East countries."[34] Home to the Khuda Baksh library, "the richest library of manuscripts on Islam in the world",[35] Bihar was the seedbed for poets such as Kazi Nazrul Islam and Ramdhari Singh Dinkar. "Bihar also produced many eminent writers, poets and critics in Urdu literature."[36] The author's pride in this tradition shows how different his class perspective is from Choudhury's. Ilias views history from the vantage point of a cultured literati which has fallen on hard times, while Choudhury's angle of vision is that of a working-class community making its way up in the world. These different perspectives helped to shape strategies for assimilation, as will be seen below, that were subtly and significantly different.

Migration Myths: Tales of Loss and Exile

Having established their singular origins in an idealised homeland, the next task for both authors is to explain why their subjects left it. Both struggle to produce a seamless narrative of migration, even though this often strains the historical evidence in their own accounts. In both works, this distinctive narrative is repeated throughout the text at regular intervals, so that it assumes a normative power – appearing to elevate and encapsulate a "truth" about the community which is truer than mere fact.

In the case of Choudhury's *Roots and Tales*, the central theme of this narrative is that *all* Bangladeshi settlers in Britain are

[34] *Biharis*, p. 17.

[35] Ibid., p. 25.

[36] Ibid.

seafarers or their descendants: "Most Bangladeshi settlers are the descendant flesh and blood of those who were lost in the seas and survived to tell their tale, so it is our duty to keep our history alive and remind everyone of who we are and why we are here."[37] This assertion is repeated three times on the very first page of the introduction. It is then rehearsed no less than *fifty* times in the book.

So how did Sylhetis, whose homeland was so far away from the water's margin, come to be seafarers? According to Choudhury, the explanation is that the River Surma – the only waterway which connected Assam to Bengal and the sea – passes through Sylhet. In consequence, Sylhet had a long tradition, beginning with the early settler-saints, of mercantile boats carrying goods from Assam to Bengal and beyond. Although Sylhet's farmers were prosperous, its "spare young men" (younger brothers and cadet sons) traditionally worked as boatmen. When the region came under British rule, things changed, particularly in the nineteenth century when the British introduced steamships and steamer stations linking Calcutta to upper Assam. Aware that "the new water way arrangement [had] hit the boatmen" hard, Choudhury argues that "the [British] steamer companies perhaps realised the need to compensate the boatmen by recruiting them mainly as engine room crew . . . This is the story of the Sylheti boatmen and how they became the steamer's crew."[38] Here again we see evidence that Choudhury would like to take a benign view of British rule in Sylhet, even though he has to admit that the Sylheti lascars began to be "ill treated and ill fed".[39] They were exploited by British navigation companies who paid them a sixth of what British crews received, he tells us, but even more by the Indian "*sarongs*" and "*bariwalas*" (or gaffers) who took a large part of

[37] *Routes and Tales*, p. ix.
[38] Ibid., p. 31.
[39] Ibid., p. 33.

their wages in return for finding them jobs on ships and housing them at ports while they waited for work. "Out of frustration, they decided to desert their ships and go wherever they would find a chance", whether in Rangoon or Singapore or London.[40] But it was only during the First World War, when, according to Choudhury, "over one thousand Bangladeshis" were brought to Britain "to replace British seamen", that a few began to settle in London.[41] And it was during the Second World War that "the Bangladeshi population began to increase in the U.K." When the war ended in 1945, and with India's Independence and Partition in 1947, more and more Sylheti seamen found themselves unemployed, and sought work in Britain to support their families. The present Bangladeshi community in Britain, Choudhury insists again and again, are all descendants and kin of these first seafaring settlers, and almost all can claim to be related to persons who fought and died in the two world wars.

This account, while superficially plausible, does not bear historical scrutiny. A few Sylheti lascars did indeed jump ship in London, and some of them, in all probability, did eventually settle in Britain. In their turn, they assisted others to do the same.[42] But it is very unlikely indeed that all of today's "Bangladeshi settlers" are their descendants. If this assertion had merit, the migrations from Sylhet to Britain would have peaked in the 1940s and 1950s, yet after Independence and Partition in 1947, very few Sylheti lascars (by Choudhury's own account, supported by other authorities) were able to find work on British ships.[43] The numbers of Bengali migrants in Britain remained tiny in this period: by the early 1950s there were perhaps no more than 300 Sylhetis in London; their numbers had grown only to about 5000 in the

[40] Ibid., p. 43.

[41] Ibid., p. 50

[42] Salter, *The Asiatic in England*; idem, *The East in the West*; see also Visram, *Ayahs, Lascars and Princes*.

[43] Balachandran, "Circulation through Seafaring".

whole of Britain by 1962.[44] It was only after this date that their numbers began to grow rapidly, a consequence not only of new British restrictions on immigration, but also of the dangers and uncertainties of life in Bangladesh during and after the civil war of 1971.[45] By 1986, when the British government published its first White Paper on Bangladeshis in Britain, it estimated that there were about 200,000 in the country.[46] By 2001, as the last census suggests, that population had grown by another 100,000 in the next fifteen years.

The point to be stressed here is that, contrary to Choudhury's account, the vast majority of Bangladeshis now settled in Britain were never lascars on British ships and were born long after the Second World War and the end of empire. The great majority of Bangladeshis who migrated to Britain did so in the two decades *after* Bangladesh achieved independence from Pakistan in 1971. So why does Choudhury repeat his unsubstantiated claim over fifty time in the course of his book? For one thing, of course, it gives the "community" a single shared history, and glosses over the deep political divisions which have long beset it.[47] It provides motley, and often divided, groups with a simple genealogy which connects today's British Bangladeshis – through the lascar seamen who served on British ships during the world wars, and through them back to the Sylheti boatmen who were recruited to work on steamships on the River Surma in Sylhet – right back to the

[44] Adams, *Across Seven Seas and Thirteen Rivers*, pp. 54, 64.

[45] In 1962, the Conservative Government enacted the Commonwealth Immigration Act, which restricted the entry to Britain of migrants from the Commonwealth by instituting a new voucher system. This led to a spurt in migration from Commonwealth countries, as many migrants from countries such as Pakistan rushed to bring close relatives over to Britain before the act came into force.

[46] *Bangladeshis in Britain*, vols 1 and 2.

[47] The community was divided by its attitude towards Pakistan before 1971; since then supporters of different regimes and parties have frequently clashed.

original band of 360 saints who accompanied Shah Jalal on his mission to spread Islam on the frontiers of Bengal. This genealogy serves both to unify "the community" as fictive kin, and gives it an intelligible history imbued with a continuing moral purpose. But no less significantly, as we shall see, it provides the foundations on which the "settlers" built their claim to rights and full membership as citizens in Britain.

In Ilias' history, the communal riots in Bihar in late 1946 are depicted as "the root cause" which explains why the "Biharis" left Bihar. Throughout the book, Ilias returns again and again to these horrific events which (in his account) claimed 50,000 lives and forced many thousands more to flee from their homes.[48] When Pakistan was established in 1947, he tells us, many of these frightened people sought and were given shelter in its eastern wing. Later on, their numbers swelled as anti-Muslim violence in India in 1950 and again in 1964 drove more and more people out. Ilias' purpose is to imprint on the reader's mind the "fact" that the people he writes about were victims of catastrophic events, refugees who, through no fault of their own, were evicted from the land of their birth and had to seek shelter elsewhere: "The Muslim minority in Bihar were . . . happy with their way of life, when India fell for communalism and Bihar became the target."[49] Even the language he uses to describe these events emphasises their passive victimhood: the Biharis were "sorted out" and "shunted off",[50] and "forced to leave their country of origin".[51] Ilias'

[48] It is always difficult to verify the numbers of those killed in riots, but 50,000 is clearly a very exaggerated figure. Lord Wavell, then the viceroy of India, guessed that between 5000 and 10,000 people lost their lives. Wavell to Pethick Lawrence, 22 December 1946, in Mansergh and Lumby, eds, *The Transfer of Power*, vol. IX, p. 140. See the discussion of numbers killed and displaced by the violence in Ghosh, *Partition and the South Asian Diaspora*, pp. 2–3.

[49] *Biharis,* p. 26.

[50] Ibid., pp. x, xi.

[51] Ibid., p. xiii.

recurrent theme is that the Biharis "are descendants of those optees and emigrants who came to East Bengal after the great divide in India in 1947."[52]

Yet there are contradictions, and a noticeable instability, in this construction of events. As Ilias himself admits, from the late nineteenth century on the British had employed large numbers of Biharis in the railways when these were extended into eastern Bengal, and also many others in "the police, judiciary and other civil departments".[53] So when the calamitous events of 1946–7 took place, there were already a large number of Biharis long settled in parts of what now became East Pakistan.[54] After Partition, some were joined by their families, but they were not refugees from violence. By Ilias' own account (which the censuses and other studies support), many of the Urdu-speaking service elites who migrated to East Pakistan after 1947 did so in fits and starts over more than two decades between 1947 and 1970, attracted by the better opportunities for employment in East Pakistan.

As we read on, then, it becomes clear why Ilias describes his "community" as "Bihari", even though he himself admits its members do not all come from Bihar, and despite the fact, as he would be the first to acknowledge, that "Bihari" has become a derogatory term in present-day Bangladesh. To call them "Urdu speakers" (arguably a more accurate appellation) would draw unwelcome attention to the question of language which sets his community apart from a national culture into which he seeks their assimilation. But more importantly, by calling them "Bihari" he fixes in the reader's consciousness an association between this migrant group and the carnage in Bihar in 1946. The Bihar riots have long been held up as "the moment when Pakistan was born", when the sheer brutality of the attacks demonstrated the

[52] Ibid., p. ix.

[53] Ibid.

[54] See Chattopadhyay, *Internal Migration in India.*

impossibility of any reconciliation or rapprochement between India's Hindus and Muslims. They hold as large a place in the collective memory of Partition in the east as do the Calcutta Killings of 1946. Used in particular contexts, the very word "Bihar" conveys all the horrors of "the deadly ethnic riot".[55] By calling his community "Biharis", Ilias seeks to recall these outrages in order to evoke the sympathy of fellow Muslims and "hosts" in Bangladesh, sympathy which his community patently deserves, despite their later "mistakes". The word "Bihari" in Ilias' book thus carries a powerful moral charge and is deployed with a clear purpose.

But at another level, the "myth" of their enforced exile from Bihar also works to provide a single straightforward common "history" for the "Bihari" community in Bangladesh today. Present-day Biharis are represented as linear descendants of those who fled the carnage. In turn, they are descended from the saintly pioneers who brought Islam to "caste-ridden" India, and all are legatees of the great revolutionaries who resisted imperial incursions. Thus, they are the standard bearers of a sacred mission with a long history and heirs of a great culture. This "history" seeks to unify the "community", sanitise and simplify its complex and multi-stranded chronicles by providing a single and intelligible "root cause" for its presence in Bangladesh. In this sense, it has much in common with the foundation myths of so many migrant groups, which typically see their migration as being the consequence of a single catastrophic event, even though historians might agree that they migrated gradually over a period of many decades, and sometimes over centuries.[56]

Both these accounts, then, simplify a complex history of migration. Choudhury ignores the fact that the great majority of

[55] Horowitz, *The Deadly Ethnic Riot*. Interestingly, the 1946 Bihar killings feature in Horowitz's book as an exemplar of this type of violence.

[56] See, for instance, the account of the foundation myths of mobile weaving communities in Roy and Haynes, "Conceiving Mobility"; and Chakrabarty, "Remembered Villages".

Sylhetis migrated to Britain during and after the upheavals of the "liberation war" in Bangladesh, and greatly exaggerates the role of lascars – typically enterprising economic migrants – in that history. For his part, Ilias plays down the long process of "economic" migration from Bihar and upper India to eastern Bengal, proposing instead that all "Biharis" were "forced migrants", victims of communal violence. These constructions enable both writers to provide a simple answer to the question "why are we here?" But, as we shall see, they deliberately privilege one particular answer to the big question over others because it suits their purposes "here" and "now". What purport to be histories are not only about the past, but about the present and about responses to contemporary challenges. They also offer prescriptions for the future.

Myths for Assimilation: Intertwining Community and "Host" Histories

In what way do these histories advance the cause of assimilation if, as has been shown, one of their purposes is vigorously to claim the unity, the integrity, and the separate identity of "the community"? I am suggesting here that people must first be "assimilated" into a community with a single story or construct about itself before it can begin to negotiate its acceptance as part of a host nation. "Ethnicity" maintenance does not prevent assimilation, as the critics of the concept have sometimes argued. Instead it is sometimes a necessary prolegomenon to it. Nor are the two processes mutually exclusive, as are the "salad bowl" and the "melting pot" views of migration and ethnicity. The reality, it would seem, is rather more complex than the conventional wisdom assumes.

The first technique our two books deploy for this work of assimilation is to insert community history into the national history of the host country. Of course, no nation has a single national history, no matter how much nationalists might claim it does. But at certain times and in certain places there may be a measure of agreement about which key historical events have crucially shaped a nation's identity, and migrant intellectuals seem to be quick to spot these areas of "national" consensus. In the case of Britain in the late 1970s, when Yousuf Choudhury began to write his book (and indeed even today, as the recent votes for Churchill as the greatest Briton suggest) the world wars, and particularly the Second World War, was one such defining event. Ordinary Britons who fought and died in these wars, as well as those who manned the "home front", are seen as having displayed national unity and national character. Courage, pluck, stoicism, and humour in the face of adversity, and "just getting on with it" came to be seen as typically "British" traits, displacing more aristocratic and more "English" gentlemanly attributes. Fighting and dying for one's country in its "finest hour", the epic struggle against Fascism, was the highest proof of Britishness.[57]

The very first page of Choudhury's *Roots and Tales* makes plain his intention to insert "the Bangladeshi settlers" into this narrative of British patriotic sacrifice, and calls to be quoted in full:

> Many people have misconceptions about the Bangladeshi settlers because they either have wrong information or lack of the same. Many do not know that the Bangladeshis were asked to come and fight for Britain in the two world wars. We fought both wars for them. We were in the warships and troop carriers when they were facing enemies. We were in British cargo-ships to bring in the vital supplies. Bangladeshis worked on the deck, went down to the bottom of the ships, and ran the engines for them. We were part of the British war power.

[57] Chris Waters and other historians of British national identity have argued that after the war British national culture was reconstructed to include the working classes in the "nation", and the war was the crucible in which this new identity was forged. See Waters, "Dark Strangers". Also idem, "J.B. Priestly"; Rose, "Race, Empire"; Weight, *Patriot.* Joanna Lumley's recent campaign in support of the Gurkhas' claim to settle in Britain also rested on their support for Britain on the battlefield.

> The ships were attacked and sunk on the high seas. Many of our men were killed, not all of their dead bodies floated to the surface of the water. The dead bodies were eaten by sharks or simply decomposed.
>
> Many dead bodies went down with their ships leaving no trace, no grave or headstone is there to be seen, so our dead Bangladeshi seamen have been forgotten for all time.
>
> Most Bangladeshi settlers are the descendent flesh and blood of those who were lost in the seas or survived to tell their tale, so it is our duty to keep our history alive and remind everyone of who we are and why we are here.[58]

This is a remarkable passage for many reasons. On the one hand, it makes very explicit the author's intention to inform people about his community's sacrifices on their behalf, and it is clear that his intended audience is the "host" society, the British. But what is particularly interesting is how he maintains the boundary between "us" and "them" ("we fought both the wars for them", etc.), even as he weaves the history of "the settlers" into the tapestry of British history.

As soon as it is recognised that Choudhury's work is not only a book about the past, but also a polemical tract staking claims in the present and for the future, many peculiarities of its language and structure become intelligible. It explains the author's decision to write the book in English rather than Bangla. It explains, for example, why the author insists repeatedly – despite compelling evidence to the contrary – that *all* "Bangladeshis" are descended from lascar seamen; it explains why his brief account of his community's origins stresses its primeval connection with the sea; why his Sylhet is literally born out of the ocean and why his community (just as its British hosts) is presented as a seafaring peoples. It explains why so much of the book is about the period of British rule over Sylhet, and why its account of British rule is so uncritical. It explains why it seeks to downplay the fierce conflicts between

[58] *Roots and Tales*, p. lx.

Sylhetis and "Britishers", positing instead a chronicle of largely cordial interdependence between rulers and ruled. It explains why it stresses the kindness and paternalism of the British owners of steamer ships, as shown when they employed the Bengali boatmen their ships had put out of business, and the decency of the British people towards them when they first arrived on their shores.[59] And of course it explains why the crucial and recurrent theme – which stresses Bangladeshi sacrifice for Britain during the wars, is the leitmotif of the work. This is the basis on which Choudhury rests his case for the community's *right* to settle in Britain. It is a right they have *earned* by their sacrifices on behalf of Britain.

But it also explains why Choudhury strives so hard to compress and simplify that history of these settlers into a single narrative. That narrative has to be controlled tightly if Choudhury is to be able to make this claim convincingly. If the true variety of histories and experiences of Bangladeshi migrants were acknowledged, it would weaken his claim to rights for the community in Britain today. The community has first to be constructed as Bangladeshi in order for it to be accepted as British. Those migrants whose stories palpably strain the unified account of the community and its origins – for instance the snobbish "Dhaka gentlemen" who turn their nose up at their more humble countrymen from Sylhet, and the "Arabic-educated" pro-Pakistanis (persons of the same group Ilias describes as Biharis) who become the imams at their new mosque – are "reconciled" with the larger Sylheti population, "gain their forgiveness", and are apparently "assimilated" into it, disappearing from the account as suddenly as they enter it.[60] It is only after this work of constructing, inventing, and assimilating migrant Bangladeshis of very different sorts into one community has been achieved by the myths of origin and migration that Choudhury begins to describe his community as "British Bangladeshi". Significantly, the term is first used only on page 196

[59] Ibid., pp. 90, 118–20.
[60] Ibid., pp. 196, 177, 179.

of a 230-page work. Thereafter, the book refers repeatedly to British Bangladeshis – their culture, but also their secular problems – particularly their underperformance in education and their politics in Britain.

But another interesting point is that the author simultaneously aligns his community with a general British past and also with *particular* sections of "British" society. His discussions of the lifestyles of the early post-war migrants – their liaisons and marriages with working-class white women, their sharing of food and lodgings with migrant workers from other parts of the world, their long shifts in the factories, their renting of premises and leasing of shops from East End Jews – identifies "Bangladeshis" with a kind of enterprising working-class cosmopolitanism that, Choudhury suggests, characterised the Britain in which they lived and worked. Palpably it is this Britain into which he seeks the incorporation of his community. In this sense, Choudhury bears out Brubaker's suggestion that assimilation must be understood as a process by which a community repositions itself with regard to many different cultural referents, rather than to a single monolithic core culture.[61]

Towards the end of the book, moreover, Choudhury begins to describe "Bengalis" as "part of the immigrant population".[62] They are represented as part of "Black" movements,[63] an integral element in the fight against racism in the 1980s: "Bangladeshis had done a lot of fighting and were still fighting for their existence and rights."[64] Increasingly he discusses their politics: their long-distance nationalism *vis-à-vis* Bangladesh (through their support of the liberation movement), but also their political activism in the local councils in Britain to improve living conditions in the inner cities.[65] He mentions certain liberal Britons as friends of

[61] Brubaker, "The Return of Assimilation", pp. 543–4.

[62] *Roots and Tales*, p. 195.

[63] Ibid., p. 192.

[64] Ibid., p. 195.

[65] On "long-distance nationalism", see Anderson, *The Spectre of Comparison;* and Schiller and Fouron, *Georges Woke Up Laughing*.

the community: the social worker and historian Caroline Adams, Ken Livingstone, and even Prince Charles, proudly reproducing a photograph of the prince's visit to Aldgate. So one can see that Choudhury is positioning his community within a certain construct of Britain and of Britishness, one that is by turns hard-working and enterprising, cosmopolitan, egalitarian, tolerant, and inclusive. In some senses, one might argue, he is constructing the Britain into which the community of Bangladeshi settlers is seeking to be assimilated quite as much as he is constructing the community itself.

Ilias adopts similar strategies in *Biharis*. He too strives to insert his community into the national history of Bangladesh. But his is a rather more difficult enterprise fraught with enormous pitfalls. It requires him repeatedly to admit his community's past mistakes and seek forgiveness for them.

The first move Ilias makes is a bold one, considering that some of the deepest differences between Biharis and their hosts revolve around the question of language: Biharis are widely believed by Bangladeshi nationalists to have looked down on the Bengali language and to have stood aloof from the Language Movement (of which more below). In the first chapter of his book, Ilias asserts that the Bengali language and "Bihari Urdu" have a common origin, that both descend from a single great linguistic tradition: that of Magadhi Prakrit.

> Bengali, Oriya and Assamese have their roots in Bihar. Bengali is a typical descendant of the great language that, under the name of Magadhi Prakrit, was the vernacular of eastern North India for many centuries. This was the official language of the great Emperor Asoka and the Buddha and Mahavira, the apostle of Jainism . . .
>
> Bihari Urdu [is] unlike the [literary] Urdu evolved in Delhi and UP, [it] was overwhelmingly plain and simple . . . Even today, most Bihari Muslims speak Magadhi, Maithili and Bhujpuri rather than Urdu . . .[66]

[66] *Biharis*, pp. 19–20.

Ilias is here seeking to construct a common linguistic heritage for "eastern north India" and place Bihar squarely inside it. His Bihari language is not a product of the courtly and aristocratic world of North India; rather it is an intrinsic part of a syncretic family of "plain and simple" spoken languages. By making this claim he seeks to defuse the tension engendered by the language question and rid Urdu as spoken in Bangladesh of its elitist and North Indian associations. He rhetorically shifts the Bihar "homeland" eastwards, in the direction of its Bengali neighbourhood and away from Upper India and Pakistan. He also pushes Bihari Urdu speakers downwards in terms of social class, associating them not with the elite or *ashraf* North Indian tradition of Persianised Urdu, but with the more lowly *atrap* or *ajlaf* everyday bazaar dialects of the eastern region.

In his next set of strategic moves, Ilias faces up squarely to the greatest obstacle to Bihari assimilation into Bangladeshi society – the charge that the community fought against the "nation" in the war of 1971, joining hands with the Pakistani army in its brutal and merciless suppression of the people's uprising. Ilias attempts to explain this in a variety of ways. The Bihari refugees from India, he admits, made grave mistakes. But they did so largely because they were misled, misguided, and ultimately betrayed by their leaders who took them into "the wilderness".[67] Despite the fact that the "local Bengali community was . . . very sympathetic towards [them]",[68] they kept themselves aloof from the locals, living apart in "reservations".[69] By adopting for themselves the title and status of "Mohajers" – the Islamic term that the Pakistani state used for refugees – they isolated themselves from other groups in society. This created in them a "psyche" which led them mistakenly to regard the cultural and political struggles of the local people as being against their interests. Instead of demanding that they be

[67] Ibid., p. 66.
[68] Ibid., p. 60.
[69] Ibid., pp. 67–8.

treated equally as citizens of Pakistan, they claimed a special status for themselves as Mohajers who had made special sacrifices for the state, and who therefore deserved special privileges and special recognition.[70] Unlike the Mohajers of Karachi and Hyderabad in West Pakistan, who were harsh critics of the Pakistani regime, the Bihari Mohajers in Bengal remained apathetic, won over by the regime through special allotments of housing and other facilities.[71] Under the martial law regime of General Ayub Khan, the Bihari Basic Democrats "were submissive to the political programmes of Ayub Khan. They performed their duty not as representatives of their community but as agents of the ruling clique."[72] Their failure to adapt and assimilate, Ilias admits, was a huge error. It was this separatist "psyche" which led to their failure to throw their weight behind the rightful political struggles of Bengalis against successive Pakistani regimes; and this was the reason for the dreadful reprisals against the Bihari community after the war ended.

These are profoundly moving passages. Like many "interested" historians of vanquished peoples, Ilias labours under the burden of having to explain why events turned out as they did, and this leads him to reflect with great seriousness on the past. In common with others in this predicament, he laments the short-sightedness of his people, but also shifts the blame to their former leaders, now deposed.[73] Again and again, he shows and regrets how the Biharis were betrayed by their leaders, misled first by the speeches of the creator of Pakistan,[74] and then by the Muslim League leadership and its "religion-based politics".[75] After Partition, they were let down by the Pakistani state, which encouraged them to cling to their refugee status as Mohajers and to their Urdu language.[76] In

[70] Ibid., p. 61.
[71] Ibid., p. 88.
[72] Ibid., p. 85.
[73] Schivelbusch, *The Culture of Defeat*, pp. 3–13.
[74] *Biharis*, p. xi.
[75] Ibid., p. 66.
[76] Ibid., p. 68.

the late 1950s they were betrayed by corrupt Bihari representatives who were too busy making money to lead the community; and in the 1960s they were exploited by Governor Monem Khan "who had very close contact with notorious [criminals]", and who used them "to create a wedge between locals and non-locals".[77] In the late 1960s, when the campaign for the autonomy of East Pakistan gained ground, they were misled by West Pakistani-based Urdu newspapers and their false propaganda against the Bengal leader Mujibur Rahman.[78] In the months before the outbreak of the civil war they were betrayed again by the media when it falsely alleged that the Mohajer Convention had called for the partition of East Bengal,[79] and after the war began they were led astray by a false prophet – Warasat Khan, the leader of the Mohajer Party – who dragged orphaned Bihari boys into the war on the side of Pakistan.[80] In the aftermath of the war, when Biharis were hunted down and killed in their thousands by the so-called Bengali "Sixteenth Divisions", they were betrayed by the Red Cross which encouraged and organised "bewildered people" to register themselves for "repatriation to Pakistan".[81] Terrified victims of grisly reprisals who huddled in makeshift camps after the war, they were exploited by the Indian soldiers who, instead of protecting them, took all their money on the false promise of getting them out of Bangladesh.[82]

This theme of betrayal is repeated so often, and at such regular intervals, that the book demands analysis of its deeper discursive intent. Arguably, it takes forward two crucially important strategic purposes. On the one hand it seeks to drive a distinction between the innocence of the general Bihari community and the culpability

[77] Ibid., p. 92.
[78] *Biharis*, p. 93.
[79] Ibid., p. 95.
[80] Ibid., p. 114.
[81] Ibid., p. 132.
[82] Ibid., p. 133.

of the "bad apples" among their leadership. By this device Ilias suggests it is right for the "soft-hearted" Bangladeshi nation to forgive these poor misguided people, in their own way as much victims of the old Pakistani order as the Bengalis on whose mercy he is throwing his community. On the other hand there is a less explicit but nonetheless potent message in this saga of betrayal, directed at the Biharis themselves. Ilias' warning to his fellow Biharis is to be wary of the siren calls of the false prophets of today. In particular, he appears to appeal to them not to be misled by the likes of Nasim Khan, the retired railway guard who organised Bihari railway employees to fight for their repatriation to Pakistan, and his organisation, the Stranded Pakistanis General Repatriation Committee (SPGRC). Since the mid 1970s, Nasim Khan and the SPGRC have waged a long and highly publicised battle to arrange the transfer of all "Stranded Pakistanis" to Pakistan, albeit with very little success.[83] Ilias describes the followers of Naseem Khan as "frustrated and uneducated and half-educated youths".[84] He clearly believes their calls for repatriation to a country they have never seen and which has repeatedly repudiated them, to be unrealistic and misguided.

Since 1980, Ahmed Ilias himself, and the "Al Falah" NGO which he directs, have worked for the rehabilitation of "Urdu-speaking Bangladeshis" living in camps.[85] His very description of them as "Urdu-speaking Bangladeshis" (as opposed to Khan's "Stranded Pakistanis") reveals his underlying purpose – to bring them out of the camps in which they have lived in a state of suspended animation and increasingly desperate poverty, and help them negotiate their assimilation into the society and polity of Bangladesh. Hence Ilias writes with approval of those individuals among the Bihari community "who are struggling for a place in the soft heart of the Bengali society", "the literate and educated,

[83] See Ghosh, *Partition and the South Asian Diaspora,* pp. 57–122.

[84] *Biharis,* p. 151.

[85] Ibid., p. 154.

representing the young generation wants to come out from the depressed situation and overcome the agony they have suffered for the last three decades."[86] The deeper intent of his whole history is to suggest that "the literate and educated" syncretists of today represent the true "progressive" spirit of the community's history, and hence represent the true leadership for the community today. Of course, in making this claim, Ilias glosses over the cracks within the community, particularly, but not exclusively those that distance Syedpur's railway workers and Dhaka's jute-mill hands from the Urdu-speaking literati. His aim is to persuade the community and their hosts alike that "Biharis" *are* in fact "Urdu-speaking Bangladeshis". The fact that this term is first used only towards the end of his book (on p. 154 of a 200-page text) suggests that through this usage Ilias seeks to transform "Biharis" into "Urdu-speaking Bangladeshis" in much the same way that Yousuf Choudhury transmutes Sylheti lascars into "British Bangladeshis".

Ilias' other objective is to provide his community of Urdu-speaking Bangladeshis with an impressive record of service to the cause of Bangladesh. He painstakingly catalogues every act by Urdu speakers, whether as individuals or groups, which displayed their loyalty to their new Bengali home and to the national ideals of Bangladesh. He notes with pride that on 21 February 1952, when Bengali students took up their celebrated protest against Pakistan's decision to enshrine Urdu as the only state language of Pakistan, the "Urdu-speaking civil servant" Hussain Haider refused to issue orders proscribing the movement and was transferred for his pains. In this way Ilias "inserts" Biharis into the history of "*Ekushey*", 21 February 1952 being symbolically the moment that Bangladeshi nationalism was born.[87] He then goes on to describe

[86] Ibid., pp. 155–6.

[87] *Ekushey*, literally "the 21st", recalls the date when Bengali students protesting against Pakistan's language policy were killed by the police. It is still commemorated as *Shaheed Dibas* (Martyr's Day) in contemporary Bangladesh. *Biharis*, p. 75. Also see Uddin, *Constructing Bangladesh.*

the contribution of "progressive" Urdu "poets, writers, journalists and students" to "the Language Movement":

> Dr. Yusuf Hasan, Arif Hushyarpuri, Ayaz Asmi, Massod Kalim, Akhtar Payami, Akhtar Hyderabadi, Adeeb Sohail, Khwaja Mohammed Ali, Qamar, Manzur Rahman, Salahuddin Mohammed, Badruddin Ahmed (Engineer), Perwez Ahmed (Barrister), Hasan Sayeed, Abu Sayeed Khan and Zainul Abedin were prominent among the supporters of the language movement. Dr. Yusuf Hasan being a member of the Urdu speaking community played a significant role in the language movement. He issued press statements on behalf of the Urdu *Progressive* Writers Association in favour of the movement. He was also selected as one of the founder members of the "*Rashtro Bhasha Sangram Parishad*" [the National Language Movement Council].
>
> At a later stage, others like Ataur Rahman Jalil, Naushad Noori, Suroor Barabankwi, Habib Ansari, Bamo Akhter Shahood, Umme Ammarah and Anwer Farhad joined the movement. It was Salahuddin Mohammed, who had even said that if Urdu and Bangla were not accepted as two state languages of Pakistan, he then would demand only for Bangla as the state language.
>
> The Language Movement also greatly influenced the *progressive* Urdu poets and writers in both wings of Pakistan . . . In East Pakistan, Urdu poet Naushad Noori wrote a very powerful poem, "*Mohenjodaro*", in Urdu . . .
>
> [Ilias then quotes the full text of the poem "Mohenjodaro", first in Urdu and then in English translation].
>
> . . . The Urdu-speaking writers expressed their solidarity with the Language Movement. *Anjuman Tarraq-e-Urdu* (Organisation for the Development of Urdu) in East Pakistan severed its tie with the All Pakistan Anjuman . . . for its support to the government on language policy . . . The *progressive* Urdu students formed *Anjuman-e-Adab*, a literary organisation in Dhaka University[,] to support the contemporary *progressive* Bengali writers for their cultural struggle . . .[88]

[88] Ibid., pp. 77–8 (emphasis added).

And so on. Later, according to Ilias, when political movements against General Ayub Khan gained momentum, "the *progressive* and pro-democratic Urdu students, youths, journalists, teachers, writers and poets" mobilised themselves in their support.[89] "The Bihari railway workers in Syedpur Railway Workshops joined the anti-Ayub movements following the directive of the Bihari labour leaders Azim Nomani and Mohammed Ibrahim."[90] On the eve of the fateful general election in 1970, Ilias tells us, "a *progressive* Urdu-speaking businessman, Mahmood Hasan of Chittagong", who had been associated with "*progressive* movements since 1952", brought out a new weekly, *Jaridah*, whose first banner headline, *Hamri Nijat Tumhari Nijat, Chey Nukat, Chey Nukat*, explicitly supported Mujibur Rahman and the Awami League's Six Point Charter of autonomy for East Pakistan.[91] In 1971, many Bihari labour leaders and journalists "joined the liberation movement".[92] He recalls that two officers in the army, Bihari Saghir Ahmed Siddiqui and the Bengali Nurul Islam, were incarcerated and killed by the Pakistani army. "Two bloods", he tells us, had "*mingled together to live in union*",[93] graphically demonstrating the hybrid character of the freedom struggle and, he suggests implicitly, the true spirit of the Bangladeshi nation.

At every stage in the history of the nation's struggles for liberation, Ilias therefore insists, Biharis had played a role. From the earliest days of the battle against British rule, Biharis had been at the forefront of every struggle. During the movement for Bangladesh's freedom, Biharis had joined with Bengalis in fighting Pakistan's oppression. While some had admittedly been misled, coerced, or inveigled into joining the Pakistani army and its

[89] Ibid., p. 94.

[90] Ibid., p. 95.

[91] Literally, the phrase means: "Our salvation, your salvation, Six Points, Six Points" (emphasis added); *Biharis,* p. 102.

[92] Ibid., p. 118.

[93] Ibid., p. 119 (emphasis added).

depredations on the people of Bangladesh, the community's true leaders – intellectuals and writers – had fought and died for the nation. So too had the hard-working Bihari masses, notably the railway workers of Syedpur. Here again we see Ilias' strategy of incorporating Bihari workers into the "progressive" history of the larger community.

So we see that Ilias skilfully weaves Biharis into the narrative of the making of the Bangladeshi nation. But also of considerable significance is the way in which he seeks to align his community with *specific* sections of Bangladesh's polity. As highlighted in the passages cited above, Ilias repeatedly uses the adjective "progressive" to describe his list of "Urdu-speaking Bangladeshi" heroes. Clearly, he is seeking to enlist the support of similarly "progressive" segments of local Bengali society to achieve the rehabilitation of his community as true members of the Bangladeshi nation. Here again we see at work the subtle and complex mechanics of assimilation. Just as Choudhury positioned his community as part of a certain kind of Britain, Ilias positions his Biharis as part of a certain kind of Bangladesh, one that is progressive in a specifically South Asian sense of that term: secular, anti-imperialist, egalitarian, tolerant, and inclusive, one that celebrates the pluralism and syncretism of South Asia's faiths and cultures. There is a subtle suggestion that this progressive vision of Bangladesh has as yet to be realised, and Ilias hints at the prospect of Urdu-speaking Bangladeshis joining with like-minded Bengalis in its construction and achievement. Just as Choudhury seeks to fashion Britain, so too Ilias constructs his community of Urdu-speaking Bangladeshis while also seeking to join with progressive elements in the host country to reconstruct "Bangladesh" itself.

The "Myth of Return" and the Context and Politics of Assimilation

The final set of questions raised by these texts has to do with their timing. Why were they written and published when they were?

What was it about that moment of their production that made them appropriate, relevant, or even possible? And if we can uncover these "conditions of production", might we be able to speculate on the conditions in which migrant groups in times past wrote histories or genealogies of their communities?

The first set of answers seems to lie in generational changes within the community. The coming of age of a generation of children who have grown up in the diaspora (in the case of Choudhury) or in camps (in the case of Ilias) is a compelling fact and a concern that animates both works. Choudhury refers directly in his introduction to these changes as one of his motives in writing his book:

> Now in 1993, most work-mates, room-mates and close friends of my earlier times have passed away. Their sons and grandsons became the family head, living in this country with their own wives and children . . . The new generation in our community need to know more about us. What we were, what we are and where we come from. It is their roots, their identity, which are unknown to many of them. That identity is vital, no matter where they live. Without it, they will be lost.[94]

Ilias is less explicit about his intention to write for the young, but he too refers repeatedly to the rise of a new generation of young people who have grown up in camps and who understand little about the causes of their situation. He seems keen not only to educate but also guide the young towards a brighter future, which he believes can only come if they embrace an Urdu-speaking Bangladeshi identity.

However, a deeper imperative behind their writing appears to come from a recognition that the "myth of return" is no longer sustainable. Choudhury writes poignantly of the gradual fading of the dream of going back "home":

> After spending ten or fifteen years here, some Bangladeshis often decided to go home to resettle. They sold their properties . . . whatever

[94] *Roots and Tales*, pp. ix–x.

> they owned, then went to Bangladesh with a lump sum of money . . . quite confident of a happy life.
>
> As the dealing . . . really started, obstacles began to emerge. He realised that, without his conscious knowledge, he himself had picked up a lot of habits from the host country and was used to another pattern of life.
>
> He found himself inexperienced in many day to day matters. He needed a guide at every step and gradually began to discover himself as a foreigner in his own home land. Still [he kept hoping] to get over it . . .
>
> As time passed on, either money or health went down, if not both. Otherwise, if he was unlucky, he might get involved with a court case . . . The people stayed on until their patience ran out.
>
> Eventually the spirit to resettle in the home land began to fade away . . . The first generation of Bangladeshi settlers might have had several tries to settle in the homeland and failed. Some are still alive . . . [Now] they grow a beard, dress up in white and attend the nearest mosque and spend hours praying . . . Although the father and son [may live] under the same roof, sharing the same food, with love, affection and care, yet in their minds they are living in different worlds.[95]

With the long, slow, and painful death of this dream, Choudhury and many of his contemporaries had to reconcile themselves to the fact that not only were their children not keen to return, but they themselves had been so changed by their years abroad that they are no longer able to slip back easily into life at "home". Perhaps (as suggested by the references to court cases and conflicts) they have also to recognise that "home" too has changed forever. It seems that the very purpose of writing this history is to come to terms with this loss, finally accepting that the Bangladeshi settlers are really here in Britain to stay.

For Ilias, too, the book signals a recognition that the dream of "repatriation" to Pakistan is just that – a dream. In a chapter

[95] Ibid., pp. 219–23.

titled "The Long March" he describes, at some length and in much painful detail, the process of disillusionment by "the step-motherly attitudes of the Pakistan government."[96] The Red Cross had raised false hopes among Bihari displacees that they would be "repatriated" to Pakistan if they signed "declarations of intention", but immediately after the Delhi Agreement of 1973 the Pakistan government made it clear that it had no intention of accepting these stranded peoples. So too did its citizens: Pakistanis in Sindh raised the slogan *Bihari na khappan* (Biharis are not wanted), "taking advantage of the known views of [Bhutto's ruling] People's Party regarding Biharis."[97] Despite the efforts of Naseem Khan and the SPGRC, and the Saudi-sponsored organisation Rabita, the Government of Pakistan had stuck to its guns that "Biharis will have to live in Bangladesh".[98] Ilias urges his community to face the harsh fact that there is no place for them anywhere else than in Bangladesh: they have been abandoned by Pakistan and forgotten by the international community. They have no choice, he suggests, but to come to terms with this fact and seek finally to settle and assimilate in Bangladesh.

So both our authors reach the same conclusion at roughly the same time, four decades after Partition and two decades after the birth of Bangladesh. The natural cycle of generations, as has been suggested above, helps to explain why this should be the case. But it would be unwise to ignore the changing political context in both "host" countries which encouraged the migrant community to take bold steps towards assimilation. The post-war decades in Britain had seen ever-harsher rhetoric against non-white immigration (Enoch Powell's "rivers of blood speech" was only one example of a wider trend) and deepening racial conflict. In 1978, Margaret Thatcher had promised in a television interview

[96] *Biharis*, p. 150.
[97] Ibid., pp. 150–1.
[98] Ibid., p. 153.

that if elected her party would "finally see an end to immigration"; in the 1980s, Asians in Thatcher's Britain had experienced "a further entrenchment of institutionalised racism, particularly in the form of immigration laws and the British Nationality Act [of 1981]."[99] These were also decades of escalating racist violence.[100] In a poignant passage Choudhury lists the names of "victims of racist attacks" killed during this period.[101] But in the early 1990s, when Choudhury wrote his book, the Poll Tax riots and the defenestration of Margaret Thatcher from the leadership of the Tory Party seemed to presage moves away from the harsh attitudes towards disadvantaged social groups in general, and immigrants in particular, which had characterised the previous decades. "New Labour" was in the process of being born, and a new alliance of the centre-left – with the support of many sections of British society including the trades unions, the church, the liberal intelligentsia and the media – was gaining ground.

In 1988, the publication of Rushdie's *Satanic Verses* prompted widespread violence among outraged Muslims in Britain's inner cities. But of no less significance (Choudhury makes no mention at all of Rushdie's book) was the publication two years earlier by the British government of the first policy document on *Bangladeshis in Britain*. This not merely revealed official concern about the

[99] Brah, *Cartographies of Diaspora*, pp. 37–8.

[100] Ibid., p. 39.

[101] "East End – Altab Ali was knifed on his way from work. Isaak Ali was murdered near his home. Southall – Gurdip Singh Chigger was stabbed to death. Newham – Akhtar Ali Baig was killed. Hackney – Michael Ferreira was murdered. Liverpool Street Station – Famous Mgutshini, an African student was knifed. Windsor – Sewa Singh was killed. Leamington Spa – racist threw petrol over an Asian woman and burnt her to death. South London – Fenton Ogbogbo lost his life. Swindon – Malcolm Chambers and Mohammed Arif were murdered by racists. Leeds – a Sikh woman burnt to death in her home when it caught fire following a racist attack. Walthamstow – Mrs Perveen Khan was sleeping in her home, with her three children, when racists set fire to the house, she and her children lost their lives . . ." *Roots and Tales*, p. 193.

continuing "backwardness" of the Bangladeshi population, it also showed beyond a doubt that their children were underachieving at school, faring far worse than Indian and Pakistani children. It is significant that Choudhury's book ends with a long discussion of the White Paper. He argues that it shocked the community, hitherto complacent about the education of its children, into action, and shows how British Bengalis began to enter local politics to seek to redress these issues. (Again, this bears out Brubaker's insight that assimilation for "secular" purposes continues to be salient for many migrant groups.[102]) Instead of focusing their energies solely on Bangladeshi politics, as they had done in the past, they increasingly saw the good reasons to seek to influence, or even to enter, local councils. Local politics appear to have become a vital arena for interaction between new spokesmen for the community and particular British people: constituency MPs, of course, but also local councillors, school head teachers, social workers, and representatives of church groups. These interactions can be seen to have created a new space – perhaps what Brah calls a "diaspora space" – in which assimilation could begin to be negotiated by certain Bangladeshis and certain individual Britons.[103] It is highly significant that Caroline Adams' path-breaking study of the community, *Across Thirteen Rivers and Seven Seas*, came out of her interaction with Bangladeshis as a social worker in the East End, and that this book "explains" the Bengali presence in Britain in precisely the same terms as Choudhury's does, recalling the sacrifice of Bengali lascars in the world wars.[104] It is also

[102] Brubaker, "The Return of Assimilation?"

[103] Brah defines it as a place of intersectionality and confluence: "where multiple subject positions are juxtaposed, proclaimed or disavowed; where the permitted and the prohibited perpetually interrogate, and where the accepted and the transgressive imperceptibly mingle even while these syncretic forms may be disclaimed in the name of purity and tradition." *Cartographies of Diaspora*, p. 208.

[104] Leach, "Caroline Adams".

significant that Choudhury's book was published by the Sylheti Social History Group in London – a small group of British liberals and left-leaning Bangladeshi community leaders such as Tassaduq Ahmed – who also is the author of the foreword to Adams' book. The fact that the preface to *Roots and Tales* was written, in a neat symmetry, by a leading Christian theologian, underlines the enabling role played by such individuals and by civil society and religious groups in the processes of Bengali assimilation.

But the most interesting feature of the last chapter of Choudhury's book which discusses the 1986 White Paper is its suggestion that assimilation (at least with the secular purpose of raising educational standards of the community, and improving their access to healthcare and housing) is a *national duty* for all British Bangladeshis. The community must encourage educational achievement, he suggests, because its failure in this regard lets the nation down. The fact that both Indian and Pakistani children had outstripped Bengalis at school is stressed again and again. It is as if Choudhury is seeking to play upon Bangladeshi anxieties about their overweening neighbours in South Asia to provoke them into taking steps to "improve" themselves in Britain. Thus we see the playing out of an apparent paradox – long-distance Bangladeshi nationalism being deployed to drive forward Bengali assimilation into *British* politics and *British* culture.

Ilias' *Biharis* must also be placed within the political context in which it was published. In 2003, months before *Biharis* came out, Bangladesh's Supreme Court ruled in the case of *Abid Khan and others vs The Government of Bangladesh* that the Urdu-speaking "Bihari" petitioners were citizens of Bangladesh by birth and could not be deprived of their political rights. This landmark judgment followed other rulings in favour of Bihari petitioners (*Mukhtar Ahmed vs Government of Bangladesh*, *Abdul Khaleque vs the Court of Settlement and Others*, and *Bangladesh vs Professor Ghulam*), where the court found that even Bihari petitioners who had acted against Bangladesh and collaborated with Pakistani soldiers during and after the civil war could not be denied their rights as citizens. In their turn, these rulings came in a context of a growing liberal pro-democracy movement, spearheaded by civil society groups such as Ain-o-Shalish Kendra, which began to challenge discrimination against Biharis, but also against Hindu minority groups and Muslim women. It was supported by sections of the academic community, notably by the Refugee Migratory Movement Research Unit (RRMRU) at Dhaka University, which published findings of research on the appalling conditions in which the Bihari camp-dwellers eked out their existence. Sections of the media took up the Bihari cause.[105] Soon after Ilias' book came out, documentary film-maker Tanvir Mokkamel portrayed in *Swapnabhumi* (The Promised Land) the community and its history in a sympathetic light. That film, made in the Bengali language, was clearly directed at the local Bengali-speaking population, and it "explained" the Biharis' predicament to local Bengalis in much the same way that Caroline Adams explained the Sylhetis' history to white British readers. The fact that Ilias mentions some of these rulings and trends in his book suggests that he was extremely aware that his goal of Bihari assimilation enjoyed the support of many "progressive" Bangladeshis.[106]

Like Choudhury, Ilias identifies the pressing need for his community to attend to its secular needs in Bangladesh. He urges it to consider the future of "the young generation" here and now, a generation that "want[s] to come out of the depressed situation and overcome the agony" instead of hankering after "repatriation" to Pakistan in an indefinite future.[107] His particular concern is that without better provision for their education in Urdu and Bengali, they would fail to improve their circumstances. But he also warns of the danger that the great Urdu literary tradition to which they

[105] See, for instance, Quddus, "Recognising Citizenship Right"; Zahur, "Enrolling Stranded Pakistanis"; "Quamruzzaman, *et al.*, "The Camp-dwelling Biharis and Bangladesh".

[106] See the chapter on "Legal Aspects", pp. 191–5, and the reference to Dr C.R. Abrar of RRMRU in *Biharis*, p. 157.

[107] *Biharis*, pp. 155-6.

are heir might die forever. Once again, we see how Ilias' Urdu/Bihari nationalism sits comfortably with his case for assimilation: indeed nationalist sentiment is deployed to advance arguments for assimilation. He sees no contradiction between the survival and persistence of the "ethnic" culture and secular incorporation into the national life of Bangladesh.

So both projects work with and through nationalisms, but in complex ways. Both identify the community with not one but *two* territorial nations (the British Isles *and* Bangladesh/Sylhet in the case of Choudhury; Bangladesh *and* Bihar/India for Ilias). But both also construct diasporic, de-territorialised "transnations".[108] British-Bangladeshi people and Urdu-speaking Bangladeshi people are both shown to have been formed, in a fundamental sense, by *repeated* migrations: they are "migrant-nations" who have successively sacralised the spaces in which they have "happened" to settle.

But it would not do to gloss over the differences between these two projects. Choudhury's shows both greater self-confidence and aspiration. It seeks to build coalitions actively to influence the direction of British national politics, by working through and with local government, the church, the "race relations industry", and other civil society groups.[109] Ilias' goals appear to be rather more modest and tentative: he seeks basic social recognition for "Urdu speakers" to supplement the very basic political rights they have finally achieved. Their respective projects for assimilation appear to work within the particular spaces their authors see as being open to them: they creatively respond to particular circumstances and negotiate particular challenges while pursuing similar (but not identical) goals.

Conclusion

In *Roots and Tales* Choudhury recalls that when he and his friends were young men working in Britain, they laughed when people

[108] As in Tololyan's "Armenian Transnation".

[109] Brah, *Cartographies of Diaspora*, p. 28.

described them as immigrants. They knew they were in Britain temporarily. They counted the money they earned in terms of Bangladeshi takas (rupees). Now, however, "their sons didn't regard his pounds as takas to invest in paddy farmland in Sylhet, as his father did. He preferred the things here – red brick houses, good carpets, modern furniture, fashionable clothes to wear, and a nice car to drive. When he got a pound he spent it as a pound in the place where it was earned and where he lived."[110]

I have tried to uncover the processes by which takas became pounds and sojourners became settlers, suggesting that the apparently clumsy and anachronistic, but in fact revealing, title of Choudhury's book – *The Roots and Tales of Bangladeshi Settlers* – provides a clue to the process by which Sylhetis became both Bangladeshis and settlers simultaneously. I have underscored their strong emotional bonds with the national project in Bangladesh while showing how they came to view assimilation (or true settlement) in Britain as a *Bangladeshi* patriotic duty. Both community histories by Choudhury and Ilias reveal the complexities and inwardness of the long-distance nationalisms of migrant groups, complexities which previous studies have tended to overlook.

Both histories suggest, moreoever, that the concept of "hybridity" calls to be refined to capture all the subtle nuances of the cultural and political processes by which migrants try to assimilate into their new homes. For our migrants, constructing and recognising their own cultural hybridity is a process replete with pain and confusion, and is part and parcel of the ending of their dreams of returning "home". Their stance towards the nation-state – whether of origin or of settlement – is also rather less critical than some authors have suggested. Most migrants (like Choudhury and Ilias) are caught up in a deeply asymmetrical relationship with the "host" society, and their tentative steps

[110] *Roots and Tales*, p. 223.

towards assimilation can only succeed if they are supported by civil society groups in the host country. They have no choice but to couch their claims for rights in terms that the host country (or sections of its political classes) deems "legitimate". The "third space" about which Bhabha has written proves, in their case at least, to be extremely constrained.

One further question arises from this effort to compare these community histories. I have investigated the circumstances in which they were written and published and concluded that both were written at the moment in the community's history when the "myth of return" could no longer be sustained. This suggests a different approach to the foundation myths of much older migrant communities. Might these older genealogies and myths – whether inscribed in copper and stone as in the case of the weavers Roy and Haynes have described, or in the Huguenot community histories Susan Lachenicht has studied, or in the tales of origin of the Goths discussed by McKitterick, Christensen and others – also have been produced at a not dissimilar juncture in their history?[111] Might they also have been constructed with similar purposes and goals? It may well prove interesting to explore further the question of *when and why* communities produce origin myths and legends. As Ilias and Choudhury's histories have hinted, such explorations in their turn might help us construct a more historically informed understanding of the mechanics of assimilation.

References

Adams, Caroline, *Across Seven Seas and Thirteen Rivers. Life Stories of Pioneer Settlers in Britain*, London, 1987.

Alexander, Claire, "Diaspora and Hybridity", in P. Hill Collins and J. Solomos, ed., *Handbook of Race and Ethnic Studies*, London, forthcoming.

Anderson, Benedict, *The Spectre of Comparison. Politics Culture and the Nation*, London, 1998.

[111] Roy and Haynes, "Conceiving Mobility"; Lachenicht, "Huguenot Immigrants"; Christensen, *Cassiodorus, Jordanes and the History of the Goths*.

Appadurai, Arjun, *Modernity at Large. Cultural Dimensions of Globalization*, Minneapolis, 1996.

Balachandran, G., "Circulation through Seafaring: Indian Seamen, 1890–1945", in Markovits, Claude, *et al.*, ed., *Mobile People* (*vide infra*).

Ballantyne, Tony, *Between Colonialism and Diaspora. Sikh Cultural Formations in an Imperial World*, Durham and London, 2006.

Bangladeshis in Britain, vols 1 and 2, UK House of Commons Home Affairs Committee, HMSO, 1986.

Bhabha, Homi, *The Location of Culture*, London, 1994.

———, "The Third Space", in J. Rutherford, ed., *Identity, Community, Culture and Difference*, London, 1990.

Brah, Avtar, *Cartographies of Diaspora*, London, 1996.

Brubaker, Rogers, "The Return of Assimilation? Changing Perspectives on Assimilation and its Sequels in France, Germany, and the United States", *Ethnic and Racial Studies*, vol. 24, no. 4, July 2001.

Chakrabarty, Dipesh, "Remembered Villages: Representation of Hindu–Bengali Memories in the Aftermath of Partition", *Economic and Political Weekly*, 1996.

Chatterji, Joya, "The Bengali Muslim. A Contradiction in Terms?", *Comparative Studies of South Asia, Africa and the Middle East*, vol. XVI, 2, 1997; republished herein and in Mushirul Hasan, ed., *Islam, Communities and the Nation*, New Delhi, 1998.

———, *The Disinherited. Migrants, Minorities and Citizenship in South Asia*, Ranikhet, forthcoming.

Chattopadhyay, Haraprasad, *Internal Migration in India. A Case Study of Bengal*, Calcutta, 1987.

Choudhury, Yousuf, *The Roots and Tales of Bangladeshi Settlers*, London, 1993.

Christensen, A.S., *Cassiodorus, Jordanes and the History of the Goths. Studies in a Migration Myth*, Copenhagen, 2002.

Clifford, James, *Routes. Travel and Translation in the Late Twentieth Century*, Cambridge, Mass., 1997.

Eaton, Richard *The Rise of Islam and the Bengal Frontier, 1204–1760*, Berkeley, 1993.

Ghosh, Papiya, *Partition and the South Asian Diaspora. Extending the Subcontinent*, London, New York, and Delhi, 2007.

Glazer, Nathan, and Daniel Moynihan, *Beyond the Melting Pot: The Negroes, Puerto Ricans, Jews, Italians and Irish of New York City*, Cambridge MA, 1963, in Brubaker, Rogers, "The Return of Assimilation" (*vide supra*).

Ho, Engseng, *The Graves of Tarim. Genealogy and Mobility across the Indian Ocean*, Berkeley, Los Angeles and London, 2006.

Horowitz, Daniel, *The Deadly Ethnic Riot*, Berkeley, 2001.

Ilias, Ahmed, *Biharis. The Indian Emigres in Bangladesh: An Objective Analysis*, Syedpur, 2003.

Lachenicht, Susanne, "Huguenot Immigrants and the Formation of National Identities, 1548–1787", *Historical Journal*, vol. 50:2 (2007).

Leach, Kenneth, "Caroline Adams: Youth Worker Devoted to the Welfare of London's Bangladeshi Community", *The Guardian* (Obituaries), 23 June 2001.

Levitt, Peggy, *The Transnational Villagers*, Berkeley and Los Angeles, 2001.

Mansergh, N., and E.R. Lumby, ed., *The Transfer of Power*, vol. IX, London, 1980.

Markovits, Claude, *et al.*, ed., *Mobile People and Itinerant Cultures in South Asia, 1750–1950*, London, 2006.

Migration: a Welcome Opportunity, RSA Migration Commission Report, 2005

Quamruzzaman, Quazi, *et al.*, "The Camp-dwelling Biharis and Bangladesh", *New Age*, 17 September 2007.

Quddus, Md Ruhul, "Recognising Citizenship Right", *The Independent* (Dhaka), 6 October 2007.

Rose, S.O., "Race, Empire and British Wartime Identity, 1939–45", *Historical Research*, vol. 74, 184 (2002).

Roy, Tirthankar, and Douglas Haynes, "Conceiving Mobility: Migration of Handloom Weavers in Precolonial and Colonial India", *Indian Economic and Social History Review*, 1999.

Salter, Joseph, *The Asiatic in England. Sketches of Sixteen Years of Work among Orientals*, London, 1873.

———, *The East in the West. Work among the Asiatics and Africans in London*, London, 1895.

Salter, Mark, *Rights of Passage: The Passport in International Relations*, Boulder, 2003.

Schiller, Nina Glick, and Georges Eugene Fouron, *Georges woke up Laughing. Long-distance Nationalism and the Search for Home*, Chapel Hill, 2001.

Schivelbusch, Wolfgang, *The Culture of Defeat. On National Trauma, Mourning and Recovery* (trans. Jefferson Chase), London, 2003.

Tololyan, Khachig, "Elites and Instituions in the Armenian Transnation", *International Migration Review*, vol. 37, 3, 2003.

Torpey, John, *The Invention of the Passport: Surveillance, Citizenship & the State*, Cambridge, 2000.

Turack, Daniel, *The Passport in International Law*, Lexington, 1972.

Uddin, Sufia M., *Constructing Bangladesh: Religion, Ethnicity, and Language in an Islamic Nation*, Chapel Hill, 2006.

Visram, Rosina, *Ayahs, Lascars and Princes. Indians in Britain 1700–1947*, London, 1986.

Waters, C., "'Dark Strangers in our Midst': Discourses on Race and Nation in Britain, 1947–63", *Journal of British Studies*, vol. 36, 2, 1997.

———, "J.B. Priestly", in Susan Pederson and Peter Mandler, ed., *After the Victorians. Private Conscience and Public Duty in Modern Britain*, London, 1994.

Weight, R., *Patriots. National Identity in Britain, 1940–2000,* London, 2003.

Zahur, A.B.M.S., "Enrolling Stranded Pakistanis", *The Daily Star*, 1 October 2007.

Zamindar, Vazira, *The Long Partition and the Making of Modern South Asia: Refugees, Boundaries, Histories*, New York, 2007.

Zolberg, Aristide, and Peter Benda, ed., *Global Migrants, Global Refugees: Problems and Solutions*, New York and Oxford, 2001.

7

Dispositions and Destinations

"Mobility Capital" and Migration in the Bengal Delta 1947–2007

In 1947, a new international border cut through the deltaic plains of Bengal. A consequence of India's Partition along religious lines, Radcliffe's border divided Bengal – the largest and most populous province of British India – between India and Pakistan. Over the next two decades, between twelve and thirteen million Hindus and Muslims crossed that border between East and West Bengal as refugees, looking to rebuild their lives in the "right" nation. Millions of others instead stayed where they were as uneasy minorities, but among them countless numbers were internally displaced.

In 1971, civil war broke out in East Bengal when Bengali nationalists fought Pakistan's army in one of the most brutal conflicts in recent times, and another ten million people fled to India.

Acknowledgements: I am grateful to the Arts and Humanities Research Council, UK, which funded the Bengal Diaspora project, of which I was principal investigator. I am indebted to my co-investigator Claire Alexander, and research assistants Annu Jalais and Shahzad Firoz. Unless otherwise specified, the interviews drawn upon here were conducted, translated, and transcribed between 2007 and 2009 by Annu Jalais. All names of interviewees have been changed, except where our respondents, such as Jinnahbhai, said they wanted to be identified.

When the war ended many were able to return home, but a second wave of violence then swept through what was now the independent nation of Bangladesh.[1] This time its target was Urdu-speaking "Biharis", most of them Partition refugees, who were believed to have collaborated with the Pakistani regime the war had overthrown.[2] Thousands of them died in grisly reprisals against their community. A few were able to escape abroad, and most of those who remained inside Bangladesh were internally displaced. To this day, many live in the makeshift camps set up by international agencies after the 1971 war.[3]

Two surges of nation-making thus tore through the fabric of Bengal in the latter half of the twentieth century, generating some of the largest migrations in recorded history. One notable feature of these upheavals was that the overwhelming majority of the refugees they produced have remained within the region. Most of those that crossed international borders went just across the Radcliffe Line to neighbouring cities, towns, and hamlets in the other part of Bengal; only between 1 and 2 per cent migrated to the West in this period, most of them to Britain.

More arresting are the patterns of movement and settlement in this diaspora. The largest numbers of the post-Partition Muslim migrants in Bengal, who are the focus here, crossed no international border and remained inside the Indian province of West Bengal. Many have been internally displaced and ghettoised.[4]

[1] "Home" often had to be wholly reconstructed, since few communities survived the war intact. Kamaluddin, "Refugee Problems in Bangladesh".

[2] The term "Bihari" has come to be used to describe all Urdu speakers in the region, though by no means do all of them come from Bihar. Rahman and van Schendel, "'I Am not a Refugee': Rethinking Partition Migration". The term has acquired pejorative connotations; hence the quote marks.

[3] Ghosh, *Partition and the South Asian Diaspora*; Ilias, *Biharis, the Indian Emigres in Bangladesh*.

[4] I have described these processes elsewhere: Chatterji, *The Spoils of Partition*, pp. 188–94. Also see Bose, *Calcutta, 1964*; and Siddiqui, *The Muslims of Calcutta*.

A considerable number gravitated close to the new border that divides India from Pakistan/Bangladesh (see Fig. 7.1).[5]

Smaller but nonetheless significant numbers of Muslims, perhaps three to four million, have migrated to East Pakistan since 1947.[6] Of these, maybe half moved to urban centres, but only to some specific towns – they shunned others.[7] Most of the rest resettled in clusters on the Pakistan side of the mainly rural border. In consequence, the border area – at 4095 kilometres one of the world's longest – has become a 100 kilometre-wide zone populated mainly by displacees and refugees (see Fig. 7.2).

Prima facie, then, the Bengal diaspora appears to lend powerful support to Aristide Zolberg's two most significant claims: first, that "nation-making is a refugee generating process",[8] and second, that the vast majority of the world's refugees since the Second World War have stayed on within their regions of origin within the developing world, with only a tiny minority migrating to the countries of the industrialised West.[9] Zolberg also observed that most of the world's refugees have remained close to the borders of their countries of origin. In this respect too, Bengali migrations exemplify these larger global patterns.

This essay, a product of an interdisciplinary and international team research project on migration in Bengal since 1947, explores why the Bengal diaspora followed these patterns. It draws on oral testimony gathered from 226 migrants in different settings

[5] Ibid., 188–9; *Census of India, 1961*, vol. 16, part I-A, book (1) (hereafter *1961 Census of India*), Delhi: Manager of Publications, 1963, p. 222.

[6] Kamaluddin, "Refugee Problems"; Rahman and van Schendel, "I Am not a Refugee".

[7] *Census of Pakistan, 1951*: vol. 3, East Bengal (hereafter *1951 Census of Pakistan*), p. 39.

[8] Zolberg, "The Formation of New States as a Refugee-Generating Process", pp. 24–38.

[9] Zolberg and Benda, eds, *Global Migrants Global Refugees*, p. 9. Also see, in the same volume, Schmeidl's quantitative evidence supporting this assertion in her paper, "Conflict and Forced Migration: A Quantitative Review".

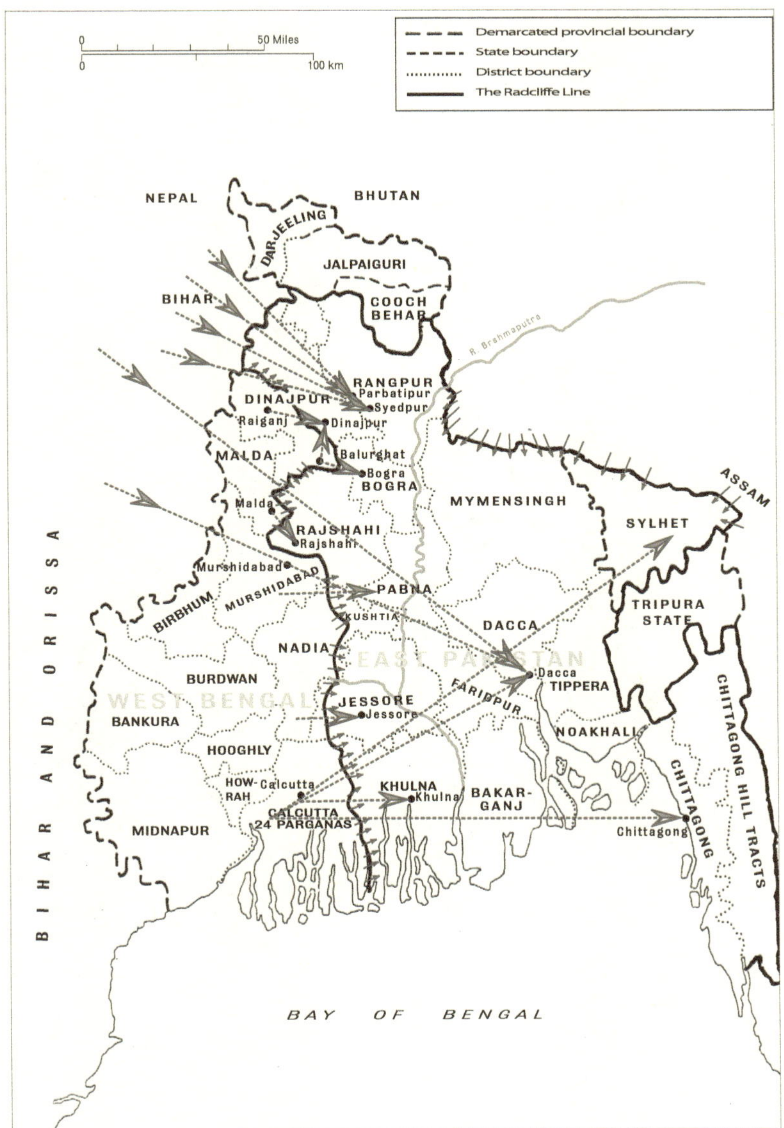

Fig. 7.1: Migration of Muslims from West Bengal, Bihar, and Assam to East Pakistan, 1946–1970

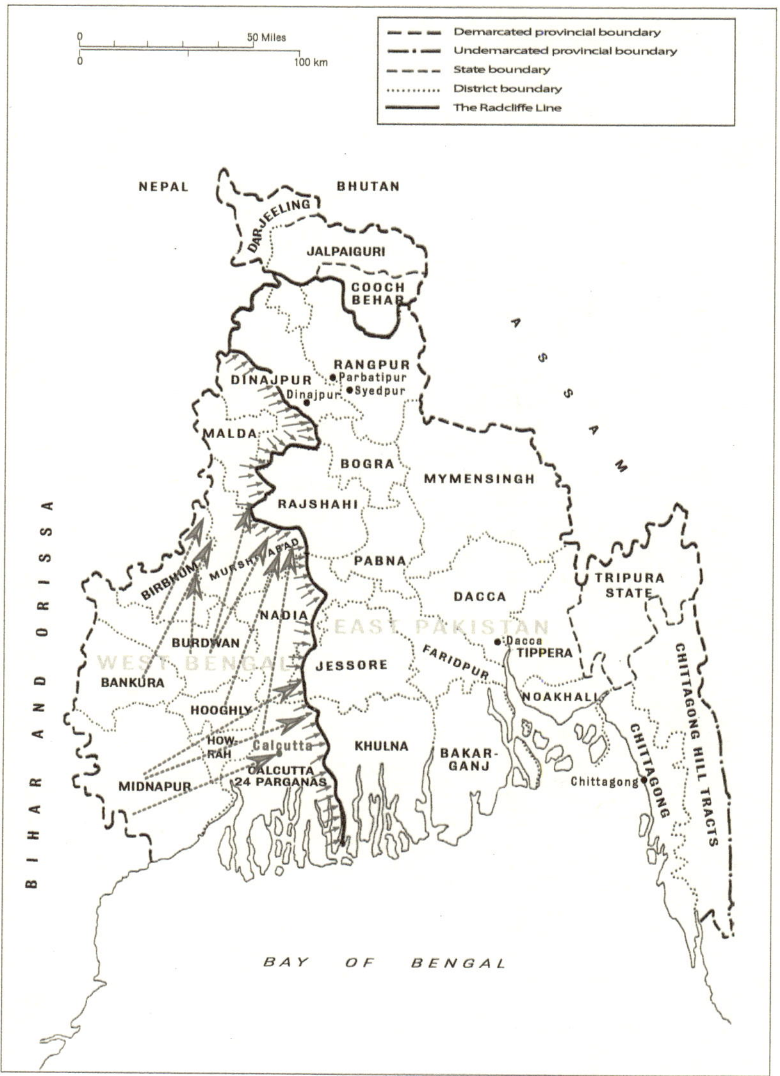

Fig. 7.2: Internal Displacement of Muslims in West Bengal

in India, Bangladesh, and Britain (see Table 7.1).[10] I will suggest why some Bengalis crossed borders and others did not; why most moved short distances within the delta; why so many huddled in the long shadows of the new national borders; and why so few embarked on a passage to faraway places in the West. I will explore the complex calculations that migrants made about whether and when to leave and where to go. By uncovering the subtle interplay between migrants' agency and structures of coercion, and between histories of mobility and attachment in the shaping of their choices, we can illuminate how the recurrent patterns identified by Zolberg were produced in a regional context of critical but unexplored significance.[11]

My aim is not simply to reinforce Zolberg's thesis. His focus is upon refugees who have crossed international borders, and that obscures other fascinating and important patterns, including those of internal displacements within new nation-states. Refugee studies have not adequately addressed a question: Why do some stay on while others flee? We need to understand the inertia of those who would or could not move during great upheavals. Hence this study is as concerned with stasis as with movement. It follows that one imperative here is better to understand the nature of the brakes upon "cumulative causation" in the migration process. In a brilliant and influential essay published in 1990, Douglas Massey argued that a dynamic interplay between processes gives migration, particularly across borders, "a strong internal momentum".[12] Massey placed migrant networks at the heart of the process of cumulative causation, since they minimised the risks and

[10] Some of the project's interviews are available on its website: "Bangla stories" at http://www.banglastories.org/.

[11] Schmeidl's data set does not consider refugee outflows produced by India's Partition, despite their scale. She does, however, include in her calculus refugee movement during the Bangladesh war: "Conflict and Forced Migration", p. 70.

[12] Massey, "Social Structure, Household Strategies", pp. 3–26 (p. 3).

Table 7.1

Field Site	*Number of Respondents*
Dhaka, Bangladesh	32
Malda/Dinajpur/Rangpur border villages, India and Bangladesh	28
Syedpur, Bangladesh	20
South, 24 Parganas/Khulna/ Sundarbans border villages, India Bangladesh	25 Bangladesh and 16 West Bengal
Calcutta, India	18
Tower Hamlets, London	30
Newham, London	20
Oldham, Greater Manchester	20
Dispersed restaurant workers, UK	17

maximised the advantages associated with migration. Yet by uncovering the forces of inertia that persuade many people to stay where they are even when they are in danger, and by highlighting the fragility of some networks, I will suggest that this persuasive model needs to be tested and qualified.

Another key question I will address is the impact that new national borders have on older forms of mobility in this region. I draw on historical research to tease out the continuing interconnections between historic patterns and micro-mobilities, and more recent regional, national, international, and trans-oceanic migrations.[13] In doing so, I challenge the assumption that "forced migrations" caused by political upheavals such as Partition are fundamentally different phenomena from the "economic migrations" driven by the demands of labour markets.

For these reasons, the unit of analysis is a region, the Bengal delta, which possessed a complex history of internal and trans-oceanic migration long before it was divided.[14] After 1947,

[13] I thus develop, in a rather different context, the research agenda outlined by Moch in "Dividing Time".

[14] Chattopadhyaya, *Internal Migration in India.*

neither government in divided Bengal took proactive steps to rehabilitate refugees, and hence this region (unlike Punjab, where the government intervened vigorously in rehabilitation) is an ideal context to study the agency of migrants as they sought to rehabilitate themselves.[15]

The migrants whose stories form the basis of this study are without exception Muslims. There are sound reasons for this focus. Almost all Bengalis who migrated to the United Kingdom after Partition were Muslims and, given that my purpose is to connect and compare international, regional, and local mobilities, a focus on Muslims enables secure comparisons to be made. Nevertheless, the conclusions are relevant for non-Muslims as well, since Bengali Hindu migration during the same period followed an almost identical pattern.[16]

In what follows I will argue that the delta's migrants tended to have very particular bundles of assets, competences, or dispositions, which are described, after Bourdieu, as "mobility capital".[17] Bengal's migrant communities were seen to display distinctive characteristics relative to the general population. These included relatively high levels of literacy or other portable skills (in many cases artisanship and hereditary craftsmanship) and some transferable assets. Migrants tended to be youthful, able-bodied, and healthy, and their numbers included more men than women. All our

[15] Randhawa, *Out of the Ashes*.

[16] Of the ten million Hindu refugees who migrated from East Pakistan to West Bengal after 1947, 40 per cent were drawn to cities, especially Calcutta, where they have tended to live in clusters. Like their Muslim counterparts, the remaining six million ended up on the Indian side of the rural border. Chatterji, *Spoils of Partition*, pp. 105–208. Those who remained in East Pakistan/Bangladesh have also been displaced in large numbers, and have tended to cluster in ever-shrinking urban ghettos or in rural borderlands close to the frontiers of India. Kamal, "The Population Trajectories of Bangladesh and West Bengal".

[17] Bourdieu, "The Forms of Capital".

migrants proved to have dense networks of contacts garnered through, and obligations earned by, personal histories of mobility. By contrast, those who stayed behind tended to lack some or all of these attributes, or were held back by complex ties or countervailing obligations. Furthermore, we will see that the make-up of a migrant's particular bundle of mobility capital influenced the trajectory of his or her movement. People with similar assets and competences tended to head towards similar destinations. Choices that puzzled observers at the time prove intelligible when viewed from this analytical perspective.

"National" Mobility: Migration to Urban Centres in the New Nation-State

Commenting on the first (1951) census of independent Pakistan, the census commissioner of East Bengal, like his counterpart in West Bengal, was baffled by the sheer numbers in which refugees flocked to a few particular towns.[18] These included Dhaka, the new capital of East Pakistan, as well as Dinajpur, Bogra, and Rajshahi, all administrative hubs close to the new border with India.[19] The railway townships of Syedpur and Parbatipur to the north were also favourite destinations, as to a lesser extent was Chittagong, a large and growing port city in eastern Bengal (see Fig. 7.1).

The commissioner might have been less mystified had he considered the fact that, long before Partition, these towns had been magnets for migrants. Since the late nineteenth century, "government bahadur", the British Raj in India, had been not only the country's biggest employer but also a powerful motor driving the wheels of Indian mobility. The public services and their specialist branches had been manned at their lower levels entirely by Indians, as were the railways and the army. Public servants

[18] *Census of India, 1951*, vol. VI, part 1-A (hereafter *1951 Census of India*), Delhi: Manager of Publications, 1953, p. 305.

[19] *1951 Census of Pakistan*, p. 39.

had typically circulated between Calcutta and the district towns in different "postings". For many decades, East Bengal's subdivisional headquarters, towns that included Dhaka, Dinajpur, Bogra, and Rajshahi, had attracted white-collar migrants.[20] In the early twentieth century, railways were extended into eastern Bengal and Assam, chiefly to transport tea to the ports at Calcutta and Chittagong, and thousands of men were recruited from North India, particularly from Bihar, to build them.[21] Large railway townships sprang up around the huge locomotive workshops at Syedpur and Parbatipur.[22] So these were not just any towns: they were towns that before Partition had drawn large numbers of migrants from the very regions that produced refugees after it.

The migrants who flocked to these towns prove to have had distinctive profiles. Before Partition, they had been overwhelmingly city-dwellers or townsfolk. Of those who headed to Dhaka, most were well educated, some were exceptionally qualified, and a significant number had worked for government as part of the North Indian Urdu-speaking service elite, about whom so much has been written.[23] After Partition, every government employee was offered the choice of serving either in India or in Pakistan, and most Muslims opted for Pakistan.[24]

It is a mistake to perceive this choice as having been wholly "free", however. The Calcutta Killings in August 1946,[25] and particularly the communal violence in Bihar in October and November that

[20] Chattopadhyaya, *Internal Migration.*

[21] Ibid., 47.

[22] Kerr, *Railways in Modern India.*

[23] The classic work remains Robinson, *Separatism among Indian Muslims.*

[24] All but one of undivided Bengal's nineteen Muslim Indian Civil Service officers opted to serve in Pakistan. Chakrabarty, *With Dr. B.C. Roy*, p. 45. Nationally, only 12 per cent of Muslim officers opted for India, and similar patterns were found in lower levels of the services. Government of India, Ministry of Home Affairs, 51(346)/48-Public.

[25] Das, *Communal Riots in Bengal.*

year,[26] had already driven thousands of Muslims from their homes, and many who had survived these horrors had lost faith in the capacity of Hindu-dominated governments to protect them. Those reluctant to move – riots notwithstanding – were "encouraged" to do so by threats, often quite naked, from Hindu vigilantes,[27] and also by more insidious persuasions from the Indian government.[28] So these Muslim "optees", as they were known in the bureaucratic jargon of the time,[29] faced subtle and not-so-subtle pressures to migrate to Pakistan. It also quickly became apparent that there were openings for them in East Bengal. In the first year after Partition, over a million upper- and middle-class (*bhadralok* or "genteel") Hindus had quit East Bengal for India.[30] In consequence, the Government of East Pakistan faced a formidable challenge in trying to fill key posts in the administration vacated by Hindu officials. This gave educated Muslims many employment opportunities in the new state. And since Dhaka, the new capital of the state, was where most of these jobs were, that was where most of these highly educated migrants headed. These were people who had traditionally worked for the state, and the nation-state now became the chief facilitator of their mobility. As with the millions of *ashraf* (elite) refugees who went to West Pakistan at this time, many of the migrants interviewed in the present study felt drawn to the project of building Pakistan, and to put their skills at its service.[31]

Migrants to nearby district towns across the border also tended

[26] Ghosh, *Partition*, pp. 6–10.

[27] In the summer of 1947, several Muslim policemen were murdered in broad daylight in Calcutta. No one was ever brought to book. Government of Bengal, Intelligence Branch, files 614/47 and 1123/47.

[28] Government of India, Ministry of Home Affairs, F.40/5/48-Appts.

[29] Rahman and van Schendel, '"I Am not a Refugee"'.

[30] Chakrabarti, *The Marginal Men*, p. 1.

[31] A classic exposition is Ali, *Emergence of Pakistan*. Also see Siddiqui, *Partition and the Making of the Mohajir Mindset*.

to have middle-class backgrounds. Their assets before Partition typically included medium-sized landholdings, some modest educational qualifications, and a little gold and cash. Several had previously held posts in these parts of eastern Bengal during their service careers, and had friends, relatives, or contacts there who could help them to migrate.

Anisa Banu is a schoolteacher at Syedpur in her early thirties. Her family's story reflects the complex mix of imperatives that informed their emigration to this particular town: "Our family is originally from Mungher [Monghyr] in Bihar. My grandfather was a railway employee and we had relatives here in Syedpur. My father's family came here in 1946 just after there were riots in Bihar. We came to the largest rail factory in Eastern India. My grandfather said, 'We're Pakistani and we're going to go to Pakistan.'" Anisa's grandfather had connections at many points along the Eastern Indian railways and had family in Syedpur, "the largest rail factory", and so there were persuasive personal and pragmatic reasons why he decided to go to Syedpur (and nowhere else) when riots broke out in Bihar. But also palpable in Anisa's testimony is her grandfather's strong identification with the idea of Pakistan, and it would be a mistake to overlook this. It remains difficult for "Biharis" in today's Bangladesh to speak of their family histories as "loyal Pakistanis", so the fact that Anisa volunteered this information is poignant and revealing.

In the early 1950s, Pakistan, like India, embarked on development designed to build a "modern" nation,[32] and families like Anisa's tied their own futures to that project. Anisa's father went on to work as a senior technician at the Power Development Board. In a suburb of Dinajpur town, not far from Syedpur, which is populated mainly by refugees, Jinnahbhai, the middle-aged and educated head of a local NGO, explained, "The place we are in

[32] The East Pakistan Industrial Development Corporation was set up in 1950. Ilias, *Biharis*, p. 61; Haines, "Concrete 'Progress'", pp. 179–200.

is a satellite town – an *uposhahr* – it has quite a few engineering and administrative offices. Every immigrant was given a small flat with an attached bathroom and kitchen. The sewage system, electrification, water supply was all very modern . . ."

The refugee rehabilitation regime, as Uditi Sen has noted, was an arena in which the Indian state forged many crucial aspects of its practices of governance,[33] and Jinnahbhai's account suggests that something of that drive – to turn refugees into model citizens of a modern state – was at work in East Pakistan. For their part, many educated *mohajirs* (as refugees in Pakistan were known) appear to have embraced the development project with enthusiasm: the very fact that Jinnahbhai's parents named him after the Quaid-i-Azam says much about the depth of their attachment to the idea of Pakistan.

But state patronage, while important, was not the only force driving this wave of migration into specific towns in East Pakistan. Twenty-six-year-old Mushirul Huq's story shows how a complex mix of connections forged in "British times", kinship networks, and access to capital enabled a family to make their move. In 1947, Mushir's family moved from the Benares region of North India to Parbatipur, a small railway town close to Syedpur:

> My maternal grandfather was an army officer [who came over] from Benaras . . . [His family] set up a confectionery shop in Parbatipur [sometime after 1947] . . . My [maternal aunt's son] was Parbatipur's Chairman . . . My paternal grandfather used to work in a train-making workshop or a "loco-set", and came from India to Parbatipur around 1947 . . . Before 1971 [when the civil war forced this "Bihari" family to flee Parbatipur] my father used to work at the Municipality or City Corporation of Parbatipur . . . he used to read and write well.

This family, which went on to become a leading light in the Bihari community in Parbatipur before 1971, had strong pre-

[33] Sen, "Refugees and the Politics of Nation-Building in India".

existing links with both the army and the railways – two well-established vectors of mobility in the region – and had relatives well connected in the municipal administration. These overlapping networks enabled them to move across the border, quickly establish themselves, and do well in their new setting. They also had enough capital to start a small business, assets typical of many other refugees who flocked to these border towns. Describing the suburb of Dinajpur where he lives, Jinnahbhai explained:

> [This] is a place of migrants – especially of rich people, many from West Bengal: first and mainly from [West] Dinajpur [which remained in India], then Malda, then Birbhum and Calcutta; quite a few came from UP and Bihar too . . . These people who came were rich; they did not necessarily "come with land" but they bought cash and gold and started businesses here. Many got government assistance like loans and land to start factories because those who came from India had the know-how, since mainly the educated and the landed came . . .

Particularly revealing is Jinnahbhai's reference to knowhow. He appears to be speaking not just of formal knowledge such as degrees and qualifications, but something more subtle and complex: worldly knowledge, about how to work the state, how to push for "loans and assistance", how to get the licences and permissions needed to set up small businesses, and a pragmatic understanding of how to deploy networks of kin, class, and caste to survive in a new place. Again, this echoes the adeptness of middle-class Hindu refugees in deploying all their connections to gain a foothold in their new setting, calling in familial and caste-based obligations as well as solidarities of class and region.[34]

When pressed to explain what he meant about refugees "who came with land", Jinnahbhai identified another trend, built around another kind of competence. This was particularly marked among refugees settled in small border towns. Many heads of migrating families were local magnates who had made deals to swap land

[34] Ibid., ch. 3.

with Hindus migrating in the other direction. Musa Ali, a young man of twenty-three who now works for a local association in Rampur, explains that his father, together with six of his brothers, migrated to East Pakistan in 1971. Musa's father was scion of a wealthy family in Malda in north-west Bengal that had owned 400 bighas, or over 100 acres, a sizeable amount in land-hungry Bengal. He had exchanged property with a local Hindu he knew who owned an estate of a similar size and who was anxious to move from East Pakistan to India during the civil war: "They came and lived with Ossini babu – he was a [Hindu] joddar [a *jotedar* or petty landlord] who had 400 bighas of land . . . We also owned 400 bighas of land in India (in Kaliaganj) so we got his land . . . and he got ours . . . We also exchanged our leases (*dalils*)."

Faruq Hussain, aged sixty-seven, now the modestly prosperous owner of a rice-husking mill, came over in the same way: "In our village [in South Dinajpur] we exchanged land with [a Hindu landholder] who used to live in Parameshpur. They had about the same amount of land as us – 45 bighas . . . We came over because . . . we were being continually harassed. [The Hindus] never let us celebrate *qurbani* [animal sacrifice] . . . they used to play the drums loudly during *namaaz* [daily prayer] time and if we ever complained they would beat us up."[35]

The success of such deals depended critically on trust between the two parties to the exchange, trust which, in times of such extreme hostility between Hindus and Muslims, was itself a remarkable phenomenon. Suraiyya Begum's father, who had been President of the Union Board in Itahar in West Dinajpur,[36] and who came over in 1956 after exchanging 450 bighas of land with Hindu landowners, "decided to settle in Borobondor because he

[35] Nakatani's finding that many immigrants had exchanged land in this way is confirmed by this data: it was common in the rural borderlands. Nakatani, "Away from Home".

[36] A Union was a group of *taluks*, the smallest unit of administration for revenue-gathering purposes in British India.

had many Hindu friends and acquaintances here. It was one of my father's Hindu friends – a high court judge – who asked him to settle here. It was he who brought [my father] to his house and oversaw everything." Migrants who were able to make such land exchanges either knew each other well, as did Suraiyya Begum's father and his friend, or were known for their probity. Their wealth was reinforced by robust local networks and reputations as "men of honour". Such attributes were as crucial as were their riches and formal qualifications in enabling their migratory ventures, particularly when this involved exchanges of property where claims to title could not be legally enforced if trust was breached.

Thus most Muslims who migrated to urban centres and small towns in East Pakistan had rich and complex bundles of assets and competences. They possessed the goods of education, land, cash, and gold in varying amounts, as well as local standing, networks of contacts, and the knowhow to deploy these assets to make their migrations viable. Indeed, they seem also ideal candidates for a move to Britain, where post-war shortages created a labour market for skilled manpower from the empire, and where pay and benefits were much higher than in the delta. But well-to-do Bengalis and Biharis seem not to have even considered this option; they chose instead to go to East Pakistan.

"Anonymous" is a landholder in his late fifties, from a modestly landed and literate family background, who left kinsfolk in India and was reluctant to reveal his name. When pressed to explain why some members of his family decided to move to Pakistan, he was expansive about their expectations in migrating to the new nation:

> My forefathers decided to come here because this was Pakistan. The main fact was that Hindustan [India] was for Hindus and Pakistan was for Muslims. Around 1965 some Muslims from our village exchanged land and hearth [with Hindus crossing in the opposite direction] to come over to this part . . . I was a student then, in class 8 . . . After putting into context the bleak future that we, as young men, would face in India, we came over. We will be able to

> claim our rights in Pakistan, we thought . . . I am at peace here. I can travel all over Bangladesh and I don't feel afraid. I can also progress . . . I can talk to our politicians, to the military – I feel I can actually go up to them and talk to them and that they will protect me if I ask them.

His words reflect one of our study's most unexpected findings, namely the strength of the sense of entitlement among these migrants to the goods of national citizenship in Pakistan, and the extent to which this influenced their decision to migrate. A surprisingly large number of our interviewees, even those from small villages, had been actively involved in politics before Partition, and they migrated not only because they wanted to place their skills at the service of "their" new nation but also because they believed they had a better chance of regaining their standing in a country that was "for Muslims". Suraiyya's story put this into sharp focus: "My parents came in 1956 . . . My father was a landowner in Itahar; he was the Union President of Itahar . . . We came over because after the country's division my father thought we would be better off in a Muslim country . . . After coming here he was selected ward chairman because he was so influential. The government gave him that position. Later my elder brother was the chairman of the municipality for two years."

Nafissa Begum's father was a highly educated schoolmaster with a Masters degree in history and an excellent command of English. He migrated after being passed over several times for promotions given to less qualified Hindus: "He repeatedly asked his colleagues why he had not been promoted and he slowly understood that this was because he was Muslim. He then realized the future would be bleak for us [his children], that we wouldn't stand a chance as equals even if we were meritorious and did well at school, and so he decided to migrate to Pakistan . . . This event happened in the 1950s, after which he resigned. We knew that in high posts in India the percentage of Muslims is practically zero." In Nafissa's testimony we see just how much it rankled middle-class

Muslims in West Bengal to see local Hindus who were "beneath" them being unjustly promoted over them. For many, it was this bitterness more than any simple cost-benefit calculation that drove them to migrate to Pakistan with their families. Their accounts lend support to Stark and Taylor's findings about the powerful role that a sense of relative deprivation plays in encouraging individuals and families to migrate.[37]

Another recurring and related theme in these migrants' stories is an obsession with their dwindling status at "home". Thus Abdul Rahim, whose landed family had come over in 1950, said that his "grandfather's elder brother . . . was the village headman [*pradhan*] but [after Partition] nobody cared whether he was headman or not." This theme also comes through in the determination these families demonstrated, when they migrated, to exchange like for like, whether in terms of their jobs, landholdings, or even specificities of bricks and mortar. Suraiyya Begum's father did not leave India immediately in 1947; he waited until he had finished the complex business of exchanging all his land, "so that he could initially have a foot in both sides whilst he moved his assets across", and he moved only after he had built in Dinajpur a house of the same style and quality as that which he was leaving behind. Nafissa's father, the schoolteacher, waited patiently "for a good opportunity to present itself in relation to the selling of his land", which he exchanged "with that of a Hindu gentleman". Because that gentleman's house was of an inferior quality ("made of mud", while his own house was a pucca, or brick structure), he made sure that he was compensated by an extra ten bighas of land in the transaction.

This context of middle-class anxieties about the loss of status and the drive to regain it is key to understanding why so many Muslims from Bengal and Bihar chose to migrate to East Pakistan

[37] Stark and Taylor, "Relative Deprivation and International Migration", pp. 1–14.

rather than to Britain, where few believed they would be adequately "respected" or "recognised". Only in Pakistan could they hope to achieve the dignity of full citizenship, and assuage their deep and painful sense of personal and communal dishonour. Of course it helped that there were vacancies they could fill in Pakistan, but the fact that so many left several years after Partition indicates that it was not just the immediate opportunities for advancement that drove them. These stories from the delta bear out Todaro's insight that in less-developed countries labour migration is driven less by wage differentials than by the probability of finding employment.[38] But they also suggest a rider, that migrants are influenced by expectations of finding employment *commensurate with their standing*, and by aspirations of upward mobility for their children. These less tangible benefits must be taken into account for a full understanding of why migrants leave home for other lands.

Blue-collar workers make up a large segment of the migrant populations in these towns and cities of East Pakistan. Many came from artisan communities and possessed skills in demand in the new "national" industries of Pakistan. They also had contacts – friends, relatives, and former colleagues – who helped them to relocate. Several had worked in the railways before Partition, and the railways were the critical pathways along which they now moved.

Mohammad Shaffiquddin's story captures the particular mix of skills and connections that made this kind of mobility possible. He is a "Bihari" who lives in Syedpur. Known locally as "Shaffiq Chacha" (Uncle Shaffiq), he is now in his seventies:

> I was born in 1935 and came here on the 17th of August 1947 with my maternal uncle. He used to work at the rail workshop of Jamalpur . . . [After he came over] he worked in a foundry workshop of the railways . . . I used to be a rail power operator – my first port of call was Khulna, which I joined in 1963. After that I was transferred to Santahar – it used to be a big junction – again as a rail power

[38] Todaro, "A Model of Labour Migration", pp. 138–48.

[electricity] operator. From there I was posted to Pakshi Rail Office and then to Amnura, then to TNG Ghat in Gaibandha district, and from there in 1971 back to Santahar.

Indeed, it was the extensive and effective network of friendships and allegiances he had formed during the course of a peripatetic life on the railways that enabled Shaffiq Chacha – unlike the many Urdu speakers who were killed at Santahar – to survive the horrors of 1971. During the riots, a former colleague gave him shelter, and later, when things were quieter, helped him get another railway job.

Another prominent group among the urban refugee population was mill-hands, including many skilled weavers who had migrated to Calcutta from upcountry long before Partition,[39] and then migrated again in the late 1940s and early 1950s to East Pakistan, after anti-Muslim riots broke out in the mill districts of Calcutta and Howrah. In 1950, the Pakistan government established the East Pakistan Industrial Development Corporation, and during the 1950s and 1960s, seventy-four jute mills, thirty-six cotton mills, and ten sugar mills were established under its aegis, as were paper mills at Khulna, Karnafuli, and Paksi.[40] This created jobs for skilled weavers and mill-hands in East Pakistan's rapidly growing industries. Under General Ayub Khan's regime (1958–69), the Pakistani state began to invest in infrastructure and housing,[41] and skilled masons, plumbers, and carpenters were much in demand. Among the refugees we interviewed was Abdul Rasul, now of Chamra Godown Camp in Niyammatpur, who migrated from Bhagalpur in India to Parbatipur after Partition. Abdul is "a carpenter, our whole *gushti* [lineage] is of carpenters." Owais, originally of Shibpur in India, was a plumber with a sideline as a marriage broker, a business through which he had forged contacts

[39] On artisanal mobility in South Asia, see Haynes and Roy, "Conceiving Mobility", pp. 35–67.

[40] Ilias, *Biharis*, 61.

[41] Daechsel, "Sovereignty, Governmentality and Development", pp. 131–57.

that facilitated his migration. During this period, Pakistan's army grew by leaps and bounds; and many of our respondents had relatives who were employed by the armed forces in various (though usually quite humble) capacities.

Most of these working-class migrants were employed by the Pakistani state in the railways or the army, or worked in state-backed private enterprises such as the jute and construction industries. Former railway workers are prominent among the group of "Bihari" people in Bangladesh who, since 1971, have described themselves as "Stranded Pakistanis" and have waged a campaign demanding "repatriation" to (West) Pakistan. They insist that they are Pakistan's "true" citizens, having migrated to East Bengal after 1947 in order to contribute to the building of the Muslim nation-state.[42] By contrast, the blue-collar migrants we interviewed made no such claims, and gave much more mundane accounts of their migration to the eastern wing of Pakistan. Their testimony suggests that they left India because Partition and communal violence had rendered them physically insecure and economically vulnerable. They moved to Pakistan as refugees because they had contacts and connections forged "in British times" through older forms of mobility, and because Pakistan appeared to offer them physical safety and some prospect of employment. They simply deployed old skills and old networks and adapted them to new circumstances. State formation and nation-building provided the context for their migration, but they appear to have been driven to move primarily by a pragmatic search for security and survival.

Migration and Displacement in the Rural Borderlands

Radcliffe's border of 1947 cut through a landscape that was overwhelmingly rural. It passed through emerald paddy fields, dense thickets of bamboo and date palm and forests of sal, across

[42] Ilias, *Biharis*, pp. 150–3; Ghosh, *Partition*, pp. 50–6.

shallow fish ponds and mangrove swamps, and along sluggish muddy rivers. Yet within a few decades of Partition this bucolic setting was transformed in astonishing fashion and beyond recognition by dense settlements of migrants.[43] Today, refugees and the displaced cluster along both sides of its length; crowded villages of refugees jostle against the settlements of people who stayed and communities of the internally displaced.[44]

Unlike the urban centres discussed above, before Partition these agrarian tracts had hardly been magnets for migration, and in fact they tended to be zones of net emigration, exporting male migrants to other parts of the region.[45] In the last fifty years, though, they have been transformed into teeming zones of immigration, a fact that the authorities on both sides regard with bemusement and unease.[46]

Since there have been few official enquiries or scholarly studies into this remarkable phenomenon, Annu Jalais, one of two research assistants on our project team, conducted over sixty interviews in villages in these borderland zones, both in West Bengal in India and in Bangladesh. Over fifteen months in 2007–8, she criss-crossed the region, travelling over dirt tracks on a motorcycle pillion, often the only motorised transport available in these parts.

One trend quickly became apparent from this extraordinary set of interviews. While almost all the migrants who cluster along Bangladesh's border with India are peasants, they tend to fall into two very distinct groups. The first is a large and very visible segment living particularly along the riverine border tracts in rural north Bengal, the so-called "maldoiyas" or "chapaiyyas", a community of mobile agriculturists. They are professional practitioners of

[43] *1961 Census of India*, p. 222.

[44] Author's interview with chief commissioner of police, Calcutta, July 2006.

[45] *1951 Census of India*, pp. 129, 248.

[46] Author's interview with chief commissioner of police, Calcutta, July 2006; van Schendel, *The Bengal Borderland.*

one of the oldest forms of migration in Bengal: reclaiming dried riverbeds and riverbanks (*diyar*: hence they are also known as *diyarias*). They also traditionally colonise for cultivation the new sandbanks and alluvial islands (*chars*) that are formed each year in the huge muddy rivers of the delta. This tradition of shifting cultivation and the colonisation of new land has been practised for many centuries in the Bengal delta and continued well into the twentieth.[47] Today, groups of Bengali cultivators, known collectively as *bhatias*, still specialise in colonising and farming richly fertile tracts of land newly created or released by Bengal's wayward rivers.[48]

A surprisingly large number of the borderland refugees turned out to be *chapaiyya* peasants. They were especially prominent in the refugee villages in northern Bengal, where the River Ganges (known locally as the Padma) forms the border between the Indian district of Murshidabad and the Bangladeshi district of Rajshahi. One of these refugees is Ghazi, who is about forty-five years old and originally from Malda in India. He told his family's story:

> As you must have realised, we are all [indicating the inhabitants of the villages in the area] from either of the two sides of the [River] Padma. The others have come from Murshidabad or Rajshahi. We have always been losing our land to the river; when that happens we move elsewhere. We were settled somewhere along the Padma, when we lost our lands [to the river] we settled in Murshidabad, from there we moved to Gangarampur, then Kaliaganj, and from there finally here in Ishwargram when we got khas land from the Pakistan government. We are all people from Chapai-Nawabganj here . . . We got this land only after we cleared this land and settled here.

In the course of the interview it transpired that the fertile land on which Ghazi and his fellow *chapaiyyas* are now settled had

[47] Iqbal, "Ecology, Economy and Society in the Eastern Bengal Delta".

[48] In different parts of the region, they often have different local names that refer to their place of "origin": *chapaiyyas* from the Chapai-Nawabganj tracts, *maldoiyas* from Malda, or *mymensinghias* from Mymensingh.

previously belonged to Hindus who had left for India. It is also evident that they have done rather well: "This place is good. You know the proverb about Dinajpur? It has 'paddy piled up high, sheds full of cows, ponds brimming with fish (*gola bhora dhan; goyal bhora goru; pukur bhora machh*).' People in this district are much happier than those in other districts; everything grows easily." His mother, Bibi Ruha, adds, "After 1947 we Indians came over. We were living in Chapai and losing our land to the river; then one of us got word that this place was a forest and that if we reclaimed it, it would belong to us."

Here, then, is a group with a distinctive form of mobility capital. They belonged to a very specific and localised network through which information about available land travelled fast. They had no formal literacy, but clearly belonged to a particular kind of information community, and they also had much experience in moving quickly and grabbing and clearing new tracts of agricultural land. Traditionally, this group lived in light bamboo huts that could be easily disassembled and reassembled. As Ghazi put it: "Our houses are usually temporary ones, look at the walls here, they are just woven bamboo bark. We can pack up and leave at the drop of a hat, whereas locals have heavy-set mud houses." Unlike most of the delta's Sunni Muslims, moreover, *chapaiyyas* did not revere the graves of their ancestors and had few religious attachments to place. In consequence, after Partition they could cross the border with relative ease, and were quick to capture much of the best land vacated by Hindus moving in the opposite direction. They were able to respond swiftly to the opportunities created by Partition and have done well. Bibi Ruha's two brothers have both been on the Hajj pilgrimage to Mecca, a sign of the family's new-found, albeit modest, affluence.

Two further points should be noted about the *chapaiyya* "refugees". They appear to be remarkably free of ideological baggage committing them to any nation, be it Pakistan, India, or Bangladesh. It is revealing that Bibi Ruha described her community, settled in East Pakistan/Bangladesh since 1947, as "we

Indians". Ghazi's daughter is married to Niaz, whom he describes as "an Indian". Niaz's brother came over to East Bengal after Partition, but then returned to India after his land was "lost to the river". They appear to be remarkably pragmatic about taking whatever land they were given by the Pakistan government, but showed themselves no less ready to leave it behind if better land turned up elsewhere in India. Secondly, it is plain that they have a lively sense of entitlement to any land that they have reclaimed from nature and cleared by their own labour, harking back to long-standing customary practice in the region.[49] The Pakistan government for its part appears to have yielded to their claims, giving post facto sanction to their actions that violate the law of property as well as crucial agreements with India.[50]

The second group of rural migrants is erstwhile smallholders clustering in the border zones, and they have been much less fortunate. Before Partition, they tended to be settled agriculturists cultivating small plots they owned or leased from others. They did not migrate to Pakistan immediately after Partition mainly because they had few elements of mobility capital – no contacts across the border, few portable skills, and few possessions they could sell. Such meagre assets as they did possess were rooted in the locality: diminutive landholdings, seldom owned outright, and to which their titles to cultivate were often insecure, and local networks of creditors who loaned them funds to invest in seeds or to tide them over lean times. Most of them were tied to "home" by a complex combination of bonds: the insecurity of their tenure, local obligations, networks of debt, and deference to local creditors and landlords. These peasants tended to leave

[49] Iqbal, "Ecology".

[50] With the Calcutta and Delhi Agreements (of 1948 and 1950, respectively), the governments of India and Pakistan agreed that land abandoned by outgoing refugees in both parts of Bengal would be held and managed for them until they were able to return. Government of India, Ministry of External Affairs, F.8-14/48-Pak1; F.8-7/48/Pak-1; and F.3(49)-BL/1950 (secret).

their homes only under conditions of extreme violence and intimidation, often when they literally had to flee for their lives. Nearly all of our interviewees in the South 24 Parganas/Khulna border areas shared this profile. They had fled across the border during the riots of 1950 and 1964.

In Tengrakhali, Jaafar Ali Faqir said that his family, together with fifty or sixty neighbouring households, had left together in 1964 when incoming Hindu refugees "started burning down our houses and fields". His neighbour, Billal Ali Chowdhury, said that his own family, together with "seven or eight other houses . . . came here when our houses started being attacked by people throwing bricks and our paddy fields were burned down." Gulam Mohammad Saif Ali of Koikhali gave a more detailed account of the circumstances under which his family took flight across the border:

> We were among about five hundred households that fled over to Bangladesh during the 1964 riots. We used to live in Kalitala in Shamsernagar, and my father was the *anchal pradhan* [headman] there. Eight of my family members were killed that night. Had the rest of us not left we would have all been killed . . . It was a Saturday and we had gone to the weekly market [*haat*] . . . [where] someone told us there was a plan to kill my father that very night . . . As soon as we arrived we pitched tents and waited for the night to end.

The land on which they happened to camp that night turned out to be a barren plot that had belonged to a Hindu landlord who fled in the opposite direction, to India. In due course, the government allotted each household three *bighas* (about an acre) of the same land on which to settle. However, life proved hard for them: "Nothing would grow on this land. We had been cultivators in India but here we couldn't cultivate anything [because] the soil was so saline, so we used to fish and work as labourers in other people's fields."

In the context of late-twentieth-century Bengal, it was typical that any "spare" land was spare precisely because it was uncultivable,[51] since any productive land vacated by emigrant Hindus had been quickly snapped up by locals or the likes of the *chapaiyyas*. Asked why, on the night of the killings, they chose to run to Koikhali and not somewhere else, Saif Ali explained, "We had a relative there, and we used to visit him as we just had to cross the river." In Saif Ali's story we see clearly the factors that predisposed people like him not to move at all or to hold on where they were for as long as possible. The world they had inhabited as agriculturists was extremely circumscribed: their relatives lived close at hand, their daughters and sisters married into homes in neighbouring villages, and their longest journeys had been to markets only a few miles away. The nearby weekly market was their connection to the outside world, and also their main source of information: it was at the Saturday market that Saif Ali's family got wind of the plans to attack his family, too late to save eight of his relatives. Such assets as they possessed – cultivation rights, potential creditors – were rooted in these localities and could not be transferred to new places. Even if they were in reasonable health, they had no skills other than as cultivators, and they could not easily turn to other work except manual labour. Their bundles of mobility capital, then, were almost non-existent. So it is hardly surprising to find that the indebted rural poor were deeply reluctant migrants, and that, as will be seen, many did not move.

Staying on: Ghettoization among "National Minorities"

Some refugees who have moved into Bangladesh's agrarian borderlands have done well, others poorly, but overall the comparison with the conditions of their co-religionists on the Indian side of the border is stark. These are mainly rural Muslims who, for a variety of reasons, could or would not move to Pakistan after 1947. They make up about 85 per cent of West Bengal's Muslim population

[51] Chatterji, "'Dispersal' and the Failure of Rehabilitation", pp. 995–1032.

of sixteen million.[52] Most have either clung on precariously where they were, albeit in ever-shrinking spaces, or have been displaced to areas within West Bengal where more of their fellow Muslims live in densely concentrated and economically depressed clusters.[53]

For these Bengali Muslims, "staying on" in India has meant a rapid downward spiral in prosperity, status, and security. Decades of communist government notwithstanding, they are among the most impoverished communities in the region. Statistics show them to be disproportionately likely to be uneducated, unemployed, or underemployed. Despite constituting about 28 per cent of West Bengal's population, Muslims hold fewer than 2 per cent of government jobs and less than 1 per cent of all service-level jobs in the private sector.[54] They tend to live in desperately overcrowded spaces, with little or no institutional support. Their children are more likely than those of other communities to remain illiterate and have shorter lives. Their daughters more often marry young and die in childbirth. Their sons, in disproportionately large numbers, fall foul of the law and spend years in prison.[55]

Members of our research team found it much more difficult to gain access to these settlements and conduct interviews there. Suspicion and even fear of our intentions were palpable. Annu Jalais was nonetheless able to conduct an extraordinary set of interviews with two branches of the same family: one branch had migrated to East Pakistan after 1947, and the other had not. The two branches had lost all contact with each other. These interviews suggest some tentative conclusions about patterns of staying on.

[52] Siddiqui, *Muslim Educational Uplift.*

[53] Chatterji, *Spoils of Partition*, pp. 181–94.

[54] Siddiqui, *Muslim Educational Uplift*, p. 7; also see Seabrook and Siddiqui, *People without History.*

[55] Volume I of papers submitted by the chief secretary of West Bengal to the (Sachar) High Level Committee on Social, Economic and Educational Status of the Muslims of India, 2005–2006, Nehru Memorial Library, Delhi.

Shahid and Jalal Gazi are brothers, originally from the village of Kalitola in the south-east corner of present-day West Bengal. After Partition, Shahid, together with many other members of the family, migrated across the border to Kalinchi in East Pakistan, but his brother Jalal did not. Today Jalal (age about ninety-five) is too ill to be able to say much, but his son Fakhruddin Gazi fills in the gaps in his story:

> We are originally from Kalitola. The Hindus expelled us from there and so we came here [Dokkhin Parghumte] where we had family. Our whole place in Kalitola used to be Muslim. Then one day [around 1950] some refugees who had come from the other side announced that Muslims would not be allowed to live there, that they would have to leave . . . They went from house to house, sometimes, raped and looted, at other times burned down our homes and our granaries . . . My elder brother . . . felt he would not be able to keep his honour and left for Khupdipur [across the border] . . . At that time all the Muslims of Jogeshganj, Parghumte, Kalitola, Samshernagar, and Gobindokati left this place . . . Our family's land used to stretch all the way to the river, now it ends with the field that surrounds our homestead . . . One by one, all of my uncles left. But my father Jalal Gazi, being the eldest, stayed back to look after the mosque and the graves of our ancestors.

Today the community is reduced to about fifty people crammed into four homesteads. It is clear that this Muslim family was once quite well-to-do, well educated, and well connected. After riots began in 1950 most of the clan went to Pakistan. Those who stayed behind did not lack contacts there, and indeed they had many close relatives and contacts that had made good on "the other side". But they stayed in India because they were bound to "home", either, as in the case of Jalal, by responsibilities to the graves of his ancestors, or by the need to care for the elderly and infirm, or by their own infirmity. Fakhruddin and Hamidullah Gazi, respectively the son and nephew of Jalal Gazi, have stayed even though there are very few opportunities for them in the locality, and even after Fakhruddin was "kicked out" of his job at the local school after being passed over for promotion in favour of a less-qualified Hindu. They have to look after the old man, who is sick and frail. "Previously," Fakhruddin said, "we all wanted to leave as our leaders all left, but it is not so now. We can't go and neither do we want to go."

As we can see, their decision to stay has resulted in a catastrophic downward spiral in their wealth and status. The landholdings of this once well-to-do clan have shrunk to one small field; the younger men in the family are either unemployed or inappropriately employed, and they are deeply pessimistic about their prospects. Interestingly, they have lost contact with their kinsfolk across the border. National borders, even ones as relatively porous as those separating India from Bangladesh, and attempts to control movement across them, have undoubtedly played a part in this. Since the Enemy Property Act came on the statute books in 1967, maintaining contact with "enemy" aliens across the border has been an enterprise fraught with danger,[56] and this may explain why two brothers, separated by Partition, had neither seen nor heard from each other for several decades. It was only when Annu Jalais took news and photographs of Jalal over to Shahid in Bangladesh that contact between them was re-established (see Fig. 7.3).

Their story reveals a critically important point overlooked by much of the literature on networks: namely, that networks atrophy and rupture in adverse circumstances. After the blood brothers lost touch with each other at a moment of upheaval and chaos, the ties between them withered. For the family members who had stayed behind, assets had been stripped, and the familial networks that might have facilitated their movement no longer existed: "We can't go and neither do we want to go." Among the less mobile, then, it seems that an initial reluctance to move can

[56] Chatterji, "South Asian Histories of Citizenship".

Fig. 7.3: In Bangladesh, Shahid Gazi sees an image of his brother Jalal for the first time in decades. The brothers had lost contact after Shahid crossed over to East Pakistan after Partition (photo by Bengal Diaspora Project).

foreclose their opportunities for migration at a later date, keeping people like Fakhruddin and Hamidullah Gazi stuck in their unenviable locations.

Our research suggests that "stayers-on" in the cities are no better off, whether in West Bengal in India or in Bangladesh, their different trajectories since Partition notwithstanding. These communities have been squeezed into ever more densely packed ghettos where they enjoy few facilities or opportunities. A recent study of Muslims in contemporary Calcutta showed that four out of every five now live in overcrowded slums, where entire households (averaging 6.65 people) sleep, eat, and work in tiny one-room shacks, averaging less than 120 sq. ft in size.[57] Their

[57] Siddiqui, *Muslim Educational Uplift*, p. 26.

levels of literacy are exceptionally low. Fewer than one in ten have any "chance of getting admitted to any kind of educational institution, [whether] recognised or unrecognised, or unaffiliated or public." Dropout rates among the few lucky children who are admitted to schools are estimated to be as high as 80 per cent. These urban communities survive mainly by self-employment in family-run businesses where they work for pitifully low returns embroidering gold thread onto cloth, making paper goods like kites, binding books, and producing cheap leather goods.[58] The communities to which the internally displaced interviewees belong have been impoverished not just by the discrimination they continue to face in the labour market, or by the loss of their properties, but by the emigration of those members who had the wherewithal to leave, taking with them such mobility capital and the economic and cultural assets that the community once possessed.

In Bangladesh, urban "stayers on" among the "Biharis" gave a vivid sense of the compulsions that persuaded them to cling on, however precariously, where they were. In the troubles of 1971, Salima's husband, who worked in the railways, was tortured by a mob and eventually died from his injuries. She was left with very young children to care for. Using her contacts, she managed to get from Syedpur to Dhaka, to the Town Hall Camp where some members of her family, including her divorced sister, had huddled together for safety. Even though Salima's father and brother migrated from Bangladesh to Pakistan, the sisters stayed behind. They live together in a tiny shack in the camp, where they do piecework as garment embroiderers to earn a few takas (or rupees) to support their families, and jointly care for their children and grandchildren, one of whom suffers from severe disabilities. Why did Salima stay? In the first instance, it was to care for her wounded husband. After his death, soon after the 1971 war ended,

[58] Ibid., pp. 23, 29.

she calculated that, as a single woman with very small children, one of them disabled, she would be better able to survive in Dhaka where she had some networks of familial support. (Even as the interview was being conducted, one of Salima's female relatives who lives nearby dropped in to help her complete her quota of piecework on time.)

Mehrunissa Khatun, a "stayer-on" in Syedpur, in 1971 also had two very young daughters, one aged three years, the other six months. The family was one of hundreds that, during the troubles, fled from a smaller railway colony of Parbatipur to the much larger neighbouring town of Syedpur, seeking safety in numbers. At this point, one of Mehrunissa's sisters was able to migrate with her husband and children to Pakistan. But Mehrunissa's own husband was bedridden ("he used to cough up blood"), and she had to care for him, as well as her children, until he died of tuberculosis in 1978. She has since managed to support her family by working as a maidservant in the house of a Canadian aid worker. Like Salima, Mehrunissa has kin in Pakistan but could not migrate because she had to care for others. She still lives in Chamra Godown Camp in extremely reduced circumstances. Neither Salima nor Mehrunissa are in contact with their relatives in Pakistan.

What stands out in these life histories is that those who stayed on despite threats to life and limb did not always lack contacts or access to networks that might have helped them to migrate. But they did lack one or more other vital dimension of mobility capital. Strikingly, most "stayers-on" we interviewed had physical disabilities or health problems that were more dramatic impediments than were any lack of literacy or skills needed for employment. Or if they were able-bodied themselves they had powerful countervailing obligations to care for the vulnerable or infirm, whether infants, the ill, the aged, or the disabled. Many, but not all, of those who stayed behind for such reasons were women.

This suggests, counterintuitively, that while networks, cash, knowhow, and skills are important elements of mobility capital, good health is vital. It also points to the role of personal, familial, and religious obligations as constraints on people's ability to join a stream of refugees. These stories indicate, moreover, that the capacity of networks to sustain cumulative patterns of migration, in and of themselves, needs to be reconsidered.

"Imperial" Mobility: Migration to Britain

Set against this backdrop, it can be seen just how exceptional an enterprise it was for peasants from Sylhet to migrate so far from home and make landfall in London. Much is already known about the migration of Bangladeshis to Britain, about how, when, and why young men from the rural central lowlands of Sylhet began to go there.[59] But I suggest that the challenge is to explain not so much why some Bengalis migrated to Britain, but rather why so few did so during this period of mass migration in the delta. To begin to understand this we must revisit some aspects of their history.

Before Partition, Sylhet was not part of Bengal but rather a district in the province of Assam in British India. Historically, however, the people of this marcher region had close ties both with Bengal to the west and Assam to the east,[60] and these had persisted and indeed been strengthened during British rule. In the late nineteenth century, demographic pressures encouraged some young Sylhetis to emigrate in two separate streams: eastwards to find jobs on the British-owned tea estates of Assam, and westwards downriver by the Surma and Kashiara to Calcutta and Hooghly to seek work as boatmen and other employment in the big city.[61] Some found work as lascars (or seafarers) in the British

[59] Adams, *Across Seven Seas*; Choudhury, *The Roots and Tales of Bangladeshi Settlers*; Balachandran, "Circulation through Seafaring".

[60] Ibid. Also see *Sylhet District Gazetteer, 1905*.

[61] Hunter, *Statistical Account of Bengal*, vol. 3, p. 284; and Chattopadhyaya, *Internal Migration*, p. 57.

Indian merchant marine, and they soon came to occupy a lowly niche as fire-stokers in the boiler rooms of steamships in a highly segmented labour market. A complex recruitment system soon sprang up that gave contracts, typically of two years, to young men from Sylhet (and which, as Ravi Ahuja acutely observes, also contrived to keep people from other parts of Bengal and India out of this monopoly."[62] That system was dominated by a troika of Sylheti hostel owners (*bariwallahs*) who put the lascars up, several to a room, while they waited in Calcutta for work on the ships; port foremen (*ghat serangs*); and ship serangs who recruited men for particular shipping lines in return for a share of their future pay. The serangs and bariwallahs were all from the same region of Sylhet, frequently from a cluster of neighbouring villages. Through this system, many lascars became embroiled in complex relationships of debt and obligation to particular bariwallahs and serangs, debts on which they could not easily renege.

For their part, ship serangs had a strong incentive to closely monitor the lascars they had recruited, since they owed their own jobs to their white employers' faith in their "customary" (and supposedly "Asiatic") command over the workforce. The serang had another powerful motive to prevent lascars from jumping ship in that "losing" one would mean the serang would also lose his cut from the absconder's future wages, and furthermore would have to square the matter with all of the other stakeholders – the ghat serangs and bariwallahs – who also owed a share of the sailor's meagre pay packet.[63] As Ahuja has shown, this complex web of bodily control, debt, and obligation – as much as the highly punitive shipping laws and immigration rules that

[62] Ahuja, "Mobility and Containment", pp. 111–41.

[63] Indian lascars earned between one-third and one-fifth of the wages that white seamen were paid for doing the same jobs. Ahuja, "Mobility and Containment". On the constraints on the power of foremen or "jobbers" over Indian workers, see Chandavarkar, "The Decline and Fall of the Jobber System", pp. 117–210.

deterred "Asiatics" from breaking their contracts or disembarking at European and American ports – explains why so few lascars jumped ship at London.[64] One must also consider the life that awaited absconders: two years of evading arrest, the challenges of surviving while on the run, and the growing racism in white seamen's unions against lascars, not to mention loneliness, London's long winters, and the ever-present spectre of destitution.[65] Sailors who weighed these against the great costs to themselves and their families of their running away had little incentive to do so. Each year between 1900 and 1947, some fifty thousand Indian seamen passed through British ports. Of these only a few dozen jumped ship and stayed in Britain, mainly in London.[66]

After Partition and Independence, however, workers from Sylhet were abruptly cut off from Assam's tea gardens, since Sylhet became part of East Pakistan and Assam was given to India. From 1948 onward, the government of Assam began to put pressure on "outsiders", particularly Muslims, to leave the state, and Sylhetis were among the thousands forced to return to East Pakistan.[67] Partition also cut Sylhet off from Calcutta, which was now the capital of the Indian state of West Bengal. India soon made it clear that Pakistanis (as the Sylhetis were now classified as being) were no longer welcome in its merchant marine.[68] As these two traditional streams of migration were disrupted by Partition, and

[64] "Lascar agreements" denied lascars shore leave in North American and African ports; shipmasters could discharge lascars only in Indian ports, and England's Merchant Shipping Act of 1894 entitled ship owners to transfer even unwilling lascars to any other vessel so long as it was bound for India. Ahuja, "Mobility and Containment"; Balachandran, "Recruitment and Control of Indian Seamen", pp. 1–18.

[65] Tabili, *"We Ask for British Justice"*.

[66] Ahuja, "Mobility and Containment".

[67] *A Study of the Report of the Commission of Enquiry (Jabbar Commission).*

[68] Government of India, Ministry of Home Affairs, C.S. Section, 36/3-c.s., 1949; and MHA/F-I section, 199-FI.

many Sylhetis were forced to return to their district, some began to consider how they might deploy their networks and knowledge of the world to migrate elsewhere in search of work. A few ended up in Britain, mainly because they had heard through the grapevine that work was to be had in the mills and factories in the north.

These migrants tended to be people who had little money or education but did possess exceptionally rich and far-flung networks established over a century of travelling on the high seas and living outside their home districts. Almost all were young, male, and able-bodied. The great majority returned home after a stint abroad. Only a handful stayed on, usually for personal and idiosyncratic reasons, for instance a love affair with an English woman, or a falling out with fathers and uncles, or getting into trouble with the authorities back at home in Sylhet.

Mohammed Fazlul Huq's family's history reflects many threads in this typical pattern. Fazlul, who claims to be 102 years old, now lives along the Dinajpur border where he owns a small plot of land. He was born in Calcutta's docklands area of Khiddirpur (formerly Kidderpore): "We were four brothers and three sisters. My father . . . was a lineman on the Indian railways. I grew up on the docks of Khiddirpur [Calcutta] – they used to moor and repair ships in front of our house, the ghat [dock] door was right in front of our house. Under the British I worked on the steamers [on the] Arenda . . . a huge ship . . . [During World War II] the Japanese blew it up." While working on the ship as an "oilman", Fazlul travelled "to London, Africa, Rangoon, Singapore, Jeddah . . . I went on the Hajj from Jedda; this was in British times."

Fazlul came from a remarkably peripatetic family. He said his forefathers were originally "Khans" (possibly Afghans); one ancestor had married a local woman in Noakhali in Bengal and settled there: "My father [was one of] six brothers. The eldest settled in Barisal and died there. The next two stayed in Noakhali and died at home in our village, [but] my father left Noakhali for Noagaon in Assam [and got a job in the railways]. The fifth died young, also in Noakhali. The youngest, Hamid Khan, worked on a steamer, married a mem [white woman] and stayed over in London. I heard they had two sons and owned a wine shop. The mem was crazy about my uncle; she never let him return." That his lascar uncle had stayed on in London was seen as an aberration by Fazlul and the rest of his family, who put it down to his infatuation with a crazy white woman.

Fazlul Huq was the only one of several siblings to have become a lascar, and like most seafarers of his generation he returned to Bengal after the war ended to set up a small business, as a tea-stall owner. The rest of his brothers also travelled in search of work, but they stayed closer home: one worked for government; a second was in private service as a clerk; and a third was a preacher, or maulvi. His sisters all married men who lived in Assam in India, where the family had established links through their father's career in the railways, and where they had moved after Partition: "I joined my parents in Assam when our house in Calcutta's Khiddirpur was taken over by the Indian Government. The Indian Government said, 'No place for Muslims here, go to Arab', and then they started burning our houses and so Jinnah said I'll break India and give a piece of it to Muslims." Later (presumably when the Assam government started to expel Bengali Muslims, soon after Independence), "We shifted to the Bengali side because they spoilt [raped] our mothers and sisters and started exploiting us and so we fought against them."

Here, then, is a family that had lived for several generations by various forms of circulatory migration. The partition of British India into two hostile countries had ruptured some of the routes along which they had traditionally moved, and closed off some of their old options. But they continued to deploy those that remained open. (So Assam, albeit in India, remained part of their shrinking canvas of opportunities.) They also developed new alternatives and diversified their strategies for survival in the changing context after 1947. Migration to the West was one of them, but it clearly was not the easiest, or only, or even the favoured option. Migration to the "right" nation-state afforded more opportunities for work in line with their aspirations and sense of status, enabling many members of the family to rise from their blue-collar backgrounds to join the lower ranks of the "respectable" service classes.

This suggests that the model of mobility capital can help explain an apparent paradox, namely the fact that after Partition the boldest migrations to the distant West were undertaken not by those with the greatest reserves of economic and cultural capital, but instead by people with little money, no literacy, and no competence in the English language, who were part of networks of far-flung connections, who had richly layered histories of mobility, and who were young and strong and had few onerous obligations back home. Even among this small, select group, staying on in the West permanently or semi-permanently was not the norm, and most harboured the dream of an eventual return home. Nor was it the case that once one member of the family or network group had established himself in Britain, the rest followed automatically in his wake, as network theorists of "cumulative causation" have suggested. For most that possessed such networks, by far the preferred strategy was to explore other, less risky avenues to achieve security and higher status in their region of origin.

Jubair Ahmed's story reinforces this point. Jubair, who runs a takeaway food business in Newham in London, is the son of a lascar who worked on the supply ships that serviced the Royal Navy during the Second World War. His father got this job through one of his own maternal uncles, who was also a lascar "in an English ship". After being discharged from the merchant marine in 1945 at the age of sixteen, Jubair's father worked for eighteen years in the steel mills at Scunthorpe, frequently returning to Sylhet to his wife and family. Jubair's grandmother and his younger uncle eventually joined Jubair's father in Britain, to look after him when his health began to fail. His older uncle stayed on in Bangladesh until his death.

Born in Sylhet in 1965, Jubair is one of four siblings. He was educated to college level in Habiganj, where the family was doing well: "My father was a good earner. Before father came here [to Britain], our financial condition was good. He multiplied it. Everyone was happy." None of his siblings wanted to move to Britain. Nor did his father intend to bring them to join him there: "We [were] not interested; my elder brother didn't want to come. My father was also not interested to bring us."

At college, however, Jubair got mixed up with student movements against the Ershad government, and his mother, concerned for his safety, urged her husband to take him to Britain:

> I was involved in politics in Bangladesh. I was not interested in coming to London. My father kept pushing me; a visa was issued, extended, and expired – once, twice, three times, five times, seven times. Last time, in 1984, during the movement against Ershad, people were being arrested in Habiganj. Everybody wrote to my father telling him to bring me to London, or else I would be sent to jail. My mother also pressured my father to bring me here . . . "You send him ticket, then you see," mother told father like this. Father sent ticket to me. Then I came, otherwise the ticket would be a loss.[69]

So Jubair ended up in Britain, essentially as a political refugee, although he moved there along a network that had been established long before by previous generations of his family who had been sojourners or "economic" migrants. His siblings did not follow him there: twenty-five years later, his older brother and sister still live in Bangladesh.

Conclusion

The aim of this study of the migration of Muslims in Bengal since 1947 has been to see whether it elucidates patterns of refugee settlement identified by Zolberg in new nations since 1945. Like many zones of migration in the late twentieth century, Bengal

[69] Interviewed by Shahzad Firoz, Newham, London, 2009.

had been administered as a single unit in the British empire, but was divided between two successor states with the transition from empire to nation. It became one of the world's most significant zones of migration after 1947, producing refugee flows on a scale rarely witnessed before or since. The essay suggests a framework for understanding these patterned flows from a comparative and global perspective.

I have proposed the concept of mobility capital to help explain patterns not only of migration, but also, significantly, of internal displacement and staying on. Most post-Partition migrants we inter-viewed had rich and complex bundles of mobility capital; all had local or supra-local contacts or connections that they deployed to facilitate their movement. All had personal prehistories of mobility, and ties of affection and obligation accrued on these journeys. Many had less easily measurable knowhow – the capacity to work the system and their assets to their best advantage. Most were knitted into knowledge communities through which they learned of both dangers and possibilities.

The migrants interviewed all possessed these different elements of mobility capital to varying degrees. Moreover, the constituent elements of each migrant's particular bundle appear crucially to have shaped his or her choice of destination: migrants with similar types of bundles tended to end up in similar places. Particular dispositions among migrants, then, appear to draw them to matching destinations. Migrants who lacked one or another dimension of mobility capital or were tied by obligations to "home", by contrast, tended to end up in impoverished communities of the internally displaced.

By comparing very different cases in a large and international study, I have tried to show that mobility capital worked as an interdependent bundle of attributes to enable successful migration. The life stories of our informants demonstrate that the lack of one or more elements of the bundle – above all, the basic fact of one's own good health or that of one's dependants – could make all the difference between staying on, being internally displaced, or moving abroad. Among the elements that make up this bundle, moreover, actual monetary resources prove not to have been as critical as we might expect, as shown by the effective moves made by the cash-poor *chapaiyya* peasant migrants we interviewed. Nor was literacy as important as one might imagine, as evidenced, again, by the stories of the *chapaiyyas*, but also by those of many lascars.

Scholars of migration will not be surprised to learn that networks played a crucial role in enabling migration in and from Bengal. Indeed, every migrant we interviewed was tied into complex webs of overlapping, historically established networks. But so too were many people who did not move at all, and were unable or reluctant so to do. It seems that networks by them-selves were insufficient to enable migration in the Bengal upheavals, let alone to produce it. This is important to recognise, given the powerful influence that "cumulative causation" and network theory have exercised over a generation of scholars of migration. These posited that once a critical mass of people from a particular source had migrated abroad, migration would continue until every member of their network joined the pioneers in the West. But when the tiny number of Bengali migrants in Britain (or indeed the few Bihari migrants in Bangladesh) is studied alongside the vast majority in the diaspora who stayed on in their region of origin, a very different picture emerges. It is plain that great numbers of people who could have (and, according to this theory, should have) moved abroad to join their kin have not done so. They have instead made highly complex personal choices to stay on in their region of origin, or not to move at all.

Looking closely at how these networks worked in practice has revealed something else: how networks could atrophy and rupture, and also how important they were in limiting and constraining migrants' choices and their trajectories of movement. The networks were not neutral spaces, easily penetrable by "outsiders", and those we studied were closed arenas in which hierarchy was perpetuated more frequently than challenged, and status was reconstituted more often than subverted. These points were well understood in many classical studies of migration, but they need to be underscored in the current intellectual context (certainly in South Asian studies), in which theories of diaspora valorise networks and "diasporic spaces" as sites of radical possibility.[70]

Finally, this research has raised doubts about one of the most persistent assumptions of migration studies by undermining the notion of a clear conceptual distinction between "forced" migrants (or refugees) and economic migrants. All the migrants we interviewed straddled this divide. All moved, or stayed on and were internally displaced, within a context of nation formation, ethnic discrimination, and religious violence, and in this sense were classic "refugees". But all of them moved in "grooves", as Adam McKeown has vividly described them,[71] created by older forms of "economic" mobility. Put differently, the "refugees" studied were all people drawn from communities that historically have been itinerant, whether for economic, political, cultural, or even environmental reasons. When faced with physical violence or threats to their livelihood and status during Partition riots and civil war, they possessed the wherewithal, often in itself partly a product of past movement, to move to safer and more propitious settings.

References

A Study of the Report of the Commission of Enquiry, Jabbar Commission on Expulsion of Pakistani Infiltrants from Tripura and Assam, New Delhi: Government of India, Ministry of Home Affairs, 1964.

Adams, Caroline, *Across Seven Seas and Thirteen Rivers: Life Stories of Sylheti Settlers in Britain*, London, 1987.

[70] Bhabha, "The Third Space"; idem., *The Location of Culture*; Brah, *Cartographies of Diaspora*; Appadurai, *Modernity at Large*.

[71] McKeown, "Global Migration 1846–1950", pp. 155–89.

Ahuja, Ravi, "Mobility and Containment: The Voyages of South Asian Seamen, c. 1900–1960", *International Review of Social History* 51, 2006, pp. 111–41.

Ali, Chaudhuri Muhammad, *Emergence of Pakistan*, New York, 1967.

Appadurai, Arjun, *Modernity at Large: Cultural Dimensions of Globalization*, Minneapolis, 1996.

Balachandran, G., "Circulation through Seafaring: Indian Seamen, 1890–1945", in C. Markovits, *et al.*, eds, *Society and Circulation: Mobile People and Itinerant Cultures in South Asia 1750–1950*, Delhi, 2003.

———, "Recruitment and Control of Indian Seamen, Calcutta, 1880–1935", *International Journal of Maritime History* 9, 1, 1997, pp. 1–18.

Bhabha, Homi, "The Third Space", in J. Rutherford, ed., *Identity: Community, Culture and Difference*, London, 1990.

———, *The Location of Culture*, London, 1994.

Bose, N.K., *Calcutta, 1964: A Social Survey*, New Delhi, 1968.

Bourdieu, Pierre, "The Forms of Capital", in J. Richardson, ed., *Handbook of Theory and Research for the Sociology of Education*, New York, 1986.

Brah, Avtar, *Cartographies of Diaspora*, London, 1996.

Chakrabarti, Prafulla, *The Marginal Men*, Calcutta, 1990.

Chakrabarty, Saroj, *With Dr. B.C. Roy and Other Chief Ministers: A Record Until 1962*, Calcutta, 1974.

Chandavarkar, Rajnarayan, "The Decline and Fall of the Jobber System in the Bombay Cotton Textile Industry, 1870–1955", *Modern Asian Studies* 42, 1, 2008, pp. 117–210.

Chatterji, Joya, "'Dispersal' and the Failure of Rehabilitation: Refugee Camp-Dwellers and Squatters in West Bengal", *Modern Asian Studies* 41, 5, 2007, pp. 995–1032.

———, "South Asian Histories of Citizenship", *Historical Journal*, 55, 4, 2012.

———, *The Spoils of Partition. Bengal and India, 1947–1967*, Cambridge, 2007.

Chattopadhyaya, Haraprasad, *Internal Migration in India: A Case Study of Bengal*, Calcutta, 1987.

Choudhury, Y., *The Roots and Tales of Bangladeshi Settlers*, London, 2003.

Daechsel, Markus, "Sovereignty, Governmentality and Development in Ayub's Pakistan: The Case of Korangi Township", *Modern Asian Studies* 44, 1, 2011, pp. 131–57.

Das, Suranjan, *Communal Riots in Bengal, 1905–1947*, Delhi, 1993.

Ghosh, Papiya, *Partition and the South Asian Diaspora: Extending the Subcontinent*, Delhi, 2007.

Haines, Daniel, "Concrete 'Progress': Irrigation, Development and Modernity in Mid-Twentieth-Century Sind", *Modern Asian Studies* 45, 1, 2011, pp. 179–200.

Haynes, Douglas E., and Tirthankar Roy, "Conceiving Mobility: Weavers' Migrations in Pre-Colonial and Colonial India", *Indian Economic and Social History Review* 36, 1, 1999, pp. 35–67.

Hunter, W.W., *Statistical Account of Bengal*, vol. 3, London, 1875–; rpnt Delhi, 1973.

Ilias, Ahmed, *Biharis, the Indian Emigres in Bangladesh: An Objective Analysis*, Syedpur, 2005.

Iqbal, K. Ifthekar, "Ecology, Economy and Society in the Eastern Bengal Delta, *c.* 1840–1943", PhD thesis, University of Cambridge, 2004.

Kamal, Nahid, "The Population Trajectories of Bangladesh and West Bengal during the Twentieth Century: A Comparative Study", PhD thesis, London School of Economics, 2009.

Kamaluddin, A.F.M., "Refugee Problems in Bangladesh", in L.A. Kosinski and K.M. Elahi, eds, *Population Redistribution and Development in South Asia*, Dordrecht, 1985.

Kerr, I.J., *Railways in Modern India*, Delhi, 2001.

Massey, Douglas, "Social Structure, Household Strategies and the Cumulative Causation of Migration", *Population Index* 56, 1, Spring 1990, pp. 3–26.

McKeown, Adam, "Global Migration 1846–1950", *Journal of World History* 15, 2, 2004, pp. 155–89.

Moch, Leslie Page, "Dividing Time: An Analytical Framework for Migration History Periodization", in Jan Lucassen and Leo Lucassen, eds, *Migration, Migration History, History: Old Paradigms and New Perspectives*, Bern, 2005.

Nakatani, Tetsuya, "Away from Home: The Movement and Settlement of Refugees from East Pakistan to West Bengal, India", *Journal of the Japanese Association for South Asian Studies* 12, 2000, n.p.

Rahman, Md. Mahbubar, and Willem van Schendel, "'I Am not a Refugee': Rethinking Partition Migration", *Modern Asian Studies* 37, 3, 2003, pp. 551–84.

Randhawa, M.S., *Out of the Ashes: An Account of the Rehabilitation of Refugees from West Pakistan in Rural Areas of East Punjab*, Punjab: Public Relations Department, 1954.

Robinson, F.C.R., *Separatism among Indian Muslims: The Politics of the United Provinces' Muslims 1860–1923*, Cambridge, 1974.

Schmeidl, Suzanne, "Conflict and Forced Migration: A Quantitative Review", in A. Zolberg and P.M. Benda, eds, *Global Migrants, Global Refugees: Problems and Solutions*, New York, 2001.

Seabrook, Jeremy, and Imran Ahmed Siddiqui, *People without History: India's Muslim Ghettos*, London, 2011.

Sen, Uditi, "Refugees and the Politics of Nation-Building in India, 1947–1971", PhD thesis, University of Cambridge, 2009.

Siddiqui, A.R., *Partition and the Making of the Mohajir Mindset: A Narrative*, Karachi, 2008.

Siddiqui, M.K.A., *Muslim Educational Uplift: How to Achieve this Goal?*, Calcutta, 2008.

———, *The Muslims of Calcutta: A Study in Aspects of their Social Organisation*, Calcutta, 1974.

Stark, Oded, and J. Edward Taylor, "Relative Deprivation and International Migration", *Demography* 26, 1, February 1989, pp. 1–14.

Tabili, Laura, *"We Ask for British Justice": Workers and Racial Difference in Late Imperial Britain*, New York, 1994.

Todaro, Michael P., "A Model of Labour Migration and Urban Development in Less Developed Countries", *American Economic Review* 59, 1, 1969, pp. 138–48.

van Schendel, Willem, *The Bengal Borderland: Beyond Nation and State in South Asia*, London, 2005.

Zolberg, A.R., "The Formation of New States as a Refugee-Generating Process", *Annals of the American Academy of Political and Social Science* 467, 1, 1983, pp. 24–38.

———, and P.M. Benda, eds, *Global Migrants, Global Refugees: Problems and Solutions*, New York, 2001.

8

Dispersal and the Failure of Rehabilitation

Refugee Camp-dwellers and Squatters in West Bengal

In September 1950, the government of West Bengal dispatched five hundred Hindu refugee families to the village of Jirat in Hooghly district. It intended to build a camp to permanently house them there. The refugees had fled from East Bengal in the turbulent aftermath of the Partition of India.

Some forty miles from Calcutta, Jirat was situated on the west bank of the River Hooghly. It had once been a substantial and prosperous village, significant enough to earn a mention in Rennell's *Atlas* of 1786 as a place where wealthy people built large homes and temples. Indeed the ancestral home of Dr Syama Prasad Mookerjee – educationist and politician, founder of the Hindu nationalist Jana Sangh Party, and ironically one of the most vociferous champions of the Hindu refugees in Bengal after Partition – was situated in the village. In the nineteenth century, however, the river had changed its course and Jirat's population was ravaged by a particularly virulent strain of the dreaded "Burdwan fever". By 1950, when the refugees arrived at Jirat, the village had long since been abandoned, its waterways choked with silt, its ponds filthy and overgrown with water hyacinth, its great buildings crumbling and derelict. A rare "empty" corner in crowded West

Bengal, this place was deemed appropriate by the government of West Bengal to house and rehabilitate 250,000 refugees: men, women, and children.

Earlier that year, in January 1950, another group of refugees from East Bengal had occupied a vacant plot in Tollygunge in the suburbs of Calcutta. Indu Ganguli, one of the ring-leaders in this enterprise, had lived in a neighbouring house since Partition, presumably with relatives or friends. He had noticed that the adjacent plot was unoccupied and untended. Together with half a dozen fellow refugees, he approached the owner of the plot with a proposal to lease it, offering to put down a deposit in advance. When the landlord turned down the offer, the refugees nevertheless went ahead and occupied it by force, dividing it into about four hundred plots of equal size. They then proceeded to distribute these plots to refugee families on a first-come first-served basis.[1] They named their new colony "Azadgarh", literally "bastion of freedom".

In 1951, the Government of India asked a team of anthropologists from the Anthropological Survey of India (ASI), led by Dr B.S. Guha and backed by experts from UNESCO, to look into the causes of "social tensions" among the Hindu refugees of West Bengal. After violent demonstrations on the streets of Calcutta and a spate of forcible occupations by refugees of properties on the outskirts of Calcutta, the West Bengal government had reluctantly been forced to recognise that "the refugee problem" was a cause for serious concern. The ASI-UNESCO study was intended to identify the reasons behind the growing disaffection among a rapidly swelling refugee population and to suggest how best to deal with it. Dr Guha's team chose to study two refugee settlements – the one established by government at Jirat, and the other by the refugees themselves at Azadgarh. Published in 1959 under the title *Memoir No. 1*, their findings provide a rich and extraordinarily detailed picture of refugee life, of the hopes, fears,

[1] Guha, *Memoir No. 1, 1954*, p. 51.

frustrations, and disappointments of those who had fled from eastern Bengal to the west. But they also highlight the striking differences between the experiences of "camp refugees", that is those who were resettled by government, and the more numerous "self-settled" refugee squatters, whose rehabilitation was entirely the result of their own efforts.

Government's efforts to rehabilitate Bengal's Hindu refugees, as scholars of Partition and modern India have come to recognise, proved to be a failure of catastrophic proportions.[2] The detailed findings of the *Memoir* were among the first to point to this conclusion. By analysing them, this essay seeks to draw conclusions about the rehabilitation of refugees and displaced peoples which may have a relevance beyond Bengal, and indeed beyond South Asia.

Government Policy in Delhi and Calcutta

The context in which the Bengal migrations took place and government policies towards refugees evolved was the outbreak of communal violence between Hindus and Muslims in the late summer of 1946. The Great Killing in Calcutta in August 1946 left at least three thousand people dead. That autumn and winter, it was followed by tit-for-tat pogroms by Hindus against Muslims in Bihar, and by Muslims against Hindus in Noakhali and Tippera in eastern Bengal. Early in 1947, savage killings in the North Indian town of Gurgaon left many thousands dead. In March 1947 the city of Rawalpindi in Punjab witnessed horrific carnage. On 15 August 1947 British India was partitioned. Two days later the Radcliffe Line, which defined the new borders between India and Pakistan and divided the provinces of Punjab and Bengal, was published. Violence now assumed genocidal proportions in Punjab and parts of North India.

[2] See, for instance, Sammadar, *The Marginal Nation*; Bose, ed., *Refugees in West Bengal*; Kudaisya and Tan, *The Aftermath of Partition*; and Chatterji, *The Spoils of Partition.*

By contrast, Bengal's partition did not spark off violence comparable with the Punjab holocaust. There was much tension between Hindus and Muslims in the two halves of truncated Bengal, but the killings tended to be sporadic and localised, and never assumed the scale of the massacres in Punjab. Early in 1950, however, there was another bout of widespread violence in East Bengal. This was followed by reprisals against Muslims in West Bengal, particularly in Howrah on the outskirts of Calcutta.

These patterns of communal violence critically influenced the flight of refugees and the directions in which they moved between India and Pakistan, as well as the government's responses to these events. Immediately after Partition, huge numbers of Hindus and Sikhs fled from West Pakistan, as did Muslims from North India more generally to the western wing of Pakistan. Between August and December 1947, some fifteen million people crossed the western borders between India and Pakistan, half of them Hindus and Sikhs seeking refuge in India, and roughly the same number of Muslims escaping to Pakistan in the opposite direction.[3] By contrast, the refugees from eastern Pakistan did not flood into India in one tidal wave. Rather, they came into India over a period of many years, sometimes in surges but more often in barely perceptible trickles.[4] In the end, however, they added up

[3] Spate and Learmonth, *India and Pakistan*, p. 130n.

[4] The table below on refugees coming into West Bengal between 1946 and 1962 is admittedly based upon official sources which always underestimated the numbers of refugees entering West Bengal, and which have only a factitious precision. Nevertheless it gives an indication of the orders of magnitude of the ebb and flow of the migration.

Migration of Refugees from East Pakistan to West Bengal 1946–1962

1946	58,602
1947	463,474
1948	490,555
1949	326,211

to an enormous total. By 1973, in the quarter of a century after Partition, six million Hindus from the east had come as refugees into West Bengal.[5] Significantly, the number of Muslims who decided to join their co-religionists in the east was much smaller: perhaps no more than a million and a half, in roughly the same period between 1947 and 1970.[6]

The sharp contrast between these migrations helps to explain why the Government of India viewed the refugee problem in the east and west in such different ways. From the start, New Delhi had accepted that Partition would result in large and irreversible transfers of population across the western border with Pakistan. The Government of India realised that refugees from the west would have to be escorted safely out of Pakistan and be fully and permanently rehabilitated in India.[7] It also swiftly decided that the

---

1950	1,172,928
1951	47,437
1952	531,440
1953	76,123
1954	121,364
1955	240,424
1956	581,000
1957	6,000
1958	4,898
1959	6,348
1960	9,712
1961	10,847
1962	13,894
Total	4,261,257 (4.26 million)

Source: Reports of the Committee of Review of Rehabilitation Work in West Bengal.

[5] See Table 1 in Pranati Chaudhuri, "Refugees in West Bengal".

[6] Chatterji, "Of Graveyards and Ghettos", p. 228.

[7] A Military Evacuation Organisation (MEO) was set up to arrange the movement of refugees across the border and was responsible for their

4.5 million acres of "evacuee" property, abandoned by Muslims who had fled to Pakistan, would be given to the refugees.[8] The transfer of Muslim property of those who left India to incoming Hindus and Sikhs became the cornerstone of official policies and programmes to rehabilitate the refugees from Punjab and western India.[9]

The influx of refugees into West Bengal was seen as a different problem altogether, both in scale and nature. Nehru was convinced that India could not cope with another refugee crisis of Punjabi proportions,[10] and, with the flawed reasoning that so often marked his response to complex problems,[11] continued to maintain, all the evidence notwithstanding, that Bengal had no refugee

---

protection en route. It also was to help civil authorities maintain law and order and protect the camps of evacuees waiting to move across the border into India. Rai, *Partition of the Punjab*, p. 78.

[8] Ibid., p. 120.

[9] The official account of the relief and rehabilitation measures for the refugees from West Pakistan is set out in *After Partition*; Tarlok Singh, *Rural Resettlement in Punjab*; Rao, *The Story of Rehabilitation*; and Luthra, *Rehabilitation*. M.S. Randhawa's *Out of the Ashes* gives an eyewitness account of these rehabilitation measures. A more scholarly assessment may be found in Rai, *Partition of the Punjab*; and Kudaisya, "The Demographic Upheaval of Partition", pp. 73–94.

[10] Nehru first referred to the Bengal refugees in his fortnightly letters to chief ministers only in April 1948. His equivocal attitude, both about India's capacity to do for the Bengalis what had been done for the refugees from the west, as well as his awareness of the potential dangers in their migration, is revealed in a letter of 1 April 1948: "We are naturally as much bound to help these refugees [from East Bengal] as any from Western Pakistan. *Nonetheless it must be remembered that it is dangerous to encourage this exodus as this may lead to disastrous consequences*." Parthasarathi, ed., *Jawaharlal Nehru. Letters to Chief Ministers 1947–64*, vol. I, p. 100 (emphasis added). A fortnight later he admitted: "We are very anxious that Hindus should not leave East Bengal. If they do so in very large numbers they will suffer greatly and *we might be wholly unable to make any arrangements for them*." Ibid., p. 108 (emphasis added).

[11] In her biography of India's first prime minister, Judith Brown describes

problem. To justify his case, Nehru insisted that conditions in East Bengal did not constitute a grave danger to its Hindu minorities. Well after the Hindu exodus had begun, he remained adamant it could be halted and even reversed. All that was needed, according to Nehru, was for the government in Dacca to deploy well-conceived "psychological measures" to restore confidence among the Hindu minorities.[12] This indeed was the aim of the Inter-Dominion Agreement of April 1948 between India and Pakistan.[13] It followed that the Government of India was against relief, let alone rehabilitation, of the Bengali refugees, since it was felt that handouts would attract economic migrants, as opposed to genuine refugees, to India.[14] Delhi also set its face firmly against redistribution of the property of Muslim evacuees from Bengal to incoming Hindu refugees. In contrast to its policies in the west, the plan was to hold their property in trust until Bengal's Muslims too returned home. Delhi's line was that refugees crossing the Bengal border in either direction should, and eventually would, be persuaded to return home. Long after it had become obvious that the refugees in Bengal were there to stay, Delhi clung to a stance where expedience triumphed over experience. The result was

---

Nehru's "inadequacy" in coping with complex administrative problems: he "could so often see the nature of the problem but could not see how to solve it." Brown, *Nehru*, p. 242.

[12] Jawaharlal Nehru to Dr B.C. Roy, 2 December 1949, cited in Chakrabarty, *With Dr B.C. Roy*, p. 144.

[13] In April 1948 the first Inter-Dominion Agreement provided for the setting up of Minorities Boards and Evacuee Property Management Boards in East and West Bengal, with members from the minority communities. Proceedings of the Inter-Dominion Conference, Calcutta, 15–18 April 1948, Government of West Bengal, Home (Political) Department Confidential File for the year 1948 (no file number), West Bengal State Archives.

[14] For a discussion of how the Indian state defined "genuine refugees" and distinguished them from "economic migrants", see Chatterji, "Right or Charity?", pp. 80–91.

that the centre, to which the constitution of 1950 had given powers to dictate rehabilitation policy throughout India,[15] did little to assist the West Bengal government to deal with its "refugee problem", even after Delhi finally and grudgingly acknowledged that such a problem did indeed exist.[16]

The government of West Bengal, however, could not afford to take such a panglossian view of the crisis. The partition of the province, by splitting the administration of West Bengal into two, crucially affected Calcutta's capacity to govern effectively. Partition had also exposed huge underlying schisms within the ruling Congress Party, as the various West Bengal factions tried to win control over an organisation which had previously been dominated by delegates from eastern Bengal. The first Congress government of West Bengal, headed by the East Bengal Gandhian Dr Prafulla Chandra Ghosh, fell in January 1948 after only six months in office, a victim of factional in-fighting. The ministry which replaced Ghosh was led by an erstwhile society doctor, Bidhan Chandra Roy, and it too was neither stable nor secure.[17] Dr Roy therefore did not have the luxury of ignoring the refugee problem and simply pretending it did not exist. By the middle of 1948, over

[15] The so-called "temporary and transitional provisions" in Article 369 of India's constitution made the centre responsible for the relief and rehabilitation of refugees. *Constituent Assembly of India. Debates*, vol. X, pp. 3–7. For a discussion of how the centre arrogated these responsibilities to itself, see Austin, *The Indian Constitution*.

[16] At the height of the 1950 riots which prompted over a million Hindus to flee from East Bengal, Nehru was still without a plan of action, while continuing to insist he was "giving the most earnest consideration to this problem of Hindus in East Bengal" and agreed with Dr B.C. Roy that "we can no longer drift". He admitted, however, that, "*this business of shifting millions of people is entirely beyond our capacity.*" Nehru to B.C. Roy, 17 February 1950, cited in Chakrabarty, *With Dr B.C. Roy*, p. 157 (author's italics).

[17] For an account of the factional conflicts which plagued the Congress in West Bengal in the first years after Independence, dividing and destabilising an already fractured party, see Sengupta, *The Congress Party in West Bengal*.

a million refugees had entered West Bengal. By the end of 1950, the number had risen threefold to almost three million. Since the entire population of West Bengal at the time of partition was twenty million, this influx of refugees in two years had driven it up by almost a sixth. In 1947, the province was already densely populated, indeed by any standards, overcrowded. By 1951 West Bengal had an average of almost 800 people per square mile,[18] and the province did not grow enough food for its own people, let alone for the incoming refugees.[19] In the critical years after Independence, West Bengal could not rely on help from the centre to cope with the traumas of Partition and with the grave problems which came in its wake. The state government had thus every reason to be desperately worried by the economic and social consequences of the continuing influx of refugees.

The initial response of the West Bengal government was to try artificially to keep down the numbers of people who were officially recognised as refugees, and therefore eligible for whatever meagre assistance government gave them.[20] To be classified as a refugee, Calcutta declared, a person had to have migrated to West Bengal before the end of June 1948; and in addition, he would have had to have been registered as a "bona fide refugee" before January 1949. Bona fide "registered" refugees, moreover, were entitled only to "relief", but not to "rehabilitation", given that that policy was based on the premise that the refugees had not arrived to stay. The next phase in the government's reactions was to cut back severely on such exiguous "relief" as was doled out, even to those relatively few refugees who had registered in time. It declared that able-bodied males who had been at a camp for more than seven days were not entitled

[18] The exact figure was 769 people per square mile. *Census of India, 1961*, vol. XVI, Part I-A, Statement II.I, p. 97.

[19] By 1941, even in a normal year, the West Bengal region had an annual per capita shortfall of 10 *seers,* or roughly 20 lbs, of rice, the main staple of the Bengali diet. Chatterjee, *Bengal in Maps*, p. 66.

[20] Chatterji, "Right or Charity?", pp. 77– 82.

to any relief,[21] this being part of its drive to shut down the relief camps as soon as it could. These policies, unbending and brutal though they were, were driven by the West Bengal government's need to limit the potentially huge financial liabilities of helping immigrants from East Bengal.[22]

Yet even as it strove to deny the "refugee" tag to as many as possible, and however loudly it protested that the refugees should go back from whence they had come, West Bengal's government could not ignore the political implications of the influx. Dr Roy was particularly alarmed by the fact that the great majority of these refugees had flocked to Calcutta, the political heart of West Bengal, and its surrounding districts.[23] Making their way to Calcutta made good sense to the refugees. Naturally they gravitated to places where they had kin and connections, and a chance to find work. Educated middle-class people, who were prominent among the first refugees,[24] were drawn to Calcutta and its suburbs because

[21] Memo No. 5610 (13) F.R., from the Secretary, Relief and Rehabilitation Department, Government of West Bengal to all district officers, 22 November 1948. This and other government memoranda cited below have been culled from the voluminous "Weekly Reports on Relief and Rehabilitation of Displaced Persons from East Bengal" contained in Government of Bengal, Intelligence Bureau (hereafter GB IB), File No. 1838/48.

[22] On the law and jurisprudence which constrained West Bengal's response to the crisis, see Sen, "The Legal Regime for Refugee Relief and Rehabilitation", pp. 49–64.

[23] The Census of 1951 discovered that most of the refugees from East Bengal ended up in just three districts of West Bengal, the 24 Parganas, Calcutta, and Nadia. In 1951, of a total of 2,099,000 refugees recorded by the census, 1,387,000, or two-thirds, were found in these three districts: 527,000 went to the 24 Parganas, 433,000 to Calcutta, and 427,000 to Nadia. *1951 Census*, vol. VI, Part I-A, p. 305. Ten years later, the Census of 1961 revealed exactly the same pattern. Refugees in West Bengal, now over three million in total, were found in the same parts of the province as a decade before. *1961 Census*, vol. XVI, Part I-A, p. 368.

[24] Of the 1.1 million refugees who had crossed the border into West Bengal by June 1948, 350,000 belonged to the urban middle classes and

it was the hub of administration, education, trade and commerce, and offered the best prospects of finding employment.[25] Calcutta also had another attraction: long before Partition, it had been home to a quarter of a million or so migrants from eastern Bengal.[26] In consequence, many of the refugees from the east came to Calcutta because they had friends, caste-fellows, and sometimes relatives in the big city who, so they hoped, would give them shelter while they looked for work and a more permanent home.[27] Artisans, who also were numerous among the refugees in the first wave, came to Calcutta for similar reasons. Many of them had traditionally worked for Hindu patrons, whether as craftsmen who fashioned idols out of clay, as bangle-makers who crafted the traditional lac and shell bangles worn by Hindu wives, or as weavers of cloth used by Brahmins for ceremonial purposes. If these skilled workers were to continue to ply their traditional trades in West Bengal, they had to make their way to the city and towns where wealthy Hindus lived and where some of their erstwhile patrons from the east had also resettled.

550,000 to their rural counterparts. Chakrabarti, *The Marginal Men*, p. 1. Saroj Chakrabarty also recalls that the first wave of refugees were "mostly" middle-class Hindus. Chakrabarty, *With Dr B.C. Roy*, p. 95.

[25] The influx of refugees, according to the census superintendent, was the main cause of the spectacular growth in population between 1941 and 1951 in districts such as the 24 Parganas, Calcutta, Jalpaiguri, Howrah, Burdwan, and Hooghly. Refugees went to places where there was industry or plantations, "neglecting agricultural parts". *1951 Census*, vol. VI, Part I-A, p. 139.

[26] The 1951 census discovered over 250,000 persons who had been born in what by then was Pakistan, but who had settled there *before* Partition: *1951 Census*, vol. VI, Part I-A, p. 248. In 1961, the census also found that one out of every five migrants from East Pakistan to Calcutta had arrived there more than two years before Partition: *1961 Census*, XVI, Part I-A, pp. 370–1.

[27] Studies of migration in Bengal before Partition have shown that there was a well-established tradition of white-collar migration from East Bengal to Calcutta and other large West Bengal towns. Chattopadhyaya, *Internal Migration in India*, p. 178.

A powerful logic thus dictated the decision of refugees to go to particular parts of West Bengal. They went to those places where they calculated they had the best chances of rebuilding their lives. But the West Bengal government found it convenient to close its eyes to this simple fact. In the thinking of the official mind, ensconced as it was in the warrens of Writers' Building, the "painful swarming" of refugees on its doorstep represented a grave threat to social and economic stability and to the ministry's very survival.[28] Unquestionably, the refugees placed an enormous strain on the already inadequate infrastructure of the city. But it was also clear that they were discontented with government. The *bhadralok* of eastern Bengal brought with them a lively tradition of political activism; indeed these refugees saw themselves as the true heirs of Bengal's nationalist legacy, the people who had made the greatest sacrifices for the Hindu homeland. Not surprisingly, they felt betrayed and angry at being received so coldly and so grudgingly by the beneficiaries of their selfless politics. B.C. Roy could see that these sentiments could be turned against his government by his many enemies, both inside and outside the Congress Party. As he explained to Nehru, the refugees were "in a state of mental excitement which enables the careerist politician to get hold of them and to utilise them for the various types of propaganda against the Government and the Congress."[29] His point was dramatically proven by the huge and heated demonstrations which met Nehru when he visited Calcutta in July 1949. Angry protesters, refugees prominent among them, hurled stones and shoes at Nehru's car and a bomb exploded at a public meeting he was addressing.[30] Nor could Roy disregard the fact that the dense concentration of refugees in relatively small clusters made them an especially numerous and dangerous constituency in the places

[28] *1951 Census*, vol. VI, Part I-A, p. 136.

[29] Dr B.C. Roy to Nehru, 17 April 1951, cited in Chakrabarty, *With Dr B.C. Roy*, p. 182.

[30] Mitra, *The New India 1948–1955*, p. 59.

where they had chosen to settle. In June 1949, the shock defeat of a Congress candidate in a by-election in South Calcutta almost brought Roy's government down.[31] From the end of 1949, another ominous trend was that refugee groups began forcibly to occupy privately owned property, as they had done at "Azadgarh", seriously alarming government and the propertied groups on whose support it relied. Whether "registered" or not, the refugees had become an awkward fact of life in Bengal with potentially serious political implications which government could no longer afford to ignore.

In February 1950, when fresh riots broke out in East Bengal and another enormous surge of refugees flooded into West Bengal, the provincial government at last gave urgent thought to their rehabilitation. Its old Canute-like stance – of trying to stem the tide of refugees by making it more and more difficult for them to enter West Bengal – had proved ineffective, although it continued to be pursued vigorously side by side.[32] The government had to recognise that something would have to be done about those who

[31] Sarat Chandra Bose, elder brother of the iconic Netaji Subhas Bose, stood as the candidate of a coalition of mainly left-wing parties and trounced the Congress candidate by 19,300 votes to 5750, a defeat which was generally believed to have been due to the large number of refugees paid to vote. Days later, in a speech given at New Delhi, Nehru expressed his opinion that Roy's ministry should resign. Chakrabarty, *With Dr B.C. Roy*, pp. 121–2.

[32] By various devices, government strove to keep down the numbers of those who were officially deemed to be refugees and therefore eligible for government assistance. One was to announce arbitrary cut-off dates, after which it declared that there would be no more refugees, or rather no more refugees who would be allowed by government to register, thereby losing entitlement to any relief or rehabilitation. In 1952, passports were made mandatory for travel between India and Pakistan in an effort to stem future inflows of refugees. In 1956, the Government of India introduced "migration certificates" to permit entry only to people "in certain special circumstances such as split families and girls coming into India for marriage etc." In December 1957, government again decreed that no assistance would be given to anyone who migrated after March 1958. Before they were granted migration certificates, those who, despite this draconian clause, still wanted to leave had to sign

had arrived in West Bengal and, as past experience amply demonstrated, were there to stay.

This was the context within which Roy's government formulated its policy of rehabilitation. It helps to explain why the central plank of that policy was to *disperse* the refugees from the areas in which they were concentrated, and in particular to get them out of Calcutta. The chief priority was to break up refugee clusters, dilute these dangerous and combustible concentrations, and drive as many of the refugees as possible out of the metropolis. The goal was to resettle them elsewhere, either in "empty" tracts as far from the city as could be contrived, or preferably to send them outside Bengal. Already in 1948, Dr Roy had mooted the idea of transporting some refugees to the infamous former penal colonies in the Andaman Islands in the Bay of Bengal.[33] Now he began to put pressure on government at the centre to persuade reluctant

---

undertakings that they would not claim any relief or rehabilitation benefits from government. *India Estimates Committee 1959–60*, p. 4. These harsh provisions remained on the statute books until 1964, when policy became even more restrictive in response to the fresh influx of about half a million refugees from East Pakistan. Government now insisted that *only those refugees who sought admission in relief camps would be offered rehabilitation.* This was intended both to limit the numbers eligible for government assistance, and also to be a measure by which the government could exert control over an increasingly recalcitrant refugee population. The second important distinguishing feature of policy after 1964 was the decision taken at this time that the border regions of West Bengal, Assam, and Tripura could receive and accommodate no more migrants; and *the new migrants would be offered rehabilitation only on the condition that they agreed to be resettled outside these border states.*

[33] As Chakrabarty has noted, in 1948 "the idea of settling refugees in the Andamans crossed the mind of the Premier. He sent there a team of eleven officials and non-officials, headed by the Relief and Rehabilitation Minister". In December 1948, the Government of West Bengal put to the prime minister of India its scheme for "the colonisation of Bengalees in the Andamans". Chakrabarty, *With Dr B.C. Roy*, p. 111.

governments in other states to accept some of Bengal's refugees.[34] Inside Bengal itself, the government embarked on a programme of setting up refugee colonies well outside Calcutta,[35] situating one or two of them in each surrounding *thana*.[36] At the same time, it made vigorous efforts to disperse the refugees to camps and colonies further away in the outlying western districts of West Bengal, particularly in Bankura, Birbhum, Midnapore, and Hooghly, where there was wasteland government could acquire. The core of the policy was to spread the "problem" as widely and thinly across the province as possible, diluting the political impact of these unwelcome "trouble-makers" by scattering them in faraway districts.

In practice, however, the policy proved easier to enunciate than to implement. Refugees showed a stubborn unwillingness to leave the camps and pavements of Calcutta for the places picked for them by the government, and demanded to have a say in where they would be rehabilitated.[37] Well before another influx in 1950 added a new and even more urgent dimension to this problem, the government's harsh response showed how seriously it took the dangers: it fell back on the ugly device of restricting the right to relief to those refugee families that fell in line with its plans.

[34] Nehru commented on the unwillingness of other states to help West Bengal in many of his letters to Dr Roy: "in spite of our efforts, it is difficult to induce most provinces to absorb more refugees. We have been pressing them to do so for some time." Nehru to Dr Roy, 16 August 1948, cited in Chakrabarty, *With Dr B.C. Roy*, p. 107.

[35] The city limits were defined by the area administered by the Calcutta Corporation; the larger surrounding urban and semi-urban agglomeration was known as the Calcutta Metropolitan District (or CMD).

[36] "Unlike the pre-1950 squatters' colonies [where refugees had settled of their own volition], these colonies were not concentrated in one or two areas", as "the Government was more interested in dispersing the refugee population throughout the C[alcutta] M[etropolitan] D[istrict], rather than allowing their concentration at one place." Chaudhuri, "Refugees in West Bengal", p. 22.

[37] Chatterji, "Right or Charity?", pp. 96–101.

Time and again in 1949, orders from Writers' Building directed camp superintendents to deny relief to "able-bodied" refugees who failed to co-operate with its plans to be sent from Calcutta for rehabilitation.[38] Memorandum after memorandum insisted that refugees could not be permitted to "hold up rehabilitation"; and stressed that "as soon as lands have been allotted and tents offered and railway warrants issued, refugees [were] expected to go to their new places of settlement."[39] By the time the riots in Khulna began to push new waves of refugees across the border into West Bengal, it was already a standard practice in the camps to starve the inmates into complying with government orders. Inevitably, it was the weakest and poorest among the camp population – refugees totally dependent for their survival on government's meagre "doles"[40] – who were most vulnerable to these pressures and became the focus of the government's drive to disperse them.

Jirat: "Rehabilitation" by Diktat

It was against this backdrop that, in September 1950, five hundred refugee families were frog-marched to the village of Jirat. All of them had fled from East Bengal in the wake of the carnage earlier in February of that year, and for more than six months they had been languishing in different "transit camps" or on the filthy platforms of Calcutta's Sealdah station. They came from many different parts of East Bengal.[41] Most were drawn from

[38] Memo No. 800 (14) R.R., from the Secretary, Relief and Rehabilitation Department, Government of West Bengal, to all District Officers, 15 February 1949, GB IB File No. 1838/48.

[39] Memo No. 8637 (13) Rehab., from J.K. Sanyal, Assistant Secretary to the Government of West Bengal, to all District Officers, 9 December 1949, GB IB File No. 1838/48.

[40] The term "doles" was used to describe free relief in cash or kind.

[41] They came from every one of East Bengal's districts other than the remote Chittagong Hill Tracts: *Memoir*, p. vii.

the entire spectrum of caste and occupational groups, including "Brahmins, Kayasthas, Baishyas, Weavers, Fishermen, Carpenters, Potters, Washermen, Barbars [*sic*], Blacksmiths, Bell-Metalsmiths, Workers and Scheduled Castes",[42] although most – seven out of ten – belonged to the higher castes.[43] Nine out of ten had been relatively well-off at home.[44] Some came from rather more modest backgrounds, but almost all had enjoyed a measure of financial security in East Bengal.[45] Three out of four of the men were literate; many had quite high educational qualifications and, remarkably, one in four of the women could read and write.[46]

In these respects, the new residents of Jirat had much the same characteristics as the general population of Bengalis who sought refuge in the west. Particularly in the first waves of migration from East to West Bengal, refugees tended to be drawn from the more privileged sectors of society. As scholars have come to recognise – although the government of the day singularly failed to accept this fact – there were good reasons why this was so.[47] The more educated and better-off the people were, the more likely they were to possess skills and movable assets which could be carried with them when they came to West Bengal, and the more probable it was that they already had kin, contacts, and connections there. In consequence, it was the better-off Hindus of East Bengal who showed themselves most ready to leave when they faced discrimination or violence at home. In contrast, the poorest were more likely to conclude that they had no option but to stand their ground since they had nothing they could take with them and literally nowhere to go.

[42] Ibid., p. 7.

[43] Sixty-eight of the hundred families randomly surveyed by Dr Guha's team were from the higher castes. Ibid., p.vii.

[44] See Table 11 in ibid., p. 19.

[45] All those interviewed had "had enough space to live in, enough food to eat and enough field[s] to earn their livelihood". Ibid., p. 20.

[46] See Table 13 in ibid., p 22.

[47] See van Hear, *New Diasporas*; and Chatterji, *The Spoils of Partition*.

But one feature distinguished the Jirat refugees from the refugee population at large: they had arrived in the camps of West Bengal utterly destitute. As the *Memoir* records, "[while the] majority of them [had] possessed a quantity of movable and immovable properties [in East Bengal] . . . these people had left Pakistan just after the incident [riots] of 1950–51 . . . [and so] they were . . . practically destitutes, having no place to live in, no income, no vocation to attend to, no hope of future recovery of the lost property . . ."[48]

Unlike many of the Hindu refugees who crossed the border in the immediate, and relatively peaceful, aftermath of the partition of Bengal (and indeed in sharp contrast to the majority of the Punjab refugees who had been escorted out of East Punjab under the protection of the Military Evacuation Organisation), the Jirat refugees had suddenly to abandon their homes in extremely turbulent circumstances, and in consequence most fled empty-handed. Some of those who had been able to take a few goods or chattels with them were robbed on their way to the border: "Their journey to India was the outcome of oppression and loss. The Muslim Ansar party, police and customs officials in the name of searching the [luggage] appropriated most of the money and things of Hindus and subjected them to torture and unjustified punishment. At railway and ferry stations Hindus were detained for days or months together causing untold misery to their families." Others were forced to hand over whatever cash or valuables they had to officials on the Pakistan side of the border checkposts "on pain of punishment and even death" before they were allowed to leave.[49] So, by the time these unfortunates reached the "transit camps" they literally possessed nothing but the clothes they were wearing.[50] And unlike the Punjab refugees, they had no prospects

[48] *Memoir*, p. 12.

[49] Ibid., p. 24.

[50] When interviewed fifty years later, one inmate who was still at Jirat recalled how she and her family left their substantial properties in Barisal with

either of recovering the assets which they had left behind or of being compensated for their losses by the government.[51]

Although the *Memoir* does not state this explicitly, it can be assumed that those who ended up in Jirat had no relatives or friends in West Bengal to whom they could turn for temporary shelter, or for help in finding work.[52] This explains why they stayed on in squalid camps for what must have seemed an interminably long wait of six months between the outbreak of the riots in February and their transportation to Jirat in September; and why, despite their range of skills and relatively high levels of literacy, they needed government "doles" to survive. They "agreed" to be sent to Jirat because the government had made it unequivocally clear that only those who did as they were told to do would continue to receive the doles and assistance. The beggars of Jirat could not be choosers: it was a question of accepting the government package or getting nothing at all.

Even so, they were ill prepared for the bleak prospects they faced when they arrived at the spot the government had chosen for them. The forest had reclaimed Jirat. The village and its surrounding areas were covered by jungle so dense "that even in broad daylight people did not dare to enter."[53] The government's plan was that able-bodied refugee males would swiftly clear the forest and build their camp. But it turned out that the work of taming

---

only one set of clothes: *"sudhu ekta dhuti-kapore oi desh chaira ei deshe ashchi."* Raychaudhuri, "Nostalgia of 'Desh'".

51 For details of the compensation schemes devised for the Punjab refugees, see Rai, *Partition of the Punjab*, pp. 145–9.

52 In the "family histories" recorded by Dr Guha's team, no mention was made of relatives or friends. In her interview with Anasua Basu Raychaudhuri, Renubaladevi recalled that her brother-in-law (presumably based in West Bengal) had helped to arrange for her and the other members of her family to be transferred from Sealdah Station to the Chandmari transit camp in Nadia. Raychaudhuri, "Nostalgia of 'Desh'".

53 *Memoir*, p. 4.

the wilderness could not begin at once because the government had yet to acquire legal title to the land: "a section of the local people" who "were unsympathetic to the refugees" had blocked the government's proposed acquisition by filing lawsuits against it.[54] It was only on 28 November, almost three months after the first families had arrived in Jirat, that work on the camp began. Under the direction of the camp superintendent, those men who were still relatively "able-bodied" after camping in a tropical forest for three months were instructed to cut down the trees and clear the scrub. In return for a daily wage of one rupee,[55] they were ordered to excavate tanks, level the land, build roads, and do the groundwork for houses and gardens. Government then gave each refugee family a house-building loan of Rs 500, repayable over five years in five equal instalments at an annual interest rate of 3 per cent. It also sold each family two bundles of corrugated iron sheets, to be paid for out of their exiguous house-building loans, to provide roofs over their heads.

The refugees had no say in the layout of their new village. Instead they had to work to a plan drawn up by a faraway Refugee Rehabilitation Department in Calcutta.[56] Even the review team could see that the mandarins sitting comfortably at their desks in Writers' Building had got it badly wrong: the plans had to be sent back to Calcutta to be redrawn "*on no less than eleven occasions*".[57] Even so, the planners still failed to get some essential matters right. Latrines were built far from the huts which they were meant to serve and too close for health to ponds and water tanks. When the rains came, the lavatories flooded and polluted the surrounding area and the water in the tanks, making it unsafe and unpotable and spreading disease among Jirat's inhabitants.[58] The planners had

[54] Ibid.

[55] Ibid., p. 7.

[56] Ibid., p. 5.

[57] Ibid. Emphasis in the original.

[58] Ibid., p. 10.

also failed to take into account the refugees' occupations when they allocated plots to them. As a result, "several families of the fisherman caste complained that the plots which were allotted to them in spite of their repeated protests" were those situated at the greatest distance from the riverside and "as such it was very inconvenient to them to carry on their trade properly from such a long distance."[59] In another piece of petty officialdom, the little despots of the Rehabilitation Department refused to allow refugees to live alongside other families from their own parts of East Bengal: "At the time of allotment of the plots, most of the inmates . . . formed into different groups according to the district they belonged to in Eastern Pakistan, and the members of each group applied for getting plots adjoining the others and were unwilling to get plots in other parts of the colony."[60]

During their unhappy stay at Jirat as well as in other "transit" camps, the refugees understandably sought to establish relationships of friendship and mutual support with others of their own kind from their own parts of East Bengal and, quite reasonably, they wanted to foster these connections in their new homes. Unlike the clerks in Calcutta, they were keenly aware that such link-ages were a vital resource: without them, they had little chance of building their lives anew in such unpropitious circumstances. But the government failed to see this. Even the anthropologists who had been called in to review the problem dismissed this sentiment as yet another form of refugee prejudice. Everyone failed to realise the obvious: without networks of mutual support and a sense of community, the refugees would be less able to achieve a measure of rehabilitation.[61]

[59] Ibid., p. 7.

[60] Ibid.

[61] Again, the stance of the Bengal government was very different from the official line on the Punjabi refugees. The desire of Punjabi refugees from one village to be resettled together "was at bottom", the government concluded, "a search for strength through social cohesion and community values", and so the government lent a hand to their efforts to get together in these ways. Punjabi

The government's idea was that once all the houses and other buildings at Jirat had been constructed, the head of each family would be given a "business loan" of up to Rs 500, which, in the same way as the house-building loan, would have to be repaid with interest over five years. Once every family had received its business loans, the government felt its job was done and deemed the population of Jirat to be permanently rehabilitated. All doles were then stopped; the government dispensary shut down and the inhabitants were left to get on with their lives as best they could in the wilderness where they had been dumped.

It was at this point that the folly of the government's policy of dispersal became apparent. Once the building works ceased and the dole was withdrawn, the refugees had to find other work in order to survive. But they were stuck literally in the middle of nowhere, Jirat being thirty-eight miles from Calcutta, and Bandel – the nearest town of any size – being too far to be reached by foot. The few fishermen among the refugees had a chance of plying their traditional vocation, since Jirat was close to the Hooghly River, but even they struggled to make a living since selling fish required customers with the wherewithal to buy them. But for the rest of Jirat's population, particularly those who had been white-collar workers, it was not at all clear how they could earn a living once the government's programme of works came to a halt.

Dr Guha's introductory remarks in the *Memoir*, in which he exhorted the refugees to "shun their old habits" and "dependence on the liberal professions" and embrace a life of "sweat and toil" suggests that the government expected the refugees to survive by cultivating the land.[62] But there was a critical flaw in this expectation. The government failed to recognise that, in contrast to East Punjab, where Muslim emigration to the west had freed up

---

refugees who were peasants with relatives in East Punjab were encouraged to settle alongside them. Rai, *Partition of the Punjab*, p. 126.

[62] *Memoir*, p. xiii.

almost 2.5 million "standard" acres of cultivable land,[63] the only "wasteland" in crowded West Bengal was land unclaimed for the good reason that it was not cultivable. The area around Jirat had been abandoned by its original inhabitants because it had become marshy, waterlogged, and malarial when the river changed course. It was no longer capable of supporting human habitation, let alone profitable agriculture. Moreover, even had the government developed the land by improving its drainage, which it failed to do, Jirat's meagre acres would have been insufficient to grow enough food to support its refugee population. At the height of Jirat's prosperity in the nineteenth century, the area had supported about 1500 people in all. The notion that it could now, in its degraded condition, produce enough to support a much larger population of 2500 was fantasy. In any event, the tiny plots the refugees had been allotted – at 10 *kottas* only about 1/6th of an acre for each family – were not capable of yielding the barest subsistence, even if the land had been exceptionally fertile, well watered, and well drained.[64] Not surprisingly, refugees who had been peasants in East Bengal and knew something about agriculture and who could do their sums, quickly decided that growing food in Jirat was a lost cause and demanded they be shifted to places less unsuited to tilling the soil.[65]

Nor were there realistic prospects of the refugees being able to supplement what they scratched out of their tiny plots by finding additional work as landless labourers, or sharecroppers on the *khas*

[63] Rai, *Partition of the Punjab*, p. 125.

[64] Even in the relatively fertile tracts of East Punjab where rural refugees were resettled, the government recognised that ten to fifteen acres was "the minimum area to meet the bare necessities of life". Ibid., p. 129.

[65] In January 1951, twenty-eight peasant families were duly sent off from Jirat to Chandipur camp in Midnapore district, where sufficient cultivable land was available under "Khasmahal". *Memoir*, p. 6. We do not know how they fared, although the omens were not good since Midnapore was historically a district which exported migrants, cultivable land there having been scarce for many decades.

(or demesne) lands of local landlords. Hooghly district already had a surfeit of landless labourers and underemployed, land-hungry, peasants of its own.[66] Naturally the local people held on fiercely to such jobs as were going. The hostility of the locals towards the refugees, on which Dr Guha remarked, had much to do with their intense competition with the outsiders in Jirat for scarce resources and even scarcer opportunities for employment. Not that the refugees had much chance of being able to snatch jobs from the locals. Landlords, creditors, and patrons preferred to employ local people whom they knew and who were integral parts of their networks of dependent, and often indebted and indentured, clients.[67] Even had there been a "free market" in agricultural labour in rural West Bengal, which there was not, the mainly high-caste and middle-class Jirat refugees were singularly unsuited to compete effectively for work requiring hard manual labour, knowledge of local conditions, and experience of cultivation. One solitary Brahmin refugee – Ananta Kumar Banerjee – broke all caste and social taboos to try his hand at farming,[68] but this was simply one man's optimism triumphing over his lack of experience.

Most refugees tried to find work in which they could deploy their traditional skills, but very few succeeded. Only twenty-two people actually found jobs outside the camp. Six found work as teachers inside the camp's one ill-equipped primary school. Forty-eight others set up as petty traders.[69] A handful took advantage of the fact that Jirat was relatively close to a busy railway line to eke out a precarious living by hawking goods on local trains.[70] A few others were even more inventive. Some joint families split into

[66] Bose, *Agrarian Bengal*, pp. 29–30.

[67] Bose shows that the use of tied labour was widespread in West Bengal, and particularly so in Hooghly district. Ibid., p. 30.

[68] *Memoir*, p. 11.

[69] The *Memoir* is not specific about this, but the small, grainy, and obscure photographs appended to it suggest that they sold coconuts, fish and vegetables. Jirat Plate V, Figures 6, 9, 10, and 12.

[70] *Memoir*, pp. 7–8.

two or more nuclear parts to enable each part to claim the housing and business loans. Others simply took the cash and disappeared altogether, no doubt returning to the big city to begin their search for work, with Rs 500 in their pockets.[71]

For the less fortunate majority who could not find sufficient paid employment and had no option but to remain in exile where the government had sent them, life was very hard indeed. The *Memoir* is an eloquent testimony to their suffering. "A very high proportion of [the camp's inmates] were on the verge of starvation and death."[72] The average income of the families was Rs 10 a week,[73] which was "not sufficient . . . to meet the daily necessities of life."[74] Many earned nothing at all.[75] Considering where the camp was situated, it was no surprise that disease was rife, particularly malaria and dysentery. During the two-month period that Dr Guha's team stayed at the camp, no fewer than twenty-one inmates died from these diseases. The camp children were without exception "undernourished"; most were ill, suffering from scabies and other ailments aggravated by malnutrition. They had a primary school for sure, but it had no walls, no pencils and textbooks, no paper or even chalk and slates: the children had to brave the elements while scratching their letters on palm leaves with bamboo reeds.[76] The faces of the adults, the *Memoir* reports, were "grave" and "full of anxiety".[77]

When asked about the causes of their "tension" – since discovering the reasons for discontent in Jirat was, after all, the study

[71] Ibid., p. 6.

[72] Ibid., p. 12.

[73] Interestingly, but not altogether surprisingly, the lower castes did slightly better, earning an average income of Rs 11 a week, since they were better able to find and hold down manual jobs. See Table 2 below.

[74] *Memoir*, p. 14.

[75] See Table 8 on p. 14, ibid.

[76] Ibid., p. 9.

[77] Ibid., p. 12.

team's brief – eight out of ten of the men and every single woman gave financial insecurity as the main cause. Nine out of ten men put having a regular source of income at the top of their wish list. As Table 8.1 below shows, the problem of how to earn a living was far and away the biggest worry of the inhabitants of Jirat. Equally unsurprisingly, concerns about ill health and the lack of even the most basic medical facilities loomed large among their concerns, as did the worrying backcloth of strained relations with local people.

Yet amazingly, despite all this evidence, nobody questioned the logic of trying to set up a rehabilitation camp for destitute, but mainly literate, refugees in the middle of a malarial swamp many miles from the nearest town. When asked for their views on their predicament, the refugees told the visiting scholars that the chief problem was the lack of employment around Jirat. But this self-evident point was dismissed out of hand by Guha and his colleagues as pathetic whingeing. Even after many of the refugees voted with their feet and ran away,[78] the government failed to recognise what lay at the root of the problems at Jirat and dubbed those who fled "deserters". The anthropologists put the blame for their troubles on the refugees themselves, berating them for being "infantile" and for their "helpless dependence" on government largesse.[79] Their study of refugees in Jirat concluded with a pseudo-scientific "analysis"which almost beggars belief in its arrogant complacency.

> The processes of regression as a consequence of accumulated tension were more visible in the subjects studied . . . a kind of primitivation [*sic*] of the behaviour of the subject seemed to be operative. His actions became less mature, more childish; the sensitivity of his discriminations and judgements diminished, his feelings and emotions became more poorly differentiated and controlled like those of

[78] By February 1951, no fewer than 64 families had already fled the camp. Ibid., p. 6.

[79] Ibid., pp. 30–2.

Table 8.1

Frequency Distribution of the Needs of Male and Female Subjects at Jirat

Needs of males (N=51)	*No. of responses*	*Per cent*
Means of livelihood	438	4.3
Financial help (including business loans)	38	74.5
Financial security	3	6
Easy life	3	6
Education	7	13.7
Sympathy from Government and local people	13	25.5
Perfect rehabilitation	10	19.6
Good social surroundings	1	2
Construction of roads etc. in the colony	3	6
Land for cultivation	3	6
Residence	4	8
Re-opening of government ration stores	1	6
Establishment of a mill	12	23.5
Medical treatment	15	29.4
Justice from government	9	17.6
Proper placement	4	6
Needs of females (N=49)	*No. of responses*	*Per cent*
Sympathy from Government officials	47	96
Regular financial and other help from government	49	100
Permanent source of income and good financial condition	17	34.6
Sympathy from local people (decent behaviour from them)	45	91.8
Easy life	2	4
Affinity of customs and social intercourse with local people	6	12
Secure future	7	14
Medical treatment	12	24.5
Education for children	6	12
Land for cultivation	8	16.3
Peaceful life	1	2

Source: Tables 15 and 17, *Memoir*, pp. 27–8.

> a child. In general, his psychological field tended spontaneously in the direction of a lower level of simplification, which is a reversal of the normal trend towards higher level complexity characteristic of the growth and maturation of the individual. Thus we find from the life histories that they were childishly dependent on the Government support. They found nothing to be done by themselves, seemed to have lost all initiative and organised efforts befitting adult persons and in its place expected that everything would be done for them by the Government. As a proof of the diminution of the sensitivity of their discrimination and judgement some subjects when asked to state their idea of rehabilitation or what Government should do for them, replied that they have lost all their power of judgement and thought, and could not answer the question and asked the interviewers to suggest these for them.[80]

This pretentious jargon allowed government conveniently to conclude that its policy of dispersal had failed not because its assumptions were misguided and its implementation shoddy and offhand, but because of the refugees' own failings. Their experience of dislocation, Guha decided, had rendered the refugees "childishly dependent on . . . Government support" and lacking "all initiative and organised efforts befitting adult persons . . ."[81] These conclusions merely encouraged Dr Roy and the government of West Bengal to strive even more officiously to rid Calcutta and West Bengal of these awkward and expendable "primitives" who had congregated on its doorstep.[82]

[80] Ibid.

[81] Ibid., p. 32.

[82] In due course, this description would develop in official discourse into a full-blown stereotype of the Bengali refugees. They were described as possessing "a certain psychological weakness or deficiency" which made them reluctant "to forgo the advantage of gratuitous relief" and disinclined "to embrace the rigorous discipline of independent existence." Rao, *The Story of Rehabilitation*, p. 155. For an analysis of the origins and implications of this stereotype, see Chatterji, "Right or Charity?"

Azadgarh: "Do-it-Yourself" Rehabilitation

The contrast between the story of Jirat and developments at Azadgarh is striking and instructive. The refugees who made their homes in the "bastion of freedom" came, interestingly, from a very similar milieu to those who were sent to Jirat. Most belonged to the higher castes (including Brahmins, Baidyas, Rishis, and Kayasthas), although some, mainly Namasudras, were drawn from lower down the Hindu hierarchy.[83] Many had been modestly well-to-do in East Bengal, although significantly more of the Azadgarh residents than the denizens of Jirat – one in three males and about half the females – described themselves as having been "poor" in their eastern Bengali homes.[84] Just as the inmates of Jirat camp, they too were moderately well educated: only one in five of the sample was totally illiterate.[85] They included some artisans, mainly carpenters. By and large they tended to have been drawn – as were the Jirat evacuees – from East Bengal's Hindu middling classes. Owning an average of 2.5 to 3 acres of land and earning an average annual per capita income of about Rs 300,[86] the Azadgarh refugees had been getting by fairly well in eastern Bengal before Partition disrupted their lives.

But at this point the tale of the two settlements diverges. The Azadgarh colonists migrated to West Bengal earlier than the Jirat inmates, and they came in more peaceful circumstances. Some indeed had left before Partition, others left soon after the division of the province, but all had arrived in West Bengal some time before largescale communal violence broke out in East Bengal in February 1950.[87] In consequence, they had been able to make the move in a more considered and orderly fashion. They had weighed the

[83] *Memoir*, p. 53.

[84] See Table 2 in ibid., p. 57, as compared with Table 11 on p. 19.

[85] Ibid., p. 57.

[86] Ibid., Appendix H.

[87] Ibid., p. 61.

pros and cons of leaving for West Bengal against their prospects as second-class citizens in a Pakistan where they would be a small, unprotected, and permanent minority. They had decided to leave not in immediate fear of their lives but after having reckoned that they would be more secure and better able to protect their values and status among their fellow-Hindus in the west.[88] They planned their move, often arranging temporary accommodation for themselves with friends or relatives in the west and, significantly, contriving to bring with them some cash and valuables when they decided to go into exile.[89] For all of them, the chosen destination was Calcutta.

They entered West Bengal at a time when the central plank in government policy was to deny refugee status to most of those coming to the west and where every device was used to get them to go back "home". The government's plan was simple: to push the refugees out of an already overcrowded metropolis. But since these particular incomers had some resources of their own and were not dependent on government handouts, the crucial difference between them and the Jirat refugees was that they had the wherewithal with which to resist Leviathan.

The "ring leaders" of the Azadgarh colonists had been staying in the Tollygunge area of Calcutta since Partition and had come to know each other at the local Taltolla club. When the government announced that all refugee camps would be shut down and the refugees would be dispersed by the end of 1949, they sprang into action.[90] Indu Ganguli had already identified a vacant six-acre

[88] Ibid., p. 64.

[89] Ibid., p. 61.

[90] In July 1949, Calcutta announced that within just three months all relief camps in West Bengal must be closed down by 31 October 1949. A little later, after a storm of protests, the deadline was grudgingly extended by sixty days to 31 December 1949, "with a clear direction that rehabilitation of the inmates of the camps be completed by that date and the camps be closed with effect from that date." Memo No. 8637 (13) Rehab., from J.K. Sanyal,

plot which would serve as the core of a new colony for his fellow refugees. Now, supported by a gang of friends, he occupied the plot by force. In the next few weeks, they took over other empty plots which were adjacent to the six-acre site or close to it. After rioting broke out in February between Hindus and Muslims, and Muslims fled from an area in which many of them had lived in the past, the refugee leaders also occupied abandoned Muslim properties. They then carved the whole area – now expanded into a sizeable holding of about forty acres in all – into plots of roughly equal size and spread the word that these plots would be given to refugees.

Azadgarh was only one of a spate of similar takeovers by refugees of empty tracts, mainly on the outskirts of Calcutta, whether owned by government or by private landlords in late 1949 and early 1950. The reaction of government and the land-lords was predictable and harsh. They sent in police and their bully boys to oust the squatters. Yet despite the threat of incurring the government's wrath, "the rush [for these plots]", the *Memoir* records, "was [so] considerable [that] many had to go back disappointed."[91] This "rush" calls to be compared with the sullen reluctance with which most refugees moved to Jirat and the other camps where government wanted them to go. Plainly, the Tollygunge area on the southern fringes of Calcutta was one where refugees were eager to settle. They had themselves found the site for their new colony and had obviously chosen well. Azadgarh was close to mills, offices, and factories and so there were jobs at hand. It was a locality where relatively well-to-do Muslims and those who served them had lived in the past,[92] but who now, in large measure had fled after

---

Assistant Secretary to the Government of West Bengal, to all District Officers, 9 December 1949, GB IB File No. 1838/48.

[91] *Memoir*, p. 51.

[92] The Nawab of Oudh and his family had settled in Ward 75; and the descendants of Tipu Sultan of Mysore in Ward 78, both in the general Tollygunge area on the southern fringes of Calcutta. Bose, *Calcutta: 1964*,

Partition and the recent rioting.[93] This left much abandoned land and also many Muslim houses up for grabs, but also jobs to be filled and services to be maintained in the broader local economy. So evident were the advantages of Azadgarh's location for refugees seeking work and shelter that, when vigorous efforts were made to dislodge them, they resisted the attacks and stood firm. Indeed they fought back with remarkable ferocity. As the *Memoir* graphically puts it, they were "a people who meet sword with sword [in . . .] their struggle with the police and the *goondas* hired by the landlords to oust them from their land."[94] This was a far cry from the acquiescence of the Jirat evacuees or, after their bitter experiences in the camp, the desperation which encouraged the more enterprising among them to run away at the first opportunity.

The two colonies were planned, developed, and organised in ways so sharply different that they seemed worlds apart. Azadgarh, unlike Jirat, was carefully planned by the refugees themselves, and swiftly and efficiently constructed. Before occupying the site, Ganguli and the other leaders had meticulously surveyed the terrain, supplementing their drawings with photographs. They plotted out the area and drew up plans before taking it over. Once they had occupied the land, they immediately set to work. All the refugees "joined their heads and hands together in setting up a self-sufficient colony by making pathways, levelling the uneven agricultural land and at certain places removing jungles infested with jackals [and] snakes";[95] they sank tube wells, built a school, and constructed a market and shops. About four hundred little

---

p. 64. Their retainers and staff followed in large numbers, as did the traders, scholars, and divines they patronised, and they had long been settled in the Tollygunge area. Siddiqui, *The Muslims of Calcutta*, p. 21.

93 Chatterji, "Of Graveyards and Ghettos", p. 222.

94 *Memoir*, pp. 72– 3.

95 Ibid., p. 51.

plots, which at 2.5 to 3 *kottas* or 1/20th of an acre each were barely a quarter of the size of those offered by government at Jirat, were handed over to individual families. Each family then proceeded to construct upon the modest plot its own home out of its own resources and according to its particular needs. Some were quite solid structures with corrugated iron or tiled roofs and brick walls; others had roofs and walls of "*hogla*" thatching, while the poorest families made huts out of thick brown paper soaked in tar to shelter themselves against the elements.

This building work was undertaken with enthusiasm and an impressive attention to detail, all refugees taking pride in their new homes, however humble. The visiting anthropologists were deeply impressed by the high morale of the Azadgarh colonists, which, as they did not fail to remark, was so different from the despair they had witnessed at Jirat.[96] They were also struck by how well organised and how cohesive the colony at Azadgarh had become. An elected central committee and three elected ward committees ran the colony. The central committee required a down-payment of Rs 15 from each plot holder; it also charged daily rents from the vendors who had stalls at the colony's market. Ward committees, in their turn, raised Rs 2 a month per family and paid a third of these local taxes into the central fund. Ward committees were responsible for looking after communal areas and pathways, for sinking tube wells and keeping them in good working order. The central committee was in charge of such key matters as sanitation and schools. It also handled the many legal cases which were instituted by landlords against the colonists, and maintained a "fighting fund" and a "fighting corps" to defend the colony, whether against litigation in the courts or attacks and harassment on the ground. There was also a "Mahasanad", or supreme council, made up of the presidents, secretaries, and other influential members of all lesser committees whose job it was to settle

[96] Ibid., p. 53.

disputes between the different committees and to make the critically important decisions which affected the colony as a whole. Barring occasional differences which cropped up, mainly on issues to do with party politics, the colony ran smoothly and had an air of "peace and tranquility",[97] a veritable oasis in the deserts of despondency in post-Partition Bengal.

By April 1951, not much more than a year after Azadgarh had been set up, its committees with only these very modest resources at their disposal had already managed to create welfare facilities for its inhabitants which were far superior to those at Jirat, with all the weight of government behind it. Azadgarh had established two schools, one for boys and one for girls, at which a hundred or so children were enrolled and received an education. The colonists had also arranged with the Dalmia Relief Committee, a local charity, to provide regular medical help: Dalmia's mobile medical van visited the colony twice a week and tended to the sick. A refugee colonist who was a trained homoeopath held a daily clinic, and all the other inhabitants of the colony took turns to ensure that the volunteer was rewarded with a square meal every day. The central committee also persuaded the Red Cross to provide the colony with free milk powder, which it distributed to infants and children below seven, to the elderly, the infirm, and pregnant women. So despite the fact that clean water remained scarce and sanitation poor – the colony was not connected to the city's main water supply or its sewage systems, its latrines being nothing more than cesspits – the Azadgarh squatters were far healthier than their counterparts in Jirat. Some of the women admittedly were reported to have been "in delicate health" from undernourishment and overwork,[98] but the visiting inspectors recorded no deaths during their two months at Azadgarh.

In addition to these basic amenities, the colonists had managed to create facilities for leisure and recreation which, at Jirat, were

[97] Ibid., p. 52.
[98] Ibid., p. 54.

"completely lacking".[99] There was a clubhouse for men and boys at Azadgarh which had daily newspapers and a room where political issues could be discussed. The clubhouse also offered games, music, and dance, and – a commentary on the embattled mentality of a colony determined to defend itself – physical training on military lines. Women and girls had a club of their own, where they received lessons in vocal and instrumental music and learned how to knit and sew. "The ladies were also found to organise processions and meetings to ventilate their grievances."[100] The clubhouses of Azadgarh evidently had become the focus of a vibrant community life.

All of this achievement depended critically on the inhabitants of Azadgarh being able to support themselves and their colony. The *Memoir*, which is full of much other fascinating information, is relatively silent on details about occupations and earnings. But it confirmed that most of the colonists managed to get by "eking [out] their livelihood" in many ways. Some ran "petty shops", which sold vegetables grown in tiny kitchen gardens or tailored garments, sewn at home by wives and daughters. Others became hawkers of the locality in cheap goods, mainly glass and brassware. A few found work as "petty hands in neighbouring mills and factories". Some wove baskets or made drums for sale. Others invested the little capital they had been able to bring with them in setting up small-scale cottage "industries", such as the manufacture of earthen ovens. A few were able to find regular employment in offices, albeit "drawing a very small salary", while others became barbers, or carpenters, or furniture polishers.[101] These businesses appear usually to have been family enterprises: indeed most Azadgarh families had more than one earning member in the workforce. In many of the families, women made a vital contri-

[99] Ibid., p. 63.
[100] Ibid., p. 53.
[101] Ibid., pp. 53, 59.

bution to the domestic economy.[102] By the combined hard work of men, women, and even children, these families somehow managed to get by, earning just enough to sustain themselves. The average weekly income of the Azadgarh families, as Table 8.3 shows, was almost twice as high as the weekly earnings of their fellow refugees at Jirat (who, it will be recalled, earned an average of only Rs 10 a week per family). While this was substantially less than they had earned in East Bengal, the gap between the world the refugees had lost and what they regained in Azadgarh was significantly smaller than the fall of income and drastic drop in standards suffered by the Jirat refugees (see Tables 8.2–8.4 below).

The conclusion is clear. In every way, the inhabitants of Azadgarh fared better than their fellow refugees at Jirat. Yet the government remained intent on forcing the inhabitants of Azadgarh out. Early in 1951, Dr Roy's government drafted legislation in secret intended to give it draconian powers to evict squatters and protect the right to private property enshrined in the 1950 constitution. In March 1951, when the clauses of the draft eviction bill were leaked to the public, Dr Roy was forced at a press conference to admit that the purpose of the bill was to

Table 8.2

Average Income of Jirat Families in East Pakistan and in Jirat Camp (in rupees, annas, and paise)

	Total annual income of all Jirat families in Pakistan		*Average income per family per week in Pakistan*		*Average income per family per week at Jirat Camp*	
	Rs	*A.P.*	*Rs*	*A.P.*	*Rs*	*A.P.*
Upper castes	88,154	00	53	00	10	10
Lower castes	26,648	00	27	80	11	130

Source: *Memoir*, Table 9, p. 14.

[102] See Azadgarh Plate IV in ibid., which shows women at work in a variety of occupations.

Table 8.3

Income of Azadgarh Refugees in 1950 (in rupees)

Caste	*No. of families*	*No. of members*	*Total income per annum*	*Average annual income per family*	*Average annual income per capita*	*Total weekly income*	*Average weekly income per family*	*Average weekly income per capita*
Higher castes	25	149	24,828	993.12	166.63	477.46	19.10	3.20
Lower castes	17	96	14,256	838.59	148.50	274.15	16.13	2.86

Source: *Memoir*, Appendix H, p. 130.

Table 8.4

Azadgarh Refugees' Income in Pakistan prior to their Migration to West Bengal (in rupees)

Caste Higher castes	*No. of families*	*No. of members*	*Total annual income*	*Annual income per family*	*Average annual income per capita*
Higher castes	16	200	52056	3253.50	260.28
Lower castes	14	89	29064	2076.00	326.58

Source: *Memoir*, Appendix H, p. 130.

enable the government to shut down refugee squatter colonies, of which Azadgarh was one of many. Faced with a sustained campaign against the eviction bill, the government of West Bengal was eventually forced to backtrack. The act when passed included a pledge that a "Displaced Person" in unauthorised occupation of land would not be evicted "until the Government provides for him other land or house . . . in an area which . . . enables the person to carry on such occupation as he may be engaged in for earning his livelihood at the time of the order."[103] Despite this caveat, the

[103] *West Bengal Act XVI of 1951. The Rehabilitation of Displaced Persons and Eviction of Persons in Unauthorised Occupation of Land Act. 1951.*

new legislation made it plain that the government intended to do what it could to "relocate", or more bluntly put, to evict, refugees in "unauthorised occupation" of property.

Having this Damocles sword of eviction constantly above them placed a huge burden of anxiety on Azadgarh's inhabitants. When Dr Guha's team visited the camp, soon after the purposes of the eviction bill had become common knowledge, it was the talk of the colony:

> Though they had acquired the zamindar's land by force and established themselves there, they did not feel any security of being there because they saw that the Government was moving in a direction which was likely to force them out because of the Eviction Bill . . . recently passed by the West Bengal Assembly. Since then they lost all peace of mind and have been living in a state of painful suspense.[104]

Understandably, the threat that Government might at any moment step in and destroy all that they had achieved at Azadgarh was their chief preoccupation. If they were to be displaced yet again, they would have nothing left to take to the new sites into which the government intended to dragoon them. They had already invested in Azadgarh whatever little they had been able to bring with them from Pakistan. If they were now forced to go elsewhere, they would be destitute and, like the inmates of Jirat, lack the capacity and resources to resist the government's orders. So, despite Guha's survey discovering that the Azadgarh refugees had done so well in so many ways, they seemed as full of "tension" as those at Jirat. Indeed they were "in a persistent state of insecurity about their continued existence at Azadgarh", so intense that it had undermined their otherwise good "group morale".[105] In this lies the terrible irony of the *Memoir*'s tale. The Jirat refugees were despondent because they could see no future for themselves in the place where the government had forced them to go, and the

[104] *Memoir*, p. 61.

[105] Ibid., p. 63.

Azadgarh refugees were desperately anxious because the government was determined to evict them from a place in which they had done well and where they wanted to remain.

Unlike Jirat, Azadgarh was an effective self-governing community. It was run much more efficiently by its elected representatives than Jirat, where an unpopular camp superintendent ruled the roost, a tinpot tyrant answerable only to faceless bureaucrats in Calcutta's secretariat. Azadgarh was governed for the refugees by the refugees. Its leaders, themselves refugees, understood what their constituents needed above all was a small space in which to live and some opportunities to earn a living. Moreover, they understood – as government did not – that refugees were keen to achieve their own rehabilitation and ready to deploy all their energies, drive, and resources to build up their little colony in Azadgarh. Refugees at Azadgarh had themselves cornered a spot which gave them the chance to earn a living. They organised, and paid for, most of the basic amenities they needed. They had created a community which provided its members with a context, with support and some protection, and above all a pride of belonging.

There is no doubt that Azadgarh's success owed much to its location on the outskirts of Calcutta; and that Jirat's failure was mainly a consequence of its situation in a malarial swamp miles distant from the nearest town. Azadgarh's inhabitants did well precisely because the colony was part of greater Calcutta, which afforded them jobs and markets at which to ply their trades, as well as access to charities which helped them in their quest to survive. As providers of cheap goods and services to the city, they were able in due course to be absorbed into its matrix.[106] Admittedly they paid a high price for being forced to enter at the bottom of the value chain, accepting low wages and having to work harder and longer hours than their competitors. But they gave all they

[106] On the processes by which another squatter colony, "Netaji Nagar", was gradually absorbed into the life of the city, see Ray, "Growing up Refugee".

had to this enterprise, deploying family labour, particularly that of women, in new ways which challenged the traditional norms of patriarchal control. They also accepted life in what, after all, was little more than an urban slum, with very little by way of basic facilities.[107] Yet in the end they transformed their colony into yet another working neighbourhood, one among so many in this teeming city of migrants,[108] but with distinctive features of its own.[109]

By contrast, Jirat presents a dismal picture. Its refugees had none of the opportunities which Azadgarh's colonists seized. They were dropped into an impoverished rural backwater, where their neighbours had been settled for generations and where local labour, already in abundant supply, was more than sufficient to meet the modest needs of a stagnant agrarian economy. Nor did Jirat provide the anonymity of a big city into which newcomers could imperceptibly merge. Jirat's indigenous communities, governed by custom and tradition, were personalised and exclusive. Its political economy was dominated by patron–client relations of long standing. This was not a context in which 2500 complete outsiders could graft themselves onto the neighbourhood's economy, or insinuate themselves into the interstices of local society.

How anyone who read the *Memoir* could have failed to conclude that Azadgarh was a more encouraging model than Jirat for the rehabilitation of West Bengal's refugees is difficult to fathom.[110]

[107] Chatterji, *Spoils of Partition.*

[108] Already during the Second World War, immigrants to Calcutta had outnumbered the local residents. *Census of India*, vol. VI, Part I-A, p. 247.

[109] Studies which suggest that Azadgarh's success was matched by other squatting refugees include Sinha, "Foundation of a Refugee Market: A Study in Self-Reliance Initiative"; Sen, "Life and Labour in a Squatters Colony"; and Chatterjee, "Midnight's Unwanted Children".

[110] Even Dr Guha, disparaging as he and his team were about the Jirat refugees' "childlike passivity", could see that the Azadgarh refugees had done

The *Memoir*'s findings were supported by other studies of West Bengal's camps and colonies commissioned by Delhi. A high-level "Fact Finding Committee" set up in 1954 by the Government of India to discover why refugees were running away from the West Bengal government's rural camps concluded that the plots given to refugee peasants were too small and situated in places "*totally unsuitable for cultivation*", while "the local population [was] able to obtain additional land or crop-share basis or supplement its income by other means, the displaced persons [were] handicapped from supplementing their income on account of *lack of local contacts*."[111] Schemes to encourage market gardening among the lower-middle classes failed for similar reasons. The camps were far from towns and cities where there was a demand for fruit and vegetables. "Many of them [the refugees] were not familiar with vegetable cultivation at all", "the soil was not suitable, irrigation facilities were lacking". Despite the obvious fact that "proximity to the market [was] very important for these colonies", "many of them were located *at a considerable distance from Calcutta* which [was] by far the most important consuming centre."[112] In trying to set up "township" colonies far from existing cities and towns, the government's plans collapsed because "the scope for finding gainful employment in business or trade . . . [was] extremely limited, and the rehabilitation of dispersed persons settled therein therefore present[ed] a very difficult problem." In contrast, the settlements which did well were those "[where] the displaced persons selected places where they felt their chances of rehabilitation were *greater*".[113] Colonies set up by refugees which

far better than those at Jirat, and was moved to recommend that, in future, refugees be allowed to take a more active role inside government camps. *Memoir*, p. 30.

[111] *Report of the Committee of Ministers for the Rehabilitation of Displaced Persons in West Bengal* (emphasis added).

[112] Ibid., p. 10 (emphasis added).

[113] Ibid. (emphasis added).

were, in effect, "adjuncts to the existing large urban towns" had "fared much better . . . as they [had] been able to settle themselves by getting gainful employment in factories, commercial firms or offices near these colonies or they [had] started small businesses or industrial establishments on their own. Many of these colonies [were] situated in the vicinity of Calcutta."[114]

The conclusions are unequivocally clear. Refugees did best in places where they had settled of their own volition; they did best of all in precisely those tracts from which the government wanted to eject them, whether by carrot or by stick. The refugees who fared worst were those who had no choice but to do as the government instructed them to do, or who were scattered like chaff, dispersed to out-of-the-way "empty" spots, far from the crowds of Calcutta or substantial district towns.

Yet the government of West Bengal resolutely ignored these findings. It continued to attempt, albeit with scant success, to throw refugees out of Calcutta and evict refugee squatters from government and private land in the city. When these efforts failed, the government chose simply to ignore these proliferating squatter colonies, allowing them to grow without regulation or amenities, without clean water, electricity, paved roads, or facilities to get rid of their garbage and sewage. At the same time, it continued every year to pay out large sums from the public purse to compensate the legal owners of the land on which the refugees were squatting. This failure of public policy continued for many decades, long after the amount paid as compensation added up to far more than what it would have cost government to resettle the refugees elsewhere with some chance of permanent success,[115] and in many cases more than it would have had to pay simply to acquire the land for the refugees in the first instance. It also pressed on with its vain efforts to disperse the refugees to distant camps outside West Bengal. It kept up pressure on the centre, and through it on

[114] Ibid. , p.12.

[115] *Report of the Committee of Review of Rehabilitation in West Bengal.*

other states of India, to take in these refugees and settle them in large camps in barren scrubland or jungles where refugees had no wish to go, where the local peoples did not want them, and where the host governments were distinctly unenthusiastic about taking on what they could see would be an unwelcome, unremitting, and intractable set of problems. And despite the many protests or "satyagrahas", which the refugees staged from time to time to back their demands to be resettled in West Bengal,[116] the government refused to budge, standing pat on the premise that there was simply no land in the homeland for refugees from the east.

It follows – official dissimulation notwithstanding – that the rehabilitation of Bengal's refugees failed not so much because too little was done for them and too late, but because the Bengal government stuck like a limpet to its disastrous principle of "dispersal". The government's policy was based on the assumption that the refugees had to be sent to places where there was empty land for them to occupy. This, as we have seen, was a fundamental error.

For its obduracy, the Government of Bengal paid a heavy price: not only in scholarly assessments about its tragic failures, but more to the point in its rejection by the electorates to which it was ultimately responsible. The government's stubborn commitment to dispersal was grounded in a particular and unique set of circumstances which West Bengal faced in the aftermath of Partition. Dr B.C. Roy's fledgling government calculated that it could not afford to alienate Calcutta's urban landlords, nor condone attacks on the sanctity of private property. Even after it became evident that the dispersal policy had failed, there were powerful arguments of political expediency for sticking to it. As refugee camps and squatter colonies in West Bengal became hotbeds of left-wing radicalism, the resolve of the provincial government to disperse refugees from Calcutta became ever stronger.

[116] For an account of the satyagraha of the "deserters" from Bettiah, see Chakrabarti, *The Marginal Men*, pp. 163–77.

Refugees were seen to be "combustible elements", as blue-touch paper capable of igniting a social and political revolution which might consume Bengal and India. Dispersal, then, had more to do with ensuring that refugees did not fracture the fragile crust of order than any genuine concern to rehabilitate them.

There is another dimension to this question which calls for comment. Policies of dispersing refugees and "asylum-seekers" still have a surprising currency today among policy-makers in other places and in other contexts. Indeed in West Bengal, even the Marxist-dominated governments whose rise to power paradoxically owed much to the support of refugee constituencies, continued to stick with this discredited policy.[117] Perhaps a clue to why this was the case can be found in the flawed assessment of the "refugee character". Those who have sought to resettle refugees have too often failed to recognise that refugees are thinking agents actively seeking to build new lives with their families in safer and more secure circumstances and surroundings. Instead they have tended to regard them as passive victims, the flotsam and jetsam of history thrust hither and yon across borders and in new places by events over which they have no control, incapable of seeing for themselves where and how to reconstruct their shattered lives.

In the case of the refugees of West Bengal, the government thought it knew better than the refugees themselves what was in their best interests, and stubbornly refused to accept any evidence to the contrary. When refugees proved reluctant to be "dispersed", government dismissed their resistance as "irrational". When the camps failed, it was not because they were the wrong solutions in the wrong places, but because the refugees had "regressed" to a state of "child-like" dependence. The government found it convenient to believe that refugees had clustered in and around Calcutta not as considered decisions based on intelligent

[117] See Jalais, "Dwelling on Morichjhanpi"; and Mallick, "Refugee Resettlement in Forest Reserves".

assessments of where they could best survive and prosper, but out of some unthinking "herd" mentality which made them huddle in urban ghettos. Likewise, the official mind brushed away the clearly expressed preference of refugees to stay on in West Bengal, or to return there from unpromising places – such as Dandakaranya on the barren borderlands of Madhya Pradesh, Orissa, and Bihar – as sentimental and irrational desires, to be taken no more seriously than the "clinging of a child to its parents". When its camps failed to deliver even a semblance of the goods of rehabilitation, the government clung against all the evidence to its view that the fault lay in the refugees' deep-seated apathy. As more and more of its camps failed, government grew more deeply convinced about the failings of the "refugee character" and more determined than ever to disperse the incoming refugees. The tragedy was that the more patently its policy failed, the more vigorously it was pursued by government. In this lie the lessons of Jirat and Azadgarh, which otherwise might merit no memorial in the greater scheme of things.

References

After Partition, Delhi: Publications Division, Government of India, Ministry of Information and Broadcasting, 1948.

Austin, Granville, *The Indian Constitution. Cornerstone of a Nation*, Oxford, 1966.

Bose, Nirmal Kumar, *Calcutta: 1964. A Social Survey* (Anthropological Survey of India), Bombay, New Delhi, Calcutta, and Madras, 1968.

Bose, Pradip Kumar, ed., *Refugees in West Bengal. Institutional Processes and Contested Identities*, Calcutta, 2000.

Bose, Sugata, *Agrarian Bengal. Economy, Social Structure and Politics, 1919–1947*, Cambridge, 1987.

Brown, J., *Nehru. A Political Life*, Yale, 2003.

Chakrabarti, Prafulla K., *The Marginal Men. The Refugees and the Left Political Syndrome in West Bengal*, Calcutta, 1990.

Chakrabarty, Saroj, *With Dr B.C. Roy and Other Chief Ministers (A Record up to 1962)*, Calcutta, 1974.

Chatterjee, N., "Midnight's Unwanted Children: East Bengal Refugees and the Politics of Rehabilitation", doctoral dissertation, Brown University, 1992.

Chatterjee, S.P., *Bengal in Maps. A Geographical Analysis of Resource Distribution in West Bengal and Eastern Pakistan*, Bombay, Calcutta, and Madras, 1948.

Chatterji, Joya, "Of Graveyards and Ghettos. Muslims in Partitioned West Bengal, 1947–67", in Mushirul Hasan and Asim Roy, eds, *Living Together Separately. Cultural India in History and Politics*, New Delhi, 2005.

———, "Right or Charity? The Debate over Relief and Rehabilitation in West Bengal, 1947– 50", in Suvir Kaul, ed., *The Partitions of Memory. The Afterlife of the Division of India*, Delhi, 2001.

———, *The Spoils of Partition. Bengal and India, 1947–67*, Cambridge, forthcoming.

Chattopadhyaya, Haraprasad, *Internal Migration in India. A Case Study of Bengal*, Calcutta, 1987.

Chaudhuri, Pranati, "Refugees in West Bengal. A Study of the Growth and Distribution of Refugee Settlements within the CMD", Calcutta: Centre for Studies in Social Sciences, Occasional Paper No. 55 (mimeograph), 1985.

Constituent Assembly of India. Debates, 1947–50, vol. X, Faridabad: Lok Sabha Secretariat, Government of India Press.

Guha, B.S., *Memoir No. 1, 1954. Studies in Social Tensions among the Refugees from Eastern Pakistan*, Calcutta: Department of Anthropology, Government of India, 1959.

India Estimates Committee 1959–60. 96th Report (Second Lok Sabha). Ministry of Rehabilitation, [Eastern Zone], New Delhi: Lok Sabha Secretariat, 1960.

Jalais, Annu, "Dwelling on Morichjhanpi. When Tigers became 'Citizens' and Refugees 'Tigerfood'", *Economic and Political Weekly*, 3 April 2005.

Kudaisya, Gyanesh, "The Demographic Upheaval of Partition: Refugees and Agricultural Resettlement in India, 1947–1967", *South Asia*, vol. XVIII, Special Issue (1995).

———, and Tai Yong Tan, *The Aftermath of Partition in South Asia*, London and New York, 2000.

Luthra, P.N., *Rehabilitation*, Publications Division, Government of India, 1972.

Mallick, Ross, "Refugee Resettlement in Forest Reserves: West Bengal Policy Reversal and the Marichjhapi Massacre", *The Journal of Asian Studies*, vol. 58, 1 February 1999.

Mitra, Asok, *The New India 1948–1955. Memoirs of an Indian Civil Servant*, Bombay, 1991.

Parthasarathi, G., ed., *Jawaharlal Nehru. Letters to Chief Ministers 1947– 64*, vol. I, New Delhi: Government of India, 1985.

Rai, Satya M., *Partition of the Punjab. A Study of its Effects on the Politics and Administration of Punjab (I), 1947–56*, New Delhi, 1965.

Randhawa, M.S., *Out of the Ashes. An Account of the Rehabilitation of Refugees from Pakistan in Rural Areas of East Punjab*, Bombay, 1954.

Rao, U. Bhaskar, *The Story of Rehabilitation*, New Delhi: Government of India, 1967.

Ray, Manas, "Growing up Refugee: On Memory and Locality", in Pradip K. Bose, ed., *Refugees in West Bengal*, Calcutta, 2000.

Raychaudhuri, Anasua Basu, "Nostalgia of 'Desh', Memories of Partition", *Economic and Political Weekly*, vol. 39, issue 52, December 2004.

Report of the Committee of Ministers for the Rehabilitation of Displaced Persons in West Bengal, Calcutta: Government of India Press, 1954.

Report of the Committee of Review of Rehabilitation in West Bengal of Displaced Persons from East Pakistan Squatting on Government and Requisitioned Properties in West Bengal, New Delhi: Ministry of Labour Employment and Rehabilitation, Government of India Press, May 1970.

Sammadar, Ranabir, *The Marginal Nation. Transborder Migration from Bangladesh to West Bengal*, New Delhi, 1999.

Sen, A., "Life and Labour in a Squatters' Colony", Occasional Paper No. 138, Calcutta: Centre for Studies in the Social Sciences (mimeograph), 1992.

Sen, Sarbani, "The Legal Regime for Refugee Relief and Rehabilitation in West Bengal, 1946–1958", in Pradip K. Bose, ed., *Refugees in West Bengal. Institutional Processes and Contested Identities*, Calcutta, 2000.

Sengupta, Prasanta, *The Congress Party in West Bengal. A Study of Factionalism 1947–86*, Calcutta, 1988.

Siddiqui, M.K.A., *The Muslims of Calcutta. A Study in Aspects of their Social Organisation* (Anthropological Survey of India), Calcutta, 1974.

Singh, Tarlok, *Rural Resettlement in Punjab*, Simla, no date.

Sinha, D., "Foundation of a Refugee Market: A Study in Self-Reliance Initiative", in P.K. Bose, ed., *Refugees in West Bengal. Institutional Processes and Contested Identities*, Calcutta, 2000.

Spate, O.H.K., and A.T.A. Learmonth, *India and Pakistan. A General and Regional Geography*, Bungay, 1967.

van Hear, Nicholas, *New Diasporas, The Mass Exodus, Dispersal and Regrouping of Migrant Communities*, London, 1988.

9

Of Graveyards and Ghettos

Muslims in West Bengal 1947–1967

THROUGHOUT THE LAST century, there has been a Muslim graveyard in Selimpore. This suburb, just south of Calcutta in the 24 Parganas,[1] was home to very many Muslims before Partition. Some were considerable landowners, part of the vanquished Muslim aristocracy settled by the British in south Calcutta in the late-eighteenth century.[2] In times past, the burial ground belonged to one such wealthy Musalman. Originally intended for the owner's family, the cemetery in time came to be used more generally by local Muslims. Spanning an acre, the unfenced plot straddled Selimpore Road and was bounded on the south by a large pond. Houses occupied by Muslims stood at its

I am very grateful to Ananya Kabir, Barbara Daly Metcalf, and Samita Sen for providing information and helpful insights; and to Anil Seal for his comments on the chapter as a whole.

[1] Selimpore has since been included in the city and now falls within Ward 92 of the Calcutta Municipal Corporation.

[2] Bose writes that "after the fall of Oudh, the Nawab was given a place of residence in Ward 75; and so were the descendants of Tippu Sultan of Mysore in Ward 78." Bose, *Calcutta, 1964*, p. 64. Their retainers and staff followed in large numbers, as did the traders, scholars, and divines they patronised, and settled in the Tollygunge area, not far from Selimpore. Siddiqui, *The Muslims of Calcutta*, p. 21.

northern edge. Beside them was a small shrine (dargah), probably the tomb of a minor *pir*.[3]

During the upheavals of Partition, Muslims left the area in large numbers. Many more fled Selimpore after the fearful Howrah riots of 1950, and squatter colonies of Hindu refugees from East Bengal sprang up in the suburb.[4] One of these colonies, Shahid-nagar, was located on the south-eastern edge of the burial ground. Others, including Bapujinagar and Adarsha Palli, formed what the police report described as "a sort of ring around the burial ground". Soon refugees from these colonies began to encroach upon the graveyard, gradually nibbling away at its edges. Once they got their foot in, they began to challenge the right of the few remaining Muslim families to use the graveyard to bury and honour their dead.

In the early 1950s the refugees repeatedly tried to get the grave-yard closed down on "health and sanitation" grounds, arguing that it was "located in a built up area . . . in the heart of refu-gee concentrations." When the Muslims refused to shut it down, Saralananda Sen, a journalist working for *Jugantar*, demanded action from the Calcutta Corporation. In March 1955, when the Muslims brought a body there for burial, Sen orchestrated a protest by the neighbouring refugees and bullied the family into burying the body instead at the graveyard at Anwar Shah Road, a couple of miles away in Tollygunge. Since burial grounds in Calcutta were intended for the exclusive use of specific Muslim

[3] Selimpore dargah does not find a place on Siddiqui's list of important *astanas* and dargahs in Calcutta. Siddiqui, *The Muslims of Calcutta*, appen-dix II, pp. 132–3.

[4] "Formerly the area was largely inhabited by Muslims, but during the riots of 1950 a good number of Muslims left the area and only a few of them have stayed there. At the moment, the area is full of refugees." Chief Administrat-ive Officer, Anjuman Mufidul Islam to Dr B.C. Roy, 3 April 1956, Govern-ment of Bengal, Intelligence Branch, file no. 2856/55 (henceforth GB IB, E No. 2856/55, and so on).

sects, ethnic, or occupational groups,[5] this is likely to have caused considerable embarrassment in Selimpore.

Two months later, a burial did take place at Selimpore. But this was only able to go ahead when a charity for burying Muslim paupers, the Anjuman Mafidul Islam, intervened. The Anjuman's head, S.M. Salahuddin, successfully petitioned the Standing Health Committee of the Calcutta Corporation for permission to conduct the burial. After this, the Muslims claimed that the refugees began to harass them in other ways as well: refugee children desecrated their graveyard by playing Holi on it, or by using some part of it as a football ground.

Matters came to a head a year later in 1956, when the Muslims tried to observe Shab-e-Baraat ceremonies at Selimpore. On *"Shobrat"*, as it is known colloquially in Bengal and Bihar, Muslims gather in burial grounds to remember their dead. The ceremony starts in the evening, when descendants of the dead bearing trays of halwa and parathas walk to the cemeteries, distributing food to the poor. All night they pray by the graves, which they adorn with flowers, incense, and candles. The festival is a vital part of the ritual calendar for Sunnis in Bengal, and these little graveyards hence are central to their spirit of continuity and community.

On this occasion, however, things went badly wrong. As the maulvi began his prayers at the Selimpore cemetery's south-eastern corner, refugees from the adjacent Shahidnagar colony gathered. Their behaviour was intimidating. Frightened, the maulvi abandoned the ceremony. Later that night, the Shab-e-Baraat was allowed to proceed but only because the police provided protective cover. When the Muslims lodged an official complaint,

[5] Siddiqui, *The Muslims of Calcutta*, p. 11. We do not know anything about this particular family's sect or ethnicity. However, the fact that the burial ground had a dargah on it, and was the site of Shab-e-Baraat ceremonies (see later in the chapter), suggests that it catered chiefly to Sunnis of the Barelvi persuasion. The Anwar Shah Road cemetery, in contrast, would have been intended mainly for the use of Shias.

the refugees countered it with the claim that they had purchased the corner of the ground on which the maulvi had conducted his prayers. The local policeman who was instructed to settle the dispute upheld the refugees' dubious claim (graveyards being *waqf* property which cannot be alienated or sold). He also dismissed as "baseless" Muslim complaints about refugee boys using the graveyard as a football field, concluding that these allegations of harassment had been "maliciously manufactured".[6]

This little tale aroused my curiosity, not least because of its striking parallels with the notorious "*pir* burial" case of 1924 in Calcutta's New Market.[7] In 1997 I went to Selimpore. There was no proper road to the site, and going down the narrow muddy track by rickshaw was like a journey to a place that time had passed by. All that now remained of the burial ground was a small corner, perhaps a sixth of the cemetery's original size, to the north of the road and adjacent to the shrine. Some elaborately carved tombstones still stood on what remained of the graveyard, decaying relics of once imposing graves of the big men who had owned the land. A few Muslim families still lived there, also to the north of the track, but in extremely reduced circumstances. When I asked the elderly *mutawalli* (custodian of the dargah), who had tended the dilapidated shrine and graves for more than half a century, he told me that for many years there had been no burials. The last, he reminisced, had taken place "under police protection . . . when Suhrawardy and Fazlul Huq were our leaders." Since then, he said, the main plot to the south of the road – which had neither a boundary wall nor masonry graves – had been encroached upon and vandalised, and was used

[6] This description of events at Selimpore is based on the lengthy report by the Additional Superintendent of Police, DIB 24 Parganas, 20 April 1956, GBIB, F No. 1010/56 (24 Parganas).

[7] For details about the heated campaign for the exhumation of the body of a fakir buried in 1924 in Calcutta's New Market, see McPherson, *The Muslim Microcosm*; and Datta, *Carving Blocs*, pp. 109–47.

as a football pitch by the neighbourhood boys.[8] This part of his story was undoubtedly correct since a makeshift goalpost stood provocatively at one end of the ground.

This vignette is a microcosm of what Partition has entailed for many Muslims of West Bengal. Recent historical work on Partition's human cost has concentrated on refugees who were driven across borders by the violence it unleashed. Partition's effect on the minorities it created on both sides of the border – minorities who for a variety of reasons chose not to emigrate to the "right" new nation – has not often been examined. This essay, which will attempt to set the Selimpore story within this wider context, is intended as a modest beginning in that direction.

I

It is now a commonplace to assert that the Muslims of the Indian subcontinent are not a homogeneous community; yet it needs forcefully to be reiterated in any discussion of West Bengal. Muslims in West Bengal were divided in many ways, by their varied ethnic origins, occupations, sects, and status, and were far more heterogeneous than their fellows in the agrarian tracts of eastern Bengal. Islam's expansion into the western tracts of Bengal has a longer and more complex history than its more recent inroads into the east. Islam first came to the west as the religion of the garrison towns and of its cosmopolitan new ruling elite: noblemen, merchants, soldiers, and saints from as far afield as Turkey, Arabia, Persia, and Abyssinia. Even after its social base grew more plebeian, Islam in these parts continued to have urban and cosmopolitan characteristics. Well into the twentieth century, the Bengali Muslim aristocracy continued to insist upon its foreign ancestry and to speak Persian or Urdu rather than Bengali. The earliest indigenous converts to Islam in western Bengal were drawn, it seems, from urban artisan castes – whether

[8] Author's interview with Khaleel on 26 May 1997, Selimpore.

the weavers (*jola*), tailors (*darji*), circumcisers (*hajam*), or bow-makers (*tirakar*) – whose function was to supply the needs of these city-based Muslim noblemen.[9]

Long after the Mughal conquest, which pushed Islam deep into the Padma delta and into reclaimed forests and marshes in the north and south-west of Bengal, in its West Bengal setting Islam remained predominantly a religion of city folk. As Calcutta developed into the East India Company's base for its transactions in Bengal and its incursions into upper India, and as a centre of industry and trade, West Bengal's Muslim population came to be even more varied. In the 1770s, for instance, Calcutta attracted Cutchi Memons from Kathiawad, and not long afterwards Muslim traders from Delhi and Lucknow. "Rankis" claiming to hail from Iraq came to monopolise the hide trade and Pathan leather merchants from the North-West Frontier set up shops around the Nakhoda mosque. In the late-nineteenth century, skilled craftsmen from distant parts of India were drawn in growing numbers to this city of opportunity; and many Muslim butchers, bakers, tailors, carpenters, cigarette makers, bookbinders, and leather workers settled in its suburbs.[10]

In the early-twentieth century, weavers from upcountry sought work in the jute mills along the Hooghly. They were followed by a much larger influx of unskilled Muslims, drawn by the lure of jobs on the shop floors of Calcutta's burgeoning industries. Another development in the twentieth century was the emergence of a small but significant Muslim middle class which came to play an increasingly visible role in the city's life. Mainly of Bengali origin, these "English-educated" matriculates and graduates moved to Calcutta and other large towns of the west when white-collar Muslims began to benefit from government patronage and its positive discrimination on their behalf. With *bhadralok*

[9] Eaton, *The Rise of Islam*, p. 101.

[10] McPherson, *The Muslim Microcosm*, pp. 9–15.

ambitions, these Muslims preferred not to live cheek by jowl with their ruder co-religionists in Calcutta's sprawling and insalubrious suburbs, and settled in the respectable central area around Park Circus.[11] Each successive wave of migration and settlement thus tended to graft another layer onto the palimpsest of Muslim Calcutta. By 1947, it had become a tessellated mosaic of "distinct sub-communal groups", each with its own unique and shifting history.[12]

By this time Muslims were to be found not only in the towns and cities but also in large numbers among the peasant communities in the countryside, particularly in the northern districts. But even here there was much variety. Not all of West Bengal's Muslim peasants were of local origin. Many, such as the Shershabadiyas, had moved to North Bengal to bring new land under the plough when the notoriously fickle Ganges changed its course, laying bare rich alluvial tracts in Malda.[13] Others were local people, converted after a fashion by the soldier-saints who proselytised in Bengal in the seventeenth and eighteenth centuries, and whose version of Islam still contained many elements of older folk religions and cults.[14] Most of these rural Muslims were Sunnis, as indeed was the vast majority of Bengal's Muslim population – the Shia communities of Murshidabad, Hooghly, and Dacca were tiny islets in a Sunni sea. The census of 1931, perhaps the most reliable enumeration of Bengal's population

[11] Ibid., p. 5.

[12] Ibid., p. 11.

[13] Legend has it that the Shershabadiyas belonged to Sher Shah's personal army and had been rewarded with land grants in Shershabad pargana. Mitra, *The New India*, p. 4.

[14] By the mid-nineteenth century, when Buchanan conducted his survey, about 70 per cent of Dinajpur's population was Muslim, but they forgot "the rules of their law on many points". Martin, *The History, Antiquities, Topography and Statistics of Eastern India*, pp. 723–6. For more details on the folk Islam of the Bengal countryside, see Eaton, *Rise of Islam*, and Roy, *The Islamic Syncretistic Tradition*.

in the first half of the century, discovered that there were more Muslims in villages than in towns in the province as a whole. But in many parts of the west, particularly in Burdwan division, it remained the case that more Muslims lived in the cities than in the countryside.[15]

Even the most cursory description of the Muslims of West Bengal at the time of Partition reveals that they were a very mixed bag indeed, containing a bewildering variety of social, ethnic, linguistic, regional, and sectarian groupings. They included the learned and the rude, *ashraf* conquerers as well as lowly converts, city men and peasants, and all manner of outsiders drawn from every corner of Hindustan and beyond. Nor were they evenly distributed throughout the land. In some districts of the west, for example in Murshidabad and undivided Nadia, Muslims outnumbered Hindus; in rural Malda, Dinajpur, Cooch Behar, the 24 Parganas, and Birbhum they formed large and visible communities. In parts of the industrial belt, among them Calcutta, Bhatpara, Dumdum, Kumarhati, and Asansol, one in four and occasionally as many as one in three of all the locals were Muslims. In Garden Reach, Muslims were as numerous as Hindus.[16] By 1947, certain parts of Calcutta had already become dominantly "Muslim" areas, notably Park Circus, Bowbazar, Ekbalpur, and Karaya. In contrast, Muslims were few and far between in other parts of western Bengal, particularly in Bankura and Darjeeling.

Partition affected this extraordinarily diverse community in ways which are complex, resistant to analysis, and, because the evidence is so elusive, incapable of precise documentation. Neither government records nor scholarly studies provide a systematic investigation of this subject. Assessing the fate of Muslims was no part of the remit of the many voluminous surveys of displaced people commissioned by the government of West Bengal. The official

[15] *Census of India, 1931*, vol. v, pt i, p. 387.

[16] See Statement viii. 3, ibid., p. 278.

record contains a single passing reference to Muslim refugees, and that was in the early days.[17] In the half-century after Partition, the decennial censuses abandoned the British practice of listing by religion the statistics of occupation, literacy, marriage, and migration. In consequence, the important changes which Partition wrought upon the Muslims of West Bengal have to be teased out from scanty, sometimes anecdotal, evidence, and their inwardness has often to be discovered in most unlikely and rebarbative sources.

In obvious ways, Partition dramatically reversed the political position of the Muslims of West Bengal. For a decade before 1947, Muslim parties had enjoyed power in united Bengal, and had asserted themselves socially and culturally even in areas where they were outnumbered by Hindus.[18] Partition reduced them to an exposed and vulnerable minority. After 1947, Muslims all over West Bengal lived in fear – hardly surprising, given the Calcutta Killings of 1946, the pogroms in Bihar, and the deadly succession of murder and intimidation in Calcutta in the months and years after Partition.[19]

Muslim reactions to their predicament, of course, were not of a piece. They could not have been. Different Muslims responded differently when they realised their lives and property were at risk. Among the many factors which determined their actions were how easily they could take their assets away with them, how effectively they could deploy their skills to earn a living in the east, what contacts they had there, and how their prospects elsewhere compared with what they might still hang on to in the west if they stayed put and tried to weather the storm. It mattered whether

[17] At the time of the 1951 census, the State Statistical Bureau conducted a survey of displaced Muslims, which is referred to in *The Survey of Unemployment* in *West Bengal, 1953*, p. 5. However, despite every effort, it has not been possible to locate this survey.

[18] Chatterji, *Bengal Divided*, pp. 213–19.

[19] There was a clear correlation between the patterns of Muslim exoduses from Bengal and the communal rioting which provoked them.

they lived in clusters or were scattered thinly in isolated pockets; it also mattered whether they were near the border or far from it.

Packing one's bags and fleeing to East Bengal was an obvious response. Yet there is no accurate record of how many Muslims crossed the border into East Pakistan. In 1951, the Pakistan census counted 700,000 Muslim "muhajirs" in East Bengal,[20] of whom two-thirds, or 486,000, were known to be refugees from the west.[21] But the number of Muslims who fled eastwards was probably much higher. The 1961 census of Pakistan mentions 850,000 people in East Bengal, who in 1951 were recorded as having been born in other parts of the subcontinent and now possessed citizenship of Pakistan, and a further 125,000 who were "non-Pakistanis from India".[22] If all of these were refugees, by 1951 Muslim refugees in East Bengal numbered about a million, of whom perhaps seven out of ten came from West Bengal. In 1964, Indian Muslims once again fled in large numbers to East Pakistan in a second wave, perhaps of roughly the same order of magnitude as the first. Most came from West Bengal and the north-east of India.[23] So rough-and-ready estimates suggest that perhaps a million and a half Muslims left West Bengal for eastern Pakistan in the two decades after Partition.

The largest Muslim exoduses from west to east were sparked off by communal violence. The biggest of them was probably from Nadia in 1950–1, which Asok Mitra – civil servant and the first census commissioner of West Bengal – describes as a movement

[20] "Muhajir" was the term used to describe persons who had moved to Pakistan "as a result of Partition and of the fear of disturbances connected therewith. Persons who came for that reason are muhajirs for census purposes, no matter from where, when or for how long a stay they have come." *Census of Pakistan,* 1951, vol. 3, p. 39.

[21] Ibid., p. 80.

[22] *Census of Pakistan Population, 1961, vol. 2, East Pakistan*, pp. 11–31.

[23] Kamaluddin, "Refugee Problems in Bangladesh", in Kosinski and Elahi, eds, *Population Redistribution and Development*, pp. 221–2.

of refugees travelling in both directions, amounting almost to an exchange of population. Namasudras driven out of East Bengal during the Jessore riots retaliated by pitchforking the entire populations of Muslim villages out of India into Pakistan. Between 100,000 and 200,000 Muslims from Nadia were tossed across the border by savage Hindu mobs baying for revenge.[24] Smaller numbers continued to escape from the latent hostility and sporadic outbursts of violence towards Muslims in Calcutta. According to the West Bengal government, by 1951 15,000 Muslims had emigrated to East Bengal from Calcutta alone "through fear of disturbances". The actual numbers were probably much higher. The 1951 census discovered 130,000 fewer Muslims in Calcutta than it expected to find.[25] It is not unreasonable to deduce that part of the explanation for this demographic anomaly was very large numbers of Muslims from the city disappearing by stealth into Pakistan (see Table 9.1). We know that large numbers of Muslims left Howrah after the riots of 1950. Thousands more migrated in the early 1960s, when a rash of anti-Muslim pogroms

[24] To the best of my knowledge, no official figures have been published on the number of Muslims who fled from Nadia in 1950. An article published in *Paigam* in 1956 stated that 60,000 Muslim families had been forced out, which would put the number of persons at roughly 240,000, given an average family of four. *Paigam,* 15 September 1956. Of course, not all of them went to East Bengal, but that many did is suggested by the Pakistan census which counted 137,000 refugees in Pakistani Nadia (renamed Kushtia) in 1951. *Census of Pakistan, 1951, vol.* 3, *East Bengal, Report and Tables*, p. 39. This is corroborated by Nakatani's study of exchanges of property between Muslims leaving for East Bengal and incoming Hindu refugees in a Nadia village. Nakatani, "Away from Home".

[25] *Census of India, 1951, vol. VI, part III, Calcutta City*, p. xvi. This figure was based on projections for "normal" growth derived from the 1931 census figures, which Asok Mitra, the author of the 1951 census, believed with good reason to be much more reliable than the count taken in wartime in 1941. If Mitra's projections for Calcutta's Muslim population had been based instead on the 1941 census, the number of "missing" Muslims would have been considerably larger.

Table 9.1

Hindus and Muslims in Calcutta 1901–1951

Year	*Hindu population*	*Muslim population*	*Muslim population as a percentage of the Hindu population*
1901	603,310	270,797	44.9
1911	672,206	275,280	41.0
1921	725,561	248,912	34.3
1931	796,628	281,520	35.3
1941	1,531,512	497,535	32.5
1951	2,125,907	305,932	14.4

Source: *Census of India, 1951, vol. VI, part III, Calcutta City*, p. xv.

broke out not only in West Bengal and Assam, but also in Madhya Pradesh and Uttar Pradesh. Every time Hindus and Muslims fell upon each other, whether in India or in Pakistan, Muslims left their homes in droves. The riots in East Bengal, the troubles over the accession of princely Hyderabad and Kashmir, and the bloodletting in Jubbulpore all pushed many Muslim families over the edge into emigrating to Pakistan. In 1964, in the wake of the serious communal rioting sparked off by the Hazratbal incident,[26]

[26] Hyderabad, the Kashmir war, and Jubbulpore led to relatively modest migrations, but the 1964 violence following the Hazratbal incident was on a much larger scale and led to very significant exoduses from both sides of the Bengal frontier. The incident which sparked off the troubles was the mysterious disappearance of the *muy-i-muqaddas* (the sacred hair of the Prophet Muhammad) from the Hazratbal shrine in Srinagar in Kashmir. (For details, see Khan, "The Significance of the Dargah of Hazratbal".) Each of these incidents of violence was usually followed by the surrender by Muslims of a "sacred space". A Calcutta police report, describing the repercussions of the violence in Karachi and Jubbulpore, speaks of "a sense of panic among some sections of Muslims at Dilkhusa Street (Park Circus) and Kalabagab areas. These Muslims apprehended that Hindus may retaliate on them on the occasion of Holi . . . S.M. Salahuddin contacted several Mohalla sardars of Phulbagan and Tantibagan in Beniapukur . . . and instructed them to ask

another 800,000 Indian Muslims left for East Bengal. Most of these migrants were from West Bengal or the north-east.[27]

Other Muslims left in a more considered way, in circumstances which were less dramatic. Government servants with the option of serving either in India or in Pakistan had six months in which to make up their minds. Many top Muslim officers understandably decided to serve in Pakistan. All but one of the nineteen Muslim Indian Civil Service officers in Bengal opted to join the Government of Pakistan.[28] In their train followed large numbers of humbler public servants – orderlies, peons, clerks, tellers, watchmen, and police constables – who left on a scale sufficiently large to cause a temporary crisis after Partition at the administrative base in West Bengal. Of course, it was not always easy to distinguish between government employees who went of their own volition and those who were persuaded to go, in other words between those who jumped and those who were pushed. There were ugly hints of a systematic campaign of intimidation launched to "persuade" Muslims in government service to quit West Bengal and go to Pakistan.[29] Nor was it uncommon for prosperous Muslims to send family members to hedge their bets in

---

Muslims of these areas to remain quiet during the Holi festival." "Repercussions in Calcutta of the incidents in Pakistan", SB note, 1 March 1961, GBIB, E No. 1278/59 (part I). "Remaining quiet" in the context of Holi would have meant allowing noisy Hindu processions to pass mosques without let or hindrance.

[27] Kamaluddin, "Refugee Problems in Bangladesh", pp. 221–2.

[28] Chakrabarty, *With Dr B.C. Roy*, p. 45.

[29] In June and July 1947, persons never identified "by the police launched a campaign of murdering Muslim policemen in Calcutta and Howrah in broad daylight, no doubt '*pour encourper les autres*'." On 26 June 1947, an upcountry Muslim constable on duty in Calcutta was shot dead at close range. No one was brought to book. GBIB, E No. 614/47. On 23 June another constable was shot at and injured while on patrol at Madhusudan Biswas Lane in Howrah. "No culprits were traced." Howrah District Report, 11 October 1947, in GBIB, E No. 614/47. On 7 July 1947, in a high-profile

Pakistan, while the heads of the households stayed on to maintain their stakes in land and business in West Bengal.[30] In some instances, Muslims who had property in West Bengal were able to make deals with propertied Hindus from the east by which they exchanged, whether legally or in less formal ways, their plots and holdings with each other.[31]

But for every Muslim who reacted to Partition by quitting India, many more stayed on. Most of those who remained were the weak and poor who had no assets, no connections and little

---

example of these trends, S.S. Huq, who was in charge of Muchipara police station, was murdered. Ibid. The army was called to quell the violence after his funeral: 40 people died and about 200 were injured. Chakrabarty, *With* Dr B.C. Roy, pp. 50–1. On 2 July 1947 two constables, one Hindu and one Muslim, were on duty at Howrah when the Muslim was shot and later died. Again "no culprit was found". GBIB, E No. 1123/47.

[30] A study of a Muslim family from Barasat, some of whose members migrated to Pakistan in 1964, is a case in point. The immediate nuclear family consisted of the parents and their nine children, of whom only three subsequently migrated to Pakistan, following their paternal uncle. One brother left Barasat for another village in West Bengal. The rest remained where they were. "There seemed too much at stake: their property for example. By this time everyone in the family was comfortably off, each with his own side business, mostly shopkeeping. That they had their own high school in the village was mentioned as a plus point. Besides no one wanted to go to a 'backward place' leaving behind their property. So the general feeling was to keep an open mind about it." This study shows how the resource base, social mobility, kinship connections, and the stage in the life cycle of individuals all played a part in determining who migrated to Pakistan and who stayed behind. Meghna Guhathakurta, "Families Uprooted and Divided".

[31] In a typical case in September 1950, a Muslim of Pulnapur "migrated to Pakistan after exchanging some properties with a Hindu." In another instance, in April 1950, a Muslim of Baramaricha in Sitalkuchi in Cooch Behar left for Paksitan in 1950, giving over his *adhiar* right to planted jute to a Hindu refugee. These, and many similar instances, are reported in the "Fortnightly Reports of Border Incidents in West Bengal" (henceforth FRBI) for 1950, GBIB, E No. 12 38A–47. Also see Nakatani, "Away from Home".

by way of skills to deploy in a new life across the border.[32] But it is significant that many of those who could most easily have migrated to Pakistan elected to remain in India. These included rank-and-file Muslim government employees, like those whom Asok Mitra found holding on to their jobs when he was posted to Malda in 1947 and later to Murshidabad in 1949.[33]

Those who stayed on in the bitterly anti-Muslim climate of post-Partition West Bengal adopted strategies of survival which varied according to circumstance.[34] But almost everyone who stayed on recognised that they had no choice but to eat humble pie, proclaim allegiance to India, and subscribe to the doctrine of a communal harmony which had ceased to exist in practice, however much people paid lip service to the principle. The literate among them would certainly have read between the lines of the Congress Working Committee's resolution which, even as it assured "the minorities in India" that the Congress government would continue to protect "to the best of its ability their citizen rights against aggression", warned them that "it would not tolerate the existence within its borders of disloyal elements" and expressed its readiness to provide "full facilities . . . to those who wish to migrate from the Indian Union."[35] In effect, Congress had thrown down the gauntlet to all Muslims who remained in India, challenging them to prove their loyalty to the new republic.

[32] As has been argued, "Migration abroad is rarely an option for the poorest households, even though they may be among the most vulnerable in terms of economic or physical security." Van Hear, "Refugee Diasporas".

[33] Mitra, *The New India*, pp. 1, 49.

[34] Describing his experiences as district magistrate in 1947 and 1948, Asok Mitra refers to the "recurrent tendency" amongst Malda's Hindus "for a witch-hunt of Muslims", and describes the list prepared by the outgoing magistrate of Murshidabad of 30,000 "undesirable Muslim families". Ibid., pp. 24, 29. The police files too are redolent of anti-Muslim attitudes, and not just in the period immediately after Partition.

[35] Congress Working Committee Resolution, 24 September 1947, All India Congress Committee Papers, First Instalment, file no. G-30 of 1946 (henceforth AICC-I, F. No. G-30/1946, and so on).

In response to this crude call for Muslims to "assimilate", even the most influential Muslims felt they had publicly to renounce their old allegiances. Once India gained Independence, former leaders of the powerful Muslim League began to dissociate themselves from it. In November 1947, Huseyn Shaheed Suhrawardy, recently premier of Bengal, convened a conference of Muslim leaders in Calcutta to discuss their future policy. Most of them took the view that the League "had ceased to exist" and that "Muslims must now independently steer their course in independent India." Their resolutions proclaimed the need for harmony and co-operation between the two governments of India and Pakistan. Reporting on the conference, the *Star of India* urged "a fusion . . . be effected between the League and the nationalist Muslim leadership", claiming that Partition had eroded every real distinction between them.[36] If political Muslims were to survive and prosper in West Bengal, they could see that the Muslim League had to be allowed to die a quiet death.

It soon became obvious, and not only to those Muslims who had truck with the Muslim League, that it was not enough simply to repudiate the League. "Allegiance and loyalty to the state" had to be displayed in more positive ways.[37]

The Muslim Conference of November 1947 in Lucknow called upon "the Mussalmans of India to be members only of non-communal political parties and advise[d] them to join the Indian National Congress."[38] Many Bengali Muslim notables saw merit in this advice and those who could, contested the 1952 elections

[36] *Star of India*, 14 November 1947, GB IB, F. No. 1045–7.

[37] Vallabhbhai Patel in his characteristically blunt style demanded "practical proof" of Muslim loyalty, insisting that mere protestations of loyalty were not enough. His comment: "You don't know what it is costing the government to protect you" was hardly calculated to reassure Muslims. Cited in Hasan, *Legacy of a Divided Nation*, p. 148.

[38] This resolution was moved by the communist S.A. Brelvi and supported by Dr Z.A. Ahmed and Humayun Kabir. AICC-I, F. No. G-23/1946–8.

on Congress tickets (see Table 9.2). For the bigwigs amongst them, this Damascene "conversion" to Congress was made easier by the factional wars within the Bengal Congress and by Dr B.C. Roy's uncertain grip over the assembly. Partition had created the anomaly of a West Bengal Congress dominated by East Bengalis, and after Partition the party witnessed a spectacular burst of fratricide as different factions struggled to capture the organization and ministry. Consequently the premier, Roy, and party boss Atulya Ghosh, were eager to welcome these Muslim grandees into their assembly party in support of their faction in the house.[39]

But bringing Leaguers into the Congress was not always a smooth process, especially at the grassroots, where many Hindu members of the Old Guard in Congress refused to become bedfellows with their enemies of yore.[40] Nor were these alliances of

[39] The factions opposed to Roy and Ghosh saw what was happening but could do little about it, as any protest could easily be denounced by the ruling group as being motivated by communal and anti-Muslim sentiments. Writing in protest against Dr B.C. Roy's admission of a Muslim to the Congress Assembly Party, Amarkrishna Ghosh declared that "the inclusion of Muslims and Anglo-Indians should be decided on a principle to be approved by the Central Parliamentary Board . . . Even in this province, if one Muslim is now admitted into the Congress Assembly Party, many others would apply for such admission and it would be difficult to resist their admission on logical grounds. And the inclusion of many Muslim members into the Party may not be advisable at this juncture of Indian politics." Amarkrishna Ghosh and eight others to Sitaramayya, 4 March 1949, All India Congress Committee Papers, Second Instalment (henceforth AICC-II), F. No. PB-3(i)/1949. In reply, B.C. Roy was quick to occupy the moral and "secular" high ground, defending the inclusion of Shamsul Huq, elected as an independent candidate "who has always been working with Congress since 1924 . . . I am perfectly sure that the Congress will not in any case countenance such a proposition that we oust an applicant simply because he happens to be a Muslim, or that the inclusion of Muslim members would be inadvisable." B.C. Roy to Kala Venkatarao, 9 April 1949, AICC-II, F. No. PB-3(i)/1949.

[40] One pamphlet lamented the fate of the Congress, demanding to know "how is it that the newly elected Deputy President [of the Malda District

Table 9.2

Party-political Profile of Muslim Candidates in General Elections in West Bengal 1952–1967*

Year	*Congress*	*Opposition parties*	*Independents*	*Total Muslim MLAs*
1952	21 [17]	14[0]	45[2]	19
1957	28 [20]	13[3]	55[2](one CPI-supported)	25
1962	31 [17]	38[4]	50[3]	24
1967	31 [18]	30[14]	48[5]	37

*Square brackets show number of victorious candidates.

Source: Dilip Banerjee, *Election Recorder*, Calcutta, 1990.

convenience seen as a boon by all Muslim nationalists. Before 1947, in resisting the blandishments of the Muslim League, they had stood against the tide and been exiled to the margins of Bengal Muslim politics.[41] Now that their party was in power in West Bengal, they might reasonably have expected their loyalty to be rewarded when the loaves and fishes were being doled out. Instead, Congress patronage now went to Muslims who could most convincingly promise to deliver the political goods, and the Muslim nationalists were not usually amongst them. For ins-

Congress Committee] Janab Latif Hussain (Arapur) who was a member of the district Muslim National Guard and who was never even a delegate of the Congress, how has he suddenly become Deputy President? . . . How has Janab Mohammad Sayyad, who was the secretary of the Malda Jila Muslim League and who never represented the Congress been appointed to the Working Committee of the Malda District Congress?" The pamphlet claimed that the lack of scruples with which Muslims of doubtful credentials were being drafted into the Congress had driven true Congressmen, including the author himself, out of the organization. Bibhuti Bhushan Chakravarti, *"Ihai ki Congress adarsh?"* (Are these really Congress ideals?), in AICC-II, F. No. PB-3/1951.

[41] Their marginality is reflected in the fact that Congress had put up only two Muslim candidates in the 1946 elections, both of whom were trounced at the polls by Muslim League rivals. See Chatterji, *Bengal Divided*, p. 130.

tance, in 1950, Jehangir Kabir, a nationalist of long standing, asked to be given the Congress ticket to a Muslim seat in the Central Legislative Assembly which the Congress Parliamentary Board had allocated to another, and more recently, recruited Muslim would-be politician. Kabir's claim rested on his own record of commitment to the party and the fact that "the other recommended gentleman never belonged to Congress and has no political past. As far as we know he is not even today an ordinary Congress member."[42] But his request was ignored. The Congress ticket went to Kabir's rival.

It was not only the ruling coterie of Congress which put realpolitik above all else: every political faction joined in the race to sign up influential Muslims regardless of their political antecedents. When by-elections were held in the 24 Parganas central Muslim constituency in 1951, Atulya Ghosh was disconcerted to fmd that Prafulla Ghosh's Krishak Majdoor Praja Party (KMPP) had put up against its man "Jenab Khairul Islam, a noted Muslim Leaguer, son of Maulana Akram Khan, ex-president of the Bengal Muslim League and present president of the Muslim League of east Pakistan." Given the ruling faction's own fallible record, its complaint against other parties "associating with noted Muslim Leaguers who are still doing all sorts of mischief against communal harmony" was a case of Atulya's sooty kettle calling Prafulla's pot black.[43]

The cynicism with which Congress welcomed prominent

[42] Jehangir Kabir to Sardar Vallabhbhai Patel, 9 September 1950, AICC-II, F. No. PB-311950.

[43] Wright has argued that Congress factionalism has not tended to work to the advantage of genuine representatives of Muslim opinion, and therefore has not been good for Muslims. There is merit in this thesis. But in the unique circumstances of divided Bengal, some Muslims were able to take advantage of Congress factionalism to gain a ticket back into the mainstream of politics. Theodore Wright, Jr, "The Effectiveness of Muslim Representation in India", p. 130.

Muslims into its fold was often mirrored by equally hard-headed calculation on the part of those Muslims who decided to join up. A typical case was that of Mahbub Huq, whose visit to Jalpaiguri in 1957, "ostensibly" to canvass support for Congress in the election, was the subject of a long and panic-stricken intelligence report.[44] According to the police, Huq had joined Congress soon after Partition, although later he was to become a citizen of Pakistan. While still in India, he kept close connections with the Mohammedan Sporting Club and gave a lot of money to the Azad Kashmir Fund. In the inspector's opinion, this was ample proof that his support for Congress was less than sincere. He had sold most of his assets in India in 1951 but continued to derive "secret earnings" from Muslim-owned tea estates, the source of the monies which paid for the "palatial" house he built for himself in Dacca. According to the police, "one of his satellites", a Hindu sanitary inspector, had helped him get his loot out of India and into Pakistan. So he was shocked to find that Huq's visit to Jalpaiguri in 1957 was "warmly backed by the President of the Jalpaiguri District Congress Committee, by a former Vice-President of the Bengal Provincial Congress Committee, by two [Hindu] MLAs and by a [Hindu] member of the Council of States."[45] This assessment was probably jaundiced by the anti-Muslim and anti-Pakistani paranoia of the officer who penned the report. But the saga does give some hint of the stratagems deployed by resourceful Muslims who were able successfully to hedge their bets, maintaining alliances, property, and connection on both sides of the border and playing both ends against the middle. Often with the connivance of the Congress establishment, well-connected Muslims were able to survive

[44] This is not the man's real name, which has been changed to protect his anonymity and to comply with the specific request of the head of the Intelligence Branch in Calcutta.

[45] Copy of the Report of the DIO, 13 February 1957, GBIB, F. No. 114–57.

Partition by these devices, and sometimes even to do well out of them.

This selective induction of some influential Muslim notables into the political establishment eased their return to prominence in West Bengal's post-Partition order, but was hardly evidence of a genuine change of heart amongst West Bengal's Hindu political elites in their underlying attitudes towards Muslims. In 1951, Dr Roy's government began to "cleanse" the border zones of Muslims, "presumably . . . because it [was] thought that they might be unreliable elements in times of trouble", a strategy which provoked a sharp reprimand from Nehru but reflected the prevailing view in Bengal that Muslims were inherently "disloyal".[46] Many Muslim politicians continued to complain about the Congress Party leadership's latent hostility towards them.[47] In 1956, one Muslim from Bengal wrote to Nehru that his people were being systematically cut out of the electoral roll, and government orders affecting their lives and times were published only in papers which most of them did not read. So "the feeling of the Minority Community [was] that they [were] being deprived of [the right to vote] intentionally and in an organised manner."[48]

Nor did the grudging acceptance of a few Muslim leaders into the Congress fold do much to improve the sense of security

[46] Jawaharlal Nehru to Dr B.C. Roy, 15 September 1951, cited in Chakrabarty, *With Dr B.C. Roy*, pp. 192–3.

[47] Zakariah asked to be allowed to "submit a memorandum to the Congress High Command about the state of affairs of the Muslims in West Bengal – who are about 26 per cent of the total population which is not a negligible number, but their position is not the same as [that] of their co-religionists living in other states . . . A large number of ours are still very staunch Congressmen but they are compelled to remain outside for the time being because of the present undesirable High Command of the West Bengal State Congress Committee." A.K.M. Zakariah to Lal Bahadur Shastri, 26 April 1952, AICC-II, F. No. PB-2111952.

[48] S.M. Salahuddin, Chief Administrative Officer, Anjuman Mufidul Islam, to Jawaharlal Nehru, 28 July 1956, AICC-II, F. No. PB-21/1956.

among the rank and file. While B.C. Roy was opening the door for Muslim bosses to enter the Congress Assembly Party, Congressmen on the ground waged petty and vicious wars against defenceless Muslims. The Congress Committee of Ward 25 in Calcutta in the Kidderpore area, for instance, gained a reputation for being "a danger to local Mohammedans". Its members once forced "22 Mahommedans to leave possession of a room and their belongings were carted away to a distant tank. Some of the men were locked up in the Congress office. Police rendered [them] no assistance . . . because [their tormentors had] Congress backing."[49] This incident was not untypical – after Partition just as before it, the hooligans who hounded Muslims wore *khadi topis* as often as khaki shorts.[50]

In significant ways, Partition helped to create new faultlines and construct new layers of stratification among West Bengal's Muslims. It created a gulf between the fortunate few who were able to find a secure place in the new order and the great majority who did not. Ordinary Muslims faced intimidation and harassment in their day-to-day lives and were particularly vulnerable whenever communal tension flared into open violence. They too tried in little ways to adopt various strategies for survival, but the options open to them were much more limited. Holding fewer court cards in their hands, staying on required them to make sacrifices, accept defeats, and absorb losses.

In much the same way as the Muslim elites who had been given lodgement by the Hindu establishment, they too tried to show they were ready and willing to assimilate, albeit lower down the social scale, and accept their minority status without ado. One way of demonstrating this was their readiness to surrender previously

[49] R. Ghosh to Sardar Vallabbhai Patel, AICC-II, F. No. PB-3(i)/1949. Ghosh resigned his Congress membership in protest against this incident.

[50] The small caps made of homespun cotton were a badge of Congress membership, just as the khaki shorts were the insignia of the Rashtriya Swayamsevak Sangh volunteers.

entrenched rights to the public observance of their religious rituals and their claims to public space. Under British rule, rights of holding public rituals were governed by precedence – a local community was permitted to perform a ceremony or hold a procession in a public place provided it had done so in the past and had established a "customary" right to do so.[51] Disputes over precedents in the conduct of festivals lay at the root of much of the communal violence in the last days of the Raj. Yet this was one British rule to which the government of independent India continued firmly to adhere. In 1948, the Home Department issued a memorandum, circulated to all district officers, which reiterated that Muslims had rights to sacrifice cows: "so far as the celebration of Bakr-Id is concerned, the principle which has always been followed in cases of dispute is that previous custom should be maintained. *No innovations should be allowed*";[52] and this rule was upheld and enshrined in the statute book in the West Bengal Animal Slaughter Control Act of 1950.[53]

It was no small concession for Muslims voluntarily to abjure precedents which assured them the continued rights, precedents which were the product of hard-fought and historic victories. It was a particularly significant step for them to renounce entrenched rights to perform the perennially controversial ritual of cow sacrifice. And yet this is what many Muslims now chose to do. Perhaps because the issue was so highly charged, so public, and so bound up with issues of power and history, this was one visible gesture humble Muslims could make which broadcast the fact

[51] For a discussion of this policy, see Chatterji, *Bengal Divided*, pp. 212–13; and Prior, "Making History".

[52] The Memorandum of 1948 is quoted in a letter dated 11 September 1950 from the Secretary to the Government of West Bengal, Home (Police) Department to all district officers of West Bengal, GBIB 1802–57 (part I). Emphasis in the original.

[53] Government of West Bengal, Department of Agriculture, Animal Husbandry and Forests, circular no. 8016-Vety., 25 June 1957, GBIB, pp. 1802–57.

that they understood their predicament and accepted the new realities. In 1947 and 1948, there were numerous occasions when police anticipated trouble at Bakr-Id, only to find that Muslims had chosen, of their own accord, or after some "persuasion", not to perform *go korbani* or cow sacrifice. In a typical instance in October 1947, police were called to the Champdany jute mill after street meetings of Hindus urged Muslims to give up *go korbani*. Expecting trouble, the police rushed in force to the area but discovered that the Muslims had decided of their own volition not to make a stand. They found that "Muslims who are in a minority are afraid of wounding the religious feeling of the Hindus by sacrificing cows. Accordingly, the Muslims of Champdany Jute Mills met together in the Champdany mosque . . . and decided not to . . . [sacrifice] any cows."[54]

Sadly, such gestures were not always enough to buy Muslims security. All too frequently, Hindus took the unbending view that Muslims no longer had any right to perform cow sacrifice *under any circumstances*. So when Muslims voluntarily, and in a considered way, gave up established rights to sacrifice cows, far from accepting this as an olive branch which required some quid pro quo, Hindus dismissed it as an inevitable sign of weakness, a gesture deserving neither recognition nor reward. Instead, they seemed intent on forcing the issue to a final solution. In 1948 and 1949, there were many occasions when Muslims were given strife for sacrificing cows even where there were well-established precedents for their doing so, and when they had taken care to perform the sacrifices well out of sight and earshot of Hindus.[55] Even after the West Bengal Animal Slaughter Control Act in 1950 laid down clear guidelines permitting *go korbani* at Id, provided it was done according to established precedent, with permission, and in a private place,[56] cow sacrifice remained an issue which

[54] SDPO Serampore's report, 21 October 1947, GBIB, F. No. 167/47.

[55] GBIB, F. No. 69A-49 (Murshidabad).

[56] Government of West Bengal, Department of Agriculture, Animal Husbandry and Forests, circular no. 8016-Vety., 25 June 1957.

continued to inflame Hindu–Muslim relations, and Muslims, step by step, were forced, sometimes covertly, sometimes by open threats and sometimes by their own decision, to give up their traditional rights. In one case, for instance, on hearing that a cow had been sold to a Muslim in a Purulia village before Bakr-Id, the local Hindus organised a public meeting "with a view to discuss their future programme over the alleged cow slaughter." The following day, the police visited the village and met the leading members of both communities. "The Hindus proposed that the Muslims should not slaughter cows any more in the village to which [a Muslim gentleman] who commands respect of the Muslims of the area agreed on behalf of local Muslims."[57] In another case, Muslims of Bil Barail, who traditionally distributed beef during Bakr-Id at a public mosque, were forced to give up the practice. In protest, they "refrained from doing Korbani on Bakr-Id day in that particular mosque."[58]

The new Hindu mood of aggressive assertiveness soon spilled over to affect other Muslim public rituals. In June 1949, for instance, a dispute erupted in Kandi between Muslims taking a *tazia* in licensed procession and Hindus who refused to allow them to trim back branches of a sacred tree which prevented the *tazia* getting past. It was the Muslims who had to back down, persuaded by one of their leaders "at a secret meeting" that the "authorities would redress their grievance in due course".[59] And once they had backed down, the new "precedent" was there to be used against them in the future. Once a traditional right to sacred space or

[57] Note of the SP DIB Purulia, 25 June 1959, GBIB. F. No. 1802/57 (part II). The name of the gentleman in question has been withheld to protect his anonymity and in accordance with the express wishes of the head of the Intelligence Branch in Calcutta.

[58] "Situation Report on the Bakr-Id festival in West Bengal", 20 June 1959, GBIB, F. No. 1802-57 (part II).

[59] Weekly Confidential Report, Murshidabad District, for the week ending 6 November 1949, GBIB 69A/49 (Murshidabad).

performing rituals had been lost, it was unlikely to be given back.

This is why the story of the graveyard at Selimpore, itself a tiny episode in the wider history of West Bengal's Muslims, warrants its place in the larger account. Calcutta's landscape is dotted with Selimpores. Most Muslim burial grounds in the city bear similar marks of retreat and defeat. Part of the burial ground for Muslim paupers at Park Circus, which had no boundary wall and no masonry graves, in 1997 (when I visited it) was being used as a football ground, despite complaints to the corporation on whose ground it stood.[60] The custodian of the burial ground at Gobra, founded in 1896 by Zillur Rahman on *waqf* land, told a similar story. The cemetery had originally covered some twenty *bighas* (about six acres) in the heart of a Muslim-dominated locality and close to a mosque on Ashgar Mistri Lane. In 1964 during the Hazratbal riots, scores of Muslims left the area and the locality was occupied by refugees from East Pakistan: "How they regularised their plots is not known." Gradually, they occupied more and more area of the paupers' graveyard, which had no boundary wall and no masonry graves, until three-quarters of the cemetery had been captured. Appeals to the corporation for permission to erect a boundary wall were unsuccessful. The new occupants have since set up a tannery on that ground, and also use part of it as a football ground. In 1989, another riot broke out over the burial ground, but no decision was taken to restore it to its Muslim owners. By 1997, all that remained of the graveyard – still beautifully tended – was about an acre of land covered with masonry graves.[61]

[60] My interview with Mushtaque Hossain, Secretary, Muslim Burial Board, 27 May 1997, Calcutta.

[61] My interview with Syeed Munir at Gobra III burial ground, Calcutta, 27 May 1997. Most of the details were confirmed by Mr Nurul Hasan of the Anjuman Mufidul Islam in his interview with me on 3 June 1997 in Calcutta. I was told a very similar story about the Raja Bazar private burial ground, where reportedly a third of the paupers' burial ground has been

Selimpore is thus but one instance of the processes by which Muslims were gradually coerced into surrendering their traditional claims to public spaces, retreating meekly into less visible and mendicant postures. As these vignettes indicate, anodyne narratives of "cultural assimilation" in the creation of secular independent India gloss over the rather harsher dynamics of intimidation, surrender, and loss which were recurring themes in the same story.

II

It was not only the boundaries of sacred and ritual space that were redrawn in the aftermath of Partition. Partition set in train a process by which the physical space occupied by Muslims was progressively reduced and rearranged. It also accelerated the process, already under way long before 1947, by which the boundaries demarcating "Muslim areas" came to be more sharply delineated. The combined effect of these twin developments was to force Muslims to huddle together in discrete pockets. If in death Muslims were deprived of their traditional graveyards, in life they were forced to live in what rapidly became Muslim ghettos.

In many ways, this "clustering" and "ghettoisation" of Muslims reflected the limitations and constraints within which efforts by ordinary Muslims to survive the traumas of Partition had to work. During riots, flight was for many the only option. Whether fleeing Muslims escaped to Pakistan or merely to safer areas in West Bengal, each exodus resulted in Muslims losing some property to dominant communities.

---

captured and turned into a football ground. If more "objective" evidence is needed of this pattern, it is provided by Nirmal Kumar Bose's survey of Calcutta in 1964. His analysis of land usage in Calcutta's wards shows that in almost every ward of Calcutta where Muslims had once been dominant, land occupied by burial grounds shrank between 1911 and 1961. "Table Showing Area Occupied by Each Kind of Land Use in 65 Wards in 1911 and 1961", Bose, *Calcutta 1964*, pp. 15–23.

When Muslims fled, many hoped to return once normalcy was restored; their exoduses were intended as temporary retreats, not permanent departures. But all too often, experience belied optimism. Notwithstanding the agreement between India and Pakistan that evacuee property in Bengal was to be held in trust until its rightful owners came back,[62] Muslim refugees were seldom able to repossess their homes and these flights invariably turned out to be one-way journeys with no points of return. When they did try to come home, Muslims usually found that their property had been grabbed by others. And it is abundantly clear, despite Prafulla Chakrabarti's protestations to the contrary, that the new occupants were usually Hindu refugees from East Bengal.[63] Police files bear eloquent testimony to the hostile reception which met Muslims who returned. In August 1950, almost four mouths after the Howrah riots, police reported that "a tense feeling is prevailing amongst the East Bengal refugees of the district who are residing in vacant Muslim houses over the question of their ejectment as many of the Muslim house owners have since returned and started cases [under section] 448 I.P.C. The refugees are trying to gain public sympathy on their behalf. Their eviction would not be an easy task unless they are rehabilitated elsewhere."[64]

In another typical incident on the Nadia border, "Muslims returning from Pakistan with their families and personal effects" in the aftermath of massive riots were attacked and looted by

[62] The Evacuee Properties Act of 1951 stated that "a migrant Muslim family from West Bengal, returning within 31 March 1951, would be entitled to re-occupy the deserted property."

[63] Chakrabarti, *The Marginal Men*, pp. 105–8: His insistence that the plight of Muslim refugees was no "great calamity in the midst of such misery" reveals a certain prejudice on this issue. It is no doubt the same mindset which lay behind the government's failure even to record the number of displaced Muslims.

[64] Report on the political activities of the refugees and corruption in the refugee camps for the week ending 20 August 1950, GBIB, F. No. 1838–48 (KW).

a party of thirty or forty refugees and were driven away from the village. "They were forced to take shelter with the Muslims of Sonadanga."[65] Yet they were not safe there either. On 23 August 1950, five Muslims in Sonadanga were driven out by refugees and their property was looted. As the police report explained: "After the migration to Pakistan of the Muslims of this village about 5000 Hindu refugees have been living here after occupying the Muslim houses either by virtue of documents of exchange or finding them vacant. The return of Muslims almost daily in large numbers has caused great commotion among the refugees who are unwilling to accommodate them."[66]

As in this instance, often Muslims coming back home would find that in their absence whole colonies of refugees had settled on their lands and taken over their houses. In Nakashipara near the Nadia border, Muslims found that Namasudra refugees had built over a hundred huts on their land in Radhanagar and Birpur *mouza*. In this case, as in so many others, once refugees had squatted on Muslim land with the support of neighbourhood leaders and their bully-boys, it was virtually impossible to prise them out.[67] In April 1950, a meeting was organised at Hanskhali under the "presidentship of Bikash Roy (Congress) [at which] he urged the refugees not to vacate Muslim houses occupied by them, nor to allow any Muslim to enter there." That same month, police reported that a volunteer group had been formed, ominously calling itself the Santan Bahini.[68] This thuggish organisation provided the threatening umbrella of muscle power

[65] Report of D/C Kotwali PS, 25 August 1950, GBIB, F. No. 1809–48 (Nadia).

[66] Report on the political activities of the refugees and corruption in the refugee camps for the week ending 3 September 1950, GBIB, F. No. 1838–48 (KW).

[67] Extract from abstract, 6 May 1950, GBIB, F. No. 1809–48 (Nadia).

[68] The volunteers in Bankim Chandra Chatterjee's famous political novel *Anandamath* called themselves "*santan*"; used in the context of post-Partition

under which refugees grabbed vacant Muslim homes. Muslims without connections were powerless to do anything about it. They had no choice but to return to Pakistan or to take refuge in Muslim ghettos where they hoped to find safety in numbers. Even when returning Muslims had the status and confidence to lodge complaints with the police against the Hindu refugees who had grabbed their property, they found that they could not get their property back, because the refugees were well organised, had established political connections, and were determined to stand their ground.[69]

Patterns of Muslim settlement and landownership were altered in other, openly aggressive, ways. Often Muslims who had chosen *not* to take flight were driven out of their homes, bag and baggage. Once again, Hindu refugees played a leading role in this deeply unattractive saga. Most cases of forcible eviction occurred in the border districts such as Nadia where refugees settled in large numbers on the property of Muslim evacuees and then tried to capture more land by intimidating the few remaining Muslim families and forcing them also to quit. In September 1950, about fifty Namasudra refugees who had settled at Paikpara near Krishnaganj in Nadia entered the Muslim part of the village and "asked" the Muslims to leave in order to make room for Hindu evacuees from East Pakistan. Overnight they put up huts on Muslim-owned land "with the object of compelling the landowners to settle the lands with them".[70] In another incident on 25 December 1950, about a hundred refugee families forced their way in the

Bengal, the name evoked powerful images of anti-Muslim vigilante violence.

[69] In Cossimbazar in July 1950, for instance, a police party was attacked when it "tried to eject refugees from a house belonging to a member of the minority community." *Hindusthan Standard*, 5 July 1950.

[70] Report on the political activities of the refugees and corruption in the refugee camps for the week ending 18 September 1949, GBIB, F. No. 1838–48 (part III).

middle of the night into the house of a Muslim of Nowdapur, P.S. Tehatta, beat him up, attacked the other Muslims in the village, "and commanded them to go away to Pakistan leaving all their properties".[71] Nadia saw the worst of these incidents, but they "were in evidence all along the dry stretches of a long rural border."[72]

There was little the overstretched rural policemen could do to protect the Muslims, even when they were minded so to do.[73] In these outlying rural border areas, state authority was

[71] Copy of radiogram message from O/C Tehatta P.S., 26 December 1950, GBIB, F. No. 1809-48 (Nadia).

[72] In May 1950, police commented on "a general tendency amongst the Namasudra evacuees, settled recently near Bongaon, to terrorise the Muslim residents of the Indian Union so that they may go away to East Pakistan by exchanging their houses and properties." Report on the political activities of the refugees and corruption in the refugee camps for the week ending 7 May 1950, GBIB, F. No. 1838–48 (part IV).

[73] One grave incident in Ranaghat in June 1950 reflects this predicament. On 25 June 1950, a party of six policemen was on its way to three Muslim villages in Ranaghat in response to a complaint that cattle belonging to Muslims had been stolen by Hindu refugees. The brave sextet was met by a crowd of "one thousand to fifteen hundred refugees" carrying *lathis*, marching towards Muslim villages: "From a distance of 150 cubits roughly, the S[ub] I[nspector] Nepal Mukherjee challenged the crowd to stop and to explain why they were proceeding in such an unusual manner and so armed. In answer to this challenge, some members of the mob reported that they would go to villages Purbanagar and Khagradanga but they did not halt to explain any further. These two villages are thick Muslim pockets. The S[ub] I[nspector] suspected that the mob was marching with [the] obvious purpose of looting the properties of the Muslims. He further shouted at the mob to halt giving them due warning. The mob did not show any sign of changing their attitude. The S[ub] I[nspector] then asked his men to load their rifles and take position. The mob became aggressive and one of them dashed against the S[ub] I[nspector]. This man was immediately arrested. At this the mob fell out in batches to round up the small police party. No alternative was then left to the police party but to open fire to protect their rifles and their lives. . . . The mob then retreated a few steps back and then reorganised there

thinly spread and deeply compromised, and the police gave Muslims little protection. For their part Muslims sometimes put up resistance, whether by fighting back,[74] or by forging factional alliances with local Hindus who had little liking for the incursions and carryings-on of the refugees,[75] or sometimes even by hiring Hindu mercenaries to protect them.[76] But as numerous abandoned Muslim villages graphically testify, these efforts had little lasting success. In Nadia, something akin to a total exchange of population between India and Pakistan took place, similar to the events in Punjab in nature if not in scale. But elsewhere Mus-

---

for fresh attack. Five shots were then fired . . . [which] wounded one man. The mob then became puzzled and fled carrying the wounded man in hot haste in different directions in the heavy rains. The police party then chased them and succeeded in arresting three others . . . The police party tried to trace the wounded man but with no result. They got help from none in the village as the inhabitants there are all refugees. There is no rural police, the village en bloc being deserted by the Muslims some time back." "Report of enquiry into the firing opened by the police against a riotous mob on 25 June 1950". GBIB, F. No. 1809–48 (Nadia).

[74] At Kalupur beside the Ichhamati river, a pitched battle was fought between the Muslims of Kalabhas village, "exclusively a Muslim pocket" and the "Kalupur people who are exclusively Namasudra refugees". Unusually the outcome was that refugees attempting to loot the Muslim village were beaten back by Muslims "armed with lathis, sharkis and other weapons". Report of the SDO Ranaghat on the Kalupur incident of 2 September 1950, U/S 148/355 IPC, GBIB, F. No. 1809–48 (Nadia).

[75] In one incident in Nadia in June 1950, when refugees of the Dhubulia camp attacked Muslims of Hansadanga village, "the Muslims resisted and were assisted by the goalas of Hansadanga. The refugees were beaten back . . . On returning to the camp, the refugees spread rumours that they had been attacked by Muslims without any provocations and that two of them had been killed." This led to widespread looting and the burning down of Muslim homes and property, even though the refugees "met with organised resistance from the goalas". Extract from abstract dated 10 June 1950, GBIB, F. No. 1809–48 (Nadia).

[76] Note, 19 April 1950, GBIB, F. No. 1238/47 (Cooch Behar).

lims who were forced to abandon their lands remained in West Bengal and took shelter in Muslim-dominated areas on the Indian side of the border.

In time, as each incident of rioting and tension sparked off a diaspora of frightened and vulnerable Muslims to safer areas, and as each temporary flight became a permanent exile, where Muslim communities had been small and less conspicuous before Partition now they either disappeared altogether or shrank into tiny little clusters. Huddled together, hemmed in by refugee colonies which sprang up around them, these tiny Muslim "pockets" were like little enclaves, surrounded and squeezed by hostile neighbours. Like Selimpore, they tended to have the air of the ghetto about them.[77]

In contrast, Muslim-dominated areas in West Bengal gradually absorbed larger and larger numbers of Muslims displaced from other parts of the state. Chiefly in northern Bengal, not surprisingly such "Muslim belts" became larger, or at least more densely settled, and ever more exclusively Muslim in their composition. There are also indications that these belts became the favoured destination of returning Muslim evacuees from East Pakistan who came back to India but were unable to go home. We do not know much about this reverse migration. Despite the terms of the Inter-Dominion Agreement of 1948 between India and Pakistan which was intended to encourage Bengali refugees on both sides of the border to return home, in fact Muslim evacuees were strongly discouraged from returning to India, and they were explicitly denied help in so doing.[78] So, by its very nature, this immi-

[77] See, for instance, Basu's *Anthropological Profile of the Muslims.* Based on fieldwork conducted in 1973 and 1974, Basu describes one (and by all accounts typical) Muslim *basti* or slum in Narikeldanga "as quite repulsive to the eye", choked with garbage, its drains filled with faeces, and its tiny hutments dark and unventilated (p. 2).

[78] There were clear directives from Delhi making it plain that the return of Muslims to India was not to be tolerated. In May 1949, a secretary at the Ministry of Rehabilitation in Delhi wrote to the chief secretary of the

gration was clandestine and few attempts were made before the mid-1970s to assess its size or scale. And yet one surviving run of the "secret Fortnightly Reports" for 1957 indicates beyond doubt that a steady flow of Muslims in this period entered West Bengal by stealth and settled there.[79]

That the process began soon after Partition is suggested by reports from Malda as early as 1949, when Muslims from Rajshahi

---

West Bengal government about the Government of India's "considerable anxiety" over the working of the permit system. "The permit system was introduced with a view to stop one-way traffic from Pakistan as the return of such Muslims was adversely affecting the rehabilitation schemes of the Government of India. Despite our request (dated 14 December 1948) that the applications for the conversion of a temporary permit into a permanent one by Muslims who came to India after 10 September 1948 should not be entertained, we are informed by our High Commissioner in Pakistan that a large number of such recommendations are being received by him . . . In this connection I am to draw your attention to my letter . . . of 18 April 1949 in which you were requested not to recommend cases for the grant of permits for permanent settlement to Muslim evacuees except in cases of genuine hardship. As you are presumably aware we have over 7 lacs of displaced people receiving free rations in camps in India. The Government of India attaches great importance to their early rehabilitation . . . Return of Muslims from Pakistan is bound to [retard] the rehabilitation of displaced persons. In the circumstances it is hoped the Provincial Governments will not allow permits for permanent settlement to Muslims wishing to come back to India till the displaced persons have been satisfactorily rehabilitated." C.N. Chandra, Government of India, Ministry of Rehabilitation to the Chief Secretary, Government of West Bengal, 9 May 1949, GBIB, F. No. 1210–48(4). This was followed by a stern reminder on 6 June 1948. Ibid.

[79] The "infiltration of Muslims into Indian territory without travel documents" was reported fortnight after fortnight all through 1957 from the border districts, from 24 Parganas, Nadia, West Dinajpur, Jalpaiguri, Darjeeling, Murshidabad, and Malda. Towards the end of the year, cases were regularly reported from these districts of Pakistani Muslims being prosecuted for "illegal entry" and for "violation of passport rules". In the first half of November 1957, twenty-one Pakistani Muslims were charged in West Dinajpur for "violation of the passport rules while in Jalpaiguri eight of

in East Bengal had reportedly begun to trickle into Malda at the rate of one or two families a week. Malda was a northern border district with a large Muslim presence. Despite the fact that "suitable steps [had] been and [were] being taken to discourage such migration", the slow, surreptitious, but steady dribble of Muslims continued, in particular into the Muslim-dominated Kaliachak area along the border.[80] That these migrants were absorbed by the Muslim communities of Malda is suggested by an undercover officer's finding in 1949 that "the Muslims who are coming to this dominion are facing very little difficulties to settle, as they are being helped by their community to settle . . . It is interesting to note that the Muslims who are coming to this end from Pakistan to settle are not begging for help from anyone else or from the Government."[81]

Again, we do not know for certain who these people were, although the report suggests that "destitutes" and "economic migrants" were mixed among returning Muslim evacuees.[82] However, it is not difficult to see that the result of this migration was a gradual increase in the size and density of the populations living in these Muslim belts, particularly those situated close to the border with Pakistan.

The cumulative impact of these displacements can be seen in the striking fact that by 1961 just under 30 per cent of West Bengal's Muslim "population lived in only fifty *thanas* or police sub-districts along the border with East Pakistan." In this handful of localities, Muslims had come to make up about 40 per cent of the total

---

them were prosecuted for the same offence. In Cooch Behar certain Pakistani Muslims . . . [were charged with] illegal entry". Secret fortnightly report for the first half of November 1957 for West Bengal, GBIB, F. No. 1210–48(4).

[80] Weekly Confidential Report for the week ending 31 December 1949, GBIB, F. No. 69A/49 (Malda).

[81] Copy of a report by the DI O (I) of Nadia district, 12 August 1949, GBIB, F. No. 1809–48 (Nadia).

[82] Ibid.

population. Their numerical weight was particularly marked in three distinct zones of "particularly strong concentration, each consisting of a chain of contiguous border police stations."[83] In each of these zones, in the border *thanas* of West Dinajpur, Malda-Murshidabad, and the 24 Parganas respectively, Muslims constituted between half and four-fifths of the total population. Significantly, Kaliachak – where the first instance of this reverse migration was discovered in 1949 – was one of these zones, and by 1961 Muslims constituted over 65 per cent of its total population. This pattern of clustering was also in evidence – though perhaps not quite so sharply – in other rural districts, such as Birbhum, where there had been a strong Muslim presence before Partition. By 1961, the Muslims of Birbhum had clustered together in the north of the district and had become the majority community there; by contrast, in south Birbhum they were less than 10 per cent of the population. It was as if Partition violently shook the great kaleidoscope of Bengali Muslim society, pushing it into a new pattern: Muslims all over West Bengal moved away from areas where they had lived in small communities and moved towards areas where they were more numerous. Small Muslim localities shrank or disappeared, large Muslim belts became larger, more densely populated, and more exclusively Muslim.

Another remarkable feature of this series of displacements is that it led to a sharp fall in the number of Muslims living in the towns and cities of West Bengal. In 1931, about three out of every ten town-bred persons in Bengal as a whole had been Muslims, and that proportion had been higher still in the west, where Muslims were "comparatively more numerous in the towns".[84] By 1971, only one out of ten city-dwellers in West Bengal was a

[83] These zones were Chopra-Islampur-Goalpokhar in West Dinajpur, Kalichak-Shamshirganj-Suti-Raghunathganj-Lalgola-Bhagawangola-Raninagar-Jalangi-Karimpur in Malda, and Murshidabad and Sarupnagar-Baduria-Basirhat in the 24 Parganas. *Census of India 1961*, vol. XVI, part I-A, p. 222.

[84] *Census of India 1931*, vol. V, part I, p. 387.

Muslim. The census of that year noted that most towns and cities, particularly those around Calcutta and on the western bank of the Hooghly, "show[ed] the effects of Partition as far as the religious composition of the population is concerned." By 1951, West Bengal's urban Muslim population had dropped sharply; and the decline continued thereafter, "steadily but rather slowly".[85] In 1964, when Nirmal Kumar Bose conducted a detailed survey of Calcutta, he found that in many wards and *mohallas* previously inhabited mainly by Muslims, refugees had edged them out and established a dominant Hindu presence.[86] Muslims long settled in these areas had left the city altogether or had "moved into greater concentration" in other wards. The net effect was a decline in the overall numbers of urban Muslims in West Bengal, and for those who hung on in the city the usual pattern was to cluster together in pockets of increasingly dense concentration.[87] When he conducted his survey of Calcutta's Muslims in 1969, Siddiqui too was struck by the way in which "recent historical events" had forced them "to cling together even more closely to meet the situation. The process that had started the withdrawal of the Muslims from South Calcutta in the mid-forties . . . has continued. This tends to concentrate them in compact areas."[88]

We do not know where all these town-bred Muslim refugees went. A certain proportion must have migrated to towns in East Pakistan. But it is interesting that the census of East Bengal taken

[85] The census commissioner concluded that this pattern of decline "reflects the greater mobility of urban populations" due to "economic factors" and no doubt such considerations played a part. *Census of India, 1971, Series 22, West Bengal, part I-A*, pp. 278–9.

[86] Bose listed wards 3, 14, 16, 34, 77, 78, 79, and 80 as areas formerly occupied by Muslim labourers and artisans, whose Muslim inhabitants had been largely replaced by refugees. Bose, *Calcutta*, p. 33.

[87] Ibid., pp. 39–40.

[88] Siddiqui, *The Muslims of Calcutta*, p. 26.

in 1951 shows that less than one out of every ten West Bengali Muhajirs settled in Dacca district, by far the most urbanised area in the east. Far greater numbers – almost two-thirds – migrated to Kushtia, Rajshahi, Rangpur, and Dinajpur: areas that were altogether more bucolic.[89] And we know that the Muslims who moved out of the cities but stayed in West Bengal gravitated towards certain Muslim-dominated clusters, all of which were rural backwaters. We also know that returning Muslim evacuees did not usually go back to their houses in the towns; they too were eventually absorbed into these rural Muslim-majority corners.

It seems impossible to escape the conclusion that West Bengal Muslim refugees after Partition mainly migrated from towns to the countryside. This is in itself a remarkable fact, since every study of migration in South Asia insists that its main direction has been citywards. Historically people in South Asia have mainly moved from villages to cities; smaller numbers have moved from one town to another or, in a minority of cases, from one rural area to another. Migration from towns to villages is almost unheard of.[90] And yet this is what West Bengal Muslims appear to have done in very considerable numbers after 1947. The significance of this fact for our understanding of migration in South Asia is potentially very great, but this is not the place to tease it out. Here it is enough to note that twenty-five years after Partition, West Bengal's Muslims were no longer the city creatures they had once been. They now lived predominantly in the countryside.

Partition thus dramatically changed the profile of the Muslim population of West Bengal. It redistributed them, and not merely spatially. Like a great earthquake, it flung them out of the cities and towns of the south, pushing them northwards to the great rural Muslim settlements along the Ganges or eastwards towards the border and beyond it. In so doing, it rubbed away some of

[89] *Census of Pakistan, 1951,* vol. III, *East Bengal, Reports and Tables*, p. 81.

[90] That migration in the Bengal area historically followed this pattern is demonstrated in Chattopadhyaya, *Internal Migration in India.*

the age-old differences between Muslims of the west – historically more urban in their setting – and their agriculturist co-religionists in East Bengal.

Even the 10 per cent who stayed on in the cities experienced upheaval and change. The communities which remained were transformed by the fact that they had to absorb refugees from more dangerous parts of the city, often into areas which had been reduced in size and usually by abandoning ritual and public space. Inevitably these communities, which had once been "distinct sub-communal groups", now became more ethnically diverse. Basu's study of Muslim bastis in Calcutta in 1974 showed that they were mainly "multi-ethnic".[91] Not surprisingly, few of the old communities had been able to survive these traumas without abandoning their hereditary trades. Not a single Ansari in Basu's survey was still a weaver in 1974; the majority lived by making *bidis*, pulling rickshaws, hawking fish, or by taking jobs as lascars. In 1974 hardly any Raiens still sold vegetables and the Sisgars had completely given up making bangles.[92] Of course, some of their members had done well, joining the urban bourgeoisie: some Ansaris and Raiens, in particular, had been able to educate themselves and enter the learned professions. But for most, the loss of old localities and old ways of life – which for most urban Muslims had revolved around hereditary skilled craftsmanship – brought poverty and hardship. For some at least, there was little choice but to join the rough-and-tumble world of the manual labouring classes.[93]

In these different ways Partition, sometimes in rushes and sometimes in imperceptible ripples, displaced and transformed

[91] Basu, *Anthropological Profile of the Muslims*, p. 5. Also see Siddiqui, "Life in the Slums of Calcutta".

[92] Basu, *Anthropological Profile of the Muslims*, pp. 14–15.

[93] Among the Sheikhjees, for instance, while almost 80 per cent still clung to their hereditary calling in trading in cattle and dairy produce, almost one in five had taken up "hard manual labour" by 1974. Ibid., p. 16.

countless Muslim communities all over western Bengal. Some left for Pakistan in the immediate aftermath of Partition, others left in fits and starts during the following decades, which were disfigured by endemic communal troubles. The many who stayed behind also suffered their share of dislocation and distress, often being forced in times of crisis to seek shelter in "safe" areas, their temporary flights usually ending up as permanent displacements. Many Muslim families who had previously lived in relative harmony cheek by jowl with Hindu neighbours gradually moved out of these mixed settlements, now opting instead to live in localities where their co-religionists had the advantage of numbers and were better insulated from their Hindu neighbours. When they left, their property was quickly seized by Hindu refugees. Others were forced out of their homes and land by Hindus, usually refugees. So large numbers of Muslims were themselves turned into refugees, whether in the formal sense of being evacuees who moved to Pakistan or as "internally displaced" persons, who had crossed no international borders but had nevertheless been dispossessed, losing their homes and their traditional means of livelihood, and being compelled to throw themselves on the mercy of their co-religionists in enclaves which increasingly became exclusively Muslim ghettos.

In time, these different processes of displacement came to impose new patterns of Muslim presence in West Bengal. Muslims now occupied considerably less land in the province than they had done before Partition and they were increasingly confined into smaller and more tightly packed locations. The extent to which these areas became sharply defined as Muslim and distinct from Hindu neighbourhoods is underlined by the way the police perceived them. From 1948 at least until 1957, the police maintained surveillance over what they described as "Mohammadan pockets", which were duly listed, with a careful record kept of any changes in their composition, right down to the number of firearms owned by their inhabitants. These clusters appear to have become relatively stable in shape and size by the mid-1950s. In 1957, only in one district, Howrah, did the Intelligence Bureau identify significant changes in the number, size, and location of these Muslim "pockets".[94] It was almost as if the larger partition of Bengal had sparked off an endless series of lesser partitions in the innumerable neighbourhoods of West Bengal, the Great Divide being mirrored in many smaller divisions in the communal topography of a changing province.

Partition thus failed to solve the root problem of the growing alienation of Muslims from Hindus in undivided Bengal. If anything, it intensified that alienation. Partition increased the social gulf as well as the physical distances separating Hindus from Muslims. It rendered more impermeable the boundaries between them. It also transformed the basic characteristics of the Muslim peoples of West Bengal, who now lost much of their historic and once highly visible presence in the towns and cities of a province whose urban profiles they had in the past done so much to shape. In those clusters where Muslims now huddled fearfully together, memories of relative prosperity and better times quickly faded in tackling the grim realities of the present and facing the even grimmer prospects of the future. Once fairly prosperous Muslim settlements were rapidly metamorphosed into slum-like ghettos of the underprivileged and the poor. In these sad communities, Muslims who were too poor and disadvantaged to migrate to Pakistan were now, in some sense, the dominant force. But in these ghettos there were other trends. Increasingly inhabited, squeezed, and crowded by Muslim outsiders from other parts of West Bengal,

[94] Memo no. D-4270, 7 February 1947, GBIB, F. No. 270/56. Sadly, the intelligence files which contained the original list of Muslim pockets (GBIB 126–48) appear to have been destroyed or lost, as also the updated full list prepared in 1951 (GBIB 2154–51). But the very fact that such a precise record was made and updated, and that such tight arrangements were made for their surveillance, indicates that these clusters were largely stable formations and regarded as such by the authorities.

who had been reduced from being skilled artisans to labourers, these Muslim neighbourhoods were a new phenomenon, ghettos which grew larger as they absorbed indigent migrants from elsewhere in Bengal and from East Pakistan itself.

Selimpore and its graveyard with which we began is a microcosm of the big picture. The visible decay of a once prosperous Muslim neighbourhood, the way it came to be a shadow of its former self, the dilapidation of its once imposing graves, the surrender by the few remaining Muslims of their rituals and rights, the suburb's lack of civic amenities, appalling even by Calcutta's inglorious standards, and the gross poverty of its denizens, all are reflections of a much broader tale or the decline of the Muslims of West Bengal. Once masters of the province, Partition pushed them both literally and figuratively – to its margins.

References

Basu, Mahadev, *Anthropological Profile of the Muslims of Calcutta,* Calcutta: Anthropological Survey of India, 1985.

Bose, Nirmal Kumar, *Calcutta, 1964: A Social Survey*, Bombay, etc.: Anthropological Survey of India, 1968.

Census of India, 1931, vol. v, pt i, Calcutta, 1933.

Census of India, 1951, vol. vi, pt iii, Calcutta City, Calcutta, 1953.

Census of Pakistan Population, 1961, vol. 2, East Pakistan, Karachi, 1964.

Census of Pakistan, 1951, vol. 3, East Bengal, Report and Tables, Karachi, n.d.

Chakrabarti, Prafulla K., *The Marginal Men: Refugees and the Left Political Syndrome in West Bengal,* Calcutta, 1990.

Chakrabarty, Saroj, *With Dr B.C. Roy*, Calcutta, 1974.

Chatterji, Joya, *Bengal Divided: Hindu Communalism and Partition, 1932–1947*, Cambridge, 1994.

Chattopadhyaya, Haraprasad, *Internal Migration in India: A Case Study of Bengal,* Calcutta, 1987.

Datta, Pradip Kumar, *Carving Blocs: Communal Ideology in Early Twentieth-century Bengal*, Delhi, 1999.

Eaton, Richard, *The Rise of Islam and the Bengal Frontier, 1204–1760*, Oxford, 1993.

Guhathakurta, Meghna, "Families Uprooted and Divided: The Case of the Bengal Partition", Unpublished paper presented at a workshop on Alternative Histories and Non-written Sources: New Perspectives from the South, La Paz, May 1999.

Hasan, Mushirul, *Legacy of a Divided Nation: India's Muslims since Independence*, Delhi, 1997.

Kamaluddin, A.F.M., "Refugee Problems in Bangladesh", in L.A. Kosinski and K.M. Elahi, eds, *Population Redistribution and Development in South Asia,* Dordrecht, 1985.

Khan, Muhammad Ishaq, "The Significance of the Dargah of Hazratbal in the Socio-religious and Political Life of Kashmiri Muslims", in Christian W. Troll, ed., *Muslim Shrines in India: Their Character, History and Significance*, Delhi, 1992.

Martin, Montgomery, *The History, Antiquities, Topography and Statistics of Eastern India: Comprisinq* the *Districts of Behar, Shabad, Bhagalpoor, Goruckpoor, Dinajepoor, Puraniya, Rungporr and Assam*, London, 1838.

McPherson, Kenneth, *The Muslim Microcosm: Calcutta 1918–1935*, Wiesbaden, 1974.

Mitra, Asok, *The New India 1948–1955*, Bombay: Popular Prakashan, 1991.

Nakatani, Tetsuya, "Away from Home: The Movement and Settlement of Refugees from East Pakistan in West Bengal, India", *Journal of the Japanese Association for South Asian Studies*, no. 12, 2000.

Prior, K., "Making History: The State's Intervention in Religious Disputes", *Modern Asian Studies,* 1993.

Roy, Asim, *The Islamic Syncretistic Tradition in Bengal,* Princeton, 1983.

Siddiqui, M.K.A., "Life in the Slums of Calcutta", *Economic and Political Weekly,* 13 December 1969.

———, *The Muslims of Calcutta: A Study in Aspects of their Social Organisation,* Calcutta: Anthropological Survey of India, 1974.

Survey of Unemployment in *West Bengal, 1953, First Interim Report,* vol. I, pt I, Government of West Bengal, 1953.

van Hear, Nicholas, "Refugee Diasporas: Trans-national Links among Displaced People in South Asia and Beyond", Unpublished paper presented at a seminar on Displaced People in South Asia, Chennai, March 2001.

Wright, P., Jr, "The Effectiveness of Muslim Representation in India", in D.E. Smith, ed., *South Asian Politics and Religion,* Princeton, 1966.

10

On Being Stuck in the Bengal Delta

Immobility in the "Age of Migration"

SCHOLARS HAVE TENDED to ignore the phenomenon of immobility.[1] I myself stumbled upon it only while researching its obverse, migration, and then only by accident. Some years ago, I came across a police report on a "fracas" at a Muslim graveyard in Calcutta, where, soon after Partition, Hindu refugees had seized the land and put a stop to burials. Out of curiosity, I tried to find the graveyard, but this proved challenging. The people of the now-affluent Hindu neighbourhood that had sprung up in the area stared blankly at me when I asked them how to get there. A few protested that no such burial ground had ever existed. Finally, I found an elderly Muslim rickshaw puller who knew where it was, and he offered to take me there. There was no pucca road leading to it, just a sodden dirt track, barely wide

[1] This essay draws on research supported by the AHRC (Arts and Humanities Research Council, UK), under the aegis of the "Bengal diaspora" project, of which I was principal investigator. I am indebted to the AHRC, to my co-investigator Claire Alexander, and research assistants Annu Jalais and Shahzad Firoz. Unless otherwise specified, the interviews drawn upon here were conducted, translated, and transcribed between 2007 and 2009 by Annu Jalais. All names of interviewees have been changed, except where respondents said they wanted to be identified.

enough for two persons to pass. When we reached the cemetery, it was like a place time had passed by. Only a dozen or so people still remained in what had been, just a few decades before, a bustling Muslim locality. They included the *mutawwali* (custodian of the shrines), and a few members of his family, who lived in the most abject poverty I had ever seen. Their crumbling huts were dark and airless. They wore rags that barely hid their skeletal bodies. The women gazed at me in silence, too listless even to brush the flies off the faces of children who neither smiled nor played.[2]

At the time, I perceived only dimly a connection between this family's immobility and their poverty; but it grew more evident in the decade that followed, as I worked on migrants in the Bengal delta. During this research project, I kept encountering their counterparts, people whom I called "stayers-on". They were quiet people like the *mutawwali*, people who had gone nowhere, people whose stories haunted me. These were not folk who had stayed on in peaceful places, in times of plenty, with pleasing prospects. Rather, they had remained where they were despite violence, impoverishment, and social boycott, which had left them culturally and politically marginalised. They had stayed on while most others around them fled, in contexts of mass migration, when the "push factors" could hardly have been more compelling.

Immobility raises awkward questions for theorists of migration. Every dominant theory (whether of the neo-classical, new economic, world systems, institutions, network, or cumulative causation variety) seeks to account for why individuals (or households) develop migration strategies, how streams of migration arise, and how these are sustained over time.[3] From the standpoint of these theories, migration is unusual behaviour that requires

[2] Also see Chatterji, "Of Graveyards and Ghettos" in this volume.

[3] For a masterful overview, see Massey, *et al.*, "Theories of International Migration", pp. 431–66.

explanation.[4] Its obverse, staying in place, is seen as the norm, an "obvious" state of affairs that calls for no accounting.

Yet, as historians are coming to recognise, assumptions about the ordinariness of immobility are insecure. For one thing, we know a great deal more about the mobile societies of early modern Asia. Between 1722 and 1776, over half of Sichuan's "poylglot society" were migrants, perhaps 3.4 million in number,[5] while in South Asia, until 1800 perhaps half of the population was mobile for much of their adult lives.[6] For another, Asian mobility in the era of high imperialism is much better understood.[7] Notwithstanding the argument by distinguished historians that, by the mid-nineteenth century, the colonial state had destroyed the last vestiges of the mobile South Asia of earlier times, forcing its habitually peripatetic communities into a sedentary mode of life rooted in village communities,[8] everyone recognises that the new economic conditions of the late nineteenth century stimulated huge new migrations to cities, plantations, mines, and factories, within India and beyond its shores. Amrith suggests that between 1834 and

[4] Neo-classical theory does not suffer from this problem, of course (although it has been challenged on other grounds), since it postulates that the migration of workers overseas is caused by differences in wage rates between countries. Migration, from this standpoint, between low-wage to high-wage-labour markets is to be expected in all cases where the costs of such migration do not outweigh the anticipated benefits. But it does suffer from the problem of explaining why people do not migrate in larger numbers, in what Malmberg describes as the "immobility paradox". Malmberg, "Time and Space in International Migration", p. 21.

[5] Kuhn, *Chinese among Others*, p. 27.

[6] Ludden, "Presidential Address".

[7] See, for instance, Amrith, *Migration and Diaspora in Modern Asia*; Northrup, *Indentured Labour in the Age of Imperialism*; Brown, *Global South Asians*; Amrith, "South Asian Migration"; Kuhn, *Chinese among Others*; and McKeown, "Global Migration 1846–1950".

[8] See, in particular, Bayly, *Indian Society and the Making of the British Empire*, pp. 136–68; and Washbrook, "Economic Depression and the Making of Traditional Society".

1940 over 28 million people left India's shores.[9] From 1926 to 1930, when overseas emigration peaked, according to Kingsley Davis some 3.2 million Indians travelled abroad.[10] Within India, in 1921, the Indian census recorded more than 15 million internal migrants,[11] a figure that underestimated the true extent of local and intra-regional movement.[12] After 1921, spurred on by unprecedented growth in population, internal migration increased still faster; and from the 1970s, these rates of growth achieved dizzying heights. By 2013, perhaps one in five of India's 1.2 billion people were internal migrants.[13] In China, between 1979 and 2009, some 340 million people moved from villages to towns.[14] In Vietnam, 4.3 million people migrated internally in the half-decade before 1999.[15] In Bangladesh, after a war that created 10 million refugees, constant migration from the countryside to towns, at a rate of over 3 per cent a year between 1975 and 2009, has led to one of the highest rates of urbanisation in the world.[16] These are staggering figures. But the broad brush of migration on the big canvas conceals higher rates still of local micro-mobility. Even in "sedentary" agricultural societies, as geographers now concur, people do not remain still: they are habitually engaged, to varying degrees, in various complex forms of spatial mobility.[17]

Yet despite these cumulative gains in our understanding of the scale of mobility in early-modern and modern Asia, and its dramatic acceleration in "the age of migration",[18] immobility

[9] Amrith, *Migration and Diaspora*, p. 32.
[10] Davis, *The Population of India and Pakistan*, p. 99.
[11] Ibid., Table XI "Birth-place", p. 497.
[12] Alexander, Chatterji, and Jalais, *The Bengal Diaspora*, ch. 1.
[13] Abbas and Varma, "Internal Labour Migration in India".
[14] Chan, "China, Internal Migration".
[15] Anh, "Migration and Poverty in Asia", p. 1718.
[16] Marshall and Rahman, *Internal Migration in Bangladesh.*
[17] Malmberg, "Time and Space in International Migration", p. 23.
[18] Castles and Miller, *The Age of Migration.*

continues to be seen as the obvious state of affairs, and few have asked questions about its causes, conditions, and histories.

Where, unusually, such questions have been raised, the emphasis has been upon the barriers built by the states of the West against South-North migration. Jorgen Carling, for instance, describes the daunting "immigration interface" that migrants who go West have to negotiate. He suggests that this interface acts not so much as a wall as a dense "jungle in which various paths are each associated with specific obstacles, costs and risks."[19] As these costs and risks have escalated in recent times, he argues, "involuntary immobility" has grown.

Yet Carling's valuable study, as well as the handful of others that have looked at this phenomenon, look exclusively at migration from the developing world to Western industrial societies.[20] This focus is problematic, however. Most of the world's migrants, and over 95 per cent of its refugees since the Second World War, have not moved to the West. They have remained within the global South, in, or close to, their regions of origin.[21] *The South is not just a "source" of migration, but its pre-eminent destination.*[22] Once this overweening fact is recognised, the "immobility paradox" takes on a quite different complexion. In the global South, the capacity of states to seal their borders is notoriously weak.[23] The costs of migration across these borders – whether material or psychological – are much lower than those of emigration to the West. The costs and risks of travel are relatively low, linguistic and cultural skills easier to acquire, and networks enabling migration often already in place. In post-colonial times, in the turbulent contexts of nation-building and minority-formation, the pressures to migrate

[19] Carling, "Migration in an Age of Involuntary Immobility", p. 26.

[20] Hammer, "Why do People Go or Stay?", p. 2.

[21] Zolberg and Benda, *Global Migrants*; Schmeidl, "Conflict and Forced Migration".

[22] Alexander, Chatterji, and Jalais, *The Bengal Diaspora.*

[23] Sadiq, *Paper Citizens.*

have been intense, particularly upon those classed as "national minorities". The *mutawwali* and his family, and others whose stories are discussed below, stayed on, but often were in fear of their very lives. They represent extreme cases, who, according to every existing theory of migration, should have left. And yet they remained.

Why did they remain? And why did this choice (if indeed it was a choice) drive them into poverty? This essay suggests some preliminary answers to these questions. Its conclusions come out of a multi-disciplinary study of the greater Bengal region in the twentieth century, and the patterns of mobility and immobility that have arisen within it.[24] In that study, the methods deployed were those of a historian and a historical ethnographer: in addition to archival research, 160 interviews were conducted amongst both Muslim migrants and stayers-on in the Bengal delta, on both sides of the border, in India and in Bangladesh. Access to interviewees was achieved by a combination of "snowballing" through community "gatekeepers", personal networks, and serendipitous meetings. We interviewed stayers-on both in urban settings (Urdu-speakers in Town Hall Camp in Dhaka, in the former railway township of Syedpur, and well as in Kolkata's Muslim neighbourhoods) and in rural areas (Bengali speakers in villages in 24 Parganas South in West Bengal). Part of our intention was to develop a historically sophisticated and ethnographically rich understanding of the processes and relationships of extreme immobility in contexts of mass migration, accelerated mobility, and violent nation creation.[25]

This article begins by analysing the impact of the intensifying links, in the late-colonial era, between Bengal and the global economy. That impact varied widely on various groups among its

[24] "Greater Bengal" refers to the latter-day Bengal Presidency, which included what is today West Bengal, Bihar, Orissa, Assam, Nagaland, Meghalaya, Arunachal Pradesh and Mizoram in India, and of course, Bangladesh.

[25] Malkki, *Purity and Exile*, p. 1.

people, in ways that had a profound bearing on their capacity to move. It identifies "deficits" – at macro, micro, and cumulative levels – each of which worked to inhibit the mobility of particular groups and individuals. It then describes "overabundances" – of obligations to people and places – that tied certain people down. Finally, it hints at the reasons why, and the ways in which, stayers-on have grown poorer.

Grids, Bottlenecks, and the Development of "Network Poverty"

In the late-nineteenth and early-twentieth century, eastern India was knitted into a new imperial system of trade and commerce, with Bengal at its centre. In the region, the interplay of private capital and the imperatives of empire – for profit, security, and cheap but safe governance – played out in specific ways. One crucial result was the creation of a particular transport grid designed to serve a distinctive labour market; and, as this section will show, their particularities made the gulf between the mobile and the immobile ever greater. Features of the transport grid, the labour market, and recruitment systems all combined to produce various (and often overlapping) forms of what might be called "network poverty". Even as the scale and pace of movement accelerated in the region, access to mobility among the people of the region became profoundly uneven.

The discovery in the region of tea, jute, and coal – three commodities that would become crucial for the imperial commerce of India – was a key factor in these processes. This, of course, is well known; but a brief recapitulation will set the context. Native varieties of tea had been discovered in Assam and Sylhet as early as 1824, with commercial production beginning in earnest only in the 1850s. By 1859, the region already had fifty-nine tea gardens, chiefly state-run enterprises, soon transferred to private (mainly European) hands on liberal terms. By 1903, these tea plantations had engrossed 820 square miles of land, producing over 200 million pounds of tea each year,[26] with Indian tea now "oust[ing] the produce of China" from British markets.[27]

Jute, a natural fibre long cultivated locally for its robustness, came into its own after the Crimean War interrupted the supply of hessian. Jute's commercial manufacture as an ideal packaging material grew with the expansion of world trade, with British-owned mills around Calcutta exploiting the region's competitive advantages. By 1903–4, India's annual jute export was valued at about twelve crore (a hundred million) rupees, and Bengal emerged not only as the world's sole supplier of raw jute, but, along with Dundee, as one of two centres where it was processed.

Neither jute nor tea would have flourished without coal. As steam replaced sail in the 1870s and '80s, ships also needed coal in huge quantities. As luck would have it, a long strip of "black country" was discovered, initially in Raniganj, and south-west Bengal and eastern Bihar became India's largest suppliers of coal. One of the first stretches of railway line in India was built to connect Calcutta to the coalfields of Raniganj. Soon afterwards, in 1894, mines in neighbouring Jharia began intensively to be opened up and were connected "to a branch line of the East India Railway", followed in quick succession by new fields at Giridih, and Bokaro, west of Raniganj.

This concatenation of developments created a voracious appetite for labour, and eastern India's transport systems were developed chiefly to carry labour, coal, and other commodities swiftly and cheaply to the points where they were in demand. By the early-twentieth century, rail, road, and steamer had linked eastern India together in a transport grid, where railways (albeit unevenly) connected the region to upper, central, and western India. Among the main railroads was the 1468-mile-long Bengal and North

[26] *Imperial Gazetteer. Vol. III. Economic*, pp. 56–62. But also see Guha, *Planter Raj to Swaraj*; and Sharma, *Empire's Garden*.

[27] *Imperial Gazetteer. Vol. III. Economic*, p. 57.

Western Railway that linked Bengal to the populous, labour-exporting districts of Oudh, Rohilkhand, Benaras, Jaunpur, and Shahbad, carrying thirteen million passengers a year by 1904.[28] The Bengal–Nagpur Railway, which connected Calcutta in the east to Bombay in the west, transporting almost eight million passengers each year, was another key link in this chain, as was the East Indian Railway from Howrah to Kalka and Simla, the distant summer capital of India, on which more than twenty-five million passengers each year jostled for standing room only. The Assam–Bengal Railway, 740 miles long, ran from Chittagong on the southeastern seaboard of Bengal, through the Surma river valley and Sylhet,[29] and across Cachar into north Assam, and transported over two million passengers a year (as well as jute and tea) by the turn of the century, while numerous smaller gauge railways criss-crossed Bengal itself, carrying local traffic over shorter distances.[30]

By the 1910s, in addition to rail, a "very complete steamer system" had begun to ply the region's waterways. The heaviest investment in the steamer system was in eastern Bengal and Assam, where topography rendered railways prohibitively expensive to build, and where connections by water were vital for the development of the (chiefly British-owned) jute and tea industries. By 1909, no less than thirteen stations in the eastern region each had at least thirty-four steamer services a month,[31] and rivers such as the Brahmaputra, previously too treacherous to navigate during the monsoons, were now regularly served by "small feeder-steamers" throughout the year.[32] The road network, admittedly the

[28] Ibid., p. 389.

[29] Khan, *History of the Port of Chittagong.*

[30] *Imperial Gazetteer. Vol. III. Economic*, p. 389. Also see *History of Railways up to 31 March 1923.*

[31] Munsi, *Geography of Transportation*, p. 66.

[32] *Imperial Gazetteer of India. Provincial Series. Eastern Bengal and Assam*, pp. 8–9.

Cinderella of Bengal's transport system, and chronically starved of funds, was also improved, although "trunk" roads, which connected the centres of British power and trade, had priority: by 1930 over a thousand miles of trunk roads had been built (or repaired) in Bengal. Some "feeder roads" were also constructed, usually as auxiliaries to the railways.

Thus, by the early-twentieth century a vast swathe of territory, stretching beyond the Chota Nagpur plateau into parts of northern Madras, the Central Provinces, Orissa, eastern UP, and Bihar had come to be linked closely with central, eastern, and North Bengal, with Assam and Burma to the east, and Nepal to the north, by a transport network built to support the new industries. The whole region had become a vast, interconnected, zonal labour market serving these different, and often competing, sectors. By 1907, Assam contained "three-quarters of a million immigrants, or one eighth of its total population . . . The drain from Bengal to Assam [was] almost counterbalanced by an influx of nearly half a million natives of the United Provinces, who come to seek employment in the mills of Calcutta and Howrah and the coal mines of Burdwan, and as earth workers, palanquin-bearers, and field labourers all over Bengal proper." By 1901, there were nearly half a million migrants in Burma.[33] In addition, a quarter of a million people had migrated from Nepal into this region, more than half settling in contiguous British districts.[34] Between 1911 and 1931, the eastern zone consistently recorded the highest numbers of internal migrants (both immigrants and emigrants) in British India. By 1931, six million persons had moved within and from the Greater Bengal region,[35] a number already twice as large as the entire Indian diaspora worldwide in 1947,[36]

[33] *Imperial Gazetteer of India. The Indian Empire. Vol. I. Descriptive*, pp. 467–8. Emphasis added.

[34] Ibid., p. 469.

[35] Ibid., pp. 69–70.

[36] Memo by B.F.H.B. Tyabji, 23 August 1952, Ministry of External Affairs (AFR II Branch)/AII/53/6491, 31 (Secret), National Archives of India.

and almost twice the size of the Chinese diaspora in the USA in 2010.

But, and this is a crucial point, access to mobility was profoundly unevenly distributed within the region, with distinct (though sometimes intertwined) kinds of "network poverty" emerging in consequence. The first arose from uneven access to the new modes of mass travel. One important factor was the conditions in the so-called "coolie class" of wagons. They were so dangerously overcrowded and unsanitary that only the strong and fit could face the grim prospect of travel in such conditions.[37] Railway staff all too frequently manhandled and abused the poor, "especially ignorant villagers",[38] and treated them "worse than brute beasts".[39] Lower-class carriages, into which passengers were stuffed like sardines into a tin, had no lighting or toilet facilities fifty years after rail travel began. Many carriages still had no seats.[40] For the elderly, the frail and the disabled, travelling by train was not a real option. Unaccompanied women and girls entrained at their peril. Even if the labour market had not increasingly denied access to women (about which more below), conditions on the "transport grid" made it a huge challenge for them even to reach it.

Another crucial axis of stratification was spatial. As Ravi Ahuja has noted, the new transport infrastructure of empire was built only in areas of commercial reward, political sensitivity, and religious significance (major pilgrimage sites increasingly were given rail and road access).[41] By the 1920s, three exceptionally well-connected clusters of transport infrastructure had emerged in the greater Bengal region. One was south-western Bengal "proper", centred around Calcutta, the jute mill townships of Hooghly and Howrah, the coal mine districts of western Bengal and Bihar, and

[37] Mukhopadhyay, "Wheels of Change".

[38] Native Newspaper Reports, cited by Mukhopadhyay in "Wheels of Change", p. 97.

[39] Ibid., p. 74.

[40] Ibid., p. 76.

[41] Ahuja, *Pathways of Empire*.

the railway hub at Asansol. The second was in eastern Bengal, with its hub at Narayanganj and Dacca, which had excellent steamer facilities. The third was the long ribbon of territory extending south to north from the port at Chittagong, through the Surma Valley in present-day Sylhet, into the tea garden districts of Assam, linked from end to end by the Assam-Bengal railway.[42] (See Figs 10.1 and 10.2.)

However, these three "hotspots" of transport infrastructure were not particularly well linked to each other. Beyond them, modern transport facilities penetrated unevenly, tentatively, or not at all. In theory, roads were intended to connect the "interior" to the "railheads", but well into the 1930s the little money that was spent on them mainly went on roads to towns that served as district or subdivisional headquarters. In 1938, of a total of 91,936 miles of road, 86,541 (94 per cent) were maintained by local authorities, about half of which were tracks and footpaths.[43] The King Report of that year concluded that "except from the system comprising the Grand Trunk Road . . . the province of Bengal has no 'Road System' in the proper sense of the term."[44] Later, during World War II, government threw vast resources at new airports and roads built to serve the war effort – Assam finally was connected to Bengal "proper" and Burma by a great new arc of metalled road, thousands of miles long.[45] In the same period, labourers built "a fine network of . . . feeder roads" to the region's 145 new aerodromes, from which South East Asia Command took the

[42] The Eastern Bengal Railway System, founded in 1884, connected the North Bengal tea-growing Dooars to Calcutta and Diamond Harbour, but had feeder lines linking it to Mymensingh, Narayanganj, Faridpore and Jessore. *History of Indian Railways*. In the Bengal Dooars system, "lines were constructed for opening up the western Dooars for the development of the tea industry." Ibid., p. 206. In the same period, many smaller and lighter tracks became part of the Bengal Provincial Railway System.

[43] Munsi, *Geography of Transportation*, p. 120.

[44] King, *Comprehensive Report on Road Development*, vol. 1, p. 91.

[45] Bhattacharya, *Propaganda and Information*, p. 19.

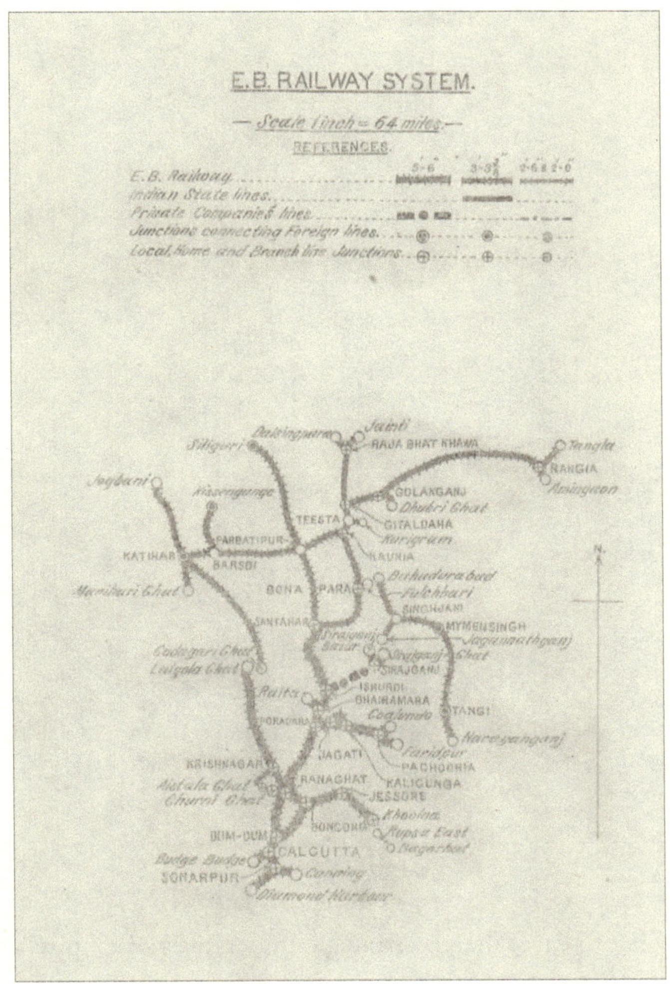

Fig. 10.1

fight to the Japanese.[46] The scale of mobilisation was such that the budget of the Engineering Department increased twenty-five-fold, from Rs 40 million in 1939–40 to Rs 1000 million by 1944.[47] Just as the logic of capital had driven the provision of infrastructure

[46] *Census of India, 1951*, pp. 75–8.
[47] Bhattacharya, *Propaganda*, p. 20, Table 1.1.

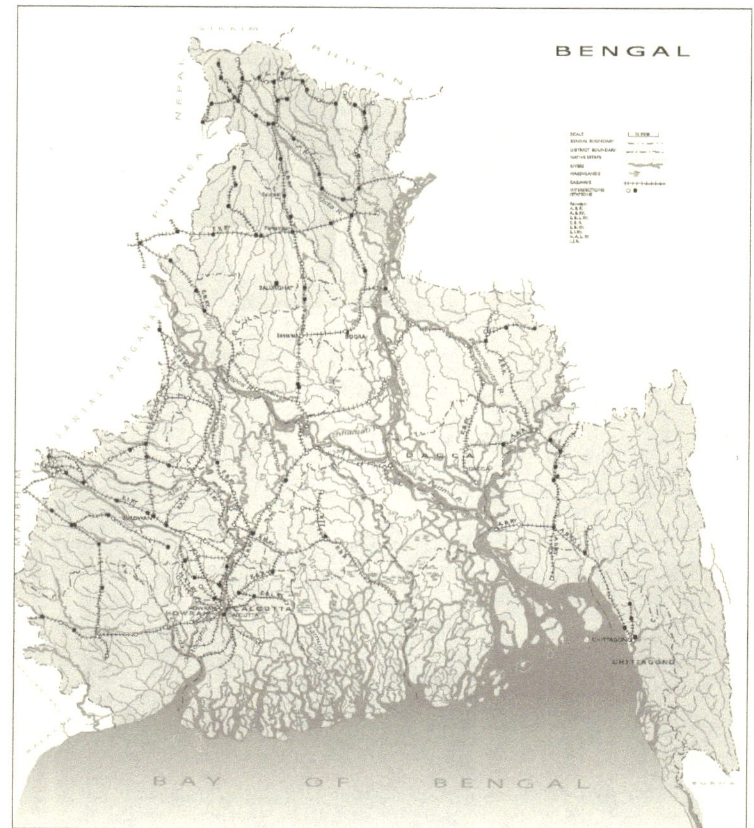

Fig. 10.2

in times of peace, the geo-strategic imperatives of empire drove it forward in times of war.

But places without claims to such importance languished: providing cheap transport to every Indian was no part of the agenda of the Raj. Comparing three districts before World War I – the first, 24 Parganas, central to the empire's commercial and political purposes, the two others, Birbhum and Palamau, more marginal to them – reveals how stark these differences were. By 1914, 24 Parganas already had 324 miles of canals, 53 ferries, over 160 miles of railways, almost 600 miles of metalled roads, and over 1000 miles of village roads.[48] Birbhum, by contrast, had no canals, no ferries, only 65 miles of "loop line" narrow railway, 180-odd miles of metalled roads, and 300 miles of unmetalled roads.[49] At the turn of the century, Palamau, probably Bengal's most isolated district, was compared by one officer "to a ship at sea running short of provisions". Even after the railway reached Daltonganj (in the coal belt) in 1902, "the interior [had] not been opened fully". Roads in the district were so few and so bad that "only a small portion of the trade [was] carried by bullock carts, and in most parts pack bullocks form[ed] the only means of transport." Inaccessibility was "particularly marked in the south, a large roadless tract mostly covered by hill, rock and jungle."[50]

Between 1942 and 1971, this grid, such as it was, suffered a series of seismic shocks. In 1942, with the Japanese threatening India's borders, the government slapped a "Boat Denial" policy onto a swathe of territory on Bengal's southern seaboard, from Chandpur in the east to Kharagpur in the west. All boats capable of carrying more than ten people were either requisitioned for military use, sunk, destroyed, or taken to reception stations where they quickly fell into disrepair. As a result, by the end of the war, only 20,417 boats remained of an original total of 66,563, and this in an area "in which communications [were] almost entirely by river".[51]

In 1947, the new boundary lines of Partition wreaked yet more havoc. Radcliffe tried, as far as he could, to preserve the integrity of major highways and railway lines while drawing the lines carving Bengal into two, but lesser roads and railway lines were torn apart. The most serious disruption for West Bengal

[48] O'Malley, *Bengal District Gazetteers. 24 Parganas*, pp. 163–70.

[49] O'Malley, *Bengal District Gazetteers. Birbhum*, pp. 79–80.

[50] O'Malley, *Bengal District Gazetteers. Palamau*, pp. 119–20.

[51] *Famine Inquiry Commission Report on Bengal*, p. 26.

was caused by North Bengal in effect being cut off from the rest of the state. To get from Malda (up north) due south to Calcutta where work was available, people now had to take a circuitous route via Rajmahal in Bihar, often involving numerous changes of trains and interminable waits.[52] The tea trade, with millions at stake, was hit hard, and only months after Partition the Indian Tea Planters' Association put in a detailed plan that would connect Jalpaiguri, Darjeeling, Malda, and West Dinajpur with Assam and the rest of West Bengal. The West Bengal government took note, and gave the reinstatement of this link urgent priority. But the challenge of reconnecting smaller roads and rail lines with markets was never addressed, producing new islands – large and small – of isolation.[53]

As for East Bengal (East Pakistan), after Partition it was left with only 300 miles of paved roads in the entire province.[54] In 1971, the Liberation War devastated an already woefully inadequate transport system: besides the destruction of railway workshops, signals and locomotives, "299 railway bridges (including the vital Hardinge and Meghna bridges) and 274 road bridges were either destroyed or damaged. Seaports and several important inland channels were blocked by sunken vessels and war debris."[55] On the achievement of Independence, "Bangladesh was left with no aircraft and no ocean-going vessels."[56]

Between 1942 and 1971, therefore, a transport grid that in the best of times had provided only the patchiest coverage, was partly destroyed or disintegrated; so badly damaged that many new

[52] Resolution passed at a public meeting at Malda on 18 February 1948, AICC-I/ G-5/1947–48. Also see the letter from Surendra Mohan Ghosh to Balvantrai Mehta (AICC General Secretary), 18 November 1953, AICC Papers Second Instalment, Parliamentary Board file no. 21 of 1953, cited in Chatterji, "The Fashioning of a Frontier".

[53] Chatterji, "The Fashioning of a Frontier".

[54] Ahmad, *A New Economic Geography of Bangladesh*, p. 157.

[55] Ibid., p. 150.

[56] Ibid.

dark spots appeared off the grid, creating localities marooned and unconnected to vibrant centres of economic activity. New bottlenecks impeded, or severed, old connections.

Colonial sources do not tell us what the "catchment area" for a road or railway station was, or list the towns or villages around the facility which used it. How close was sufficiently close? How far was too far, putting the grid beyond people's reach?

However, two studies conducted in the 1970s give some hint of the answers. The first compared three villages in Bangladesh in the 1970s, soon after the Liberation War. The first village was on a metalled road. The second was 1.5 miles away from such a road, and the third was six miles away from an all-weather road. In the first village, half the respondents had seen a government official in the preceding three months. In the third village only one in seven (or 14 per cent) had had that dubious privilege.[57] If officers, with the resources of government at hand, still struggled to get to parts of their jurisdictions which were off the beaten track, the challenge to ordinary people in isolated villages to reach market towns or railheads, or to places even further away where labour was in demand, can be easily imagined.

The second study, conducted in India, draws on data gathered by the National Sample Survey in 1977–8. Its conclusions are even more startling. In the late 1970s, three of every four (72.3 per cent) journeys of over one kilometre in rural India were made *on foot.* (This compared with only 34.8 per cent of such journeys in urban areas, where, of course, there was much more public transport.[58]) Village dwellers used bicycles for only one in ten of their journeys, and railways even more rarely. For most of rural India, motorised travel by road was either not available or not affordable. So most people had to walk, most of the time, because they had no other option.

As a consequence, they could not travel far. Inevitably, the

[57] Abedin, *Local Administration and Politics.*

[58] *The Demand for Personal Transport*, p. 4.17.

shortest distances travelled overall (in the whole of India) were by those who lived in "backward" areas (from the perspective of infrastructure provision) such as Arunachal, Tripura, and Manipur.[59] In Assam and Bihar, "it took [on average] three households, each with more than five persons, to find one person who took a trip of more than one kilometre in the reference week."[60]

Compare these findings with the millions of travellers who, for the past century, had journeyed to work, sometimes going many hundreds of miles because the grid linked their homes by rail to distant workplaces, and the stunning differences between living "on the grid" and living off it begin to be clear. People who lived "off the grid" had little or no experience of the dramatic effects of 'space-time compression" of modern modes of travel. As Ahuja has argued, late-colonial "development" opened up new lines of inequality *within* regions,[61] and, as these studies suggest, post-colonial states have done relatively little to redress them. The inequities, unevennesses (and eccentricities) of the grid have not merely compounded and reshaped older differences of wealth and status, they have created an altogether new type of inequality – measured by access (or lack of access) to mobility.

These problems of asymmetrical access to mobility were compounded by the idiosyncrasies of the labour market, which, for all its size, evolved in ways that allowed only certain kinds of people entry. For one, opportunities for work increasingly came to be restricted by region of origin, with a marked tendency towards an ethnicisation of the labour force. This pattern emerged organically as employers (in every sector) concluded that migrant *"pardesis"* (foreigners) were more "reliable" and "amenable to discipline". As Kerr has noted, long-distance migrants who had travelled too far from their villages and fields to be drawn back

[59] Ibid., pp. 4.16–17.

[60] Ibid., pp. 4.9.

[61] Ahuja, *Pathways of Empire.*

into the annual cycle of sowing and harvesting, or were not trapped by forms of servitude to local agrarian elites, soon emerged as the "modern" employee of choice.[62]

In time, however, recruiting practices that had evolved in response to irregular labour supply hardened, in tune with the mood music of the times, into racial stereotypes. Local people everywhere were deemed to be "lazy", whereas certain immigrant "races" and "peoples" were by contrast considered good workers. The tea gardens in Darjeeling thus recruited "Gurkha" workers from the hill populations of Nepal, and also relied on Santal labour from Champaran to the west. The Assam tea gardens soon became notorious for their unscrupulous recruiting of workers from Chotanagpur, Bihar, and the United Provinces, who were then forced to stay on, despite the brutal conditions of work and life in the plantations.[63] Most millhands in the jute industry were also migrants from upper India, particularly from Bihar and the United Provinces, and also from famine-prone parts of northern Orissa and the Madras Presidency.[64]

As decades passed, these stereotypes became more elaborate, so that particular forms of labour within each industry came to be deemed appropriate only for people from a particular place, and supposedly of a specific type. Santals were favoured by tea planters for their hardiness in withstanding the humid climate and harsh conditions of the Assam gardens; allegedly they were immune to malaria, willing to work long hours, and above all, docile. Santal women and children were deemed to have the build

[62] Kerr, *Building the Railways of the Raj*, p. 90.

[63] Behal, "Power Structure, Discipline and Labour in Assam", pp. 143–72; Sharma, "'Lazy' Natives, Coolie Labour", pp. 429–55; Sen, "Questions of Consent", pp. 231–60.

[64] This point has long been recognised by historians of labour in the jute industry. See, for instance, Sen, *Women and Labour in Late Colonial India*, pp. 21–54. Also see Chakrabarty, *Rethinking Working Class History*; Basu, *Does Class Matter?*

best suited to the plucking of tea. Assamese workers, by contrast, were irredeemably lazy in the planters' eyes, and as a result, by 1884 only five per cent of all workers in Assam's plantations were local people.[65] "Poorbeas" (men from eastern UP and Bihar) were preferred in the jute mills. In the coalfields, the "bulk of the colliers belong[ed] to the Kamia class of landless labourer", although some were "agriculturists holding land at a distance from the coalfields."[66] (Both groups, for reasons that of course had nothing to do with "race", were unlikely to "abscond" back to the fields in the harvesting season.) Poorbeas soon came to dominate the regular staff on the railways, and, as Parth Shil's work shows, Bengal's constabulary as well.[67] Men from Noakhali and Sandwip in East Bengal were ubiquitous on Calcutta's docks. Sylhetis soon came to monopolise the boiler rooms of steamships. And so on.

This process of ethnicisation was also consolidated by systems of labour recruitment, which (as is well known) relied heavily on sirdars or jobbers of various kinds. Sirdars enlisted men from their own caste, community, kinship group, and village, and this hardened the links between particular areas of recruitment and specific sectors of the economy. Even within these recruitment "hotspots", opportunities for movement came to be restricted to particular networks, access to which sirdars sought tightly to control. In time, therefore, the "segmentary" labour market in these "modern" sectors of the economy became less open to the population at large, even when recruitment swelled to record levels.[68]

As Chandavarkar has shown for Bombay, the power of jobbers waned in the latter half of the twentieth century.[69] But access to jobs is still, in the 21st century, dominated by networks. Those

[65] Sharma, *Empire's Garden*, p. 83.

[66] *Imperial Gazetteer. Vol. III. Economic*, p. 164.

[67] Shil, "Police Labour and State Formation in Bengal".

[68] Ahuja, "Mobility and Containment".

[69] Chandavarkar, "Decline and Fall of the Jobber System".

historically excluded from such networks continue to find it hard to break into these employments. Anirudh Krishna's study of poverty in 35 villages in North India, conducted in 2002, bears this out. In 309 cases where young men had successfully diversified household income by migrating to the city, he discovered, 198 had relied upon a contact, "a friend, or more often a relative, already established in the city."[70] But others, "equally well qualified in most other respects have not been equally able to take advantage of these opportunities." Krishna cites one respondent, Pratap Singh:

> I am educated [to high school level] and eager to get a job in the city, but I have no way of knowing what jobs exist. I have no one in the city who can find out and tell me. It is very expensive for me to live there waiting for a job, and my family cannot afford these expenses. Some day, I hope, I will get a job and help my family. I wish I had an uncle or cousin in . . . [the nearest city] who could help me, just as Gopi Singh's brother-in-law helped him to find a job.

Everyone in this vignette is male. Pratap Singh is a man, as is Gopi Singh and his helpful brother-in-law. Pratap Singh bemoans his lack of uncles and (male) cousins who might have been able to help him. Women do not enter his narrative of work and the routes to mobility at all.

This is because gender was, and remains, another crucially important axis of differentiation, *which cuts across regions and even networks*, in ways that the next section will discuss more fully. But here the historical backcloth is relevant. In every industry, as historians have shown single, able-bodied men dominated the migrant working population from the start, and that dominance grew with every passing decade. Even if women had been able easily, say, to hop onto a train, which they could not, employers grew ever more reluctant to hire them as the perceived costs of doing so rose with increasing regulation, as

[70] Krishna, "Escaping Poverty and Becoming Poor", p. 130.

Samita Sen has shown for the jute industry.[71] The coal industry hired some women and children well into the twentieth century, but paid them lower wages for carrying coal to the tubs and the mineshafts. The industry became increasingly reluctant to hire them from the 1930s, when the prohibition on employing women for underground work came into force, leaving 60 per cent of women in mining centres unemployed.[72] Tea plantations were an exception – women and children continued to be employed – but this was chiefly in plucking and hand-weeding, tasks that were deemed "unskilled" and poorly paid. Colonial legal regimes made matters worse. In 1901, the Assam Labour Emigration Act denied married women the legal capacity to enter into labour contracts without their husbands' consent.[73] Of course, historians of labour know all this. But the point here is that women's ability to move to seek work was curtailed in numerous, intertwined ways. "Network poverty" had profoundly gendered characteristics.

Admittedly, labour conditions in these sectors of the economy were exploitative in the extreme. Employers paid as little as they could and workers endured appalling hardship. Yet scholars of migration cannot ignore the fact that the mobility afforded by these new industries – mobility that in times of famine, epidemic, or riot, made the difference between life and death – was tilted heavily in favour of men and was asymmetrically distributed.

With the end of empire and Partition, the implications of being stuck, always grave, became even more profound. As I have shown elsewhere, the mass migrations after Partition followed in grooves of mobility carved out in colonial times.[74] People who had access to mobility used prefigured routes and connections

[71] Sen, *Women and Labour, passim.*

[72] *Imperial Gazetteer. Vol. III. Economic*, p. 164. Also see Sen, "'Without his Consent?'", p. 86.

[73] Sen, "'Without his Consent?'"

[74] Chatterji, "Dispositions and Destinations".

to get out when times were hard or, indeed, impossible. In these ways the "economic migrants" in the labour markets of empire became the refugees of post-Independence South Asia. This is the context in which the predicament of the immobile presents itself in stark relief.

Deficits and Overabundances

In an important study, three economists recently tried to get to the heart of why people in Rangpur district in Bangladesh, notoriously prone to annual famines called *monga*, did not migrate during these famines despite knowing the potential benefits of getting away and the dire consequences of staying in place. Fears of failed migration, insufficient savings, and poor information about the opportunities on offer, so they discovered, did not adequately explain this reluctance to migrate. The authors described the behaviour of respondents as "something of a puzzle", admitting that "there is some element [here] that we do not understand."[75]

This section suggests some answers to this conundrum, using oral history interviews with "stayers on". The interviews took place in three locations where "stayers on" had clustered. Two of the sites were in urban Bangladesh, in Dhaka and Syedpur respectively, where our interviewees were Urdu or Bhojpuri speakers of the so-called "Bihari" community who stayed on in Bangladesh after 1971, despite the virulent climate there of hostility and violence against them.[76] The third location was a rural settlement in the south-west corner of West Bengal, close to the Bangladesh border to the east, and the Bay of Bengal to the south. Here we

[75] Byran, Chowdhury, and Mobarak, "Underinvestment in a Profitable Technology", p. 1693. I am grateful to Abhijit Banerjee for pointing me in the direction of this paper.

[76] For details, see Ghosh, *Partition and the South Asian Diaspora*; Redclift, *Statelessness and Citizenship*; and Alexander, Chatterji, and Jalais, *The Bengal Diaspora*.

interviewed Bengali-speaking rural Muslim families who had stayed on in West Bengal in India despite intense pressures on them to leave after Partition.

These interviews suggest some conclusions about patterns of staying on that are best expressed in terms of overabundances and deficits of certain attributes, albeit in different combinations. Strikingly, the main deficit proved not to be a lack of education, cash, or even access to networks (although these were significant), but *physical frailty*. The overabundances – "sticky" qualities that lead to inertia – are perhaps less surprising, but nonetheless revealing: they have to do with deeply internalised, albeit socially constituted, *obligations of care*.

Salima (Fig. 10.3) is a widow, now in her fifties, who has lived in one tiny room in Town Hall Camp in Dhaka for over thirty years.

A small, thin, bespectacled woman, she shares the room with her adult son and his wife, her daughter, and grandchildren of

Fig. 10.3: Salima

whom one, Taukir, about fourteen years of age, is disabled. Salima's husband used to work in the railways, but during the troubles of 1971 he was tortured and eventually succumbed to his injuries. For several months, Salima nursed him and tended their children. After his death she went to Dhaka as she had relatives in the city. She became a squatter in what would eventually become the Camp: "This was then a market place. It was empty. We put jute curtains up and started to live here. Things were very difficult. There were no fans – only light bulbs tied to bamboo poles, one providing light to a few families together."

This room is now one of a hundred similar rooms in Town Hall Camp, itself one of several "Bihari" camps in Dhaka. Salima's room is completely without ventilation. When we interviewed her, the stale air smelt strongly of kerosene. None of her children have had any education. She works as a cleaner for a local NGO and supplements her meagre income doing piecework for garment manufacturers.

One by one, most of Salima's male relatives, including her father and brother, left for Pakistan, where the family had kin and connections. Interestingly, Salima is still in contact with her father. But he was unable (or unwilling) to take his widowed daughter and grandchildren over to Pakistan to live with him, and she seems equally unable to consider moving.

Why did Salima stay on? In the first instance, to care for her fatally wounded husband. After his death soon after the war ended, as a single woman with very small children, one of whom was disabled, she calculated that she (and her vulnerable dependants) would be better able to survive in Dhaka where she had some networks of (mainly female) familial support. (Indeed, even as the interview was being conducted, one of Salima's female relatives, who lived close by, dropped in to help Salima – whose eyesight is beginning to fail – complete her quota of piecework on time.) As a squatter in Town Hall Camp, with 36 square feet which she occupies but does not own, she is tied to place. She is also pinned down by her responsibilities for her daughter (who was abandoned by her own husband), and for her disabled grandson Taukir. With all others who might have shared these responsibilities with her having emigrated long ago, they weigh heavily on her shoulders.

Also in Town Hall Camp lives Sairun (Fig. 10.4), a 45-year-old widow. She occupies a small room with her nephew, his wife and their two-year-old child.

She was born in Old Dhaka, and, as with Salima, her family had links with the railways. But in March, 1971, her husband died.

Fig. 10.4: Sairun

"What happened to him?" we asked.

"He left for his business as usual one morning and never returned. He must have been killed."

During or after the 1971 war, every single one of Sairun's male relatives – her son, her brother (and his wife and children) – left for Pakistan, where they now live in Orangi township in Karachi. But Sairun stayed on in Dhaka. This was because one of her sisters fell sick and eventually died, leaving behind two small children. Sairun, who had nursed her bedridden sister, brought these two orphans up along with her own two children. She never travels anywhere, so she tells us. Even though she is in touch with her Pakistani family, she has not seen her son, now an adult, since 1971. None of her children is educated, even though Sairun herself can read and write – she occasionally supplements her insubstantial income as a maid by giving tuitions in Arabic.

Or take the story of Mehrunissa Khatun, a stayer-on who lives in Chamra Godown Camp in Syedpur, where we interviewed her. Syedpur was once the site of the largest railway workshop of the Assam–Bengal Railway, which previously employed thousands of "Urdu-speaking" upcountry migrants, who were so numerous that they once made up three out of four of the town's population. But both Syedpur, as well as neighbouring Parbatipur and Santahar, came under vicious attack during and after the Liberation War, and thousands fled for their lives. Mehrunissa's family was one of hundreds which, during the trouble (*gondogol* is the Bengali word our informants used to describe these events), fled from Parbatipur – a smaller railway colony – to the larger town of Syedpur, seeking safety in numbers.

Like Salima and Sairun, Mehrunissa had two very young children, daughters (aged three years and five months respectively). She says: "Here I had three more children. One baby died at the age of ten months. Then I had another daughter and she is now in Pakistan . . . My eldest daughter is called Shah Jahan and is married to a man who works in the trucks as a coolie . . . He is parentless so he lives here with us in Syedpur. They [her daughter and son-in-law] have five children."

In 1978 Mehrunissa's own husband, who was bedridden for years – "he used to cough up blood" – died. Mehrunissa continued to care for all her surviving children, and, when her oldest daughter married, for her son-in-law as well as her many grandchildren. Times were so hard that they often had nothing to eat. But somehow they struggled on. In 1985, one of Mehrunissa's sisters was able to migrate with her own husband and children to Pakistan. She took Mehrunissa's younger daughter, Sabra, with her to Pakistan, marrying her off to her own son, to relieve her sister of the burden of one more mouth to feed.

Since then, Mehrunissa managed to support her family by working as a maid in the house of a Canadian aid-worker. Like Salima, Mehrunissa had kinsfolk in Pakistan (her sister and daughter). She longs to see Sabra but will not herself migrate, because she has responsibilities to her other children and grandchildren. She still lives in the same place in Chamra Godown Camp, in extremely reduced circumstances.

Maryam also lives in Syedpur.

She is perhaps sixty years old, and the head of a household of nine people, whom she supports also by working as a maid, and occasionally sewing garments. She has lived here since the 1971 war began, when she moved with her husband from the neighbouring railway colony at Parbatipur. Her husband, a mechanic in the railways, was ailing "with some stomach-related illness", and she looked after him (as well as her children) until his death in 1975.

The details of Hanifa's story are distressing, but not unusual in this milieu. She lived in the railway township of Santahar in Bogra before the war, where "Urdu speakers" experienced some of the worst violence. "When the war started," she said,

> I was picked up and beaten up. I had two ribs and my skull broken. My husband, two sons, three daughters and grandchild were killed

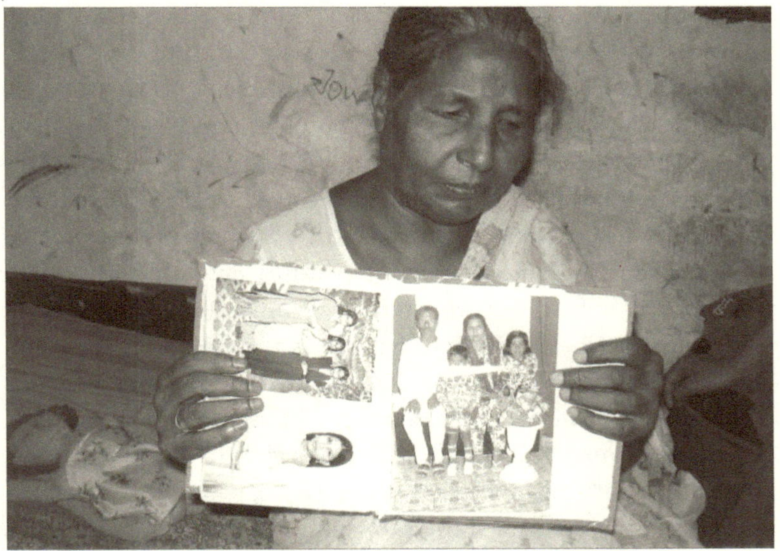

Fig. 10.5: Maryam

> that night . . . Then, taking us all for dead, they left . . . When I regained consciousness I realised that my young son Habib was still alive, and that my baby Zafar, despite the deep gash he had on his stomach, was alive. So I rushed them both to the doctor . . . A kindly [person] treated the children and saved them. After that we survived by eating frogs and grass and mud and wearing coarse cloth made of jute.

These stories all have a common narrative thread. The stayers-on who hung on despite threats to life and limb did not always, in the first instance, lack access to networks that might have helped them migrate. On the contrary, everyone we interviewed in this context belonged to the Bhojpuri-speaking labour diaspora connected with the railways, and they all had rich and far-flung networks across India, Pakistan, and Bangladesh, and indeed, further afield.[77] Nor did they lack skills – many were literate and some were moderate-

[77] See, for instance, Mohapatra, "'Following Custom?'"; Ghosh, *Partition*

ly well-off before 1971. But they lacked other elements of what I have elsewhere defined as "mobility capital", the bundle of assets and competences that makes moving possible.[78] Above all, they lacked health. Or if they were able-bodied themselves, they had powerful countervailing obligations to care for the vulnerable and infirm, whether infants, the ill, the aged or the disabled, for whom they felt responsible. Most in this category were women.

This suggests – somewhat counter-intuitively – that while networks, cash, knowhow, and skills are important elements of mobility, good health is vital. So also is the "freedom" to leave others behind, to abandon (socially constructed) duties of care. The women we interviewed seemed to practise what Sara Ruddick describes as "maternal thinking", responding to the "prolonged physical fragility and therefore prolonged dependence" not only of children, but of fragile others, by taking responsibility for their care.[79] Even at times of grave danger to themselves (graphically demonstrated by Hanifa's story), many women chose not to flee, but to stay where they were to try to ensure that their children survived. Those who were already carers of children took on the responsibility first to care for sick and disabled relatives, and then (as with Sairun and her sister) to look after those orphaned by the death of these relatives. They tended the fragile, the sick, and the vulnerable among their kin, even if this put them in danger. If this held them back and meant they had to pass over opportunities to migrate in the bargain, they did this with a sense of resignation. None, other than Hanifa, expressed bitterness or regret. Indeed, few described it as a decision at all.

Sickness and frailty stalk these narratives. Husbands, children, sisters, and sons-in-law fell ill and died of diseases our informants

---

and the South Asian Diaspora; and Alexander, Chatterji, and Jalais, *The Bengal Diaspora*, ch. 6.

78 Chatterji, "Dispositions and Destinations".

79 Ruddick, *Maternal Thinking*, p. 19.

could not name. They merely described their most graphic symptoms – "he used to cough up blood" or "he had some stomach ailment", or 'she was bedridden", or "his mind went wrong".

These life stories, and others of their ilk, suggest that sickness, disease, and disability are surely part of the answer to the puzzle of the "immobility paradox". Further, given the strong correlation between poverty and illness, and the dynamic relationship between illness, dependency, and care – they point to a vicious circle that traps the ill, the dependent, and their carers in lives of immobility and poverty.

However, while most examples of staying on can be explained by this cycle of dependency, not all can. There are those who had overabundant obligations produced by deeply held religious beliefs, responsibilities to graves and to ancestors. They were usually eldest sons. My final story throws light on the description of the graveyard with which I began.

Shahid and Jalal Gazi are brothers, originally from the village of Kalitola in the south-east corner of present-day West Bengal. The village was "off the grid", served neither by rail nor steamer. But it happened to be just a few miles away from the Radcliffe Line that now divided West Bengal in India from eastern Pakistan. After Partition, faced with violence and intimidation, Shahid, the younger brother, together with many other members of the family, migrated just across the border. Carrying small bundles of possessions over their shoulders, they trekked by foot on land and by small boat over water, to Khupdipur in East Pakistan. But his brother Jalal did not leave. Today Jalal (aged about 95) is too ill and confused to be able to say much. His son, Fakhruddin, fills in the gaps in his story:

> We are originally from Kalitola. The Hindus kicked us away from there so we came here [Dokkhin Parghumte] where we had family. Our whole place in Kalitola used to be Muslim. Then one day [around 1950] some refugees who had come from the other side announced that Muslims wouldn't be allowed to live there, that they

> would have to leave . . . They went from house to house, sometimes, raped and looted, at other times burned down our homes and our granaries . . . My elder brother . . . felt he wouldn't be able to keep his honour and left for Khupdipur [across the border] . . . At that time all the Muslims of Jogeshganj, Parghumte, Kalitola, Samshernagar, Gobindokati left this place . . . Our family's land used to stretch all the way to the river, now it ends with the field which surrounds our homestead . . . One by one all of my uncles left. But my father Jalal Gazi, being the eldest, stayed back to look after the mosque and the graves of our ancestors.

Today their community of Muslims is reduced to about fifty people, cramped into only four homesteads. The Gazi family had clearly once been modestly prosperous. After riots broke out in 1950, many members of the clan went to Pakistan. Those who were left behind did not lack contacts in Pakistan – indeed, they had many close relatives and contacts who had made good on "the other side". But they stayed on in India because they were bound to "home", either, as in the case of Jalal, the eldest son, by responsibilities to the graves of his ancestors, or by infirmity, or by the need to care for the elderly and infirm. Fakhruddin and Hamidullah Gazi, respectively the son and nephew of Jalal Gazi, have stayed even though there are very few opportunities for them in the locality, and despite the fact that the former was "kicked out" of his job at the local school, after being passed over for promotion by a less qualified Hindu. They felt obliged to look after the old man, who is sick, disoriented, and frail.

"Previously," Fakhruddin continued, "we all wanted to leave as our leaders all left, but it is not so now. We can't go and neither do we want to go."

Their decision to stay has resulted in a catastrophic downward spiral in wealth and status. The landholdings of this clan have shrunk to one small field. The younger men in the family are either unemployed or inappropriately employed, and they are deeply pessimistic about their prospects. Interestingly, they have lost contact with their kin across the border. National borders, even ones as relatively porous as those between India and Bangladesh, and attempts to control movement across them have undoubtedly played a part in this. Since the Enemy Property Act came on the statute book in 1967, maintaining contact with "enemy" aliens across the border has been fraught with danger,[80] and this may explain why two brothers, separated by Partition, had neither seen nor heard from each other for several decades. It was only when we took news and photographs of Jalal over to Shahid in Bangladesh that contact between them was re-established.

Their story reveals a critically important point overlooked by much of the literature on networks: namely, that networks atrophy and rupture in adverse circumstances. After the blood brothers

Fig. 10.6: In Bangladesh, Shahid Gazi sees an image of his brother Jalal for the first time in decades. The brothers had lost contact after Shahid crossed over to East Pakistan after Partition (photo by Bengal Diaspora Project).

[80] Chatterji, "South Asian Histories of Citizenship", pp. 1049–71.

lost touch with each other at a time of upheaval and chaos, the ties between them withered. For the family members who had stayed behind, this meant a cumulative decline in their capacity to move, with assets stripped and familial networks that might once have facilitated their movement gradually disintegrating: "We can't go and neither do we want to go." Among the less mobile, then, it seems that an initial reluctance to move could foreclose their options for migration at a later date, keeping people like Fakhruddin and Hamidullah Gazi stuck in their unenviable situations.

Conclusion

In his study of North Indian villages, Anirudh Krishna concludes that most of those who escaped poverty had done so by "building a bridge to the city". Very few of those who remained where they were in rural areas were able to break free of the destitution in which they lived.[81] Similarly, the study of villages in famine-prone Rongpur shows that those who migrated (to areas where wages were higher) significantly improved the lives of their families back in the village (as measured by consumption of calories and expenditure on children's education).[82] Migration, the authors show, is a "profitable technology".[83] It is also, as we know, a "technology" that, in times of upheaval, provides a means of "escape from violence".[84]

This essay has drawn attention to the phenomenon of immobility, insisting that it demands greater attention in an age of ever-increasing migration. It suggests that for many people this immobility has arisen historically as a result of being left out, or left off, the grid, rendering them unable (for reasons of age, health,

[81] Krishna, "Escaping Poverty", p. 129.

[82] Bryan, *et al.*, "Underinvestment in a Profitable Technology", p. 1681.

[83] Ibid., *passim.*

[84] Zolberg, Suhrke, and Aguayo, *Escape from Violence.*

or gender) to use it safely. Spatial differences were very significant – for many people who lived off the grid, the costs and risks of movement were simply too great, with these inhibiting factors having remained essentially unchanged since early-modern times. Even within regions that were connected to the grid, access to mobility tended to be restricted to healthy male members of the "right" ethnic group, caste, or kinship network. Deficits of these enabling qualities led to different forms of "network poverty", which, for some unfortunate people, overlapped, with one factor reinforcing others to leave them stuck in their localities.

And even among members of the "right" ethnic group, caste, or kinship network, some individuals were far more stuck than others. As the second part of this essay shows, the most inert are sometimes people who, at least on the face of it, are not "network deprived" in these ways. Among them, however, were the most vulnerable – the sick and the disabled, the very old and very young – and those (all women) who looked after them. The women whose stories we heard were all from richly networked railway families, but they were held back by the fragility of those for whom they felt responsible. As Livingston has observed in her study of disability in Botswana, "debility . . . troubles, mobilizes and intensifies social relations", and indeed, "the moral imagination".[85] Sickness and dependency generated overabundant obligations, responsibilities from which some people, mainly women, could not, and would not, walk away.

Furthermore, having made the initial choice to stay, many of these people found their capacity to move eroded as the years passed by. Address books got lost (many women wept as they told us this), the emigrants among their kin got on with their new lives, and the ties that once bound those who left to those who stayed behind weakened as time went by. Thus networks that might have enabled migrations at a later date withered and died,

[85] Livingston, *Debility and the Moral Imagination*, p. 3, and *passim*.

and any notion of moving grew more and more unrealistic. So stayers-on remained where they were, while the world around them moved on, moved more, and moved more rapidly.

This choice (as well as the conditions that led to it in the first place) appear to have combined to propel these households into a downward spiral towards poverty. While the interviews cited here are mainly with "Biharis" in Bangladesh, whose political status is in many respects extremely precarious, Muslim stayers-on in rural West Bengal appear to have fared little better. Decades of communist government notwithstanding, they are among the most impoverished communities in the region. Statistics show them to be disproportionately likely – compared to the rest of the population – to be uneducated, unemployed, or under-employed. Despite constituting about 28 per cent of West Bengal's total population, Muslims hold less than 2 per cent of government jobs, and less than 1 per cent of all "service-level" jobs in the private sector.[86] They tend to live in desperately overcrowded spaces, with little or no institutional support. Their children are more likely than those of other communities to remain illiterate and have shorter lives. Their daughters are more likely to marry young and die in childbirth. Their sons, in disproportionately large numbers, fall foul of the law and spend years in prison.[87] A recent study of Muslim stayers-on in contemporary Calcutta showed that four out of every five now live in overcrowded slums, where entire households (an average size of 6.65 persons) sleep, eat, and work in tiny one-room shacks,[88] the average size of which is less than 120 square feet.[89] Their literacy is exceptionally low.

[86] Siddiqui, *Muslim Educational Uplift*, p. 7; and Seabrook and Siddiqui, *People Without History*.

[87] Vol. I of papers submitted by the Chief Secretary of West Bengal to the (Sachar) High Level Committee on Social, Economic and Educational Status of the Muslims of India, 2005–6, Nehru Library, Delhi.

[88] Siddiqui, *Muslim Educational Uplift*, p. 26.

[89] Ibid.

More than nine out of ten have no "chance of getting admitted to any kind of educational institution [whether] recognised or unrecognised, or unaffiliated or public." Drop-out rates among the few lucky children who are admitted to schools are estimated to be as high as 80 per cent. These urban communities survive mainly by self-employment in family-run sweatshops where they work for pitifully low returns embroidering gold thread onto cloth, making paper goods like kites, binding books, and making cheap leather goods.[90]

The history of immobility in South Asia, and its intricate relationship with poverty, is complex, and as yet little understood. Much remains to be done. These stories, it is hoped, will help stimulate more research, while giving us some insight into why, and in what ways, mobility has become "a scarce and unequally distributed commodity", and one of the "main stratifying factors of our late modern or post modern times."[91]

References

Abbas, Rameez, and Divya Varma, "Internal Labour Migration in India Raises Integration Challenges for Migrants", *Migration Policy Institute Newsletter*, 2013 http://www.migrationpolicy.org/article/internal-labor-migration-india-raises-integrationchallenges-migrants, accessed 18 March 2015.

Abedin, Najmul, *Local Administration and Politics in Modernising Societies, Bangladesh and Pakistan*, Dacca: National Institute of Public Administration, 1973.

Ahmad, Nafis, *A New Economic Geography of Bangladesh*, New Delhi: Vikas Publishing House, 1976.

Ahuja, Ravi, "Mobility and Containment: The Voyages of Indian Seamen, *c.* 1900–1960", *International Review of Social History*, 51 (Supplement), 2006.

———, *Pathways of Empire. Circulation, "Public Works" and Social Space in Colonial Orissa, c. 1780–1924*, Hyderabad: Orient BlackSwan, 2009.

[90] Ibid., pp. 23, 29.

[91] Bauman, *Globalisation*, p. 2.

Alexander, Claire, Joya Chatterji, and Annu Jalais, *The Bengal Diaspora. Rethinking Muslim Migration*, London: Routledge, 2015.

Amrith, Sunil, *Migration and Diaspora in Modern Asia*, Cambridge: Cambridge University Press, 2011.

———, "South Asian Migration, *c.* 1800–1950", in Jan Lucassen and Leo Lucassen, eds, *Globalising Migration History: The Eurasian Experience*, Leiden: Brill Publishers, 2014.

Anh, D.N., "Migration and Poverty in Asia: With Reference to Bangladesh, China, the Philippines and Vietnam", *Ad hoc Expert Group Meeting on Migration and Development*, Economic and Social Commission for Asia and the Pacific: Bangkok, 2003.

Basu, Subho, *Does Class Matter? Colonial Capital and Workers' Resistance in Bengal, 1890–1937*, New Delhi: Oxford University Press, 2004.

Bauman, Zygmunt, *Globalisation: The Human Consequences*, 1998; rpnt Cambridge: Polity Press, 2012.

Bayly, C.A., *Indian Society and the Making of the British Empire*, Cambridge: Cambridge University Press, 1988.

Behal, Rana P., "Power Structure, Discipline and Labour in Assam Tea Plantations under Colonial Rule", *International Review of Social History*, 51 (Supplement) 2006.

Bhattacharya, Sanjoy, *Propaganda and Information in Eastern India. A Necessary Weapon of War*, London: Curzon.

Brown, Judith, *Global South Asians. Introducing the Modern Diaspora*, Cambridge: Cambridge University Press, 2006.

Byran, Gharad, Shyamal Chowdhury, and Ahmed Mushfiq Mobarak, "Underinvestment in a Profitable Technology: The Case of Seasonal Migration in Bangladesh", *Econometrica*, vol. 82, no. 5, September 2014.

Carling, Jorgen, "Migration in an Age of Involuntary Immobility: Theoretical Reflections and Cape Verdean Experiences", *Journal of Ethnic and Migration Studies* vol. 28, no. 1, January 2002.

Castles, Stephen, and Mark Miller, *The Age of Migration: International Population Movements in the Modern World*, 4th edn, Basingstoke: Palgrave Macmillan, 2009.

Chakrabarty, Dipesh, *Rethinking Working Class History: Bengal 1890 to 1940*, New Jersey: Princeton University Press, 1989.

Chan, Kam Wing, "China, Internal Migration", in Immanuel Ness & Peter Bellwood, eds, *The Encyclopedia of Global Migration*, Oxford: Blackwell, 2013.

Chandavarkar, Rajnarayan, "The Decline and Fall of the Jobber System in the Bombay Cotton Textile Industry, 1870–1955", *Modern Asian Studies*, 42, 1, 2008.

Chatterji, Joya, "Dispositions and Destinations: Refugee Agency and 'Mobility Capital' in the Bengal Diaspora, 1947–2007", *Comparative Studies in Society and History*, vol. 55, no. 2, 2013.

———, "Of Graveyards and Ghettos. Muslims in West Bengal, 1947–67", in Mushirul Hasan and Asim Roy, eds, *Living Together Separately. Cultural India in History and Politics*, Delhi: Oxford University Press, 2005.

———, "South Asian Histories of Citizenship, 1946–1970", *The Historical Journal*, 55, 4 (December) 2012.

———, "The Fashioning of a Frontier: The Radcliffe Line and Bengal's Border Landscape, 1947–1952", *Modern Asian Studies*, 33, 1, 1999.

Davis, Kingsley, *The Population of India and Pakistan*, Princeton, NJ: Princeton University Press, 1951.

Demand for Personal Transport in Developing Countries, World Bank: Infrastructure and Urban Development Department Report by Angus Deaton, with Duncan Thomas, Janet Neelin, and Nikhilesh Bhattacharya, 1987.

Famine Inquiry Commission Report on Bengal (Chairman, Sir John Woodhead), Government of India: Department of Food, 1945.

Ghosh, Papiya, *Partition and the South Asian Diaspora. Extending the Subcontinent*, Delhi: Routledge, 2007.

Guha, Amalendu, *Planter Raj to Swaraj*, New Delhi: Indian Council of Historical Research, 1977.

Hammer, Tomas, "Why do People Go or Stay?", in T. Hammer and Grete Brochmann, eds, *International Migration, Immobility and Development: Multidisciplinary Perspectives*, Oxford: Berg, 1997.

Imperial Gazetteer of India. Provincial Series. Eastern Bengal and Assam, Calcutta: Superintendent of Government Printing, 1909.

Imperial Gazetteer of India. The Indian Empire. Vol. I. Descriptive, Oxford: Clarendon Press, 1907.

Imperial Gazetteer of India. The Indian Empire. Vol. III, Economic, Oxford: Clarendon Press, 1907.

Kerr, Ian, *Building the Railways of the Raj, 1850–1900*, New York: Oxford University Press, 1995.

Khan, Misbahuddin, *History of the Port of Chittagong*, Dhaka: Dana Publishers, 1990.

King, A.J., *Comprehensive Report on Road Development Projects in Bengal*, vol. 1, Calcutta: Government of Bengal.

Krishna, Anirudh, "Escaping Poverty and Becoming Poor: Who Gains, Who Loses and Why?" *World Development*, vol. 32, no. 1.

Kuhn, Philip, *Chinese among Others. Emigration in Modern Times*, Lanham: Rowman and Littlefield, 2009.

Livingston, Julie, *Debility and the Moral Imagination in Botswana*, Bloomington: Indiana University Press, 2005.

Ludden, David, "Presidential Address: Maps in the Mind and the Mobility of Asia", *Journal of Asian Studies*, 62, 4, 2003.

Malkki, Lisa, *Purity and Exile. Violence, Memory and National Cosmology among Hutu Refugees in Tanzania*, Chicago and London: University of Chicago Press, 1995.

Malmberg, Gunnar, "Time and Space in International Migration", in Tomas Hammar, Grete Brochmann, Kristof Tamas, and Thomas Faist, eds, *International Migration, Immobility and Development. Multidisciplinary Perspectives*, Oxford and New York: Berg, 1997.

Marshall, Richard, and Shibaab Rahman, *Internal Migration in Bangladesh: Character, Drivers and Policy Issues*, Bangladesh: UNDP, 2013, http://www.undp.org/content/dam/bangladesh/docs/Publications/Pub-2013/Internal%20Migration%20in%20Bangladesh%20UNDP%20Final.pdf.

Massey, Douglas S., Joaquin Arango, Graeme Hugo, Ali Kouaouci, Adela Pellegrino, and J. Edward Taylor , "Theories of International Migration: A Review and Appraisal", *Population and Development Review*, vol. 19, no. 3, September 1993.

McKeown, Adam, "Global Migration 1846–1950", *Journal of World History*, 15, 2, 2004.

Mohapatra, Prabhu, "'Following Custom'? Representations of Community among Indian Immigrant Labour in the West Indies", in R.P. Behal and P. van der Linden, eds, *Coolies, Capital and Colonialism: Studies in Indian Labour History*, Cambridge: Cambridge University Press, 2006.

Mukhopadhyay, Aparajita, "Wheels of Change: Impact of Railways in Colonial North Indian Society", Unpublished doctoral dissertation, School of Oriental and African Studies, 2013.

Munsi, Sunil Kumar, *Geography of Transportation in Eastern India under the British Raj*, Calcutta: K.P. Bagchi, 1980.

Northrup, David, *Indentured Labour in the Age of Imperialism, 1834–1922*, Cambridge: Cambridge University Press, 1995.

O'Malley, L.S.S., *Bengal District Gazetteers. 24 Parganas*, Calcutta: The Bengal Secretariat Depot, 1914.

———, *Bengal District Gazetteers. Birbhum*, Calcutta: The Bengal Secretariat Depot, 1910.

———, *Bengal District Gazetteers. Palamau*, Calcutta: The Bengal Secretariat Depot, 1907.

Redclift, Victoria, *Statelessness and Citizenship: Camps and the Creation of Political Space*, Abingdon: Routledge, 2013.

Ruddick, Sara, *Maternal Thinking. Towards a Politics of Peace*, New York: Ballantine Books, 1989.

Sadiq, Kamal, *Paper Citizens: How Illegal Immigrants Acquire Citizenship in Developing Countries*, Oxford, 2009.

Schmeidl, Susan, "Conflict and Forced Migration: A Quantitative Review" in Aristide Zolberg & Peter Benda, eds, *Global Migrants, Global Refugees*, New York: Berghahn, 2001.

Seabrook, Jeremy, and Imran Ahmed Siddiqui, *People Without History. India's Muslim Ghettos*, London: Pluto Press, 2011.

Sen, Samita, "Questions of Consent: Women's Recruitment for Assam Tea Gardens", *Studies in History*, 2, 2002.

———, "'Without his Consent?' Marriage and Women's Migration in Colonial India", *International Labour and Working-Class History*, 65 (Spring) 2004.

———, *Women and Labour in Late Colonial India: The Bengal Jute Industry*, Cambridge: Cambridge University Press, 1999.

Sharma, Jayeeta, *Empire's Garden. Assam and the Making of India*, Durham and London: Duke University Press, 2011.

———, "'Lazy' Natives, Coolie Labour and the Assam Tea Industry", *Modern Asian Studies*, 46, 6, 2009.

Shil, Partha Pratim, "Police Labour and State Formation in Bengal *c.* 1860 to 1950", University of Cambridge, forthcoming doctoral dissertation.

Siddiqui, M.K.A., *Muslim Educational Uplift. How to Achieve this Goal?*, Calcutta: Institute of Objective Studies, 2008.

Washbrook, David, "Economic Depression and the Making of Traditional Society in Colonial India, 1820–1855", *Transactions of the Royal Historical Society*, Sixth Series, II, 1993.

Zolberg, Aristide, and Peter Benda, eds, *Global Migrants, Global Refugees: Problems and Solutions*, New York: Berghahn, 2001.

Zolberg, Aristide, Astri Suhrke, and Segio Aguayo, *Escape from Violence. Conflict and the Refugee Crisis in the Developing World*, Oxford: Oxford University Press, 1989.

11

From Subjecthood to Citizenship

Migration, Nationality, and the Post-imperial Global Order

THE FALL OF GREAT empires has often prompted migration. But in the past these were, by all accounts, relatively small flows made up chiefly of soldiers, skilled artisans, and comprador elites who had failed to forge fresh strategic alliances with new rulers at home and who migrated abroad in search of political patrons.[1] The fall of the great European empires, in contrast, and the rise of nation-states in the twentieth century were accompanied by mass migrations on a wholly unprecedented scale.

Why was this the case, and what have been the implications of these massive flows for the new global order? Here I will follow Zolberg in arguing that nation-formation is a "refugee-generating process", and explore the global consequences of the mass migrations which complicated Britain's retreat from its erstwhile imperial possessions.[2] India's Independence and Partition in 1947, the Independence of Ceylon and Burma in 1948, the wave of nation-formation in Anglophone Africa in the 1950s and 1960s, and the breakaway of Bangladesh from Pakistan in 1971 provoked

[1] Claire Davies lent invaluable help with research on the evolution of British and American migration controls after World War II.

For related accounts of migration, see Roy and Haynes, "Conceiving Mobility"; and Nichols, *A History of Pashtun Migration.*

[2] Zolberg, "The Formation of New States".

both vast migrations and drives by states to fortify their frontiers. The new nation-states of the later twentieth century – not least those of the Indian subcontinent – were more concerned than their imperial predecessor had been with controlling flows across borders. They also had far more pressing reasons to define who was, and who was not, a citizen.

This essay will highlight the central role that India and Pakistan, and their South Asian neighbours, played in this process. In their drive to manage and control mass migration, the new states of South Asia developed concepts of citizenship that rolled back the hitherto dominant idea of British imperial subjecthood. In its stead they erected an ethnically defined model of nationality founded on the right to enter, the right to remain, and the right to return. In due course, this model spread throughout the erstwhile British empire, eventually being adopted in 1971 by the former metropole itself.

First, however, a few words about "British subjecthood" and what it had come to mean by the mid-twentieth century. As Caitlin Anderson has argued, British subjecthood was founded upon the doctrine of allegiance, a complicated and "quasi-mythical" idea whose antecedents date back to the medieval period. According to this doctrine, subjecthood derived from an individual's loyalty to the crown; and because that relationship was founded in natural law ("written with the finger of God in the heart of man"), it was indelible and unalterable by either sovereign or subject.[3] Since 1608, when Sir Edward Coke, in *Calvin's Case*, had insisted that all the king's subjects were equal, subjecthood had also implied the equal legal status of all those born within the king's dominions.[4] This was the celebrated principle of *jus soli*, or subjecthood by virtue of birth in the realm.[5]

[3] Anderson, "Aliens at Home, Subjects Abroad".

[4] Parry, *British Nationality Including Citizenship*; Kim, *Aliens in Medieval Law*.

[5] Parry, *British Nationality*.

By the end of the nineteenth century, this principle of legal equality had been eroded in practice, and "natural born" Britons had come to enjoy greater rights and protections than those born in the empire.[6] All British subjects did not enjoy equal and unfettered rights to move wherever they wanted within an empire on which the sun never set. Some Indian migrants enjoyed greater freedom of mobility than others. The "passenger" classes who paid their own fares and were, in the main, traders, were, in theory at least, free to travel when they pleased. Indentured coolies were legally obliged to serve out their contracts abroad, and "assisted" migrants recruited by agents known as *kanganis* were shackled even more firmly by the bonds of debt: by the late nineteenth century, over a million Indians working in labour-hungry tropical plantations all over the empire found themselves tied down in a variety of ways.[7] During World War I, moreover, passports were introduced in India, and thereafter all private travellers leaving India by sea had to carry this document. By this time, several British dominions had devised racially inflected stratagems for barring unwanted persons from South Asia: notably Australia's Immigration Restriction Act of 1901 that used a dictation test to exclude the unwanted; Canada's exclusionary head tax aimed at non-whites; and South Africa's Immigrants Regulation Act of 1913 which prohibited persons whose "standards and habits of life" rendered them "unsuited to the requirements of the Union."[8] By the 1930s, even the imperial territories of the Indian Ocean rim had begun to restrict the immigration of Indians: Malaya and the Straits Settlement now imposed controls. After its separation from India in 1937, Burma too began negotiations for a

[6] Anderson, "Aliens at Home, Subjects Abroad".

[7] Tinker, *A New System of Slavery*, esp. pp. 61–115.

[8] Mongia, "Race, Nationality, Mobility", pp. 527–57; *Question of Treatment of Indians in the Union of South Africa before the United Nations. Documents and Proceedings*, Government of India Press, Simla, 1947, Ministry of External Affairs, India (henceforth MEAI), F. 3-1/OSI-1948.

treaty to limit Indian migration; and in 1939 Ceylon banned it altogether.[9]

Nor was entry into India itself unregulated. Wars in the twentieth century generated a regime of controls designed to keep out of India those seen as a threat to imperial security. With the Great War, even "troublemakers" of Indian origin were denied ingress into India; and the Passport Act of 1920 made travel documents compulsory for all wishing to travel to India.[10] In 1939, "the needs of the war emergency" justified the enactment of a Foreigners Ordinance and an Enemy Foreigners Order, giving the imperial state powers to detain and expel foreigners.[11]

The British imperial past was thus not some halcyon age of unrestricted mobility for all His Majesty's subjects; and nor was that subjecthood equal in practice. Yet there is no doubt that British decolonisation and the emergence of new nations ushered in a new migration regime whose interlocking and overlapping laws, policies, and practices are a crucial dimension of the new global order.

Partition and Independence in India and Pakistan

The most dramatic and far-reaching changes were first witnessed in India and Pakistan. In 1947, when the high politics of decolonisation culminated in the decision to divide Britain's Indian empire into India and Pakistan, the contentious boundary between them was drawn on the basis of religion: contiguous Muslim-majority districts in the north-west and east were carved out to produce Pakistan. In the negotiations for the transfer of power,

[9] Amrith, "Indians Overseas?", pp. 231–61.

[10] Singha, "A 'Proper Passport'".

[11] "Statement of Objectives and Reasons", *The Foreigners Act, 1946 (Act No. 31 of 1946). An Act to Confer upon the Central Government Certain Powers in Respect of Foreigners.*

Britain was able to persuade India and Pakistan to stay within the Commonwealth. The architects of the complex Partition agreements assumed that citizens of India and Pakistan would remain British subjects, and as such continue to have "free" access to the other dominion and all parts of the empire.[12] Astonishing as it may seem in retrospect, in August 1947 the leaders of India and Pakistan still believed that, Partition notwithstanding, the peoples of the subcontinent would stay where they were. The consensus was that open borders between the two states would facilitate the orderly transfer of power to two separate dominions, with little or no social and economic disruption.

This proved a vain hope. The fires of civil violence that broke out on 15 August 1947 spread rapidly across the western plains of the subcontinent. Massive migrations began and millions of ordinary Hindus, Sikhs, and Muslims stranded on the wrong side of the border had to flee their homes in terror. As the humanitarian catastrophe unfolded, India and Pakistan acted in concert to set up a Military Evacuation Organisation (MEO) to protect "stranded refugees" and escort them across the new border. By the end of 1947 it had evacuated five million refugees across the borders between India and Pakistan in each direction.[13] By 1951, some twenty million refugees had crossed the borders in both directions.

The MEO was a response to an emergency that neither state was equipped to handle on its own; but it proved to be the first step down a slippery slope, towards a new policy with far-reaching ramifications. If Partition's refugees in their millions were to be allowed to move across borders between India and Pakistan (and indeed to be assisted by the MEO in so doing), this raised the question of what was to happen to the property they left behind. Who was to protect it and by what means? Both India and Pakistan

[12] Statement on Partition by the Deputy Prime Minister in the Constituent Assembly, 12 December 1947, MEAI/ F. 9-2/48-Pak I.

[13] Randhawa, *Out of the Ashes*.

started out with the firm intention of protecting the property of the emigrants (or "evacuees", as they were labelled), guaranteeing their continued rights of ownership. Both governments appointed Custodians of Evacuee Property "to take possession of the property and effects of evacuees and to take such measures as he considers necessary or expedient for preserving such property or effects."[14]

But problems soon arose about how to deal with incoming refugees who had occupied property abandoned by evacuees during the riots. Everywhere, incoming refugees had begun to break into and squat in any vacant property they could find, resolutely (and often violently) resisting efforts to oust them. Local policemen proved reluctant to take action to evict refugees of their own faith. Increasingly, the Indian government began to draw a distinction between refugees and "ordinary looters", acknowledging the special claims of refugees.[15] However, this in turn raised another conundrum. What would happen if Muslim evacuees came back home to India once order was restored (and many were known to want to return)?[16] Where would they go if their houses had been taken over by refugees? And what would happen to Hindu and Sikh refugees who wanted to return to homes in Pakistan?

In early 1948, Nehru's government came to the momentous conclusion that the only way forward was to prevent evacuees from returning to reclaim their homes. The Influx from Pakistan (Control) Ordinance held that "no person shall enter India from any place in Pakistan, whether directly or indirectly unless . . . he is in possession of a permit."[17] A year later, when it had become plain that the permit system was impossible to enforce in a society

[14] See the introduction to the *Government of East Punjab Evacuees (Administration of Property) Act, 1947 (Act XIV of 1947).*

[15] Jawaharlal Nehru to Sardar Vallabhbhai Patel, 6 October 1947, in Durga Das, ed., *Sardar Patel's Correspondence, 1945–50,* vol. 4, p. 400.

[16] Ibid.

[17] Ordinance XXXIV of 1948, NAI/MEACR/F.26-189/48-Pak I (Secret).

where few people had any identity documents, the Evacuee Property Ordinance came onto the statute book. This draconian ordinance empowered provincial governments in every part of India (except in the eastern states of West Bengal, Assam, and Tripura) to acquire evacuee property "as it may need for a public purpose which may include the rehabilitation of refugees . . . or payment of fair compensation [to them]."[18] At a stroke, the ordinance effectively nationalised *all* evacuee Muslim property, adding it to the pool of resources out of which India hoped to rehouse and rehabilitate incoming Hindu and Sikh refugees. Pakistan's officials protested vociferously and with justification that these measures effectively "disinherited" India's Muslim displacees. But very soon it followed with its own identical legislative and executive measures.[19] Faced with a situation in which India had slammed the door shut on Muslim refugees and made it impossible to recover their properties, Pakistan could see that it had little option but to appropriate all abandoned evacuee Hindu and Sikh property in its turn.

These measures repudiated the fundamental doctrines of British subjecthood: namely, that it was forged by birth within the realm, and that it was an indelible and unalterable bond. The "permit system" stripped partition's refugees of the right to return to the land of their birth.[20] The Evacuee Property ordinances made their flight an irrevocable step. Once the very act of leaving one's home rendered it liable to seizure, people were forced to stay where they

[18] The reasons for the exclusion of West Bengal, Assam, and Tripura from the emerging evacuee property regime is a complex subject in itself which cannot, for reasons of space, be discussed here.

[19] Pakistan promulgated a central Evacuee Property Ordinance in October 1949. "The Problem of Evacuee Property and Efforts Made to Solve It", enclosure in Memo from the Indian Ministry of External Affairs to India's Permanent Representative at the UN, 31 December 1949, MEAI/11(21)/49-Pak III (Secret).

[20] Zamindar, *The Long Partition.*

were. And those who had already left had no alternative but to remain where they now found themselves, or to seek some new destination outside South Asia where they could settle. Migration was endowed with a new finality and novel political resonances. Muslim migrants to Pakistan were deemed by India to have chosen citizenship of Pakistan by the very act of moving there, and to have renounced forever their right to Indian citizenship. Hindu and Sikh refugees born in Pakistan, likewise, were banned from returning to their homes there. The imperatives of responding to mass migrations that neither had desired or anticipated pushed both nations towards redefining nationality in ethnoreligious terms.

These regulatory regimes had a profound impact upon South Asia. They effectively sealed the western borders between India and Pakistan. The eastern borders between them, too, were gradually closed. After 1952, passports and visas were required for travel between India and East Pakistan. The Enemy Property Acts of 1967, promulgated by both countries, applied to *all* their territories, bringing East Pakistan, West Bengal, Assam, and Tripura (hitherto excluded from the purview of the evacuee property regime) firmly within its remit. These acts not only made it more difficult than ever to cross the borders, it also made it hazardous for people even to maintain contact with relatives on the other side, since fraternising with "the enemy" across the border rendered property liable to seizure.[21] In 1972, after its secession from Pakistan in a war which produced ten million refugees, Bangladesh too enacted its own Vested Property Ordinance. This mirrored the provisions of the evacuee property acts of its neighbours, with calamitous implications for its large Hindu populations, and also for its Urdu-speaking minorities.[22] Today,

[21] Chatterji, *The Disinherited.*

[22] Barkat, *et al.*, *Political Economy of the Vested Property Act*; Farooqui, *Law of Abandoned Property*; Ghosh, *Partition and the South Asian Diaspora.*

South Asia's borders are among the most violently policed frontiers in the world.[23]

The impact of these upheavals was not restricted to the subcontinent. They had a ripple effect that soon touched South Asians in the diaspora. By 1947 there were three million people of South Asian origin scattered over fifty-eight countries. Perhaps one in three of these "overseas Indians" was a Muslim.[24] Many of these Muslims came from parts of the subcontinent that after Partition went to India, not Pakistan, and they had relatives and properties there. Questions were now raised about their nationality. The External Affairs Ministry was much exercised, for instance, by the case of one Mr Gardee, a Muslim of Indian origin and long-time resident of Johannesburg. Mr Gardee, reputedly one of South Africa's richest men, came from Bombay, where he had substantial properties. Indian officials believed (with no definite evidence to support their belief) that he had "pro-Pak leanings" and travelled to Pakistan to buy property there. This led to a move to enlarge the scope of the Evacuee Property Act whereby it could apply to overseas Indian Muslims of "doubtful loyalty".[25] Mr Gardee's properties in Bombay were seized by the Custodian of Evacuee Property, as were the properties of many other Indian Muslims living abroad.[26]

Not surprisingly, finding themselves in a similar position to Mr Gardee, many overseas Indians rushed to register themselves as Indian citizens. The position of those whose homes were in the erstwhile princely states was further complicated by the passage of the British Nationality Act of 1948 (of which more later), which

[23] van Schendel, "The Wagah Syndrome".

[24] Memo by BFHB Tyabji dated 23 August 1952, MEA (AFR II Branch)/AII/53/6491, 31 (Secret).

[25] MEA/AII/52/6423/31 (1952, Secret).

[26] File note dated 20 April 1950, MEA/17-39/49-AFRI (Secret).

extended British nationality to all former British Indian subjects. Since inhabitants of the princely states had technically never been British Indian subjects – owing allegiance first and foremost to their own rulers rather than the British king-emperor – they now found themselves at risk of being rendered stateless by the new legislation.[27] This prompted a flood of applications for Indian citizenship, to which many were technically entitled under the Indian constitution of 1950.

However, this rush among diasporic South Asians for Indian citizenship did not play well in their host countries. Ethno-nationalists in East and South Africa now seized on the phenomenon as proof that Indian migrants had no loyalty to their countries of adoption.[28] In South Africa, where the Afrikaner National Party had long been pressing for the repatriation of "Asiatics", the question had more delicate ramifications. If South Africa's "Asiatics" *were* Indian nationals, the National Party claimed, it was well within South Africa's rights to ask them to leave. If, on the other hand, they were South African citizens by virtue of birth and domicile, then India had no business interfering in South Africa's internal affairs and proselytising in the UN on their behalf.[29]

For its part, the Indian government began now to see compelling reasons why its diasporic peoples should be encouraged to take on the citizenship of their host countries. This would allow India to sidestep the sticky question of who, among these three million or so people abroad, was entitled to Indian citizenship; who among them was a "closet" Pakistani; and whom it was safe to allow back home. It would also – or so the officials in New

[27] Technically, they were "British Protected Persons". After the Nationality Act of 1948, they could become citizens of the UK and Colonies by naturalisation, but did not get this citizenship automatically, as did other British Indian subjects. Parry, *British Nationality*, p. 95.

[28] MEA/17-39/49-AFRI (Secret) and MEA/AII/52/6423/31 (1952, Secret).

[29] India had been campaigning against the Asiatic Land Tenure Act since its promulgation in 1946, and took the matter to the United Nations.

Delhi's South Block hoped – give these people more secure claim to political rights in their host nations than if they were deemed to be migrants.[30] It would, furthermore, prevent a flood of returning migrants seeking shelter back in India at a time when its government was stretched to the limit by the challenge of rehabilitating millions of Partition refugees. But, as subsequent events would show, this policy was no guarantee that the "host" countries would accept Indian migrants as their own people.

Nationality in the Neighbourhood and Wider Empire

In 1948, Burma and Ceylon gained independence and stood forward as new nations. Both countries immediately set about drafting new citizenship laws that distinguished between "ethnic" citizens and immigrants. In August 1949, Ceylon enacted an Indian and Pakistani Residents (Citizenship) Act which allowed persons of Indian and Pakistani origin to register, within two years of the passage of the act, for citizenship of Ceylon. But it distinguished between citizens "by descent" and citizens by registration – who were not entitled, as defined by various new development initiatives, to the "goods" of development.[31] According to the Indian Mission in Colombo, Ceylonese officials had no intention of making registration easy for Indian migrants, "deliberately dragging their feet in registration of Indians as citizens of their voting rights."[32] Already in 1939 the further migration of Tamil

[30] Note by M.L. Mehta dated 5 April 1950, GOI/MEAI/7/49/BCI (C) (Secret).

[31] No Indian (or Pakistani) registered under the act would have rights under the Land Development Ordinance, the Fisheries Ordinance, and the Omnibus Licensing Ordinances, designed to promote the welfare of Ceylonese citizens. Note by M.L. Mehta dated 5 April 1950, MEAI/7/49/BCI (C) (Secret).

[32] Ministry of External Affairs (CAP Branch), file note dated ?/5/1951, MEAI/ 7/49-BCI (C).

plantation workers to Ceylon had been banned. But among the seven or eight hundred thousand Tamils who had already migrated to Ceylon before this date, many had left their wives and children behind in South India. This population, for the most part unlettered and unorganised (few independent unions were allowed to operate on the plantations), had now to negotiate the complex business of acquiring Ceylonese citizenship for themselves and their families.[33] As the Indian Mission in Colombo concluded, "the best thing would be for all Indians who were qualified to be Ceylonese citizens to apply for citizenship without hesitation."[34]

For its part, in 1948 Burma defined its own nationality law on frankly ethnic grounds, giving citizenship only to persons deemed to belong to an "indigenous race" or having one grandparent from an "indigenous race". Indians who had lived in British Burma since before 1942 could register as citizens, but were soon to be victims of government drives forcibly to acquire their land without fair compensation.[35] This generated a new wave of migration (or repatriation), as Indians from Burma began to trickle into India as refugees and, in the case of Arakanese Muslims, to East Pakistan. Neither India nor Pakistan – both still struggling to rehabilitate millions of refugees – was able to do much to help them, beyond allowing them (with greater or lesser degrees of reluctance) the right to enter and remain in their countries of origin. In the case of "Anglo-Indian" residents of Burma, even this was rather more than the Indian government was prepared to do: the Indian Mission in Burma was advised to issue them only with temporary papers, rather than register them as full-fledged Indian citizens. Because of their doubtful claims to ethnic Indian antecedents, their loyalty to India was deemed suspect.[36] The rising tides of ethnically defined nationalisms throughout the Indian Ocean region meant that

[33] Peebles, *The Plantation Tamils of Ceylon.*

[34] Note by M.L. Mehta dated 5 April 1950, MEAI/7/49/BCI (C) (Secret).

[35] "Note on Land Nationalisation in Burma", GOI/ MEA/F. 9-8/ 48-0.s.II/1948.

[36] Indian Ministry of Home Affairs (MHAI)/33/32/49-FII (1949).

the Anglo-Indians too would now have to seek new destinations in other parts of the world where their British subjecthood still allowed them entry, in yet another new stream of migration in the South Asian diaspora.

The Decline, Revival, and Fall of "British Subjecthood"

By 1948, Canada and Australia too had adopted their own citizenship laws. Even as they paid lip service to the idea of a shared British subjecthood in the empire and Commonwealth, they reaffirmed their commitment to keeping non-white migrants – whether from the Commonwealth or elsewhere – out from their territories. Australia and Canada stuck obstinately to this position, invoking their sovereign right to determine who could and could not enter their territories, and they held fast, until the mid-1960s, to an immigration policy in which colour and race were the determinants. "British imperial subjecthood" was beginning to look like a tattered inheritance, its contradictions exposed to the world.

These were the circumstances under which London brought the British Nationality Act onto the statute book in 1948. The act introduced the new legal statuses of "Citizens of the UK and Commonwealth" (CUKC) and "Citizens of Independent Commonwealth Countries" (CICC).[37] It allowed both categories (CUKCs and CICCs) free entry into the UK, with the right to find employment, while citizens of the old (white) dominions, were given the right to register as British citizens after a year's residence.[38] It therefore extended, on paper at least, free access to the UK to all citizens of both the "old" and "new" Commonwealth, and hence to Indians, Pakistanis, and Ceylonese.

[37] The act created five different categories of citizens. In addition to CUKC and CICC, these included "Irish British subjects", "British subjects without citizenship", and "British Protected Persons". The latter category included former subjects of Indian princely states.

[38] Hansen, *Citizenship and Immigration*, pp. 46-7.

Enacted at a time of cross-party consensus about the importance of defending the traditional ideal of British subjecthood and on the necessity of maintaining close relations with the Commonwealth, the act was passed before immigration from the "new" Commonwealth had become a concern in Britain. But the context changed almost immediately with the arrival on British shores of 492 Jamaicans on board the *Empire Windrush* in June 1948. After this "incursion" (as Attlee famously described it), every UK government would face demands that Britain's doors be closed to "coloured immigrants".[39]

Between 1948 and 1962, Whitehall resisted pressures to introduce controls that were openly discriminatory and hung on to what remained of the common subjecthood in the empire and Commonwealth. But it is not the case, as is often claimed, that Britain in this period remained open to all comers. Interestingly, Britain now used its good offices with governments in the "source" countries to encourage them to introduce their own controls to prevent unregulated emigration from their shores. In the mid-1950s, when South Asian migrants replaced those from the Caribbean as the prime focus of official concern, Britain asked India and Pakistan not to issue their citizens with passports for travel to the UK. They agreed to deny passports to their own people if they lacked adequate resources, and if they could not prove adequate literacy and knowledge of English. Both countries instituted police checks into the character and antecedents of would-be migrants. For its part, by unpublicised arrangements with the UK Home Office, India began to weed out applications for passports from "low class citizens", checking their claims that they had secured work and accommodation in Britain.[40] It was only in 1960, when India's

[39] Ibid., p. 57.

[40] Pakistan agreed, in addition, to give publicity to the difficulties encountered by Pakistanis in finding work in Britain. Cabinet Memorandum on Commonwealth Immigrants, Memorandum by the Lord President of the Council, 20 June 1958, PRO/CAB/129/93.

Supreme Court declared it to be discriminatory that this strange practice – of "outsourcing" of UK migration controls against Indians to India – came to an end.[41] In 1961, Pakistan too lifted its own restrictions on emigration to the UK.[42]

Finally, after a decade of mounting domestic pressure for restrictions, the Commonwealth Immigrants Act went onto the statute book in 1962.[43] Although it did not openly discriminate on the grounds of race, it was specifically designed to restrict the admission of "coloured immigrants", and this was the outcome in practice. Prospective migrants from South Asia now had to obtain employment vouchers from the Ministry of Labour before being allowed into Britain. These were given mainly to people who had specific jobs to go to in Britain, or to those who had particular skills and qualifications which Britain wanted. Only the wives and children of migrants already in Britain still had an absolute right of entry into the UK.

Since 1962, the immigration laws of Britain have become ever more complex and restrictionist, even, for a brief and inglorious episode in the 1980s, subjecting migrant brides from South Asia to virginity tests. Space does not permit a detailed discussion of these laws, but two points need to be noted. In 1963, Kenya gained independence, and four years later, in 1967, passed an Immigration Act that obliged all those without Kenyan citizenship to acquire work permits. It also introduced laws that deliberately targeted South Asians in business and trade. This followed a drive to "Africanise" the newly independent national government and economy of Kenya. Uganda followed suit, setting up a committee to Africanise commerce and industry in 1968, and introducing discriminatory

[41] Pakistan agreed, in addition, to give publicity to the difficulties encountered by Pakistanis in finding work in Britain. Cabinet Memorandum on Commonwealth Immigrants, Memorandum by the Lord President of the Council, 20 June 1958, PRO/CAB/129/93.

[42] Brown, *Global South Asians*, p. 42.

[43] Kershaw and Pearsall, *Immigrants and Aliens*.

systems of trade licences and work permits in 1969. Many of the South Asians who left East Africa at this time were British citizens, having opted to retain their CUKC status in 1963. In 1968, Britain passed a new Commonwealth Immigration Act which restricted the number of Asian families from East Africa permitted to enter the UK to 1500. This broke an explicit pledge, given in 1963 to East African Asians who retained their CUKC status, that they would have unrestricted rights of entry into the UK. It also meant that Britain now had denied the right of return to a specific class of *Britain's own citizens.*

In 1971, a Conservative government passed an Immigration Act which introduced "patriality" as a condition for the right of abode in the UK. This was a thinly disguised form of ethnic qualification – "patriality" being "indigenous" antecedents by another name. Commonwealth citizens were now deemed to have the same status as "aliens" in Britain. After a quarter of a century of prevarication, with this step Britain repudiated its own historic conception of subjecthood. Faced with the triple challenge of economic and geopolitical decline and potentially huge post-colonial immigration, as Joppke has suggested,[44] Britain refashioned itself from a "civic" to an "ethnic" nation, in which membership is defined by the tests of birth and ancestry. Finally, as the last vestiges of its empire faded away, Britain joined the new world of ethnic nation-states as a full-fledged member, abandoning its legacy as architect of a liberal and (in this matter) universalist empire and turning upon itself to keep outsiders at bay.

The World of the "Green Card-Holder", "Gulf" Subordination, and Human Trafficking

Since the mid-1960s, the international migration regime (as it affects South Asians) has been dominated by two main trends. The first is the move – heralded by the passage of the Hart-Celler Act

[44] Joppke, "Multiculturalism and Immigration".

by the United States in 1965 – explicitly to embrace a hierarchy of preferences for certain *types* of migrants within a system of controls which caps overall numbers but does not bar certain peoples or races. In the US, preference has been given to two groups.[45] The first, based on the notion of "family reunion", are the children and dependants of migrants who are already legal permanent residents. The second is for highly accomplished migrants whose skills match the needs of the domestic economy. By and large, with local and temporal variations, these preferences have also guided the immigration policies of the developed countries of the English-speaking West since the 1970s. Australia, Canada, and Britain have all adopted this model. Although the common perception is that Britain "closed" her doors to South Asians at the same time that the rest of the world began to welcome them,[46] the facts point to a different conclusion: different regimes have converged since the 1960s and 1970s upon a broadly common ground.

The second trend has been the re-emergence – side by side with a rapidly growing global labour market – of familiar forms of subordination among poor and unskilled migrants. These migrants are predominantly young and able-bodied men, and they have been joined increasingly by large numbers of single women working as cooks, maids, child-minders, or sex-workers. The oil-rich Gulf emirates are merely the most visible parts of a labour market segmented by race and hierarchy, in which a few highly skilled and paid elite migrants enjoy freedoms and mobility, while poorer South Asian workers are employed on astonishingly illiberal terms.[47] These new helots enjoy few, if any, rights.[48] The noxious practice of employers confiscating the passports of "labour-class" employees has become common-

[45] Refugees and asylum seekers are the third category of migrants who still have access under these systems, but for reasons of space they cannot be discussed here.

[46] Shukla, *India Abroad*, p. 49, for instance.

[47] Ballard, "The Political Economy of Migration".

[48] Nichols, *Pashtun Migration*.

place. Gang-masters lure poor migrants to destinations all the way from Malaysia or Dubai to Britain with great expectations of pay and good working conditions, only to confiscate their (often forged) papers on arrival, withhold pay, and in effect incarcerate them until they have worked enough notionally to pay off the costs of their passage. The brutalities of human trafficking in the twenty-first century recall many of the horrors of indenture and *kangani* in the 1900s.

On the face of it, then, the migration regimes of the twenty-first century bear an uncanny resemblance with those of the old imperial world. Just as the old order was stratified by class and status, with a clear legal distinction between the self-funded free "passenger class" and "assisted" unfree "coolie class", the new order is characterised by the chasm that separates the legal status of increasingly hyper-mobile "green-card holders" (and their ilk), and trafficked or otherwise "assisted" migrants drawn from larger poor communities that are "stuck".[49]

But there are important distinctions, and I will conclude by pointing to them. In the nineteenth century it was well understood that free and "assisted" migrants alike would usually leave families behind, remitting monies home and returning periodically. Now the tendency for Western governments is to promote "family reunion". It would be churlish to deny that this bias owes something to genuine humane concerns in receiving states. But it would be no less naïve to believe that when Western governments endorse "family reunion", they are not concerned to ensure that those few migrants whom they have been forced to accept as permanent inhabitants have all their eggs in one national basket, and that is the basket which the host controls. These states are anxious to ensure that migrants deposit all their emotional ties and loyalties safely within the borders of the nation-state in which they now live.

[49] Williams, "On Being Stuck".

The final distinction between the old and the new is the preference today for "permanent settlement", by those chosen few deemed eligible for entry and who have "earned" their right to stay in Western industrialised nation-states. To get a "green card" in the US, the applicant has to demonstrate *continuous unbroken residence* and legal employment. In Britain, those with "leave to remain" have not only to demonstrate an unbroken stretch of domicile before they are granted that leave, but also cannot leave the UK for any length of time *without losing that entitlement.* The paradox for today's "green-card migrants" is that they can only regain their freedom to come and go by taking the ultimate step, of applying for the citizenship of their host country and renouncing affiliation with their homeland. Only by professing loyalty to the adopted nation through ever more elaborate rituals of citizenship can today's migrants regain the right freely to leave it. And yet, ironically, the technologies of today also enable them ever more easily to resort to the many forms of subversion of the nation-state that are collectively understood as "transnationalism".

Conclusion

The imperatives behind the passage of the Hart-Celler Act have been debated; some argue persuasively that it had much to do with the civil rights revolution at home in the United States.[50] But few would deny that it was as much a response to the new international context of decolonisation and the Cold War, and to America's assumption of leadership of the "free world". America's imperial role required, as did every successful empire earlier, that it elaborate a universalist and inclusive discourse. Restrictionist policies in the pre-World War II era – with their emphasis on national quotas that favoured "assimilable" Western Europeans, their espousal of an "Asiatic Barred Zones", and measures to prevent

[50] Joppke, "Multiculturalism and Immigration", pp. 292–9.

Chinese and Japanese immigration – were at odds with America's image as the beacon of liberty, and had to be abandoned.[51] Older liberal republican traditions of civic citizenship, which promised that anyone could become an American if they embraced its love of liberty, were instead revived and reworked as the ideological underpinning of the free world.

One question which the decline of Britain's imperium poses for the future of America is this: will America, like Britain before it, retreat from its confident universalism? Just as Britain retreated from a universalist liberal notion of subjecthood to a narrow, increasingly ethnically understood conception of national citizenship, might America's view of itself (however rose-tinted) as a multi-cultural nation of migrants be challenged by the realities of its economic decline? Buffeted by globalisation, the exodus of capital, the multiplicity of allegiances of migrants in a global labour market, will America be pushed, like Britain before her, into embracing a revived nativism? Can America respond to the challenge of refashioning its citizenship in ways that do not alienate or exclude sections of its post-imperial plural society? When this essay was first written, this remained an open question. Now, under Donald Trump's presidency, the wind is blowing in the direction of extreme exclusion. Calls to "build the wall" and policies which incarcerate immigrant children surely mark a new turning point in the history of "drawing the global colour line".[52]

References

Amrith, Sunil, "Indians Overseas? Governing Tamil Migration to Malaya, 1870–1941", *Past and Present*, 208 (August 2010).

Anderson, Caitlin, "Aliens at Home, Subjects Abroad: British Nationality Law and Policy, 1815–1870", University of Cambridge, PhD thesis, 2008.

[51] Bernard, "Immigration: History of U.S. Policy".

[52] Lake and Reynolds, *Drawing the Global Colour Line.*

Ballard, Roger, "The Political Economy of Migration: Pakistan, Britain and the Middle East", in J. Eade, *Migrants, Workers and the Social Order*, London: Tavistock, 1987.

Barkat, Abul, *et al.*, *Political Economy of the Vested Property Act in Rural Bangladesh*, Dhaka: ALRD, 1997.

Bernard, William, "Immigration: History of U.S. Policy", in David Jacobson, ed., *The Immigration Reader: America in Multidisciplinary Perspective*, Oxford: Blackwell, 1998.

Brown, Judith, *Global South Asians. Introducing the Modern Diaspora*, Cambridge: Cambridge University Press, 2004.

Chatterji, Joya, *The Disinherited. Migrants, Minorities and Citizenship in South Asia*, Cambridge: Cambridge University Press, forthcoming.

Das, Durga, ed., *Sardar Patel's Correspondence, 1945–50*, vol. 4.

Farooqui, M.I., *Law of Abandoned Property*, Dhaka: Khaja Art Press, 2000.

Ghosh, Papiya, *Partition and the South Asian Diaspora. Extending the Subcontinent*, London, New York, and Delhi: Routledge, 2007.

Hansen, Randall, *Citizenship and Immigration in Postwar Britain: The Institutional Origins of a Multicultural Nation*, Oxford, 1999.

Joppke, Christian, "Multiculturalism and Immigration: A Comparison of the United States, Germany and Great Britain", in David Jacobson, ed., *The Immigration Reader: America in Multidisciplinary Perspective*, Oxford: Blackwell, 1998.

Kershaw, Roger, and Mark Pearsall, *Immigrants and Aliens. A Guide to Sources on UK Immigration and Citizenship*, Kew: PRO, 2004.

Kim, Keechang, *Aliens in Medieval Law. The Origins of Modern Citizenship*, Cambridge, 2004.

Mongia, Radhika, "Race, Nationality, Mobility: A History of the Passport", *Public Culture*, 11, 3, Fall 1999.

Nichols, Robert, *A History of Pashtun Migration 1775–2006*, Oxford, 2008.

Parry, Clive, *British Nationality Including Citizenship of the United Kingdom and Colonies and the Status of Aliens*, London: Steven and Sons, 1951.

Peebles, Patrick, *The Plantation Tamils of Ceylon*, London, 2001.

Question of Treatment of Indians in the Union of South Africa before the United Nations. Documents and Proceedings, Simla: Government of India Press, 1947.

Randhawa, M.S., *Out of the Ashes; An Account of the Rehabilitation of Refugees from West Pakistan in Rural Areas of East Punjab* (1954).

Roy, Tirthankar, and Douglas Haynes, "Conceiving Mobility: Weavers' Migrations in Pre-colonial and Colonial India", *Indian Economic and Social History Review*, 36, 1, 1999.

Shukla, Sandhya, *India Abroad*, Princeton, 2003.

Singha, Radhika, "A 'Proper Passport' for the Colony: Border Crossing in British India, 1882–1920", unpublished paper.

Tinker, Hugh, *A New System of Slavery. The Export of Indian Labour Overseas 1830–1920*, London: Hansib, 1974.

van Schendel, Willem, "The Wagah Syndrome: Territorial Roots of Contemporary Violence in South Asia", in Amrita Basu and Srirupa Roy, eds, *Violence and Democracy in India*, Calcutta, 2007.

Williams, Robert Gooding, "On Being Stuck", in *Reading Rodney King, Reading Urban Uprising*, New York, 1993.

Zamindar, Vazira F., *The Long Partition and the Making of Modern South Asia. Refugees, Boundaries, Histories*, New York: Columbia University Press, 2007.

Zolberg, Aristide, "The Formation of New States as a Refugee-generating Process", *Annals*, 467, May 1983.

12

Princes, Subjects, and Gandhi

Alternatives to Citizenship at the End of Empire

This essay harks back to the period when B.R. Nanda, an outstanding student at Lahore University and subsequently a government servant in the railways, began to write history. Nanda's first and least-known work, published under a pseudonym, was on the Partition of India. This was not a book about great men, Nanda's subsequent preoccupation, but of ordinary people uprooted. Like him, I write of their actions during the upheavals of 1947. Gandhi is part of my story, but he is not the main focus, for I am not a scholar of Gandhi. Yet Gandhi's words and actions at this crucial juncture reveal unexplored dimensions of the Mahatma's moral politics that call for deeper and more sustained investigation.

The mass migrations after Partition immediately conjure up images of refugee caravans crossing the Radcliffe Line between India and Pakistan. We assume that the frightened people who fled their homes faced a clear and binary choice between two republics – India and Pakistan – and between two alternative "modern" postcolonial sovereignties. This is the official narrative of the new nations, and no historian who has studied refugees has challenged it.

However, the story was far more complex and far more intriguing than that narrative. In 1947, thousands of people made other choices that did not involve flight to "the other dominion", choices that reveal a deep lack of trust in *both* the new republics. They escaped to princely states, seeking the protection of rajas, raosahebs, jamsahebs, nizams, and nawabs. Just when the constituent assemblies of India and Pakistan were debating the terms of national citizenship, their would-be citizens fled in search of subjecthood.

This essay attempts to piece together this little-known history from fragmentary and scattered sources. It first discusses the patterns of migration to give a sense of their scope and scale. Next it teases out some of the hopes and expectations that animated the migrants, and the princes' responses to them. Finally, it touches briefly upon Gandhi's engagement with these migrants and the princes whose shelter they sought. The very fact that many people of the subcontinent sought alternatives to republican citizenship, I argue, demands our attention. As things turned out, these aspirations for post-imperial subjecthood failed. Nonetheless, they are deeply significant in ways I hope to elucidate in my concluding remarks.

I

In 1947, undivided India contained 562 princely states which varied enormously in size. The largest, Hyderabad, was about half the size of France and boasted seventeen million subjects in the mid-twentieth century; the smallest was less than one square mile, with a population of barely two hundred.[1] Together these

[1] I thank the trustees of the B.R. Nanda Trust for the privilege of being able to acknowledge the debt of gratitude that every historian of modern India owes to B.R. Nanda, and to pay tribute to his role as founder-director of one of India's great institutions, the Nehru Memorial Museum and Library. Founded in 1964, Teen Murti is a mecca for every historian of modern India.

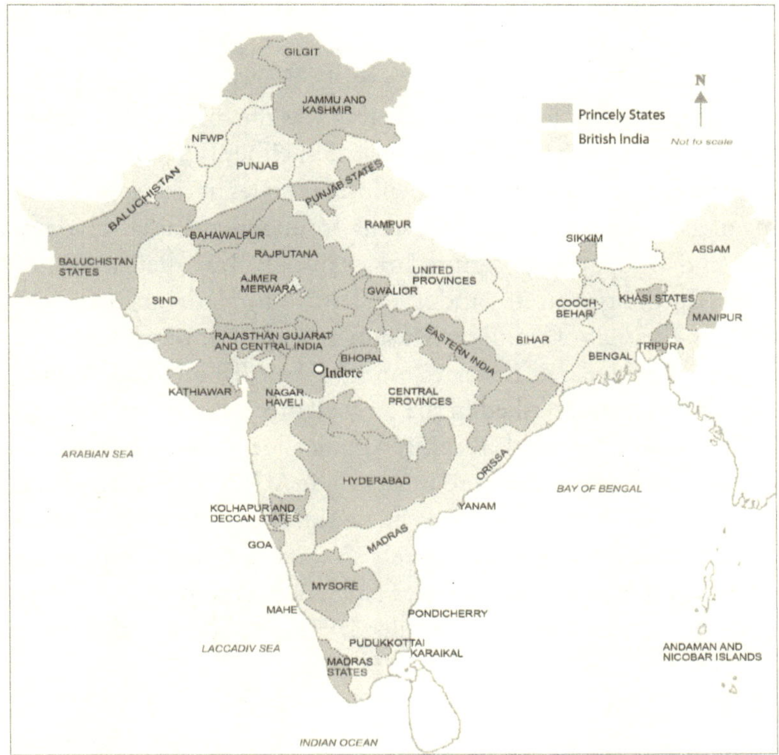

Fig. 12.1: Map of Undivided India in 1947, Showing Princely States

Source: Prepared by Tina Bone.

Note: This is a historical map and is included here for representative purposes. The international boundaries, coastlines, denominations, and other information shown do not necessarily imply any judgement concerning the legal status of any territory or the endorsement or acceptance of such information. For current boundaries, readers may refer to the Survey of India maps. Map not to scale.

It holds the world's most impressive archive – at the time of writing almost a million pages of manuscripts – on modern India, an unrivalled newspaper collection, and photographic records. Its library, now being digitised, will soon preserve a priceless heritage of more than nine million documents. As

principalities covered roughly a third of India's territory and accounted for one in four of its people.

In broad terms, migrations to subjecthood, as they might be described, were of four types. The first was the flight from territories of former British India (now places in either India or Pakistan) to princely states. Prominent peninsular states acted as powerful magnets to panic-stricken Muslims from across India. Hyderabad and Bhopal were significant examples, but they were not alone. In the run-up to, and after, Partition, Hyderabad attracted three-quarters of a million Muslim migrants.[2] Immediately after Partition, refugees also started pouring into Bhopal, an Afghan successor state established in the early eighteenth century.[3] Nawab Hamidullah of Bhopal, recently Chancellor of the Chamber of Princes,[4] had a "position and prestige", in V.P. Menon's jaundiced view, "out of all proportion to the size and revenue of his State".[5] Bhopal was one of the last princely states to accede to India – the other laggards being Travancore, Hyderabad, Dholpur, and Indore (not all of which had Muslim rulers).[6] Bhopal city was about five

---

its first director, Nanda laid the foundations on which the Museum and Library were built. The values that prompted Nanda to take up his pen after Gandhi's assassination in 1948 are under siege once again today. So also, it seems, is the independence of Teen Murti, and indeed of the historical profession itself. Perhaps there has never been a more appropriate moment to laud B.R. Nanda's contribution and legacy, and to recall the ideals of tolerance that were close to his heart.

Government of India, *White Paper on Hyderabad*, p. 2; Ramusack, *The Indian Princes and their States*, p. 3.

[2] "Note on the Refugee Problem of Hyderabad", National Archives of India (NAI), MoS/F. 10(27)-H/49, 1949.

[3] Ramusack, *The Indian Princes and their States*, p. 28.

[4] Menon, *Integration of the Indian States*, p. 97.

[5] Ibid., p. 347.

[6] Mansergh, ed., *Transfer of Power*, vol. 12, Doc. 302, "Viceroy's Personal Report No. 15, L/PO/6/123:ff 208–22".

hundred miles due south of Delhi; and from late August 1947 thousands of Indian Muslims from the Central Provinces, the United Provinces, Gwalior, and East Punjab made a beeline for it. Notably, these people chose to head south to Bhopal rather than migrate west across the border into West Pakistan, which for many of these migrants was just as close as Bhopal, if not closer. By mid October, 160,000 refugees had gathered in Bhopal, and more would continue to flow in.[7]

The sources make it clear that if Bhopal could not absorb them, the refugees were ready to march further south to Hyderabad, but they had no intention of going back to their homes, now in a new republican entity called India. As C.C. Desai of the States Department admitted, about 100,000 "Muslim refugees were clustered

Table 12.1

Refugees Registered in Bhopal State up to 16 October 1947

Location	*Origin*	*Numbers*
In Bairagarh camp	From Central Provinces	32,225
	From United Provinces	6,896
	From other provinces	750
	From Gwalior	23,279
	From other states	9,000
	Total in Bairagarh	**72,150**
In Bhopal city	Unsorted	12,000
Unregistered arrivals since 16 October	-ditto-	4,000
Elsewhere in Bhopal, in Begumganj, Sehore, Budni and smaller thanas and tehsils	-ditto-	4,000
Total in Bhopal State		**92,150**

Source: NAI, MoS/F.16-G(R)/47 (Secret).

[7] H.H. Hamidullah of Bhopal to Vallabhbhai Patel, 6 October 1947, NAI, MoS/F.16-G(R)/47 (Secret). The table shows only the number of people registered.

at Bhopal station" in appalling conditions because the Government of India had advised Bhopal's nawab not to let them in; significantly the "refugees refuse[d] to get into [trains]" leaving Bhopal for destinations in India.[8] The Nizam of Hyderabad's government was sympathetic to the plight of these refugees and put on special trains within the state's borders for them,[9] but this only made the Indian government more suspicious of Hyderabad's intentions, and it did all it could to prevent the movement of Muslim refugees from India, as well as from other states such as Bhopal, into the nizam's territories.[10] But its attempts to stem these flows were ineffectual. Between August 1947 and September 1948, that is, between Partition and the "police action" that ended Hyderabad's brief show of independence, Indian Muslims continued to migrate to Hyderabad.[11]

Refugees were attracted not only to "important" states with vocal leaders. For reasons that are unfathomable to us today, they rushed to the smallest of principalities and to a multitude of "little kingdoms".[12] As the Nawab of Pataudi wrote in September 1947, "refugees and wounded are pouring in as Pataudi town is the only place they feel safe."[13] Malerkotla, a small state in Punjab ruled by the Afghan Sherwani dynasty, which famously remained peaceful during Partition,[14] was the destination for 40,000–60,000 refugees fleeing the massacres in surrounding East Punjab.[15] Mahmudabad, a minor Shia state near Lucknow, also drew hundreds of thousands

[8] File Note by C.C. Desai, 18 October 1947, NAI, MoS/F.16-G (R)/47 (Secret).

[9] Ibid.

[10] Ibid.

[11] "Note on the Refugee Problem in Hyderabad", NAI, MoS/F.10(27)/H-49. Also see Sherman, *Muslim Belonging in Secular India*, p. 24.

[12] Cohn, "Political Systems in Eighteenth Century India", pp. 313–14.

[13] H.H. Pataudi to Major General Rajkumar Rajindersinghji, 5 September 1947, NAI, MoS/F.2(13)-PR/47 (Secret).

[14] Bigelow, *Sharing the Sacred.*

[15] NAI, MoS/F.2(19)PR-47.

of refugees, both Shia and Sunni, from the surrounding districts of the United Provinces.[16]

Nor was it the case that Muslim refugees only went to states with Muslim rulers (although this was the dominant pattern). By 10 October 1947, the tiny state of Dholpur, whose "conservative" Hindu maharaja had long been the bane of the States Ministry, had already received about 20,000 Muslims. The maharaja then agreed to absorb even more Muslim evacuees from amongst the unfortunates gathered at Bhopal station, an action that led one intelligence officer to remark on his strange "soft corner for these fellows".[17] The maharaja, for his part, defended his actions in the name of "our precious national *RAJNITI* [politics] from our great cultures and outlook", and "King Dharma".[18]

The second stream was of refugees who abandoned their homes in one princely state to seek shelter in another. In this quest they often passed through dominion territory, whether Indian or Pakistani, but carried on by foot, cart, or train until they reached the princely state of their choice. One example was the flight of Muslims from Ajmer, Bharatpur, and Alwar – where communal violence, particularly against people of the Meo community,[19] achieved horrific proportions – to Tonk,[20] a small state due south of Jaipur founded in 1818 by Amir Khan, a prominent Pindari leader. By mid-November 1947 "some 20,000" Muslims had arrived in Tonk, chiefly from Alwar and Bharatpur.[21] Another was the "unaccountable exodus of Muslims, in large numbers, particularly of weavers and other artisans", from the Holkar state of

[16] Personal interview with Suleiman Khan of Mahmudabad, Delhi, September 2014.

[17] NAI, MoS/2(42)-PR/47, 1947.

[18] Ibid.

[19] Copland, "The Further Shores of Partition", pp. 203-39; Mayaram, *Resisting Regimes*.

[20] NAI, MoS/F.2(23)-PR/1947.

[21] "Tonk Affairs", D.O. No. 296-P, NAI, MoS/F.2(23)-P.R.

Indore to Hyderabad.[22] A third, as we saw in the case of Bhopal, was the flight of some 25,000 refugees from Gwalior, the Maratha state south of Agra and the Chambal river,[23] to Bhopal state.[24] All these refugees were Muslims who had previously lived peaceably as subjects of a Hindu ruler, but who now sought the protection of a Muslim nawab or nizam (albeit in states which had Hindu majorities). Once again, they chose to go to these states rather than to Pakistan, although their homes were relatively close to Pakistan's borders.

A third form of migration to subjecthood involved crossing the Radcliffe Line between India and Pakistan. But here some refugees, instead of seeking the protection of the other dominion, specifically sought to reach neighbouring principalities instead. One major stream of this kind was of Sindhi Hindu refugees from the Khanate of Kalat in Balochistan to the Rajputana states in India. Another was the emigration of refugees into Bahawalpur, a largely barren desert state on the left bank of the Indus in Pakistan,[25] chiefly from East Punjab and Rajputana. We know a fair amount about this particular example because Penderel Moon, who took up an appointment in Bahawalpur just months before Partition, left a detailed record in his celebrated memoir, *Divide and Quit*. The refugees were mainly from Ferozepur district in Indian (East) Punjab,[26] and also from Bikaner.[27] Moon says his "heart sank at the vast numbers" of refugees, "a column that stretched all the way from MacLeodganj Road to Bahawalnagar." He recalls: "I was at a loss to understand why

[22] Prime Minister, Indore, to C.C. Desai, 14 October 1947, NAI, MoS/F.16-G (R)/47 (Secret).

[23] Malcolm, *A Memoir of Central India*; Gordon, *The Marathas 1600–1818*.

[24] See Table 12.1 above.

[25] Ramusack, *The Princes of India*, p. 40; and Bennett, "The Greening of Bahawalpur", *Indo-British Review*, pp. 5–14.

[26] Moon, *Divide and* Quit, p. 179.

[27] Ibid., p. 229.

they had entered Bahawalpur instead of crossing the Sutlej into the [West] Punjab. They all said that Indian troops had scared them away from the road leading to the bridge over the river at Suleimanke and that they had therefore been compelled to turn aside into Bahawalpur."[28] But Moon's account is inconsistent. While suggesting that "some of them with connections in the West Punjab still wanted to get there",[29] Moon admits that "we could pick and choose among the refugees who actually entered our borders, passing onto the Punjab [only] those whom we did not like or were too numerous for us to absorb. But we could not control or even influence the movement of refugees from India and so determine which of them would enter Bahawalpur territory." He also confesses to "pushing" refugees "of very poor stuff", those who were likely to be "a drag on the economy", into West Punjab.[30] Clearly, Bahawalpur was an attractive destination for refugees and most were reluctant to leave it.

Another flow of this kind, albeit moving in the opposite direction – chiefly from Hyderabad in Sindh – headed to Jodhpur state, which by the end of September 1947 had received upwards of 45,000 refugees.[31] All the bordering princely states clearly faced a refugee crisis: in late September, the Ministry of States wrote to the prime ministers not only of Jodhpur, but also Bikaner, Patiala, Jind, Malerkotla, Kapurthala, Faridkot, and Nabha, demanding information on refugee numbers in their states: "[S]uch information [is] essential for planning movement programmes."[32] Just as the officials of the ministry in late 1947, so today's investigators cannot establish the numbers that had flowed

[28] Ibid., p. 179.

[29] Ibid.

[30] Ibid., p. 229.

[31] Report by A.S. Dhawan, 29 September 1947, NAI, MoS/ F.32-G(R)/47 (Secret).

[32] Ministry of States to Prime Ministers, 19 September 1947, NAI, MoS/ F.32-G(R)/47(Secret).

into each state along the border, but the panicky communications suggest they were not insignificant.

The fourth stream were refugees who first sought help from a dominion government, whether India or Pakistan – and when that failed them, marched on to a princely state. One such example was the migration of Muslims from Badwani state in Central India to Dhulia in the Bombay Presidency. There "the Congress Leaders" apparently "encouraged" them to return home, which they obediently did. But when they faced further attacks "at home", they decided to seek refuge in Hyderabad.

It is all but impossible to produce a reliable estimate of a total number for the people who joined one or other of these four streams. Few states kept records as precise as those of Bhopal, or if they did and survive they remain scattered across five hundred mainly unarchived private collections. These movements took place before the census of 1951, by which time most states had disappeared, having been integrated into larger provinces. But two sources hint at their consistency and scale. In his study of Sindhi culture, Thakur notes that while the largest numbers of Sindhi refugees went to Bombay, the substantial remainder who did not concentrated in Jaipur, Ajmer, Jodhpur, Udaipur, Kotah, Bhilwarah, Tonk, Alwar and Bharatpur, and the "old State[s] of Madhya Pradesh" (see Table 12.2).[33]

By October 1948 the trend was even clearer: more refugees were heading for princely territories (see Table 12.3).

Even more revealing is the Government of India's White Paper on States, published in 1950. This suggests that these trends had been so widespread, and so marked, that the distribution of India's minorities changed dramatically between 1947 and 1950 with *a marked clustering of minorities in princely territories*. By 1950, in under three years since Partition, the proportion of India's Muslim population concentrated in princely territories had risen from

[33] Thakur, *Sindhi Culture*, p. 32.

Table 12.2

Distribution of Sindhi Refugees, 1948

Ajmer Merwara at Deoli	10,200
Bombay	216,500
Baroda	10,700
Bikaner State	8,900
Jaipur State	33,200
Jodhpur State	11,800
Madhya Bharat	3,400
Former Rajasthan	15,800
Saurashtra Union	45,500
Vindhya Pradesh	15,400
Madhya Pradesh	81,400
Total	**452,800**

Source: Thakur, *Sindhi Culture*, p. 31.

Table 12.3

Distribution of Sindhi Refugees, October 1948

Ajmer Merwara	92,799
Bombay	264,023
Baroda State	21,138
C.P. and Berar	91,507
Jaipur State	51,795
Jodhpur State	45,060
Madhya Bharat Union	59,333
Rajasthan Union	32,544
Matsya Union	53,034
Saurashtra Union	35,891
Vindhya Pradesh	12,945

Source: Thakur, *Sindhi Culture*, p. 103.

16 per cent to 26 per cent; of Christians from 46 per cent to 50 per cent; and of Sikhs from 27 per cent to 36 per cent.[34] These patterns of clustering demand an explanation.

[34] White Paper on Indian States (1950), p. 18.

The migrations make one fact abundantly clear. At the end of empire, the people of the subcontinent were aware of the multiple sovereignties around them which coexisted in uneasy juxtaposition. When they migrated, they believed they had real options between meaningful polities of very different kinds. For many, startling though it may seem today, neither "India" nor "Pakistan" was their first choice of destination.

II

Why was this? I now suggest some tentative answers.

A part of the answer must surely be the fact that these states – large and small – appeared to offer a measure of constancy in a terrifying world of change. In no small measure, this was a consequence of British policies of indirect rule: the British had propped up subsidiary allies after 1818, and after the Rebellion of 1857 ensured that no state, however small, was allowed to fail. Hence many ruling dynasties, which might otherwise have collapsed or been absorbed into other polities, survived, and their very longevity seems to have fostered the popular belief in 1947 that even the tiniest of little kingdoms would somehow endure, even as large parts of British India dissolved in chaos. However "hollow" were the crowns worn in miniature principalities such as the tiny Kathiawad states, or indeed Puddukottai in the South, the migrants seemed to think the heads which wore them would not tumble.

Indeed, these huge movements of people demand that we re-examine the metaphor of the "hollow crown".[35] In 1947, in a moment of profound danger and crisis, would-be subjects cherished significant expectations of these polities and their rulers, expressed in petitions like this one from Abdul Wahid Khan, the former postmaster of Okara, to "Her Highness, Rani Sahiba,

[35] Dirks, *The Hollow Crown.*

Kalsia state": "Owing to this loss of lives and property, we the remaining four members . . . of my family are quite destitute and helpless, and in the name of justice we demand from your kind highness that full justice may please be meted out by taking the culprits to task and granting us compensation of the full loss. Hoping full justice and early reply."[36] Above all, the migrants expected *protection* and *justice* – the postmaster uses the word "justice" three times in his two sentences.

To explain this dynamic, I draw on Sanjay Subrahmanyam and Muzaffar Alam's account of the successor states of the eighteenth century, which argues that these polities used a regional idiom consistently and successfully. The authors show that these polities "dug deep into the mythic resources of regions"; they also argue that "the regional identities that were formed . . . were . . . the product of a complex interaction between region and empire."[37] They referred, of course, to the Mughal empire. But I suggest that these regional, often quasi-ethnic identities (and their mythic resources and idioms), continued to evolve in the nineteenth and twentieth centuries in no less complex interactions with the British empire.

I also borrow Timothy Mitchell's concept of the "state effect".[38] Mitchell argues that the state exists not only in a material sense, as a set of institutions, but also as an idea. Put simply, people "imagine" the state in ways that are often more coherent than the state as it is materially practised. This "coherence" in the popular imagination of what the state was – "the state effect" – I suggest, was at play in princely states too, even if it was the product of different processes. Thomas Blom Hansen has developed Mitchell's concept by distinguishing between the "sublime" and "profane"

[36] Abdul Wahid Khan to Rani Sahiba, Kalsia State, 25 October 1947, NAI, MoS/PR Branch, 2(51)-PR/47.

[37] Alam and Subrahmanyam, eds, "Introduction", in *The Mughal State*, p. 68.

[38] Mitchell, "The Limits of the State", pp. 77-96.

dimensions of the "state effect", showing how, when "a public order upset by riots" in Bombay exposed the state's everyday corruption and its "profane" qualities, the Srikrishna Commission, which drew upon "the rhetoric of the state as a moral entity",[39] restored some sense of its existence as a sublime, ethical whole. For reasons that have partly to do with the sublime "state effect" nurtured quite deliberately in these kingdoms, I suggest, would-be subjects *believed* that nawabs, rajas, and ranis could and would protect them more effectively than the Indian army, in whom as Pataudi wrote, they had lost "all confidence",[40] despite the fact that most princely states had no armies whatsoever.[41]

Migrants to the states thus had powerful expectations of justice – *ad'l* – a central tenet of kingship, which, as Richard Eaton has argued, had taken powerful root throughout the subcontinent by the eighteenth century.[42] They voiced these expectations forcefully in innumerable petitions which asked for relief, compensation, and even full-scale rehabilitation.

Were these hopes fuelled by their awareness of contemporaneous practices of "modern" kingship? It seems very likely. Recent scholarship suggests that despite British attempts to bend the principalities to their purposes, and to rule them firmly (if indirectly), rajas and nawabs found ways of resisting British intrusion in many areas of courtly life, religious affairs, and secular patronage, adapting or "inventing" new institutions, traditions, and duties of kingship – *rajdharma* – by which they entrenched a sort of "monarchical modernity" or established new forms of "minor sovereignty" over their subjects.[43] Indeed, many of them sought to project their influence beyond the boundaries of their

39 Hansen, "Governance and Myths of State in Mumbai", pp. 51–2.

40 Nawab of Pataudi to Major General Rajkumar Rajindersinghji, 5 September 1947, NAI, MoS/F.2(13)-P.R./47.

41 Chamber of Princes Questionnaire 1928, *passim*.

42 Eaton, "Theorizing Historical Space in Pre-colonial India".

43 Beverley, *Hyderabad, British India and the World*.

kingdoms. As the Indian government admitted in its White Paper of 1950, "In almost all the States, owing to the smallness of the size and the compact nature of the territory, the existence of autocratic government had made for *easy co-ordination and quick solution* of such problems as attracted the Ruler's attention and interest."[44] This speedy dispensation of justice by the durbars compared favourably with the lumbering, opaque, and expensive courts of British India where justice was, if not denied, endlessly delayed. While most states did not have laws recorded in codes accessible to the people (often simply borrowing the laws of British India *mutatis mutandis* and applying them where needed), they administered justice decisively and above all swiftly. If in most cases "the decree of the Ruler was law, in a number of cases the Ruler not only constituted the source of justice but also personally administered it in actual practice."[45] The postmaster of Okara's appeal to the ranisaheba for justice is intelligible when viewed through this lens.

Another crucial development was the hugely expanded worship of tutelary deities in princely states over more than a century, and the patronage of religious festivals, notably Dasara and Muharram, in the performance of which the kings and courts played a central part, and which, as Pamela Price has noted, enabled these kingdoms to be perceived as a "*divinely protected area[s]*".[46] The proper, and ever more public, performance of these festivals by the nawab, raosaheb, or ranisaheba was intended to reassure subjects that the kingdom would be protected by the divine grace of god or the regional tutelary deity. In Mysore, for instance, Dasara – during which the tutelary deity Chamundeshwari slays the demon Mahisasura – grew increasingly elaborate as the nineteenth century drew to a close. As the Resident observed in 1889,

[44] White Paper (1950), p. 102. Emphasis added.

[45] Ibid., p. 116.

[46] Price, *Kingship and Political Practice in Colonial India*, p. 138.

"The Maharaja sits as a God to be worshipped by the people . . . he assumes a sacred character, and if not God himself, is held to represent for a time a kingly divinity . . . In this capacity he . . . presents himself to the homage, if not the adoration, of the people."[47] The numbers who came to Mysore city to view this spectacle and take part in the Dasara festival rose sharply in the early twentieth century. By 1941 the festival is said to have drawn 150,000 visitors to a town whose regular population had been recorded in 1931 as only 107,000.[48]

In addition, princes patronised artists and artisans, they maintained mosques and madrassas and endowed temples – and not merely within their own kingdoms. Princely prestation supported the bathing ghats at Benaras, the Golden Temple at Amritsar, and the holy places in Mecca and Medina.[49] Other beneficiaries of what

Fig. 12.2: The Dasara Festival
Source: Archives of the Centre of South Asian Studies, University of Cambridge. Used with permission.

[47] St John, "Note on Dusserah Durbar at Mysore 1889", cited in Ikegame, *Princely India Re-Imagined*, p. 153.

[48] Ikegame, *Princely India Re-Imagined*, p. 158.

[49] Ramusack, *The Princes of India*, p. 141.

Pamela Price has called "dharmic largesse" included the Shiromani Gurdwara Prabandhak Committee, Aligarh College, Benares Hindu University, the Deccan Educational Society, and Khalsa College, to name a few well-known "national" institutions.[50] By the mid-1920s, several princes had become adept at projecting their influence and reputation well beyond the boundaries of their states.[51]

The notion that kings were personally courageous was another message routinely disseminated by princes while making their presence felt within their states – usually done by "touring", in conjunction with hunting excursions or shikar – which offered opportunities to display royal skills,[52] and conspicuous devotion to their subjects. In one of several such stories that litter accounts of shikar, Mordaunt Pemberton describes going, in January 1933, on a hunt with "H.H." of Jhalawar, a tiny principality not far from Indore: "Soon after breakfast a shikar officer arrived from the jungle, where he had been tracking the pugmarks of the big panther, with a badly bitten arm. The animal had attacked him from behind . . . We went to the [nearest] dispensary *where H.H. personally began to tend to him . . .*"[53] Shikar is usually seen through the prism of craven collaboration with "hunting-shooting" white residents, but, as Julie Hughes shows, these were also occasions which allowed monarchs to display ethical attitudes to the land and the environment, and indeed towards their subjects.[54] Here again, if we read between the lines, we can see how princes adapted older traditions, norms, and the symbolism of shikar to the new setting of empire and evolving conceptions of monarchical modernity.

50 Price, *Kingship and Political Practice in Colonial India, passim.*

51 Ramusack, *The Princes of India*, p. 141.

52 Ibid., p. 134.

53 M. Pemberton Papers, Box 1, diary entry, Tuesday, 17 January 1933, Centre of South Asian Studies, Cambridge.

54 Hughes, "Royal Tigers and Ruling Princes".

Fig. 12.3: Princes Setting Off for Shikar.
Source: Archives of Centre of South Asian Studies, University of Cambridge. Used with permission.

The role of the "colonial-modern" king as benevolent patron of the poor, the needy, and the distressed is another pertinent aspect of this reconstitution of modern kingship. By the time of his death in 1868, Krishnaraja Wodeyar III of Mysore had racked up huge debts. When these were investigated, it turned out that the "bad habit" which had put him into the clutches of the moneylenders was distributing rice to the poor, his largest single creditor being a grain supplier in Mysore city, one Naga Shetty.[55] Kingly beneficence, as Dirks has shown, had been central to the conceptions of sovereignty of the Vijayanagara kings, their duties being to protect dharma and preside over a prosperous realm "where the people, unafflicted by calamities, were continually enjoying festivals."[56] Modern monarchs, it seems, adapted these notions of beneficence to late-colonial circumstances. Relief in

[55] Ikegame, *Princely India Re-Imagined*, p. 24.
[56] Dirks, *The Hollow Crown*, p. 37.

times of ecological crisis and famine was a central arena of princely activity, and as famine grew more frequent and more deadly in the nineteenth and twentieth centuries, princes engaged more and more prominently in famine relief in ways that differed markedly from those of their British neighbours and overlords. Among the largest monuments to the princes' engagement with famine relief is the Awadh nawab's Great Imambara complex in Lucknow, completed as early as 1791, which is believed to have cost a million rupees.[57] Another is (the arguably less beautiful Beaux-Art or "Indo-Deco" style) Umaid Bhavan palace in Jodhpur, built between 1929 and 1944 to provide work to the famished poor. Indore's royal family created the Gangajali Fund "for use in grave emergency such as famine".[58] Hyderabad's famine relief works are particularly well known, signalling as they did the distinctive political ethics of a patrimonial state in stark contrast to its British colonial counterpart. As Bhangya Bhukya and Eric Beverley tell us, an important preoccupation of the nizam's government was giving relief to the Indian victims of the late nineteenth century's "Victorian holocausts".[59] In British India, famine relief was given on the cheap in return for hard labour. Asaf Jah Hyderabad instead wrote off land revenue demands and other taxes and debts. Recognising that, by definition, victims weakened by famine were unable to work on heavy jobs such as road building, the nizam's government offered paid work for lighter tasks such as the repair of tanks and irrigation channels. As well as the free provision of victuals to those unable to work, the state of Hyderabad provided food to those who were unable to migrate to relief sites, and even offered land for grazing and cultivation to new migrants.[60] Indeed, so extensive and successful were the Asaf Jah state's famine relief policies that people began to migrate to Hyderabad in the late

[57] Cole, *Roots of North Indian Shi'ism in Iran and Iraq*, p. 95.

[58] White Paper on Indian States (1950), p. 66.

[59] Bhukya, "Between Tradition and Modernity".

[60] Beverley, *Hyderabad*, p. 175.

nineteenth century to take advantage of them.[61] And crucially, the nizam's relief policy – about which his government was never slow to boast – was that it was given on exactly the same terms to immigrants from British India as to his own subjects. Hyderabad's officials took great pains, moreover, to ensure that these charitable deeds received the widest publicity within the state as well as beyond. In volumes of photographs published between 1885 and 1902, the nizam commissioned the famous photographer Lala Deen Dayal to document his "Good Works". This backcloth helps explain why refugees might have expected both protection and succour in princely states in 1947.

There is a further point to consider. As Bérénice Guyot- Réchard has recently shown, "borderlanders" living in the vicinity of rival sovereignties after decolonisation "were comparing what each one brought them, in both positive and negative terms."[62] Her work speaks of the anxiety-fuelled encounter between Independent India and the People's Republic of China along their eastern Himalayan border, and the migration of people between these two competing states, but her analysis has a relevance to the situation in the entire subcontinent in 1947, where huge *internal* border zones connected princely states and republican dominions, as well as their subjects. When, as Ishan Mukherjee has noted, both the sacred and profane dimensions of "state effect" in India collapsed in 1947 in the face of riots, mass migration, looting, and disorder,[63] it is not impossible to understand why so many inhabitants of these internal borderlands chose the protection of princely states that seemed – at the time – both more stable, more "sublime", and more likely to offer protection and justice than two dominions which had yet to prove their capacity to govern.

Numerous kings and queens seized on the opportunity and

[61] Ibid., pp. 172–5.

[62] Guyot-Réchard, *Shadow States*, p. 25.

[63] Mukherjee, "Agitations, Riots and the Transitional State in Calcutta, 1945–50".

responded energetically to these expectations, albeit in the idioms of "modern" monarchical patronage. Hyderabad sheltered and fed huge numbers of those who migrated to the state, spending Rs 1,25,00,000 (1.25 crore) on "maintaining camps, providing houses, and settling them on lands."[64] A full year after Partition, at the time of India's "police action", Hyderabad's relief camps were still looking after refugees long after India had shut down most of its own camps. Hamidullah of Bhopal also refused to turn the refugees away, despite intense pressure from the Government of India to do so, and long after the state's ability to absorb and feed these extra mouths had been overwhelmed by the size of the refugee influx.[65] The nawab, interestingly, also refused to put his tiny military force at India's disposal "to compel these refugees to get into the trains" headed back to India. He gave Patel his reasons, in words that are deeply revealing: "[it is] extremely difficult . . . [for a Ruler] to exturn [*sic*] people who have entered its territories in great distress and in a condition of physical exhaustion, and who are seeking refuge and protection in parts of the country where they feel they might receive sympathy and kindness." Bhopal also stressed how badly his own subjects would react if he acted otherwise: "Any force used against such persons is likely to excite the local populations who might with justification blame their Government for ruthless and non-humanitarian policies."[66]

Concerns about how refugee flows – both inwards and outwards – would affect their kingdoms also preoccupied the rulers of princely states. The Nawab of Bahawalpur was desperately upset that his "loyal Hindu subjects" had been "encouraged" (by Penderel Moon) to emigrate to India while he was away in

[64] "Note on the Refugee Problem of Hyderabad", NAI, MoS/10(27)/H-49, 1949.

[65] H.H. Hamidullah of Bhopal to Vallabhbhai Patel, 24 September 1947, NAI, MoS/F.16-G(R)/47 (Secret).

[66] H.H. Hamidullah of Bhopal to Vallabhbhai Patel, 24 September 1947, NAI, MoS/F.16-G(R)/47 (Secret).

Europe on his annual tour, and looked askance at many of the Muslim refugees who had arrived in their stead.[67] Significantly, the nawab expressed the wish that *only refugees from Indian princely states* should be received and settled in Bahawalpur, since these people, "being accustomed to personal rule, would more readily accommodate themselves to (local) conditions and develop a loyalty to the Ruler."[68] He was not alone in attempting to bolster, and indeed refashion, a princely order deemed suitable for postcolonial times by recruiting, after the British departure, loyal new subjects of the "right type". Dholpur, a Hindu maharaja, for his part sought to strengthen his position by absorbing those Muslim refugees who could not be accommodated in Bhopal, thereby bolstering his reputation as a *dharmic* ruler who cared for *all* his subjects, Hindu and Muslim alike, and tended the needy.[69] Hyderabad also sought to attract Muslim artisans, notably weavers. The Rajputana, Punjab, and western Indian states were particularly keen to invite Hindu refugee merchants from Sindh to make their states their chosen destination. Gwalior offered to accept 400–500 refugee families, but only on the condition that they were "well-to-do".[70] And perhaps most bold of all these princely manoeuvres was that of Bharatpur, who – having driven out Meo Muslims in large numbers – began to invite members of the Jat community from Rohtak and surrounding areas to settle in Bharatpur, offering them key positions in the state. "The Bharatpur government", a States Department official alleged, was "dreaming of a Jatistan".[71]

[67] Moon, *Divide and Quit*, p. 228.

[68] Ibid., p. 229.

[69] Central Intelligence Officer's Report, 27 October 1947, NAI, MoS/2 (42)-PR/47.

[70] Uttara Shahani, personal communication. I am deeply grateful to Uttara for her practical help with this project, for being a critical interlocutor and a guide to elusive sources.

[71] Superintendent, Eastern Rajputana States Agency to Ministry of States, 2 December 1947, NAI, MoS/2 (30)-P.R./47.

III

By now it might well be asked: what does this have to do with Gandhi, a tragic, Lear-like figure in the last days of his life?

A certain amount, as it turns out. The sources on this period reveal fascinating hints that, for Gandhi, the princely states had a key role to play after Independence, both in the protection of minorities and the rehabilitation of refugees.

Two particularly poignant stories, which relate to the last weeks of the Mahatma's life, will make the point. The first has to do with Hindus who remained in Bahawalpur state after Partition, but where in late November and December fierce attacks on Hindu villages drove thousands out of the state into India. By December 1947 a call for the mass evacuation of all Hindus from Bahawalpur to India was becoming louder, and Penderel Moon argued that this would be for the best, since the state's tiny (and, according to Moon, unruly) army and police force could not guarantee their safety. But Gandhi intervened, urging Bahawalpur's Hindus to stay put. He had spoken with the nawab, Gandhi told them, and had received "the word of the Ruler that . . . the remaining Hindus could live in peace and safety, and [that] no one would interfere with their religion."[72] When pressure for evacuation continued to mount, Gandhi agreed to send a personal emissary to Bahawalpur. So, in the third week of January 1948, Sushila Nayyar arrived in the state bearing a message from the Mahatma to the state's Hindus, urging them to stay on and rely on the nawab's reassurances. After touring the state herself, Nayyar concluded that Gandhi's position was delusional: too much blood had been spilled, too many Hindus had left, and too many Hindu homes had already been occupied by incoming refugees, or locals, for the Mahatma's message to have any chance of succeeding. By the time she returned to Delhi a week later, however, the Mahatma was dead. Until his last, then, Gandhi continued to have faith

[72] Moon, *Divide and Quit*, p. 243.

not only the capacity but the will of a Muslim ruler of a princely state in Pakistan to protect his Hindu subjects.

The second vignette speaks volumes about Gandhi's concern, by late September 1947, about the rehabilitation of Sindhis. To begin with, his particular preoccupation was the condition of "Harijans" (Dalits) who had remained behind in Sindh in Pakistan, and whom the government of Sindh was reluctant to give permission to leave. Gandhi believed that they were in great distress and wrote letters urging the owners of Sindhi shipping firms to evacuate them to ports in Kathiawad.[73] This broadened into a wider engagement, on Gandhi's part, with the question of where Sindhi refugees should be settled. The Mahatma concluded that his home region of princely Kathiawad would be the best place of refuge for them. To achieve this, he set about persuading the Maharao of Kutch to donate land for the creation of a large Sindhi Hindu settlement. Within no time, he succeeded. The Maharao agreed to donate 15,000 acres of land abutting the (then small) port at Kandla. The grant was gazetted on 29 January 1948. On the morning of 30 January, just hours before he was assassinated, Gandhi received a telegram from the Dewan of Kutch informing him of the Maharao's grant.[74] The township established on the site is named Gandhidham in his memory.

Here again we see evidence of Gandhi's belief that princes, whether as patrons of refugees or as protectors of minorities, had a part to play in the postcolonial future of South Asia.

In this matter, as in other matters of the moment, Gandhi was sharply at odds with his coadjutors in the Congress leadership, not least Nehru, whose view of the states was deeply unsympathetic, and who was clear that the rehabilitation of refugees was the job not of the princes but of the government of India's new republic.

[73] Gandhi to Shantikumar N. Morarjee, 25 September 1947 (from *Gujarati*, vol. 89, p. 235); Motilal Jotwani, ed., *Gandhiji on Sindh and the Sindhis*, Delhi: Sindhi Academy, ND (courtesy Uttara Shahani).

[74] Gandhidham, *Bombay: The Sindhu Resettlement Corporation*, 1952. I thank Uttara Shahani for generously sharing this document with me.

Fig. 12.4: Gandhidham Samadhi[75]
Source: Photograph by Uttara Shahani.
Used with permission.

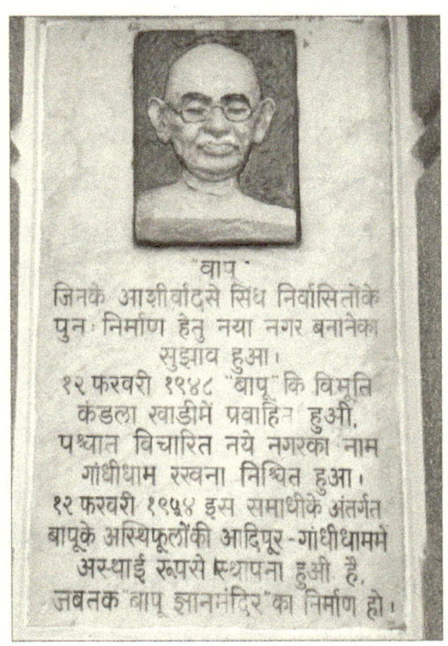

Fig. 12.5: Detail of Gandhidham Samadhi
Source: Photograph by Uttara Shahani.
Used with permission.

[75] The translation of the commemorative text reads, "Bapu, by whose blessing it was swiftly resolved to construct a new township for the denizens of Sindh. On 12 February 1949, Bapu's ashes/blessings were immersed in Kandla, and so it was resolved to call the new township Gandhidham . . ."

Let me underline that these interventions by the Mahatma came *after* Gandhi's much-better-known support of satyagrahas against many aspects of princely rule in the late 1930s and 1940s. I am not suggesting some false revision by which Gandhi is metamorphosed into an uncritical admirer of India's princes. My hypothesis – and it is no more than that – is that the Mahatma had a different and more nuanced understanding of what Janaki Nair describes as "monarchical modernity",[76] and with princely experiments with a different "truth".

Gandhi himself was, of course, a princely subject born and bred. His knowledge of parts of princely India, or "Indian India" as it was often described in the late nineteenth century, was foundational and intimate. He had been raised in Kathiawad, a region dotted with small states in one of which his father was the dewan (or chief minister) of the ruler. He spent most of his later life in western India, a vast internal borderland region in which princely states were more numerous and prominent than in any other part of India. These polities were thus in no sense exotic or unfamiliar to him. At the start of his political career in South Africa, Gandhi's work (as that of so many nationalists and social reformers) had been funded by leading Indian princes: Bikaner, Mysore, and Hyderabad.[77] In his first recorded thoughts on princes, he writes of being moved by their plight, dressed up like *khansamas* (or head waiters) at Lord Curzon's durbar.[78] Seeing them attired "like women" in silk *achkans*, pearl necklaces, and bracelets revealed to him the depth of their "slavery" and emasculation.[79] Arguably, then, for Gandhi, the rajas and nawabs were *Indians*. He was influenced by their own self-image as being oppressed – albeit in very particular ways – by British power. This was a viewpoint that many

[76] Nair, *Mysore Modern*.

[77] Brown, *Gandhi: Prisoner of Hope*, p. 54.

[78] Gandhi, *The Indian States' Problem*. Also see Gandhi, *Autobiography*, vol. I, pt III, ch. 16, *passim*.

[79] Gandhi, *The Indian States' Problem*, p. 4.

began to articulate more openly after Lord Reading's viceroyalty, and it lay behind the princes' move to join the proposed Indian federation, which eventually failed, in 1935.

In 1925, addressing the Kathiawad Political Conference, Gandhi put forward his first serious and detailed thesis on kingship. In it, he argued that trusteeship was the ethical basis of kingship: "If the institution of kingship has a moral basis, Princes are not independent proprietors but only trustees of their subjects for revenue received from them. It can therefore be spent for them only as trust money . . . [as in] the English Constitution."

This resembled, of course, Gandhi's much better known and much criticised thesis on the responsibilities of the ideal capitalist, and the correct relationship between captains of industry and workers. As with the mill-owning capitalists, he urged restraint on the princes, asking them to "observe our ancient tradition that revenue is intended only for popular welfare", and to abolish the practice (ancient or otherwise) of extracting cesses from their subjects. "*My ideal of Indian states is Ram Rajya*", the Mahatma declared – a condition he believed the princes could achieve and that should be their goal.[80] In an interesting twist, Gandhi also referred to "ideal caliphs" such as Abubakar and Hazrat Umar – who would "know public opinion by intuition".[81] Intriguingly, as late as 1936, Gandhi described Mysore under Wodeyar rule as "Ramrajya".[82]

I offer these preliminary thoughts on Gandhi, princes, and subjecthood to provoke discussion. Scholarship on a few individual states has, in the twenty-first century, begun to recognise how some princes had engaged, in distinctive ways, with modernity, and elaborated new practices and discourses of legitimacy within the framework of indirect rule. Perhaps the time has also come

[80] *Young India*, 8 January 1925.

[81] Ibid.

[82] *The Hindu*, 1 January 1936. Also cited in Ikegame, *Princely India Re-Imagined.*

to re-frame our understanding of Gandhi to take on board the influence of "monarchical modernity" on his ethical politics. Perhaps Ramrajya was more than just a metaphor for Gandhi. Certainly, until his last breath, he believed the well-run princely state to be viable, legitimate, and to have a postcolonial future. For him, the flight of refugees to these kingdoms after Partition made perfect sense. For his colleagues in the Congress, by contrast, these movements were completely unintelligible. The governments of both India and Pakistan regarded these migrations as profoundly dangerous. In its Whiggish course, history was not on Gandhi's side; nor was it on the side of refugees in search of subjecthood.

These aspirations – whether princely, popular, or Gandhian – failed. But "success" is not, and should not be, the only subject of history (if that were our yardstick, there would be little material outside the chronicles of the victors for historians to study). These events represent a brief moment when alternative outcomes were imagined and deemed possible; and they challenge – and make briefly strange – the teleological histories of the nation with which we are so familiar. They call to mind Frederick Cooper's account of the end of empire in Africa,[83] a story rich and strange, with many possible endings, not all of them resulting in the nation-state. Just as the inhabitants of West Africa, so also the people of the subcontinent dreamt different dreams in 1947. For a great many more than we have previously realised, the survival and flourishing of princely sovereignty seemed a distinct and meaningful possibility.

In the period between 1947 and 1956, the princely states emerged as potentially powerful regional polities with distinct and embedded alternative claims to legitimacy. Some challenged and even threatened the very premises of the nation-state, and this was not restricted to Hyderabad. "Language movements" admittedly

[83] Cooper, *Colonialism in Question.*

also began to articulate regional identities in other ways. But I suggest that the ideas of the linguistic region and of ethical kingship were not separate but were powerfully conjoined by late-colonial monarchical practice and popular perception. This is why they came to be seen as such an immediate threat to India's survival as a nation-state.

After Partition, the mass migration of refugees to these princely states, and their emergence as a potential focus of alternative notions of sovereignty, legitimacy, and belonging, helps to explain why national governments in India were uncompromisingly insistent on dismantling them so rapidly and so ruthlessly between 1948 and 1950. This account makes it easier to understand why the instruments of accession the princes signed (which in any event made few concessions to them) were rapidly torn up by the Government of India, why the states were swiftly bundled into larger provinces, and why the Indian constitution of 1950 is shot through with tense republicanism, in no mood to make concessions to India's monarchical past. Another conundrum – the sudden ubiquity of language movements and regionalisms arising apparently out of nowhere in 1947 – also begins to make sense when viewed from this perspective, and offers us another entry point into the story of States Reorganisation in 1956.

There are many possible ways, then, in which the actions of these frightened refugees who fled to states ruled by princes and ranis who received them with regal beneficence might help us to rethink the early history of the new nation. The Mahatma's last-minute interventions in these affairs, likewise, shed new and unfamiliar light on his vision of its future.

References

Alam, Muzaffar, and Sanjay Subrahmanyam, eds, Introduction, in *The Mughal State, 1526–1750*, New Delhi: Oxford India Publications, 1998.

Bennett, Richard R., "The Greening of Bahawalpur", *Indo-British Review*, vol. 15, 1988.

Beverley, Eric Lewis, *Hyderabad, British India and the World: Muslim Networks and Minor Sovereignty, c. 1850–1950*, Cambridge: Cambridge University Press, 2015.

Bhukya, Bhangya, "Between Tradition and Modernity: Nizams, Colonialism and Modernity in Hyderabad State", *Economic and Political Weekly*, vol. XLVIII(48), November 2013.

Bigelow, Anna, *Sharing the Sacred: Practicing Pluralism in Muslim North India*, Oxford: Oxford University Press, 2010.

Brown, Judith M., *Gandhi: Prisoner of Hope*, Delhi: Oxford University Press, 1990.

Cohn, Bernard S., "Political Systems in Eighteenth Century India: The Benares Region", *Journal of the American Oriental Society*, 1962.

Cole, J.R.I., *Roots of North Indian Shi'ism in Iran and Iraq: Religion and State in Awadh, 1722–1859*, Berkeley: University of California Press, 1988.

Cooper, Frederick, *Colonialism in Question: Theory, Knowledge, History*, Berkeley: University of California Press, 2005.

Copland, Ian, "The Further Shores of Partition: Ethnic Cleansing in Rajasthan", *Past & Present* (160), August 1998.

Dirks, Nicholas, *The Hollow Crown: Ethnohistory of an Indian Kingdom*, Cambridge: Cambridge University Press, 1987.

Eaton, Richard, "Theorizing Historical Space in Pre-colonial India: Sovereignty, Religion, Literary Networks", Birkbeck Lecture presented at Trinity College, Cambridge, October 2015.

Gandhi, M.K., *Autobiography*, vol. I, pt III, translated from the original in Gujarati by Pyarelal and Mahadev Desai, Ahmedabad: Navajivan Trust, 1958 edn (first published 1927).

———, *The Indian States' Problem*, Ahmedabad: Navajivan Trust, 1941.

Gordon, Stewart, *The Marathas 1600–1818: The New Cambridge History of India, II.4*, Cambridge: Cambridge University Press, 1993.

Government of India, *White Paper on Hyderabad*, Delhi: Manager of Publications, 1948.

Guyot-Réchard, Bérénice, *Shadow States: India, China and the Himalayas, 1910–1962*, Cambridge: Cambridge University Press, 2017.

Hansen, Thomas Blom, "Governance and Myths of State in Mumbai", in C.J. Fuller and Veronique Benei, eds, *The Everyday State in Modern India*, London: Hurst, 2001.

Hughes, Julie E., "Royal Tigers and Ruling Princes: Wilderness and Wildlife Management in the Indian Princely States", *Modern Asian Studies*, vol. 49, pt 4, July 2015.

Ikegame, Aya, *Princely India Re-Imagined: A Historical Anthropology of Mysore from 1799 to the Present*, Abingdon: Routledge, 2013.

Jotwani, Motilal, ed., *Gandhiji on Sindh and the Sindhis*, Delhi: Sindhi Academy, ND (courtesy Uttara Shahani).

Malcolm, Sir John, *A Memoir of Central India Including Malwa and Adjoining Provinces*, 2 vols, 1823.

Mansergh, Nicholas, E.W.R. Lumby and Penderel Moon, eds, *Transfer of Power*, vol. 12, London: HMSO, 1982.

Mayaram, Shail, *Resisting Regimes: Myth, Memory and the Shaping of a Muslim Identity*, Delhi: Oxford University Press India, 1997.

Menon, V.P., *Integration of the Indian States*, Mumbai: Orient Longman, 1956; rpntd 1999.

Mitchell, Timothy, "The Limits of the State: Beyond Statist Approaches and Their Critics", *American Political Science Review*, vol. 85(1), March 1991.

Moon, Penderel, *Divide and Quit: An Eyewitness Account of the Partition of India*, New Delhi: Oxford India Paperbacks, 1998.

Mukherjee, Ishan, "Agitations, Riots and the Transitional State in Calcutta, 1945–50", Unpublished PhD dissertation, University of Cambridge, 2017.

Nair, Janaki, *Mysore Modern: Rethinking the Region Under Princely Rule*, Minneapolis and London: University of Minnesota Press, 2011.

Price, Pamela, *Kingship and Political Practice in Colonial India*, Cambridge: Cambridge University Press.

Ramusack, Barbara, *The Indian Princes and Their States: The New Cambridge History of India III.6*, Cambridge: Cambridge University Press, 2004.

Sherman, Taylor C., *Muslim Belonging in Secular India: Negotiating Citizenship in Postcolonial Hyderabad*, Cambridge: Cambridge University Press, 2015.

St John, Oliver (Resident), "Note on Dusserah Durbar at Mysore 1889", in Aya Ikegame, *Princely India Re-Imagined: A Historical Anthropology of Mysore from 1799 to the Present*, Abingdon: Routledge, 2013.

Thakur, U.T., *Sindhi Culture*, Delhi: Sindhi Academy, 1959.

White Paper on Indian Sates (1950), *Government of India Ministry of States*, New Delhi: Manager of Publications, 1950.

13

South Asian Histories of Citizenship 1946–1970

Scholars have tended to locate the origins of modern notions of citizenship at the conjuncture of political, intellectual, and legal currents in early-modern Europe,[1] looking at citizenship beyond the European world from a rather modular and diffusionist perspective. Just as colonies were once thought to have all adopted one or other of the European models of nationalism described by Benedict Anderson, so notions of citizenship are believed to have borrowed or adapted one of a small stock of European-authored "ideal types". For more than sixty years, political science has been dominated by Hans Kohn's typology, which contrasts "ethnic" and "civic" models of nationhood,[2] the latter sub-divided into "liberal" and "republican", where influences of British subjecthood and French Jacobinism respectively hold

I am grateful to Sunil Amrith, David Feldman, John Lonsdale, Fiona McConnell, and David Washbrook for their detailed comments on an earlier version of this article; to Tim Harper for kindly organising a workshop to discuss its main themes; to Jasdeep Brar for summarising the rich case law on the permit system; to the Newton Trust which provided a small grant for that purpose; to Newal Osman who procured rare published sources from Karachi and Islamabad; and to the Arts and Humanities Research Council (UK), which funded the early stages of this research.

[1] See, for instance, Kim, *Aliens in Medieval Law.*

[2] Kohn, *The Idea of Nationalism*, *passim.*

sway.[3] The new nation-states which emerged in the twentieth century are all assumed to have based their own citizenship laws on one or other of these models, often drawing upon the traditions of their imperial rulers. In a new account of Indian citizenship, Ornit Shani argues that independent India drew, at different times and in different combinations, on all these components of the European tradition, but her revisions share certain diffusionist assumptions.[4]

When non-Western citizenship has been a subject of research, much of that (mainly anthropological) work has focused, as Niraja Jayal notes, on the distance between *de jure* and *de facto* citizenship.[5] Scholars have tended to take formal membership for granted, assuming that newly sovereign nation-states bestowed this automatically on all persons who inhabited their territories. Seeing the problem to be the failure of non-Western states properly to uphold their citizenship laws, they have concentrated on struggles by formal members to achieve substantive or "thick" citizenship, understood as "the substantive distribution of the rights . . . to those deemed citizens".[6] Yet, the question of whether full formal citizenship was actually extended to all members of these states, and how it was created, qualified, or denied in specific historic locations and circumstances, has not sufficiently been investigated.

In the scholarship on South Asian citizenship, two further themes are apparent. One is a persistent assumption that India and Pakistan adopted contrasting citizenship models, the former civic or liberal, the latter ethnoreligious. Indeed, many academics regard the apparently "great divergence" in their respective trajectories as a linear consequence of these different choices. Another powerful strand sees citizenship as a wholly alien concept, foisted from above

[3] Walzer, "Citizenship".

[4] Shani, "Conceptions of Citizenship", pp. 145–73.

[5] Jayal, "Genealogies of Rights".

[6] Holsten, *Insurgent Citizenship*, p. 7.

upon an unsuspecting populace by the small elite minority that constituted civil society, with little purchase beyond it.[7]

This article challenges, or qualifies, these assumptions. It suggests that distinctive forms of legal citizenship were pioneered in the subcontinent during the upheavals that followed Independence and Partition. Lawmakers and leaders were not the sole architects of these regimes, although they played a part in the story. South Asian citizenship was produced, on the contrary, as a result of complex interactions between a bewildering plethora of actors: above all, by the actions of millions of people who became stranded minorities as a consequence of Partition and Independence, and whose decisions to flee, stay on, or return to their homes were posited on notions of where they belonged and where they were entitled to protection. This article will argue that these actions – small but decisive acts of agency by countless ordinary people firmly convinced of the justice of their claims – posed new questions of the states whose protection they sought, and elicited novel answers from them.

This article will thus challenge the post-colonial view, recently forwarded by Vazira Zamindar, that the states of South Asia imposed citizenship from above upon the people of the subcontinent, forcing their fluid and multiple affiliations into neat national boxes, producing "with some force, bounded citizens of two nation-states".[8] Instead, it argues that the process was complex, messy, and often ugly, and that refugees were active agents in it. They exerted considerable pressure on the functionaries charged with dealing with them, who were in their turn members of a bitterly divided society, and whose actions were shaped by their own norms and beliefs. In consequence, these men – local constables, non-commissioned soldiers, and spies, as well as railway guards and ship's captains who handled the flow of migrants – often took steps that had

[7] Chatterjee, *Politics of the Governed.*

[8] Zamindar, *The Long Partition*, p. 7 and *passim.*

no sanction from above, and that did not accord with any tenet of the official law.[9] As Taylor Sherman has shown in her study of Afghans in Hyderabad after the 1948 "police action", these officials made their own assumptions about citizenship and belonging,[10] which in turn informed the ad hoc measures they devised to manage migrants and rehabilitate refugees. But while the Afghans in Sherman's story ducked, weaved, and evaded officialdom when policy contradicted their own sense of what was best for them – understandably since their place in India was at best precarious – the refugees discussed below robustly, even violently, resisted government. Hence, officials had to backpedal, to improvise and revise strategies to deal with rapidly changing realities on the ground.

This article will argue that the citizenship regimes which emerged out of these complex interactions were not only different from the leaders' "original blueprints",[11] they were distinct, in critical ways, from models derived from the West. It will show too that the citizenship regimes of India and Pakistan shared remarkably significant (and hitherto unnoticed) symmetries. Both produced the new figure of "the minority citizen", neither citizen nor alien, but a hybrid subject of new national regimes of identification and law. This status, it will argue, is not simply a matter of the routine *de facto* deprivations of "inclusive" but "inegalitarian citizenship", in Holsten's cumbersome but useful phrase.[12] This was a *de jure* status of a new and particular kind. It will also suggest that practices of citizenship forged in the subcontinent travelled beyond the subcontinent through the South Asian diaspora, influencing norms and practices of citizenship in the wider world.

[9] Migdal, *State in Society*, p. 23.

[10] Sherman, "Migration, Citizenship and Belonging", pp. 81–107.

[11] Migdal, *State in Society*, p. 12.

[12] Holsten, *Insurgent Citizenship*, p. 7.

I

The processes by which South Asian citizenship was constructed can best be tracked by looking first at the "original blueprints" for citizenship devised by the leaders of the new nation-states. When the Constituent Assembly of India first met in December 1946, it had immediately to take a view on who India's citizens were to be. Who were "the people of India", in Nehru's uplifting prose, who were "giving themselves" a constitution? Until this defining moment, the leaders of the all-India Congress had been wont to invoke "the people of India" and even "the citizens of India", but had taken a very broad-brush approach to who was included in that category.[13] Now that question demanded careful consideration since, to paraphrase Benhabib,[14] self-determination requires self-constitution.

The Constituent Assembly acted swiftly. On 24 January 1947, it set up an advisory committee on minorities and fundamental rights to examine the question. Its chairman was Sardar Vallabhbhai Patel, strong man of the Congress Party, then home minister in the interim government. The very name of the committee reveals that when they began their deliberations, the lawmakers saw "minority rights" and "fundamental rights" as allied matters. Its minutes reveal that at this early stage its members were unanimous in regarding minority rights as *additional* "safeguards" that were to be enjoyed by certain communities, *over and above* the fundamental rights that all citizens would enjoy in equal measure.[15]

[13] The "Constitution of India Bill" of 1895 merely stated that all "those born in India" or naturalised therein would be Indian citizens. Rao, ed., *The Framing of India's Constitution*, I, p. 6. The Nehru Report of 1928 took a similar line. Ibid., p. 59.

[14] Benhabib, *The Rights of Others*.

[15] See the responses to the questionnaire "safeguards" sent on 28 February 1947 to the subcommittees on fundamental rights and minority rights. Rao, ed., *India's Constitution*, II, pp. 391–2. Also see Pant's speech on the subject

On 23 April 1947 the committee reported back to the Assembly with a formula for Indian citizenship which was both simple and elegant. "Clause 3" of its draft proposal suggested that "every person born in the Union or naturalised according to its laws and subject to the jurisdiction thereof shall be a citizen of the Union".[16] The committee had taken the principle in English law of *jus soli*, or birth within the realm, as the basis for citizenship of independent India.

There is much to suggest that in proposing this formula, the committee had been influenced by the legacy of British subjecthood and imperial citizenship,[17] quite as much as by the Congress Party's long-standing commitment to liberal constitutionalism.[18] Patel explained that the committee had deliberately eschewed the more "racial" or "ethnic" notions of citizenship of continental Europe; *jus soli* was, in its view, the most "democratic",[19] "enlightened", and "civilised"[20] model of citizenship to be found anywhere in the world.[21] Two world wars and the Holocaust also cast their long shadow over the constitution-makers in Delhi: Pandit Pant of the United Provinces reminded the Assembly that treaty arrangements by the Associated Powers had failed to protect minorities after the First World War.[22] It is no part of my argument, then, that in

---

in the Constituent Assembly on 24 January 1947. *Constituent Assembly of India: Debates* (hereafter *CAID*), II, p. 328.

[16] *CAID*, III, p. 417.

[17] Banerjee, *Becoming Imperial Citizens*; Tabili, *"We Ask for British Justice"*, *passim*.

[18] For the numerous iterations of this sentiment by Congress since 1985, see Rao, ed., *India's Constitution*, I. The Sapru Report (1945) also held firm to this notion of citizenship.

[19] See K.M. Munshi's speech in defence of Clause 3 on 29 April 1947. *CAID*, III, p. 424.

[20] See Patel's defence of Clause 3 made minutes later on the same day, ibid.

[21] Ibid., p. 526.

[22] See Pant's speech on 24 January 1947, *CAID*, II, p. 424.

tackling the issue of citizenship, South Asia's leaders were parochial and ignorant of global intellectual currents. On the contrary, when the Assembly's distinguished constitutional adviser, Sir B.N. Rau, drafted his preliminary notes in September 1946, he drew upon an impressive range of international precedents.[23] Well before Rau launched on his tour to study constitutions in other parts of the world,[24] India's leaders were alert to the wider global contexts and implications of their deliberations.

Those who opposed Clause 3 were also aware of these considerations, albeit from a different angle of vision. They were led by Dr Rajendra Prasad, a leading figure in the Congress high command, president of the Constituent Assembly, and soon to be president of the new republic. "Suppose," he bluntly enquired, "a Jap by birth is travelling through the country and while travelling a child is born to him. What happens?"[25] Others raised concerns about the position of children of Indian parents who had been born abroad. Would they be denied citizenship?[26] In their different ways, these questions derived from the notion that the claims of descent (*jus sanguinus*), of Indian ethnicity or blood, should determine citizenship. This "continental" conception of Indian citizenship had vociferous supporters in the Assembly, some of whom – like Prasad – were powerful figures. But Patel stood firm against them. He pointed out that it would be inconsistent for the Congress leadership to push for "narrow nationality" given that it had demanded full rights of citizenship for Indians born in South Africa. He rebuked Prasad for seeking to introduce "racial phraseology" into the constitution on account of "a few foreigners coming here".[27]

[23] "Note on fundamental rights by B.N. Rau, 2 September 1946", in Rao, ed., *India's Constitution*, II, pp. 21–55.

[24] Rau, *India's Constitution in the Making*, *passim*.

[25] *CAID*, III, p. 419.

[26] See R.V. Dhulekar's question on this subject. Ibid., p. 421.

[27] Ibid., p. 423.

Patel's remark shows, beyond a shadow of doubt, that at this point the Congress leaders had not entertained the possibility of admitting large and permanent migrant populations into India in the event of a partition that looked increasingly likely. By this stage, it had the imprimatur of the Congress high command. In March 1947 the Congress leadership had settled for a limited partition of India; and by the beginning of May, it had persuaded Mountbatten that partition on these terms was the only way out of the constitutional impasse. Even though it remained unclear which precise territories would be included in the Indian Union and which would go to Pakistan, some of the Assembly's members had begun to recognise the implications of a partition for the citizenship question. Despite Patel's brisk attempts to cut short further debate on the matter,[28] they refused to be silenced. Significantly, it was R.K. Sidhwa, a Parsi member from Sindh – a Muslim-majority province that would soon become part of Pakistan – who asked the critically important question: "I am born in Sindh. Supposing Sindh is not going to be part of the Union, what will be my position? Am I to lose my citizenship of the Union [of India]?"[29]

After this, no one could ignore the proverbial elephant in the room. Sidhwa's question brought into the open, for the first time, the thorny issue of what would happen to non-Muslims who would be "stranded", by virtue of their place of birth and domicile, in Pakistan. Were they entitled to Indian citizenship? If so, on what basis? Immediately it became apparent, as Pandey has also remarked, that many members of the Assembly strongly believed that these people were "obviously" Indians, and hence "patently" entitled to Indian citizenship.[30] In its turn, this notion ran a coach and horses through the tidy territorial definition of

[28] See his remark urging K. Santhanam to withdraw his proposed amendment to this new clause. Ibid.

[29] *CAID*, III, p. 527.

[30] See the remarks by B.R. Ambedkar and C. Rajagopalachariar on

citizenship and nationality that Patel and his supporters had striven to impose. It soon became apparent that the issue could not easily be resolved, and so discussion of the citizenship clause was postponed. In consequence, on 15 August 1947, when India achieved independence, the vital decision of who its citizens were to be had not yet been settled.

On the other side of the fence, discussions about citizenship in Pakistan only began after Attlee's announcement of 3 June 1947 that British India would be divided into two successor states. It followed that a separate Constituent Assembly for Pakistan had to be set up, and that Assembly first met on 10 August 1947, just five days before Partition and the transfer of power. Nevertheless, it immediately set to work to tackle the question of citizenship, and its deliberations are of great significance. Jinnah's historic speech of 11 August 1947, promising "equal rights, privileges and obligations" to all citizens, regardless of their religion, is well known.[31] Yet, its inwardness has not been understood: Indian historians, in particular, have tended to question Jinnah's sincerity of purpose. In fact, Jinnah had come to see the logic of a territorial definition of citizenship immediately after Attlee's announcement. On 9 June 1947, addressing the general assembly of the All-India Muslim League, he had urged Muslims who would be left in India after Partition to "stick to their respective homeland[s]", live as Indian citizens, and avoid the "temptation" to migrate.[32] He stuck to this position in the face of vigorous opposition from many members of the Pakistan Assembly who wanted the new nation's constitution to be based on Islamic foundations.[33] Jinnah

2 May 1947. *CAID*, III, p. 527; and Pandey, "Can a Muslim be an Indian?", pp. 608–29.

[31] *Constituent Assembly of Pakistan: Debates* (hereafter *CADP*), I, no. 2, pp. 16–20.

[32] Jinnah's speech, "Those Who Gave Great Sacrifices", 9 June 1947, cited in Naqvi, "The Politics of Commensuration", p. 56.

[33] *CADP*, I, no. 2, p. 16.

underlined his seriousness of intent by setting up, and chairing, a committee on fundamental rights of citizens and minorities. Just as in India, Pakistan's lawmakers saw these two subjects as being intertwined; and just as in India, they regarded minority rights as additional protections that were to be enjoyed by certain minorities, over and above the fundamental rights enjoyed by all citizens.

It is not surprising that historians have struggled to make sense of Jinnah's apparent "U-turn" on this vital question. They agree that Jinnah's conception of Pakistan (and indeed that of many of his followers) was imprecise and de-territorialized, and that until he was forced to accept the "moth-eaten" Pakistan that Partition gave him, his pronouncements on Pakistan had been deliberately vague. Jinnah's declaration in the Assembly reveals, however, that as soon as it became clear that Pakistan was to be a sovereign, territorial, nation-state, he concluded that its citizenship had to be defined on a territorial basis.

So, contrary to the legend of their inherently different personalities, based in turn upon their distinctive nationalisms, both India and Pakistan started out with *jus soli* as the basis of citizenship. Both appear to have done so in response to the same imperatives: to restore confidence among their fearful minority populations and prevent mass migrations from one partitioned country to the other. But by the time their respective advisory committees came back with their recommendations on citizenship several months after Partition, Jinnah was dead, and so was Gandhi; and mass migrations across the new borders had transformed the situation.

II

So far, this account of the debates on South Asian citizenship is compatible with received wisdom. Indeed, the story does appear to be one of "borrowing" and "adapting" existing European models. The leaders of India and Pakistan had looked at many constitutions and definitions of citizenship around the world, and decided that the British liberal conception of *jus soli* would work best for them. But it departs from conventional accounts in one important respect: it underlines the similarity, in the frantic weeks before Partition, of Indian and Pakistani leaders' responses to the question, emphasising the pragmatic concerns that informed this common stance.[34] As the rest of this article will show, once the mass migrations had begun, questions of citizenship in both countries were complicated by the problematic status, and the decisive actions, of refugees, emigrants, and stayers-on. Both countries responded to the crisis in surprisingly similar ways.

On 17 August 1947, violence on an unprecedented scale broke out in the divided province of Punjab and spread to many parts of North India and western Pakistan. Gripped by panic, countless people began to flee from their homes. Thousands tried to cross the new border to seek the protection of the "right" nation-state, but found themselves vulnerable to attack in their refugee convoys and camps. Huge numbers abandoned their homes to cluster in localities on the same side of the border where their co-religionists tended to be concentrated, seeking safety in numbers. Many hoped to return home when "normality" returned. But "normality" never did return to the subcontinent. In the weeks and months after Partition, officials on the ground devised a series of *ad hoc* administrative measures to deal with the pressing problems and exigencies which mass migration brought in its train. These measures, as much as the acts of migrants themselves, were informed by common-sense notions about citizenship, belonging, justice, and entitlement.[35] In a remarkable series of developments,

[34] Bajpai's perceptive new discussion of the Indian Constituent Assembly debates focuses on the content of the speeches and the ideas that underpinned them, disregarding context outside the Assembly. Bajpai, *Debating Difference*. This article, in contrast, interprets the significant shifts in the Assembly's line towards minorities in the light of the rapidly evolving political situation outside it.

[35] Sherman, "Migration, Citizenship and Belonging".

these conceptions swiftly came to push, stretch, and reshape policy, and eventually to inform law, constituting a new regime that, once put into place, could not be undone. The "state of exception", to use Agamben's evocative phrase,[36] would become the new order.

The plight of "stranded refugees" prompted the first of these emergency measures. Desperate to flee across the border but unable to do so for want of transport, many hundreds of thousands of migrants huddled together in makeshift camps, terrified at the prospect of being attacked by marauding gangs, or by refugees crossing in the opposite direction thirsty for revenge. Immediately after Partition, social workers and local officials began to bombard ministers in India and Pakistan with telegrams warning that the very soldiers and policemen who were supposed to protect these refugees were implicated in the violence that had prompted their flight. On 24 August 1947, Sushila Nayyar, one of Gandhi's closest aides and disciples, sent an urgent message to Delhi from Wah near Rawalpindi in Pakistan, alerting India's leaders to the fact that "Muslim troops and police [were] cooperating in [the] disturbances".[37] On 25 August 1947, as Ian Talbot has shown, soldiers of the 3rd Baluch regiment perpetrated what was perhaps the single most gruesome act of violence during Partition, mowing down in cold blood 3000 Hindu and Sikh refugees in Sheikhpura in West Punjab.[38] After this incident, Sampuran Singh, newly appointed deputy high commissioner for India in Pakistan, wrote to Patel predicting genocide: "Fifty thousand Hindus and Sikhs are daily butchered by the military and the police here. No high commissioner can save them. All Hindus and Sikhs in West Punjab will be finished."[39] Evidently, there were slippages between Singh's

[36] Agamben, *State of Exception.*

[37] Telegram from Patel to the Governor of East Punjab, 24 August 1947, in Das, ed., *Sardar Patel's Correspondence* (hereafter *SPC*), IV, p. 249.

[38] Talbot, "The August 1947 Violence".

[39] Telegram from Sampuran Singh to Patel, 27 August 1947, *SPC*, IV, p. 256.

official role as India's spokesman in Pakistan and his personal sense of obligation to "save" his co-religionists in that country. But it is important to recognize that Singh was responding to floods of appeals from "stranded" Hindus and Sikhs in West Pakistan who expected the Indian high commission to help them: the fortnightly reports from the commission in Karachi are full of references to members of these communities turning up at the commission's headquarters at Damodar Mahal, demanding help and protection.[40]

On the Indian side of the border, the situation was much the same. On 28 August, Lt Col. P.N. Kirpal told Mountbatten that "Indian officers and men had become . . . affected with the communal virus."[41] During these terrible weeks, Jinnah too heard news that Indian policemen and soldiers had joined in the bloodletting against Muslims. On 22 August 1947, Salma Tasasaddaque Hussain,[42] social worker and secretary of the Central Punjab Muslim League, wrote of "the most gruesome, inhuman and brutal assaults by Sikhs and non-Muslim soldiers" on "innocent Muslims".[43] The Punjab Boundary Force, hastily put together in July 1947 specifically to keep the peace in the border districts,[44] had not only failed spectacularly in its task, some of its members had joined members of their own community in committing atrocities against the other. This was the context in which, in September 1947, the two embattled prime ministers of India and Pakistan set up the Military Evacuation Organization

[40] Government of India, Ministry of External Affairs Papers, National Archives of India (hereafter MEAI), F./2–1/48-Pak I (vol. I).

[41] Note from Lt Col. Kirpal to the Joint Defence Council, 28 August 1947, Mountbatten Papers (Mountbatten Papers Database, University of Southampton), section I (MBI), D/46/3.

[42] The role played by social workers in shaping policy will be discussed in the larger work on which this article is based: Chatterji, *The Disinherited*.

[43] Salma Tasasaddaque Hussain to M.A. Jinnah, 22 August 1947, in Zaidi, ed., *Jinnah Papers*, v, p. 90.

[44] Kamran, "The Unfolding Crisis in Punjab", pp. 203–39.

(MEO). Its task was to protect refugees and escort them across the border. But since the army from which it was drawn (itself in the process of being partitioned) was largely recruited from the Punjab, and since its soldiers had apparently succumbed to the "contagion" of communalism which had gripped that province, Nehru and Liaquat Ali Khan agreed that Muslim refugees should be protected and evacuated by Muslim troops, and that Hindu and Sikh refugees, would, in their turn, be protected by soldiers *of the same faith*. In consequence, early in September 1947, Muslim troops from Baluchistan (in Pakistan) were brought in to Delhi (in India) to protect Muslim Meo refugees who had fled from the unfolding carnage in Rajasthan (in India),[45] and were charged with the task of escorting across the border those who wished to leave for Pakistan.[46] Within a month of achieving sovereignty, driven by similar concerns to protect minorities, both India and Pakistan had thus conceded that the troops of the other dominion could enter its territory to rescue and protect its "own" refugees.[47] Initially intended to be restricted to disturbed areas in the Punjab and Delhi, the MEO's operations were soon extended to Sindh, after representations to Patel from Sindhi Congressmen.[48] In October 1947, after the Sikh leader Baldev Singh urged Patel to mount an operation to rescue "non-Muslim girls" abducted by Muslim youths in Pakistan, and suggested that "some dominion military might also be allowed in the other dominion for this work",[49] the two dominions also took on the role of protectors of "their" respective women in the other state.[50]

[45] Copland, "The Further Shores of Partition", pp. 203–39.

[46] See Rajendra Prasad to Patel, 10 September 1947; and Patel's reply to Prasad, 12 September 1947, *SPC*, IV, pp. 340–1.

[47] See Patel's directions of 3 October 1947 that "we should insist that our motor transport convoys bring in our refugees", ibid., p. 308.

[48] Enclosure in Jairamdas Doulatram to Patel, 24 September 1947, *SPC*, IV, p. 373.

[49] Baldev Singh to Patel, 6 October 1947, ibid., pp. 348–9.

[50] Menon and Bhasin, *Borders and Boundaries*.

Of course, much is already known about the work of the MEO,[51] and about the recovery of abducted women.[52] But what calls to be underlined here is that these measures had far-reaching implications for citizenship in South Asia. Until this point, India and Pakistan had recognised – indeed insisted upon – ground rules which placed the responsibility for ensuring the protection and welfare of minorities within their own territories upon themselves, not on the other. Each had expressed grave concerns about the fate of minorities in the other dominion, but had restricted its role to exhorting the other to do more effectively to protect them.[53] Establishing the MEO represented a decisive shift from this stance. Implicit in its remit was an admission that Hindus and Sikhs "stranded" by virtue of their birth in Pakistan had to be protected by the Indian nation-state, and vice versa.

By December 1947, the MEO had evacuated most of the refugees in the two Punjabs, Sindh, and Delhi,[54] and it appeared that the crisis was finally over. Yet, no sooner had things begun to settle down in the north-west than violence broke out in divided Bengal in the east, sparking off fresh exoduses across the eastern border between India and Pakistan. This was the context in which India and Pakistan held their first inter-dominion conference in Calcutta in April 1948. The fascinating details of how the two countries reached an agreement about the treatment of minorities in their respective dominions is the subject of another paper;[55] but what calls to be noted here is that at the Calcutta conference both India and Pakistan accepted that the high commissioner of the

[51] E.g. Jeffrey, "The Punjab Boundary Force", pp. 491–520; Kamran, "The Unfolding Crisis".

[52] E.g. Menon and Bhasin, *Borders and Boundaries*.

[53] See, for instance, Nehru to Liaquat Ali Khan, 9 August 1947, and Liaquat Ali Khan to Nehru, 22 August 1947, *SPC*, IV, pp. 247–8.

[54] Randhawa, *Out of the Ashes*.

[55] Chatterji, "Mutuality and Cooperation in South Asia".

other dominion should formally be deemed the "proper channel" through which oversight over the protection of minorities was to be exercised.[56]

What this meant in practice was the two countries agreed to adopt a bizarre procedure for the redress of the grievances of minorities. If, say, a Hindu girl was abducted in East Pakistan, her family had to report the matter to the deputy high commissioner for India in Dacca. This member of India's foreign service would then take the matter up with Pakistan's ministry of external affairs; which would pass the case on to Pakistan's interior ministry to investigate the charges. Whatever information the interior ministry gathered about the truth or falsity of the claim, and any action that had been taken by way of redress, would then be relayed, by the same circuitous route, back to India's high commission via its external affairs ministry in Delhi.[57] The impromptu and *ad hoc* actions of the first Indian high commissioners and their deputies (the likes of Sampuran Singh, mentioned above) – who took it upon themselves to respond to urgent calls from refugees for help, and to agitate on their behalf – was now, by this agreement, given formal sanction.

By agreeing to these measures, India and Pakistan further compromised their stated commitment to the principles of *jus soli* and territorial citizenship. They did this, moreover, in tandem: responding to common pressures, with common aims and common purposes.

III

But these were only the first steps down a slippery slope, straying from the *via tuta* of *jus soli*. Once refugees moved across borders

[56] MEAI/ F.8–15/48/Pak-i (Secret); for Pakistan, see memo by A. Rashid Ibrahim, 25 May 1948, REF no. 315-Cord/48, MEAI/F.8–48-Pak-i (Secret); and MEAI/F. 10(9)/Pak (A)/1949.

[57] Such cases run into the thousands. See, for instance, MEAI/F.9–10/48-Pak i.

in large numbers (and indeed were assisted by "national" troops in so doing), this raised the question of what was to happen to their property in the country they were leaving behind. Who was to protect it and by what means?

Once again, both nations started out with the firm intention of protecting the vacant properties of emigrants (designated "evacuees") within their own territories. Both declared that they were determined to keep out looters and squatters, to preserve the "property and effects of evacuees", and to guarantee their continued rights of ownership over these properties, whether moveable or immoveable. On 9 September 1947, by emergency ordinance, the West Punjab government in Pakistan appointed a custodian of evacuee property, charged with the duty of taking "possession of the property and effects of evacuees" and "[taking] such measures as he considers necessary or expedient for preserving such property or effects". Indian East Punjab followed suit.[58]

In turn, this posed the urgent but intractable problem of how to deal with the innumerable refugees who had already occupied evacuee property in the first few weeks after Partition. The problem was complicated by the fact that many thousands of these refugee squatters had left homes not in former British India but in princely territories. They had been ruled by Hindu rajas and Muslim nawabs who had distinctive ideas about the duties of king and subject, and had been governed by regimes of law and property that differed substantially from those of British India.[59] All over India, and indeed Pakistan, the refugees, who had by now grabbed and squatted in any vacant land or buildings they could find,[60] held diverse views about their duties and entitlements, often at odds with the liberal policies of their respective governments.

[58] See the introduction to the Government of East Punjab Evacuees (Administration of Property) Act, 1947 (Act XIV of 1947).

[59] See, for instance, *Administration of the Dhar State*; *Ruling Princes and Chiefs of India*.

[60] Zamindar, *The Long Partition*, *passim*; Chatterji, *The Spoils of Partition*, ch. 3; Ansari, *Life after Partition*, *passim*.

By definition, in India, much of this illegally acquired property had previously been owned by Muslims who had abandoned their homes during the violence. Hindu and Sikh refugee squatters now refused, point-blank, to vacate these properties. Instead, they displayed a "threatening" attitude towards landlords, intimidated policemen charged with enforcing the ordinance, and cowed remaining Muslim families who tried to remonstrate with them.[61] In a letter to the district commissioner of Delhi, one Chandni Chowk landlord wrote of refugees squatting in his property: "They are not paying any attention towards my request of vacating . . . and are now threatening me and are causing . . . much anxiety in the entire *mohalla* [neighbourhood]."[62] In another case, a Muslim landowner wrote repeatedly to the custodian of evacuee property in Delhi, begging for his help to recover property that had been forcibly occupied by Sikh refugees: "All my buildings have been unauthorisingly [sic] trespassed by these trespassers and [I have] been deprived of my birthright, income and peaceful living . . . It will not be out of place to mention here that I am a peaceful, loyal and faithful citizen of Delhi and well-wisher of our Benign Government of India."[63]

But policemen all over North India and Pakistan reported that when they tried to enforce the ordinance, they encountered fierce resistance in thousands of such cases. All too frequently, these confrontations ended in violence: refugees fighting pitched battles against the police and landlords.[64]

[61] For examples from West Bengal, see Government of Bengal Intelligence Bureau (Calcutta; hereafter GB IB), 1838–48 (KW) and GB IB 1809–48 (Nadia). For instances in Delhi, see Delhi State Archives (hereafter DSA), 16/48/DC, and DSA, DCO/259/47.

[62] M.L. Mehra to the District Commissioner of Delhi, 9 October 1948, DSA, DC, 16/48.

[63] Noor Ahmed to J.M.L. Prabhu (Custodian of Evacuee Property), New Delhi, 13 November 1947, DSA, DC, 191/1947.

[64] For an account of one celebrated battle by the refugees of "Azadgarh" squatter colony south of Calcutta, see Guha, *Memoir No. I*; and Chatterji, "'Dispersal' and the Failure of Rehabilitation", pp. 955–1032.

In this pattern of action and response, the refugees' powerful sense of entitlement comes across forcefully. Hindu and Sikh refugees plainly believed that they belonged in India, and that its government was obliged to protect them. They also felt that they had a moral claim to the property of Muslim evacuees. As Sarah Ansari's study of Karachi shows, Muslim refugees there felt similarly entitled.[65] Refugee squatters were remarkably effective, furthermore, at persuading "the public" of their rights. The manner in which the refugees stood their ground in the face of police action allows us to see these encounters as true "acts of citizenship", which *changed* and *shaped* the political landscape *from below*. Engin Isin has described these as acts by which "subjects become claimants when they are least expected or anticipated to do so", "under surprising conditions"; acts which over a "short period of time" rupture existing notions of order, creating new norms that enable the actors "to remain at the scene", standing their ground "rather than fleeing it".[66] In the thousands of local battles refugees fought across India and Pakistan at this time, we see instances of such rapid but profound shifts, as illegal acts of forcible appropriation quickly gained legitimacy in the eyes of "a public" that sided with intransigent refugees. Instead, it was usually the local havildar who had to flee, taking his eviction orders with him. One frightened constable in Calcutta, for instance, reported how his efforts to "eject" Hindu refugees from Muslim-owned houses evoked a "threatening response", with the refugees succeeding in gaining "public sympathy on their behalf. Their eviction", he concluded, "would not be an easy task."[67]

The local policemen sent on these unenviable missions were themselves drawn from the very "public" they confronted in these encounters; and, unsurprisingly, they soon showed signs of being swayed by its sympathy towards the refugees. Again and again,

[65] Ansari, *Life after Partition*, *passim*.

[66] Isin, "Theorising Acts of Citizenship", pp. 17, 26.

[67] GB IB File no. 1838–48 (KW).

Hindu and Sikh policemen showed themselves to be reluctant to take any action to evict refugees of their own faith from Muslim-owned properties across North India. Increasingly, they dragged their feet about evicting refugees in any circumstances, even when they were squatting on public roads and footpaths. For example, when the Delhi municipal committee tried to get the police to remove refugee hawkers from pavements in the business areas of Old Delhi, the superintendent of police told his boss that he was "not in favour of removing these hawkers who are at present earning their livelihood by fair means and they are putting no burden on the Indian Dominion".[68] Here, he made explicitly normative claims, not only about the refugees' absolute right to shelter in India, but also their right to livelihood "by fair means".

Senior officers quickly came to be persuaded by these sentiments. Commenting on the continuing lawlessness in Delhi in the winter of 1947, the deputy inspector general of police warned his superiors that "unless a satisfactory solution of the refugees' problems [could] be found there [could] be no permanent peace in Delhi". He pointed out that "a large number of Muslim houses and shops [were] vacant and the general feeling amongst the public [was] that refugees should be permitted to occupy these houses and shops." He put forward what he felt was the obvious solution: the refugees should be allowed to occupy vacant Muslim-owned properties instead of being prevented from so doing.[69]

The temper and norms of "the public" then – the refugees, their numerous sympathisers in local communities, as well as lower-level state functionaries drawn from those communities – were pitted against the official policies and laws of the sarkar. This climate of opinion began, with surprising speed, to influence the Indian government. Nehru, who six weeks before had been determined

[68] Superintendent of Police to Deputy Inspector General of Police, Delhi, 20 December 1947, DSA, DC, 259/47.

[69] Deputy Inspector General of Police to Chief Commissioner, Delhi, 20 December 1947, DSA, DC, 259/47.

to protect all Muslim evacuee properties against all squatters, by October 1947 had begun to prevaricate on the issue. He began increasingly to draw a normative distinction between refugees and "ordinary looters". Writing to Patel on 6 October 1947, he insisted that it was only the latter category, squatters who were simply looters "profiteering at the expense both of the original owner of the house and the Punjabi refugee", who called to be evicted and punished.[70]

However, these equivocations raised yet another conundrum. What would happen if Muslim evacuees came back home to India once order was restored? Many were known to want to return: Nehru himself estimated that perhaps half of Old Delhi's Muslim evacuees wished to return to their own homes and neighbourhoods, and had no desire to migrate to Pakistan.[71] But where were they to go if their homes had been captured by refugees? And what would happen to Hindu and Sikh refugees who wanted, in their turn, to return to homes in Pakistan?

It was in response to this quandary that Nehru's government came to a historic conclusion: it had to prevent Muslim evacuees from returning to reclaim their homes. The "Influx from Pakistan (Control) Ordinance", promulgated in January 1948, laid down that "no person shall enter India from any place in [West] Pakistan, whether directly or indirectly unless . . . he is in possession of a permit."[72] These permits were to be issued by the Indian high commission in Karachi only if officials had satisfied themselves of one of two conditions: either that the applicant had never intended permanently to migrate to Pakistan, or that he was a Pakistani national wishing to make a short trip to India on legitimate business.[73] The intention was plain. Muslim refugees who

[70] Nehru to Patel, 6 October 1947, *SPC*, IV, p. 400.

[71] Ibid.

[72] Ordinance XXXIV of 1948, MEAI/ F.26–189/48-Pak I (Secret).

[73] "Rules Regarding Permit System Introduced between India and Pakistan", Notification no. II(55)/48-General, *Gazette of India*, 14 September 1948.

had fled to Pakistan were not to be readmitted into India. In October 1948, Pakistan followed suit with its own ordinance laying down the same conditions.[74]

Zamindar insists that the permit system was the product of a "bureaucratic discourse" that "gathered force" in 1948, driven by a "bureaucratic rationality" that saw returning refugees as a challenge to governance.[75] This article argues, on the contrary, that while official concerns about law and order played a part in these events, it would be a mistake to ignore the relentless pressure that refugees themselves exerted on government from below. In fact, both India and Pakistan retreated from their liberal commitment to uphold the law and to protect the property of evacuees. But they did so because they recognised that they had already lost the argument on the ground.

IV

The permit system, however, proved impossible to administer. Not merely was it liable to gross abuse, as Zamindar has shown: it was impossible to enforce. The governments of both India and Pakistan lacked the wherewithal to police the length of the western border, so the actual business of checking whether people had the right permit devolved to the petty functionaries who manned the transport networks in the border regions. Railway guards, ticket collectors, and ship's captains now began to demand that passengers who, from their common-sense perspective, did not look like "bona fide nationals" produce their permits for inspection, with all the inequities that make such stop-and-search procedures notorious. And for their part, the targets of their haphazard surveillance found plenty of ways of evading it. Holders of temporary permits simply tore them up, claiming never to have left India in the first place, leaving the police "with no means whatever

[74] Zamindar, *The Long Partition*, p. 82.

[75] Ibid., pp. 79–95.

to identify [them]".[76] Very quickly, a flourishing trade sprang up in counterfeit permits. By October 1948, the intelligence agencies were reporting that "we suspect fake permits are being issued", while pointing out how difficult it was to distinguish between fake and genuine papers.[77] As Kamal Sadiq has recently remarked, the "ways and means" by which illegal immigrants acquire citizenship in developing countries are many and strange,[78] and countless people caught up in the permit system took recourse to them. In December 1948, the Government of India was forced to instruct all state governments to stop issuing any permits for permanent resettlement. Stern reminders were sent in April 1949, and again in May 1949, but to no avail.[79]

Even where officials succeeded in catching "permit dodgers" and tried to deport them, their efforts often foundered. In India, the system provoked thousands of appeals from Muslims facing deportation who insisted that they had never intended permanently to migrate to Pakistan. Judges struggled to establish the required state of mind (*animus manendi*) to prove that the appellants had not intended to renounce their Indian citizenship by travelling to Pakistan, and for their part, appellants struggled to produce evidence sufficient to prove such a state of mind. Take the case of Fazal Dad (*alias* Sardar Khan Fateh Ali), who was arrested in 1953. Fazal Dad claimed to have lived in a village in Madhya Pradesh (Central India) for forty years, where he owned "considerable immovable property". According to his deposition, he went to Pakistan on a temporary visit in 1948 to attend a marriage and

[76] V.D. Moray, Bombay CID, to A. Jayaram, 14 September 1948, MEAI/Pak-I Section, F. 26–189/48-Pak I (Secret).

[77] See, for instance, the lengthy discussions about whether the permits of Noor Mohamed and Ishaque Khan, two Muslims "found" in Nagpur, were fake or authentic. Ibid.

[78] Sadiq, *Paper Citizens*.

[79] C.N. Chandra, Secretary, Ministry of Rehabilitation, to all Chief Secretaries, 9 May 1949, GB IB 1210–48 (4).

to bring his children back to India. He had to stay on in Pakistan until 1953 for reasons beyond his control, when he re-entered India using a Pakistani passport. In court, he argued that he "has always been a citizen of India and that he could not, on account of his allegedly temporary visit to Pakistan . . . be deemed to have lost his rights as a citizen of this country." The case dragged on for almost a decade. Finally, in November 1962, Justices Krishnan and Sharma finally ruled that he was a Pakistani citizen and his petition to be allowed to stay in India was dismissed.[80] Of course, these rulings tended to be biased against the plaintiffs; and, of course, less fortunate Muslims who had no papers or property were seldom given the benefit of the doubt.[81] But the point here is that thousands of people charged with violating the permit rules challenged the system in the courts; and their appeals continued to clog the sclerotic arteries of the Indian judicial system long after the permit laws were repealed in 1952, when passports were introduced for travel between the two countries.

This was the context for the promulgation of the Evacuee Property Ordinance in June 1949.[82] This draconian ordinance effectively nationalised, at a stroke, all property vacated by Muslims in India, outside Bengal, Assam, and the north-eastern states.[83] Such property, the ordinance stated, was to be deployed by the government for the rehabilitation of refugees, and for other "public purposes". Any property, or part of a property, which had been

[80] *AIR* 1964 MP 272 Bench: H. Krishnan, P. Sharma.

[81] For the difficulties appellants faced in proving their claims, see any of the 6000-odd cases fought in the Indian courts; e.g. *The State of Mysore v. Abdul Salam* in July 1951; or *Nazir Hussain v. The State* on 13 December 1951, in which the judge described the plaintiff 's case as "balderdash".

[82] "An Ordinance to Provide for the Administration of Evacuee Property and for Certain Matters Connected Therewith", Ordinance no. xxvii of 1949, *Gazette of India*, 18 October 1949, MEAI, F. 17–39/49-AFRI.

[83] The reasons why India excluded West Bengal, Assam, and Tripura from the evacuee property regime are addressed in Chatterji, *The Disinherited.*

abandoned, or appeared to have been abandoned, by its Muslim owners was liable to be attached, on the presumption that its owners had migrated to Pakistan. Whether or not this was actually the case, the ordinance gave the custodian absolute authority to vest ownership of such property in the state.

As with the permit system, the identification of Muslims as evacuees depended on a subjective assessment by an official about their "state of mind". A ruling by the custodian that a Muslim was "an intending evacuee" would be virtually impossible to challenge. But now, with the bitter experience of being mired in the courts with thousands of permit cases, the Indian government decided to arm itself with more wide-ranging powers. Chapter 7 of the Evacuee Property Act expressly denied the jurisdiction of civil or revenue courts to adjudicate on whether or not "any property or any right to or any interest in any property is or is not evacuee property." It also refused the courts the power "to question the legality of any action taken by the Custodian General or the Custodian under this Act."[84]

Evacuee property was thus made an area of governance outside the rule of law: a true state of exception where executive authority was wholly unchecked. The significance of this for the status and rights of India's Muslim citizens can hardly be exaggerated. Even as T.H. Marshall was writing his classic account of citizenship in 1950, which argued that access to courts was a vital attribute of "civil citizenship",[85] in India this access was being denied to one category of citizen. As Keechang Kim has shown, access to "helpe and protection by the king's law" was the very basis of *jus soli* since Calvin's case of 1608, which held that the plaintiff, once deemed to be a subject of the king, could not arbitrarily be deprived of his property.[86] The fact that Muslims were denied these protections

[84] Ordinance No. XXVII of 1949.

[85] Marshall, "Citizenship and Social Class".

[86] Kim, *Aliens in Medieval Law*, *passim*; Anderson, "Britons Abroad, Aliens at Home", *passim*.

by sweeping actions of the executive is a commentary on their legal status in India. When the constitution-makers first met early in 1947, they had agreed that minorities needed *additional* safeguards, over and above the fundamental rights enjoyed by all citizens. Now, less than three years later, the act stripped them of a key fundamental right – the right to property – and also of the right of appeal against their dispossession. This meant that they enjoyed substantially *fewer* rights and protections than "ordinary" citizens.

Officials in Pakistan protested, with justification, that these harsh measures "disinherited" India's Muslim "displacees". But very soon, in October 1949, they followed with their own measures appropriating all evacuee Hindu and Sikh property abandoned in Pakistan.[87] In October 1954, India formalised its own arrangements with the Displaced Persons (Compensation and Rehabilitation) Act, which subsumed all Muslim evacuee property in a "compensation pool" to pay for the rehabilitation of Hindu and Sikh refugees.[88] Pakistan followed suit with its own laws and rules to misappropriate Hindu and Sikh property.[89] Evacuee property was thus established as the cornerstone of refugee rehabilitation, and, by extension, of the new post-Partition order.

These regulatory regimes had a profound impact upon South Asia. In a region where mobility and circulation had for centuries been a way of life,[90] they stopped the legitimate movement of populations, forcing them into an unnatural stability. They sealed the western borders between India and Pakistan much more effectively than any wall or fence. A series of measures followed,

[87] Pakistan promulgated a central Evacuee Property Ordinance in October 1949. "The Problem of Evacuee Property and Efforts Made to Solve It", MEAI/II(21)/49-Pak III (Secret).

[88] (India) Act XXXXIV of 1954, 9 October 1954.

[89] Syed, ed., *Edition 2008*.

[90] Markovits, Pouchepadass, and Subrahmanyam, eds, *Society and Circulation*.

which gradually extended their remit (see Table 13.1). In 1955, India enacted citizenship laws which created a hierarchy of rights, ruling out citizenship for persons who had at any point migrated to Pakistan or been domiciled there; Pakistan having legislated along the same lines in 1951. In 1965, India and Pakistan fought a brief war, and in 1968 both promulgated enemy property ordinances

Table 13.1

Key Legislation and Agreements Regarding Refugees and Evacuees in India, Pakistan, and Bangladesh, 1947–1972

Declarations establishing custodians of evacuee property	India, September 1947	Pakistan, September 1947
Joint Defence Council decision to establish the MEO	India, September 1947	Pakistan, September 1947
Calcutta inter-dominion agreement	India, April 1948	Pakistan, April 1948
Permit ordinances	India, 14 July 1948	Pakistan, 15 October 1948
Evacuee Property Ordinance	India, June 1948	Pakistan, October 1948
Karachi Agreement	India, January 1949	Pakistan, January 1949
Evacuee Property Act	India, April 1950	Pakistan, April 1950
Liaquat-Nehru Pact	India, 1950	Pakistan, 1950
Passports	India, October 1952	Pakistan, October 1952
Displaced Persons (Compensation) Act	India, 1954	Pakistan (National Database and Registration Authority Rules), 1949–55
Enemy Property Act	India, 1968	(Ordinance) Pakistan, 1969
Vested Property Ordinance		Bangladesh, 1972

which gave the state draconian powers to seize property owned by an "enemy". India defined "an enemy" as any Muslim who had migrated from India to Pakistan in the wake of Partition, and Pakistan, for its part, as any Hindu or Sikh who had migrated to India. Both governments extended the scope of the enemy acts to cremation and burial sites, temples, and shrines: sacred spaces which had hitherto been spared from the sweeping power of the custodians. The enemy acts applied, moreover, to all their territories, bringing East Pakistan, West Bengal, Assam, and Tripura within their remit. Long after the wars of 1965 and 1971 ended, the acts in both countries continued to be strengthened by amendment; they remain in force to this day. These new acts made it even more difficult than before for minorities to move. They also made it hazardous for people to maintain contact with relatives on the other side, since fraternizing with "the enemy" across the border could render their property liable to seizure.[91] Just as the evacuee property acts before them, the enemy acts were deliberately placed outside the purview of the courts. In 1972, after its secession from Pakistan in a war that produced ten million refugees, Bangladesh too enacted its own Vested Property Ordinance, mirroring the provisions of the evacuee and enemy property acts of its neighbours, with calamitous implications for its large Hindu populations, and also for its Urdu-speaking (so-called Bihari) minorities.[92]

These developments had a ripple effect on the South Asian diaspora worldwide. By this time, over three million people of South Asian origin were scattered throughout the world, most of them descendants of earlier generations of indentured and *kangani* (assisted) labour migrants, and of merchants who had travelled across the British empire in search of new opportunities.

[91] Chatterji, *The Disinherited.*

[92] Barkat, *et al.*, *Political Economy of the Vested Property Act*; Farooqui, *Law of Abandoned Property* (Dhaka, 2000); Ghosh, *Partition and the South Asian Diaspora.*

Perhaps one in three was a Muslim.[93] Many came from parts of the subcontinent that after Partition became a part of India, not Pakistan, and had family and property in India. Questions were now raised about their nationality. Mandarins in the external affairs ministry in Delhi urged government to enlarge the scope of the evacuee property act to apply it to overseas Muslims of "doubtful loyalty". Their campaign failed because the law ministry would not support it;[94] but despite this, and despite the fact that the great majority of these people had migrated abroad many decades before the birth of Pakistan, the custodian went ahead and seized the properties in India of several overseas Indian Muslims.[95] Not surprisingly, scores of people in this position tried to register themselves as Indian citizens to protect their familial property in India. But this did them few favours in their host countries. In Ceylon, as in East and South Africa, the phenomenon was seen as proof that Indian migrants had no loyalty to their countries of adoption.[96] In South Africa, where the Afrikaner National Party had long been pressing for the repatriation of "Asiatics", this issue had dangerous ramifications for South Asians long settled in the Republic. If South Africa's "Asiatics" were Indian nationals, the National Party claimed, it was well within South Africa's rights to ask them to leave. If, on the other hand, they were South African citizens by virtue of birth and domicile, then India had no business interfering in South Africa's internal affairs and proselytising, in the United Nations or elsewhere, on their behalf.

For its part, the Indian government began now to see compelling reasons why its diasporic peoples should be encouraged to take up the citizenship of their host countries. If it could not extend

[93] Memo by B.F.H.B. Tyabji, 23 August 1952, MEAI (AFR II Branch)/AII/52/6491/31 (Secret).

[94] MEAI/AII/52/6423/31 (1952) (Secret).

[95] File note 20 April 1950, MEAI/17–39/49-AFRI (Secret).

[96] MEAI/17–39/49-AFRI (Secret) and MEAI/AII/52/6423/31 (1952, Secret).

the evacuee property laws worldwide, it had to try and prevent by other means the return to India of "undesirables" who might claim title to such property. It did so by setting its face against granting citizenship to overseas Indians on the basis of descent, and firmly rejecting any calls for dual nationality. This would allow the Indian government to sidestep the awkward question of who, among these three million or so people abroad, was entitled to Indian citizenship, who among them was a "closet" Pakistani, and who, if they were allowed to return home, could disrupt the precarious arrangements arrived at about evacuee property.

This was another significant shift. Time was when Indian nationalists had loudly voiced their concerns about their brethren in other parts of the British empire, whether South Africa, Burma, Malaya, or Ceylon.[97] Now suddenly they were more muted. India's missions in these countries began actively to encourage the descendants of Indian migrants to register themselves as citizens of their host countries, to assimilate, and to settle for whatever terms – however unequal – the governments of their adopted countries offered them.[98] Pakistan's citizenship act of 1951, likewise, provided for an extremely narrow interpretation of citizenship by descent, extending this only to persons whose parents, at the time of their birth, were Pakistani citizens.[99]

As the history of the late-twentieth century has shown, this policy gave no guarantees that the "host" countries would accept South Asian migrants as full citizens. But the point is that not only did India and Pakistan retreat from *jus soli* principles of citizenship, they set their face simultaneously against *jus sanguinus*, which would have transmitted citizenship of India and Pakistan

97 Fischer-Tine, "Indian Nationalism and the World Forces", pp. 325–44.

98 So in 1949, India advised that "in the changed political circumstances of the two countries . . . the best thing would be for all Indians who were qualified to be Ceylon citizens to apply for [Ceylonese] citizenship without hesitation." MEAI/F.7/49–8Ci (C) (Secret).

99 Syed, ed., *The Citizenship Laws*, p. 14.

to millions of persons of South Asian descent who had been born abroad. In consequence, a hitherto disparate and dispersed diaspora now shared a common predicament, and a liminal legal status, both in their "home" country and their "host" states. In these ways, forms of partial citizenship pioneered in the Indian subcontinent in the aftermath of Partition travelled to many parts of the erstwhile British empire where there were significant populations of Indian origin, complicating and compromising their status, while producing new forms of quasi-citizenship in their wake.

V

After Partition, minorities in South Asia emerged as a distinct legal category of citizens who were not fully protected by the states within which they lived. Their fundamental right to property was taken out of the jurisdiction of the courts. By executive action, they were deprived of their freedom of mobility. They were stripped of the right to return – a vital attribute of citizenship. They were rendered liable to lose their property if suspected of harbouring the intention of moving. Maintaining transnational networks was fraught with danger, since it laid them open to the charge of fraternising with the enemy. The power of South Asia's nation-states over their "minority-citizens" far exceeds their sovereignty over ordinary citizens, and the capacity of "minority-citizens" to resist this power was broken, as this article has shown, by a series of draconian executive actions.

Ong has recently put forward the notion of "flexible citizenship": the capacity of certain transnational groups to exercise their rights of membership flexibly and opportunistically so as to maximize advantage in the global marketplace.[100] The minorities of South Asia, by contrast, have a form of citizenship which is profoundly

[100] Ong, *Flexible Citizenship*.

inflexible, a "bare citizenship" which renders them uniquely immobile, and hence uniquely vulnerable, in an age of predatory global capitalism and ever-intensifying state power.

But minority citizenship was not simply a product of "bureaucratic rationality", as some have suggested, or even of "governmentality". On the contrary, it was produced by complex, often violent, interactions between government and a range of non-state actors, who forced their own ideas of nationality, justice, and entitlement on to the statute books. Citizenship in South Asia thus proves to have a complex parenthood, with the "civil" and the "political" more entangled, and mutually constituted, than some theorists would have us believe. India and Pakistan continued to be bound together by migrants and migration even as their discursive claims seemed to pull them ever further apart.

The striking similarities which this article has revealed in India's and Pakistan's citizenship practices challenge many stereotypes about the early history of the two states. But potentially they also help us better to understand the history of citizenship in the wider world. Since Brubaker argued that contrasting citizenship laws in France and Germany derived from their contrasting nationalisms – the one "civic" and the other "ethnic"[101] – scholars have assumed that national movements determine the citizenship models nation-states are likely to adopt. Our story suggests caution in assuming a simple linear connection. Just as many small acts of agency and much realpolitik intervened in South Asia to mould citizenship in surprising, and counterintuitive, ways, it is likely that complex histories of agency, process, and politics helped to form European "models" as well; and if this were the case, they cease to be models in any meaningful sense.

Finally, the brief discussion here of the ways in which South Asian citizenship practices travelled beyond the subcontinent, affecting the status of overseas Indians and having an impact

[101] Brubaker, *Citizenship and Nationhood.*

upon the citizenship norms of the countries where they lived, suggests another conclusion. The diffusion of ideas and practices regarding citizenship have flowed in more than one direction. The history of citizenships in different parts of the world may be far more multi-sited, entangled, and intertwined than historians have previously assumed.

References

Administration of the Dhar State for 1939–1940, Dhar, 1940.

Agamben, Giorgio, *State of Exception*, trans. Kevin Attrell, Chicago, Il, 2005.

Anderson, Caitlin, "Britons Abroad, Aliens at Home: Nationality Law and Policy in Britain, 1815–1870", Doctoral dissertation, Cambridge, 2004.

Ansari, Sarah, *Life after Partition: Migration, Community and Strife, 1947–1962*, Oxford, 2004.

Bajpai, Rochana, *Debating Difference: Group Rights and Liberal Democracy in India*, New Delhi, 2011.

Banerjee, Sukanya, *Becoming Imperial Citizens: Indians in Late-Victorian Empire*, Durham, NC, and London, 2010.

Barkat, Abul, *et al.*, *Political Economy of the Vested Property Act in Rural Bangladesh*, Dhaka, 1997.

Benhabib, Seyla, *The Rights of Others: Aliens, Residents and Citizens*, Cambridge, 2004.

Brubaker, Rogers, *Citizenship and Nationhood in France and Germany*, Cambridge MA, 1992.

Chatterjee, Partha, *The Politics of the Governed*, New York, NY, 2004.

Chatterji, Joya, "'Dispersal' and the Failure of Rehabilitation: Refugee Camp-dwellers and Squatters in West Bengal', *Modern Asian Studies*, 41 (2007).

———, "Mutuality and Cooperation in South Asia: An Alternative History of India–Pakistan relations", Unpublished lecture, Royal Asiatic Society, March 2012.

———, *The Disinherited: Migrants, Minorities and Citizenship in South Asia, 1946–1970* (forthcoming).

———, *The Spoils of Partition. Bengal and India, 1947–1967*, Cambridge, 2007.

Constituent Assembly of India: Debates, 12 vols, Faridabad, 1947–51.

Constituent Assembly of Pakistan: Debates, 16 vols, Karachi, 1947–54.

Copland, Ian, "The Further Shores of Partition: Ethnic Cleansing in Rajasthan, 1947", *Past and Present*, 160 (1998).

Das, Durga, ed., *Sardar Patel's Correspondence*, 10 vols, Ahmedabad, 1971.

Farooqui, M.I., *Law of Abandoned Property*, Dhaka, 2000.

Fischer-Tine, Harald, "Indian Nationalism and the World Forces: Transnational and Diasporic Dimensions of the Indian Freedom Movement on the Eve of the First World War", *Journal of Global History*, (2007).

Ghosh, Papiya, *Partition and the South Asian Diaspora: Extending the Subcontinent*, Delhi, 2007.

Guha, B.S., *Memoir No. I, 1954. Studies in Social Tensions among the Refugees from Eastern Pakistan*, Calcutta, 1959.

Holsten, James, *Insurgent Citizenship: Disjunctions of Democracy and Modernity in Brazil*, Princeton, NJ, 2008.

Isin, Engin F., "Theorising Acts of Citizenship", in Engin F. Isin and Greg M. Neilson, eds, *Acts of Citizenship*, London, 2008.

Jayal, Niraja Gopal, "Genealogies of Rights", Unpublished lecture.

Jeffrey, Robin, "The Punjab Boundary Force and the Problem of Order, 1947", *Modern Asian Studies*, 8 (1974).

Kamran, Tahir, "The Unfolding Crisis in Punjab, March–August, 1947: Key Turning Points and British Responses', *Journal of Punjab Studies*, 14 (2007).

Kim, Keechang, *Aliens in Medieval Law: The Origins of Modern Citizenship*, Cambridge, 2000.

Kohn, Hans, *The Idea of Nationalism: A Study in its Origins and Background*, 1944; rpntd New Brunswick, NJ, 2005.

Markovits, C., J. Pouchepadass, and S. Subrahmanyam, eds, *Society and Circulation: Mobile people and Itinerant Cultures in South Asia, 1750–1950*, Delhi, 2003.

Marshall, T.H., "Citizenship and Social Class" (1950), in J. Manza and M. Sander, eds, *Inequality and Society*, 1950; rpntd New York, NY, 2009.

Menon, Ritu, and Kamla Bhasin, *Borders and Boundaries: Women in India's Partition*, New Delhi, 1998.

Migdal, Joel S., *State in Society: Studying how States and Societies Transform and Constitute One Another*, Cambridge, 2009.

Naqvi, Tahir Hasnain, "The Politics of Commensuration: The Violence of Partition and the Making of the Pakistani State", *Journal of Historical Sociology*, 20 (2007).

Ong, Aihwa, *Flexible Citizenship: The Cultural Logics of Transnationality*, Durham, NC, 1999.

Pandey, Gyanendra, "Can a Muslim be an Indian?", *Comparative Studies in Society and History*, 41 (1999).

Randhawa, M.S., *Out of the Ashes: An Account of the Rehabilitation of Refugees from West Pakistan in Rural Areas of East Punjab*, Chandigarh, 1954.

Rao, B. Shiva ed., *The Framing of India's Constitution: Select Documents*, 5 vols, New Delhi, 1966.

Rau, B.N., *India's Constitution in the Making*, Calcutta, 1960.

Ruling Princes and Chiefs of India: A Brief Historical Record of the Leading Princes and Chiefs in India Together with a Description of Their Territories and Methods of Administration, Bombay, 1930.

Sadiq, Kamal, *Paper Citizens: How Illegal Immigrants Acquire Citizenship in Developing Countries*, Oxford, 2009.

Shani, Ornit, "Conceptions of Citizenship in India and the 'Muslim Question'", *Modern Asian Studies*, 44 (2010).

Sherman, Taylor C., "Migration, Citizenship and Belonging in Hyderabad (Deccan), 1946–1956", *Modern Asian Studies*, 45 (2011).

Syed, Nazar Abbas, ed., *Edition 2008: The Citizenship Laws with NADRA Laws*, Lahore, 2008.

Tabili, Laura, *'We Ask for British Justice': Workers and Racial Difference in Late Imperial Britain*, New York, NY, 1994.

Talbot, Ian, "The August 1947 Violence in Sheikhpura City", Unpublished paper, Honolulu (April 2011).

Walzer, Michael, "Citizenship", in Terence Ball, James Farr, and Russell L. Hanson, eds, *Political Innovation and Conceptual Change*, Cambridge, 1995.

Zaidi, Z.H., ed., *Jinnah Papers: First Series* (18 vols), Islamabad, 1998–2011.

Zamindar, Vazira F., *The Long Partition and the Making of Modern South Asia: Refugees, Boundaries, Histories*, New York, NY, 2007.

Index

www.ingramcontent.com/pod-product-compliance
Lightning Source LLC
LaVergne TN
LVHW050145080826
844660LV00002B/88
* 9 7 8 1 4 3 8 4 8 3 3 3 7 *